Proceedings of the
First USENIX Symposium

on

Operating Systems Design and Implementation
(OSDI)

Co-sponsored by ACM SIGGOPS and IEEE TCOS

November 14-17, 1994
Monterey, California, USA

Table of Contents

First Symposium on Operating Systems Design and Implementation

November 14-17, 1994
Monterey, California

Tuesday, November 15

Opening Remarks, *Jay Lepreau, University of Utah*
Keynote Address, *David Patterson, University of California, Berkeley*

SCHEDULING AND MOBILITY

FILE SYSTEMS

DISTRIBUTED SHARED MEMORY I

Wednesday, November 16

NETWORKING AND MULTIPROCESSING

STEPS TO EXTENSIBILITY

Thursday. November 17

DISTRIBUTED SHARED MEMORY II

MEMORY MANAGEMENT

Program Committee

Jay Lepreau, Program Chair, *University of Utah*
Brian Bershad, *University of Washington*
David Black, *OSF Research Institute*
Paul Leach, *Microsoft Corp.*
Jim Lipkis, *Chorus Systémes*
Karin Petersen, *Xerox PARC*
Larry Peterson, *University of Arizona*
Karsten Schwan, *Georgia Institute of Technology*
Michael Scott, *University of Rochester*
Willy Zwaenepoel, *Rice University*

Message from the Program Chair

Creating a new symposium is a major effort that in OSDI's case required a year and a half of attention, commitment, and negotiation from many in the community. Starting from observing the overlap of the three USENIX symposia on Mach, Microkernels, and SEDMS, we have come a long way. From now on, OSDI should occur every two years, sponsored by USENIX, with co-sponsorship by ACM SIGOPS and IEEE TCOS. My baby is born; from now on it's up to others to raise it well.

The birthing process was arduous. The review process was intended to encourage submissions of timely work, minimizing the time from submission to publication, while retaining high quality. It was all of: short, intense, stressful, massive — but despite and because of that, high quality. I would not repeat it! An intense five week process culminated in choosing the 21 titles you find here. The original extended abstracts averaged about 10 pages in length, with a total of 178 submitted. This was considerably more than expected, so we scrambled, recruiting a large number of outside referees, and squeezing in a second one-week round of reviews for the top 80 papers. My gratitude to all of the referees and committee members who responded to our calls for last minute reviews. In the short review time, people contributed 736 formal ratings and reviews. More often than not, the reviews were lengthy and thorough. Besides aiding the selection process, these were major factors in helping the authors improve their papers. The median number of reviews for the second round papers was 5.5. Every paper was read by at least two program committee members, and usually three. Nearly every paper of the entire 178 had at least three reviews.

We accepted three papers co-authored by program committee members, out of 12 submitted. Committee authors did not see reviews or rankings of their own papers until the mass mailing after the meeting, did not know the fate of their papers until nearly the whole program had been selected, and of course were not present when their papers were discussed. In other cases of obvious conflict of interest, the affected members were to remain silent unless I asked them to speak.

Finally, every accepted paper was shepherded by a member of the program committee, with this interaction often resulting in substantially improved presentations or more extensive results.

This conference could not have been created without the efforts of a vast number of people. Even without the detail each deserves, listing them all approaches Academy Award level excitement for the reader. Above all, the small 10-person program committee did an outstanding job, generously giving their expertise, their time, and their prestige. Great thanks also to the referees, some of whom reviewed a large number of papers in a very short time. The authors of all submitted papers were the most important contributors of all, and took a greater chance than usual, on a new conference.

On the committee, Karin Petersen deserves special thanks for help in recruiting referees, as does Willy Zwaenepoel for being a source of excellent advice and help. I thank Dave Black, Ellie Young, Lori Grob, Steve Johnson, and the entire USENIX board for their confidence in me, and their support in merging the three small symposia and creating OSDI. Thanks to Lori for her excellent help throughout most of the process, as board liaison. Hank Levy was a valuable mentor to me throughout the process, especially regarding conflict of interest procedures. My thanks also go to Hank and the SIGOPS board for co-sponsoring OSDI, and, with USENIX's help, publishing the proceedings for the SIGOPS membership. I am grateful to Darrell Long, chair of TCOS, for their co-sponsorship and other aid, and to Margo Seltzer, for general advice.

Being program chair for a USENIX-sponsored event is normally easier than for most other conferences, because the USENIX professional staff are so excellent. First and foremost is Ellie Young, who was wonderful, and wonderfully effective, in every way. Judy DesHarnais is the other key person, whose huge experience ensures the conference mechanics go smoothly. I much appreciate their remarkable good humor in dealing with me and the stress I brought. Carolyn Carr deserves a medal for patience in dealing with the proceedings and my last minute ways. Toni Veglia and others at USENIX helped in a variety of important ways, as always. Dan Klein and the tutorial presenters are crucial in making this conference of broad appeal. Rob Kolstad and Jeff Mogul contributed the software we used to run the review process. I am sure there are several others to thank that elude me this moment.

Finally, special thanks go to some great people at Utah: above all, my kitchen cabinet of Doug Orr, Bryan Ford, and Mike Hibler, who digested vast numbers of papers. I am grateful to Sean O'Neill for support of the review software and mechanics, to Joe Hitchens for a long night designing a snazzy cover (that unfortunately, USENIX did not use), and to Loretta Cruse, Steve Clawson, and Linus Kamb for administrative support. Finally, my best care, thanks, and apologies to all who lived and worked with me while I spent too much of my life on this. You know who you are.

Jay Lepreau
October, 1994

AUTHOR INDEX

External Referees

The following people wrote often extensive reviews for one or more of the submitted papers, greatly assisting the papers' authors and the Program Committee.

Sarita Adve
Vikram Adve
Mustaque Ahamad
Richard Alpert
David P. Anderson
Tom Anderson
Francois Armand
Mary Baker
John Bennett
Nina T. Bhatti
Ricardo Bianchini
Mats Bjorkman
Ben A. Blake
Matt Blaze
Hans-J. Boehm
Bill Bolosky
Ivan Boule
Mic Bowman
Lawrence S. Brakmo
Allan Bricker
Vinny Cahill
John Carter
David Chaiken
John Chapin
Jeffrey Chase
Peter M. Chen
David Cheriton
Michal Cierniak
Stephen Clawson
David L. Cohn
Alan Cox
Mark Crovella
David E. Culler
Helen Davis
Thomas W. Doeppner
Michelle Dominijanni
Fred Douglis
Richard Draves
Peter Druschel
Dan Duchamp
Kenneth Duda
Sandhya Dwarkadas
Maria Ebling

Jan Edler
Amr El Abbadi
Carla Ellis
Elmootazbellah Elnozahy
Dawson R. Engler
Ed Felten
Jean-Marc Fenart
Marc E. Fiuczynski
Brett D. Fleisch
Bryan Ford
Alessandro Forin
Vincent W. Freeh
Jean-loup Gailly
Garth Gibson
David Golub
Burra Gopal
Ganesh Gopalakrishnan
Prabha Gopinath
Allan Gottlieb
Jim Griffioen
Thomas Gross
John Hartman
Carl Hauser
Rob Haydt
Debra Hensgen
Mike Hibler
Peter Honeyman
Antony L. Hosking
Wilson Hsieh
Kevin Jeffay
David B. Johnson
Mike Jones
Hasnain Karampurwala
Pete Keleher
Jay Kistler
David Kotz
Orran Krieger
Rick LaRowe
Alan Langerman
Jeff Law
Hank Levy
Wei Li
Kai Li

Jochen Liedtke
Beng-Hong Lim
Luke Lin
Gary Lindstrom
John Robert LoVerso
Susan LoVerso
Darrell Long
David Lowenthal
Honghui Lu
Rod MacDonald
Chris Maeda
Timothy Mann
Michael Marchetti
Brian Marsh
Henry Massalin
Steven McCanne
Kathryn S. McKinley
Marshall Kirk McKusick
Dylan McNamee
Wagner Meira
P. M. Melliar-Smith
John M. Mellor-Crummey
Dejan S. Milojicic
Jeffrey Mogul
David Mosberger-Tang
Louise Moser
Eliot Moss
Jishnu Mukerji
Bodhisattwa Mukherjee
Durriya Netterwala
Scott M. Nettles
Rob Netzer
David Nichols
Brian Noble
Hilarie Orman
Douglas Orr
Tom Page
Przemyslaw Pardyak
Joseph Pasquale
Simon Patience
Rob Pike
David L. Presotto
Sanjay Ranka

Herman Rao
Franklin Reynolds
Dennis Rockwell
Mendel Rosenblum
Paul Roy
Frederic Ruget
Vince Russo
Francois Saint-Lu
M. Satyanarayanan
Stefan Savage
Bill Schilit
Bart Sears
Margo Seltzer
Jonathan S. Shapiro
Marc Shapiro
Liuba Shrira
Jaswinder Pal Singh
Emin Gun Sirer
Christopher Small
David Steere
Michael Stumm
Mark Swanson
Douglas B. Terry
Marvin Theimer
Vicraj Thomas
James O'Toole
Franco Travostino
Chau-Wen Tseng
Robbert van Renesse
Raj Vaswani
Yi-Min Wang
Don Waugaman
Bruce W. Weide
Brent Welch
Bob Wheeler
John Wilkes
Bob Wisniewski
Michael Wu
Weimin Yu
Matthew J. Zekauskas
Hongyi Zhou
Benjamin Zorn

Lottery Scheduling: Flexible Proportional-Share Resource Management

Carl A. Waldspurger *   William E. Weihl *

MIT Laboratory for Computer Science
Cambridge, MA 02139 USA

Abstract

This paper presents *lottery scheduling*, a novel randomized resource allocation mechanism. Lottery scheduling provides efficient, responsive control over the relative execution rates of computations. Such control is beyond the capabilities of conventional schedulers, and is desirable in systems that service requests of varying importance, such as databases, media-based applications, and networks. Lottery scheduling also supports modular resource management by enabling concurrent modules to insulate their resource allocation policies from one another. A *currency* abstraction is introduced to flexibly name, share, and protect resource rights. We also show that lottery scheduling can be generalized to manage many diverse resources, such as I/O bandwidth, memory, and access to locks. We have implemented a prototype lottery scheduler for the Mach 3.0 microkernel, and found that it provides flexible and responsive control over the relative execution rates of a wide range of applications. The overhead imposed by our unoptimized prototype is comparable to that of the standard Mach timesharing policy.

1   Introduction

Scheduling computations in multithreaded systems is a complex, challenging problem. Scarce resources must be multiplexed to service requests of varying importance, and the policy chosen to manage this multiplexing can have an enormous impact on throughput and response time. Accurate control over the quality of service provided to users and applications requires support for specifying relative computation rates. Such control is desirable across a wide spectrum of systems. For long-running computations such as scientific applications and simulations, the consumption of computing resources that are shared among users and applications of varying importance must be regulated [Hel93]. For interactive computations such as databases and media-based applications, programmers and users need the ability

*E-mail: {carl, weihl}@lcs.mit.edu. World Wide Web: http://www.psg.lcs.mit.edu/. The first author was supported in part by an AT&T USL Fellowship and by a grant from the MIT X Consortium. Prof. Weihl is currently supported by DEC while on sabbatical at DEC SRC. This research was also supported by ARPA under contract N00014-94-1-0985, by grants from AT&T and IBM, and by an equipment grant from DEC. The views and conclusions contained in this document are those of the authors and should not be interpreted as representing the official policies, either expressed or implied, of the U.S. government.

to rapidly focus available resources on tasks that are currently important [Dui90].

Few general-purpose schemes even come close to supporting flexible, responsive control over service rates. Those that do exist generally rely upon a simple notion of *priority* that does not provide the encapsulation and modularity properties required for the engineering of large software systems. In fact, with the exception of hard real-time systems, it has been observed that the assignment of priorities and dynamic priority adjustment schemes are often ad-hoc [Dei90]. Even popular priority-based schemes for CPU allocation such as *decay-usage scheduling* are poorly understood, despite the fact that they are employed by numerous operating systems, including Unix [Hel93].

Existing *fair share* schedulers [Hen84, Kay88] and *microeconomic* schedulers [Fer88, Wal92] successfully address some of the problems with absolute priority schemes. However, the assumptions and overheads associated with these systems limit them to relatively coarse control over long-running computations. Interactive systems require rapid, dynamic control over scheduling at a time scale of milliseconds to seconds.

We have developed *lottery scheduling*, a novel randomized mechanism that provides responsive control over the relative execution rates of computations. Lottery scheduling efficiently implements *proportional-share* resource management — the resource consumption rates of active computations are proportional to the relative shares that they are allocated. Lottery scheduling also provides excellent support for modular resource management. We have developed a prototype lottery scheduler for the Mach 3.0 microkernel, and found that it provides efficient, flexible control over the relative execution rates of compute-bound tasks, video-based applications, and client-server interactions. This level of control is not possible with current operating systems, in which adjusting scheduling parameters to achieve specific results is at best a black art.

Lottery scheduling can be generalized to manage many diverse resources, such as I/O bandwidth, memory, and access to locks. We have developed a prototype lottery-scheduled mutex implementation, and found that it provides flexible control over mutex acquisition rates. A variant of lottery scheduling can also be used to efficiently manage space-shared resources such as memory.

In the next section, we describe the basic lottery scheduling mechanism. Section 3 discusses techniques for modular resource management based on lottery scheduling. Implementation issues and a description of our prototype are presented in Section 4. Section 5 discusses the results of several quantitative experiments. Generalizations of the lottery scheduling approach are explored in Section 6. In Section 7, we examine related work. Finally, we summarize our conclusions in Section 8.

2 Lottery Scheduling

Lottery scheduling is a randomized resource allocation mechanism. Resource rights are represented by lottery *tickets*.[1] Each allocation is determined by holding a *lottery*; the resource is granted to the client with the winning ticket. This effectively allocates resources to competing clients in proportion to the number of tickets that they hold.

2.1 Resource Rights

Lottery tickets encapsulate resource rights that are abstract, relative, and uniform. They are *abstract* because they quantify resource rights independently of machine details. Lottery tickets are *relative*, since the fraction of a resource that they represent varies dynamically in proportion to the contention for that resource. Thus, a client will obtain more of a lightly contended resource than one that is highly contended; in the worst case, it will receive a share proportional to its share of tickets in the system. Finally, tickets are *uniform* because rights for heterogeneous resources can be homogeneously represented as tickets. These properties of lottery tickets are similar to those of money in computational economies [Wal92].

2.2 Lotteries

Scheduling by lottery is *probabilistically fair*. The expected allocation of resources to clients is proportional to the number of tickets that they hold. Since the scheduling algorithm is randomized, the actual allocated proportions are not guaranteed to match the expected proportions exactly. However, the disparity between them decreases as the number of allocations increases.

The number of lotteries won by a client has a binomial distribution. The probability p that a client holding t tickets will win a given lottery with a total of T tickets is simply $p = t/T$. After n identical lotteries, the expected number of wins w is $E[w] = np$, with variance $\sigma_w^2 = np(1 - p)$. The coefficient of variation for the observed proportion of wins is $\sigma_w/E[w] = \sqrt{(1 - p)/np}$. Thus, a client's throughput is proportional to its ticket allocation, with accuracy that improves with $\sqrt{n}$.

---

[1]A single physical ticket may represent any number of logical tickets. This is similar to monetary notes, which may be issued in different denominations.

The number of lotteries required for a client's first win has a geometric distribution. The expected number of lotteries n that a client must wait before its first win is $E[n] = 1/p$, with variance $\sigma_n^2 = (1 - p)/p^2$. Thus, a client's average response time is inversely proportional to its ticket allocation. The properties of both binomial and geometric distributions are well-understood [Tri82].

With a scheduling quantum of 10 milliseconds (100 lotteries per second), reasonable fairness can be achieved over subsecond time intervals. As computation speeds continue to increase, shorter time quanta can be used to further improve accuracy while maintaining a fixed proportion of scheduler overhead.

Since any client with a non-zero number of tickets will eventually win a lottery, the conventional problem of starvation does not exist. The lottery mechanism also operates fairly when the number of clients or tickets varies dynamically. For each allocation, every client is given a fair chance of winning proportional to its share of the total number of tickets. Since any changes to relative ticket allocations are immediately reflected in the next allocation decision, lottery scheduling is extremely responsive.

3 Modular Resource Management

The explicit representation of resource rights as lottery tickets provides a convenient substrate for modular resource management. Tickets can be used to insulate the resource management policies of independent modules, because each ticket probabilistically guarantees its owner the right to a worst-case resource consumption rate. Since lottery tickets abstractly encapsulate resource rights, they can also be treated as first-class objects that may be transferred in messages.

This section presents basic techniques for implementing resource management policies with lottery tickets. Detailed examples are presented in Section 5.

3.1 Ticket Transfers

Ticket transfers are explicit transfers of tickets from one client to another. Ticket transfers can be used in any situation where a client blocks due to some dependency. For example, when a client needs to block pending a reply from an RPC, it can temporarily transfer its tickets to the server on which it is waiting. This idea also conveniently solves the conventional priority inversion problem in a manner similar to priority inheritance [Sha90]. Clients also have the ability to divide ticket transfers across multiple servers on which they may be waiting.

3.2 Ticket Inflation

Ticket inflation is an alternative to explicit ticket transfers in which a client can escalate its resource rights by creating more lottery tickets. In general, such inflation should be disallowed, since it violates desirable modularity and load insulation properties. For example, a single client could easily monopolize a resource by creating a large number of lottery tickets. However, ticket inflation can be very useful among mutually trusting clients; inflation and deflation can be used to adjust resource allocations without explicit communication.

3.3 Ticket Currencies

In general, resource management abstraction barriers are desirable across logical trust boundaries. Lottery scheduling can easily be extended to express resource rights in units that are local to each group of mutually trusting clients. A unique *currency* is used to denominate tickets within each trust boundary. Each currency is backed, or *funded*, by tickets that are denominated in more primitive currencies. Currency relationships may form an arbitrary acyclic graph, such as a hierarchy of currencies. The effects of inflation can be locally contained by maintaining an *exchange rate* between each local currency and a *base* currency that is conserved. The currency abstraction is useful for flexibly naming, sharing, and protecting resource rights. For example, an access control list associated with a currency could specify which principals have permission to inflate it by creating new tickets.

3.4 Compensation Tickets

A client which consumes only a fraction f of its allocated resource quantum can be granted a *compensation ticket* that inflates its value by $1/f$ until the client starts its next quantum. This ensures that each client's resource consumption, equal to f times its per-lottery win probability p, is adjusted by $1/f$ to match its allocated share p. Without compensation tickets, a client that does not consume its entire allocated quantum would receive less than its entitled share of the processor.

4 Implementation

We have implemented a prototype lottery scheduler by modifying the Mach 3.0 microkernel (MK82) [Acc86, Loe92] on a 25MHz MIPS-based DECStation 5000/125. Full support is provided for ticket transfers, ticket inflation, ticket currencies, and compensation tickets.[2] The scheduling quantum on this platform is 100 milliseconds.

4.1 Random Numbers

An efficient lottery scheduler requires a fast way to generate uniformly-distributed random numbers. We have implemented a pseudo-random number generator based on the

[2]Our first lottery scheduler implementation, developed for the *Prelude* [Wei91] runtime system, lacked support for ticket transfers and currencies.

total = 20
random [0 .. 19] = 15

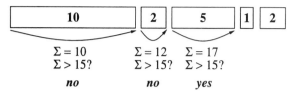

Figure 1: **Example Lottery.** Five clients compete in a list-based lottery with a total of 20 tickets. The fifteenth ticket is randomly selected, and the client list is searched for the winner. A running ticket sum is accumulated until the winning ticket value is reached. In this example, the third client is the winner.

Park-Miller algorithm [Par88, Car90] that executes in approximately 10 RISC instructions. Our assembly-language implementation is listed in Appendix A.

4.2 Lotteries

A straightforward way to implement a centralized lottery scheduler is to randomly select a winning ticket, and then search a list of clients to locate the client holding that ticket. This requires a random number generation and $O(n)$ operations to traverse a client list of length n, accumulating a running ticket sum until it reaches the winning value. An example list-based lottery is presented in Figure 1.

Various optimizations can reduce the average number of clients that must be examined. For example, if the distribution of tickets to clients is uneven, ordering the clients by decreasing ticket counts can substantially reduce the average search length. Since those clients with the largest number of tickets will be selected most frequently, a simple "move to front" heuristic can be very effective.

For large n, a more efficient implementation is to use a tree of partial ticket sums, with clients at the leaves. To locate the client holding a winning ticket, the tree is traversed starting at the root node, and ending with the winning client leaf node, requiring only $O(\lg n)$ operations. Such a tree-based implementation can also be used as the basis of a distributed lottery scheduler.

4.3 Mach Kernel Interface

The kernel representation of tickets and currencies is depicted in Figure 2. A minimal lottery scheduling interface is exported by the microkernel. It consists of operations to create and destroy tickets and currencies, operations to fund and unfund a currency (by adding or removing a ticket from its list of backing tickets), and operations to compute the current value of tickets and currencies in base units.

Our lottery scheduling policy co-exists with the standard timesharing and fixed-priority policies. A few high-priority threads (such as the Ethernet driver) created by the Unix server (UX41) remain at their original fixed priorities.

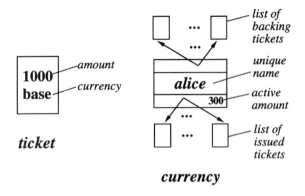

ticket   **currency**

Figure 2: **Kernel Objects.** A *ticket* object contains an amount denominated in some currency. A *currency* object contains a name, a list of tickets that back the currency, a list of all tickets issued in the currency, and an active amount sum for all issued tickets.

4.4 Ticket Currencies

Our prototype uses a simple scheme to convert ticket amounts into base units. Each currency maintains an active amount sum for all of its issued tickets. A ticket is *active* while it is being used by a thread to compete in a lottery. When a thread is removed from the run queue, its tickets are deactivated; they are reactivated when the thread rejoins the run queue.[3] If a ticket deactivation changes a currency's active amount to zero, the deactivation propagates to each of its backing tickets. Similarly, if a ticket activation changes a currency's active amount from zero, the activation propagates to each of its backing tickets.

A currency's value is computed by summing the value of its backing tickets. A ticket's value is computed by multiplying the value of the currency in which it is denominated by its share of the active amount issued in that currency. The value of a ticket denominated in the base currency is defined to be its face value amount. An example currency graph with base value conversions is presented in Figure 3. Currency conversions can be accelerated by caching values or exchange rates, although this is not implemented in our prototype.

Our scheduler uses the simple list-based lottery with a move-to-front heuristic, as described earlier in Section 4.2. To handle multiple currencies, a winning ticket value is selected by generating a random number between zero and the total number of active tickets in the *base* currency. The run queue is then traversed as described earlier, except that the running ticket sum accumulates the value of each thread's currency in *base* units until the winning value is reached.

---

[3] A blocked thread may transfer its tickets to another thread that will actively use them. For example, a thread blocked pending a reply from an RPC transfers its tickets to the server thread on which it is waiting.

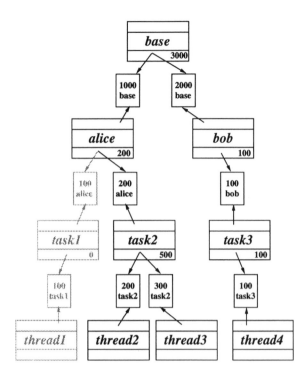

Figure 3: **Example Currency Graph.** Two users compete for computing resources. Alice is executing two tasks: *task1* is currently inactive, and *task2* has two runnable threads. Bob is executing one single-threaded task, *task3*. The current values in base units for the runnable threads are *thread2* = 400, *thread3* = 600, and *thread4* = 2000. In general, currencies can also be used for groups of users or applications, and currency relationships may form an acyclic graph instead of a strict hierarchy.

4.5 Compensation Tickets

As discussed in Section 3.4, a thread which consumes only a fraction f of its allocated time quantum is automatically granted a compensation ticket that inflates its value by $1/f$ until the thread starts its next quantum. This is consistent with proportional sharing, and permits I/O-bound tasks that use few processor cycles to start quickly.

For example, suppose threads A and B each hold tickets valued at 400 base units. Thread A always consumes its entire 100 millisecond time quantum, while thread B uses only 20 milliseconds before yielding the processor. Since both A and B have equal funding, they are equally likely to win a lottery when both compete for the processor. However, thread B uses only $f = 1/5$ of its allocated time, allowing thread A to consume five times as much CPU, in violation of their $1:1$ allocation ratio. To remedy this situation, thread B is granted a compensation ticket valued at 1600 base units when it yields the processor. When B next competes for the processor, its total funding will be $400/f = 2000$ base units. Thus, on average B will win the processor lottery five times as often as A, each time consuming $1/5$ as much of its quantum as A, achieving the desired $1:1$ allocation ratio.

4.6 Ticket Transfers

The mach_msg system call was modified to temporarily transfer tickets from client to server for synchronous RPCs. This automatically redirects resource rights from a blocked client to the server computing on its behalf. A transfer is implemented by creating a new ticket denominated in the client's currency, and using it to fund the server's currency. If the server thread is already waiting when mach_msg performs a synchronous call, it is immediately funded with the transfer ticket. If no server thread is waiting, then the transfer ticket is placed on a list that is checked by the server thread when it attempts to receive the call message.[4] During a reply, the transfer ticket is simply destroyed.

4.7 User Interface

Currencies and tickets can be manipulated via a command-line interface. User-level commands exist to create and destroy tickets and currencies (mktkt, rmtkt, mkcur, rmcur), fund and unfund currencies (fund, unfund), obtain information (lstkt, lscur), and to execute a shell command with specified funding (fundx). Since the Mach microkernel has no concept of user and we did not modify the Unix server, these commands are setuid root.[5] A complete lottery scheduling system should protect currencies by using access control lists or Unix-style permissions based on user and group membership.

5 Experiments

In order to evaluate our prototype lottery scheduler, we conducted experiments designed to quantify its ability to flexibly, responsively, and efficiently control the relative execution rates of computations. The applications used in our experiments include the compute-bound Dhrystone benchmark, a Monte-Carlo numerical integration program, a multithreaded client-server application for searching text, and competing MPEG video viewers.

5.1 Fairness

Our first experiment measured the accuracy with which our lottery scheduler could control the relative execution rates of computations. Each point plotted in Figure 4 indicates the relative execution rate that was observed for two tasks executing the Dhrystone benchmark [Wei84] for sixty seconds with a given relative ticket allocation. Three runs were executed for each integral ratio between one and ten.

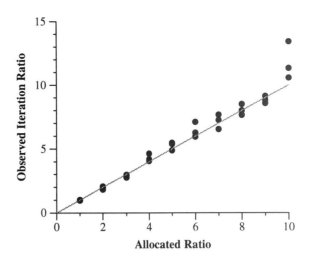

Figure 4: **Relative Rate Accuracy.** For each allocated ratio, the observed ratio is plotted for each of three 60 second runs. The gray line indicates the ideal where the two ratios are identical.

With the exception of the run for which the $10:1$ allocation resulted in an average ratio of $13.42:1$, all of the observed ratios are close to their corresponding allocations. As expected, the variance is greater for larger ratios. However, even large ratios converge toward their allocated values over longer time intervals. For example, the observed ratio averaged over a three minute period for a $20:1$ allocation was $19.08:1$.

Although the results presented in Figure 4 indicate that the scheduler can successfully control computation rates, we should also examine its behavior over shorter time intervals. Figure 5 plots average iteration counts over a series of 8 second time windows during a single 200 second execution with a $2:1$ allocation. Although there is clearly some variation, the two tasks remain close to their allocated ratios throughout the experiment. Note that if a scheduling quantum of 10 milliseconds were used instead of the 100 millisecond Mach quantum, the same degree of fairness would be observed over a series of subsecond time windows.

5.2 Flexible Control

A more interesting use of lottery scheduling involves dynamically controlled ticket inflation. A practical application that benefits from such control is the Monte-Carlo algorithm [Pre88]. Monte-Carlo is a probabilistic algorithm that is widely used in the physical sciences for computing average properties of systems. Since errors in the computed average are proportional to $1/\sqrt{n}$, where n is the number of trials, accurate results require a large number of trials.

Scientists frequently execute several separate Monte-Carlo experiments to explore various hypotheses. It is often desirable to obtain approximate results quickly whenever a new experiment is started, while allowing older experiments to continue reducing their error at a slower rate [Hog88].

---

[4] In this case, it would be preferable to instead fund all threads capable of receiving the message. For example, a server task with fewer threads than incoming messages should be directly funded. This would accelerate all server threads, decreasing the delay until one becomes available to service the waiting message.

[5] The fundx command only executes as root to initialize its task currency funding. It then performs a setuid back to the original user before invoking exec.

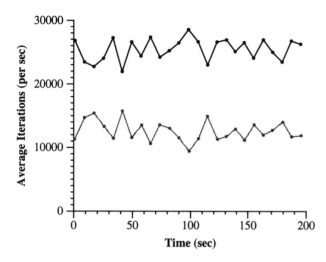

Figure 5: **Fairness Over Time.** Two tasks executing the Dhrystone benchmark with a 2:1 ticket allocation. Averaged over the entire run, the two tasks executed 25378 and 12619 iterations/sec., for an actual ratio of 2.01:1.

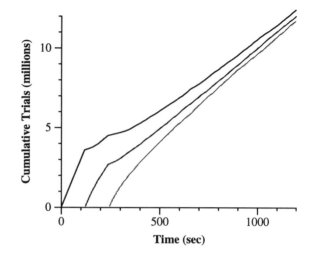

Figure 6: **Monte-Carlo Execution Rates.** Three identical Monte-Carlo integrations are started two minutes apart. Each task periodically sets its ticket value to be proportional to the square of its relative error, resulting in the convergent behavior. The "bumps" in the curves mirror the decreasing slopes of new tasks that quickly reduce their error.

This goal would be impossible with conventional schedulers, but can be easily achieved in our system by dynamically adjusting an experiment's ticket value as a function of its current relative error. This allows a new experiment with high error to quickly catch up to older experiments by executing at a rate that starts high but then tapers off as its relative error approaches that of its older counterparts.

Figure 6 plots the total number of trials computed by each of three staggered Monte-Carlo tasks. Each task is based on the sample code presented in [Pre88], and is allocated a share of time that is proportional to the square of its relative error.[6] When a new task is started, it initially receives a large share of the processor. This share diminishes as the task reduces its error to a value closer to that of the other executing tasks.

A similar form of dynamic control may also be useful in graphics-intensive programs. For example, a rendering operation could be granted a large share of processing resources until it has displayed a crude outline or wire-frame, and then given a smaller share of resources to compute a more polished image.

5.3 Client-Server Computation

As mentioned in Section 4.6, the Mach IPC primitive mach_msg was modified to temporarily transfer tickets from client to server on synchronous remote procedure calls. Thus, a client automatically redirects its resource rights to the server that is computing on its behalf. Multithreaded servers will process requests from different clients at the rates defined by their respective ticket allocations.

We developed a simple multithreaded client-server application that shares properties with real databases and information retrieval systems. Our server initially loads a 4.6 Mbyte text file "database" containing the complete text to all of William Shakespeare's plays.[7] It then forks off several worker threads to process incoming queries from clients. One query operation supported by the server is a case-insensitive substring search over the entire database, which returns a count of the matches found.

Figure 7 presents the results of executing three database clients with an 8:3:1 ticket allocation. The server has no tickets of its own, and relies completely upon the tickets transferred by clients. Each client repeatedly sends requests to the server to count the occurrences of the same search string.[8] The high-priority client issues a total of 20 queries and then terminates. The other two clients continue to issue queries for the duration of the entire experiment.

The ticket allocations affect both response time and throughput. When the high-priority client has completed its 20 requests, the other clients have completed a total of 10 requests, matching their overall 8:4 allocation. Over the entire experiment, the clients with a 3:1 ticket allocation respectively complete 38 and 13 queries, which closely matches their allocation, despite their transient competition with the high-priority client. While the high-priority client is active, the average response times seen by the clients are 17.19, 43.19, and 132.20 seconds, yielding relative speeds of 7.69:2.51:1. After the high-priority client terminates,

---

[6] Any monotonically increasing function of the relative error would cause convergence. A linear function would cause the tasks to converge more slowly; a cubic function would result in more rapid convergence.

[7] A disk-based database could use lotteries to schedule disk bandwidth; this is not implemented in our prototype.

[8] The string used for this experiment was lottery, which incidentally occurs a total of 8 times in Shakespeare's plays.

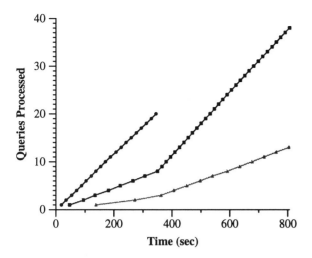

Figure 7: **Query Processing Rates.** Three clients with an 8 : 3 : 1 ticket allocation compete for service from a multithreaded database server. The observed throughput and response time ratios closely match this allocation.

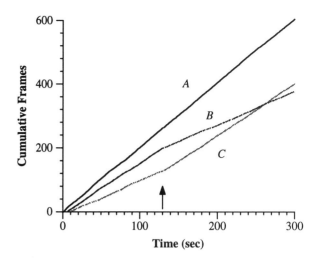

Figure 8: **Controlling Video Rates.** Three MPEG viewers are given an initial $A:B:C = 3:2:1$ allocation, which is changed to $3:1:2$ at the time indicated by the arrow. The total number of frames displayed is plotted for each viewer. The actual frame rate ratios were $1.92:1.50:1$ and $1.92:1:1.53$, respectively, due to distortions caused by the X server.

the response times are 44.17 and 15.18 seconds, for a 2.91 : 1 ratio. For all average response times, the standard deviation is less than 7% of the average.

A similar form of control could be employed by database or transaction-processing applications to manage the response times seen by competing clients or transactions. This would be useful in providing different levels of service to clients or transactions with varying importance (or real monetary funding).

5.4 Multimedia Applications

Media-based applications are another domain that can benefit from lottery scheduling. Compton and Tennenhouse described the need to control the quality of service when two or more video viewers are displayed — a level of control not offered by current operating systems [Com94]. They attempted, with mixed success, to control video display rates at the application level among a group of mutually trusting viewers. Cooperating viewers employed feedback mechanisms to adjust their relative frame rates. Inadequate and unstable metrics for system load necessitated substantial tuning, based in part on the number of active viewers. Unexpected positive feedback loops also developed, leading to significant divergence from intended allocations.

Lottery scheduling enables the desired control at the operating-system level, eliminating the need for mutually trusting or well-behaved applications. Figure 8 depicts the execution of three mpeg_play video viewers (A, B, and C) displaying the same music video. Tickets were initially allocated to achieve relative display rates of $A:B:C = 3:2:1$, and were then changed to $3:1:2$ at the time indicated by the arrow. The observed per-second frame rates were initially $2.03:1.59:1.06$ ($1.92:1.50:1$ ratio), and then $2.02:1.05:1.61$ ($1.92:1:1.53$ ratio) after the change.

Unfortunately, these results were distorted by the round-robin processing of client requests by the single-threaded X11R5 server. When run with the -no_display option, frame rates such as $6.83:4.56:2.23$ ($3.06:2.04:1$ ratio) were typical.

5.5 Load Insulation

Support for multiple ticket currencies facilitates modular resource management. A currency defines a resource management abstraction barrier that locally contains intra-currency fluctuations such as inflation. The currency abstraction can be used to flexibly isolate or group users, tasks, and threads.

Figure 9 plots the progress of five tasks executing the Dhrystone benchmark. Let *amount.currency* denote a ticket allocation of *amount* denominated in *currency*. Currencies A and B have identical funding. Tasks $A1$ and $A2$ have allocations of $100.A$ and $200.A$, respectively. Tasks $B1$ and $B2$ have allocations of $100.B$ and $200.B$, respectively. Halfway through the experiment, a new task, $B3$, is started with an allocation of $300.B$. Although this inflates the total number of tickets denominated in currency B from 300 to 600, there is no effect on tasks in currency A. The aggregate iteration ratio of A tasks to B tasks is $1.01:1$ before $B3$ is started, and $1.00:1$ after $B3$ is started. The slopes for the individual tasks indicate that $A1$ and $A2$ are not affected by task $B3$, while $B1$ and $B2$ are slowed to approximately half their original rates, corresponding to the factor of two inflation caused by $B3$.

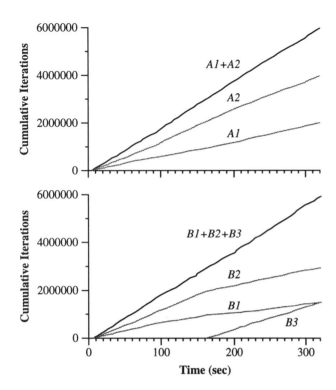

Figure 9: **Currencies Insulate Loads.** Currencies A and B are identically funded. Tasks $A1$ and $A2$ are respectively allocated tickets worth $100.A$ and $200.A$. Tasks $B1$ and $B2$ are respectively allocated tickets worth $100.B$ and $200.B$. Halfway through the experiment, task $B3$ is started with an allocation of $300.B$. The resulting inflation is locally contained within currency B, and affects neither the progress of tasks in currency A, nor the aggregate $A:B$ progress ratio.

5.6 System Overhead

The core lottery scheduling mechanism is extremely lightweight; a tree-based lottery need only generate a random number and perform $\lg n$ additions and comparisons to select a winner among n clients. Thus, low-overhead lottery scheduling is possible in systems with a scheduling granularity as small as a thousand RISC instructions.

Our prototype scheduler, which includes full support for currencies, has not been optimized. To assess system overhead, we used the same executables and workloads under both our kernel and the unmodified Mach kernel; three separate runs were performed for each experiment. Overall, we found that the overhead imposed by our prototype lottery scheduler is comparable to that of the standard Mach timesharing policy. Since numerous optimizations could be made to our list-based lottery, simple currency conversion scheme, and other untuned aspects of our implementation, efficient lottery scheduling does not pose any challenging problems.

Our first experiment consisted of three Dhrystone benchmark tasks running concurrently for 200 seconds. Compared to unmodified Mach, 2.7% fewer iterations were ex-

ecuted under lottery scheduling. For the same experiment with eight tasks, lottery scheduling was observed to be 0.8% slower. However, the standard deviations across individual runs for unmodified Mach were comparable to the absolute differences observed between the kernels. Thus, the measured differences are not very significant.

We also ran a performance test using the multithreaded database server described in Section 5.3. Five client tasks each performed 20 queries, and the time between the start of the first query and the completion of the last query was measured. We found that this application executed 1.7% faster under lottery scheduling. For unmodified Mach, the average run time was 1155.5 seconds; with lottery scheduling, the average time was 1135.5 seconds. The standard deviations across runs for this experiment were less than 0.1% of the averages, indicating that the small measured differences are significant.[9]

6 Managing Diverse Resources

Lotteries can be used to manage many diverse resources, such as processor time, I/O bandwidth, and access to locks. Lottery scheduling also appears promising for scheduling communication resources, such as access to network ports. For example, ATM switches schedule virtual circuits to determine which buffered cell should next be forwarded. Lottery scheduling could be used to provide different levels of service to virtual circuits competing for congested channels. In general, a lottery can be used to allocate resources wherever queueing is necessary for resource access.

6.1 Synchronization Resources

Contention due to synchronization can substantially affect computation rates. Lottery scheduling can be used to control the relative waiting times of threads competing for lock access. We have extended the Mach CThreads library to support a lottery-scheduled mutex type in addition to the standard mutex implementation. A lottery-scheduled mutex has an associated *mutex currency* and an *inheritance ticket* issued in that currency.

All threads that are blocked waiting to acquire the mutex perform ticket transfers to fund the mutex currency. The mutex transfers its inheritance ticket to the thread which currently holds the mutex. The net effect of these transfers is that a thread which acquires the mutex executes with its own funding plus the funding of all waiting threads, as depicted in Figure 10. This solves the priority inversion problem [Sha90], in which a mutex owner with little funding could execute very slowly due to competition with other threads

---

[9]Under unmodified Mach, threads with equal priority are run round-robin; with lottery scheduling, it is possible for a thread to win several lotteries in a row. We believe that this ordering difference may affect locality, resulting in slightly improved cache and TLB behavior for this application under lottery scheduling.

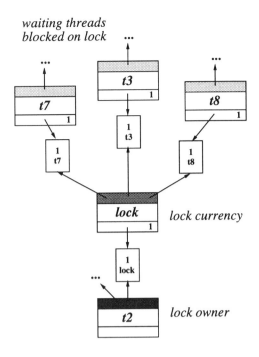

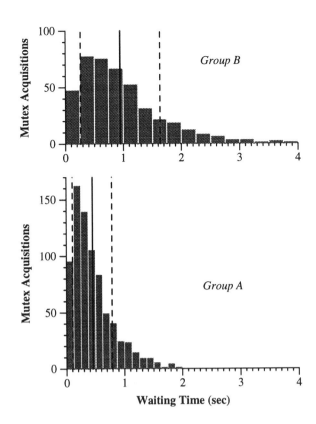

Figure 10: **Lock Funding.** Threads *t3*, *t7*, and *t8* are waiting to acquire a lottery-scheduled lock, and have transferred their funding to the lock currency. Thread *t2* currently holds the lock, and inherits the aggregate waiter funding through the backing ticket denominated in the lock currency. Instead of showing the backing tickets associated with each thread, shading is used to indicate relative funding levels.

Figure 11: **Mutex Waiting Times.** Eight threads compete to acquire a lottery-scheduled mutex. The threads are divided into two groups (A, B) of four threads each, with the ticket allocation $A : B = 2 : 1$. For each histogram, the solid line indicates the mean (μ); the dashed lines indicate one standard deviation about the mean ($\mu \pm \sigma$). The ratio of average waiting times is $A : B = 1 : 2.11$; the mutex acquisition ratio is $1.80 : 1$.

for the processor, while a highly funded thread remains blocked on the mutex.

When a thread releases a lottery-scheduled mutex, it holds a lottery among the waiting threads to determine the next mutex owner. The thread then moves the mutex inheritance ticket to the winner, and yields the processor. The next thread to execute may be the selected waiter or some other thread that does not need the mutex; the normal processor lottery will choose fairly based on relative funding.

We have experimented with our mutex implementation using a synthetic multithreaded application in which n threads compete for the same mutex. Each thread repeatedly acquires the mutex, holds it for h milliseconds, releases the mutex, and computes for another t milliseconds. Figure 11 provides frequency histograms for a typical experiment with $n = 8$, $h = 50$, and $t = 50$. The eight threads were divided into two groups (A, B) of four threads each, with the ticket allocation $A : B = 2 : 1$. Over the entire two-minute experiment, group A threads acquired the mutex a total of 763 times, while group B threads completed 423 acquisitions, for a relative throughput ratio of $1.80 : 1$. The group A threads had a mean waiting time of $\mu = 450$ milliseconds , while the group B threads had a mean waiting time of $\mu = 948$ milliseconds, for a relative waiting time

ratio of $1 : 2.11$. Thus, both throughput and response time closely tracked the specified $2 : 1$ ticket allocation.

6.2 Space-Shared Resources

Lotteries are useful for allocating indivisible time-shared resources, such as an entire processor. A variant of lottery scheduling can efficiently provide the same type of probabilistic proportional-share guarantees for finely divisible space-shared resources, such as memory. The basic idea is to use an *inverse lottery*, in which a "loser" is chosen to relinquish a unit of a resource that it holds. Conducting an inverse lottery is similar to holding a normal lottery, except that inverse probabilities are used. The probability p that a client holding t tickets will be selected by an inverse lottery with a total of n clients and T tickets is $p = \frac{1}{n-1}(1 - t/T)$. Thus, the more tickets a client has, the more likely it is to avoid having a unit of its resource revoked.[10]

For example, consider the problem of allocating a physical page to service a virtual memory page fault when all

---

[10]The $\frac{1}{n-1}$ factor is a normalization term which ensures that the client probabilities sum to unity.

physical pages are in use. A proportional-share policy based on inverse lotteries could choose a client from which to select a victim page with probability proportional to both $(1 - t/T)$ and the fraction of physical memory in use by that client.

6.3 Multiple Resources

Since rights for numerous resources are uniformly represented by lottery tickets, clients can use quantitative comparisons to make decisions involving tradeoffs between different resources. This raises some interesting questions regarding application funding policies in environments with multiple resources. For example, when does it make sense to shift funding from one resource to another? How frequently should funding allocations be reconsidered?

One way to abstract the evaluation of resource management options is to associate a separate *manager* thread with each application. A manager thread could be allocated a small fixed percentage (*e.g.*, 1%) of an application's overall funding, causing it to be periodically scheduled while limiting its overall resource consumption. For inverse lotteries, it may be appropriate to allow the losing client to execute a short manager code fragment in order to adjust funding levels. The system should supply default managers for most applications; sophisticated applications could define their own management strategies. We plan to explore these preliminary ideas and other alternatives for more complex environments with multiple resources.

7 Related Work

Conventional operating systems commonly employ a simple notion of *priority* in scheduling tasks. A task with higher priority is given absolute precedence over a task with lower priority. Priorities may be static, or they may be allowed to vary dynamically. Many sophisticated priority schemes are somewhat arbitrary, since priorities themselves are rarely meaningfully assigned [Dei90]. The ability to express priorities provides absolute, but extremely crude, control over scheduling, since resource rights do not vary smoothly with priorities. Conventional priority mechanisms are also inadequate for insulating the resource allocation policies of separate modules. Since priorities are absolute, it is difficult to compose or abstract inter-module priority relationships.

Fair share schedulers allocate resources so that users get fair machine shares over long periods of time [Hen84, Kay88]. These schedulers monitor CPU usage and dynamically adjust conventional priorities to push actual usage closer to entitled shares. However, the algorithms used by these systems are complex, requiring periodic usage updates, complicated dynamic priority adjustments, and administrative parameter setting to ensure fairness on a time scale of minutes. A technique also exists for achieving service rate objectives in systems that employ *decay-*

usage scheduling by manipulating base priorities and various scheduler parameters [Hel93]. While this technique avoids the addition of feedback loops introduced by other fair share schedulers, it still assumes a fixed workload consisting of long-running compute-bound processes to ensure steady-state fairness at a time scale of minutes.

Microeconomic schedulers [Dre88, Fer88, Wal92] use auctions to allocate resources among clients that bid monetary funds. Funds encapsulate resource rights and serve as a form of priority. Both the *escalator algorithm* proposed for uniprocessor scheduling [Dre88] and the distributed *Spawn* system [Wal89, Wal92] rely upon auctions in which bidders increase their bids linearly over time. The *Spawn* system successfully allocated resources proportional to client funding in a network of heterogeneous workstations. However, experience with *Spawn* revealed that auction dynamics can be unexpectedly volatile. The overhead of bidding also limits the applicability of auctions to relatively coarse-grain tasks.

A market-based approach for memory allocation has also been developed to allow memory-intensive applications to optimize their memory consumption in a decentralized manner [Har92]. This scheme charges applications for both memory *leases* and I/O capacity, allowing application-specific tradeoffs to be made. However, unlike a true market, prices are not permitted to vary with demand, and ancillary parameters are introduced to restrict resource consumption [Che93].

The *statistical matching* technique for fair switching in the AN2 network exploits randomness to support frequent changes of bandwidth allocation [And93]. This work is similar to our proposed application of lottery scheduling to communication channels.

8 Conclusions

We have presented lottery scheduling, a novel mechanism that provides efficient and responsive control over the relative execution rates of computations. Lottery scheduling also facilitates modular resource management, and can be generalized to manage diverse resources. Since lottery scheduling is conceptually simple and easily implemented, it can be added to existing operating systems to provide greatly improved control over resource consumption rates. We are currently exploring various applications of lottery scheduling in interactive systems, including graphical user interface elements. We are also examining the use of lotteries for managing memory, virtual circuit bandwidth, and multiple resources.

Acknowledgements

We would like to thank Kavita Bala, Eric Brewer, Dawson Engler, Wilson Hsieh, Bob Gruber, Anthony Joseph, Frans Kaashoek, Ulana Legedza, Paige Parsons, Patrick

Sobalvarro, and Debby Wallach for their comments and assistance. Special thanks to Kavita for her invaluable help with Mach, and to Anthony for his patient critiques of several drafts. Thanks also to Jim Lipkis and the anonymous reviewers for their many helpful suggestions.

References

[Acc86]   M. Accetta, R. Baron, D. Golub, R. Rashid, A. Tevanian, and M. Young. "Mach: A New Kernel Foundation for UNIX Development," *Proceedings of the Summer 1986 USENIX Conference*, June 1986.

[And93]   T. E. Anderson, S. S. Owicki, J. B. Saxe, and C. P. Thacker. "High-Speed Switch Scheduling for Local-Area Networks," *ACM Transactions on Computer Systems*, November 1993.

[Car90]   D. G. Carta. "Two Fast Implementations of the 'Minimal Standard' Random Number Generator," *Communications of the ACM*, January 1990.

[Che93]   D. R. Cheriton and K. Harty. "A Market Approach to Operating System Memory Allocation," Working Paper, Computer Science Department, Stanford University, June 1993.

[Com94]   C. L. Compton and D. L. Tennenhouse. "Collaborative Load Shedding for Media-based Applications," *Proceedings of the International Conference on Multimedia Computing and Systems*, May 1994.

[Dei90]   H. M. Deitel. *Operating Systems*, Addison-Wesley, 1990.

[Dre88]   K. E. Drexler and M. S. Miller. "Incentive Engineering for Computational Resource Management" in *The Ecology of Computation*, B. Huberman (ed.), North-Holland, 1988.

[Dui90]   D. Duis and J. Johnson. "Improving User-Interface Responsiveness Despite Performance Limitations," *Proceedings of the Thirty-Fifth IEEE Computer Society International Conference (COMPCON)*, March 1990.

[Fer88]   D. Ferguson, Y. Yemini, and C. Nikolaou. "Microeconomic Algorithms for Load-Balancing in Distributed Computer Systems," *International Conference on Distributed Computer Systems*, 1988.

[Har92]   K. Harty and D. R. Cheriton. "Application-Controlled Physical Memory using External Page-Cache Management," *Fifth International Conference on Architectural Support for Programming Languages and Operating Systems*, October 1992.

[Hel93]   J. L. Hellerstein. "Achieving Service Rate Objectives with Decay Usage Scheduling," *IEEE Transactions on Software Engineering*, August 1993.

[Hen84]   G. J. Henry. "The Fair Share Scheduler," *AT&T Bell Laboratories Technical Journal*, October 1984.

[Hog88]   T. Hogg. Private communication (during *Spawn* system development), 1988.

[Kan89]   G. Kane. *Mips RISC Architecture*, Prentice-Hall, 1989.

[Kay88]   J. Kay and P. Lauder. "A Fair Share Scheduler," *Communications of the ACM*, January 1988.

[Loe92]   K. Loepere. *Mach 3 Kernel Principles*. Open Software Foundation and Carnegie Mellon University, 1992.

[Par88]   S. K. Park and K. W. Miller. "Random Number Generators: Good Ones Are Hard to Find," *Communications of the ACM*, October 1988.

[Pre88]   W. H. Press, B. P. Flannery, S. A. Teukolsky, and W. T. Vetterling. *Numerical Recipes in C: The Art of Scientific Computing*. Cambridge University Press, Cambridge, 1988.

[Sha90]   L. Sha, R. Rajkumar, and J. P. Lehoczky. "Priority Inheritance Protocols: An Approach to Real-Time Synchronization," *IEEE Transactions on Computers*, September 1990.

[Tri82]   K. S. Trivedi. *Probability and Statistics with Reliability, Queuing, and Computer Science Applications*. Prentice-Hall, 1982.

[Wal89]   C. A. Waldspurger. "A Distributed Computational Economy for Utilizing Idle Resources," Master's thesis, MIT, May 1989.

[Wal92]   C. A. Waldspurger, T. Hogg, B. A. Huberman, J. O. Kephart, and W. S. Stornetta. "Spawn: A Distributed Computational Economy," *IEEE Transactions on Software Engineering*, February 1992.

[Wei84]   R. P. Weicker. "Dhrystone: A Synthetic Systems Programming Benchmark," *Communications of the ACM*, October 1984.

[Wei91]   W. Weihl, E. Brewer, A. Colbrook, C. Dellarocas, W. Hsieh, A. Joseph, C. Waldspurger, and P. Wang. "Prelude: A System for Portable Parallel Software," Technical Report MIT/LCS/TR-519, MIT Lab for Computer Science, October 1991.

A Random Number Generator

This MIPS assembly-language code [Kan89] is a fast implementation of the Park-Miller pseudo-random number generator [Par88, Car90]. It uses the multiplicative linear congruential generator $S' = (A \times S) \bmod (2^{31} - 1)$, for $A = 16807$. The generator's ANSI C prototype is: `unsigned int fastrand(unsigned int s).`

```
fastrand:
    move    $2, $4            | R2 = S (arg passed in R4)
    li      $8, 33614         | R8 = 2 × constant A
    multu   $2, $8            | HI, LO = A × S
    mflo    $9                | R9 = Q = bits 00..31 of A × S
    srl     $9, $9, 1
    mfhi    $10               | R10 = P = bits 32..63 of A × S
    addu    $2, $9, $10       | R2 = S' = P + Q
    bltz    $2, overflow      | handle overflow (rare)
    j       $31               | return (result in R2)

overflow:
    sll     $2, $2, 1         | zero bit 31 of S'
    srl     $2, $2, 1
    addiu   $2, 1             | increment S'
    j       $31               | return (result in R2)
```

Scheduling for Reduced CPU Energy

Mark Weiser, Brent Welch, Alan Demers, Scott Shenker

Xerox PARC
3333 Coyote Hill Road
Palo Alto, CA 94304
{weiser,welch,demers,shenker}@parc.xerox.com

Abstract

The energy usage of computer systems is becoming more important, especially for battery operated systems. Displays, disks, and cpus, in that order, use the most energy. Reducing the energy used by displays and disks has been studied elsewhere; this paper considers a new method for reducing the energy used by the cpu. We introduce a new metric for cpu energy performance, millions-of-instructions-per-joule (MIPJ). We examine a class of methods to reduce MIPJ that are characterized by dynamic control of system clock speed by the operating system scheduler. Reducing clock speed alone does not reduce MIPJ, since to do the same work the system must run longer. However, a number of methods are available for reducing energy with reduced clock-speed, such as reducing the voltage [Chandrakasan *et al* 1992][Horowitz 1993] or using reversible [Younis and Knight 1993] or adiabatic logic [Athas *et al* 1994].

What are the right scheduling algorithms for taking advantage of reduced clock-speed, especially in the presence of applications demanding ever more instructions-per-second? We consider several methods for varying the clock speed dynamically under control of the operating system, and examine the performance of these methods against workstation traces. The primary result is that by adjusting the clock speed at a fine grain, substantial CPU energy can be saved with a limited impact on performance.

1 Introduction

The energy use of a typical laptop computer is dominated by the backlight and display, and secondarily by the disk. Laptops use a number of techniques to reduce the energy consumed by disk and display, primarily by turning them off after a period of no use [Li 1994][Douglis 1994]. We expect slow but steady progress in the energy consumption of these devices. Smaller computing devices often have no disk at all, and eliminate the display backlight that consumes much of the display-related power. Power consumed by the CPU is significant; the Apple Newton designers sought to maximize MIPS per WATT [Culbert 1994]. This paper considers some methods of reducing the energy used for executing instructions. Our results go beyond the simple power-down-when-idle techniques used in today's laptops.

We consider the opportunities for dynamically varying chip speed and so energy consumption. One would like to give users the appearance of a 100MIPS cpu at peak moments, while drawing much less than 100MIPS energy when users are active but would not notice a reduction in clock rate. Knowing when to use full power and when not requires the cooperation of the operating system scheduler. We consider a number of algorithms by which the operating system scheduler could attempt to optimize system power by monitoring idle time and reducing clock speed to reduce idle time to a minimum. We simulate their performance on some traces of process scheduling and compare these results to the theoretical optimum schedules.

2 An Energy Metric for CPUS

In this paper we use as our measure of the energy performance of a computer system the MIPJ, or millions of instructions per joule. MIPS/WATTS = MIPJ. (Of course MIPS have been superseded by better metrics, such as Specmark: we are using MIPS to stand for any such workload-per-time benchmark). MIPJ is not improving that much for high-end processors. For example, a 1984 2-MIPS 68020 consumed 2.0 watts (at 12.5Mhz), for a MIPJ of 1, and a 1994 200-MIPS Alpha chip consumes 40 watts, so has a MIPJ of 5. However, more recently lower speed processors used in laptops have been optimized to run at low power. For example, the Motorola 68349 is rated at 6 MIPS and consumes 300 mW for 20 MIPJ.

Other things being equal, MIPJ is unchanged by changes in clock speed. Reducing the clock speed causes a linear reduction in energy consumption, but a similar reduction in MIPS. The two effects cancel. Similarly, turning the computer off, or reducing the clock to zero in the "idle-loop", does not effect MIPJ, since no instructions are being executed. However, a reduced clock speed creates the opportunity for quadratic energy savings; as the clock speed is reduced by n, energy per cycle can be reduced by n^2. Three methods that achieve this are voltage reduction, reversible logic, and adiabatic switching. Our simulations assume n^2 savings, although it is really only important that the energy savings be greater than the amount by which the clock rate is reduced in order to achieve an increase in MIPJ.

Voltage reduction is currently the most promising way to save energy. Already chips are being manufactured to run at 3.3 or 2.2 volts instead of the 5.0 voltage levels commonly used. The intuition behind the power savings comes from the basic energy equation that is proportional to the square of the voltage.

$$E/clock \propto V^2$$

The settling time for a gate is proportional to the voltage; the lower the voltage drop across the gate, the longer the gate takes to stabilize. To lower the voltage and still operate correctly, the cycle time must be lowered first. When raising the clock rate, the voltage must be increased first. Given that the voltage and the cycle time of a chip could be adjusted together, it should be clear now that the lower-voltage, slower-clock chip will dissipate less energy per cycle. If the voltage level can be reduced linearly as the clock rate is reduced, then the energy savings per instruction will be proportional to the square of the voltage reduction. Of course, for a real chip it may not be possible to reduce the voltage linear with the clock reduction. However, if it is possible to reduce the voltage at all by running slower, then there will be a net energy savings per cycle.

Currently manufacturers do not test and rate their chips across a smooth range of voltages. However, some data is available for chips at a set of voltage levels. For example, a Motorola CMOS 6805 microcontroller (cloned by SGS-Thomson) is rated at 6 Mhz at 5.0 Volts, 4.5 Mhz at 3.3 Volts, and 3 Mhz at 2.2 Volts. This is a close to linear relationship between voltage and clock rate.

The other important factor is the time it takes to change the voltage. The frequency for voltage regulators is on the order of 200 KHz, so we speculate that it will take a few tens of microseconds to boost the voltage on the chip.

Finally, why run slower? Suppose a task has a deadline in 100 milliseconds, but it will only take 50 milliseconds of CPU time when running at full speed to complete. A normal system would run at full speed for 50 milliseconds, and then idle for 50 milliseconds (assuming there were no other ready tasks). During the idle time the CPU can be stopped altogether by putting it into a mode that wakes up upon an interrupt, such as from a periodic clock or from an I/O completion. Now, compare this to a system that runs the task at half speed so that it completes just before its deadline. If it can also reduce the voltage by half, then the task will consume 1/4 the energy of the normal system, even taking into account stopping the CPU during the idle time. This is because the same number of cycles are executed in both systems, but the modified system reduces energy use by reducing the operating voltage. Another way to view this is that idle time represents wasted energy, even if the CPU is stopped!

3 Approach of This Paper

This paper evaluates the fine grain control of CPU clock speed and its effect on energy use by means of trace-driven simulation. The trace data shows the context switching activity of the scheduler and the time spent in the idle loop. The goals of the simulation are to evaluate the energy savings possible by running slower (and at reduced voltage), and to measure the adverse affects of running too slow to meet the supplied demand. No simulation is perfect, however, and a true evaluation will require experiments with real hardware.

Trace data was taken from UNIX workstations over many hours of use by a variety of users. The trace data is described in Section 4 of the paper. The assumptions made by the simulations are described in Section 5. The speed adjustment algorithms are presented in Section 6. Section 7 evaluates the different algorithms on the basis of energy savings and a delay penalty function. Section 8 discusses future work, including some things we traced but did not fully utilize in our simulations. Finally, Section 9 provides our conclusions.

4 Trace Data

Trace data from the UNIX scheduler was taken from a number of workstations over periods of up to several hours during the working day. During these times the workloads included software development, documentation, e-mail, simulation, and other typical activities of engineering workstations. In addition, a few short traces were taken during specific workloads such as typing and scrolling through documents. Appendix I has a summary of the different traces we used.

Table 1: Trace Points

SCHED	Context switch away from a process
IDLE_ON	Enter the idle loop
IDLE_OFF	Leave idle loop to run a process
FORK	Create a new process
EXEC	Overlay a (new) process with another program
EXIT	Process termination
SLEEP	Wait on an event
WAKEUP	Notify a sleeping process

The trace points we took are summarized in Table 1. The idle loop events provide a view on how busy the machine is. The process information is used to classify different programs into foreground and background types. The sleep and wakeup events are used to deduce job ordering constraints.

In addition, the program counter of the call to sleep was recorded and kernel sources were examined to determine the nature of the sleep. The sleep events were classified into waits on "hard" and "soft" events. A hard event is something like a disk wait, in which a sleep is done in the kernel's biowait() routine. A soft event is something like a select that is done awaiting user input or a network request packet. The goal of this classification is to distinguish between idle time that can be eliminated by rescheduling (soft idle) and idle that is mandated by a wait on a device (hard idle).

Each trace record has a microsecond resolution time stamp. The trace buffer is periodically copied out of the kernel, compressed, and sent over the network to a central collection site. We used the trace data to measure the tracing overhead, and found it to range from 1.5% to 7% of the traced machine.

5 Assumptions of the Simulations

The basic approach of the simulations was to lengthen the runtime of individually scheduled segments of the trace in order to eliminate idle time. The trace period was divided into intervals of various lengths, and the runtime and idletime during that interval were used to make a speed adjustment decision. If there were excess cycles left over at the end of an interval because the speed was too slow, they were carried over into the next interval. This carry-over is used as a measure of the penalty from using the speed adjustment.

The ability to stretch runtime into idle periods was refined by classifying sleep events into "hard" and "soft" events. The point of the classification is to be fair about what idle time can be squeezed out of the simulated schedule by slowing down the processor. Obviously, running slower should not allow a disk request to be postponed until just before the request

completes in the trace. However, it is reasonable to slow down the response to a keystroke in an editor such that the processing of one keystroke finishes just before the next.

Our simulations did not reorder trace data events. We justify this by noting that only if the offered load is far beyond the capacity of the CPU will speed changes affect job ordering significantly. Furthermore, the CPU speed is ramped up to full speed as the offered load increases, so in times of high demand the CPU is running at the speed that matches the trace data.

In addition, we made the following assumptions:

The machine was considered to use no energy when idle, and to use energy/instruction in proportion to n^2 when running at a speed n, where n varies between 1.0 and a minimum relative speed. This is a bit optimistic because a chip will draw a small amount of power while in standby mode, and we might not get a one-to-one reduction in voltage to clock speed. However, the baseline power usages from running at full speed (reported as 1.0 in the graphs) also assume that the CPU is off during idle times.

It takes no time to switch speeds. This is also optimistic. In practice, raising the speed will require a delay to wait for the voltage to rise first, although we speculate that the delay is on the order of 10s of instructions (not 1000s).

After any 30 second period of greater than 90% idle we assumed that any laptop would have been turned off, and skipped simulating until the next 30 second period with less than 90% idle. This models the typical power saving features already present in portables. The energy savings reported below does not count these off periods.

There was assumed to be a lower bound to practical speed, either 0.2, 0.44 or 0.66, where 1.0 represents full speed. In 5V logic using voltage reduction for power savings, these correspond to 1.0 V, 2.2 V and 3.3V minimum voltage levels, respectively. The 1.0 V level is optimistic, while the 2.2 V and 3.3V levels are based on several existing low power chips. In the graphs presented in section 7, the minimum voltage of the system is indicated, meaning that the voltage can vary between 5.0 V and the minimum, and the speed will be adjusted linearly with voltage.

6 Scheduling Algorithms

We simulated three types of scheduling algorithms: unbounded-delay perfect-future (OPT), bounded-delay limited-future (FUTURE), and bounded-delay limited-past (PAST). Each of these algorithms adjust the CPU clock speed at the same time that scheduling decisions are made, with the goal of decreasing time wasted in the idle loop while retaining interactive response.

OPT takes the entire trace, and stretches all the run times to fill in the idle times. Periods when the machine was "off" (more that 90% idle over 30 seconds) were not considered available for stretching runtimes into. This is a kind of batch approach to the work seen in the trace period: as long as all that work is done in that period, any piece can take arbitrarily long. OPT power savings were almost always limited by the minimum speed, achieving the maximum possible savings over the period. This algorithm is both impractical and undesirable. It is impractical because it requires perfect future knowledge of the work to be done over the interval. It also assumes that all idle time can be filled by stretching runlengths and reordering jobs. It is undesirable because it produces large delays in runtimes of individual jobs without regard to the need for effective response to real-time events like user keystrokes or network packets.

FUTURE is like OPT, except it peers into the future only a small window, and optimizes energy over that window, while never delaying work past the window. Again, it is assumed that all idle time in the next interval can be eliminated, unless the minimum speed of the CPU is reached. We simulated windows as small as 1 millisecond, where savings are usually small, and as large as 400 seconds, where FUTURE generally approaches OPT in energy savings. FUTURE is impractical, because it uses future knowledge, but desirable, because no realtime response is ever delayed longer than the window.

By setting a window of 10 to 50 milliseconds, user interactive response will remain high. In addition, a window this size will not substantially reduce a very long idle time, one that would trigger the spin down of a disk or the blanking of a display. Those decisions are based on idle times of many seconds or a few minutes, so stretching a computation out by a few tens of milliseconds will not affect them.

PAST is a practical version of FUTURE. Instead of looking a fixed window into the future it looks a fixed window into the past, and assumes the next window will be like the previous one. The PAST speed setting algorithm is shown at the top of the next column.

There are four parts to the code. The first part computes the percent of time during the interval when the

Speed Setting Algorithm (PAST)

`run_cycles` is the number of non-idle CPU cycles in the last interval.

`idle_cycles` is the idle CPU cycles, split between hard and soft idle time.

`excess_cycles` is the cycles left over from the previous interval because we ran too slow. All these cycles are measured in time units.

```
idle_cycles = hard_idle + soft_idle;
run_cycles += excess_cycles;
run_percent = run_cycles /
   (idle_cycles + run_cycles);

next_excess = run_cycles -
   speed * (run_cycles + soft_idle)
IF excess_cycles < 0. THEN
   excess_cycles = 0.

energy = (run_cycles - excess_cycles) *
   speed * speed;

IF excess_cycles > idle_cycles THEN
   newspeed = 1.0;
ELSEIF run_percent > 0.7 THEN
   newspeed = speed + 0.2;
ELSEIF run_percent < 0.5 THEN
   newspeed = speed -
      (0.6 - run_percent);

IF newspeed > 1.0 THEN
   newspeed = 1.0;
IF newspeed < min_speed THEN
   newspeed = min_speed;

speed = newspeed;
excess_cycles = next_excess;
```

CPU was running. The `run_cycles` come from two sources, the runtime in the trace data for the interval, and the `excess_cycles` from the simulation of the previous interval.

The `excess_cycles` represents a carry over from the previous interval because the CPU speed was set too slow to accommodate all the load that was supplied during the interval. Consider:

```
next_excess = run_cycles -
   speed * (run_cycles + soft_idle)
```

The `run_cycles` is the sum of the cycles presented by the trace data and the previous value of `excess_cycles`. This initial value is reduced by the soft idle time and the number of cycles actually performed at the current speed. This calculation represents the ability to squeeze out idle time by lengthening the runtimes in the interval. Only "soft" idle, such as waiting for keyboard events, is available for elimination of idle. As the soft idle time during an interval approaches zero, the excess cycles approach:

```
run_cycles * (1 - oldspeed)
```

The energy used during the interval is computed based on an n^2 relationship between speed and power consumption per cycle. The cycles that could not be serviced during the interval have to be subtracted out first. They will be accounted for in the next interval, probably at a higher CPU speed.

The last section represents the speed setting policy. The adjustment of the clock rate is a simple heuristic that attempts to smooth the transitions from fast to slow processing. If the system was more busy than idle, then the speed is ramped up. If it was mostly idle, then it is slowed down. We simulated several variations on the code shown here to come up with the constants shown here.

7 Evaluating the Algorithms

Figure 1 compares the results of these three algorithms on a single trace (Kestrel March 1) as the adjustment interval is varied. The OPT energy is unaffected by the interval, but is shown for comparison. The vertical access shows relative power used by the scheduling algorithms, with 1.0 being full power. Three sets of three lines are shown, corresponding to three voltage levels which determine the minimum speed, and the three algorithms, OPT, FUTURE, and PAST. The PAST and FUTURE algorithms approach OPT as the interval is lengthened. (Note that the log scale for the X axis.) For the same interval PAST actually does better than FUTURE because it is allowed to defer excess cycles into the next interval, effectively lengthening the interval. The intervals from 10 msec to 50 msec are considered in more detail in other figures.

Figure 2 shows the excess cycles that result from setting the speed too slow in PAST when using a 20 msec adjustment interval and the same trace data as Figure 1. Note that the graph uses log-log scales. Cycles are measured in the time it would take to execute them at full speed. The data was taken as a histogram, so a given point counts all the excess cycles that were less than or equal that point on the X axis, but greater than the previous bucket value in the histogram. Lines are used to connect the points so that the spike at zero is evident. The large spike at zero indicates that most intervals have no excess cycles at all. There is a smaller peak near the interval length, and then the values drop off.

As the minimum speed is lowered, there are more cases where excess cycles build up, and they can accumulate in longer intervals. This is evident Figure 2

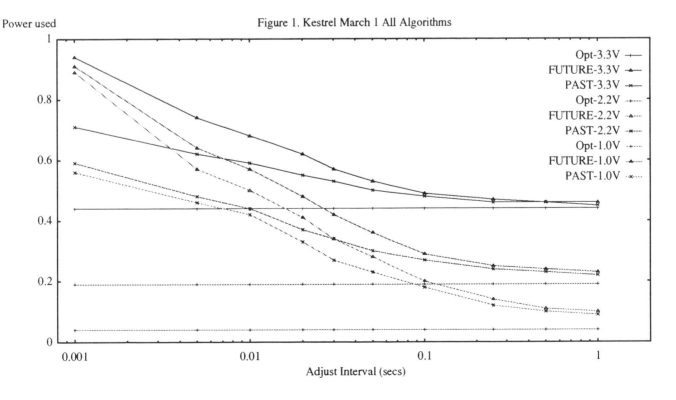

Figure 1. Kestrel March 1 All Algorithms

Power used

Adjust Interval (secs)

where the points for 1.0 V are above the others, which indicates more frequent intervals with excess cycles, and the peak extends to the right, which indicates longer excess cycle intervals.

Figure 3 shows the relationship between the interval length and the peak in excess cycle length. It compares the excess cycles with the same minimum voltage (2.2 V) while the interval length varies. This is from the same trace data as Figures 1 and 2. The main result here is that the peak in excess cycle lengths shifts right as the interval length increases. All this means is that as a longer scheduling interval is chosen, there can be more excess cycles built up.

Figure 4 compares the energy savings for the bounded delay limited past (PAST) algorithm with a 20 msec adjustment interval and with three different min-

imum voltage limits. In this plot each position on the X access represents a different set of trace data. The position corresponding to the trace data used in Figures 1 to 3 is indicated with the arrow.

While there is a lot of information in the graph, there are two overall points to get from the figure: the relative savings for picking different minimum voltages, and the overall possible savings across all traces.

The first thing to look for in Figure 4 is that for any given trace the three points show the relative possible energy savings for picking the three different minimum voltages. Interestingly, the 1.0 V minimum does not always result in the minimum energy. This is because it. has more of a tendency to fall behind (more excess cycles), so its speed varies more and the power consumption is less efficient. Even when 1.0 V does

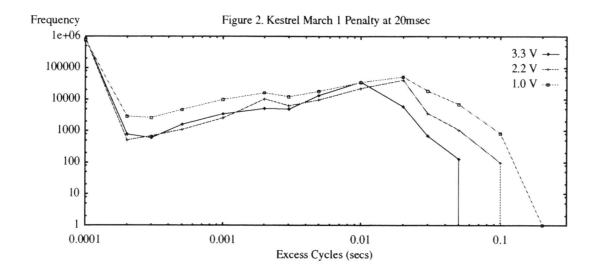

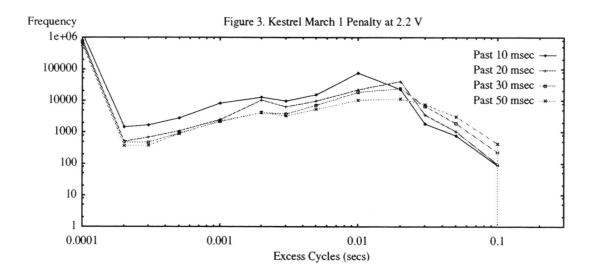

provide the minimum energy, the 2.2 V minimum is almost as good.

The other main point conveyed by Figure 4 is that in most of the traces the potential for energy savings is good. The savings range from about 5% to about 75%, with most data points falling between 25% to 65% savings.

Figure 5 fixes the minimum voltage at 2.2 V and shows the effect of changing the interval length. The OPT energy savings for 2.2 V is plotted for comparision. Again, each position on the X axis represents a different trace. The position corresponding to the trace data used in Figures 1 to 3 is indicated with the arrow.

In this figure the main message to get is the difference in relative savings for a given trace as the interval is varied. This is represented by the spread in the points plotted for each trace. A longer adjustment period results in more savings, which is consistent with Figure 1.

Figures 6 and 7 show the average excess cycles for all trace runs. These averages do not count intervals with zero excess cycles. Figure 6 shows the excess cycles at a given adjustment interval (20 msec) and different minimum voltages. Figure 7 shows the excess cycles at a given minimum voltage (2.2 V) and different intervals. Again, the lower minimum voltage

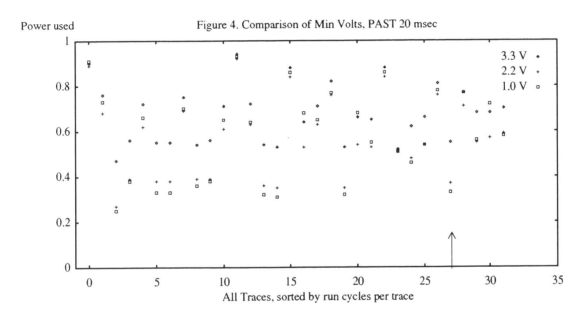

Figure 4. Comparison of Min Volts, PAST 20 msec

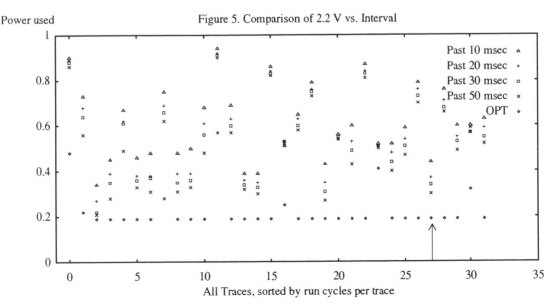

Figure 5. Comparison of 2.2 V vs. Interval

results show more excess cycles, and the longer intervals accumulate more excess cycles.

There is a trade off between the excess cycles penalty and the energy savings that is a function of the interval size. As the interval decreases, the CPU speed is adjusted at a finer grain and so it matches the offered load better. This results in fewer excess cycles, but it also does not save as much energy. This is consistent with the motivating observation that it is better to execute at an average speed than to alternate between full speed and full idle.

8 Discussion and Future Work

The primary source of feedback we used for the speed adjustment was the percent idle time of the system. Another approach is to classify jobs into background, periodic, and foreground classes. This is similar to what Wilkes proposes in his schemes to utilize idle time [Wilkes 95]. With this sort of classification the speed need not be ramped up when executing background tasks. Periodic tasks impose a constant, measurable load. They typically run for a short burst and then sleep for a relatively long time. With these tasks there is a well defined notion of "fast enough",

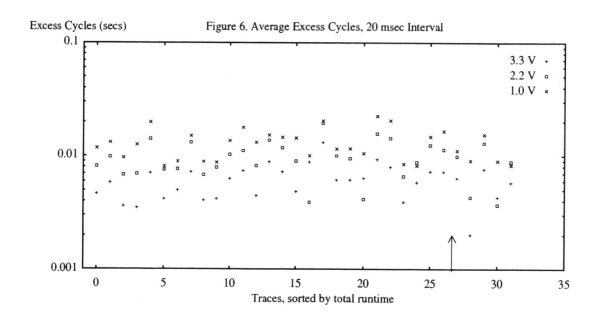

Figure 6. Average Excess Cycles, 20 msec Interval

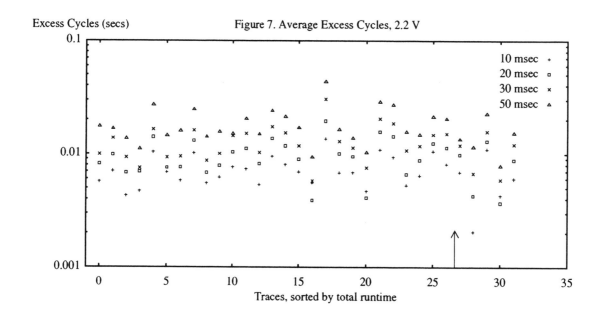

Figure 7. Average Excess Cycles, 2.2 V

and the CPU speed can be adjusted to finish these tasks just in time. When there is a combination of background, periodic, and foreground tasks, then the standard approach is to schedule the periodic tasks first, then fit in the foreground tasks, and lastly fit in the background tasks. In this case there would be a minimum speed that would always execute the periodic tasks on time, and the system would increase the speed in response to the presence of foreground and background tasks.

The simulations we performed are simplified by not reordering scheduling events. In a real rate-adjusting scheduler, the change in processing rates will have an effect on when jobs are preempted due to time slicing and the order that ready jobs are scheduled. We argue that unless there is a large job mix, then the reordering will not be that significant. Our speed adjustment algorithm will ramp up to full speed during heavy loads, and during light loads the reordering should not have a significant effect on energy.

In order to evaluate more realistic scheduling algorithms, it would be interesting to generate an abstract load for the simulation. This load includes CPU runs with preemption points eliminated, pause times due to I/O delays preserved, and causal ordering among jobs preserved. Given an abstract load, it would be possible to simulate a scheduler in more detail, giving us the ability to reorder preemption events while still preserving the semantics of I/O delays and IPC dependencies.

We have attempted to model the I/O waits by classifying idle time into "hard" and "soft" idle. We think this approximation is valid, but it would be good to verify it with a much more detailed simulation.

9 Conclusions

This paper presents preliminary results on CPU scheduling to reduce CPU energy usage, beyond the simple approaches taken by today's laptops. The metric of interest is how many instructions are executed for a given amount of energy, or MIPJ. The observation that motivates the work is that reducing the cycle time of the CPU allows for power savings, primarily by allowing the CPU to use a lower voltage. We examine the potential for saving power by scheduling jobs at different clock rates.

Trace driven simulation is used to compare three classes of schedules: OPT that spreads computation over the whole trace period to eliminate all idle time (regardless of deadlines), FUTURE that uses a limited future look ahead to determine the minimum clock

rate, and PAST that uses the recent past as a predictor of the future. A PAST scheduler with a 50 msec window shows power savings of up to 50% for conservative circuit design assumptions (e.g., 3.3 V), and up to 70% for more aggressive assumptions (2.2 V). These savings are in addition to the obvious savings that come from stopping the processor in the idle loop, and powering off the machine all together after extended idle periods.

The energy savings depends on the interval between speed adjustments. If it is adjusted at too fine a grain, then less power is saved because CPU usage is bursty. If it is adjusted at too coarse a grain, then the excess cycles built up during a slow interval will adversely affect interactive response. An adjustment interval of 20 or 30 milliseconds seems to represent a good compromise between power savings and interactive response.

Interestingly, having too low a minimum speed results in less efficient schedules because there is more of a tendency to have excess cycles and therefore the need to speed up to catch up. In particular, a minimum voltage of 2.2 V seems to provide most of the savings of a minimum voltage of 1.0 V. The 1.0 V system, however, tends to have a larger delay penalty as measured by excess cycles.

In general, scheduling algorithms have the potential to provide significant power savings while respecting deadlines that arise from human factors considerations. If an effective way of predicting workload can be found, then significant power can be saved by adjusting the processor speed at a fine grain so it is just fast enough to accommodate the workload. Put simply, the tortoise is more efficient than the hare: it is better to spread work out by reducing cycle time (and voltage) than to run the CPU at full speed for short bursts and then idle. This stems from the non-linear relationship between CPU speed and power consumption.

Acknowledgments

This work was supported in part by Xerox, and by ARPA under contract DABT63-91-C-0027; funding does not imply endorsement. David Wood of the University of Wisconsin helped us get started in this research, and provided substantial assistance in understanding CPU architecture. The authors benefited from the stimulating and open environment of the Computer Science Lab at Xerox PARC.

Appendix I. Description of Trace Data

The table on the next page lists the characteristics of the 32 traces runs that are reported in the figures. The table is sorted from shortest to longest runtime to match the ordering in Figures 4 through 7. The elapsed time of each trace is broken down into time spent running the CPU on behalf of a process (Runtime), time spent in the idle loop (IdleTime), and time when the machine is considered so idle that it would be turned off by a typical laptop power manager (Offtime). The short traces labeled mx, emacs, and fm are of typing (runs 1 and 2) and scrolling (run 3) in various editors. The remaining runs are taken over several hours of everyday use

References

William C. Athas, Jeffrey G. Koller, and Lars "J." Svensson. "An Energy-Efficient CMOS Line Driver Using Adiabatic Switching", 1994 IEEE Fourth Great Lakes Symposium on VLSI, pp. 196-199, March 1994.

A. P. Chandrakasan and S. Sheng and R. W. Brodersen. "Low-Power CMOS Digital Design". JSSC, V27, N4, April 1992, pp 473--484.

Michael Culbert, "Low Power Hardware for a High Performance PDA", *to appear* Proc. of the 1994 Computer Conference, San Francisco.

Fred Douglis, P. Krishnan, Brian Marsh, "Thwarting the Power-Hungry Disk", Proc. of Winter 1994 USENIX Conference, January 1994, pp 293-306

Mark A. Horowitz. "Self-Clocked Structures for Low Power Systems". ARPA semi-annual report, December 1993. Computer Systems Laboratory, Stanford University.

Kester Li, Roger Kumpf, Paul Horton, Thomas Anderson, "A Quantitative Analysis of Disk Drive Power Management in Portable Computers", Proc. of Winter 1994 USENIX Conference, January 1994, pp 279-292.

S. Younis and T. Knight. "Practical Implementation of Charge Recovering Asymptotically Zero Power CMOS." 1993 Symposium on Integrated Systems (C. Ebeling and G. Borriello, eds.), Univ. of Washington, 1993.

Wilkes, John "Idleness is not Sloth", *to appear*, proc. of the 1995 Winter USENIX Conf

Table 2: Summary of Trace Data

I	Trace	Runtime	Idle	Elapsed	Offtime
0	feb28klono	0.906	29.094	9H 24M 20S	33828.9
1	idle1	1.509	28.653	39S	9.05
2	heur1	7.043	3.103	10S	0
3	emacs2	7.585	31.719	40S	0
4	emacs1	8.060	32.273	40S	0
5	mx2	8.362	30.916	39S	0
6	mx1	9.508	30.871	41S	0
7	fm1	9.544	10.594	20S	0
8	em3	11.669	27.580	40S	0
9	fm2	16.679	23.770	41S	0
10	mx3	20.738	18.642	39S	0
11	feb28dekanore	30.548	541.045	9H 24M 40S	33307.8
12	fm3	30.626	9.942	41S	0
13	mar1klono	41.822	1011.251	9H 55M 46S	34690.6
14	feb28mezzo	61.940	449.717	9H 24M 20S	33346.1
15	mar1cleonie	214.656	1321.591	9H 50S	30913.0
16	feb28kestrel	510.259	3362.222	1H 4M 33S	0
17	feb28corvina	524.248	768.857	9H 24M 41S	32588.0
18	mar1mezzo	686.340	673.204	9H 55M 36S	34375.7
19	mar1egeus	695.409	4774.911	9H 55M 35S	30263.6
20	feb28ptarmigan	1497.908	2207.005	1H 1M 41S	0
21	feb28fandango	1703.037	3489.760	9H 24M 17S	28665.0
22	feb28zwilnik	4414.429	29448.058	9H 24M 21S	0
23	mar1zwilnik	4914.787	30823.917	9H 55M 38S	0
24	mar1kestrel	5135.297	30599.364	9H 55M 34S	0
25	feb28siria	6714.109	27146.678	9H 24M 20S	0
26	mar1siria	8873.114	26868.738	9H 55M 37S	0
27	feb28egeus	9065.477	13500.028	6H 16M 6S	0
28	mar1corvina	10898.545	24648.883	9H 55M 57S	210.202
29	mar1ptarmigan	12416.924	23319.178	9H 55M 34S	0
30	mar1fandango	20101.182	15638.594	9H 55M 38S	0
31	mar1dekanore	25614.651	14168.562	9H 55M 58S	7191.81

Storage Alternatives for Mobile Computers*

Fred Douglis[†]
AT&T Bell Laboratories

Ramón Cáceres
AT&T Bell Laboratories

Frans Kaashoek
Massachusetts Institute of Technology

Kai Li
Princeton University

Brian Marsh
D.E. Shaw & Co.

Joshua A. Tauber
Massachusetts Institute of Technology

Abstract

Mobile computers such as notebooks, subnotebooks, and palmtops require low weight, low power consumption, and good interactive performance. These requirements impose many challenges on architectures and operating systems. This paper investigates three alternative storage devices for mobile computers: magnetic hard disks, flash memory disk emulators, and flash memory cards.

We have used hardware measurements and trace-driven simulation to evaluate each of the alternative storage devices and their related design strategies. Hardware measurements on an HP OmniBook 300 highlight differences in the performance of the three devices as used on the Omnibook, especially the poor performance of version 2.00 of the Microsoft Flash File System [11] when accessing large files. The traces used in our study came from different environments, including mobile computers (Macintosh Power-Books) and desktop computers (running Windows or HP-UX), as well as synthetic workloads. Our simulation study shows that flash memory can reduce energy consumption by an order of magnitude, compared to magnetic disk, while providing good read performance and acceptable write performance. These energy savings can translate into a 22% extension of battery life. We also find that the amount of unused memory in a flash memory card has a substantial impact on energy consumption, performance, and endurance: compared to low storage utilizations (40% full), running flash memory near its capacity (95% full) can increase energy consumption by 70–190%, degrade write response time by 30%, and decrease the lifetime of the memory card by up to a third. For flash disks, asynchronous erasure can improve write response time by a factor of 2.5.

1 Introduction

Mobile computer environments are different from traditional workstations because they require light-weight, low-cost, and low-power components, while still needing to provide good interactive performance. A principal design challenge is to make the storage system meet these conflicting requirements.

Current storage technologies offer two alternatives for file storage on mobile computers: magnetic hard disks and flash memory. Hard disks provide large capacity at the lowest cost, and have high throughput for large transfers. The main disadvantage is that they consume a lot of energy and take seconds to spin up and down. Flash memory consumes relatively little energy, and has low latency and high throughput for read accesses. The main disadvantages of flash memory are that it costs more than disks—$30–50/Mbyte, compared to $1–5/Mbyte for magnetic disks—and that it requires erasing before it can be overwritten. It comes in two forms: flash memory cards (accessed as main memory) and flash disk emulators (accessed through a disk block interface).[1] These devices behave differently, having varying access times and bandwidths.

This paper investigates three storage systems: magnetic disk, flash disk emulator, and directly accessed flash memory. All of these systems include a DRAM file cache. Our study is based on both hardware measurements and trace-driven simulation. The measurements are "micro-benchmarks" that compare the raw performance of three different devices: a typical mobile disk drive (Western Digital Caviar Ultralite CU140), a flash disk (SunDisk 10-Mbyte SDP10 PCMCIA flash disk [21], sold as the Hewlett-Packard F1013A 10-Mbyte/12-V Flash Disk Card [6]), and a flash memory card (Intel 10-Mbyte Series-2 flash memory card [8]). The measurements provide a baseline comparison of the different architectures and are used as device specifications within the simulator. They also point out specific performance issues, particularly with the Microsoft Flash File System (MFFS) version 2.00 [11].

---

*This work was performed at Panasonic Technologies, Inc.'s Matsushita Information Technology Laboratory.

[†]Email: douglis@research.att.com

[1]In this paper, we use *flash disk* to refer to block-accessed flash disk emulators. We use *flash (memory) card* to refer to byte-accessible flash devices. When we wish to refer to the generic memory device or either of the above devices built with it, we refer to *flash memory* or a *flash device*. Note that the flash disk is actually a flash memory card as well, but with a different interface.

Flash memory is significantly more expensive than magnetic disks, but our simulation results show that flash memory can offer energy reduction by an order of magnitude over disks—even with aggressive disk spin-down policies that save energy at the cost of performance [5, 13]. Since the storage subsystem can consume 20–54% of total system energy [13, 14], these energy savings can as much as double battery lifetime. Flash provides better read performance than disk, but worse average write performance. The maximum delay for magnetic disk reads or writes, however, is much higher than maximum flash latency due to the overhead of occasional disk spin-ups.

We also show that the key to file system support using flash memory is erasure management. With a flash card, keeping a significant portion of flash memory free is essential to energy conservation and performance. With a flash disk, decoupling write and erase latency can improve average write response by a factor of 2.5.

In total, our paper uses both hardware measurements and simulation to contribute two key results: a quantitative comparison of the alternatives for storage on mobile computers, taking both energy and performance into account, and an analysis of techniques that improve on existing systems.

The rest of this paper is organized as follows. The next section discusses the three storage architectures in greater detail. Section 3 describes the hardware microbenchmarks. Section 4 describes our traces and the simulator used to perform additional studies. After that come the results of the simulations. Section 6 discusses related work, and Section 7 concludes.

2 Architectural Alternatives

The three basic storage architectures we studied are magnetic disks, flash disk emulators, and flash memory cards. Their power consumption, cost, and performance are a function of the workload and the organization of the storage components. Each storage device is used in conjunction with a DRAM buffer cache. Though the buffer cache can in principle be write-back, in this paper we consider a write-through buffer cache: this models the behavior of the Macintosh operating system and until recently the DOS file system.

An idle disk can consume 20–54% or more of total system energy [13, 14], so the file system must spin down the disk whenever it is idle. Misses in the buffer cache will cause a spun-down disk to spin up again, resulting in delays of up to a few seconds [5, 13]. Writes to the disk can be buffered in battery-backed SRAM, not only improving performance, but also allowing small writes to a spundown disk to proceed without spinning it up. The Quantum Daytona is an example of a drive with this sort of buffering. In this paper, we give magnetic disks the benefit of the doubt by simulating this deferred spin-up policy except where noted.

The flash disk organization replaces the hard disk with a flash memory card that has a conventional disk interface. With the SunDisk SDP series, one example of this type of device, transfers are in multiples of a sector (512 bytes). In contrast, the flash card organization removes the disk interface so that the memory can be accessed at byte-level. The flash card performs reads faster than the flash disk, so although the instantaneous power consumption of the two devices during a read is comparable, the flash card consumes less energy to perform the operation.

A fundamental problem introduced by flash memory is the need to *erase* an area before it can be overwritten. The flash memory manufacturer determines how much memory is erased in a single operation. The SunDisk devices erase a single 512-byte sector at a time, while the Intel Series-2 flash card erases one or two 64-Kbyte "segments." There are two important aspects to erasure: *flash cleaning* and performance. When the segment size is larger than the transfer unit (i.e., for the flash card), any data in the segment that are still needed must be copied elsewhere. Cleaning flash memory is thus analogous to segment cleaning in Sprite LFS [19]. The cost and frequency of segment cleaning is related in part to the cost of erasure, and in part to the segment size. The larger the segment, the more data that will likely have to be moved before erasure can take place. The system must define a policy for selecting the next segment for reclamation. One obvious discrimination metric is segment utilization: picking the next segment by finding the one with the lowest utilization (i.e., the highest amount of memory that is reusable). MFFS uses this approach [4]. More complicated metrics are possible; for example, eNVy considers both utilization and locality when cleaning flash memory [24].

The second aspect to erasure is performance. The SunDisk SDP flash disks couple erasure with writes, achieving a write bandwidth of 75 Kbytes/s. The time to erase and write a block is dominated by the erasure cost. The Intel flash card separates erasure from writing, and achieves a write bandwidth of 214 Kbytes/s—but only after a segment has been erased. Because erasure takes a large fixed time period (1.6s) regardless of the amount of data being erased [8], the cost of erasure is amortized over large erasure units. (The newer 16-Mbit Intel Series 2+ Flash Memory Cards erase blocks in 300ms [9], but these were not available to us during this study.) The two types of flash memory have comparable erasure bandwidth; to avoid delaying writes for erasure it is important to keep a pool of erased memory available. It becomes harder to meet this goal as more of the flash card is occupied by useful data, as discussed in Section 5.2.

Another fundamental problem with flash memory is its limited endurance. Manufacturers guarantee that a particular area within flash may be erased up to a certain number of times before defects are expected. The limit is 100,000 cycles for the devices we studied; the Intel Series

2+ Flash Memory Cards guarantee one million erasures per block [9]. While it is possible to spread the load over the flash memory to avoid "burning out" particular areas, it is still important to avoid unnecessary writes or situations that erase the same area repeatedly.

3 Hardware Measurements

We measured the performance of the three storage organizations of interest on a Hewlett-Packard OmniBook 300. The OmniBook 300 is a 2.9-pound subnotebook computer that runs MS-DOS 5.0 and contains a 25-MHz 386SXLV processor and 2 Mbytes of DRAM. The system is equipped with several PCMCIA slots, one of which normally holds a removable ROM card containing Windows and several applications. We used a 40-Mbyte Western Digital Caviar Ultralite CU140 and a 10-Mbyte SunDisk SDP10 flash disk, both of which are standard with the OmniBook, and a PCM-CIA 10-Mbyte Intel Series 2 Flash Memory Card running the Microsoft Flash File System [11]. The Caviar Ultralite CU140 is compatible with PCMCIA Type III specifications, and weighs 2.7 ounces, while the flash devices are PCMCIA Type II cards weighing 1.3 ounces. Thus one may consider two 10-Mbyte flash devices as equivalent in size and weight to a single 40-Mbyte hard disk. However, in our simulations we treated the flash devices as though they too stored 40 Mbytes, since their capacities are increasingly rapidly and the difference in energy consumption and performance between individual flash devices of different capacities using the same technology are minimal. Cost does scale with capacity, of course, and must be taken into account. Finally, the CU140 and SDP10 could be used directly or with compression, using DoubleSpace and Stacker, respectively. Compression is built into MFFS 2.00.

We constructed software benchmarks to measure the performance of the three storage devices. The benchmarks repeatedly read and wrote a sequence of files, and measured the throughput obtained. Both sequential and random accesses were performed, the former to measure maximum throughput and the latter to measure the overhead of seeks. For the CU140 and SDP10, we measured throughput with and without compression enabled; for the Intel card, compression was always enabled, but we distinguished between completely random data and compressible data. The compressible data consisted of the first 2 Kbytes of Herman Melville's well-known novel, *Moby-Dick*, repeated throughout each file (obtaining compression ratios around 50%). The Intel flash card was completely erased prior to each benchmark to ensure that writes from previous runs would not cause excess cleaning.

Table 1 summarizes the measured performance for 4-Kbyte reads and writes to 4-Kbyte and 1-Mbyte files, while Figure 1 graphs the average latency and instantaneous throughput for 4-Kbyte writes to a 1-Mbyte file. These numbers all include DOS file system overhead. There are

several interesting points to this data:

- Without compression, throughput for the magnetic disk increases with file size, as expected. With compression, small writes go quickly, because they are buffered and written to disk in batches. Large writes are compressed and then written synchronously.

- Compression similarly helps the performance of small file writes on the flash disk, resulting in write throughput greater than the theoretical limit of the SunDisk SDP10.

- Read throughput of the flash card is much better than the other devices for small files, with reads of uncompressible data obtaining about twice the bandwidth of reads of compressible data (since the software decompression step is avoided). Throughput is unexpectedly poor for reading or writing large files. This is due to an anomaly in MFFS 2.00[11], whose performance degrades with file size. The latency of each write (Figure 1(a)) increases linearly as the file grows, apparently because data already written to the flash card are written again, even in the absence of cleaning. This results in the throughput curve in Figure 1(b).

Comparing the different devices, it is obvious that the Caviar Ultralite CU140 provides the best write throughput, since the disk is constantly spinning; excluding the effects of compression, the flash card provides better performance than the flash disk for small files on an otherwise empty card, while its read and write performance are both worse than the flash disk for larger files.

In Table 2 we include the raw performance of the devices, and power consumed, according to datasheets supplied by the manufacturers. As shown, the hard disk offers the best throughput of the three technologies, but consumes many times the power of the flash-based technologies. With regard to the two flash-based devices, the flash card offers better performance than the flash disk, while both devices offer comparable power consumption.

4 Trace-Driven Simulation

We used traces from several environments to do trace-driven simulation, in order to evaluate the performance and energy consumption of different storage organizations and different storage management policies under realistic workloads. This section describes the traces and the simulator, while Section 5 describes the simulation results.

4.1 Traces

We used four workloads, MAC, PC, HP, and SYNTH. For the MAC trace, we instrumented a pair of Apple Macintosh PowerBook Duo 230s to capture file system workloads from a mobile computing environment. The traces are file-level: they report which file is accessed, whether the operation is a read or write, the location within the file, the size

Device	Operation	Throughput (Kbytes/s) Uncompressed		Throughput (Kbytes/s) Compressed	
		4–Kbyte file	1–Mbyte file	4–Kbyte file	1–Mbyte file
Caviar Ultralite CU140	Read	116	543	64	543
	Write	76	231	289	146
SunDisk SDP10	Read	280	410	218	246
	Write	39	40	225	35
Intel flash card	Read	645	37	345	34
	Write	43	21	83	27

Table 1: Measured performance of three storage devices on an HP OmniBook 300.

Device	Operation	Latency (ms)	Throughput (Kbytes/s)	Power (W)
Caviar Ultralite CU140	Read/Write	25.7	2125	1.75
	Idle	—	—	0.7
	Spin up	1000.0	—	3.0
SunDisk SDP10	Read	1.5	600	0.36
	Write	1.5	50	0.36
Intel flash card	Read	0	9765	0.47
	Write	0	214	0.47
	Erase	1600	70	0.47

Table 2: Manufacturers' specifications for three storage devices. Latency for read/write operations indicates the overhead from a random operation, excluding the transfer itself (i.e., controller overhead, seeking, or rotational latency). The Intel erasure cost refers to a separate operation that takes 1.6s to erase 64 or 128 Kbytes (in this case latency and throughput are analogous).

of the transfer, and the time of the access. This trace did not record deletions. The traces were preprocessed to convert file-level accesses into disk-level operations, by associating a unique disk location with each file.

We used DOS traces collected by Kester Li at U.C. Berkeley [12], on IBM desktop PCs running Windows 3.1, also at file-level. They include deletions. The traces were similarly preprocessed.

We used disk-level traces collected by Ruemmler and Wilkes on an HP workstation running HP-UX [20]. These traces include metadata operations, which the file-level traces do not, but they are below the level of the buffer cache, so simulating a buffer cache would give misleading results (locality within the original trace has already been largely eliminated). Thus the buffer cache size was set to 0 for simulations of HP. The trace includes no deletions.

Finally, we created a synthetic workload, called SYNTH, based loosely on the *hot-and-cold* workload used in the evaluation of Sprite LFS cleaning policies [19]. The purpose of the synthetic workload was to provide both a "stress test" for the experimental testbed on the OmniBook, and a series of operations that could be executed against both the testbed and the simulator. (Unfortunately, none of our other traces accessed a small enough dataset to fit on a 10-Mbyte flash device.) The comparison between measured and simulated results appears in Section 5.1. The trace consists of 6 Mbytes of 32-Kbyte files, where $\frac{7}{8}$ of the accesses go to $\frac{1}{8}$ of the data. Operations are divided 60% reads, 35% writes, 5% erases. An erase operation deletes an entire file; the

next write to the file writes an entire 32-Kbyte unit. Otherwise 40% of accesses are 0.5 Kbytes in size, 40% are between .5 Kbytes and 16 Kbytes, and 20% are between 16 Kbytes and 32 Kbytes. The interarrival time between operations was modeled as a bimodal distribution with 90% of accesses having a uniform distribution with a mean of 10ms and the remaining accesses taking 20ms plus a value that is exponentially distributed with a mean of 3s.

Though only the MAC trace comes from a mobile environment, the two desktop traces represent workloads similar to what would be used on mobile computers, and have been used in simulations of mobile computers in the past [12, 13, 15]. Table 3 lists additional statistics for the nonsynthetic traces.

4.2 Simulator

Our simulator models a storage hierarchy containing a buffer cache and non-volatile storage. The buffer cache is the first level searched on a read and is the target of all write operations. The cache is write-through to non-volatile storage, which is typical of Macintosh and some DOS environments[2]. A write-back cache might avoid some erasures at the cost of occasional data loss. When the secondary store is magnetic disk, an intermediate level containing battery-backed SRAM can buffer writes; in this case, a write-through DRAM buffer cache especially makes sense, since writes to SRAM are fast. In addition, the buffer cache

---

[2]DOS supports a write-back cache, but after users complained about losing data, write-through caching became a user-configurable option.

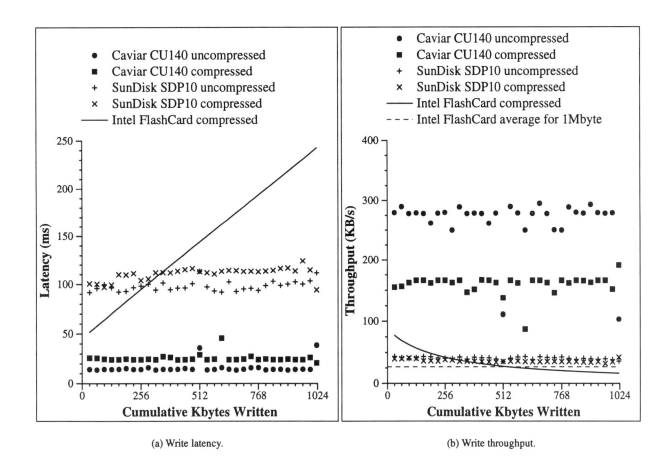

| (a) Write latency. | (b) Write throughput. |

Figure 1: Measured latency and instantaneous throughput for 4-Kbyte writes to a 1-Mbyte file. To smooth the latency when writing via DoubleSpace or Stacker, points were taken by averaging across 32-Kbytes of writes. Latency for an Intel flash card running the Microsoft Flash File System, as a function of cumulative data written, increases linearly. Though writes to the first part of the file are faster for the flash card than for the flash disk, the average throughput across the entire 1-Mbyte write is slightly worse for the flash card. The flash card was erased prior to each experiment. Also, because the CU140 was continuously accessed, the disk spun throughout the experiment.

can have zero size, in which case reads and writes go directly to non-volatile storage. A zero-sized buffer cache is applicable only to the HP-UX trace, which has an implicit buffer cache.

We simulated the disk, flash disk, and flash card devices with parameters for existing hard disk, flash memory disk emulator, and flash memory card products, respectively. Each device is described by a set of parameters that include the power consumed in each operating mode (reading, writing, idle, or sleeping) and the time to perform an operation or switch modes. The power specifications came from datasheets; two different set of performance specifications were used, one from the measured performance and one from datasheets.

In addition to the products described in Section 3, we used the datasheet for the NEC μPD4216160/L 16-Mbit DRAM chip [17]. In the case of the SunDisk device, the simulation using raw (nonmeasured) performance numbers is based upon the SunDisk SDP5 and SDP5A devices, which

are newer 5-volt devices [3]. Lastly, we also simulated the Hewlett-Packard Kittyhawk 20-Mbyte hard disk, which we refer to as KH, based on its datasheet [7]. In order to manage all the traces, we simulated flash devices larger than the 10-Mbyte PCMCIA flash devices we had for the Omni-Book. Based on the characteristics of different-sized Intel flash cards, the variation in power and performance among flash cards of different size are insignificant.

For each trace, 10% of the trace was processed in order to "warm" the buffer cache, and statistics were generated based on the remainder of the trace.

The simulator accepts a number of additional parameters. Those relevant to this study are:

Flash size	The total amount of flash memory available.
Flash segment size	The size of an erasure unit.
Flash utilization	The amount of data stored, relative to flash size. The data

	MAC			DOS			HP		
Applications	Finder, Excel, Newton Toolkit			Framemaker, Powerpoint, Word			email, editing		
Duration	3.5 hours			1.5 hours			4.4 days		
Number of distinct Kbytes accessed	22000			16300			32000		
Fraction of reads	0.50			0.24			0.38		
Block size (Kbytes)	1			0.5			1		
Mean read size (blocks)	1.3			3.8			4.3		
Mean write size (blocks)	1.2			3.4			6.2		
	Mean	Max	σ	Mean	Max	σ	Mean	Max	σ
Inter-arrival time (s)	0.078	90.8	0.57	0.528	713.0	10.8	11.1	30min	112.3

Table 3: Summary of (non-synthetic) trace characteristics. The statistics apply to the 90% of each trace that is actually simulated after the warm start. Note that it is not appropriate to compare performance or energy consumption of simulations of different traces, because of the different mean transfer sizes and durations of each trace.

are preallocated in flash at the start of the simulation, and the amount of data accessed during the simulation must be no greater than this bound.

Cleaning policy
On-demand cleaning, as with the SunDisk SDP5, and asynchronous cleaning, as with the Flash File System running on the Intel flash card. Flash cleaning is discussed in greater detail below.

Disk spin-down policy
A set of parameters control how the disk spins down when idle and how it spins up again when the disk is accessed.

DRAM size
The amount of DRAM available for caching.

We made a number of simplifying assumptions in the simulator:

- All operations and state transitions are assumed to take the average or "typical" time, either measured by us or specified by the manufacturer.

- Repeated accesses to the same file are assumed never to require a seek (if the transfer is large enough to require a seek even under optimal disk layout, the cost of the seek will be amortized); otherwise, an access incurs an average seek. Each transfer requires the average rotational latency as well. These assumptions are necessary because file-level accesses are converted to disk block numbers without the sophistication of a real file system that tries to optimize block placement.

- For flash file systems, while file data and metadata that would normally go on disk are stored in flash, the data structures for the flash memory itself are managed by the simulator but not explicitly stored in flash or DRAM. In the case of the SunDisk SDP5 flash device, there is no need for additional data structures beyond what the file system already maintains for a magnetic disk and the flash disk maintains internally for block remapping. For the Intel flash card, the flash metadata includes state that must be frequently rewritten, such as linked lists.

- For the flash card, the simulator attempts to keep at least one segment erased at all times, unless erasures are done on an as-needed basis. One segment is filled completely before data blocks are written to a new segment. Erasures take place in parallel with reads and writes, being suspended during the actual I/O operations, unless a write occurs when no segment has erased blocks.

5   Results

We used the simulator to explore the architectural trade-offs between disks, flash disks, and flash cards. We focussed on four issues: the basic energy and performance differences between the devices; the effect of storage utilization on flash energy consumption, performance, and endurance; the effect of combined writes and erasures on a flash disk; and the effect of buffer caches, both volatile and nonvolatile, on energy and performance.

5.1   Basic Comparisons

Tables 4(a)–(c) show for three traces and each device the energy consumed, and the average, mean, and standard deviations of the read and write response times. As mentioned in Section 4.2, the input parameters for each simula-

Device	Parameters	Energy (J)	Read Response (ms)			Write Response (ms)		
			Mean	Max	σ	Mean	Max	σ
CU140	measured	8,854	2.75	3535.3	50.5	0.93	3505.5	38.1
CU140	datasheet	8,751	2.04	3516.2	48.7	0.77	3493.6	37.8
KH	datasheet	9,945	8.70	1675.0	94.6	1.03	1536.2	30.2
SDP10	measured	1,516	0.50	1001.7	7.6	26.74	586.3	45.6
SDP5	datasheet	1,190	0.35	619.9	4.7	16.07	350.4	27.3
Intel flash card	measured	1,746	0.35	665.6	5.0	32.30	1787.9	78.8
Intel flash card	datasheet	888	0.12	105.2	0.9	5.65	147.3	9.9

(a) MAC trace

Device	Parameters	Energy (J)	Read Response (ms)			Write Response (ms)		
			Mean	Max	σ	Mean	Max	σ
CU140	measured	1,495	9.82	2746.1	58.7	0.42	5.6	0.4
CU140	datasheet	1,466	6.80	2717.6	57.4	0.42	5.6	0.4
KH	datasheet	1,786	17.35	1560.9	131.2	4.56	1476.5	77.3
SDP10	measured	733	2.94	120.2	5.6	36.60	317.6	19.7
SDP5	datasheet	606	1.98	77.5	3.6	21.88	190.6	11.8
Intel flash card	measured	731	1.96	80.8	3.8	38.41	939.0	21.5
Intel flash card	datasheet	451	0.51	17.0	0.8	7.85	459.7	5.2

(b) DOS trace

Device	Parameters	Energy (J)	Read Response (ms)			Write Response (ms)		
			Mean	Max	σ	Mean	Max	σ
CU140	measured	21,370	57.26	3537.4	145.3	30.46	3505.9	152.7
CU140	datasheet	20,659	38.65	3505.2	142.5	22.60	3475.1	151.6
KH	datasheet	28,887	81.96	1620.9	277.0	107.06	1552.9	362.2
SDP10	measured	4,972	10.50	40.4	6.9	138.96	5734.4	101.0
SDP5	datasheet	4,448	6.40	24.9	4.2	82.80	3412.5	60.1
Intel flash card	measured	3,865	6.58	24.8	4.4	155.52	7143.9	182.7
Intel flash card	datasheet	2,167	0.42	1.6	0.3	36.72	1922.9	118.5

(c) HP trace

Table 4: Comparison of energy consumption and response time for different devices, using the MAC, DOS, and HP traces. There was a 2-Mbyte DRAM buffer for MAC and DOS but no DRAM buffer cache in the HP simulations. Disk simulations spun down the disk after 5s of inactivity. Flash simulations were done with flash memory 80% utilized.

tion were either based on measurements on the OmniBook (labeled "measured") or manufacturers' specifications (labeled "datasheet"). Note that it is not appropriate to compare response time numbers between the tables, because of the different mean transfer sizes of each trace. Simulations of the magnetic disks spun down the disk after 5s of inactivity, which is a good compromise between energy consumption and response time [5, 13]. Simulations using the flash card were done with the card 80% full.

Based solely on the input parameters from the datasheets, one may conclude that the Intel flash card consumes significantly less energy than either the Caviar Ultralite CU140 or the SunDisk SDP5. It provides better read performance than either of the other devices, and better write performance than the SunDisk SDP5, but much worse write performance than a Caviar Ultralite CU140 or KH with an SRAM write buffer. This latter discrepancy suggests that an SRAM write buffer is appropriate for flash memory as well, something that we have not explored so far but that is an integral part of the eNVy architecture [24].

When using the numbers for measured performance as input to the simulator, the flash card does not perform as well as the flash disk. In particular, its write performance is worse than the simulated write performance based on the SunDisk SDP10, across all three traces. This discrepancy suggests that when choosing between a flash disk emulator and a flash memory card, one must consider both the hardware and software characteristics of the environment.

We verified the simulator by running a 6-Mbyte synthetic trace both through the simulator and on the OmniBook, using each of the devices. The trace was smaller than the ones described above, in order to fit on the 10-Mbyte flash devices. We used the measured micro-benchmark performance to drive the simulator and then compared against actual performance. All simulated performance numbers were within a few percent of measured performance, with the exception of flash card reads and Caviar Ultralite CU140 writes. The measured mean performance for flash card reads was four times worse than the simulated performance; we believe this is due to overhead from cleaning and from decompression, which are more severe in practice than during the controlled experiments described in Section 3. Measured write performance for the CU140 was about twice as slow in practice as in simulation; we believe this is due to our optimistic assumption about avoiding seeks.

5.2 Flash Storage Utilization

For the Intel flash card, there is a substantial interaction between the storage utilization of flash memory and the behavior of the flash when the flash is frequently written. To examine this behavior, we simulated each trace with 40% to 95% of flash memory occupied by useful data. To do this, we set the size of the flash to be large relative to the size of the trace, then filled the flash with extra data blocks that reduced the amount of free space by an appropriate amount. Under low utilization, energy consumption and

performance are fairly constant, but as the flash fills the behavior of the flash degrades, resulting in much greater energy consumption, worse performance, and more erasures per unit time (thus affecting flash endurance). This is because the system must copy "live" data from one erasure unit to another to free up an entire erasure unit. By comparison, the flash disk is unaffected by utilization because it does not copy data within the flash.

Figure 2 graphs simulated energy consumption and write response time as a function of storage utilization for each trace, using the specifications from the Intel flash card datasheet and a 2-Mbyte DRAM cache (no DRAM cache for the HP trace). At a utilization of 95%, compared to 40% utilization, the energy consumption rises by up to 150%, while the average write time increases up to 30%. For the MAC trace, the maximum number of erasures for any one segment over the course of the simulation increases from 7 to 34, while the mean erasure count goes up from 0.9 to 1.9 (110%). For the HP trace the erasure count tripled. Thus higher storage utilizations can result in "burning out" the flash two to three times faster under this workload.

In addition, experiments on the OmniBook demonstrated significant reductions in write throughput as flash memory was increasingly full. Figure 3 graphs instantaneous throughput as a function of cumulative data written, with three amounts of "live" data in the file system: 1 Mbyte, 9 Mbytes, and 9.5 Mbytes. Each data point corresponds to 1 Mbyte of data being overwritten, randomly selected within the total amount of live data. The flash card was erased completely prior to each experiment, so that any cleaning overhead would be due only to writes from the current experiment and the experiments would not interfere with each other. The drop in throughput over the course of the experiment is apparent for all three configurations, even the one with only 10% space utilization, presumably because of MFFS 2.00 overhead. However, throughput decreased much faster with increased space utilization.

5.3 Asynchronous Cleaning

The next generation of SunDisk flash products, the SDP5A, will have the ability to erase blocks prior to writing them, in order to get higher bandwidth during the write [3]. Erasure bandwidth is 150 Kbytes/s regardless of whether new data are written to the location being erased; however, if an area has been pre-erased, it can be written at 400 Kbytes/s. We simulated to compare the SDP5A with and without asynchronous cleaning. Asynchronous cleaning has minimal impact on energy consumption, but it decreases the average write time for each of the traces by 56–61%.

The improvement experienced by asynchronous erasure on the SunDisk demonstrates the effect of small erasure units on performance. Considering again the simulated write response of the SunDisk SDP5 and Intel flash card shown in Tables 4(a)–(c), if the SunDisk SDP5 write response decreased by 60% it would be comparable to the flash card. But as storage utilization increases, flash card

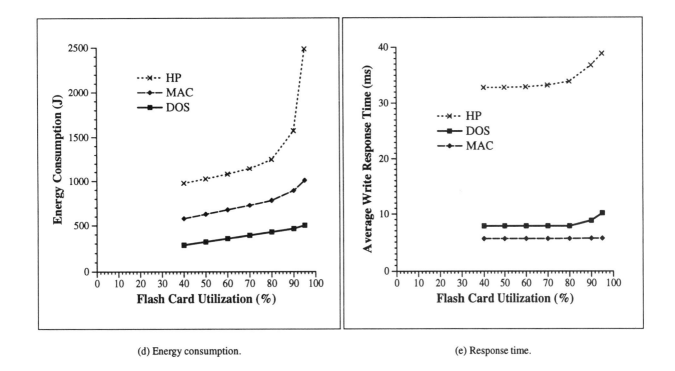

(d) Energy consumption.

(e) Response time.

Figure 2: Energy and write response time as a function of flash storage utilization, simulated based on the datasheet for the Intel flash card, with a segment size of 128 Kbytes. Each of the traces is shown. Energy consumption increases steadily for each of the traces, due to increased cleaning overhead, but the energy consumed by the HP trace increases the most dramatically with high utilization. Write response time holds steady until utilization is high enough for writes to be deferred while waiting for a clean segment; even so, the MAC trace has constant mean write response. It has a higher fraction of reads, so the cleaner keeps up with writes more easily. The size of the DRAM buffer cache was 2 Mbytes for MAC and DOS and no DRAM was used for HP.

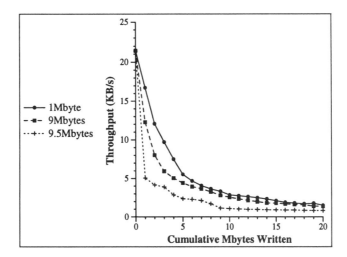

Figure 3: Measured throughput on an OmniBook using a 10-Mbyte Intel flash card, for each of 20 1-Mbyte writes (4 Kbytes at a time). Different curves show varying amounts of live data. Throughput drops both with more cumulative data and with more storage consumed.

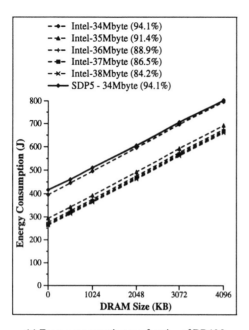

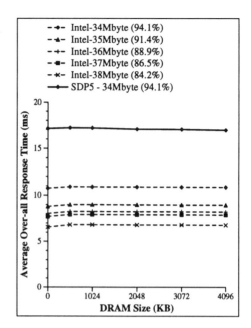

(a) Energy consumption as a function of DRAM size and flash size.

(b) Response time as a function of DRAM size and flash size.

Figure 4: Energy consumption and average over-all response time as a function of DRAM size and flash size, simulated for the DOS trace. We simulated multiple flash sizes for the Intel flash card, which shows a benefit once it gets below 80% utilization. Each line represents a 1-Mbyte differential in flash card size, similar to moving along the x-axis by 1 Mbyte of DRAM. Increasing the DRAM buffer size has no benefit for the Intel card. The SunDisk has no benefit due to increased flash size (not shown), and here for this trace it shows no benefit from a larger buffer cache either.

write performance will degrade although the performance of the flash disk will remain constant.

5.4 DRAM Caching

Since flash provides better read performance than disk, the dynamics of using DRAM for caching file data change. DRAM provides better performance than flash but requires more power and is volatile. Unlike flash memory, DRAM consumes significant energy even when not being accessed. Thus, while extremely "hot" read-only data should be kept in DRAM to get the best read performance possible, other data can remain in flash rather than DRAM. One may therefore ask whether it is better to spend money on additional DRAM or additional flash. In order to evaluate these trade-offs, we simulated configurations with varying amounts of DRAM buffer cache and flash memory. (As is the case with all our simulations, they do not take into account DRAM that is used for other purposes such as program execution.) We began with the premise that a system stored 32 Mbytes of data, not all of which necessarily would be accessed, and considered hypothetical flash devices storing from 34–38 Mbytes of data. (Thus total storage utilization ranged from 94% with 34 Mbytes of storage down to 84% with 38 Mbytes.) In addition, the system could have from 0–4 Mbytes of DRAM for caching.

Figure 4 shows the results of these simulations, run against the DOS trace using specifications from the datasheets. For the Intel flash card, increasing the amount of flash available by 1 Mbyte, thereby decreasing storage utilization from 94.1% to 91.4%, reduces energy consumption by 25% and average over-all response time by 18%. The incremental benefit on energy consumption of additional flash beyond the first Mbyte is minimal, though adding flash does help to reduce response time. Adding DRAM to the Intel flash card increases the energy used for DRAM without any appreciable benefits: the time to read a block from flash is barely more than the time to read it from DRAM.

Only one curve is shown for the SunDisk SDP5 because increasing the size of the flash disk has minimal effect on energy consumption or performance. In fact, for this trace, even a 500-Kbyte DRAM cache increases energy consumption for the SunDisk SDP5 without improving performance. With the MAC trace, which has a greater fraction of reads, a small DRAM cache improves energy consumption and performance for the SunDisk SDP5, while the Intel flash card shows a less pronounced benefit from lower utilization. Thus the trade-off between DRAM and flash size is dependent both on execution characteristics (read/write ratio) and hardware characteristics (the difference in performance between DRAM and the flash device).

5.5 NVRAM Caching

So far we have assumed that magnetic disks are configured with an SRAM write buffer that allows the disk to stay spun down if a small write is issued. In practice, SRAM write buffers for magnetic disks are relatively commonplace, though we are unaware of products other than the Quantum Daytona that use the write buffer to avoid spinning up an idle disk. Here we examine the impact of nonvolatile memory on write performance, the effects of deferring spin-up, and the cost-effectiveness of the write buffer. We base our results on a NEC 32Kx8-bit SRAM chip, part μPD43256B, with a 55ns access time [18]. We assume that writes to SRAM can be recovered after a crash, so synchronous writes that fit in SRAM are made asynchronous with respect to the disk.

A 32-Kbyte SRAM write buffer costs only a few dollars, which is a small part of the total cost of a disk system. Under light load, this buffer can make a significant difference in the average write response time, compared to a system that writes all data synchronously to disk. Although SRAM consumes significant energy itself, by reducing the number of times the disk spins up, the SRAM buffer can potentially conserve energy. However, if writes are large or are clustered in time, such that the write buffer frequently fills, then many writes will be delayed as they wait for the disk. In this case, a larger SRAM buffer will be necessary to improve performance, and it will cost more money and consume more energy.

Figure 5 graphs normalized energy consumption and write response time as a function of SRAM size for each of the traces. The values are normalized to the case without an SRAM buffer. As with the other experiments, DRAM was fixed at 2 Mbytes for MAC and DOS and not used for HP;[3] the spin-down threshold was fixed at 5s. For the first two traces, using a 32-Kbyte SRAM buffer improves average write response by a factor of 20 or more, with no difference from larger buffers; for the HP trace a 32-Kbyte buffer only halves the average write response time, but a 512-Kbyte buffer reduces it by another 20%. A small SRAM buffer reduces energy by a much less dramatic amount: 21% for the MAC trace, 15% for DOS, and just 4% for HP, with another 4% reduction with 512 Kbytes of SRAM.

6   Related Work

In addition to the specific work on flash file systems mentioned previously, the research community has begun to explore the use of flash memory as a substitute for, or an ad-

dition to, magnetic disks. Cáceres et al. proposed operating system techniques for exploiting the superior read performance of flash memory while hiding its poor write performance, particularly in a portable computer where all of DRAM is battery-backed [2]. Wu and Zwaenepoel discussed how to implement and manage a large non-volatile storage system, called eNVy, composed of NVRAM and flash memory for high-performance transaction processing. They simulated a system with Gbytes of flash memory and Mbytes of battery-backed SRAM, showing it could support the I/O corresponding to 30,000 transactions per second using the TPC-A database benchmark [23]. They found that at a utilization of 80%, 45% of the time is spent erasing or copying data within flash, while performance was severely degraded at higher utilizations [24]. Marsh et al. examined the use of flash memory as a cache for disk blocks to avoid accessing the magnetic disk, thus allowing the disk to be spun down more of the time [15]. SunDisk recently performed a competitive analysis of several types of flash memory on an HP Omnibook 300 and found that the Sun-Disk SDP5-10 flash disk emulator was nearly an order of magnitude faster than an Intel Flash card using version 2 of the Flash Files System [22]. They also found that performance of the Intel Flash card degraded by 40% as it filled with data, with the most noticeable degradation between 95% and 99% storage utilization.

Other researchers have explored the idea of using non-volatile memory to reduce write traffic to disk. Baker et al. found that some 78% of blocks written to disk were done so for reliability. They found that a small amount of NVRAM on each client was able to reduce client-server file write traffic by half, and NVRAM on the file server could reduce writes to disk by 20% [1]. However, the benefits of NVRAM for workstation clients did not justify its additional cost, which would be better applied toward additional DRAM. This contrasts with our results for a mobile environment, in which larger amounts of DRAM are not so cost effective, but a small amount of NVRAM helps energy consumption and performance. Ruemmler and Wilkes also studied how well NVRAM could absorb write traffic, finding that 4 Mbytes of NVRAM was sufficient to absorb 95% of all write traffic in the systems they traced [20].

Finally, segment cleaning in Rosenblum and Ouster-hout's Log-Structured File System (LFS) [19] has a number of similarities to flash cleaning when the flash segment size is a large multiple of the smallest block size. The purpose of Sprite LFS is to amortize write overhead by writing large amounts of data at once; to do so requires that large amounts of contiguous disk space be emptied prior to a write. However, cleaning in LFS is intended to amortize the cost of seeking between segments anywhere on the disk, while flash cleaning is a requirement of the hardware. Kawaguchi et al. [10] recently designed a flash memory file system for UNIX based on LFS, with performance comparable to the 4.4BSD Pageable Memory based File Sys-

---

[3] For this experiment, one should discount the result from the HP trace by comparison to the other two traces. This is because the HP simulation has no DRAM cache, so reads cause the disk to spin up more than with the other simulations (except those reads that are serviced from recent writes to SRAM). The effect of SRAM on energy and response time in the HP environment bears further study.

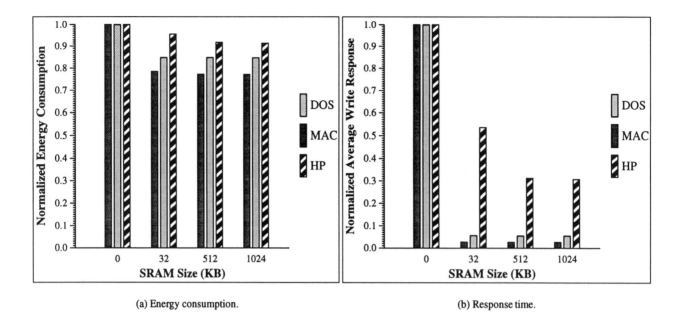

(a) Energy consumption.

(b) Response time.

Figure 5: Normalized energy and write response time as a function of SRAM size for each trace. Results are normalized to the value corresponding to no SRAM. While a 32-Kbyte SRAM write buffer improves energy and response time for each of the traces, the improvement is more significant for MAC and DOS than for HP. Only the HP trace significantly benefits from an SRAM cache larger than 32 Kbytes. Disks were spun down after 5s of inactivity. The size of the DRAM buffer cache was 2 Mbytes for MAC and DOS and and no DRAM was used for HP.

tem [16]. They found that cleaning overhead did not significantly affect performance, but they need more experience with cleaning under heavier loads.

7 Conclusions

In this paper we have examined three alternatives for file storage on mobile computers: a magnetic disk, a flash disk emulator, and a flash memory card. We have shown that either form of flash memory is an attractive alternative to magnetic disk for file storage on mobile computers. Flash offers low energy consumption, good read performance, and acceptable write performance.

The main disadvantage of using magnetic disk for file storage on mobile computers is its great energy consumption. To extend battery life, the power management of a disk file system spins down the disk when it is idle. But even with power management, a disk file system can consume an order of magnitude more energy than a file system using flash memory.

Our trace simulation results, using a SunDisk SDP5 and a Caviar Ultralite CU140, show that the flash disk file system can save 59–86% of the energy of the disk file system. It is 3–6 times faster for reads, but its mean write response is a minimum of four times worse. Adding a nonvolatile SRAM write buffer to a flash disk should enable it to compete with newer magnetic disks that are coupled with SRAM buffers.

The flash memory file system (using the Intel flash card) has the most attractive qualities with respect to energy and performance, though its price and capacity limitations are still drawbacks. Even in the presence of disk power management, the flash memory file system can save 90% of the energy of the disk file system, extending battery life by 20–100%. Furthermore, in theory the flash memory file system can provide mean read response time that is up to two orders of magnitude faster than the disk file system. However, its mean write response time varies from 50% to an order of magnitude worse than a CU140 magnetic disk with an SRAM write buffer. Again, adding SRAM to flash should dramatically improve performance, except in situations where flash performance is dominated by cleaning costs.

In practice, hardware measurements showed that there is a great discrepancy between the rated performance of each of the storage media and their performance in practice under DOS. This is especially true with the flash card using MFFS 2.00, whose write performance degrades linearly with the size of the file. Some of the differences in performance can be reduced with new technologies, in both hardware and software. One new technique is to separate the write and erase operations on a flash disk emulator, as the next generation of the SunDisk flash disk will allow. Another hardware technique is to allow erasure of more of a flash memory card in parallel, as the newer 16-

Mbit Intel flash devices allow [9]. Newer versions of the Microsoft Flash File System should address the degradation imposed by large files, and in order to take advantage of asynchronous flash disk erasure, file systems for mobile computers must treat the flash disk more like a flash card than like a magnetic disk.

Finally, in our simulation study, we found that the erasure unit of flash memory, which is fixed by the hardware manufacturer, can significantly influence file system performance. Large erasure units require a low space utilization. At 90% utilization or above, an erasure unit that is much larger than the file system block size will result in unnecessary copying, degrading performance, wasting energy, and wearing out the flash device. In our simulations, energy consumption rose by as much as 190%, the average write response increased up to 30%, and the rate of erasure as much as tripled. Flash memory that is more like the flash disk emulator, with small erasure units that are immune to storage utilization effects, will likely grow in popularity despite being at a disadvantage in basic power and performance.

Acknowledgments

We are grateful to P. Krishnan, who did much of the work on the storage simulator used in this study. We also thank W. Sproule and B. Zenel for their efforts in gathering trace data and/or hardware measurements. J. Wilkes at Hewlett-Packard and K. Li at U.C. Berkeley graciously made their file system traces available. Thanks to R. Alonso, M. Dahlin, C. Dingman, B. Krishnamurthy, P. Krishnan, D. Milojičić, C. Northrup, J. Sandberg, D. Stodolsky, B. Zenel, W. Zwaenepoel, and anonymous reviewers for comments on previous drafts. We thank the following persons for helpful information about their products: A. Elliott and C. Mayes of Hewlett-Packard; B. Dipert and M. Levy of Intel; and J. Craig, S. Gross, and L. Seva of SunDisk.

References

[1] Mary Baker, Satoshi Asami, Etienne Deprit, John Ousterhout, and Margo Seltzer. Non-volatile memory for fast, reliable file systems. In *Proceedings of the Fifth International Conference on Architectural Support for Programming Languages and Operating Systems*, pages 10–22, Boston, MA, October 1992. ACM.

[2] Ramón Cáceres, Fred Douglis, Kai Li, and Brian Marsh. Operating Systems Implications of Solid-State Mobile Computers. In *Proceedings of the Fourth Workshop on Workstation Operating Systems*, pages 21–27, Napa, CA, October 1993. IEEE.

[3] Jeff Craig, March 1994. Personal communication.

[4] Brian Dipert and Markus Levy. *Designing with Flash Memory*. Annabooks, 1993.

[5] Fred Douglis, P. Krishnan, and Brian Marsh. Thwarting the Power Hungry Disk. In *Proceedings of 1994 Winter USENIX Conference*, pages 293–306, San Francisco, CA, January 1994.

[6] Hewlett-Packard. *HP 100 and OmniBook Flash Disk Card User's Guide*, 1993.

[7] Hewlett-Packard. *Kittyhawk HP C3013A/C3014A Personal Storage Modules Technical Reference Manual*, March 1993. HP Part No. 5961-4343.

[8] Intel. *Mobile Computer Products*, 1993.

[9] Intel. *Flash Memory*, 1994.

[10] Atsuo Kawaguchi, Shingo Nishioka, and Hiroshi Motoda. A flash-memory based file system. In *Proceedings of the USENIX 1995 Winter Conference*, New Orleans, January 1995. To appear.

[11] Markus Levy. Interfacing Microsoft's Flash File System. In *Memory Products*, pages 4–318–4–325. Intel Corp., 1993.

[12] Kester Li. Towards a low power file system. Technical Report UCB/CSD 94/814, University of California, Berkeley, CA, May 1994. Masters Thesis.

[13] Kester Li, Roger Kumpf, Paul Horton, and Thomas Anderson. A Quantitative Analysis of Disk Drive Power Management in Portable Computers. In *Proceedings of the 1994 Winter USENIX*, pages 279–291, San Francisco, CA, 1994.

[14] B. Marsh and B. Zenel. Power Measurements of Typical Notebook Computers. Technical Report 110-94, Matsushita Information Technology Laboratory, May 1994.

[15] Brian Marsh, Fred Douglis, and P. Krishnan. Flash Memory File Caching for Mobile Computers. In *Proceedings of the 27th Hawaii Conference on Systems Sciences*, pages 451–460, Maui, HI, 1994. IEEE.

[16] Marshall Kirk McKusick, Michael J. Karels, and Keith Bostic. A pageable memory based file system. In *USENIX Conference Proceedings*, pages 137–144, Anaheim, CA, Summer 1990. USENIX.

[17] NEC. *Memory Products Data Book, Volume 1: DRAMS, DRAM Modules, Video RAMS*, 1993.

[18] NEC. *Memory Products Data Book, Volume 2: SRAMS, ASMs, EEPROMs*, 1993.

[19] Mendel Rosenblum and John Ousterhout. The design and implementation of a log-structured file system. *ACM Transactions on Computer Systems*, 10(1):26–52, February 1992. Also appears in Proceedings of the 13th Symposium on Operating Systems Principles, October 1991.

[20] Chris Ruemmler and John Wilkes. UNIX disk access patterns. In *Proceedings of the Winter 1993 USENIX Conference*, pages 405–420, San Diego, January 1993.

[21] SunDisk Corporation. *SunDisk SDP Series OEM Manual*, 1993.

[22] SunDisk Corporation, 3270 Jay Street, Santa Clara, CA 95054. *Competitive Analysis 80-40-00002 Rev. 1.0*, 1994.

[23] Transaction Processing Performance Council. *TPC Benchmark A Standard Specification Rev 1.1*.

[24] Michael Wu and Willy Zwaenepoel. eNVy: a Non-Volatile, main memory storage system. In *Proceedings of the Sixth International Conference on Architectural Support for Programming Languages and Operating Systems*, San Jose, CA, October 1994. To appear.

Opportunistic Log: Efficient Installation Reads
in a Reliable Storage Server

James O'Toole   Liuba Shrira

Laboratory for Computer Science
Massachusetts Institute of Technology
Cambridge, MA 02139 {james,liuba}@lcs.mit.edu

Abstract

In a distributed storage system, client caches managed on the basis of small granularity objects can provide better memory utilization then page-based caches. However, object servers, unlike page servers, must perform additional disk reads. These *installation reads* are required to install modified objects onto their corresponding disk pages. The *opportunistic log* is a new technique that significantly reduces the cost of installation reads. It defers the installation reads, removing them from the modification commit path, and manages a large pool of pending installation reads that can be scheduled efficiently.

Using simulations, we show that the opportunistic log substantially enhances the I/O performance of reliable storage servers. An object server without the opportunistic log requires much better client caching to outperform a page server. With an opportunistic log, only a small client cache improvement suffices.

Our results imply that efficient scheduling of installation reads can substantially improve the performance of large-scale storage systems and therefore introduces a new performance tradeoff between page-based and object-based architectures.

1 Introduction

A distributed storage system provides long-lived data objects accessed by clients over a network. As such systems scale to support many clients they tend to become I/O bound.

A fundamental design decision concerns the granularity of the data exported by the server to the clients. The server can export small-granularity *objects* (units semantically meaningful to the application), or it can export large fixed-size *pages* (the unit of disk transfer). The relative merits of this fundamental design choice are still the subject of debate [2, 3, 4, 7].

Client caches managed on the basis of small granularity objects can provide better memory utilization than page-based caches because pages are likely to include unneeded data that cannot be discarded from the cache [3, 4, 7, 14, 21]. On the other hand, object servers may need to do extra I/O when a modified object needs to be updated on disk. If the containing page is not in the object server cache, this page has to be read back from the disk. The modified object is then installed in the page, and the page can be written out. These extra *installation reads* do not happen in page servers because the whole page with the modified objects is sent back from the client.

We expect many object modifications to require installation reads in large-scale client-server storage systems. There will be many clients using the server, so the pages containing the combined working set of the clients will not fit inside of the server cache memory.

In this paper, we introduce a simple new approach for organizing I/O that substantially enhances the I/O performance of object servers. A standard technique to make updates atomic is to record them in a stable write-ahead log [10]. We keep this log of modifications in memory and defer installation reads from the commit path. This allows the accumulation of a large pool of pending installation reads that can be scheduled efficiently using well-known disk scheduling techniques [13, 25].

How does one evaluate the impact of scheduled installation reads on the overall performance of an object storage system? One way is to study how it affects the performance tradeoffs between object and page-based architectures. The comparison of the I/O performance of the object and page architectures depends crucially on the difference in how well the respective client caches perform. One extreme is if the loads generated by the client caches are exactly the same, in which case the page server has an advantage. At

This research was supported in part by the Advanced Research Projects Agency of the Department of Defense, monitored by the Office of Naval Research under contract N00014-91-J-4136, in part by the National Science Foundation under Grant CCR-8822158, and in part by the Department of the Army under Contract DABT63-92-C-0012.

the other extreme, if the object architecture makes the client cache more effective, this should decrease the server load, giving the advantage to the object server. Between these two extremes there is a break even point where the two systems have equivalent performance.

We construct a simple performance model that focuses on the I/O costs in object and page servers. Using simulations, we study the effect of scheduled installation reads on the break even point. The results show that when server I/O performance is a bottleneck our techniques have a dramatic effect on the competition between page servers and object servers. Without scheduled installation reads, break even requires a substantial improvement in the client cache performance. With our techniques only a small improvement suffices.

Although there exists substantial work on optimizing deferred writes [13, 20, 25], and read-ahead is used to optimize sequential reads, we are the first (to our knowledge) to take advantage of the opportunity to optimize the installation reads that are important in object servers. We think that file systems could also benefit from optimized installation reads when performing updates to file system meta-data and very small files. Conventional file systems do perform installation reads in these and other situations, but because they do not have a log they cannot defer the installation reads and schedule them efficiently.

Previous studies [2, 7] compared the communication and concurrency control cost of page-based and object-based architectures. Our study is the first to identify the fundamental I/O performance tradeoff between the efficiency of object cache and the cost of installation reads. Our results imply that efficient scheduling of installation reads can substantially improve the performance of large-scale object systems, and hence, our techniques affect the performance tradeoffs between page-based and object-based architectures.

In the following sections, we introduce the basic reliable object server design (Section 2) and describe the opportunistic log design (Section 3). We then describe our experimental setup, presenting the experimental server configurations and the simulation model (Section 4). We present simulation results that illustrate the value of our techniques (Section 5). Finally, we discuss related research (Section 6) and our conclusions (Section 7).

2 Reliable Object Servers

This section introduces the basic design of a reliable object server. A reliable object server provides transactional updates to persistent objects. Objects managed by the server are grouped into *pages* on disk. Objects are small, and a single page can contain many objects. Pages are the unit of disk transfer and caching at the server. We assume that objects on disk are updated in place.[1]

For concreteness in this presentation, we assume optimistic concurrency control and in-memory commit. These features of our object server architecture are derived from the Thor [17] persistent object system. Nevertheless, we believe that the new technique we are proposing is independent of these two assumptions.

Fetching

Clients fetch objects to a local client cache as objects are read, update objects in their cache as they are written, and send back updated objects in a commit request to the server. To improve performance, the client prefetches objects. We assume for simplicity that the prefetching unit is the page containing the object that the client is reading.

Committing

The clients and the server together execute a concurrency control and cache consistency protocol that ensures all transactions are serializable and all client caches are "almost" up-to-date. Since we use an optimistic concurrency control scheme, a client transaction may read an out-of-date value, in which case it will be aborted by the server when it sends its commit request. We assume the need to abort is detected at the server using a validation phase that does not require any disk accesses; see Adya [1] for the details.

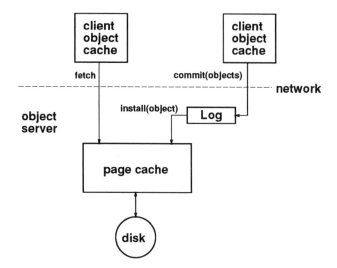

Figure 1: Clients using an object-based server.

When the client sends a commit request, the server records a commit record in a stable log, as shown in Figure 1. The commit record contains the objects modified by the client. A client's transaction is considered committed once its commit entry is present in the log.

---

[1] An alternative log-structured disk organization for objects would also be possible and is considered by Ghemawat [9].

Installing

After a transaction commits, modifications from the log are applied to the appropriate pages; we call this update process *installation*. Note that an install may require a disk read if the page to be updated is not currently cached. This is an important point, and throughout the paper we are careful to distinguish between disk reads initiated by a client fetch request and reads initiated by an install in the object server. Installs are synchronized with fetch requests, to ensure that fetches retrieve the current committed object state.

Writing

Installations modify pages in the cache, but the dirty pages are not immediately written to disk. We assume that dirty pages are accumulated to permit efficient disk arm scheduling when writing.

3 The Opportunistic Log

We suggest that the server may substantially improve disk I/O performance by opportunistically choosing log entries for installation. We expect opportunistic log processing to reduce the disk I/O requirements of an object server in several ways. The benefits of this method may be so substantial as to justify allocating a large fraction of server primary memory to the log.

When an updated object is to be installed onto its containing page, that page must be read from the disk if it is not already in the server cache. Installation reads can represent a significant source of disk load in an object server (see Section 4). By delaying the installation and performing installation reads opportunistically on the basis of disk head position, we can expect to dramatically reduce the expected cost of an installation read.

There is substantial previous work on delayed processing of disk write operations [13, 25]. Some methods applied to delayed disk writes involve writing pages at new locations [5, 8, 22] and would not work with disk reads. However, standard disk scheduling methods based on head position apply equally well to read operations. In particular, Seltzer et. al. [25] have shown that when a pool of 1000 operations is available, greedy algorithms can reduce the cost of individual operations to a fraction of the normal random-access cost.

3.1 Basic Tradeoffs

In addition to reducing the *cost* of installation reads, we expect to reduce the *number* of installation reads. With enough object modifications waiting in the log, there will sometimes be multiple object modifications that belong in the same page. In this case, by installing these modifications together, only a single installation read will be required. It might even make sense to preferentially choose installation reads that will combine multiple pending log entries in this way.

An installation read will also be avoided when a client fetch operation requires a fetch read of a page for which there exists a pending installation. Note however, that such a fetching read needs to be serviced right away since the client is waiting for it, and cannot benefit as much from efficient disk arm scheduling. This indicates that when a large fraction of the installation reads is avoided by preceding fetch reads, the benefit of scheduling installations is reduced.

In these examples, the installation reads are being avoided when installations occur nearby in time to each other or to a fetch request involving the same disk page. Even without opportunistic log processing, the cache memory in the server would help avoid installation reads when temporal locality is present. However, the object modification log should enlarge the window of opportunity for exploiting temporal locality because the log can store modified objects more compactly than the page cache.

However, there is a tradeoff between allocating memory to the page cache and allocating it to the log. The page cache provides a pool of dirty pages for writing and the log provides a pool of dirty objects that require installation reads. These disk operations will have lower individual costs when a larger pool of candidate operations is available to the scheduler. If too much memory is allocated to one pool, then the disk cost of the operations selected from the other pool will increase.

3.2 Prototype Design

We have described how a large in-memory log of delayed object installations can offer optimization opportunities. We must choose a simple prototype design that can be used in our simulation experiments. The reliable object server must maintain a log of object updates that have not yet been installed onto corresponding pages. Here, for simplicity, we will assume that the server memory is non-volatile.

Thus, the opportunistic server can use a simple scheduler that considers only disk position information to select delayed installations for processing, as shown in Figure 2. The scheduler is free to process and discard the log entries in an arbitrary order. The prototype design will use a greedy scheduler that always selects the delayed installation read that has the shortest positioning time, based on the most recent disk head position. The scheduler uses a branch-and-bound implementation of the shortest positioning time algorithm [25]. We estimate that a good branch-and-bound implementation would make approximate shortest positioning time calculations over thousands of disk operations feasible in current disk controllers.

Without non-volatile memory, the server would need to write the log to a stable disk to commit transactions. The log entries would also be retained in volatile memory for installation processing. The installation processing would

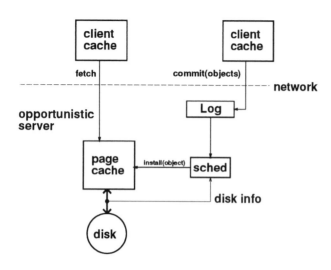

Figure 2: Object Server with Opportunistic Log

be somewhat complicated by the need to bound length of the log, as in a conventional databases with a write-ahead log [10]. In this case the opportunistic log might need to use an age-weighted scheduling algorithm.

4 Experimental Evaluation

To evaluate our technique we studied the effect of the opportunistic log on the performance of a persistent object system. We focus here on the I/O requirements of the persistent object system because these systems tend to become disk bound when they scale to support many clients. Moreover, the current hardware trend towards processor performance outstripping I/O performance appears likely to exacerbate this problem in the foreseeable future.

We performed a series of experiments by simulating a system of clients and a reliable server. The goal of our simulations is not to predict the actual performance of the system precisely but to compare fairly the disk I/O requirements of the system with and without the prototype opportunistic log.

In our simulations we use a simplified server workload with a uniform access pattern and fairly large objects. A workload generated by real client applications would probably exhibit a skewed access pattern and some temporal locality. However, in a large-scale system the server will observe the workloads of many clients mixed together. With enough clients, the server memory will not be large enough to extract much benefit from the locality present in an individual client's request stream. The combined working set of all the clients will not fit in the server cache memory in pages, so the pages fetched by a client will be quickly displaced by other traffic passing through the server cache.

We assume large objects because this is a worst-case scenario for our proposed opportunistic log design. With smaller objects, the in-memory log will store more pending installations per page of memory used.

We use a simplistic client model with a single parameter directly controlling how much work the client can do out of his local cache. The performance of a client cache should be reflected in the number of fetch operations in the request mix observed by the server, so we choose the *fetch ratio* as our workload parameter. The fetch ratio is defined as the ratio of the number of fetch operations generated by the client cache system to the number of transaction commit operations. Traditionally studies like ours have focused on the cache hit ratio, but this measure is not very useful in a system with prefetching.

4.1 Impact of the Opportunistic Log

Our first experiments investigate the impact of the opportunistic log on the performance of a reliable object server. In these experiments, the client behavior is fixed. First, we isolate the two main effects of the opportunistic log: eliminating installation reads through absorption and reducing installation read cost through disk scheduling.

To isolate these two effects we implement three object server configurations and compare their throughput. An *opportunistic server* implements the design presented in 3.2 and therefore benefits from both absorption and disk scheduling. A *basic server* uses the log to defer and schedule disk writes but does not defer or schedule installation reads. This configuration represents an object server with an in-memory log [18]. An *absorbing server* defers installations but does not use intelligent disk scheduling for installation reads. This configuration benefits from absorption only. Section 5.1 presents and analyses these results.

To understand the impact of the opportunistic log on server cache performance, we explore the tradeoffs involved in choosing the log size. We compare the throughput of an opportunistic server with widely varying log sizes and show the tension between more efficient disk arm scheduling for installation reads and for writes. Section 5.2 presents and analyses these results.

4.2 Comparison with Page Server

Our next experiments investigate the impact of the opportunistic log on the overall performance of an object storage system. The opportunistic log optimizes the installation reads that occur in object servers. Since installation reads do not occur in page based servers, optimization of installation reads affects the performance tradeoffs between page-based and object-based systems.

Several studies have indicated that object caching at the client can provide better utilization of client memory [3, 4, 14, 21] than page caching because the cache can hold more objects that are useful to the client. Improved client memory utilization translates into fewer fetch operations, and therefore reduced I/O load at the server. Therefore, object servers might outperform page servers when client object caching reduces their fetch ratio enough to compensate for the added I/O load of installation reads.

To examine how opportunistic I/O affects the competition between page servers and object servers, we implement a page server and compare the throughput of the servers while varying the client fetch ratio. We measure how much the fetch ratio of the object cache must decrease to make the object server outperform the page server. Section 5.3 presents and analyses the results of these experiments.

When considering the choice between page and object servers we are deliberately ignoring the question of whether the server uses page level or object level concurrency control. The choice of concurrency control granularity, though very important in absolute terms, is orthogonal to the question of the relative I/O costs of the object and page server architectures. Using our validation techniques [1], either page or object level concurrency control can be used with both object and page servers.

4.3 Server Designs

We implemented four reliable server designs within the simulation model. The first section below describes the common features of the reliable server designs. The following sections describe how the four servers process transaction commits and object modifications.

Common Server Model

The server processes fetch and commit requests from clients by reading and writing relevant database pages that are stored on an attached disk. The server maintains a cache of pages that is used to respond to client fetch requests and to buffer transaction modifications that must later be written to disk. The server supports prefetching by sending to the client the whole page containing the requested object. Since we assume the use of non-volatile memory in the server, there is no disk logging cost. However, we would not expect the cost of logging to a dedicated disk to be a limiting factor in system throughput, so ignoring the logging cost is a safe assumption.

When the number of clean pages in the cache drops below the *WriteTrigger* threshold, the server writes one dirty page to the disk. The page is selected using the shortest positioning time algorithm [25].

In the object-based server, the simulator models the transaction log as a collection of modified objects. A portion of the non-volatile primary memory is statically allocated to hold log entries. The *Objects-per-page* parameter defines the number of log entries that can be stored per page of memory allocated. We chose to set *Objects-per-page* to 2 because this seems to be a very conservative choice.

Concurrency control at the server is described by the *ValidationTime* parameter, which defines the cpu time required to validate a transaction. We chose not to model transaction aborts because they are indistinguishable from read-only

Server	
Database size (full disk)	335,500 pages
Page size	4 Kbytes
Objects-per-page	2
Server memory (10% of database)	33,550 pages
ValidationTime	5 μsecs
InstallationTime	1 msec
WriteTrigger	< 1000 clean pages
IReadTrigger	< 50 empty log entries

Table 1: Server Parameters

transactions for our purposes. The object servers differ from each other in how they install object modifications onto pages (see Section 4), but in all cases the installation uses *InstallationTime* cpu time. Table 1 shows the server simulation parameters.

Basic Object Server

In the basic object server, only the modified object is included in the transaction commit message sent by the client. The server adds the modified object to the log and sends a confirming message to the client. If the page containing the modified object is not in the cache, then the server immediately initiates a disk read for that page. When the page is available, the modified object is installed onto the page. Then the page is marked dirty and the log entry is removed.

Absorbing Object Server

In the absorbing object server, as before, the modified object is added to the log when a transaction commits. The confirming message is then sent to the client. If the page containing the object is in the cache, then the object is installed immediately. However, if the page is not in the cache, then the installation is postponed.

When the number of empty log entries decreases below the *IReadTrigger* threshold the server issues an installation read to obtain the page needed for a pending log entry. Whenever a page is read from the disk, whether due to a fetch read or an installation read, all modified objects that belong to that page are installed onto it.

Opportunistic Object Server

The opportunistic object server postpones installations as in the absorbing server design. However, when the *IReadTrigger* is invoked the server selects a pending installation from the log opportunistically, using the shortest positioning time algorithm, as described in Section 3.2.

Client Workload Parameters	
Access pattern	Uniform
WriteRatio	20%
FetchRatio	20%
ClientThinkTime	200 msec
Number of clients	20 . . . 70

Table 2: Workload Parameters

Page Server

In the page server, the whole page containing the modified object is included in the transaction commit message sent by the client. The server primary memory is non-volatile and the page-based server therefore does not require a log. In systems without non-volatile memory, the page server might have a greater logging cost than the object servers if the page server logs entire pages. However, we would not expect the log disk to be a limiting factor, and in any case modern page-based systems have techniques that allow them to do object-based logging. The page server also uses optimistic concurrency control and in-memory commit. The server stores the page into non-volatile cache memory and marks it dirty. The server then sends a confirming message to the client.

4.4 System Parameters

The simulated system is described by the parameters shown in Table 3. In general, the hardware parameters reflect our assumption that future processor and network speeds will increase substantially relative to disk seek latency. We discuss the simplifications and assumptions in the sections that follow.

Client Workload

The simulated clients each contain a cpu and a local memory for caching either objects or pages depending on the type of server in use. Each client executes a sequence of transactions. Each transaction accesses a single object in the database. If necessary, the client fetches the object from the server. Then the client computes for *ClientThinkTime* and possibly modifies the object (*WriteRatio*). Finally the client ends the transaction by sending a commit request to the server. After the commit is confirmed by the server, the client immediately starts its next transaction.

The workload parameters are shown in Table 2. They are based loosely on similar parameters in other studies of object servers [2, 7]. We chose not to model the contents of the client cache because only the workload presented to the servers is relevant to our comparisons. Therefore we simply use the *FetchRatio* parameter to control the workload. The *FetchRatio* is defined as the ratio of the number

Network	
Message latency	1 msec
Per-message cpu overhead	100 μsecs
Disk (HP97560)	
Rotational speed	4002 rpm
Sector size	512 bytes
Sectors per track	72
Tracks per cylinder	19
Cylinders	1962
Head switch time	1.6 msec
Seek time ($\leq$ 383 cylinders)	$3.24 + 0.4\sqrt{d}$ ms
Seek time ($>$ 383 cylinders)	$8.00 + 0.008d$ ms

Table 3: System Parameters

of fetch operations generated by the client cache system to the number of transaction commit operations.

Network

The network model provides unlimited bandwidth and a fixed message delivery latency. Each message transmission also incurs a small cpu overhead. We chose to ignore network contention because we do not expect network bandwidth to be the limiting factor in the performance of reliable servers.

An unlimited bandwidth network favors page-based architectures because they send larger commit messages (containing whole pages). Thus, this is a convenient and safe simplification when analyzing the disk I/O requirements of competing server designs.

Disk

The disk modeled by the simulator provides FIFO servicing of requests issued by the server. The disk geometry and other performance characteristics are taken from the HP97560 drive, as described by Wilkes [23]. We chose the HP97560 model because it is simple, accurate, and available. We believe that newer and faster drives will make opportunistic I/O even more important because transfer time is decreasing much faster than seek time [23]. That trend should increase the relative value of locality-based optimizations.

5 Simulation Results

In the sections that follow we first examine the relative performance of the object server designs. Then we explore the tradeoffs involved in choosing the log size. Finally we show how opportunistic I/O affects the competition between page-based and object-based servers.

We use auxiliary metrics to examine the impact of installation reads on server performance. To produce the simulation results we randomly generated several transaction traces for each workload. We sampled the behavior of each server over intervals so large that we observed no significant variation, and then averaged the results.

5.1 Opportunistic I/O

To test the value of opportunistic log processing we compare the performance of the object servers. For the moment, we arbitrarily choose to allocate 1500 pages to the log in the absorbing and opportunistic servers.

Figure 3 shows the throughput of all three servers plotted versus the number of clients in the simulation. Note that with fewer than 30 clients the disk is not saturated and the throughput rises linearly. However, when the system is fully loaded, we can see that the opportunistic server performs significantly better than the other two servers. In this simulation opportunistic scheduling of installation reads increased the maximum server throughput by over 40%.

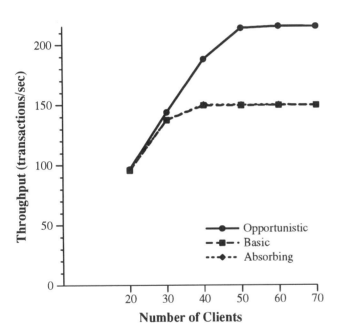

Object Server	tx/sec	I-Abs.	ICost	IDsk
Basic	150	28%	19.0 ms	41%
Absorbing	150	29%	19.0 ms	40%
Opportunistic	214	29%	4.8 ms	15%

Figure 3: Opportunistic I/O Improves Throughput

The table in Figure 3 provides throughput, installation absorption, and installation read disk costs for all three servers. The installation absorption figure (*I-Abs.*) indicates the percentage of installations that did not require an installation read. The absorbing server did not actually increase absorption very much; 28% of installations are absorbed even in the base system just because of fetch operations and expected server cache hits. Of course, this result reflects our workload: 20% of the modifying transactions fetch and therefore have no installation reads, and 10% of the remaining modifications hit in the server cache.

The installation read cost (*ICost*) is the average number of milliseconds that the disk arm was occupied (seek, rotate, and transfer) by an individual installation read operation. The aggregate cost of all installation reads (*IDsk*) gives the percentage of time that the disk arm was in use by all installation read operations in total. From these numbers we see that because the opportunistic server can choose installation reads from a pool of about 3000 log entries, it is able to reduce the average installation read cost nearly fourfold. Essentially all of the performance improvement shown in Figure 3 is due to this.

5.2 Log Size

We examine the performance of the opportunistic server with widely varying log sizes in Table 4. Here we see the throughput, the installation metrics, and corresponding write metrics. Note that for the log size used in the previous section (1500 pages), the remaining page cache contains over 30,000 pages. The server writes when this cache is almost fully dirty, and the opportunistic choice among 30,000 dirty pages leads to a very attractive write cost of only 3.0 milliseconds.

These measurements show that increasing the log is initially very valuable as the installation read cost drops rapidly. However, later improvements are smaller and require much greater increases in log size. Of course, this is the effect we expected, as described by Seltzer [25].

Metrics for 50 clients, fetch ratio 20%

Log	tx/s	I-Abs.	ICost	IDsk	WCost	WDsk
26	159	28%	16.2ms	37%	3.0ms	9%
60	195	28%	8.2ms	23%	3.0ms	11%
325	207	28%	6.0ms	18%	3.0ms	11%
1500	214	29%	4.8ms	15%	3.0ms	12%
6000	217	33%	3.8ms	11%	3.2ms	12%
12000	217	36%	3.3ms	9%	3.4ms	13%

Table 4: Opportunistic server performance and log size

It is important to note that in this simulation, there was not much increase in total throughput from increasing the log size beyond 1500 pages. There was actually no improvement between the last two rows of the table even though the installation cost dropped. This is explained by the increase in write cost. When the log grew by 6000 pages, the available pool of dirty pages dropped enough to increase

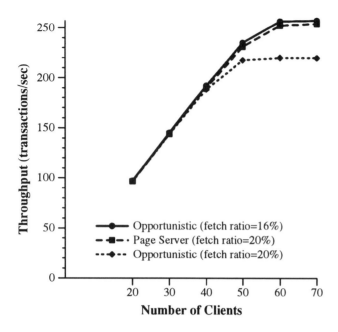

Figure 4: Opportunistic Object Server vs. Page Server

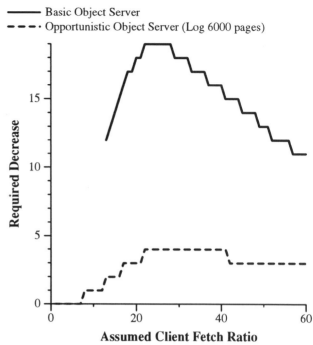

Figure 5: Object Caching vs. Page Caching

the write cost by 0.2ms. Although not shown here, the increase in log size also reduced the server cache hit ratio by 2 percentage points. The combined increase in disk usage due to these two effects effectively canceled out the other improvements.

5.3 Objects vs. Pages

Now that we have identified a good log size for the opportunistic object server (6000 pages), we would like to compare its performance to the page server. As we discussed in Section 4, the two servers face essentially identical concurrency control costs. And although the page server might consume more network bandwidth, this is not included in our simulation model. Therefore, we expect the page server to have higher throughput because it does not need to perform installation reads.

However, if object-based client caching provides better client cache performance, then the object server might be superior because it would have a lower fetch ratio. The difference in performance will depend on the FetchRatio, the WriteRatio, the server memory size, and the actual cost of installations and fetches. We varied the client FetchRatio and found that a 4 percentage point decrease in the fetch ratio was required for the opportunistic object server to surpass the page server. Figure 4 shows the throughput of the opportunistic server (for 20% and 16% fetch ratios) and the page server (20% only).

We see from this example that when the client fetch ratio is 20%, the opportunistic server requires a 4 point fetch ratio decrease to surpass the throughput of the page server. Each fetch read avoided compensates for roughly four installation reads, because installation reads are less

costly than fetch reads (compare the smallest and largest values of *ICost* in Table 4). In this configuration, about 16% of all transactions require an installation read, so removing fetches from 4% of all transactions will compensate for the disk cost of installation reads.

To determine the required fetch ratio decrease over a wide range of client cache performance, we simulated the basic object server, the opportunistic object server, and the page server while varying the client fetch ratio between 1% and 60%, using a 50 client workload. Figure 5 plots the decrease in client fetch ratio required by the two object servers in order to equal the throughput of the page server system. Note that below the 20% fetch ratio, the required decrease is much lower because in this range the 50 client workload is not fully loading the disk arm.

The reduced installation cost we saw in Table 4 makes the object server worthwhile if client object caching reduces the fetch ratio on the server by just a few percentage points. In contrast, when installation reads are treated the same as fetch reads, object caching is not advantageous for this workload unless it decreases the client fetch ratios by at least 10–20 percentage points. We believe these results are indicative of the importance of optimizing the asynchronous disk read operations that will be required in object-based systems.

6 Related Work

To put our work in perspective we consider other persistent object systems, systems that use a log for efficient disk

---

access, work on disk scheduling, and studies that compare object and page architectures for persistent object systems.

Many persistent object systems use the more traditional page based architecture [11, 19, 12]. Other systems [6, 15] use object server architectures but have not specifically addressed the problem of installation reads.

There is an enormous literature on centralized and distributed databases (see Jim Gray's book [10] for an excellent survey). Most modern databases use a stable log to store modifications to insure durability of updates. The log is not used as a source of updates to the database during normal operations, since database code modifies the pages directly in memory. Therefore there are no installation reads.

RVM [24] is a portable package that provides durable updates to virtual memory regions. RVM stores the modifications to VM regions in a stable write-ahead log on disk, propagates the modifications from the log to an (additional) persistent copy of the data on disk, and performs installation reads when containing pages are not in memory. However, portability concerns, the assumption that the persistent data fits in primary memory, and the fact that clients fetch data from one disk copy while stable updates are propagated to another disk copy of the database, make RVM performance considerations very different from our work.

Harp [18] is a replicated NFS server that uses a replicated in-memory write-ahead log to store durable modifications to Unix files. The log defers and propagates the modifications efficiently. However, since Harp is implemented on top of the Unix file system, it does not access the disk directly and does not deal with installation reads.

Much earlier effort has been invested in optimizing disk scheduling and so widening the performance gap between unoptimized and optimized disk access. Read-ahead is widely used to optimize sequential reads [16]. Recent studies by Seltzer, Chen and Ousterhout [25] and by Jacobson and Wilkes [13] aggressively take advantage of large memories to efficiently schedule deferred writes. Our techniques capitalize on this disk scheduling work. We are not aware of any other work besides ours that is directly concerned with efficient scheduling of deferred reads.

Several studies have investigated the design choices for persistent object system architecture. Dewitt et. al. [7] focuses on the question of distributing the functionality of a persistent object system between the client and the server. Day [4] studies whether to fetch data on a page or an object basis. Cheng and Hurson [3] demonstrated how object server architecture can enable more efficient client cache utilization. Carey et. al. [2] studied concurrency control issues in object, page and hybrid servers. None of these studies considered installation reads. However, in our recent work [21] we have investigated further the I/O performance tradeoffs related to the granularity of caching in large-scale object storage systems. We explored a hybrid design that selectively caches at the client either objects or pages, trading fetch reads for (optimized) installation reads.

Our work on deferred reads would also relate to work on prefetching, if prefetching reads were treated more like installation reads. The opportunistic log reduces the expected cost of installation reads by taking advantage of the fact that they are asynchronous (non-blocking) reads. It also seems possible that the lower cost of asynchronous reads should be considered when evaluating the cost of prefetching for clients. Prefetch requests could be treated as asynchronous read operations and scheduled opportunistically, as long as the client is not currently waiting for their results.

7   Conclusion

Persistent object systems combine the flexibility of modern programming languages with the efficiency and reliability of modern databases. Modern programming languages support variable size objects of user defined types. Databases support efficient access to large collections of a fixed set of system defined types. We believe persistent object systems will become increasingly important as applications scale in size and complexity.

It is still an open question what is the best architecture for a large-scale persistent object system. Should the server export fixed size pages (the unit of disk transfer) or should it export objects (units semantically meaningful to the application)?

In this paper, we introduced the opportunistic log method for organizing I/O. The opportunistic log substantially enhances the performance of object servers. This new technique uses an in-memory log to provide opportunities for scheduling asynchronous reads.

The opportunistic log is applicable to any disk cache manager that must handle large numbers of partial-block updates, as in file systems. If a block being partially updated is not in the cache, then the block must be read from disk before the update can be processed (by "installing" the updated bytes in the block and writing it back to disk). Seeks and transfers for these "installation reads" make partial block updates expensive. Client caching makes the problem worse by reducing the likelihood that a block to be updated will be resident in the server's cache: Although the needed block would have been read into the cache in order to handle the client's request to read the data, the block is likely to have been flushed from the server cache by the time the client's request to modify the data arrives.

The opportunistic log technique devotes a portion of the server cache memory to holding a pool of unprocessed partial-block update requests. As the pool grows, installation reads needed to process these updates can be scheduled greedily, assuming the disk head can be scheduled effectively by the software.

To investigate the performance advantage provided by the opportunistic log, we built a simplified simulation model that focuses on the I/O costs in page and object servers, and captures the important characteristics of a large-scale object storage system. We investigated and found that the optimal log size should balance the improved cost of scheduled installation reads against the improved cost of scheduled writes. We then studied how our new technique affects the performance payoff from a more efficient client cache. Our results show that the opportunistic log technique affects the break even point between object and page server performance. Without the opportunistic log, an object server must have a much more efficient client cache to outperform a page server. With the opportunistic log a small improvement suffices.

In contrast to previous studies that compared object and page systems, our work is the first to identify and explore the fundamental tradeoff between the efficiency of an object cache and the cost of installation reads. Although there exists substantial work on intelligent disk scheduling of deferred writes, we are the first to take advantage of the opportunity to schedule the large pool of installation *reads* that are important to the performance of object servers.

Modern storage systems have not paid sufficient attention to optimizing installation reads. Our simulation results strongly suggest that this previously overlooked factor should be considered in future storage architectures.

Acknowledgments

We would like to thank the ASPLOS and OSDI referees for their comments. Thanks especially to referee #6, for one paragraph of our conclusion, and to Karsten Schwan, for serving as the shepherd for our paper. We also thank our readers: Brian Bershad, Gregory Ganger, David Gifford, Maurice Herlihy, Barbara Liskov, and John Wroclawski.

References

[1] Atul Adya. A Distributed Commit Protocol for Optimistic Concurrency Control. Master's thesis, Massachusetts Institute of Technology, February 1994.

[2] M. Carey, M. Franklin, and M. Zaharioudakis. Fine-Grained Sharing in a Page Server OODBMS. In *Proceedings of SIGMOD 1994*, 1994.

[3] Jia-bing R. Cheng and A. R. Hurson. On the Performance Issues of Object-Based Buffering. In *Proceedings of the Conference on Parallel and Distributed Information Systems*, pages 30–37, 1991.

[4] M. Day. *Managing a Cache of Swizzled Objects and Surrogates*. PhD thesis, MIT-EECS, In preparation.

[5] W. de Jonge, F. Kaashoek, and W. Hsieh. The Logical Disk: A New Approach to Improving File Systems. In *Proc. of the 14th Symposium on Operating Systems Principles*, Asheville, NC, December 1993. ACM.

[6] O. Deux et al. The Story of O$_2$. *IEEE Trans. on Knowledge and Data Engineering*, 2(1):91–108, March 1990.

[7] David J. DeWitt, Philippe Futtersack, David Maier, and Fernando Velez. A Study of Three Alternative Workstation-Server Architectures for Object Oriented Database Systems.

[8] R. English and A. Stepanov. Loge: a Self-Organizing Disk Controller. In *Proceedings of Winter USENIX*, 1992.

[9] S. Ghemawat. *Disk Management for Object-Oriented Databases*. PhD thesis, MIT-EECS, In preparation.

[10] J. Gray and A. Reuter. *Transaction Processing: Concepts and Techniques*. Morgan Kaufmann, 1993.

[11] M. Hornick and S. Zdonik. *A Shared, Segmented Memory System for an Object-Oriented Database*, pages 273–285. Morgan Kaufmann, 1990.

[12] Object Design Inc. An Introduction to Object Store, Release 1.0. Burlington, Massachusetts, 1989.

[13] David M. Jacobson and John Wilkes. Disk Scheduling Algorithms Based on Rotational Position. Technical Report HPL-CSP-91-7, Hewlett-Packard Laboratories, February 1991.

[14] Alfans Kemper and Donal Kossman. Dual-Buffering Strategies in Object Bases. In *Proceedings of the 20th Conference on Very-Large Databases*, Santiago, Chile, 1994.

[15] W. Kim et al. Architecture of the ORION Next-Generation Database System. *IEEE Trans. on Knowledge and Data Engineering*, 2(1):109–124, June 1989.

[16] Samuel J. Leffler, Marshall Kirk McKusick, Michael J. Karels, and John S. Quarterman. *The Design and Implementation of the 4.3bsd UNIX Operating System*. Addison-Wesley, 1989.

[17] B. Liskov, M. Day, and L. Shrira. Distributed Object Management in Thor. In M. Tamer Özsu, Umesh Dayal, and Patrick Valduriez, editors, *Distributed Object Management*. Morgan Kaufmann, San Mateo, California, 1993.

[18] B. Liskov, S. Ghemawat, R. Gruber, P. Johnson, L. Shrira, and M. Williams. Replication in the Harp File System. In *Proceedings of the 13th ACM Symposium on Operating Systems Principles*, 1991.

[19] D. Maier and J. Stein. Development and Implementation of an Object-Oriented DBMS. In B. Shriver and P. Wegner, editors, *Research Directions in Object-Oriented Programming*. MIT Press, 1987.

[20] Jeffrey C. Mogul. A Better Update Policy. In *USENIX Summer Conference, Boston*, 1994.

[21] James O'Toole and Liuba Shrira. Hybrid Caching for Large-Scale Object Systems. In *Proceedings of the 6th Workshop on Persistent Object Systems*, Tarascon, France, September 1994. ACM.

[22] M. Rosenblum and J.K. Ousterhout. The Design and Implementation of a Log Structured File System. In *Proc. of the 13th Symposium on Operating Systems Principles*, Pacific Grove, CA, October 1991. ACM.

[23] Chris Ruemmler and John Wilkes. Modelling Disks. Technical Report HPL-93-68rev1, Hewlett-Packard Laboratories, December 1993.

[24] M. Satyanarayanan, H. Mashburn, P. Kumar, D. Steere, and J. Kistler. Lightweight Recoverable Virtual Memory. In *Proc. of the 14th Symposium on Operating Systems Principles*, Asheville, NC, December 1993. ACM.

[25] M. Seltzer, P. Chen., and J. Ousterhout. Disk Scheduling Revisited. In *Proceedings of Winter USENIX*, 1990.

In the reference [7] continued text:
In *Proceedings of the 16th Conference on Very Large Data Bases*, pages 107–121, Brisbane, Australia, 1990.

Metadata Update Performance in File Systems

Gregory R. Ganger, Yale N. Patt
Department of EECS, University of Michigan
ganger@eecs.umich.edu

Abstract

Structural changes, such as file creation and block allocation, have consistently been identified as file system performance problems in many user environments. We compare several implementations that maintain metadata integrity in the event of a system failure but do not require changes to the on-disk structures. In one set of schemes, the file system uses asynchronous writes and passes ordering requirements to the disk scheduler. These **scheduler-enforced** ordering schemes outperform the conventional approach (synchronous writes) by more than 30 percent for metadata update intensive benchmarks, but are suboptimal mainly due to their inability to safely use delayed writes when ordering is required. We therefore introduce **soft updates**, an implementation that asymptotically approaches memory-based file system performance (within 5 percent) while providing stronger integrity and security guarantees than most UNIX file systems. For metadata update intensive benchmarks, this improves performance by more than a factor of two when compared to the conventional approach.

1 Introduction

File system metadata updates traditionally proceed at disk speeds rather than processor/memory speeds [Ousterhout90, McVoy91, Seltzer93], because synchronous writes are used to properly order stable storage changes. This update sequencing is needed to maintain integrity in the event of a system failure (e.g., power loss).[1] For example, the *rename* operation changes the name of a file by adding a link for the new name and removing the old link. If the system goes down after the old directory block has been written (with the link removed) but before the new one is written, neither name for the file will exist when the system is restarted. To protect metadata consistency, the new directory entry must reach stable storage before the old directory block. We refer to this ordering requirement as an update *dependency*, as writing the old directory block *depends* on first writing the new block. The ordering constraints essentially map onto three simple rules: (1) Never reset the old pointer to a resource before the new pointer has been set (when moving objects), (2) Never re-use a resource before nullifying all previous pointers to it, and (3) Never point to a structure before it has been initialized.

Synchronous[2] writes are used for metadata update ordering by many variants of both the original UNIX[TM] file system [Ritchie78] and the Berkeley fast file system (FFS) [McKusick84]. The performance degradation can be so dramatic that many implementations choose to ignore certain update dependencies. For example, a pointer to a newly allocated block should not be added to a file's inode before the block is initialized on stable storage. If this ordering is not enforced, a system failure could result in the file containing data from some previously deleted file, presenting both an integrity weakness and a security hole. However, *allocation initialization* with synchronous writes can degrade performance significantly. As a result, most UNIX file system implementations, including FFS derivatives, either do not force initialization or force initialization only for newly allocated directory blocks in order to protect the integrity of the directory hierarchy. We investigate the performance cost of allocation initialization in our comparison of different ordering schemes.

Previous schemes that address the performance penalty of update ordering generally entail some form of logging (e.g., [Hagmann87, Chutani92, Journal92]) or shadow-paging (e.g., [Chamberlin81, Ston87, Chao92, Seltzer93]). While these approaches have been successfully applied,

---

[1] For complete integrity, each individual update must also be atomic (not partially written to disk). This can be achieved by forcing each critical structure to be fully contained by a single disk sector. Each disk sector is protected by error correcting codes that will almost always flag a partially written sector as unrecoverable. This may result in loss of structures, but not loss of integrity. In addition, many disks will not start laying down a sector unless there is sufficient power to finish it.

[2] There are three types of UNIX file system writes: *synchronous, asynchronous* and *delayed*. A write is synchronous if the process issues it (i.e., sends it to the device driver) immediately and waits for it to complete. A write is asynchronous if the process issues it immediately but does not wait for it to complete. A delayed write is not issued immediately; the affected buffer cache blocks are marked dirty and issued later by a background process (unless the cache runs out of clean blocks).

there is value in exploring implementations that do not require changes to the on-disk structures (which may have a large installed base).

The remainder of this paper is organized as follows. Section 2 describes our experimental setup, measurement tools and base operating system. Sections 3 and 4 describe several approaches to "safe" metadata updates, including our implementations of each. Section 3 describes schemes in which the file system uses asynchronous writes and passes any ordering restrictions to the disk scheduler with each request. Section 4 describes soft updates, a file system implementation that safely performs metadata updates with delayed writes. Section 5 compares the performance of the different schemes. Section 6 compares important non-performance characteristics, such as user-interface semantics and implementation complexity. Section 7 draws some conclusions and discusses avenues for future research. The appendix describes some low-level details of our soft updates implementation.

2   Experimental apparatus

All experiments were performed on an NCR 3433, a 33MHz Intel 80486 machine equipped with 48 MB of main memory (44 MB for system use and 4 MB for a trace buffer). The HP C2447 disk drive used in the experiments is a high performance, 3.5-inch, 1 GB SCSI storage device [HP92]. Our base operating system is UNIX SVR4 MP, AT&T/GIS's production operating system for symmetric multiprocessing. We use the *ufs* file system for our experiments, which is based on the Berkeley fast file system [McKusick84]. The virtual memory system is similar to that of SunOS [Gingell87, Moran87], and file system caching is well integrated with the virtual memory system. The scheduling code in the device driver concatenates sequential requests, and the disk prefetches sequentially into its on-board cache. Command queueing at the disk is not utilized.

One important aspect of the file system's reliability and performance is the *syncer daemon*. This background process executes at regular intervals, writing out dirty buffer cache blocks. The syncer daemon in UNIX SVR4 MP operates differently than the conventional "30 second sync"; it awakens once each second and sweeps through a fraction of the buffer cache, marking each dirty block encountered. An asynchronous write is initiated for each dirty block marked on the previous pass. This approach tends to reduce the burstiness associated with the conventional approach.

We run all experiments with the network disconnected and with no other non-essential activity. We obtain our measurements from two sources. The UNIX *time* utility provides total execution times and CPU times. We have also instrumented the device driver to collect I/O traces, including per-request queue and service delays. The traces are collected in the 4 MB trace buffer mentioned above and copied to a separate disk after each experiment. The

timing resolution is approximately 840 nanoseconds, and the tracing alters performance by less than 0.01 percent (assuming that the trace buffer could not be otherwise used).

In section 5, we use several benchmarks to compare the performance of the metadata update schemes described in the next two sections. To concisely quantify the performance impacts of some of the implementation decisions, however, it will be useful to provide small amounts of measurement data with the descriptions. For this purpose, we use the results from two metadata update intensive benchmarks. In the N-user copy benchmark, each "user" concurrently performs a recursive copy of a separate directory tree (535 files totaling 14.3 MB of storage taken from the first author's home directory). In the N-user remove benchmark, each "user" deletes one newly copied directory tree. Each datum is an average of several independent executions, with coefficient of variation (standard deviation / mean) below 0.05.

3   Scheduler-enforced ordering

With scheduler-enforced ordering, the responsibility for properly sequencing disk writes is shifted to the disk scheduler (generally part of the device driver). The file system uses asynchronous writes and augments each request with any ordering requirements. We examine two levels of ordering information: a simple flag and a list of specific dependencies.

3.1   Ordering flag

A straight-forward implementation of scheduler-enforced ordering attaches a one-bit flag to each disk request (as suggested in [McVoy91]). Write requests that would previously have been synchronous for ordering purposes (i.e., writes that may require ordering with respect to subsequent updates) are issued asynchronously with their ordering flags set. Of course, the disk scheduler must also be modified to appropriately sequence flagged requests.

The most significant implementation issue is the semantic meaning of the flag, which represents a contract between the file system and the disk scheduler. The ordering semantics determine which subsequent requests can be scheduled before a flagged request and which previous requests can be scheduled after a flagged request. With the most restrictive semantics, a flagged request acts as a barrier. Less restrictive meanings offer the disk scheduler more freedom but may require the file system to set the flag more frequently, reducing scheduling flexibility. In general, we find that less restrictive flag semantics result in improved performance. In particular, allowing read requests to bypass the list of writes waiting on ordering constraints[3] can improve performance significantly without endangering metadata integrity.

---

[3] Unless the read requests are for locations to be written, of course.

We compare four meanings for the ordering flag: *Full*, *Back*, *Part* and *Ignore*. In *Full*, a flagged request acts as a full barrier (i.e., all previous requests must complete before it is scheduled and no subsequent requests can bypass it). *Back* prevents requests issued after a flagged request from being scheduled before it or any previous request, but allows the flagged request to be re-ordered freely with previous non-flagged requests. This scheme is less restrictive than *Full* but still allows several requests to be ordered with respect to a later request with only the last such request issued with the flag set. *Part* further relaxes the constraints by requiring only that requests issued after a flagged request not be scheduled before it (i.e., previous non-flagged requests can be re-ordered freely with subsequent requests and the flagged request). With this flag meaning, all requests that require ordering with respect to any subsequent request must have the flag set. The addition of *-NR* to any scheme indicates that the disk scheduler allows non-conflicting read requests to bypass the list of writes waiting because of ordering restrictions.[4] Finally, *Ignore* re-orders requests freely, ignoring the flag. This scheme does not protect metadata integrity and we include it only for comparison.

For the 4-user copy benchmark (figure 1), performance improves with each reduction in the flag's restrictiveness. Reducing the number of requests with the flag set should improve performance by increasing the disk scheduler's freedom to re-order. Such cases do occur, but too infrequently to counter the increased restrictiveness of the flag's meaning. We also found that allowing reads to bypass flag-pending writes improves performance significantly. The disk access times (figure 1b) directly display the impact of allowing the scheduler greater freedom. The elapsed times (figure 1a) show how this translates into overall performance. This trend, less restrictive flag semantics results in higher performance, holds for most of our benchmarks, and the comparisons in section 5 utilize *Part-NR*.

The 1-user remove benchmark (figure 2) is an exception to this rule. The elapsed times (figure 2a) are system response times observed by the benchmark "user." As the write requests that remove the directory tree are issued, a very large queue builds up in the scheduler. This effect is evident from the average driver response times (i.e., the times from when requests are issued to the device driver to when they complete, including both queue times and disk access times) of 5+ seconds shown in figure 2b. When read requests bypass this queue, the "user" process wastes very little time waiting for I/O, and the benchmark completes without waiting for the driver queue to empty (the writes fit into main memory). Given the *-NR* option, the **more** restrictive flag semantics result in lower user-observed response times, because fewer requests interfere with read requests

<hr />

[4]Note that this could reasonably be viewed as an implementation decision rather than part of the flag semantics. The ordering required for metadata integrity pertains only to writes.

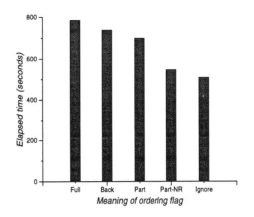

(a) Elapsed time (seconds)

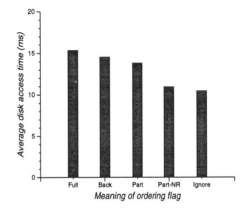

(b) Average disk access time (ms)

Figure 1: Performance impact of ordering flag semantics for the 4-user copy benchmark.

for service. This demonstrates the performance advantage, in sub-saturation bursts of activity, of giving preference to those requests which block processes [Ganger93]. However, tying the disk scheduler's hands is a poor way of realizing this performance improvement and does not behave well when system activity exceeds the available memory (as shown above).

3.2 Scheduler chains

Even with the least restrictive semantics for the ordering flag, requests are often constrained unnecessarily by flagged writes. By tagging each disk request with a unique identifier and a list of requests on which it depends (i.e., a list of requests that must complete before it can be scheduled), such "false" dependencies can be avoided. We refer to this approach as *scheduler chains*. Similar approaches exist in other systems. The MPE-XL^{TM} file system provides support for ordered sequences of user writes, although write-

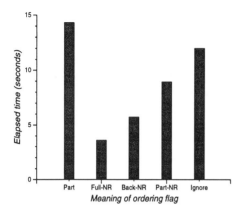

(a) Elapsed time (seconds)

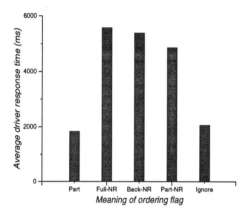

(b) Average driver response time (ms)

Figure 2: Performance impact of ordering flag semantics for the 1-user remove benchmark.

ahead logging protects the metadata [Busch85, Kondoff88]. [Cao93] describes a method for supporting request dependencies in an intelligent storage controller (or a device driver). As we are not dealing with multiple hosts and an interconnection network, our disk scheduler support can be less complete. In particular, we do not allow requests to depend on future requests; a new request can depend only on previously issued requests. In addition to the increased scheduler complexity, the file system must maintain information regarding which dirty blocks depend on which outstanding requests. In most cases, this is straight-forward because newly updated blocks depend on just-issued requests.

The exception to this rule is block de-allocation. A de-allocated block should not be re-used before the old pointer has been re-initialized on stable storage. Generally, the de-allocation is independent of subsequent re-use; at the least, they usually occur during separate system calls. We examined two approaches to maintaining the required or-

dering. The first falls back on the flag-based approach. The asynchronous write of the inode (or indirect block) is issued as a *Part-NR* barrier (i.e., no subsequent write request is scheduled before it completes). The second approach maintains information about recently freed blocks until the re-initialized pointer reaches the disk. The blocks can be re-allocated at any time and the new owner (inode or indirect block) becomes dependent on the write of the old owner. In fact, we make the newly allocated block itself dependent on the old owner. This prevents new data from being added to the old file due to untimely system failure. The barrier approach is obviously simpler to implement, but can cause unnecessary dependencies and thereby reduce performance. As with the comparison of flag meanings, we find that the less restrictive approach provides superior performance (e.g., 16 percent for the 4-user remove benchmark). Therefore, the second approach was used for the scheduler chains data reported in section 5.

3.3 Avoiding write locks

Our initial implementation of scheduler-enforced ordering revealed that, although metadata writes are no longer synchronous, processes still wait for them in many cases. This occurs when multiple updates to given file system metadata occur within a short period of time. When a write request is issued to the device driver, the source memory block(s) are write-locked until the request completes.[5] This prevents subsequent updates from occurring while the I/O subsystem hardware may be accessing the data. As a result, a second update must wait for the first to reach stable storage. One solution is to make a second (temporary) in-memory copy of the memory block(s) before issuing the first request. This copy becomes the source for the first write request, obviating the need to write-lock the original at the cost of a block copy operation.[6] To avoid unnecessary overhead for the special case of allocation initialization, we reserve a zero-filled memory block when the system is booted. This block becomes the source for initialization writes.[7]

Figure 3 compares four different implementations of the *Part* ordering flag scheme described above: with no options, with the *-NR* option, with the block copying (*-CB*) and with both. With both (*Part-NR/CB*), user processes spend the least time waiting for disk requests. Failing to include either enhancement greatly reduces the benefit. For this

---

[5] "Less critical" source data, such as file blocks and virtual memory pages, often bypass this safety precaution. For file blocks in particular, this is a difficult performance vs. reliability trade-off/judgment call made by system implementors.

[6] Copy-on-write would clearly be a superior approach. We plan to investigate this alternative, but do not expect substantially improved throughput (the increase in CPU usage caused by the memory copying is a small fraction of the total time). However, the copy-on-write approach should be more "memory-friendly."

[7] A better approach would utilize an "erase" I/O operation (e.g., the *WRITE SAME* SCSI command [SCSI93]), initializing the disk sectors without wasting a block of memory or transferring a block of zeroes from host memory to disk.

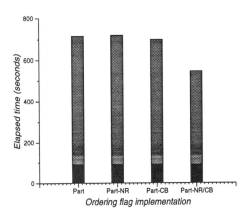

(a) Elapsed time (seconds)

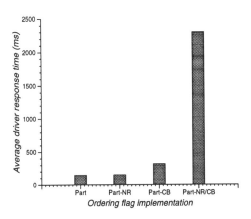

(b) Average driver response time (ms)

Figure 3: Implementation improvements for ordering flags for the 4-user copy benchmark. *Part-NR* allows reads to bypass writes waiting due to ordering restrictions. *Part-CB* uses the block copy scheme to avoid write locks. *Part-NR/CB* combines these two enhancements. The dark region of each elapsed time bar represents the total CPU time charged to the four benchmark processes.

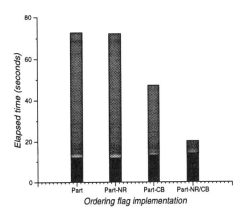

(a) Elapsed time (seconds)

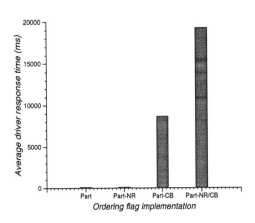

(b) Average driver response time (ms)

Figure 4: Implementation improvements for ordering flags for the 4-user remove benchmark. *Part-NR* allows reads to bypass writes waiting due to ordering restrictions. *Part-CB* uses the block copy scheme to avoid write locks. *Part-NR/CB* combines these two enhancements. The dark region of each elapsed time bar represents the total CPU time charged to the four benchmark processes.

reason, the performance comparisons in earlier subsections used the block copying implementation. The CPU time increases caused by the block copying are small and tend to use time that was otherwise idle (processes waiting for disk I/O). Figure 3b shows the driver response times for each of the implementations. Again we find that the queue grows very large as processes generate requests much more quickly than the disk can service them. The 4-user remove benchmark (figure 4) follows the same general trends, but the performance differences are more substantial. Also, the queueing delays are much larger (almost 20 seconds for *Part-NR/CB*).

We also observe the same general behavior with scheduler chains. The block copying (*-NR* holds no meaning with

scheduler chains) reduces the elapsed time by 26 percent for the 4-user copy benchmark and 57 percent for the 4-user remove benchmark.

4   Delayed metadata writes

Delayed metadata writes associate additional information with the in-memory metadata, detailing any ordering constraints on stable storage updates. To complete a structural change, the file system modifies the in-memory copies of the affected metadata (via delayed writes) and updates the corresponding dependency information. The dirty metadata blocks are later flushed by the syncer daemon as described in section 2. Of course, the ordering constraints must be upheld in the process. Delayed metadata writes can substantially improve performance by combining multiple updates into a much smaller quantity of background disk writes. The savings come from two sources: (1) multiple updates to a given metadata component (e.g., removal of a recently added directory entry), and more significantly, (2) multiple independent updates to a given block of metadata (e.g., several files added to a single directory). The next subsection briefly describes our original approach (which is flawed), and the following subsection describes our current implementation.

4.1 Cycles and aging problems

When we began this work, we envisioned a dynamically managed DAG (Directed, Acyclic Graph) of dirty blocks for which write requests are issued only after all writes on which they depend complete. In practice, we found this to be a very difficult model to maintain, being susceptible to cyclic dependencies and aging problems (blocks could consistently have dependencies and never be written to stable storage). Most of the difficulties relate to the granularity of the dependency information. The blocks that are read from and written to disk often contain multiple metadata structures (e.g., inodes or directory fragments), each of which generally contains multiple dependency causing components (e.g., block pointers and directory entries). As a result, originally independent metadata changes can easily cause dependency cycles and excessive aging. Detecting and handling these problems increases complexity and reduces performance.

4.2 Soft updates

Having identified coarse-grain dependency information as the main source of cycles and aging, our most recent implementation (which we refer to as *soft updates*) maintains dependency information at a very fine granularity. Information is kept for each individual metadata update indicating the update(s) on which it depends. A block containing dirty metadata can be written at any time, so long as any updates within that block that have pending dependencies are first temporarily "undone" (rolled back). Thus, the block as written to disk is consistent with respect to the current on-disk state. When the disk write completes, any undone updates are re-established before the in-memory block can be accessed. With this approach, aging problems do not occur because new dependencies are not added to existing update sequences. Dependency cycles do not occur because no single sequence of dependent updates is cyclic. In fact, the sequences are the same as in the original synchronous write approach.

There are four main structural changes requiring sequenced metadata updates: (1) block allocation (direct and indirect), (2) block de-allocation, (3) link addition (e.g.,

file creation), and (4) link removal. We implement block allocation and link addition with the undo/redo approach outlined above. For block de-allocation and link removal, we defer the freeing of resources until after the newly reset pointer has been written to stable storage. In a sense, these deferred updates are undone until the disk writes on which they depend complete.

When a disk write completes, there is often some processing needed to update/remove dependency structures, redo undone changes, and deal with deferred work, such as block de-allocation and file removal. An implementation of soft updates requires some method of performing these small tasks in the background. Very simple changes can be made during the disk I/O completion interrupt service routine (ISR), which calls a pre-defined procedure in the higher-level module that issued the request. However, any task that can block and wait for a resource (e.g., a lock or, worse yet, an uncached disk block) cannot be handled in this way. Such a task must be handled outside of the ISR, preferably by a background process. We use the syncer daemon (described in section 2) for this purpose. Any tasks that require non-trivial processing are appended to a single *workitem* queue. When the syncer daemon next awakens (within one second), it services the workitem queue before its normal activities.

The appendix describes our soft updates implementation in detail, including how each of the four main structural changes is supported.

5 Performance comparison

In the following subsections, we compare the performance of five different ordering schemes. As a baseline (and a goal), we ignore ordering constraints (*No Order*) and use delayed writes for all metadata updates. This baseline has the same performance and lack of reliability as the delayed mount option described in [Ohta90]. It is also very similar to the memory-based file system described in [McKusick90]. The *Conventional* scheme uses synchronous writes to sequence metadata updates. The *Scheduler Flag* data represent the *Part-NR/CB* scheduler-enforced ordering flag scheme. The *Scheduler Chains* data represent the best performing scheme described in section 3.2. Both scheduler-enforced ordering schemes use the block copying enhancement described in section 3.3. The *Soft Updates* data are from our current implementation.

5.1 Metadata throughput

Figure 5 compares the metadata update throughput supported by the five implementations as a function of the number of concurrent "users." Each "user" works in a separate directory. As a result, create throughput improves with the number of "users" because less CPU time is spent checking the directory contents for name conflicts. *Scheduler*

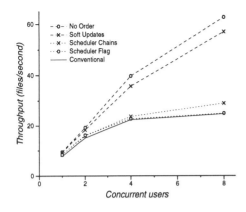

(a) 1KB file creates

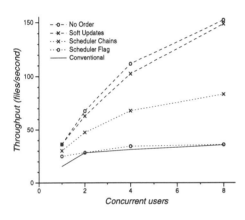

(b) 1KB file removes

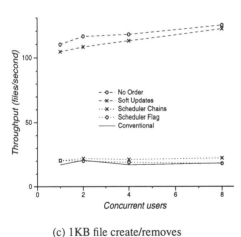

(c) 1KB file create/removes

Figure 5: Metadata update throughput (files/second). Each data point (10,000 files split among the "users") is an average of several independent executions. All coefficients of variation are less than 0.05. Allocation initialization is enforced only for *Soft Updates*.

Flag reduces metadata update response times compared to *Conventional*, but does not substantially improve throughput. *Scheduler Chains* does better, more than doubling file removal throughput with 8 "users." *No Order* and *Soft Updates* both outperform the other schemes, and the differences increase with the level of concurrency. The power of delayed metadata writes can be seen in figure 5c, where each created file is immediately removed. *No Order* and *Soft Updates* proceed at memory speeds, achieving over 5 times the throughput of the other three schemes. In all cases, *Soft Updates* performance is within 5 percent of *No Order*.

5.2 Metadata intensive benchmarks

Table 1 shows performance data for the 4-user copy benchmark. *No Order* decreases elapsed times by 20 percent and the number of disk requests by 12 percent when compared to *Conventional* with no allocation initialization. *Scheduler Flag* and *Scheduler Chains* decrease the elapsed times by 2 and 4 percent, respectively, but do not affect the number of disk requests. Performance for *Soft Updates* is within a few percent of *No Order* in both elapsed time and number of disk requests. The performance cost of allocation initialization for this benchmark ranges from 3.8 percent for *Soft Updates* to 87 percent for *Conventional*.

The performance differences are more extreme for file removal (table 2), which consists almost entirely of metadata updates. Note that *Soft Updates* elapsed times are lower than *No Order* for this benchmark. This is due to the deferred removal approach used by *Soft Updates*. The order of magnitude decrease in disk activity (e.g., *Soft Updates* verses *Scheduler Chains*) demonstrates the power of delayed metadata writes. The lengthy response times for the scheduler-enforced ordering schemes are caused by the large queues of dependent background writes that form in the device driver.

5.3 Andrew benchmark

Table 3 compares the different schemes using the original Andrew file system benchmark [Howard88]. It consists of five phases: (1) create a directory tree, (2) copy the data files, (3) examine the status of every file, (4) read every byte of each file, (5) compile several of the files.

As expected, the most significant differences are in the metadata update intensive phases (1 and 2). The read-only phases (3 and 4) are practically indistinguishable. The compute intensive compile phase is marginally improved (5-7 percent) by the four non-*Conventional* schemes. The compile phase dominates the total benchmark time because of aggressive, time-consuming compilation techniques and a slow CPU, by 1994 standards.

Ordering Scheme	Alloc. Init.	Elapsed Time (seconds)	Percent of No Order	CPU Time (seconds)	Disk Requests	I/O Response Time Avg (ms)
Conventional	N	390.7	123.9	72.8	36075	293.3
	Y	732.3	232.3	82.4	51419	140.1
Scheduler Flag	N	381.3	120.9	72.8	36038	477.3
	Y	545.7	173.1	90.0	51028	2297
Scheduler Chains	N	375.1	119.0	76.0	36019	304.1
	Y	530.6	168.3	86.0	51248	423.8
Soft Updates	N	319.8	101.4	69.6	31840	368.7
	Y	330.9	104.9	80.0	31880	262.1
No Order	N	315.3	100.0	68.4	31574	304.1

Table 1: Scheme comparison using 4-user copy. Each datum is an average of several independent executions. The elapsed times are averages among the "users", with coefficients of variation less than 0.05. The CPU times are sums among the "users", with coefficients of variation less than 0.1. The disk system statistics are system-wide, with coefficients of variation less than 0.2.

Ordering Scheme	Elapsed Time (seconds)	Percent of No Order	CPU Time (seconds)	Disk Requests	I/O Response Time Avg (ms)
Conventional	80.24	1050	12.68	4600	68.02
Scheduler Flag	24.97	326.8	13.64	4631	22173
Scheduler Chains	31.03	406.2	14.80	4618	2495
Soft Updates	6.71	87.83	5.64	391	73.53
No Order	7.64	100.0	7.44	278	84.03

Table 2: Scheme comparison using 4-user remove. Each datum is an average of several independent executions. The elapsed times are averages among the "users", with coefficients of variation less than 0.05. The CPU times are sums among the "users", with coefficients of variation less than 0.1. The disk system statistics are system-wide, with coefficients of variation less than 0.2.

Ordering Scheme	(1) Create Directories	(2) Copy Files	(3) Read Inodes	(4) Read Files	(5) Compile	Total
Conventional	2.49 (0.50)	4.07 (0.71)	4.08 (0.27)	5.91 (0.31)	295.8 (1.53)	312.4 (1.98)
Scheduler Flag	0.54 (0.50)	4.45 (0.77)	4.09 (0.28)	5.91 (0.29)	279.1 (1.50)	294.1 (1.96)
Scheduler Chains	0.53 (0.50)	3.72 (0.74)	4.09 (0.27)	5.86 (0.35)	280.6 (0.78)	294.8 (1.36)
Soft Updates	0.34 (0.47)	2.77 (0.60)	4.25 (0.43)	5.84 (0.86)	276.3 (0.86)	289.5 (1.32)
No Order	0.37 (0.48)	2.74 (0.52)	4.14 (0.34)	5.84 (0.38)	276.6 (2.58)	289.7 (2.76)

Table 3: Scheme comparison using Andrew benchmark. Each value is in seconds and represents an average of 100 independent executions. The values in parens are the standard deviations. Allocation initialization was enforced only for *Soft Updates*.

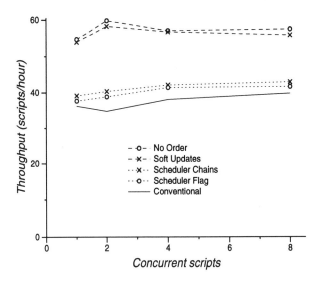

Figure 6: Scheme comparison using Sdet. Each data point is an average of 3 independent executions and all coefficients of variation are less than 0.02. Allocation initialization is enforced only for *Soft Updates*.

5.4 Sdet

Figure 6 compares the five schemes using Sdet, from the SPEC SDM suite of benchmarks. This benchmark [Gaede81, Gaede82] concurrently executes one or more *scripts* of user commands designed to emulate a typical software-development environment (e.g., editing, compiling, file creation and various UNIX utilities). The scripts are generated randomly from a predetermined mix of functions. The reported metric is scripts/hour as a function of the script concurrency.

Scheduler Flag outperforms *Conventional* by 3-5 percent. *Scheduler Chains* provides an additional one percent improvement. *No Order* outperforms *Conventional* by 50-70 percent, and *Soft Updates* throughput is within 2 percent of *No Order*.

6 Non-performance comparisons

6.1 File system semantics

The use of synchronous writes to sequence metadata updates does not imply synchronous file system semantics. In general, the last write in a series of metadata updates is asynchronous or delayed. In many cases, when a file system call returns control to the caller, there is no guarantee that the change is persistent. For link addition and block allocation, the last update adds the pointer to the directory block, inode or indirect block. So, the requested change is not permanent when the system call returns.[8] For link removal and block de-allocation, however, the last update modifies the free maps. When the system call returns, the link is permanently removed and/or the blocks have been freed and are available for re-use. With the scheduler-enforced ordering schemes, freed resources are immediately available for re-use, but links and pointers are not permanently removed when the system call returns. For soft updates, neither is true. In particular, freed resources do not become available for re-use until the re-initialized inode (or indirect block) reaches stable storage.

Some calls have a *SYNCIO* flag that tells the file system to guarantee that changes are permanent before returning. All of the schemes we have described support this interface (although the scheduler-enforced ordering schemes will encounter lengthy delays when a long list of dependent writes has formed). It may be useful to augment additional file system calls (e.g., link addition and link removal) with such a flag in order to support lock files.

6.2 Implementation complexity

Of the schemes we compare, the conventional synchronous write approach is clearly the most straight-forward to implement. Moving to an ordering flag scheme is also straight-forward; the synchronous writes become asynchronous with the flag set. Our changes to the device driver required less than 50 lines of C code. Scheduler-enforced ordering with specific request dependencies is considerably more difficult. Our implementation required about 550 lines of C code for the device driver support and 100 lines for the file system changes. The support for specific remove dependencies adds an additional 150 lines of code. The block-copy enhancement described in section 3.3 required an additional 50 lines of code. Our implementation of soft updates consists of 1500 lines of C code and is restricted to the file system and buffer cache modules. Having learned key lessons from an initial implementation, the first author completed the soft updates implementation in two weeks, including most of the debugging.

7 Conclusions and Future Work

The use of synchronous writes to order metadata updates has been identified as a file system performance problem [Ousterhout90, McVoy91, Seltzer93]. By direct measurement, we have compared several alternative implementations. Schemes in which the file system relies on the disk scheduler to appropriately order disk writes outperform the conventional approach by more than 30 percent in many cases (up to a maximum observed difference of 500 percent). Even with this improvement, however, these schemes

---

[8] Software locking schemes that use lock files may encounter surprises because of this.

fail to achieve the performance levels available using delayed writes.

Therefore, we have introduced a new mechanism, soft updates, that approaches memory-based file system performance (within 5 percent) while providing stronger integrity and security guarantees (e.g., allocation initialization) than most UNIX file systems. This translates into a performance improvement of more than a factor of 2 in many cases (up to a maximum observed difference of a factor of 15).

The implementations compared in this paper all prevent the loss of structural integrity. However, each requires assistance (provided by the *fsck* utility in UNIX systems) when recovering from system failure or power loss. Unfortunately, the file system can not be used during this often time-consuming process, reducing data and/or system availability. We are investigating how soft updates can be extended to provide faster recovery.

While our experiments were performed on a UNIX system, the results are applicable to a much wider range of operating environments. Every file system, regardless of the operating system, must address the issue of integrity maintenance. Many (e.g., MPE-XL^{TM}, CMS^{TM}, Windows NT^{TM}) use database techniques such as logging or shadow-paging. Others (e.g., OS/2^{TM}, VMS^{TM}) rely on carefully ordered synchronous writes and could directly use our results.

Because the soft updates mechanism appears so promising, we plan to compare it to other popular methods of protecting metadata integrity, such as non-volatile RAM (NVRAM), logging and shadow-paging. NVRAM can greatly increase data persistence and provide slight performance improvements as compared to soft updates (by reducing syncer daemon activity), but is very expensive. Write-ahead logging provides the same protection as soft updates, but must use delayed group commit to achieve the same performance levels. Using shadow-paging to maintain integrity is difficult to do with delayed writes. Combined with soft updates, however, late binding of disk addresses to logical blocks [Chao92] could provide very high performance. The log-structured file system [Seltzer93] is a special case of shadow-paging that provides integrity by grouping many writes atomically (with a checksum to enforce atomicity). The large writes resulting from log-structuring can better utilize disk bandwidth, but the required cleaning activity reduces performance significantly.

We hope to make the non-proprietary components of our implementations available in the near term. If interested, please contact the authors.

8 Acknowledgements

We thank Jay Lepreau ("shepherd" for our paper), John Wilkes, Bruce Worthington and the anonymous reviewers for directly helping to improve the quality of this paper. We also thank our "remote hands" during the summer months, Carlos Fuentes. Finally, our research group is very fortunate to have the financial and technical support of several industrial partners, including AT&T/GIS, Hewlett-Packard, Intel, Motorola, SES, HaL, MTI and DEC. In particular, AT&T/GIS enabled this research with their extremely generous equipment gifts and by allowing us to generate experimental kernels with their source code. The high performance disk drives used in the experiments were donated by Hewlett-Packard.

References

[Busch85] J. Busch, A. Kondoff, "Disc Caching in the System Processing Units of the HP 3000 Family of Computers", *HP Journal*, 36 (2), February, 1985, pp. 21-39.

[Cao93] P. Cao, S. Lim, S. Venkataraman, J. Wilkes, "The Ticker-TAIP Parallel RAID Architecture", *ACM ISCA Proceedings*, May 1993, pp. 52-63.

[Chamberlin81] D. Chamberlin, M. Astrahan, et. al., "A History and Evaluation of System R", *Communications of the ACM*, 24 (10), 1981, pp. 632-646.

[Chao92] C. Chao, R. English, D. Jacobson, A. Stepanov, J. Wilkes, "Mime: A High-Performance Parallel Storage Device with Strong Recovery Guarantees", Hewlett-Packard Laboratories Report, HPL-CSP-92-9 rev 1, November 1992.

[Chutani92] S. Chutani, O. Anderson, M. Kazar, B. Leverett, W. Mason, R. Sidebotham, "The Episode File System", *Winter USENIX Proceedings*, January 1992, pp. 43-60.

[Gaede81] S. Gaede, "Tools for Research in Computer Workload Characterization", *Experimental Computer Performance and Evaluation*, 1981, ed. by D. Ferrari and M. Spadoni.

[Gaede82] S. Gaede, "A Scaling Technique for Comparing Interactive System Capacities", *13th International Conference on Management and Performance Evaluation of Computer Systems*, 1982, pp. 62-67.

[Ganger93] G. Ganger, Y. Patt, "The Process-Flow Model: Examining I/O Performance from the System's Point of View", *ACM SIGMETRICS Proceedings*, May 1993, pp. 86-97.

[Gingell87] R. Gingell, J. Moran, W. Shannon, "Virtual Memory Architecture in SunOS", *Summer USENIX Proceedings*, June 1987, pp. 81-94.

[Hagmann87] R. Hagmann, "Reimplementing the Cedar File System Using Logging and Group Commit", *ACM SOSP Proceedings*, 1987, pp. 155-162, published by ACM as *Operating Systems Review*, 21 (5), November 1987.

[HP92] Hewlett-Packard Company, "HP C2244/45/46/47 3.5-inch SCSI-2 Disk Drive Technical Reference Manual", Edition 3, September 1992, Part No. 5960-8346.

[Howard88] J. Howard, M. Kazar, S. Menees, D. Nichols, M. Satyanarayanan, R. Sidebotham, M. West, "Scale and Performance in a Distributed File System", *IEEE Transactions on Computer Systems*, 6 (1), February 1988, pp. 51-81.

[Journal92] NCR Corporation, "Journaling File System Administrator Guide, Release 2.00", NCR Document D1-2724-A, April 1992.

[Kondoff88] A. Kondoff, "The MPE XL Data Management System: Exploiting the HP Precision Architecture for HP's Next Generation Commercial Computer Systems", *IEEE Compcon Proceedings*, 1988, pp. 152-155.

[McKusick84] M. McKusick, W. Joy, S. Leffler, R. Fabry, "A Fast File System for UNIX", *ACM Transactions on Computer Systems*, August 1984, pp. 181-197.

[McKusick90] M. McKusick, M. Karels, K. Bostic, "A pageable memory based filesystem", *UKUUG Summer Conference*, pub. United Kingdom UNIX systems User Group, Buntingford, Herts., July 1990, pp. 9-13.

[McVoy91] L. McVoy, S. Kleiman, "Extent-like Performance from a UNIX File System", *Winter USENIX Proceedings*, January 1991, pp. 1-11.

[Moran87] J. Moran, "SunOS Virtual Memory Implementation", *EUUG Conference Proceedings*, Spring 1988, pp. 285-300.

[Ohta90] M. Ohta, H. Tezuka, "A fast /tmp file system by delay mount option", *Summer USENIX Proceedings*, June 1990, pp. 145-150.

[Ousterhout90] J. Ousterhout, "Why Aren't Operating Systems Getting Faster As Fast as Hardware?", *Summer USENIX Proceedings*, June 1990, pp. 247-256.

[Ritchie78] D. Ritchie, K. Thompson, "The UNIX Time-Sharing System", *Bell System Technical Journal*, 57 (6), July/August 1978, pp. 1905-1930.

[Ruemmler93] C. Ruemmler, J. Wilkes, "UNIX Disk Access Patterns", *Winter USENIX Proceedings*, January 1993, pp. 405-420.

[SCSI93] "Small Computer System Interface-2", ANSI X3T9.2, Draft Revision 10k, March 17, 1993.

[Seltzer93] M. Seltzer, K. Bostic, M. McKusick, C. Staelin, "An Implementation of a Log-Structured File System for UNIX", *Winter USENIX Proceedings*, January 1993, pp. 201-220.

[Ston87] M. Stonebraker, "The Design of the POSTGRES Storage System", *Very Large DataBase Conference*, September 1987, pp. 289-300.

A Soft updates implementation details

This appendix provides some low-level details about our soft updates implementation. It assumes the information in section 4.2 has already been read.

We use a basic structure for storing dependency information, containing two sets of next/previous pointers for internal indexing purposes, a unique identifier, a type (we currently use 11 types), and space for several additional type-specific values (currently 9). We found it useful to have "organizational" dependency structures for inodes and general file blocks (i.e., pages in our system) and to keep these **separate** from the actual file system metadata. This allows the file blocks and in-core inode structures to be re-used without losing or corrupting the dependency information. Whenever a directory block or inode is accessed, we check for an outstanding dependency structure (stored in a hash table) and make certain that any undone updates

are reflected in the copy visible to users. Two of the dependency structure types serve this purpose. Three of the type-specific values identify the "owner": the pointer to the virtual file system (VFS) structure, the inode number[9], and the logical block number within the file (or -1 for the inode itself). Each organizational structure also heads two lists of dependency structures: those that are simply waiting for the metadata to be written to disk and those that support undo/redo on portions of the "owner."

Block allocation

When a new block/fragment (direct or indirect) is allocated for a file, the new block pointer should not be written to stable storage until after the block has been initialized. This is the allocation initialization dependency described in the introduction. At the time of allocation, we update the metadata in the normal fashion and allocate[10] an *allocsafe* dependency structure for the new block (for which initialized memory is also allocated) and an *alloc* dependency structure (*allocdirect* or *allocindirect*, as appropriate) for the metadata containing the block pointer (inode or indirect block). The one *allocsafe*-specific value is a pointer to its companion *alloc* structure. There are several *alloc*-specific values: the exact location of the block pointer within the metadata structure, the new value for the pointer, the old value for the pointer (NULL, unless a fragment is being extended), the new and old size of the newly allocated block (necessary for fragment extension), a pointer to the corresponding *allocsafe* structure and a state. The state indicates whether or not the dependency is outstanding and whether or not the in-memory copy is up-to-date (always true for allocation dependencies).

At this point, the implementations for direct and indirect pointers differ; we first describe the support for pointers located in the inode. When the initialized block has been written to disk, the *allocdirect* state is modified accordingly and the corresponding *allocsafe* structure is freed. The next time the inode is written, the *allocdirect* structure will also be freed. If the inode is written **before** the newly allocated block has been initialized, the allocation must first be undone. This is accomplished by replacing the new block pointer with the old and, in the case of fragment extension, reducing the file length appropriately. These values can be changed in the buffer cache block without modifying the *in-core*[11] inode structure. "Redo" operations are only necessary if an in-core structure holding an inode with pending *allocdirect* dependencies is re-used by the file

---

[9] The inode number uniquely identifies the inode within a file system.

[10] We use a simple, fast management policy for the dependency structures. When more are needed, we allocate a page of kernel memory and break it into a list of structures. Freeing a structure consists of adding it to this list, and allocation simply takes the next structure off the list.

[11] The file system always copies an inode's contents from the buffer cached into an *in-core* (or internal) inode structure before accessing them. So, the inode structure manipulated by the file system is always separate from the corresponding source block for disk writes.

system. When the inode is again brought in-core, the new values replace the old and the inode is marked dirty. If this does not happen within 15 seconds, the inode dependency structure is added to the workitem queue. The service function consists simply of bringing the inode in-core.

For pointers in indirect blocks, we implement things differently. An indirect block can contain many block pointers, making it inefficient to traverse a list of per-pointer structures to undo/redo updates. We associate an *indirdep* dependency structure with each indirect block that has pending allocation dependencies. A block of memory equal in size to the indirect block is allocated with this structure, and initialized with a copy of the "safe" contents. When writing the indirect block to disk, this "safe" block is used as the source. When a newly allocated disk block has been initialized, its *allocsafe* structure is freed, and the corresponding *allocindirect* structure is used to update the "safe" copy and then freed. If there are no remaining dependencies when the indirect block is next written, the *indirdep* structure and the "safe" block are freed. Because indirect blocks generally represent a very small fraction of the cache contents, we force them to stay resident and dirty while they have pending dependencies. This allows us to avoid additional undo/redo embellishments.

Block de-allocation

A de-allocated block should not be re-used before the previous pointer to it has been permanently reset. We achieve this by not freeing the block (i.e., setting the bits in the free map) until the reset block pointer reaches stable storage. When block de-allocation is required, the old block pointer values are placed in a *freeblocks* dependency structure, together with the size of the last fragment, if appropriate. Outstanding *alloc* and *allocsafe* dependencies for de-allocated blocks are freed at this point, since they no longer serve any purpose. The block pointers are then reset in the inode (or indirect block) to release the blocks. After the modified metadata has been written to disk, the *freeblocks* structure is added to the workitem queue. For the special case of extending a fragment by moving the data to a new block, and thus de-allocating the original fragment, we do not consider the inode appropriately "modified" until the *allocdirect* dependency clears. The blocks are freed by the syncer daemon using the same code paths as the original file system. Any dependency structures "owned" by the blocks are considered complete at this point and handled accordingly; this applies only to directory blocks.

Link addition

When a new link is added to a directory block, it should not be written to disk until the pointed-to inode (possibly new) has reached stable storage with its link count[12] incremented. We use an undo/redo approach, as with allocation initialization, to provide this protection. The in-memory copies of the directory block and inode are modified in the normal fashion. In addition, an *addsafe* dependency structure is allocated for the inode and an *add* structure is allocated for the directory block. The one *addsafe*-specific value is a pointer to the new *add* structure. There are several *add*-specific values: the offset of the new directory entry within the block, the pointed-to inode number, a pointer to the *addsafe* structure and a state.

The state serves the same purposes described above for allocation initialization. When the inode has been written, the *addsafe* structure is freed and the state is modified appropriately. When the directory block is next accessed, the *add* structure is freed. If the directory block is written **before** the inode reaches stable storage, the link addition is first undone by replacing the inode number in the directory entry with zero (indicating that the entry is unused). After the directory block write completes, the correct inode number again replaces the zero. Because the directory block's contents are out-of-date, we inhibit all accesses (reads and writes) during the disk write. Also, we do not mark the directory block as dirty immediately after the disk write completes. Rather we allow the system to re-use the cache block (i.e., VM page) if necessary. When the directory block is next accessed, we make certain that all directory entries are up-to-date. If it is not accessed within 15 seconds, its dependency structure is added to the workitem queue. The service function simply accesses the directory block and marks it dirty.

Link removal

When a link is removed, the link count in the inode should not be decremented before the modified directory block reaches the disk. We provide this protection with a deferred approach, like that used for block de-allocation. The directory entry is removed in the normal fashion. If the directory entry has a pending link addition dependency, the *add* and *addsafe* structures are removed and the link removal proceeds unhindered (the add and remove have been serviced with no disk writes!). Otherwise, a *remove* dependency structure is allocated for the directory block. The two *remove*-specific values are the inode number and a pointer to the VFS structure, allowing the previously pointed-to inode to be identified later. When the directory block has been written to disk, the *remove* structure is added to the workitem queue. Its service function consists of decrementing the link count. If the link count becomes zero, the inode is freed using the normal code paths and its blocks are de-allocated as described above.

---

[12]The link count identifies the number of directory entries pointing to the inode.

Disk-directed I/O for MIMD Multiprocessors

David Kotz

Department of Computer Science
Dartmouth College
Hanover, NH 03755
dfk@cs.dartmouth.edu

Abstract

Many scientific applications that run on today's multiprocessors, such as weather forecasting and seismic analysis, are bottlenecked by their file-I/O needs. Even if the multiprocessor is configured with sufficient I/O hardware, the file-system software often fails to provide the available bandwidth to the application. Although libraries and enhanced file-system interfaces can make a significant improvement, we believe that fundamental changes are needed in the file-server software. We propose a new technique, *disk-directed I/O*, to allow the disk servers to determine the flow of data for maximum performance. Our simulations show that tremendous performance gains are possible. Indeed, disk-directed I/O provided consistent high performance that was largely independent of data distribution, obtained up to 93% of peak disk bandwidth, and was as much as 16 times faster than traditional parallel file systems.

1   Introduction

Scientific applications like weather forecasting, aircraft simulation, seismic exploration, and climate modeling are increasingly being implemented on massively parallel supercomputers. Applications like these have intense I/O demands, as well as massive computational requirements. Recent multiprocessors have provided high-performance I/O hardware, in the form of disks or disk arrays attached to I/O processors connected to the multiprocessor's interconnection network, but effective file-system software has yet to be built.

Today's typical multiprocessor has a rudimentary parallel file system derived from Unix. While Unix-like semantics are convenient for users porting applications to the machine, the performance is often poor. Poor performance is not surprising because the Unix file system was designed for a general-purpose workload [OCH+85], rather than for a parallel, scientific workload. Scientific

---

This research was funded by Dartmouth College.

applications, on the other hand, use larger files and have more sequential access [MK91, GGL93, PP93]. *Parallel* scientific programs access the file with patterns not seen in uniprocessor or distributed-system workloads, in particular, complex strided access to discontiguous pieces of the file [KN94, NK94]. Finally, scientific applications use files for more than loading raw data and storing results; files are used as scratch space for very large problems as application-controlled virtual memory [CK93]. In short, multiprocessors need new file systems that are designed for parallel scientific applications.

In this paper we describe a technique that is designed specifically for high performance on parallel scientific applications. It is most suited for MIMD multiprocessors that have no remote-memory access, and that distinguish between I/O Processors (IOPs), which do file-system processing, and Compute Processors (CPs), which do mostly application processing. The IBM SP-2, Intel iPSC, Intel Paragon, KSR/2, Meiko CS-2, nCUBE/2, and Thinking Machines CM-5 all use this model; the CS-2 and the SP-2 allow IOPs to double as CPs. Furthermore, our technique is best suited to applications written in a single-program-multiple-data (SPMD) or data-parallel programming model. With our technique, *disk-directed I/O*, CPs collectively send a single request to all IOPs, which then arrange the flow of data to optimize disk, buffer, and network resources.

We begin by advocating a "collective-I/O" interface for parallel file systems. Then, in Sections 3 and 4, we consider some of the ways to support collective I/O and our implementation of these alternatives. Section 5 describes our experiments, and Section 6 examines the results. We contrast our system to related work in Section 7, and summarize our conclusions in Section 8.

2   Collective I/O

Consider programs that distribute large matrices across the processor memories, and the task of loading such a matrix from a file.[1] From the point of view of a traditional file system, each processor independently requests its portion of the data, by reading from the file into its local memory. If that processor's data is not logically contiguous in the file, as is often the case [KN94], a separate file-system call is needed for each contiguous chunk of the file. The file system is thus faced with concurrent small requests from many processors, instead of the single large request that would have occurred on a uniprocessor. Indeed, since most multiprocessor file systems [CF94, FPD93, Pie89, Roy93, DdR92, LIN+93, BGST93, Dib90, DSE88] decluster file data across many disks, each application request may be broken into even smaller requests that are sent to different IOPs. It is difficult for the file system, which is distributed across many I/O processors, to recognize these requests as a single coordinated request, and to use that information to optimize the I/O. Valuable semantic information — that a large, contiguous, parallel file transfer is in progress — is lost through this low-level interface. A *collective-I/O interface*, in which all CPs cooperate to make a single, large request, retains this semantic information, making it easier to coordinate I/O for better performance [dBC93, Nit92, PGK88].

Collective I/O need not involve matrices. Many out-of-core parallel algorithms do I/O in "memoryloads," that is, they repeatedly load some subset of the file into memory, process it, and write it out [CK93]. Each transfer is a large, but not necessarily contiguous, set of data. Traditional caching and prefetching policies, geared for sequential access, would be ineffective or even detrimental for this type of I/O.

Unfortunately, few multiprocessor file systems provide a collective interface. Most have an interface based on simple parallel extensions to the traditional read/write/seek model, focusing on coordination of the file pointer. Vesta [CF94] and the nCUBE file system [DdR92] support logical mappings between the file and processor memories, defining separate "subfiles" for each processor. Although these mappings remove the burden of managing the file pointer from the programmer, and allow the programmer to request noncontiguous data in a single request, there is no support for collective I/O. CM-Fortran for the CM-5 does provide a collective-I/O interface, which leads to high performance through cooperation among the compiler, runtime, operating system, and hardware. ELFS [GP91] provides an object-oriented interface that encourages operations on large objects, and could lead to support for collective I/O. Finally, there are several interfaces for collective matrix I/O [GGL93, BdC93, BBS+94]. For example, to

read a two-dimensional matrix of integers in the notation of [GGL93], every processor executes the following code:

```
/* describes my part of matrix */
PIFArrayPart mypart[2] =  ... ;
/* memory for my part */
int *A = malloc(...);
PIFILE *fp = PIFOpen(...);
PIFReadDistributedArray(fp, NULL,
    sizeof(int), mypart, 2,
    A, MSG_INT);
```

Thus, the groundwork for collective I/O exists. The challenge is to provide mechanisms that use the semantic-information content of collective operations to improve performance.

3 Collective-I/O implementation alternatives

In this paper we consider collective-read and -write operations that transfer a large matrix between CP memories and a file that is declustered, block by block, over many IOPs and disks. The matrix is distributed among the CPs in various ways, but within each CP the data is contiguous in memory. We discuss three implementation alternatives: traditional caching, two-phase I/O, and disk-directed I/O. The latter two require a collective-I/O interface similar to that of Galbreath et al [GGL93], above.

Traditional caching. This alternative mimics a "traditional" parallel file system like Intel CFS [Pie89], with no explicit collective-I/O interface and with IOPs that each manage a file cache. Figure 1a shows the function called by the application on the CP to read its part of a file, and the corresponding function executed at the IOP to service each incoming CP request. Recall that each application process must call ReadCP once for each contiguous chunk of the file, no matter how small. Each IOP attempts to dynamically optimize the use of the disk, cache, and network interface.

Two-phase I/O. Figure 1b sketches an alternative proposed by del Rosario, Bordawekar, and Choudhary [dBC93, BdC93], which permutes the data among the CP memories before writing or after reading. Thus, there are two phases, one for I/O and one for an in-memory permutation. The permutation is chosen so that requests to the IOPs "conform" to the layout of the file, that is, the requests are for large contiguous chunks.

Disk-directed I/O. We go further by having the CPs pass the collective request on to the IOPs, which then arrange the data transfer as shown in Figure 1c. This *disk-directed* model, which essentially puts the disks (IOPs) in control of the order and timing of the flow of data, has several potential performance advantages:

---

[1]This scenario arises in many situations. The file may contain raw input data or may be a scratch file written in a previous phase of the application. The matrix may be the whole data set, or may be a partition of a larger data set, for example, a 2-d slice of a 3-d matrix. Furthermore, the operation may be synchronous, with the application waiting for I/O to complete, or asynchronous, perhaps as the result of a compiler-instigated prefetch request.

a) Traditional caching

```
ReadCP(file, read parameters, destination address):
    for each file block needed to satisfy request
        compute which disk holds that file block
        if our previous request to that disk is still outstanding,
            wait for response and deposit data into user's buffer
        send new request to that disk's IOP for this (partial) block
    end
    wait for all outstanding requests.
```

```
ReadIOP(file, read parameters):
    look for the requested block in the cache
    if not there
        find or make a free cache buffer
        ask disk to read that block into cache buffer
    reply to CP, including data from cache buffer
    consider prefetching or other optimizations
```

b) Two-phase I/O

```
CollectiveReadCP(file, read parameters, destination address):
    Barrier (CPs using this file), to ensure that all are ready
    decide what portion of the data this processor should read
        (conforming to the file layout)
    for each contiguous chunk of the file this processor should read
        ReadCP(file, one chunk)
    Barrier (CPs using this file), to wait for all I/O to complete
    run permutation algorithm to send data to correct destination
    Barrier (CPs using this file), to wait for permutation to complete
```

```
ReadIOP (as above)
```

c) Disk-directed I/O

```
CollectiveReadCP(file, read parameters, destination address):
    arrange for incoming data to be stored at destination address
    Barrier (CPs using this file), to ensure that all buffers are ready
    any one CP:
        multicast (CollectiveRead, file, read parameters) to all IOPs
    wait for all IOPs to respond that they are finished
    Barrier (CPs using this file), to wait for all I/O to complete
```

```
CollectiveReadIOP(file, read parameters):
    determine the set of file data local to this IOP
    determine the set of disk blocks needed
    sort the set of disk blocks to optimize disk movement
        using double-buffering for each disk,
        request blocks from the disk
        as each block arrives from disk,
            send piece(s) to the appropriate CPs
    when complete, send message to original requesting CP
```

Figure 1: Pseudo-code for collective-read implementations. Collective writes are similar.

- The I/O can conform not only to the logical layout of the file, as in two-phase I/O, but to the physical layout on disk.

- The disk-I/O phase is integrated with the permutation phase.

- There is only one I/O request to each IOP; subsequent communication uses only low-overhead data-transfer messages.

- Disk scheduling is improved, possibly across megabytes of data: in Figure 1c, the IOPs presort the block list for each disk.

- Prefetching and write-behind require no guessing, and thus make no mistakes.

- Buffer management is perfect, needing little space (two buffers per disk per file), and capturing all potential locality advantages.

- No additional memory or memory-memory copying is needed at the CPs for buffering, message-passing, or permuting data.

- There is no communication among the IOPs and none, other than barriers, among the CPs. The cost of these barriers is negligible compared to the time needed for a large file transfer.

4 Evaluation

We implemented both a traditional-caching system and a disk-directed-I/O system on a simulated MIMD multiprocessor (see below). We did not implement two-phase I/O because, as we discuss in Section 7.1, disk-directed I/O obtains all the benefits of two-phase I/O, and more. In this section, we describe our simulated implementation; more details can be found in [Kot94].

Files were striped across all disks, block by block. Each IOP served one or more disks, using one I/O bus. Each disk had a thread permanently running on its IOP, that controlled access to the disk.

Disk-directed I/O. Each IOP received one request, creating one new thread. The new thread computed the list of disk blocks involved, sorted the list by location, and informed the relevant disk threads. It then allocated two one-block buffers for each local disk, and created a thread to manage each buffer. While not absolutely necessary, the threads simplified programming the concurrent activities. These buffer threads repeatedly transferred blocks, letting the disk thread choose which block to transfer next. When reading, they used a special "Memput" message to move data from the IOP memory to the CP memory, using DMA to and from the network. When writing, they

sent a "Memget" message to the CP, causing it to reply with a message containing the requested data, again using DMA. When possible the thread sent concurrent Memget or Memput messages to many CPs.

Traditional caching. Our code followed the pseudo-code of Figure 1a. CPs did not cache or prefetch data, so all requests involved communication with the IOP. The CP sent concurrent requests to all the relevant IOPs, with up to one outstanding request per disk per CP. This limit was a compromise between maximizing concurrency and the need to limit the potential load on each IOP.[2]

At the IOP, each incoming request was handled by a new thread. Each IOP managed a cache that was large enough to double-buffer an independent stream of requests from each CP to each disk.[3] The cache used an LRU-replacement strategy, prefetched one block ahead after each read request, and flushed dirty buffers to disk when they were full (i.e., after n bytes had been written to an n-byte buffer [KE93]).

We transferred data as a part of request and reply messages, and used DMA for all message-passing. Thus, the reply to a read request contained up to one block of data, which was deposited directly in the user buffer before waking the CP. Write-request messages also contained up to one block of data, which was deposited directly into a new thread's buffer. Later, the thread copied the data into a cache buffer, the only memory-memory copy we used.[4]

While our cache implementation does not model any specific commercial cache implementation, we believe it is reasonable and better than most, and thus a fair competitor for our disk-directed-I/O implementation.

4.1 Simulator

The implementations described above ran on top of the Proteus parallel-architecture simulator [BDCW91], which in turn ran on a DEC-5000 workstation. We configured Proteus using the parameters listed in Table 1. These parameters are not meant to reflect any particular machine, but a generic machine of current technology.

We added a disk model, a reimplementation of Ruemmler and Wilkes' HP 97560 model [RW94, KTR94]. We validated our model against disk traces provided by HP, using the same technique and measure as Ruemmler and Wilkes. Our implementation had a demerit percentage of 3.9%, which indicates that it modeled the 97560 accurately.

---

[2]More aggressive strategies would require either more buffer space or the addition of dynamic flow control, without a substantial improvement in parallelism.

[3]While two cache buffers per disk *per CP* is not scalable, it is reasonable in most situations (e.g., only 16 MB per IOP for 2 local disks, 512 CPs, and an 8 KB block size). Note that this is much more than the space needed for disk-directed I/O, two buffers per disk.

[4]We chose this design because it was similar to traditional systems. In any case, we believe that avoiding the memory-memory copy by using Memgets and dataless request messages would be unlikely to justify the extra round-trip message traffic, particularly for small writes.

Table 1: Parameters for simulator. Those marked with a *
were varied in some experiments.

MIMD, distributed-memory	32 processors
Compute processors (CPs)	16 *
I/O processors (IOPs)	16 *
CPU speed, type	50 MHz, RISC
Disks	16 *
Disk type	HP 97560
Disk capacity	1.3 GB
Disk peak transfer rate	2.34 Mbytes/s
File-system block size	8 KB
I/O buses (one per IOP)	16 *
I/O bus type	SCSI
I/O bus peak bandwidth	10 Mbytes/s
Interconnect topology	6×6 torus
Interconnect bandwidth	200×10^6 bytes/s bidirectional
Interconnect latency	20 ns per router
Routing	wormhole

5 Experimental Design

We used the simulator to evaluate the performance of disk-directed I/O, with the throughput for transferring large files as our performance metric. The primary factor used in our experiments was the file system, which could be one of three alternatives: traditional caching, disk-directed, or disk-directed with block-list presort (defined in Figure 1c). We repeated this experiment for a variety of system configurations; each configuration was defined by a combination of the file-access pattern, disk layout, number of CPs, number of IOPs, and number of disks. Each test case was replicated in five independent trials, to account for randomness in the disk layouts and in the network. To be fair, the total transfer time included waiting for all I/O to complete, including outstanding write-behind and prefetch requests.

The file and disk layout. Our experiments transferred a one- or two-dimensional array of records. Two-dimensional arrays were stored in the file in row-major order. The file was striped across disks, block by block. The file size in all cases was 10 MB (1280 8-KB blocks). While 10 MB is not a large file, preliminary tests showed qualitatively similar results with 100 and 1000 MB files. Thus, 10 MB was a compromise to save simulation time.

Within each disk, the blocks of the file were laid out according to one of two strategies: *contiguous*, where the logical blocks of the file were laid out in consecutive physical blocks on disk, or *random-blocks*, where blocks were placed at random physical locations. A real file system would be somewhere between the two. As confirmed by our own preliminary tests, it would have performance somewhere between the two.

The access patterns. Our read- and write-access patterns differed in the way the array elements (records) were mapped into CP memories. We chose to evaluate the array-distribution possibilities available in High-Performance Fortran [HPF93, dBC93], as shown in Figure 2. Thus, elements in each dimension of the array could be mapped entirely to one CP (NONE), distributed among CPs in contiguous blocks (BLOCK; note this is a different "block" than the file system "block"), or distributed round-robin among the CPs (CYCLIC). We name the patterns using a shorthand beginning with r for reading and w for writing; the r names are shown in Figure 2. There was one additional pattern, ra (ALL, not shown), which corresponds to all CPs reading the entire file, leading to multiple copies of the file in memory. A few patterns are redundant in our configuration (rnn ≡ rn, rnc ≡ rc, rbn ≡ rb) and were not actually used.

We chose two different record sizes, one designed to stress the system's capability to process small pieces of data, with lots of interprocess locality and lots of contention, and the other designed to work in the most-convenient unit, with little interprocess locality or contention. The small record size was 8 bytes, the size of a double-precision floating point number. The large record size was 8192 bytes, the size of a file-system block and cache buffer. These record-size choices are reasonable [KN94]. We also tried 1024-byte and 4096-byte records, leading to results between the 8-byte and 8192-byte results; we present only the extremes here.

6 Results

Figures 3 and 4 show the performance of our disk-directed-I/O approach and of the traditional-caching method. Each figure has two graphs, one for 8-byte records and one for 8192-byte records. Disk-directed I/O was usually at least as fast as traditional caching, and in one case was *16 times* faster.

Figure 3 displays the performance on a random-blocks disk layout. Three cases are shown for each access pattern: traditional caching (TC), and disk-directed I/O (DDIO) with and without a presort of the block requests by physical location. Throughput for disk-directed I/O with presorting consistently reached 6.2 Mbytes/s for reading and 7.4–7.5 Mbytes/s for writing. In contrast, traditional-caching throughput was highly dependent on the access pattern, was never faster than 5 Mbytes/s, and was particularly slow for many 8-byte patterns. Cases with small chunk sizes were the slowest, as slow as 0.8 Mbytes/s, due to the tremendous number of requests required to transfer the data. As a result, disk-directed I/O with presorting was up to 9.0 times faster than traditional caching.

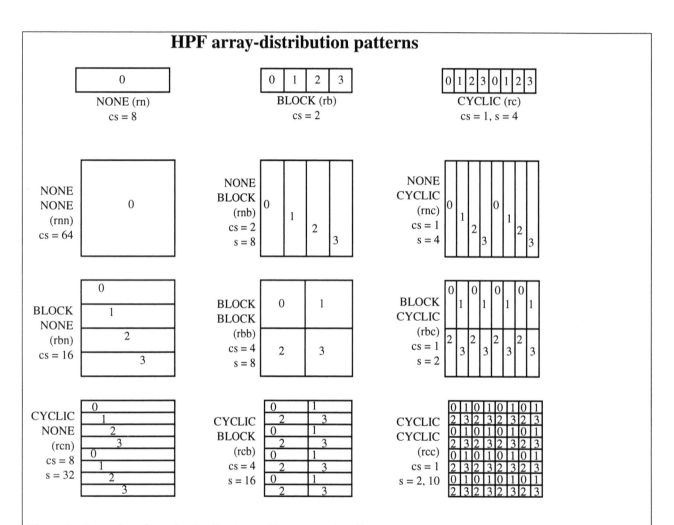

Figure 2: Examples of matrix distributions, which we used as file-access patterns in our experiments. These examples represent common ways to distribute a 1x8 vector or an 8x8 matrix over four processors. Patterns are named by the distribution method (NONE, BLOCK, or CYCLIC) in each dimension (rows first, in the case of matrices). Each region of the matrix is labeled with the number of the CP responsible for that region. The matrix is stored in row-major order, both in the file and in memory. The *chunk size* (cs) is the size of the largest contiguous chunk of the file that is sent to a single CP (in units of array elements), and the *stride* (s) is the file distance between the beginning of one chunk and the next chunk destined for the same CP, where relevant.

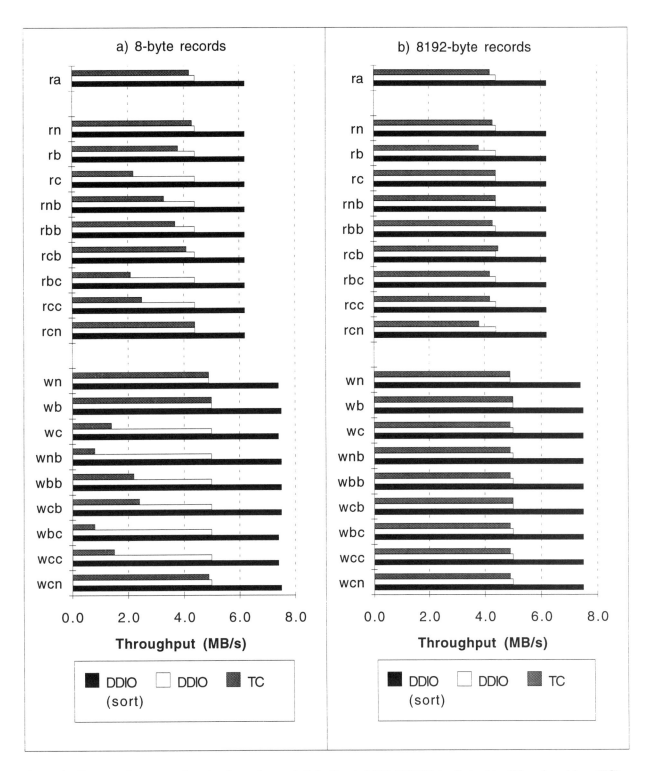

Figure 3: Two graphs comparing the throughput of disk-directed I/O (DDIO) to that of traditional caching (TC), on a **random-blocks** disk layout. `ra` throughput has been normalized by the number of CPs. Each point represents the average of five trials of an access pattern on both methods (maximum coefficient of variation (*cv*) is 0.14).

Figure 3 also makes clear the benefit of presorting disk requests by physical location, an optimization available in disk-directed I/O to an extent not possible in traditional caching or, for that matter, in two-phase I/O. Nonetheless, disk-directed I/O without presorting was still faster than traditional caching in most cases. At best, it was 6.1 times faster; at worst, there was no noticeable difference. Disk-directed I/O thus improved performance in two ways: by reducing overhead and by presorting the block list.

To test the ability of the different file-system implementations to take advantage of disk layout, and to expose other overheads when the disk bandwidth could be fully utilized, we compared the two methods on a contiguous disk layout (Figure 4). I/O on this layout was much faster than on the random-blocks layout, by avoiding the disk-head movements caused by random layouts and by benefiting from the disks' own caches when using the contiguous layout. In most cases disk-directed reading moved about 32.8 Mbytes/s, and disk-directed writing moved 34.8 Mbytes/s, which was an impressive 93% of the disks' peak transfer rate of 37.5 Mbytes/s. The few cases where disk-directed I/O did not get as close to the peak disk transfer rate were affected by the overhead of moving individual 8-byte records to and from the CPs. Further tuning of the disk-directed-I/O code may alleviate this problem, but the real solution would be to use gather/scatter Memput and Memget operations.

Traditional caching was rarely able to obtain the full disk bandwidth, and had particular trouble with the 8-byte patterns. Although there were cases where traditional caching could match disk-directed I/O, traditional caching was as much as 16.2 times slower than disk-directed I/O. Traditional caching failed in a few critical ways:

- When the CPs were active at widely different locations in the file (e.g., in rb or rcn), there was little inter-process spatial locality. In the contiguous layout, the multiple localities defeated the disk's internal caching and caused extra head movement, both a significant performance loss. Furthermore, the lost locality could hamper the performance of IOP caching and prefetching, although our caches were large enough to avoid this factor.

- In some patterns, IOP-prefetching mistakes caused extraneous disk reads. At the end of the rb pattern, for example, one extra block is prefetched on most disks; this one block is negligible in large files, but accounts for most of traditional caching's poor performance on rb in Figure 3.

- When the CPs were using 8-byte CYCLIC patterns, many IOP-request messages were necessary to transfer the small non-contiguous records, requiring many (expensive) IOP-cache accesses. In addition, the success of interprocess spatial locality was crucial for performance.

- The high data rates of the contiguous disk layout expose the cache-management overhead in traditional caching, unable to match disk-directed I/O's performance except for wn.

6.1 Sensitivity

To evaluate the sensitivity of our results to some of the parameters, we independently varied the number of CPs, number of IOPs, and number of disks. It was only feasible to experiment with a subset of all configurations, so we chose a subset that would push the limits of the system by using the contiguous layout, and exhibit most of the variety shown earlier, by using the patterns ra, rn, rb, and rc with 8 KB records. ra throughput was normalized as usual. For more details and other variations, see [Kot94].

We first varied the number of CPs (Figure 5), holding the number of IOPs and disks fixed, and maintaining the cache size for traditional caching at two buffers per disk *per CP*. Note that disk-directed I/O was unaffected. Multiple localities hurt rb as before, but the most interesting effect was the poor performance of traditional caching on the rc pattern. With 1-block records and no buffers at the CP, each CP request can only use one disk. With fewer CPs than IOPs, the full disk parallelism was not used. Finally, cache-management overhead, which grew with cache size and contention by multiple CPs, reduced the performance of traditional caching on all four patterns.

We then varied the number of IOPs (and SCSI busses), holding the number of CPs, number of disks, and total cache size fixed (Figure 6). Performance decreased with fewer IOPs because of increasing bus contention, particularly when there were more than two disks per bus, and was ultimately limited by the 10 MB/s bus bandwidth. As always, traditional caching had difficulty with the rb pattern. Cache-management overhead contributed to traditional caching's inability to match disk-directed I/O.

We then varied the number of disks, using one IOP, holding the number of CPs at 16, and maintaining the traditional-caching cache size at two buffers per CP *per disk* (Figures 7 and 8). Performance scaled with more disks, approaching the 10 MB/s bus-speed limit. The relationship between disk-directed I/O and traditional caching was determined by a combination of factors: disk-directed I/O's lower overhead and better use of the disks, and traditional caching's better use of the bus (sometimes the "synchronous" nature of disk-directed I/O caused bus congestion on the contiguous layout).

Summary. These variation experiments showed that while the relative benefit of disk-directed I/O over traditional caching varied, disk-directed I/O consistently provided excellent performance, at least as good as traditional caching, often independent of access pattern, and often close to hardware limits.

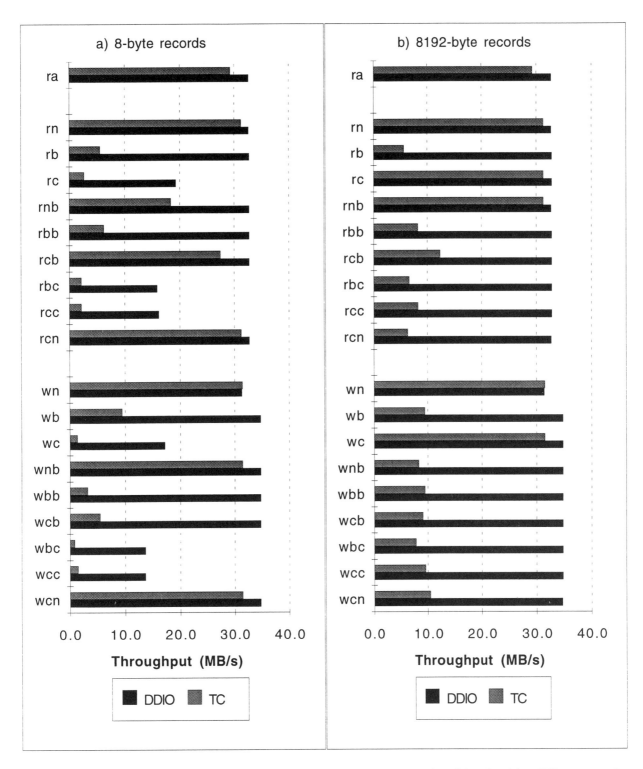

Figure 4: Two graphs comparing the throughput of disk-directed I/O (DDIO) and traditional caching (TC), on a **contiguous** disk layout. `ra` throughput has been normalized by the number of CPs. Each point represents the average of five trials of an access pattern on both methods (maximum *cv* is 0.13). Note that the peak disk throughput was 37.5 Mbytes/s.

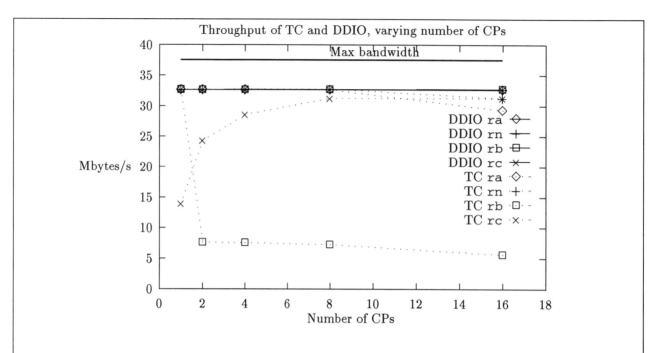

Figure 5: A comparison of the throughput of disk-directed I/O (DDIO) and traditional caching (TC), as the **number of CPs varied**, for the ra, rn, rb, and rc patterns (ra throughput has been normalized by the number of CPs). All cases used the contiguous disk layout, and all used 8 KB records.

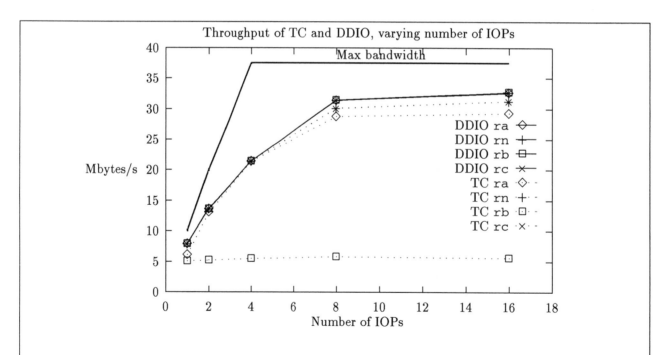

Figure 6: A comparison of the throughput of disk-directed I/O (DDIO) and traditional caching (TC), as the **number of IOPs (and busses) varied**, for the ra, rn, rb, and rc patterns (ra throughput has been normalized by the number of CPs). All cases used the contiguous disk layout, and all used 8 KB records. The maximum bandwidth was determined by either the busses (1–2 IOPs) or the disks (4–16 IOPs).

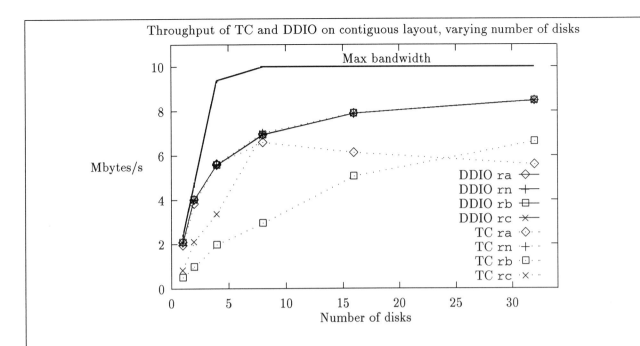

Figure 7: A comparison of the throughput of disk-directed I/O (DDIO) and traditional caching (TC), as the **number of disks varied**, for the `ra`, `rn`, `rb`, and `rc` patterns (`ra` throughput has been normalized by the number of CPs). All cases used the contiguous disk layout, and all used 8 KB records. The maximum bandwidth was determined either by the disks (1–4 disks) or by the (single) bus (8–32 disks).

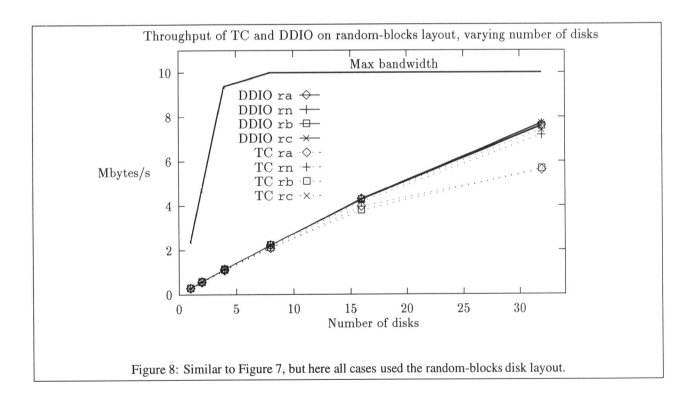

Figure 8: Similar to Figure 7, but here all cases used the random-blocks disk layout.

7 Related work

Disk-directed I/O is somewhat reminiscent of the PIFS (Bridge) "tools" interface [Dib90], in that the data flow is controlled by the file system rather by than the application. PIFS focuses on managing *where* data flows (for memory locality), whereas disk-directed I/O focuses more on *when* data flows (for better disk and cache performance).

Some parallel database machines use an architecture similar to disk-directed I/O, in that certain operations are moved closer to the disks to allow for more optimization. In the Tandem NonStop system [EGKS90] each query is sent to all IOPs, which scan the local database partition and send only the relevant tuples back to the requesting node. The Super Database Computer [KHH+92] has disk controllers that continuously produce *tasks* from the input data set, which are consumed and processed by CPs as they become available. While this concept is roughly similar to our disk-directed I/O, it is primarily a speed-matching buffer used for load balancing.

The Jovian collective-I/O library [BBS+94] tries to coalesce fragmented requests from many CPs into larger requests that can be passed to the IOPs. Their "coalescing processes" are essentially a dynamic implementation of the two-phase-I/O permutation phase.

Our model for managing a disk-directed request, that is, sending a high-level request to all IOPs which then operate independently under the assumption that they can determine the necessary actions to accomplish the task, is an example of *collaborative execution* like that used in the TickerTAIP RAID controller [CLVW93].

Finally, our Memput and Memget operations are not unusual. Similar remote-memory-access mechanisms are supported in a variety of distributed-memory systems [WMR+94, CDG+93].

7.1 Comparison to Two-phase I/O

The above results clearly show the benefits of disk-directed I/O over traditional caching. Two-phase I/O [dBC93] was designed to avoid the worst of traditional caching while using the same IOP software, by reading data in a "conforming distribution," then permuting it among the CPs. At first glance, disk-directed I/O is two-phase I/O implemented by rewriting IOP software so the IOPs do both phases simultaneously. In fact, disk-directed I/O has many advantages over two-phase I/O:

- There is no need to choose a conforming distribution. Our data indicates that it would be a difficult choice, dependent on the file layout, access pattern, record size, and cache management algorithm. The designers of two-phase I/O found that an `rb` distribution was appropriate for a matrix laid out in row-major order, but our results show that `rb` was rarely the best choice.

- There is the opportunity to optimize disk access with disk-request presorting, in our case obtaining a 41–50% performance boost.

- Smaller caches are needed at the IOPs, there are no prefetching mistakes, and there is no cache thrashing.

- No extra memory is needed for permuting at the CPs.

- No extra time is needed for a permutation phase; the "permutation" is overlapped with I/O.

- Each datum moves through the interconnect only once in disk-directed I/O, and typically twice in two-phase I/O.

- Communication is spread throughout disk transfer, not concentrated in a permutation phase.

Thus, although we did not simulate two-phase I/O, it should be slower than disk-directed I/O because it cannot optimize the I/O as well and because the I/O and permutation phases are not overlapped. Two-phase I/O could be faster than disk-directed I/O in some patterns if the network were much slower than the disks, *and* two-phase I/O were able to use a smart permutation algorithm not available to the more dynamically scheduled disk-directed I/O.

8 Conclusions

Our simulations showed that disk-directed I/O avoided many of the pitfalls inherent in the traditional caching method, such as cache thrashing, extraneous disk-head movements, excessive request-response traffic between CP and IOP, inability to use all the disk parallelism, inability to use the disks' own caches, overhead for cache management, and memory-memory copies. Furthermore, disk-directed I/O presorted disk requests to optimize head movement, and had smaller buffer space requirements. As a result, disk-directed I/O could provide consistent performance close to the limits of the disk hardware. Indeed, it was in one case more than 16 times faster than the caching method, and was never substantially slower. More importantly, its performance was nearly independent of the distribution of data to CPs.

Our results also reaffirm the importance of disk layout to performance: throughput on the contiguous layout was about 5 times that on a random-blocks layout. Multiprocessor file systems for scientific applications should definitely consider extent-based layouts or other techniques to increase physical contiguity.

As presented here, disk-directed I/O would be most valuable when making large, collective transfers of data between multiple disks and multiple memories, whether for loading input data, storing result data, or swapping data to a scratch file in an out-of-core algorithm. Indeed, the data need not be contiguous; our random-blocks layout also simulates a request for an arbitrary subset of blocks from a large file. The concept of disk-directed I/O can be extended to other environments, however. Non-collective I/O access (e.g., our rn and wn patterns) can benefit, although the gain is not as dramatic. Our Memput and Memget operations would fit in well on a shared-memory machine with a block-transfer operation. Although our patterns focused on the transfer of 1-d and 2-d matrices, we expect to see similar performance for higher-dimensional matrices and other regular structures. Finally, there is potential to implement transfer requests that are more complex than simple permutations, for example, selecting only a subset of records that match some criterion.

Our results emphasize that simply layering a new interface on top of a traditional file system will not suffice. For maximum performance the file-system interface must include collective-I/O operations, and the file-system software (in particular, the IOP software) must be redesigned to use mechanisms like disk-directed I/O to support collective I/O. Nonetheless, there is still a place for caches. Irregular or dynamic access patterns involving small, independent transfers and having substantial temporal or interprocess locality will still benefit from a cache. The challenge, then, is to design systems that integrate the two techniques smoothly.

Future work

There are many directions for future work in this area:

- design an appropriate collective-I/O interface,

- find a general way to specify a collective, disk-directed access request to IOPs,

- reduce overhead by allowing the application to make "strided" requests to the traditional caching system,

- optimize network message traffic by using gather/scatter messages to move non-contiguous data, and

- optimize concurrent disk-directed activities.

Acknowledgements

Thanks to Song Bac Toh and Sriram Radhakrishnan for implementing and validating the disk model; to Chris Ruemmler, John Wilkes, and Hewlett Packard Corporation for allowing us to use their disk traces to validate our disk model, and for their help in understanding the details of the HP 97560; to Denise Ecklund of Intel for help understanding the Paragon interconnection network; to Eric Brewer and Chrysanthos Dellarocas for Proteus; to Tom Cormen, Keith Kotay, Nils Nieuwejaar, the anonymous reviewers, and especially Karin Petersen for feedback on drafts of this paper.

References

[BBS+94] Robert Bennett, Kelvin Bryant, Alan Sussman, Raja Das, and Joel Saltz. Jovian: A framework for optimizing parallel I/O. In *Proceedings of the 1994 Scalable Parallel Libraries Conference*. IEEE Computer Society Press, October 1994. To appear.

[BdC93] Rajesh Bordawekar, Juan Miguel del Rosario, and Alok Choudhary. Design and evaluation of primitives for parallel I/O. In *Proceedings of Supercomputing '93*, pages 452–461, 1993.

[BDCW91] Eric A. Brewer, Chrysanthos N. Dellarocas, Adrian Colbrook, and William E. Weihl. Proteus: A high-performance parallel-architecture simulator. Technical Report MIT/LCS/TR–516, MIT, September 1991.

[BGST93] Michael L. Best, Adam Greenberg, Craig Stanfill, and Lewis W. Tucker. CMMD I/O: A parallel Unix I/O. In *Proceedings of the Seventh International Parallel Processing Symposium*, pages 489–495, 1993.

[CDG+93] David E. Culler, Andrea Drusseau, Seth Copen Goldstein, Arvind Krishnamurthy, Steven Lumetta, Thorsten von Eicken, and Katherine Yelick. Parallel programming in Split-C. In *Proceedings of Supercomputing '93*, pages 262–283, 1993.

[CF94] Peter F. Corbett and Dror G. Feitelson. Design and implementation of the Vesta parallel file system. In *Proceedings of the Scalable High-Performance Computing Conference*, pages 63–70, 1994.

[CK93] Thomas H. Cormen and David Kotz. Integrating theory and practice in parallel file systems. In *Proceedings of the 1993 DAGS/PC Symposium*, pages 64–74, Hanover, NH, June 1993. Dartmouth Institute for Advanced Graduate Studies. Revised from Dartmouth PCS-TR93-188.

[CLVW93] Pei Cao, Swee Boon Lim, Shivakumar Venkataraman, and John Wilkes. The TickerTAIP parallel RAID architecture. In *Proceedings of the 20th Annual International Symposium on Computer Architecture*, pages 52–63, 1993.

[dBC93] Juan Miguel del Rosario, Rajesh Bordawekar, and Alok Choudhary. Improved parallel I/O via a two-phase run-time access strategy. In *IPPS '93 Workshop on Input/Output in Parallel Computer Systems*, pages 56–70, 1993. Also published in Computer Architecture News 21(5), December 1993, pages 31–38.

[DdR92] Erik DeBenedictis and Juan Miguel del Rosario. nCUBE parallel I/O software. In *Eleventh Annual IEEE International Phoenix Conference on Computers and Communications (IPCCC)*, pages 0117–0124, April 1992.

[Dib90] Peter C. Dibble. *A Parallel Interleaved File System*. PhD thesis, University of Rochester, March 1990.

[DSE88] Peter Dibble, Michael Scott, and Carla Ellis. Bridge: A high-performance file system for parallel processors. In *Proceedings of the Eighth International*

Conference on Distributed Computer Systems, pages 154–161, June 1988.

[EGKS90] Susanne Englert, Jim Gray, Terrye Kocher, and Praful Shah. A benchmark of NonStop SQL Release 2 demonstrating near-linear speedup and scaleup on large databases. In *Proceedings of the 1990 ACM Sigmetrics Conference on Measurement and Modeling of Computer Systems*, pages 245–246, May 1990.

[FPD93] James C. French, Terrence W. Pratt, and Mriganka Das. Performance measurement of the Concurrent File System of the Intel iPSC/2 hypercube. *Journal of Parallel and Distributed Computing*, 17(1–2):115–121, January and February 1993.

[GGL93] N. Galbreath, W. Gropp, and D. Levine. Applications-driven parallel I/O. In *Proceedings of Supercomputing '93*, pages 462–471, 1993.

[GP91] Andrew S. Grimshaw and Jeff Prem. High performance parallel file objects. In *Sixth Annual Distributed-Memory Computer Conference*, pages 720–723, 1991.

[HPF93] High Performance Fortran Forum. *High Performance Fortran Language Specification*, 1.0 edition, May 3 1993.

[KE93] David Kotz and Carla Schlatter Ellis. Caching and writeback policies in parallel file systems. *Journal of Parallel and Distributed Computing*, 17(1–2):140–145, January and February 1993.

[KHH+92] Masaru Kitsuregawa, Satoshi Hirano, Masanobu Harada, Minoru Nakamura, and Mikio Takagi. The Super Database Computer (SDC): System architecture, algorithm and preliminary evaluation. In *Proceedings of the Twenty-Fifth Annual Hawaii International Conference on System Sciences*, volume I, pages 308–319, 1992.

[KN94] David Kotz and Nils Nieuwejaar. Dynamic file-access characteristics of a production parallel scientific workload. In *Proceedings of Supercomputing '94*, November 1994. To appear.

[Kot94] David Kotz. Disk-directed I/O for MIMD multiprocessors. Technical Report PCS-TR94-226, Dept. of Computer Science, Dartmouth College, July 1994.

[KTR94] David Kotz, Song Bac Toh, and Sriram Radhakrishnan. A detailed simulation model of the HP 97560 disk drive. Technical Report PCS-TR94-220, Dept. of Computer Science, Dartmouth College, July 1994.

[LIN+93] Susan J. LoVerso, Marshall Isman, Andy Nanopoulos, William Nesheim, Ewan D. Milne, and Richard Wheeler. *sfs*: A parallel file system for the CM-5. In *Proceedings of the 1993 Summer USENIX Conference*, pages 291–305, 1993.

[MK91] Ethan L. Miller and Randy H. Katz. Input/output behavior of supercomputer applications. In *Proceedings of Supercomputing '91*, pages 567–576, November 1991.

[Nit92] Bill Nitzberg. Performance of the iPSC/860 Concurrent File System. Technical Report RND-92-020, NAS Systems Division, NASA Ames, December 1992.

[NK94] Nils Nieuwejaar and David Kotz. A multiprocessor extension to the conventional file system interface. Technical Report PCS-TR94-230, Dept. of Computer Science, Dartmouth College, September 1994.

[OCH+85] John Ousterhout, Hervé Da Costa, David Harrison, John Kunze, Mike Kupfer, and James Thompson. A trace driven analysis of the UNIX 4.2 BSD file system. In *Proceedings of the Tenth ACM Symposium on Operating Systems Principles*, pages 15–24, December 1985.

[PGK88] David Patterson, Garth Gibson, and Randy Katz. A case for redundant arrays of inexpensive disks (RAID). In *ACM SIGMOD Conference*, pages 109–116, June 1988.

[Pie89] Paul Pierce. A concurrent file system for a highly parallel mass storage system. In *Fourth Conference on Hypercube Concurrent Computers and Applications*, pages 155–160, 1989.

[PP93] Barbara K. Pasquale and George C. Polyzos. A static analysis of I/O characteristics of scientific applications in a production workload. In *Proceedings of Supercomputing '93*, pages 388–397, 1993.

[Roy93] Paul J. Roy. Unix file access and caching in a multicomputer environment. In *Proceedings of the Usenix Mach III Symposium*, pages 21–37, 1993.

[RW94] Chris Ruemmler and John Wilkes. An introduction to disk drive modeling. *IEEE Computer*, 27(3):17–28, March 1994.

[WMR+94] Stephen R. Wheat, Arthur B. Maccabe, Rolf Riesen, David W. van Dresser, and T. Mack Stallcup. PUMA: An operating system for massively parallel systems. In *Proceedings of the Twenty-Seventh Annual Hawaii International Conference on System Sciences*, 1994.

Many of these papers can be found at
`http://www.cs.dartmouth.edu/pario.html`

The disk-model software can be found at
`http://www.cs.dartmouth.edu/`
    `cs_archive/diskmodel.html`

Message-Driven Relaxed Consistency in a Software Distributed Shared Memory

Povl T. Koch   Robert J. Fowler   Eric Jul

Department of Computer Science, University of Copenhagen (DIKU)
Universitetsparken 1, 2100 Copenhagen, Denmark
{koch,fowler,eric}@diku.dk

Abstract

Message-passing and distributed shared memory have their respective advantages and disadvantages in distributed parallel programming. We approach the problem of integrating both mechanisms into a single system by proposing a new *message-driven coherency* mechanism. Messages carrying explicit causality annotations are exchanged to trigger memory coherency actions. By adding annotations to standard message-based protocols, it is easy to construct efficient implementations of common synchronization and communication mechanisms. Because these are user-level messages, the set of available primitives is extended easily with language- or application-specific mechanisms. CarlOS, an experimental prototype for evaluating this approach, is derived from the lazy release consistent memory of TreadMarks. We describe the message-driven coherency memory model used in CarlOS, and we examine the performance of several applications.

1 Shared Memory and Messages

We present an approach to distributed parallel computation that combines user-level message-passing with a software distributed shared memory (DSM) based on a relaxed model of memory consistency. Specifically, messages carrying *causality annotations* are used explicitly to drive and control a set of memory-consistency mechanisms derived from the *lazy release consistent* (LRC) protocol [12]. Some annotations allow messages to be transmitted without incurring memory-consistency overhead, while others force the receiver to a state consistent with the sender.

This approach is a simple and sound architectural basis for the construction of hybrid systems that provide both shared memory and message-passing. In particular, this strategy permits and encourages the use of efficient message-based protocols to build a user-extensible set of interprocess coordination (synchronization, scheduling, and communication) mechanisms for controlling an underlying abstraction of shared memory. We present the message-driven memory model, the problems that it ad-

dresses, and examples of its use. The model is compatible with hardware- as well as software implementations. We describe a software prototype called CarlOS that was built by applying extensive modifications to the TreadMarks DSM system [11].

There are advantages and disadvantages to message-passing as well as to shared memory. Message-passing gives programmers and compilers explicit control over the choice of data communicated and over the time of transmission. With appropriate interfaces and protocols, it is relatively easy to overlap computation with communication. The explicit nature of message-passing is perceived also as its main weakness; programmers and compilers need to plan and to program explicitly every communication action. Such planning is especially difficult for applications that use complex, pointer-based data structures. When exact access patterns are not known, performance is affected by compromises among the volume of data communicated, the number of messages sent, and the amount of time that processes must wait for messages to be delivered.

In contrast, shared memory is often viewed as a simpler and more intuitive abstraction. In hardware implementations of distributed shared memory, communication occurs without the overhead of processor interrupts, context switching, and software network protocols, even when the system is based on a low-level message-passing network. Mechanisms to reduce or hide memory latencies [9], including update-based coherence protocols [20], are intended specifically to allow memory operations to be overlapped with computation. Related techniques can be used in software implementations to control the overhead of using shared memory by delaying and coalescing communication overhead [3, 12].

1.1 Shared Memory: Problems and Fixes

There are many common operations whose shared-memory implementations perform worse than do their message-based equivalents. Mismatches in alignment and size between the system's memory blocks and user data structures

---

reduce the control that memory-based protocols have over *which* data are communicated. Multiple memory operations are needed to transfer a data structure when it spans two or more blocks. On the other hand, transferring a large block is inefficient when only a small part of it is needed. There is also the false sharing problem: even when the values of individual variables only need be communicated infrequently, co-locating several variables on a large block increases the chance that there will be fine-grain sharing of the block.

There are additional problems specific to the "lazy, demand-driven communication" model implicit in invalidation-based protocols. To propagate a newly computed value from one processor to another, a shared-memory approach needs at least two (cache-miss, data) messages, and the requesting process will be blocked until the reply arrives. If invalidations and acknowledgements are counted, it takes three or more messages. In contrast, message-passing offers an "eager, producer-driven communication" model that allows data to be delivered as soon as it is ready and that overlaps communication with computation. The memory-based protocol requires a separate synchronization protocol, whereas message delivery combines data transfer and synchronization.

Interprocess coordination operations (synchronization and scheduling) are especially important, so many systems, whether hardware- or software-based, supplement their shared-memory implementations with additional mechanisms for synchronization. Additional incentives to give synchronization special treatment are provided by models of memory consistency [1, 6, 8, 12] that require that synchronization operations be identified to the memory coherence mechanism. On message-based hardware, this often means that the implementation of shared memory relies on a set of message-based synchronization mechanisms. In our message-driven consistency strategy, we make those mechanisms visible at the user-level.

Many of the problems with shared memory can be mitigated by using improved implementation techniques. Relaxed models of memory consistency have been used effectively to overlap communication and computation, thus reducing and hiding the latencies of *writes* and of coherence operations. The read-latency problem has been addressed by using update-based protocols [20], by augmenting invalidation-based protocols with prefetching[17], and by multithreading. See [9] for a comparative evaluation of these alternatives.

Software DSMs have fewer opportunities to use buffering and pipelining to overlap computation with communication. Even so, the LRC protocol delays or eliminates many memory-related communication events, update-based protocols can decrease read latencies, and multiple-writer protocols [3] greatly reduce the impact of false sharing.

Although sophisticated implementation techniques improve some aspects of the performance of shared memory, there still are many cases in which message-passing retains its advantages. If one adds message-passing to the user interface of a shared-memory system, however, it has to be done so that message-based protocols and the state of memory are consistent with one another. A conceptually simple approach is to deliver user messages only after all preceding memory operations have been performed.[1] Several groups [13, 14, 15] are working on systems that combine some form of message-passing with shared memory at the hardware level. By using the same pipelines to carry user messages and memory-system messages in these designs, in-order delivery can be ensured without adversely affecting the performance of the memory subsystem.

In some systems, allowing messages to bypass pending memory operations may offer substantial performance advantages. In particular, the strategy underlying the LRC protocol delays performing memory-related communication as long as possible. It also buffers and coalesces such operations. Since many uses of message-passing are intended to avoid the overhead of memory coherence, implicitly forcing memory consistency every time a message is delivered would be counterproductive. The message-driven memory consistency model is intended to provide a means of guaranteeing memory consistency when it is required, while permitting messages to bypass the consistency mechanisms.

2 Message-Driven Memory Consistency

The message-driven consistency model is intended for systems in which there is an underlying message-passing layer on top of which all synchronization and communication mechanisms are built, including the shared-memory abstraction and a user-level message-passing interface. Since everything is built on top of messages anyway, we give up the pretence that synchronization can or should be based on access to variables in shared memory. *All* reasoning, whether formal or informal, about the ordering of memory events is expressed in terms of an ordering relation induced by passing user-level, synchronizing messages. Specifically, if processor A sends a synchronizing message m to processor B, any modifications to shared memory visible on A before m was sent become visible to B when B receives m. If all messages are synchronizing messages, the ordering of memory events is consistent with "happened before" as defined by Lamport [16] for message-passing systems. Since all reasoning is in terms of synchronizing messages, they are the only mechanism needed to drive the memory system into consistent states. A consequence of

---

[1] In-order point-to-point delivery of messages is not a sufficient condition for correctness. A user-level message might be delivered via the shortest route, whereas a memory coherence operation might be delivered first to another node, e.g. the node that holds the relevant directory entry, before being delivered to the final destination(s).

this strategy is that any message-based protocol for coordinating processes will ensure memory consistency automatically, so long as the protocol can be proven correct using techniques consistent with Lamport's model.

Forcing memory coherence on every message has several side effects that can affect performance adversely. Consider Figure 1. Processors $P1$ and $P2$ share variable x. Processor $P1$ has written x while holding a lock and $P2$ wants to read x. $P2$ sends a "get lock" message to $P1$ and will get a "release lock" message in reply. Since memory is kept consistent with the happened-before (henceforth denoted $\rightarrow$) relation on messages, the "release lock" message correctly ensures that the value of x written by $P1$ is visible at $P2$. If all messages induce $\rightarrow$ on memory, this protocol induces an *unintended symmetry*, because the request message from $P2$ to $P1$ also causes $P1$ to become consistent with $P2$. Furthermore, the transitivity of the $\rightarrow$ means that this unintended and unnecessary consistency will involve other processors. Thus, although there is no intention to induce an ordering between $e3$ and $e4$, that ordering is required by the model because of the (dashed) message from $P3$ to $P2$. This transitivity will extend to every processor with which P1 communicates in the future.

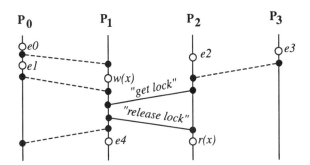

Figure 1: Memory consistency induced by messages. The desired outcome is that a lock protocol (solid lines) make the value of x written by P_1 visible when x is read at P_2. If all messages force "happened before" constraints, then the system becomes overly consistent.

To avoid overhead associated with forcing memory consistency on every message, we propose relaxing the event ordering model so that only designated messages induce $\rightarrow$ on memory. This is accomplished by marking each message with a memory-consistency annotation. In the example of Figure 1, we can eliminate the unintended symmetry and its consequences by marking the "get lock" message such that it does not induce memory consistency.

While the transitivity of $\rightarrow$ is required to capture correctly the notion of potential causality, the actual chains of causality may be more restricted. In Figure 1, for example, events $e0$ and $e1$ on processor $P0$ both happened before the "release lock" message was sent, so the model requires that their effects should be visible on node $P2$ when it reads x. On the other hand, only $e0$ happened before the $w(x)$ on

$P(1)$, so if the only real communication between $P1$ and $P2$ is through the value of x, it is not necessary to propagate the effects of $e1$. Furthermore, if the value of x does not depend upon $e0$, its effects also need not be propagated.

We leave for further research a general solution to the problem of limiting the transitivity in message-driven memory consistency models. Our interim approach is to use synchronization protocols that avoid inducing unnecessary memory consistency. We also define an annotation that explicitly limits transitivity by propagating only those changes to shared memory that were performed by the sender. This mechanism is used in the implementation of the global barrier primitive in TreadMarks. A node arriving at a barrier sends consistency information in a system-level message to a barrier manager. When all nodes have arrived, the manager merges the consistency information and sends it back out in the message that signals that the barrier has fallen. Because the union of the individual contributions produces a globally consistent view, it is sufficient for each node to send only a description of its own actions. We include the limited transitivity message in the model specifically for use in implementing barriers, because one of our goals is to always do at least as well as TreadMarks.

2.1 Message Annotations in CarlOS

To implement the memory consistency model described above, each user-level message in CarlOS carries one of these annotations:

RELEASE messages are synchronizing messages. In terms of release consistency memory models, the operation of sending a RELEASE message is a *release* event and the operation of accepting it at the receiver is a matching *acquire* event. Any program that mixes message-passing and shared memory will be consistent if all messages are marked RELEASE, but performance may suffer because the system will be kept overly consistent.

REQUEST messages are non-synchronizing. While it does not hurt to include this annotation in any message, it is intended to be used when a RELEASE message will be returned. CarlOS appends a description of the sending node's knowledge of the state of shared memory so that a precisely-tailored RELEASE message can be sent in response.

NONE messages are non-synchronizing. They are intended to be used when the expected response is not a RELEASE message. They do not interact with the memory consistency mechanisms in any way.

RELEASE_NT messages are the non-transitive form of the release messages.

NONE and REQUEST messages are semantically equivalent, but they have different costs. Using a REQUEST message entails the overhead of including and processing status information. Using a NONE message risks the possibility that a subsequent RELEASE message will contain more consistency information than necessary.

2.2 Forwarding of Release Messages

In many protocols, messages are sent to intermediaries that relay the message contents to their ultimate destination. For example, requests for a mobile resource often are sent to a fixed "home node" or "manager". The manager then forwards each request to the current location of the resource. In CarlOS, protocols that forward NONE or REQUEST messages are relatively easy to manage, because there is no problem with unintended side-effects on memory consistency.

There also are cases in which a RELEASE message is relayed through an intermediary. Consider the problem of implementing a shared task queue. In a typical shared-memory style implementation, the queue is protected by a lock. In addition to the overhead of locking and of migrating some part of the queue's representation to the node currently accessing the queue, the locking mechanism guarantees that the node will become consistent with a past state of every processor that has touched the queue.

To avoid the cost of locking and migration, Carter experimented with an RPC-based queue implementation using a fixed manager [2]. Because the items in the queue could contain references to shared memory, each node explicitly forced memory into a consistent state by performing a `flush` operation before accessing the queue. A similar implementation in CarlOS uses a RELEASE message in each of the *enqueue* and *dequeue* operations to ensure that the eventual recipient of a queued item becomes memory-consistent with the node that created the item. In a straightforward implementation, the queue manager node becomes consistent with every node that enqueues items. Whenever a node dequeues an item, it will be made consistent with the manager and, transitively, with *all* of the nodes that enqueued the items currently in the queue.

We provide a forwarding mechanism to avoid unnecessarily propagating consistency information through intermediaries like the queue manager. When a message marked RELEASE arrives, low-level code that first receives the message is allowed to inspect the message before any memory consistency actions are performed. This code must perform one of three actions on the message. If it *accept*s the message, the required memory consistency operations are performed. It also may *forward* the message and its encapsulated consistency information to another node, or it may use a *store* operation to indicate that the final disposition of this message has been deferred. For the purposes of the memory consistency model, a message is not considered to have been *delivered* to user-level until the *accept* operation is performed.

3 Use of Annotated Messages

Because CarlOS does not include any built-in synchronization beyond messages, the first order of business was to allow the system to function as a conventional DSM. We therefore used simple message-based protocols to provide several different types of lock, two kinds of barrier, and a centralized manager for shared work queues.

The standard CarlOS lock uses a simple distributed queue protocol. To acquire a lock, a node sends a REQUEST message to the lock's manager node, which in turn forwards the message to the node that last requested the lock, *i.e.* the node at the tail of the queue. If the lock is not held, then the previous holder sends a RELEASE message immediately. Otherwise, the requesting node joins the request queue. When the lock is released, the node at the head of the queue is notified using a RELEASE message. Semaphores and condition variables have similar implementations.

Each TreadMarks-style barrier is assigned a manager node. Clients arriving at a barrier send RELEASE messages to the manager. If this is a global barrier, RELEASE_NT messages can be used. The manager node accepts the arrival messages to make itself consistent with all of the client nodes. To signal the fall of the barrier, the manager sends departure messages marked RELEASE to the client nodes. When each client accepts the departure message, it becomes consistent with the manager and, hence, with all of the other clients.

High-level coordination mechanisms also have straightforward implementations. Stacks and queues for shared work are built using the fixed manager strategy described in the previous section. Enqueue requests and dequeue replies are marked RELEASE, while the dequeue request messages are marked REQUEST. The manager code acts as a forwarding agent for the messages in the queue; it never accepts any RELEASE messages.

Many numerical applications have communication patterns amenable to message-passing. Prominent examples include hydrodynamics and engineering codes that iteratively solve partial differential equations using finite difference or finite element techniques. Small amounts of data are easy to include in a message. If the data are numerous or difficult to marshall, it is easier to use a shared-memory style of communication combined with a notification message marked RELEASE sent to the node that will use the data. If the underlying memory coherence mechanism uses update rather than invalidation, the actual data transmission occurs eagerly and asynchronously when the notification message is sent.

4 Design and Implementation

CarlOS ("Commodity Architecture Research Laboratory Operating System") is being developed as a platform for research in distributed parallel computing on workstation networks. The current hardware configuration consists of four Digital AXP workstations running DEC OSF/1 and connected via Ethernet. Future expansion will include the addition of a second Ethernet to support experiments with very low-cost network upgrades, a high-performance network (ATM), and more nodes.

A major goal of the CarlOS project is to explore hybrid distributed computing environments that integrate aspects of distributed shared memory based on "flat" memory spaces with aspects of distributed object-based languages [10]. This objective affects the design in several ways. In particular, the development of our message-driven memory consistency model was motivated by the need to combine explicit user-controlled object migration, function shipping in the form of remote invocation, and a flat, coherent address space.

Currently, CarlOS runs entirely in Unix user mode and uses the standard Unix system interface. The implementation strategy is evolutionary and will entail some kernel-level support, particularly in the network drivers. We began with the TreadMarks [11] code. While the basic mechanisms of lazy release consistency are intact, data structures and internal protocols have been restructured extensively to support the internal concurrency and asynchrony implicit in the message-driven consistency model. Other modifications include support for fine-grain user-level multithreading.

4.1 Address Space

Applications see an address space containing three disjoint regions. First, each node has a *private memory* region. This is used internally by CarlOS. Applications can use it for node-local private data structures that are not shared. Second, we provide a *non-coherent shared memory* region in which address mappings are kept consistent across all nodes. Although CarlOS does not maintain the consistency of this region, the single address map provides a consistent interpretation for pointers to objects in this region. The intention is that memory consistency for this region will be provided by run-time libraries using message-passing protocols such as those used in Amber [4]. Third, the *coherent shared memory* region contains user-allocated data kept consistent with the message-driven coherency mechanism.

4.2 Memory Consistency Mechanisms

In both TreadMarks[2] and CarlOS, the execution history of each node is divided into an indexed sequence of *in-*

---

[2] In discussing the low-level memory coherence mechanisms in CarlOS, we often use descriptions that also apply to TreadMarks. Our presentation focuses on the differences between the systems, and space limitations prevent us from including too much detail that has appeared elsewhere. A detailed description of the TreadMarks implementation can be found in [11].

tervals whose endpoints occur at the acquire and release events executed on that node. In TreadMarks, these occur within the execution of built-in synchronization primitives. In CarlOS, they occur when RELEASE messages are sent and accepted, respectively (see Section 4.3). The memory-consistency state of each node is summarized by a *vector timestamp*, each element of which is the index of the most recently seen interval from the corresponding node. Each interval is summarized by a list of *write notices*, one for each page that was modified in the interval.

Modifications to pages in shared memory are detected using the Unix virtual memory protection facility (mprotect) and a SIGSEGV handler. All clean shared pages are marked read-only. On a write-access fault to a protected page, a copy (a *twin*) is created and the page is marked read-write. When the node receives a write-notice for a modified page, or when another node requests the page or its modifications, the page is compared with its twin and the modifications are recorded in a run-length encoded *diff* structure. Then, the twin is removed, and the page is marked read-only. Invalid pages that have not been discarded can be brought up to date by applying an appropriate sequence of diffs, perhaps from multiple writers. Modifications can be requested from another node using a *diff request* message. A node also can request an entire page if it does not hold a copy.

4.3 Annotated Messages

Sending a CarlOS message is an asynchronous operation. CarlOS messages currently are implemented using UDP/IP datagrams supplemented with a sliding window protocol to assure reliable, in-order delivery. The CarlOS message interface defines a form of *active messages* [19]. Each message contains a pointer to a handler function that is invoked when the message is received and to which the body of the message is passed as an argument. Although using active messages has a negligible performance advantage in the current implementation on top of OSF/1 and UDP/IP, it is still a useful structuring technique for building multithreaded systems. Future versions of CarlOS built closer to the underlying hardware and using faster, lower-latency networks should be able to realize a substantial performance advantage.

A memory consistency annotation is a user-visible component of the message. Any consistency information appended by CarlOS is invisible at the user level. A NONE message does not interact with the memory consistency mechanisms. Currently, CarlOS piggybacks the vector timestamp of the sending node onto a REQUEST message. In the future, it also may include additional information to guide a hybrid update/invalidate protocol.

When sending a RELEASE message, CarlOS creates a new interval on the sending node. It then appends to the message a vector timestamp that represents the minimum timestamp required for a recipient to become consistent on the basis of other information in the message. This timestamp is necessary to handle forwarding correctly. The consistency information appended to the message comprises interval descriptions that the sender has determined are needed to make the immediate receiver consistent. If an invalidation-based consistency strategy is used, the interval descriptions contain only write notices. If an update or hybrid strategy [7] is used, the message also will contain a set of diffs. Thus far, we have used only the invalidation strategy in CarlOS.

When a node accepts a RELEASE message, it performs the actions required by an acquire event in LRC. This entails creating a new interval, applying all of the write notices in the message, and updating its vector timestamp. Using the invalidation strategy, applying the write notices means invalidating the named pages. Using the update or hybrid strategies, pages to which a "complete" set of diffs can be applied remain valid. Occasionally, a forwarded message does not contain enough consistency information. This is checked by comparing the accepting node's current vector timestamp with the required vector timestamp in the message. If the required vector timestamp is "later" in any dimension, the consistency information in the message is inadequate. In such cases, the accepting node requests additional information from the original sender of the message.

Compared with TreadMarks, additional care is required in CarlOS for the creation, propagation, and application of consistency information. This is due to the concurrency and asynchrony implicit in the existence of unsolicited RELEASE messages and of multiple outstanding requests from multithreaded nodes.

The RELEASE and RELEASE_NT annotations differ in that messages marked with the latter contain only consistency information about intervals created at the sending node. The correct vector timestamps are sent, however, so the receiving node is able to determine whether it has been left with an inconsistent view of memory. The inconsistency can be resolved by requesting additional consistency information.

When a user-level message is delivered by the sliding window protocol, control is passed to the handler function specified in the message. As in most implementations of active messages, message handlers are intended to be low-level code that perform a limited amount of processing as an extension to an interrupt-handling function. They are not allowed to block, nor should they touch coherent shared memory. Critical sections between the message handlers and higher-level code are handled by blocking the delivery of incoming messages. The handler is allowed to inspect the message. Before the handler terminates, it must either inform CarlOS that the message has been stored for later disposition or it must dispose of the message, either by accepting it or by forwarding it to another node. Forwarding or accepting the message frees the message buffer.

4.4 Support for multithreading

The current implementation of TreadMarks allocates only one thread of control per physical node. This means that a node blocks on a page or diff fault until it receives the needed reply. This blocking leads to high idle times. Multiprogramming is the classic technique for hiding the latencies of blocking operations, so CarlOS is designed to support multiple user threads per node. We take the position that each language implementor should be able to build a customized thread package, so we have designed support for building thread packages on top of CarlOS. We provide a hook to make an upcall to a user-level scheduler to prevent user code from blocking on remote coherent shared memory operations (page requests, diff requests, etc.).

The message-driven memory consistency mechanism is available to implement inter-node synchronization and scheduling. The upcall interface is available to schedule or to reschedule threads when they block or unblock, thereby masking remote latencies. Upcalls out of handlers for active messages provide a mechanism for building remote invocation and other interfaces to thread schedulers on remote nodes. The non-coherent shared memory region is ideal for the allocation of thread control blocks and stacks, because it allows pointers to be used to name these structures while allowing message handlers to access them safely.

To support user-level multithreading, we reimplemented all of the internal message-passing in TreadMarks to use the CarlOS message interface and its reliable message delivery facility. This eliminates blocking of Unix receive calls. We also modified the internal data structures so that multiple page and diff requests can be left outstanding.

5 Performance Measurements

In this section, we report our early experiences with the performance of CarlOS. The performance measurements were made on a cluster of DEC 3000/300 workstations with 150 MHz Alpha AXP processors running DEC OSF/1 v1.3 on an isolated Ethernet segment. Timings were obtained using a fine-grain low-overhead timing facility based on AXP architecture's processor cycle counter [5].

We examine at least two versions of each of three applications running on CarlOS: TSP, Quicksort, and Water. One version of each application is a "strictly shared memory" program that runs on TreadMarks and is synchronized using locks and barriers. The other versions are hybrids that still keep data in coherent shared memory, but that use message-passing for high-level process coordination. We start out by providing an overview of the results. Each of the applications is described and analyzed in more detail in a later section.

We first compared the unmodified applications running on TreadMarks and running on CarlOS to examine the impact of replacing the built-in synchronization mechanisms with similar implementations using annotated messages.

For the TSP and Quicksort application, the performance penalty is a 5-6% increase in total execution time. This is mainly due to the generality of CarlOS message handling. Both of these programs have high contention for locks and suffer from a large increase in acquisition latency. Water performed as well on CarlOS as on TreadMarks.

Figure 2 summarizes the average execution times on CarlOS of the two versions of each of the three applications. The original lock and barrier versions of the applications are marked '/lock' and the hybrid versions are marked '/hybrid'. The execution times have been broken down into application computations (marked User), the cost of OSF/1 calls (Unix), all CarlOS message-passing and shared memory overhead (CarlOS), and time spent waiting for remote operations to complete (Idle).

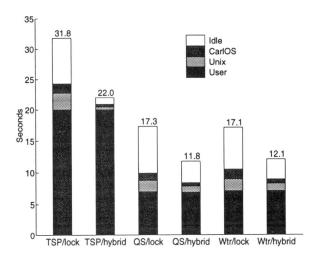

Figure 2: Execution breakdown for the TSP, Quicksort, and Water applications on four nodes.

Since the algorithms are unchanged in each variation, the user times in each pair of applications are almost identical. The main benefit from using the hybrid strategies is a reduction in communication costs. The hybrid programs all use far fewer messages than the original versions. Although message size increases, the total volume of data communicated decreases. All three components of overhead are reduced. The largest benefits are in the reduction of the idle-time components of overhead. Even using the hybrid strategies, the idle-time components remain large compared to the CarlOS and Unix components.

5.1 The TSP Application

The Traveling Salesman Problem application (TSP) uses a branch-and-bound algorithm to find the shortest path through 19 cities. In the original version of TSP, a lock is used to provide mutual exclusion among writers trying to update the current bound ("best tour") and another lock is used to protect a shared work queue. Since the bound is updated with a single instruction, it is not necessary to provide mutual exclusion between readers and writers.

We replaced the above lock-based implementation of the queue with a centralized implementation using messages. While the changes to the source code were small, the modifications did change the locations at which some parts of the computation are performed. The manager node on which the queue is located is responsible for generating the queued tours, and it also participates in the search for the best tour. To request a tour index from the queue, a client node sends a REQUEST message to the manager, which then sends its reply in a RELEASE message. The tour descriptors are kept in coherent shared memory. In the CarlOS version, the client nodes never touch the queue directly, so the representation of the queue is never propagated to the clients. As in the lock version, the first step in updating the bound in the CarlOS version is to test the value on the client node. If a better bound has been found, it is posted to the master in a REQUEST message. The master writes the value to shared memory and replies with a RELEASE message. The new value becomes visible to each client when the latter next accepts a RELEASE message from the manager. Message-passing is used only to implement the shared work queue. Shared memory is used to distribute the current bound and the tour descriptions. While better performance could have been obtained easily by transferring the data in messages, the point of this example is to explore the impact of alternative synchronization mechanisms.

Execution times and communication statistics for TSP are presented in Table 1. The columns display the number of nodes (N), the execution time speedups,[3] the total number of messages sent, their average size in bytes, and an estimate of network utilization.[4] The network utilization figure is included to illustrate the degree to which the Ethernet is a bottleneck.

Version	N	Time (s)	Speed-up	Messages #	Messages Size	Net Util.
Lock	2	52.3	1.64	5,838	133	1%
	3	39.7	2.16	8,626	168	3%
	4	31.8	2.69	10,403	219	6%
Hybrid	2	44.9	1.91	1,204	356	1%
	3	31.0	2.76	1,916	426	2%
	4	22.0	3.89	2,198	498	4%

Table 1: The TSP application on CarlOS using coherent shared memory and either locks or message-passing.

The hybrid version of TSP obtains much better speedup than does the lock version (3.89 versus 2.69 on four nodes). The performance problem with the lock implementation of TSP is that the shared work queue migrates among all the

---

[3] Speedups are calculated relative to the single-node execution of the same application.

[4] Calculated assuming an ideal 10 Mbit/sec. Ethernet. (Ethernet and UDP headers are **not** included, so the network utilization estimate is conservative.)

nodes that manipulate it. Although the network load is light (1-5%), relatively slow message delivery contributes to the high idle times. See Figure 2. The hybrid version sends less than one-fourth as many messages. The average message size increases in the hybrid version because many small messages are eliminated, and some of the consistency information that they would have carried appears in the remaining messages.

5.2 The Quicksort Application

The Quicksort application sorts an array of 256K integers in shared memory. When subarrays get smaller than 1K elements, the nodes use a local Bubblesort. Initially, a shared stack contains a descriptor for the whole array. In each step of the algorithm, a node pops a descriptor off the queue and sorts the corresponding subarray. If the subarray is bigger than the threshold of 1K elements, the node partitions the array, pushes a descriptor for the smaller subarray on the queue, and recursively Quicksorts the larger subarray. When the whole array has been sorted, a barrier is used to collect all of the sorted subarrays, thereby making all nodes consistent.

In the lock version of this program, the shared work stack is protected by a lock, so each operation on it requires that a lock be acquired and released. The shared work stack thus migrates among all of the nodes that manipulate it, and each node that manipulates the stack becomes consistent with all of the previous manipulators of the stack. The use of diffs ensures that only data near the top of the stack is actually communicated.

In a hybrid version of Quicksort (named Hybrid-1), we used a non-migrating shared work queue. The node that hosts the queue manager code also participates in the sorting. The manager node represents the queue as a list of pointers to "enqueued" messages that have been stored. When a remote node issues a dequeue request, the stored message at the head of the queue is forwarded. If the request for work comes from the manager node, the message is accepted. Note that a client node waits for the reply message in a dequeue operation, but that enqueue operations are completely asynchronous.

To measure the impact of using correct annotations and the use of the CarlOS forwarding mechanism, we created two minor variations of the hybrid version of Quicksort. In one variation, all messages for accessing the shared work queue are RELEASE messages. This is the Hybrid-2 program. In another variation, the forwarding mechanism is not used. The performance of this program is nearly identical to that of Hybrid-2.

The performance of the lock and hybrid versions of Quicksort is summarized in Table 2. This Quicksort program is communication-intensive; a four-node execution consumes half of the gross bandwidth of the Ethernet for user data. The request-reply pattern of communication in the lock version limits the possible overlap of computation

Version	N	Time (s)	Speed-up	Messages		Net Util.
				#	Size	
Lock	2	19.6	1.36	2,426	1,209	12%
	3	18.6	1.44	5,144	1,446	32%
	4	17.3	1.54	6,866	1,560	50%
Hybrid-1	2	17.5	1.53	1,406	1,704	11%
	3	13.9	1.93	2,282	2,265	30%
	4	11.8	2.27	2,870	2,564	50%
Hybrid-2	4	14.2	1.89	4,361	2,254	55%

Table 2: The Quicksort application on CarlOS using coherent shared memory and either locks or message-passing.

and communication. This is reflected in a speedup of 1.54 on four nodes. In contrast, the Hybrid-1 program gains a speedup of 2.27. This is partly due to a 58 percent decrease in the number of messages sent and a 31 percent decrease in data communicated. It requires substantial overlap of communication and computation, however, to get a speedup of over two with a network utilization of at least 50 percent. The asynchrony of the "enqueue" operation in the hybrid program provides this.

The correct use of consistency annotations and of forwarding reduces the amount of consistency overhead, as measured in the numbers of diffs created and of diff requests sent. This overhead is paid in the form of the immediate costs of creating intervals and diffs as well as in the cost of communicating them in messages. There is also a delayed cost in the form of a global garbage collection of these data structures.[5] Thus, Hybrid-1 consumes resources more slowly than does the original program. On this problem instance, Hybrid-1 avoids a garbage collection that the original program required. For much larger, longer-running problem instances, the difference would not be whether there is a garbage collection, but rather how many garbage collections are necessary.

The messages in Hybrid-2 are all RELEASE messages, so it creates many more intervals and diffs than does Hybrid-1. Thus, while Hybrid-2 still benefits from the message-based queue, it also pays for the added diffs. This increases the volume of data communicated, and it represents a large relative increase in the amount of consistency overhead. The relatively small contribution of consistency overhead to total execution time, however, limits the magnitude of the effect.

5.3 The Water Application

Water is a molecular dynamics simulation application from the SPLASH suite [18]. Each iteration of the program consists of several phases separated by barriers. In a problem instance with P processors and N molecules, each processor is assigned N/P molecules. In the most

---

[5]CarlOS uses TreadMarks' memory management mechanisms for system data structures (intervals, diffs, etc.). When the free space for system structures falls below a threshold, a global garbage collection is performed, thereby forcing more messages to be sent.

communication-intensive phase of each iteration, the processors compute the intermolecular forces for all pairs of molecules. While pairs are examined in this phase, non-zero forces are computed only if the molecules are close to each other. The resulting force vectors acting on each molecule and on each atom within the molecule are accumulated in a net force vector that is part of the molecule's representation. This computation on molecule pairs is partitioned among the processors by making each processor responsible for computing the interactions between its set of molecules and half of the remaining molecules. Since several processors contribute to the force computation for each molecule, it is necessary to coordinate their updates. Using a fine-grain approach, each processor could update the force vector of each of its own molecules as many as $N(1-P)/2P$ times and that of each of the other molecules N/P times. Since the net force on each molecule is the vector sum of the individual contributions, the SPLASH report suggests reducing the amount of interprocess interaction by having each processor accumulate its own contributions and then perform a single update to the force vector of each molecule. The lock version of Water does this by accumulating all of the forces in a private array in the first part of the phase and by updating the molecules in the second part of the phase. To ensure that the updates are applied correctly, each molecule is protected with a lock.

The hybrid version of the program was derived from the lock version by defining an update function to replace the lock-update-unlock sequence for each molecule. The node that generates the update information sends a NONE message to the node that owns the molecule to invoke the update function. The sequential delivery property of CarlOS messages guarantees that the updates are applied atomically, thus eliminating the need to use locks on individual molecules.

Version	N	Time (s)	Speed-up	Messages #	Size	Net Util.
Lock	2	23.3	1.34	6,920	368	9%
	3	19.4	1.61	11,348	374	17%
	4	17.3	1.81	15,423	379	27%
Hybrid	2	18.4	1.70	2,546	889	10%
	3	14.4	2.20	4,155	876	20%
	4	12.1	2.58	5,634	871	32%

Table 3: The Water application on CarlOS using coherent shared memory and either locks or message-passing.

We ran the lock and hybrid version of Water for 343 molecules for five steps. The results are summarized in Table 3. For four nodes, the hybrid version sends about a third less data than does the lock version. Idle time is reduced from 6.7 to 3.3 seconds per node. This is a 51 percent reduction.

In the hybrid versions of the other two programs, we used function shipping to implement process coordination mechanisms. In this case, messages are used to eliminate ex-

plicit synchronization by using user-level function shipping to eliminate both the need to migrate data in shared memory and the need to perform explicit synchronization.

5.4 Choice of Annotations

One important issue is whether or not all of the consistency annotations in the model are necessary. For example, the extra overhead of a REQUEST message compared to that of a NONE message in the current implementation is the cost of handling a vector timestamp at the sender and receiver. Currently, this adds two bytes per node to the message. It incurs a direct cost of between 750 and 2350 extra processor cycles, about 5 and 15 microseconds, respectively. Since variation is most likely due to cache misses, an accurate accounting of the total cost should include the additional cache misses incurred to bring back the data that were replaced. In our current environment, these costs are dwarfed by the costs of system calls on OSF/1, the UDP/IP protocol stack, and message latencies on the Ethernet. On the other hand, these times are a substantial fraction of the time necessary to pass a small message on a current-generation multicomputer interconnect or on a streamlined ATM. Furthermore, while the vector timestamp is small compared to typical Ethernet packets, it is a large part of an ATM frame. Thus, while making the distinction between NONE and REQUEST is overkill in our current environment, we believe it is worth retaining in the design.

Similarly, it would eliminate a potential source of programming errors if all user-level messages were RELEASE messages. In our current implementation, the additional overhead of a RELEASE message compared to that of a NONE message is about 30 microseconds plus the time to process the write notices that the message contains. The overhead per write notice has a wide variation, depending on how much work needs to be done. For the lock and hybrid versions of TSP, the average costs per write notice are 42 and 52 microseconds, respectively. For the two versions of Quicksort, the costs are 125 and 141 microseconds, and for Water, they are 94 and 95 microseconds. These costs are large enough that they result in measurable differences when all messages are marked RELEASE in these programs. On systems with high-performance interconnects, the additional overhead will be more important.

Our experiments with Quicksort showed a significant, but not crippling, penalty when all messages were marked RELEASE. Running the hybrid versions of the TSP and Water applications with all messages marked RELEASE, however, increased execution times by only 2.4% and 1.4%, respectively.[6] The explanation is that most of the time the only benefit of not using a RELEASE message is the 30-microsecond fixed overhead. This is because, in these

---

[6] For TSP, it meant sending twice as much data, because RELEASE messages are bigger than REQUEST messages. Since the messages were small in the first place, this had no significant effect on the total execution time.

applications, most of the write notices will be transmitted eventually, so avoiding the use of a RELEASE message in one place merely delays the transmission of some number of write notices until a later RELEASE message is sent. This effect would occur in Figure 1 if it were extended with a request for a lock from $P1$ to $P2$ followed by a RELEASE message from $P2$ to $P1$ in reply. The savings realized by marking the first request from $P2$ REQUEST rather than RELEASE are illusory because the same write notices will be piggybacked onto the later RELEASE message. In the programs that we studied, the cost of acting on a specific write notice does not change much over time, and all nodes do become mutually consistent, so there cannot be a large impact.

There will be a high penalty for using RELEASE messages unnecessarily in cases in which there is fine-grain false sharing and a frequent exchange of messages that do not need to synchronize memory. Despite the multiple-writers protocol, the synchronizing effect of using RELEASE annotations on the non-synchronizing messages will force the shared pages constantly to be invalidated and "unnecessary" diffs to be requested. Thus, we know that artificial examples can be constructed to illustrate the importance of non-synchronizing messages to the message-driven consistency model. We have not yet seen such an example arise in practice.

6 Discussion and Conclusions

The message-driven memory consistency model is intended to provide a foundation for constructing systems that integrate message-passing and shared memory such that each of these abstractions can be used for purposes for which it is best suited. Message-passing provides an explicit communication mechanism that is especially well suited for constructing process coordination mechanisms. The shared memory abstraction provides a single global name space for shared data. Coherent caching techniques provide an implicit communication mechanism to move and replicate data to the processors that access them. Our early experiences with CarlOS indicate that the model has fulfilled our expectations.

We report performance measurements for CarlOS based on our early experiences with a few applications and a very small cluster of high-performance workstations connected by Ethernet. The main benefit from using our message-driven consistency model is derived from the use of high-level process synchronization and scheduling mechanisms. Compared to locks and barriers, using these mechanisms reduces the number of messages exchanged. While message sizes increase, there is a net reduction in the total amount of data transferred. The asynchrony of message transmission also helps to overlap computation and communication. Even then, there still is a substantial amount of idle time associated with remote operations. CarlOS is designed to support user-level multithreading to address this problem as well as to improve the distributed programming model by providing function shipping and thread migration mechanisms in a well structured user interface. We currently have two multithreading packages under construction.

The message-driven consistency model provides several annotations that are intended to provide a means of limiting "unnecessary consistency". Our initial experiences with a few applications running on our prototype have shown limited benefit to this strategy. To a certain extent, this is an example of Amdahl's law in action. Given high overheads and latencies in the operating system and network, the memory consistency code itself does not contribute much to overall execution time for the applications that we measured. Even doubling this consistency overhead would have a small effect. In other contexts, such as more modern networks and finer-grain applications, consistency code overhead may be a larger part of overall execution time, and the choice of annotations will become more important.

While synchronizing (RELEASE) messages have substantially higher overhead than non-synchronizing ones, using more than the required number of RELEASE messages had a smaller-than-expected effect on execution time in our experiments. In these cases, the choice of annotation mostly affects *when* a particular consistency operation is performed rather than *whether* it is performed. Even for these programs, however, the choice of annotations gives the programmer some degree of control over when the program will incur consistency overhead. We currently are investigating alternative implementations of synchronization mechanisms designed to move consistency operations out of the critical path.

The performance figures that we report were measured on a very small, four-node cluster of powerful workstations connected by Ethernet. Our immediate plans include evaluating the performance of CarlOS on larger clusters and more modern networks.

Acknowledgements

We are very grateful to Alan Cox and Willy Zwaenepoel of Rice University for giving us access to TreadMarks. The equipment was provided by a grant from The Faculty of Natural Sciences, University of Copenhagen. Lars Jarnbo Pedersen profiled CarlOS using fine-grained timers. The anonymous reviewers and our shepherd, Michael Scott, provided very valuable comments. Special thanks to Niki Fowler for weeding out phrases too literally translated from Danish and for smoothing out the text in general. We would also like to thank Marc Shapiro and Julien Maisonneuve at INRIA Rocquencourt (France) for granting us access to their computing facility.

References

[1] Sarita V. Adve and Mark D. Hill. A unified formalization of four shared-memory models. *IEEE Transactions on Parallel and Distributed Systems*, 4(6):613–624, June 1993.

[2] John B. Carter. Efficient distributed shared memory based on multi-protocol release consistency. Ph.D. thesis, Rice University, September 1993.

[3] John B. Carter, John K. Bennett, and Willy Zwaenepoel. Techniques for reducing consistency-related communication in distributed shared memory systems. *ACM Transactions on Computer Systems*. To appear.

[4] Jeffrey S. Chase, Franz G. Amador, Edward D. Lazowska, Henry M. Levy, and Richard J. Littlefield. The Amber system: Parallel programming on a network of multiprocessors. In *Proceedings of the 12th ACM Symposium on Operating System Principles*, pages 147–158, December 1989.

[5] Digital. Alpha architecture handbook. Digital Press, 1992.

[6] M. Dubois, C. Scheurich, and F.A. Briggs. Memory access buffering in multiprocessors. In *Proceedings of the 13th Annual International Symposium on Computer Architecture*, pages 434–442, May 1986.

[7] Sandhay Dwarkadas, Pete Keleher, Alan L. Cox, and Willy Zwaenepoel. Evaluation of release consistent software distributed shared memory on emerging network technology. In *Proceedings of the 20th Annual International Symposium on Computer Architecture*, pages 244–255, May 1993.

[8] Kourosh Gharachorloo, Daniel Lenoski, James Laudon, Phillip Gibbons, Anoop Gupta, and John Hennessy. Memory consistency and event ordering in scalable shared-memory multiprocessors. In *Proceedings of the 17th Annual International Symposium on Computer Architecture*, pages 15–26, May 1990.

[9] A. Gupta, J. Hennessy, K. Gharachorloo, T. Mowry, and W.-D. Weber. Comparative evaluation of latency reducing and tolerating techniques. In *Proceedings of the 18th Annual International Symposium on Computer Architecture*, pages 254–263, May 1991.

[10] E. Jul, H. Levy, N. Hutchinson, and A. Black. Fine-grained mobility in the Emerald system. *ACM Transactions on Computer Systems*, 6(1):109–133, February 1988.

[11] Peter Keleher, Alan L. Cox, Sandhya Dwarkadas, and Willy Zwaenepoel. TreadMarks: Distributed shared memory on standard workstations and operating systems. In *Proceedings of the 1994 Winter USENIX Conference*, pages 115–132, January 1994.

[12] Peter Keleher, Alan L. Cox, and Willy Zwaenepoel. Lazy release consistency for software distributed shared memory. In *Proceedings of the 19th International Symposium on Computer Architecture*, pages 13–21, May 1992.

[13] D. Kranz, K. Johnson, A. Agarwal, J. Kubiatowicz, and B-H. Lim. Integrating message-passing and shared-memory: Early experience. In *Proceedings of the Fourth ACM SIGPLAN Symposium on Principles and Practice of Parallel Programming*, pages 54–63, San Diego, May 1993.

[14] John Kubiatowicz and Anant Agarwal. Anatomy of a message in the Alewife multiprocessor. In *Proceedings of the 1993 ACM International Conference on Supercomputing*, pages 195–206, July 1993.

[15] Jeffrey Kuskin, David Ofelt, Mark Heinrich, John Heinlein, Richard Simoni, Kourosh Gharachorloo, John Chapin, David Nakahira, Joel Baxter, Mark Horowitz, Anoop Gupta, Mendel Rosenbaum, and John Hennessy. The Stanford FLASH multiprocessor. In *Proceedings of the 21st Annual International Conference on Computer Architecture*, pages 302–313, April 1994.

[16] Leslie Lamport. Time, clocks, and the ordering of events in a distributed system. *Communications of the ACM*, 21(7):558–565, July 1978.

[17] T. Mowry and A. Gupta. Tolerating latency through software-controlled prefetching in shared-memory multiprocessors. *Journal of Parallel and Distributed Computing*, 12:87–106, June 1991.

[18] J. Singh, W. Weber, and A. Gupta. SPLASH: Stanford parallel applications for shared memory. *Computer Architecture News*, 20(1):5–44, March 1992.

[19] Thomas von Eicken, David E. Culler, Seth Copen Goldstein, and Karl Erik Schauser. Active messages: A mechanism for integrated communication and computation. In *Proceedings of the 19th Annual International Symposium on Computer Architecture*, pages 256–266, May 1992.

[20] Larry D. Wittie, Gudjun Hermannsson, and Ai Li. Eager sharing for efficient massive parallelism. In *1992 International Conference on Parallel Processing*, pages 251–255, St. Charles, IL, August 1992.

Software Write Detection for a Distributed Shared Memory

Matthew J. Zekauskas   Wayne A. Sawdon
School of Computer Science
Carnegie Mellon University
5000 Forbes Avenue
Pittsburgh, PA 15213
{mattz,wsawdon}@cs.cmu.edu

Brian N. Bershad
Department of Computer Science
and Engineering FR-35
University of Washington
Seattle, WA 98185
bershad@cs.washington.edu

Abstract

Most software-based distributed shared memory (DSM) systems rely on the operating system's virtual memory interface to detect writes to shared data. Strategies based on virtual memory page protection create two problems for a DSM system. First, writes can have high overhead since they are detected with a page fault. As a result, a page must be written many times to amortize the cost of that fault. Second, the size of a virtual memory page is too big to serve as a unit of coherency, inducing false sharing. Mechanisms to handle false sharing can increase runtime overhead and may cause data to be unnecessarily communicated between processors.

In this paper, we present a new method for write detection that solves these problems. Our method relies on the compiler and runtime system to detect writes to shared data without invoking the operating system. We measure and compare implementations of a distributed shared memory system using both strategies, virtual memory and compiler/runtime, running a range of applications on a small scale distributed memory multicomputer. We show that the new method has low average write latency and supports fine-grained sharing with low overhead. Further, we show that the dominant cost of write detection with either strategy is due to the mechanism used to handle fine-grain sharing.

1 Introduction

A distributed shared memory (DSM) system provides the abstraction of a shared memory multiprocessor to a program running on multiple processors that do not physically share

---

This research was sponsored in part by the Advanced Research Projects Agency under the title "Software System Support for High Performance Multicomputing", contract number DABT63-93-C-0054. Sawdon was partially supported by a grant from the International Business Machines Corporation.

The views and conclusions contained in this document are those of the authors and should not be interpreted as representing the official policies, either expressed or implied, of ARPA, IBM, or the U.S. Government.

memory. Software DSM systems implement this abstraction entirely in software, relying on an explicit message-passing network for communication [Li & Hudak 89, Carter et al. 91, Bershad et al. 93, Keleher et al. 94]. The primary service provided by these systems is *cache management*, which enables processors to cache recently accessed data items in local memory. Cache management requires that the DSM system detect writes to shared memory so that a consistency protocol can be activated.

In this paper, we examine the performance implications of two strategies – one relying on virtual memory page protection (VM-DSM) and one relying on the compiler and runtime (RT-DSM) – to detect and collect writes to shared data in a software-based DSM system. We show that RT-DSM has lower overhead than VM-DSM for three reasons. First, RT-DSM tends to have lower average update latency because it can avoid the operating system altogether. Second, RT-DSM directly supports variable sized objects eliminating *false-sharing* and the overhead necessary to accommodate it. Third, RT-DSM efficiently provides a detailed update history, which allows it to minimize the data transferred to maintain consistent memory.

1.1 Motivation

Most DSM systems use virtual memory page protection to detect writes to shared memory. The runtime relies on virtual memory write faults to detect updates to a program's address space. VM-DSM systems are attractive because they allow an application to use shared memory in a transparent fashion using native compilers and libraries [Li & Hudak 89]. There are, however, some disadvantages. Virtual memory operations, even in an optimized system, have a high cost [Appel & Li 91, Thekkath & Levy 94] relative to that of an instrumented write, as we show in this paper. More importantly, the large virtual memory page size creates problems with false sharing [Bennett et al. 90]. To support sharing at the sub-page level, an additional mechanism such as page "diffing" is required [Carter et al. 91]. Such mechanisms are generally memory reference intensive, and

---

therefore expensive. Moreover, mechanisms that deal with false sharing at the page level do not efficiently reveal a fine-grained history of updates to shared data, resulting in either the transfer of excess data or a more complicated data consistency algorithm.

In contrast to VM-DSM, RT-DSM relies on the compiler and runtime to detect writes entirely in software at user-level. No virtual memory operations are required. Each memory store operation is instrumented by the compiler to update a locally maintained *dirtybit* associated with the stored address. This approach offers low overhead and supports fine-grain sharing since the unit of coherency is not tied to the virtual memory page size. Fine-grain dirtybits can be used directly to record the history of updates to a particular line of shared memory. This history enables the RT-DSM system to perform an update at a processor exactly once, thereby minimizing the data communicated between processors.

A potential disadvantage with the RT-DSM approach is that the overhead of write detection occurs on every write. Multiple stores to the same item incur the same overhead each time. In contrast, with VM-DSM, only the first store to a page must be detected with a page fault. Others can proceed at full speed, thereby amortizing the initial overhead. The amortization period lasts until another processor attempts to access the new data or its containing page. The page must then be write protected to detect the next store.

This paper explores the tradeoffs between the two approaches to detecting writes in a DSM system. We base our comparison on the observed behavior of applications running on top of Midway [Bershad et al. 93], a DSM system for a network of workstations that can be configured as either a VM-DSM or an RT-DSM for parallel C programs.

1.2   Related work

Most software DSM work has focused on improving the performance of page-based DSM systems [Minnich & Farber 89, Bryant et al. 91, Carter et al. 91, Keleher et al. 94]. A few parallel programming environments support shared memory, but do not rely on hardware page protection, such as Orca, Amber and Emerald. Orca [Bal et al. 92] implements an update-based protocol based on language-specific objects. The protocol is implemented as part of the compiler for the Orca language. Data is globally replicated and updates are broadcast as they occur, so write detection and consistency management occur as a single operation. Emerald [Jul et al. 88] and Amber [Chase et al. 89] are object-oriented systems that detect writes by way of runtime support. However, these systems only support data migration, not replication, so write detection and consistency management are combined.

There are a few efforts to distill shared memory into its basic operations. Tempest [Reinhardt et al. 94] is an interface definition for a hardware DSM that could be realized in software. Tempest requires both write *and* read detection.

A software implementation, Blizzard-S [Schoinas et al. 94], has been done for the CM-5. However, Blizzard-S more closely emulates a hardware DSM and uses a more complex scheme for fine-grain detection than the scheme presented here. SAM [Scales & Lam 94] provides shared objects, not general shared memory, with new kinds of data called *accumulators* and *values*. A compiler can issue operations on these kinds of data much like our compiler instrumenting writes.

The languages community has explored the tradeoffs between runtime and page-based support for access detection within a single-node program [Hosking & Moss 93, Appel & Li 91]. The majority of these studies have concentrated on the use of write detection to implement efficient garbage collection in object-oriented and type-safe languages. Recently, software write detection has been investigated for other purposes, such as debugger breakpoints [Wahbe 92] and fault isolation [Wahbe et al. 93].

Our experiments, which are based on parallel programs running on a DSM system, differ from previous work in the choice of language used, whether or not the language is compiled or interpreted, style of programming (parallel vs. sequential), the existence of sharing and synchronization patterns, communication (bandwidth and latency) overheads, and the presence of fine-grained sharing.

The rest of this paper

In the next section we discuss the role of write detection in software-based DSM systems, and provide more details on the tradeoffs between RT-DSM and VM-DSM. In Section 3 we describe our implementation of both detection mechanisms in Midway. In Section 4 we compare the performance of a suite of benchmark applications using the two methods. Finally, in Section 5 we present our conclusions.

2   Reference detection and consistency protocols

Low-latency reads and writes represent the primary goal for any DSM system. To provide the abstraction of a single address space, software-based DSM systems must detect updates to shared memory and propagate the changes. Whether reads must also be detected depends on the consistency protocol. Read latency is decreased to local memory latency if an update protocol is used, since there are no read misses. An update-based protocol can increase the amount and frequency of communication between processors [Dwarkadas et al. 93]. Two techniques can be used to counter this effect. First, an update can be tied to a program's use of synchronization, enabling the updates to be coalesced and piggybacked on top of the necessary synchronization messages. The linking of synchronization to updates is accomplished by basing the DSM system on a weakly consistent memory model [Adve & Hill 93, Mosberger 93] as implemented in several systems [Carter et al. 91, Bershad et al. 93, Keleher et al. 94]. Second, the propagation of updates can be restricted to those processors that require the new data, rather than all processors, by taking advantage of the causal communication ordering revealed by a program's synchronization pattern [Keleher et al. 92, Bershad et al. 93, Keleher et al. 94]. Given that read latency can be minimized by an efficient update protocol, the problem becomes one of minimizing write latency, that is, detecting writes.

It might appear that write detection in an RT-DSM system is not as efficient as in a VM-DSM system because there is a constant overhead for each write. However, there are a number of factors to consider:

- The relative cost of a page fault is much greater than that of an individual write [Appel & Li 91, Hosking & Moss 93, Wahbe et al. 93, Thekkath & Levy 94]. In contrast, a write to shared memory can be instrumented with an overhead of just a few instructions.

- The virtual memory page size is too large for many applications, resulting in *false sharing* [Bennett et al. 90]. False sharing occurs when two data items share the same memory block, but are updated independently by two different processors, causing the memory block to be repeatedly transferred between the two processors. RT-DSM systems do not suffer from false sharing because the size of the unit of coherency can be set to meet the needs of the application.

- The number of instrumented writes in an RT-DSM system can be decreased by observing that shared memory parallel programs often have regions of memory dedicated to a particular processor, with just a few key data structures and variables shared among the processors. There is no need to instrument writes to memory that will not be referenced by other processors.

Whether RT-DSM or VM-DSM systems offer lower average write latency depends on a program's reference and synchronization pattern. For a coarse-grained program that exhibits little actual sharing, a VM-DSM system may be advantageous. In contrast, for a program that synchronizes (communicates) frequently, an RT-DSM system may be better. We consider these aspects of performance in Section 4.

3 Implementing write detection

In this section we describe the implementation of two write detection facilities, one using runtime support and one using virtual memory page protection. We have implemented both facilities in the context of Midway, a distributed shared memory system for a network of workstations to run parallel C programs. Our algorithms for page management under the VM-based strategy follow those described in the literature for other systems [Li & Hudak 89, Carter et al. 91, Keleher et al. 94].

Midway is a DSM system that provides the programmer with a weakly-consistent memory model called *entry consistency* [Bershad et al. 93]. Using entry consistency, processes synchronize explicitly via locks or barriers. Locks may be acquired in exclusive (for writing) or non-exclusive mode (for reading). When a processor acquires a lock that was last acquired on another processor, the first processor (the requester) must send a message to the second processor (the releaser) explicitly requesting the lock. A reply to this message represents a point of synchronization between the processors. The programmer provides the association between a lock or barrier and the data that the lock or barrier protects. At a synchronization point, entry consistency ensures that the data protected by the requested synchronization object reflects the most recent write to that data at the requesting processor. In practice, this requires that the DSM system determine the set of updates which have been performed at all other processors that have yet to be applied at the requesting site.

There are two aspects of each write detection scheme to consider. First, a write to shared memory must be trapped to ensure that the write can be later propagated to other processors. Second, at each synchronization point, a DSM system must collect the set of writes to be performed at the requesting processor. This set includes those actually issued on the releasing processor, and those writes issued on processors that had previously released the synchronization object. In the next two sections, we discuss in detail these two aspects, called *write trapping* and *write collection*, for both implementations.

3.1 Write trapping in RT-DSM

In Midway's RT-DSM implementation, write trapping is done entirely in user-level software. Every shared address cached on a processor has a dirtybit elsewhere in that processor's memory that reflects whether or not the address has been written. After each write to a shared address, the program sets a dirtybit associated with the modified address.

The strategy for write trapping relies on the careful arrangement of shared data and dirtybits in a processor's virtual memory. The application's virtual address space is partitioned into large, fixed size *regions*, as is illustrated in Figure 1. Data within a single region is either shared between all processors or private to each processor. The data within a shared region is divided into software *cache lines* and each cache line has a single dirtybit per processor. All cache lines in a region are the same size, although different regions may have different cache line sizes. The first page of each region contains a code template that updates the dirtybits for all data within that region. This code is tailored specifically for each region to contain the cache line size and location of the dirtybits as constants. The code template is generated when memory within the region is first allocated and write protected to prevent inadvertent modification.

To set a dirtybit, the compiler generates code that zeroes the low-order bits of the memory address being modified to produce the address of the dirtybit update code template. The generated code then calls the template passing the offset of the modified data within the region. The dirtybit update code computes the address of the dirtybit corresponding to the modified data, sets the dirtybit and returns. The compiler treats the call as a built-in and does not clobber temporary registers. Using common code for a region limits the inline code expansion and minimizes the perturbation in the processor's instruction cache. The code template also enables library code, such as *bcopy* and *scanf*, to be compiled only once and used on both shared and private memory.

Midway uses a modified version of the GCC compiler to emit the call to set the dirtybit after each write to shared memory. The compiler classifies program memory as either *shared* or *private*. By default, the program's static data is classified as shared and data stored on the program's stack is private. Memory referenced via a pointer is, by default, also classified as shared. All writable memory has a dirtybit template at the base of its region. The template for private memory returns to the caller without side-effects, although on our platform there is a six instruction penalty associated with misclassifying memory. The programmer can annotate the code with explicit `shared` or `private` attributes to change the classification of a type, a variable or a single assignment statement. These attributes are type-checked by the compiler and warnings are generated for mismatched assignments. In practice, it is relatively easy to accurately classify all memory, with misclassifications occurring quite infrequently.

We have found that the most frequently occurring type of write involves a doubleword store to a doubleword cache line. On a DECstation 5000/200 (MIPS R3000 [Kane 87]), this common case requires nine instructions (360 nanoseconds), of which four are generated inline by the compiler and five are in the dirtybit update code stored in the region's template. There are no load instructions which could miss in the cache and only one store instruction, which does not stall the processor given a sufficiently deep writebuffer. Instruction sequences for the dirtybit update code on a MIPS R3000 are shown in Appendix A.

3.2 Write collection in RT-DSM

Midway's RT-DSM implementation uses the dirtybits to collect the data to transfer at each synchronization point. There are two aspects to write collection: determining the data that the local processor has modified, and determining the data that has been previously modified, but has not been updated at the requesting processor. RT-DSM uses the dirtybits for both functions. A dirtybit is actually a timestamp that records the time of the most recent modification

to each cache line. When a processor modifies a shared data item, it sets the associated dirtybit to the processor's local time.[1] The processor's local time is maintained as a *Lamport clock* [Lamport 78] to provide an ordering on the updates to an individual cache line.

The dirtybits allow RT-DSM to send the minimum number of updates necessary to maintain consistent memory. Updates are never performed more than once at a processor. The algorithm for collecting the minimal set of prior modifications is as follows. The first time a processor, P_1, acquires a lock (or crosses a barrier) it obtains all data bound to the lock, all dirtybits associated with the data, and the current logical time of the releasing processor. When the lock is subsequently transferred to another processor, P_1 updates the dirtybit timestamps for the data it modified to its current logical time. This time is also recorded by P_1 as the logical time at which the lock's data was consistent in the local cache. P_1 includes this time in a subsequent request to reacquire the lock from a remote processor, P_2. To make P_1's local cache consistent again, all data bound to the requested lock that has changed since P_1 last held the lock must be included in the reply message. The releasing processor, P_2, collects this set of data by scanning its dirtybits associated with the requested lock. Any dirtybit value greater than P_1's last timestamp indicates P_1's version of the associated data is inconsistent and must be updated. The new value and its timestamp are included in the lock reply message.

3.3 Write trapping in VM-DSM

Midway's VM-DSM implementation is similar to that of many systems using hardware page faults to detect writes to shared memory. VM-DSM uses Mach's external pager [Young et al. 87] to receive page fault notifications. The application's shared address space is mapped to allow a Midway runtime thread to service the application's paging requests. Initially all shared pages are mapped for read-only access and marked as clean. On the first store to each page, a write fault occurs and Midway creates a *twin* by saving a copy of the page. The page is marked as dirty, and write access is granted. The application's store is then completed and the faulting thread resumed. Subsequent writes to the page are not trapped and incur no additional overhead.

3.4 Write collection in VM-DSM

A reply message to a synchronization request must include any changes made by the releasing processor, as well as earlier changes by other processors that have not been performed at the requester. Each time a lock or barrier is transferred, its *incarnation number* is incremented and an

---

[1] In practice, the dirtybit timestamp is zeroed and lazily set to the processor's local time when the guarding synchronization object is transferred to another processor.

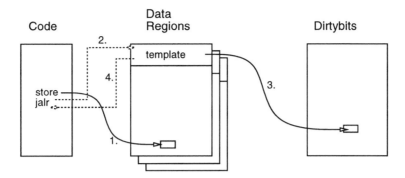

Figure 1: *This figure schematically represents a shared memory write. First the write is done. Based on the address of the modified data, a jump is made to the template for that region. The template computes the dirtybit address and stores a zero to mark the cacheline as dirty.*

update is created to encapsulate the modifications made to the data during that incarnation. The incarnation number imposes an ordering on the updates to the data bound to each synchronization object. In this sense, the incarnation number is similar to the cache line timestamps in the RT-DSM implementation. Each synchronization request includes the associated incarnation number at the last time it was held by the requester. Only updates with an incarnation number larger than the one indicated by the requester are transferred.

Midway's VM-DSM collects the data modified by the local processor by using the entry consistency binding information to locate the pages containing data bound to the requested lock or barrier. If any data on the page has been modified, the page will have been marked as dirty and a twin allocated. The contents of the page are compared against the original contents stored in the twin to create a *diff*. The diff is a succinct description of all modifications to the page. Modified data that is bound to the requested lock or barrier is collected into an update and shipped to the requesting processor. The diff created for each page is saved and may be reused to transfer other data on the page bound to different synchronization objects. When all modified data on the page has been shipped to other processors, the page is considered clean and its diff and twin deallocated. At the site which requested the lock, the incoming updates are applied to the shared data and the updates are saved. If the page being updated is currently marked as dirty, the update is applied to both the primary page and to the twin. Updating the twin ensures that the update will not be treated as a new modification by the local processor.

Updates from prior incarnations may either be combined by the releasing processor, or sent in their entirety and applied in incarnation order at the requester. The releasing processor has available the complete set of prior updates, because it saves the updates it receives when acquiring each lock. When subsequently releasing the lock, all prior updates required by the requesting processor are included in the reply message. There are no additional messages to

other processors to obtain prior updates. However, Midway's implementation of VM-DSM does not save all the updates, nor does it combine updates from different incarnations. For example, if a memory location is written during incarnation 7 and then again during incarnation 8, any processor requesting a lock with a "last seen" incarnation number less than 7 would receive both writes. If the size of the concatenated updates exceeds the size of the data, a new update containing all of the bound data is sent instead. Combining updates requires that each address in the combined set reflect the most recent incarnation at which the address was written. We could maintain a finer-grained history by associating an incarnation number with each update to every shared address in the VM-DSM (as we do in RT-DSM), but have chosen not to do so. This scheme would incur at least the same data collection overhead as the RT-DSM (scan the incarnation numbers) and it would incur the additional overhead of trapping and detection for VM-DSM (write fault, twin, and diff).

3.5 Alternative approaches

The strategies described above represent points in the possible design space of write detection and collection mechanisms. There are alternate approaches that require neither software dirtybits nor virtual memory page faults to ensure consistency. For example, we could implement entry consistency by simply "blasting" all data associated with a synchronization object during interprocessor synchronization. There would be no need to detect writes at all (either with dirty bits or with page faults), since the guarantees of the consistency model could be provided through a conservative update protocol. This approach, although simple and having no immediate write overhead, would transfer data unnecessarily when synchronization objects guard large data objects being sparsely written.

A twinning and differencing algorithm, similar to our implementation for VM-DSM, could be used to reduce the amount of data transferred by the simple "blasting" approach described above. As data arrived on a processor, the processor would keep a second copy of each data item. At each synchronization point, all data bound to the synchronization object would be compared with its copy to determine which addresses have been modified. This approach avoids the cost of write detection, but increases the storage requirements (every shared data item must be twinned on any processor which writes it), and the synchronization overhead of the consistency mechanism (to diff unmodified data and to maintain the twin). Moreover, this approach would still require management of the update incarnations to ensure that a chain of processor updates are correctly propagated. As we show in the next section, data twinning and write collection constitute a significant portion of system overhead compared to the actual page fault time. Strategies that reduce the number of page faults by increasing the amount of data diffed cannot minimize the total cost of write detection.

Other memory models

A *targetted* memory consistency model delimits the addresses that must be made consistent whenever processors communicate. In contrast, an *untargetted* consistency model requires that the entire shared address space be made consistent. Entry consistency is a targetted model because only the data explicitly bound to the synchronization object is made consistent when processors synchronize using that object. Other consistency models, such as release consistency [Gharachorloo et al. 89], are untargetted. The consequence of an untargetted model is that a different style of bookkeeping is necessary during write trapping to delimit the scope of subsequent consistency operations. For example, Midway's RT-DSM strategy, when used with an untargetted memory model, would require scanning the dirtybit for every line cached in the processor's local memory. Implementations of write detection for untargetted models are more likely to rely on data structures better suited for sparseness.

There are two straightforward ways that Midway's RT-DSM strategy could be extended to support untargetted memory models. Both approaches slightly increase the write trapping overhead to reduce the subsequent write collection overhead. One approach is to use an update queue rather than a dirtybit array. Many updates are sequential, allowing a simple heuristic to substantially reduce the queue size. Although an update queue roughly triples the cost of write trapping, it keeps the cost of write detection proportional to the amount of dirty data, rather than the amount of shared data. An alternative approach is to represent dirtybits in a two level structure. Each dirtybit at the first level can "cover" a large number of dirtybits at the second. On a write to a shared address, the dirtybit at both levels associated with the written address is set. When synchronizing between processors, the first level dirtybits are scanned. If the first level bit has not been set, then no data in the

second level is dirty and scanning of the second level bits can be avoided. Two-level dirtybits can be implemented with one additional store instruction in the write detection path, increasing its length by about 10%. Virtual memory page protection could also be used to implement the first level dirtybits. The second level dirtybits could be write protected so that a write to any one of them causes a page fault. The fault would result in the associated first level dirtybit being set and the page on which the second level bits are stored being made writable. As we show in the next section, write collection, and not write trapping, is the more expensive operation, therefore this seems like a practical approach.

Other memory consistency protocols invalidate cached memory rather than updating the data values. For applications that exhibit little write sharing, an invalidation protocol may reduce the total amount of data communicated. A consequence of invalidated memory is that reads, as well as writes, to shared data must be detected. Software read detection incurs a higher overhead than write detection, since read detection is more complicated and generally invoked more often than write detection. Applications with little write sharing also exhibit infrequent accesses to the invalidated data. By minimizing the cost of the common case and using the hardware to detect the exceptional events, we expect a VM-DSM system to incur lower overhead than an RT-DSM system. Of course, if the VM-DSM system exhibits a large number of read misses, than an update-based protocol is in order.

4 Experiments

In this section we describe the results of experiments using implementations of RT-DSM and VM-DSM described in the previous section. All experiments were run on a cluster of eight DECstation 5000/200's connected through Fore Systems TCA-100 TURBOchannel interface cards to a 140 MBit/sec ForeRunner ASX-100 ATM switch. The workstations run Mach 3.0 [Accetta et al. 86], have 25MHz MIPS R3000 processors, a 4KB page size, and 64 MBs of memory (no paging occurs during program execution). Our communication protocols use the ATM AAL3/4 adaptation layer directly, bypassing the Unix server [Brustoloni 94].

The experiments are intended to answer three questions:

1. Do programs using RT-DSM execute more quickly than when run under VM-DSM?

2. How does the cost of write trapping using RT-DSM compare to that using VM-DSM?

3. How much overhead is required during processor synchronization to collect the set of modified data that must be transferred?

We selected and ran five applications to answer these questions. These applications have sharing and computation patterns that are representative of a range of parallel programs. The applications were modified to use entry consistency and to run on both the RT-DSM and VM-DSM systems.

The first application, water, is a N-body molecular dynamics simulation from the Splash application suite [Singh et al. 92]. The program evaluates forces and potentials for a system of 343 water molecules in a liquid state for 5 steps. It exhibits medium-grained sharing. Our version of water has the optimization suggested in [Singh et al. 92], which collects changes to the molecules in private memory during a time step, updating the shared molecules only at the end of each time step.

The second application, quicksort, is one of the TreadMarks applications [Keleher et al. 94]. It sorts an array of 250, 000 integers using a parallel quicksort algorithm until the partition size is less than a threshold of 1000 elements and then sorts locally using a bubblesort algorithm. This program exhibits medium to coarse-grain sharing, but does little computation between writes to shared memory (the inner loop does a compare and swap of adjacent elements in the array). The array is partitioned dynamically, so the lock binding the data to the task queue element is rebound to a new range of addresses for every task created.

The matrix-multiply application exhibits coarse grain sharing with a high computation to communication ratio. This program multiplies two 512×512 floating point matrices. The matrix-multiply program is of interest because its data is partitioned to minimize the amount of sharing and because it writes every word on every page of the result matrix. The large number of writes to each page helps the VM-DSM system best amortize the cost of the initial page fault. By minimizing the amount of fine-grain sharing, the program also minimizes the cost of twinning and diffing. This represents the expected best case for VM-DSM, and the worst case for RT-DSM. For the RT-DSM system, every write incurs the overhead to set the associated dirtybit.

The application sor implements a red-black successive over-relaxation algorithm to calculate the steady state temperature of a two-dimensional rectangular plate, given a fixed temperature at each edge. The program iteratively computes new values for each element in a 1000×1000 matrix of floating point values. The matrix data is laid out with red and black elements adjacent in memory and is not partitioned to match the peculiarities of the memory system. Only data at the edges of each partition are shared between processors. The interior elements are initialized to random values to maximize the changed elements per iteration. The program runs for 25 iterations and exhibits medium-grain sharing.

The final application, cholesky, is from the Splash application suite and performs a parallel Cholesky factorization of a sparse matrix. Given a positive definite matrix A, the program finds a lower triangular matrix L, such that

$A = LL^T$. This program exhibits fine-grain sharing.

Overall performance

The graphs in Figure 2 show the execution time and the amount of data transferred for each application under both RT-DSM and VM-DSM. The graphs show that VM-DSM dominates RT-DSM only for quicksort. The other programs run either faster, or no slower when using run time detection. quicksort frequently changes the association between locks and data. When a lock binding changes under RT-DSM, the dirtybits must still be scanned for every lock transfer. Under VM-DSM, the incarnation number is incremented which causes all data bound to the lock to be sent without performing a diff. Since this application modifies nearly all of the bound data on every transfer, the VM-DSM approach is better. Although the matrix-multiply program has expected worst-case performance for RT-DSM and best-case performance for VM-DSM, the graphs show only a minor difference between the two approaches. The medium and fine-grained programs, water, sor, and cholesky, all exhibit lower execution times and transmit less data under RT-DSM than under VM-DSM.

The graphs in Figure 2 also show the execution time for a standalone, uniprocessor version of each application. The standalone version contains no code for write detection or synchronization, which is included in both the RT-DSM and VM-DSM versions, and thus executes faster than either version. The uniprocessor times for water under RT-DSM, VM-DSM and a standalone system are 110.1, 109.1, and 104.2 seconds, respectively. The execution time for the uniprocessor RT-DSM version is highest since it pays the entire cost for write detection. The VM-DSM version pays for a single write fault on each shared page. It never diffs or write protects a page, since the data is never transferred. Thus its overhead is lower than the RT-DSM version. Once the application runs in parallel, the cost of write collection becomes important and we see RT-DSM outperform VM-DSM.

4.1 The cost of write trapping

The previous section presented overall program performance. In this and the next section, we discuss the performance of a write detection mechanism's two components: write trapping and write collection. We determine the cost of write trapping by examining the frequency and cost of the primitives required for its implementation under RT-DSM and VM-DSM. The primitive operations for RT-DSM are (1) set a dirty bit after a shared write and (2) set a dirty bit after a private write. For VM-DSM, the primitive operations are (1) field a write fault, (2) twin a page, and (3) set the page protection. The measured cost of each primitive operation is given in Table 1. Table 2 summarizes the invocation counts for each application as a per processor

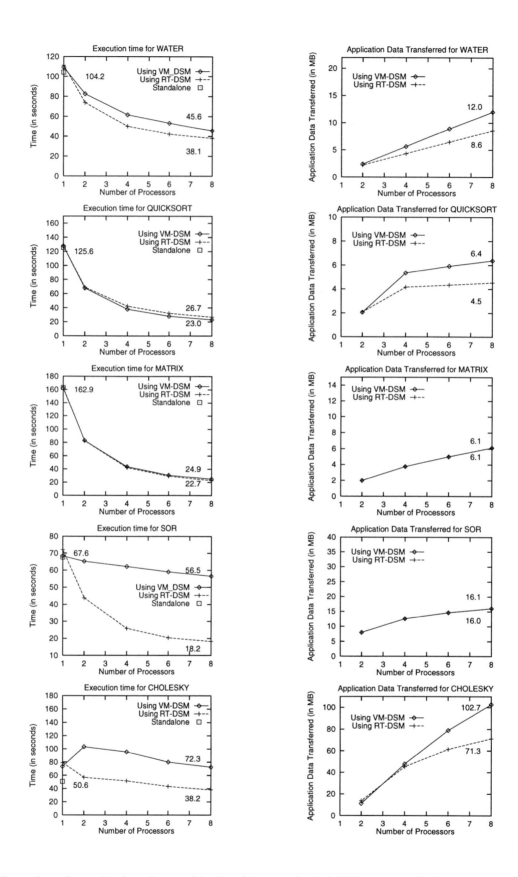

Figure 2: *Comparison of execution times (in seconds) and total data transferred (in MB) for our applications. The graphs represent an average over 5 runs of each application. The average value of the standalone execution time, eight processor execution time, and data transferred in an eight processor execution are also shown.*

System	Primitive Operation	Time (μsecs)	Cycles
RT-DSM	dirtybit set time		
	for a word write	0.360	9
	for a doubleword write	0.360	9
	for writing to private memory	0.240	6
	dirtybit read time		
	for each "clean" dirtybit read	0.217	5
	for each "dirty" dirtybit read	0.187	4
	dirtybit write time		
	for each dirtybit updated	0.067	2
VM-DSM	page write fault		
	includes page copy & protection call	1,200	30,000
	page diff time		
	if none or all of the data changed	260	7,000
	if every other word changed	1,870	46,750
	page protection call		
	to allow read-write access	125	3,125
	to allow read-only access	127	3,175
	memory block copy time		
	for each KB of data in a cold cache	84	2,100
	for each KB of data in a warm cache	26	650

Table 1: *Execution times for primitive operations on a 25MHz MIPS R3000 processor running Mach 3.0. The page size is 4 KB. All times are measured averages and are given in microseconds.*

		Applications				
System	Operation	Water	Quicksort	Matrix	SOR	Cholesky
RT-DSM	dirtybits set	43,180	220,804	98,311	348,516	1,284,004
	dirtybits misclassified	0	124	11	1	28
	clean dirtybits read	48,552	98,190	135,776	19,185	2,568,269
	dirty dirtybits read	11,280	108,939	94,217	261,097	739,625
	dirtybits updated	35,676	147,896	200,849	262,987	1,132,009
	data transferred (in KB)	1,096	579	784	2,053	9,128
	percent dirty data	55.7	62.7	87.4	98.1	29.3
VM-DSM	write faults	258	156	74	468	2,916
	pages diffed	253	27	120	674	3,107
	pages write protected	253	27	120	674	3,107
	data updated in twins (in KB)	976	418	15	47	5,114
	data transferred (in KB)	1,543	816	784	2,058	13,144

Table 2: *Per processor invocation counts of the primitive operations. All numbers are averages for all processors in an 8-way run. The "data transferred" number measures only application data, it does not include protocol overhead.*

average. By multiplying the counts in Table 2 by the time for each primitive operation from Table 1, we can estimate the cost for write trapping in each system. A summary of the write trapping costs for each applications is presented in Table 3. For example, we compute the write trapping cost for water as follows: under RT-DSM, each processor set 43,180 dirtybits (none were misclassified), requiring 0.360 μsecs each for a total time of 16 msecs; under VM-DSM, each processor incurred 258 write faults, requiring 1200 μsecs each to handle the fault, make a twin and set the page protection, for a total time of 310 msecs. Times for the other programs can be similarly determined.

The impact of fast exceptions

Midway's VM-DSM implementation uses Mach's external pager, which is relatively expensive, to trap writes. A write exception, though, can be delivered in as few as 18 μsecs on the hardware used by Midway [Thekkath & Levy 94]. Despite this, the VM-DSM fault handler must still copy the 4KB page to its twin, increasing the best-case time to service a write fault to 122 μsecs. We can estimate the contributed cost of write trapping when using a fast exception handler. The graph in Figure 3 shows this cost for a range of write trapping overheads, comparing against the write trapping cost for an RT-DSM system. Each application is represented by a horizontal line showing the effect of varying the page fault service time between 122 μsecs and 1200 μsecs. The

System	Operation	Applications				
		Water	Quicksort	Matrix	SOR	Cholesky
RT-DSM	write trapping time	15.6	79.5	35.4	125.5	485.3
VM-DSM	write trapping time	309.6	187.2	88.8	561.6	3,499.2
RT-DSM trapping advantage		**294.0**	**107.7**	**53.4**	**436.1**	**3,103.9**

Table 3: *Summary of the time for write trapping. All times are in milliseconds and are computed by measuring the costs of the primitive operations and multiplying by the average per-processor number of invocations for each application.*

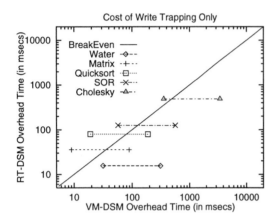

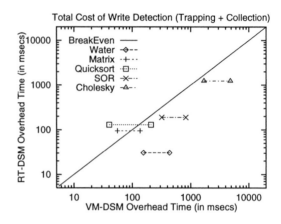

Figure 3: *The effect of varying page fault cost on write detection. Each application is a line with the left end represents the costs incurred by VM-DSM with a time to service a page fault of 122 μsecs using Thekkath and Levy's fast exception handler. The right end represents the costs with a page fault service time of 1200 μsecs using Mach's external pager. The diagonal line represents the break even point between VM-DSM and RT-DSM. Points beneath the line show a lower cost for RT-DSM.*

Figure 4: *The effect of varying page fault cost on the total cost of write detection, including both trapping and collection. The graph is interpreted as in Figure 3. The break even cost for handling a page fault is 650 μsecs for* matrix-multiply *and 696 μsecs for* quicksort.

break even line for the cost of write detection is shown as the diagonal line. All points beneath the diagonal line indicate that write trapping overhead will be lower when using RT-DSM as opposed to VM-DSM. If the line for the application crosses the break even point, write trapping for that application will be less expensive when using a VM-DSM system with a fast exception mechanism.

The graph shows that most applications span the break even point. This indicates the cost of write trapping under VM-DSM is strongly dependent on the cost of the platform's exception handler. For the coarse-grained applications, matrix-multiply and quicksort, the actual overhead is small and neither system outperforms the other. For the medium and fine-grained applications, the costs are higher and tend to favor the RT-DSM approach.

4.2 The cost of write collection

The cost of trapping writes is only one part of the total cost for write detection. We must also account for the cost of collecting modified data at each synchronization point. We can determine this cost by examining the frequency and cost of the primitive operations required for its implementation under RT-DSM and VM-DSM. The primitives for

RT-DSM are (1) read a dirtybit when collecting data, (2) reset the dirtybit for modified data, and (3) update a dirtybit with a new timestamp value for data updated at the requesting processor. For VM-DSM, the primitive operations are (1) compare a page during diffing, (2) change the page protection, and (3) update twinned data at the requesting processor. The measured cost of each primitive operation is given in Table 1.

The count of invocations of each primitive operation is summarized in Table 2. By multiplying the counts in Table 2 by the time for each primitive operation from Table 1, we can estimate the average cost per processor for write collection in each system. The results are summarized in Table 4. We see that, with the exception of quicksort where diffing is not performed due to the lock rebinding, write collection with VM-DSM is more expensive than with RT-DSM. Furthermore, the cost of write collection increases with the amount of write sharing; fine-grained applications incur a higher percentage overhead than coarse-grained ones.

The break even point between VM-DSM and RT-DSM for write collection is a function of the percentage of data that has been modified by the local processor. It does not depend on page fault overhead. If none of the data bound to the requested synchronization object has been modified, nor has any of the data on the containing pages, then VM-DSM can avoid the cost of diffing. The RT-DSM system,

System	Operation	Applications				
		Water	Quicksort	Matrix	SOR	Cholesky
RT-DSM	clean dirtybits read	10.5	21.3	29.5	0.5	557.3
	dirty dirtybits read	2.0	19.2	16.6	46.0	138.3
	dirtybits updated	2.4	9.9	13.5	17.6	75.8
	Total	14.9	50.4	59.6	64.1	771.4
VM-DSM	pages diffed	65.8	7.0	31.2	175.2	807.8
	pages write protected	32.1	3.4	15.2	85.6	394.6
	data updated in twins	25.4	10.9	0.4	1.2	133.0
	Total	123.3	21.3	46.8	262.0	1,335.4
RT-DSM collection advantage		108.4	-29.1	-12.8	197.9	564.0

Table 4: *Summary of the cost for write collection as a per-processor average. All times are in milliseconds and are computed by measuring the costs of the primitive operations and multiplying by the average number of per-processor invocations for each application.*

however, must still scan all of the dirtybits bound to the requested object. In practice, we found that often much of the bound data is modified, nullifying this possible advantage. Table 2 shows the percentage of dirty data bound to the synchronization object for each of the applications.

The graph in Figure 4 shows the accumulated cost of write trapping and write collection for each application across a range of page fault times. Like Figure 3, the break even line for the total cost is shown as the diagonal line. All points beneath the diagonal indicate a lower overhead when running under RT-DSM than under VM-DSM. If the application's line crosses the break even line, the application will have a lower total cost using a VM-DSM system with the fast exception mechanism, but a higher cost using VM-DSM on our system. The coarse-grained applications do not exhibit sufficient sharing to be strongly affected by either approach and are again near the break even line. The `quicksort` application favors VM-DSM since its calls to rebind data to locks allow VM-DSM to avoid the overhead of diffing. The medium and fine-grain applications have moved substantially to the right. This indicates that the cost of write collection is significant, and that even with an optimized exception handler RT-DSM dominates VM-DSM.

Memory reference activity

Collecting writes is memory intensive. We can partially account for the cost differential between RT-DSM and VM-DSM by observing the number of additional memory references required with each approach. For example, under VM-DSM the number of memory references is equal to twice the number of words per twinned page (read the original, write the twin), plus twice the number of words per diffed page (read the original, read the twin), plus the number of words applied to each twin during update. Under RT-DSM, it is the sum of the dirtybits set, clean dirtybits read, dirty dirtybits read (times 2 to store the timestamp in the dirtybit value), and the dirtybits updated to set the timestamps at the requesting processor. We can compare the number of memory references incurred by each ap-

proach using the primitive operation counts in Table 2. Table 5 shows that for medium and fine-grain applications, RT-DSM incurs substantially fewer memory references, primarily because it avoids the page twin and diff operations. As memory reference times continue to increase relative to CPU cycle time, we expect the impact of this difference will grow.

Data transferred

The graphs and figures show that Midway's implementation of RT-DSM transfers less data than VM-DSM, although both use the same consistency protocol. As previously mentioned, the difference stems from how the two implementations maintain update histories. An exact history, like that made possible by the RT-DSM's dirtybit timestamps, is necessary to minimize the total data transferred. The amount of redundant data transferred can be substantial. For example, `water` sent an extra 441 KB/processor (40%), and `cholesky` sent an extra 4015 KB/processor (44%). As network bandwidth increases, the impact of the additional data load on the network may decrease, however it will still remain necessary to construct the packets containing the excess data, and to needlessly reapply the updates at the requesting processor's local cache.

4.3 Summary

Our analysis divides the cost of write detection into two components, write trapping and write collection. For the VM-DSM system, the cost of write trapping depends on the platform's cost for exception handling. Even for systems with fast exceptions, an RT-DSM system has comparable or lower write trapping overhead for most applications. The total cost of write trapping is relatively low, and write collection (which is memory intensive) is the dominant component of write detection. The dirtybit scheme used by RT-DSM has low fixed overheads and naturally accommodates fine-grain sharing. The RT-DSM dirtybit scheme also provides an update history, reducing both the overhead and the data sent at each synchronization point.

System	Operation	Applications				
		Water	Quicksort	Matrix	SOR	Cholesky
RT-DSM	write trapping	43	221	98	349	1,349
	write collection	96	355	431	526	4,440
	Total	139	576	529	875	5,788
VM-DSM	write trapping	510	358	262	1,264	5,767
	write collection	768	162	250	1,392	7,672
	Total	1,278	521	512	2,656	13,439
RT-DSM memory reference advantage		**1,139**	**-55**	**-17**	**1,781**	**7,651**

Table 5: *Total memory references incurred for write detection under RT-DSM and VM-DSM. All counts are in units of* 1000 *and are per-processor averages.*

5   Conclusions

We have presented a new technique for detecting writes in a distributed shared memory system, and have compared its performance to a page-based strategy. A system using run-time write detection in conjunction with an update-based protocol can exhibit lower overhead when compared to a page-based system. The base cost of servicing a page fault is only one factor in the total overhead, the dominant cost is the mechanism to ● upport fine-grain sharing. The overhead incurred using runtime write detection does not depend on the granularity of sharing, allowing runtime detection to more efficiently support fine-grained applications. Our compiler-based detection mechanisms are currently being used in the Midway distributed shared memory system at Carnegie Mellon University.

Acknowledgments

José Brustoloni implemented the network drivers for our Mach 3.0 Fore ATM interfaces. Dave McKeown has been invaluable in obtaining the resources we used, as well as providing a user's perspective. Finally, Willy Zwaenepoel helped us clarify much of this paper's presentation.

References

[Accetta et al. 86] Accetta, M. J., Baron, R. V., Bolosky, W., Golub, D. B., Rashid, R. F., Avadis Tevanian, J., and Young, M. W. Mach: A New Kernel Foundation for Unix Development. In *Proceedings of the 1986 Summer USENIX Conference*, pages 93–113, July 1986.

[Adve & Hill 93] Adve, S. V. and Hill, M. D. A Unified Formalization of Four Shared-Memory Models. *IEEE Transactions on Parallel and Distributed Systems*, 4(6):613–624, June 1993.

[Appel & Li 91] Appel, A. W. and Li, K. Virtual Memory Primitives for User Programs. In *Proceedings of the Fourth ACM Conference on Architectural Support for Programming Languages and Operating Systems*, pages 96–107, April 1991.

[Bal et al. 92] Bal, H. E., Kaashoek, M. F., and Tanenbaum, A. S. Orca: A Languange For Parallel Programming of Distributed Systems. *IEEE Transactions on Software Engineering*, 18(3):190–205, March 1992.

[Bennett et al. 90] Bennett, J. K., Carter, J. B., and Zwaenepoel, W. Adaptive Software Cache Management for Distributed Shared

Memory Architectures. In *Proceedings of the 17th Annual Symposium on Computer Architecture*, pages 125–134, May 1990.

[Bershad et al. 93] Bershad, B. N., Zekauskas, M. J., and Sawdon, W. A. The Midway Distributed Shared Memory System. In *Proceedings of the 1993 IEEE CompCon Conference*, pages 528–537, February 1993.

[Brustoloni 94] Brustoloni, J. C. Exposed Buffering and Sub-Datagram Flow Control for ATM LANs. In *Proceedings of the 19th Annual Conference on Local Computer Networks*. IEEE Computer Society, September 1994.

[Bryant et al. 91] Bryant, R., Carini, P., Chang, H.-Y., and Rosenburg, B. Supporting Structured Shared Virtual Memory under Mach. In *Proceedings of the Second Mach USENIX Symposium*, pages 59–76, November 1991.

[Carter et al. 91] Carter, J., Bennett, J., and Zwaenepoel, W. Implementation and Performance of Munin. In *Proceedings of the 13th ACM Symposium on Operating Systems Principles*, pages 152–164, October 1991.

[Chase et al. 89] Chase, J. S., Amador, F. G., Lazowska, E. D., Levy, H. M., and Littlefield, R. J. The Amber System: Parallel Programming on a Network of Multiprocessors. In *Proceedings of the 12th ACM Symposium on Operating Systems Principles*, pages 147–158, December 1989.

[Dwarkadas et al. 93] Dwarkadas, S., Keleher, P., Cox, A. L., and Zwaenepoel, W. Evaluation of Release Consistent Software Distributed Shared Memory on Emerging Network Technology. In *Proceedings of the 20th Annual Symposium on Computer Architecture*, pages 144–155, May 1993.

[Gharachorloo et al. 89] Gharachorloo, K., Lenoski, D., Laudon, J., Gibbons, P., Gupta, A., and Hennessy, J. Memory Consistency and Event Ordering in Scalable Shared Memory Multiprocessors. In *Proceedings of the 16th Annual Symposium on Computer Architecture*, pages 15–26, May 1989.

[Hosking & Moss 93] Hosking, A. L. and Moss, J. E. B. Protection Traps and Alternatives for Memory Management of an Object-Oriented Language. In *Proceedings of the 14th ACM Symposium on Operating Systems Principles*, pages 106–119, December 1993.

[Jul et al. 88] Jul, E., Levy, H., Hutchinson, N., and Black, A. Fine-Grained Mobility in the Emerald System. *ACM Transactions on Computer Systems*, 6(1):109–133, February 1988.

[Kane 87] Kane, G. *MIPS R2000 RISC Architecture*. Prentice Hall, 1987.

[Keleher et al. 92] Keleher, P., Cox, A. L., and Zwaenepoel, W. Lazy Release Consistency for Software Distributed Shared Memory. In *Proceedings of the 19th Annual Symposium on Computer Architecture*, pages 13–21, May 1992.

[Keleher et al. 94] Keleher, P., Cox, A. L., Dwarkadas, S., and Zwaenepoel, W. TreadMarks: Distributed Shared Memory on Standard Workstations and Operating Systems. In *Proceedings of the 1994 Winter USENIX Conference*, pages 115–132, January 1994.

[Lamport 78] Lamport, L. Time, Clocks and the Ordering of Events in a Distributed System. *Communications of the ACM*, 21(7):558–565, July 1978.

[Li & Hudak 89] Li, K. and Hudak, P. Memory Coherence in Shared Virtual Memory Systems. *ACM Transactions on Computer Systems*, 7(4):321–359, November 1989.

[Minnich & Farber 89] Minnich, R. and Farber, D. The Mether System: A Distributed Shared Memory for SunOS 4.0. In *Proceedings of the 1989 Summer USENIX Conference*, June 1989.

[Mosberger 93] Mosberger, D. Memory Consistency Models. Technical Report TR 93/11, Department of Computer Science, University of Arizona, 1993.

[Reinhardt et al. 94] Reinhardt, S. K., Larus, J. R., and Wood, D. A. Tempest and Typhoon: User-Level Shared Memory. In *Proceedings of the 21st Annual Symposium on Computer Architecture*, pages 325–336, April 1994.

[Scales & Lam 94] Scales, D. J. and Lam, M. S. The Design and Evaluation of a Shared Object System for Distributed Memory Machines. In *Proceedings of the First Symposium on Operating Systems Design and Implementation*, November 1994.

[Schoinas et al. 94] Schoinas, I., Falsafi, B., Lebeck, A. R., Reinhardt, S. K., Larus, J. R., and Wood, D. A. Fine Grained Access Control for Distributed Shared Memory. In *Proceedings of the Sixth ACM Conference on Architectural Support for Programming Languages and Operating Systems*, October 1994.

[Singh et al. 92] Singh, J. P., Weber, W.-D., and Gupta, A. SPLASH: Stanford Parallel Applications for Shared Memory. *Computer Architecture News*, 20(1):2–12, March 1992.

[Thekkath & Levy 94] Thekkath, C. A. and Levy, H. M. Hardware and Software Support for Efficient Exception Handling. In *Proceedings of the 6th International Conference on Architectural Support for Programming Languages and Operating Systems*, October 1994.

[Wahbe 92] Wahbe, R. Efficient Data Breakpoints. In *Proceedings of the Fifth ACM Conference on Architectural Support for Programming Languages and Operating Systems*, pages 200–212, September 1992.

[Wahbe et al. 93] Wahbe, R., Lucco, S., Anderson, T. E., and Graham, S. L. Efficient Software-Based Fault Isolation. In *Proceedings of the 14th ACM Symposium on Operating Systems Principles*, pages 203–216, December 1993.

[Young et al. 87] Young, M., Tevanian, A., Rashid, R., Golub, D., Eppinger, J., Chew, J., Bolosky, W., Black, D., and Baron, R. The Duality of Memory and Communication in the Implementation of a Multiprocessor Operating System. In *The Proceedings of the 11th Symposium on Operating System Principles*, November 1987.

Appendix A: Dirtybit Update Code

Every dirtybit update is handled by two separate code sequences. The compiler generates the first sequence of code inline, immediately following the store to shared memory. The exact instruction sequence depends on the alignment of data and the amount of data written (eg. byte, word, doubleword). The instructions compute the address of the second code sequence, stored at the base of the region of memory being modified. The second code sequence actually sets the dirtybit to mark the cache line as "dirty."

All writable memory is logically divided into regions. The first page of the region is write protected and contains the code to update the dirtybits for data within that region. When the region is first allocated, a template of the dirtybit update code is copied to the base of the region and is modified to include as constants in the instruction stream the cache line size and the location of the dirtybits. Each template contains five entry points to set the dirtybit for a store of a byte, halfword, word, doubleword and an arbitrary sized range of bytes, called an "area". For shared regions, the template depends on the cache line size, allowing an optimization for word and doubleword size cache lines. For private regions, each entry point in the template simply returns.

For floating point applications, the common case is a doubleword store to doubleword size cache line. On the MIPS R3000 this requires 9 instructions, 4 generated inline by the compiler and 5 in the dirtybit update template. The exact sequence is shown in Figure 5. The mask for computing the base of the region is a constant and the compiler may allocate a register to it and avoid reloading it for subsequent stores. The compiler treats the dirtybit update call as a built-in and will only clobber registers a0, a1, and ra.

For integer applications, the common case is a single word store to a word size cache line. This is shown in Figure 6. The compiler must generate one extra instruction inline to compute the address of the entry point within the template for the dirtybit code for word writes. The code in the template saves an instruction, since the offset in the data region equals the offset in the dirtybits.

The most expensive case is when writing an unaligned object or for area operations, such as structure assignments. The compiler must generate an extra instruction to pass the size of the object modified as an argument to the dirtybit code. The inline code is shown in Figure 7. The code stored in the template allocates a stack frame, saves the temporary registers, and then calls a higher-level routine to perform the actual work. This sequence is rarely invoked. It was called only once by one of the applications presented.

If the compiler misclassifies a write to private memory, it will generates a call to the dirtybit update code for that region. The code for all entry points for private memory simply returns to the caller and is shown in Figure 8.

```
#
# Code generated inline by the compiler for a doubleword write
#
        sw      <val_lo>, 0(rx)         # original store instruction of low order word
        sw      <val_hi>, 4(rx)         # original store instruction of high order word
        lui     a0, <mask_for_template> # load mask for start of region address
        and     at, a0, rx              # generate addr for dirtybit template
        jalr    at                      # jump to dirtybit update code
        sub     a0, rx, a0              #  compute offset w/in region (jump delay slot)
#
# Code stored in template for a doubleword write to a doubleword size cache line
#
        lui     at,<dbit_address>       # load addr of start of dbits for region
        srl     a1, a0, 1               # divide offset by 2 to get dbit offset
        addu    at, a1, at              # generate address of dbit
        jr      ra                      # and return
        sw      zero, 0(at)             #  zero dbit to mark as ``dirty''
```

Figure 5: *Doubleword write to a doubleword size cache line.*

```
#
# Code generated inline by the compiler for a word write
#
        sw      <val>, 0(rx)            # original store instruction of word
        lui     at, <mask_for_template> # load mask for start of region addr
        and     a0, at, rx              # generate addr for dirtybit template
        or      at, a0, <entryW_offset> # gen addr for entry point w/in template
        jalr    at                      # jump to dirtybit update code
        sub     a0, rx, a0              #  compute offset within region
#
# Code stored in template for a word writes to a word size cache line
#
        lui     at,<dbit_address>       # load addr of start of dbits for region
        addu    at, a1, at              # generate address of dbit
        jr      ra                      # and return
        sw      zero, 0(at)             #  zero dbit to mark as ``dirty''
```

Figure 6: *Word write to a word size cache line.*

```
        sw      <val>, 0(rx)            # example of original store instuction
        lui     at, <mask_for_template> # load mask for start of region address
        and     a0, at, rx              # generate addr for dirtybit template
        or      at, a0, <entryA_offset> # generate addr for entry point w/in template
        addi    a1, zero, <object_size> # arg1 is size of the object written
        jalr    at                      # jump to dirtybit update code
        sub     a0, rx, a0              #  arg0 is the offset w/in region (jump delay slot)
```

Figure 7: *Code generated inline by the compiler, following an unaligned write or a write to an object larger than a doubleword.*

```
        jr      ra                      # simply return to caller
        nop                             #  fill jump delay slot
```

Figure 8: *Code stored in template for all writes to unshared memory.*

The Design and Evaluation of a Shared Object System for Distributed Memory Machines

Daniel J. Scales and Monica S. Lam

Computer Systems Laboratory
Stanford University, CA 94305
{scales,lam}@cs.stanford.edu

Abstract

This paper describes the design and evaluation of SAM, a shared object system for distributed memory machines. SAM is a portable run-time system that provides a global name space and automatic caching of shared data. SAM incorporates mechanisms to address the problem of high communication overheads on distributed memory machines; these mechanisms include tying synchronization to data access, chaotic access to data, prefetching of data, and pushing of data to remote processors. SAM has been implemented on the CM-5, Intel iPSC/860 and Paragon, IBM SP1, and networks of workstations running PVM. SAM applications run on all these platforms without modification.

This paper provides an extensive analysis on several complex scientific algorithms written in SAM on a variety of hardware platforms. We find that the performance of these SAM applications depends fundamentally on the scalability of the underlying parallel algorithm, and whether the algorithm's communication requirements can be satisfied by the hardware. Our experience suggests that SAM is successful in allowing programmers to use distributed memory machines effectively with much less programming effort than required today.

1 Introduction

Distributed memory systems, especially in the form of networks of workstations, are an important computational resource. However, programming distributed memory machines using commonly available message-passing libraries is a difficult process. The necessary communication and synchronization in an application must be reduced to low-level message-passing calls that require coordination between the senders and receivers. The difficulties become even greater for applications that have highly irregular parallelism and communication. The single address space provided by shared memory machines significantly eases the

This research was supported in part by DARPA contract DABT63-91-K-0003.

process of programming these kinds of applications. Shared data are easily accessed via the shared address space without regard to where data are currently located in the system. In addition, cache-coherent shared memory multiprocessors reduce the cost of accesses to shared data by automatically caching recently accessed data locally.

Our thesis is that it is possible to build a portable software layer that provides the shared memory programming model in a distributed memory environment, while providing mechanisms to help tolerate the relatively high cost of communication on these machines. In this paper we describe the design and evaluation of a shared object system called SAM which we have implemented that supports this thesis. Shared data items in SAM are accessed via a global name space and are automatically cached in the main memory of each processor to exploit the locality of reference in applications. For efficiency reasons, shared data are accessed and managed only at the level of user-defined data types. By requiring that programmers signify how data will be used when it is accessed, SAM can combine synchronization and data access and reduce communication. In addition, SAM provides operations that allow the programmer to explicitly optimize communication when desired. SAM is intended to be used in exploiting task-level parallelism; we believe that the parallelism inherent in operations on regular data structures, such as arrays, is most effectively exploited by parallelizing compilers.

SAM has been implemented as a C library on a variety of platforms: on the CM-5, Intel iPSC/860, Intel Paragon, and IBM SP1, and on heterogeneous networks of workstations using PVM [26]. To evaluate the effectiveness of SAM, we have chosen a number of complex scientific applications that have previously been developed by other researchers either for machines with hardware shared memory support or for distributed memory machines using the message-passing style. We have implemented these applications on distributed memory machines using SAM; each application runs unchanged across the various platforms. We then attempt to evaluate the usefulness of the SAM system by analyzing the performance, programming difficulty, and SAM overheads of these applications, and comparing with the original implementations on shared memory multiprocessors or using message passing.

In the following section, we describe the SAM design rationale and discuss some related work. Next, we describe the basic SAM primitives. Then we describe the applications, explain some of the aspects of programming these applications using SAM, and give performance numbers on all the machines. We also give figures on the various costs of parallelizing these applications, including the SAM software overhead. We then describe the effects of various aspects of SAM's design on the performance of the applications, and conclude.

2 Design Rationale

In this section, we give background on some existing software distributed shared memory systems and describe the basic SAM design principles.

2.1 Background

There have been a number of software systems for distributed memory machines that give the user the illusion of a shared memory and provides automatic caching of shared data. Shared virtual memory (SVM) systems such as Ivy [18] apply the concepts of hardware caching to virtual memory pages. Such systems transparently support the view of a single address space across processors. However, the use of pages as the unit of coherence can result in extensive false sharing; unnecessary communication occurs because of the placement of unrelated shared data on the same page, which may be difficult to avoid in applications with complex data structures. In addition, the protocols for maintaining cache consistency may produce excess communication, since the system treats the entire memory uniformly. Processes use lock and unlock operations to synchronize with each others' data accesses. The system must guarantee that *all* memory updates preceding a synchronization operation are observable by all processors when the synchronization completes, though most updates may be relevant to only a few processors.

Munin [15] and Treadmarks [16] address the problem of false sharing by allowing multiple processors to write to a page and merging changes at the next synchronization point. In addition, Treadmarks attempts to alleviate the problems of excess consistency messages by implementing lazy release consistency, in which the modifications or invalidations to data are not sent until a processor acquires a lock that requires that it see those modifications. Cox et al. [12] compare the performance of several applications on a network of eight workstations running Treadmarks and on a hardware shared-memory multiprocessor. Some of the applications perform comparably under the two systems, but several do not scale well for certain inputs and

one application must be restructured to get speedups under Treadmarks. It remains undemonstrated as to how these approaches perform for applications with more demanding communication patterns.

To provide the user with control over the granularity of communication and avoid false sharing, systems such as Amber [11], Prelude [28], Orca [1], Midway [3], and Linda [5, 7] communicate data at the level of user-defined data types (or *objects*), rather than virtual-memory pages. Amber, Prelude, and Orca provide access to shared data in the context of object-oriented languages. Amber and Prelude primarily provide access to shared objects by moving tasks to the processor containing the data. Orca and Midway allow for replication of shared objects across processors. One Orca implementation replicates objects on all the processors and uses an update protocol to maintain the consistency of shared data. Such a protocol works well for some applications, but can cause performance problems in many other applications. Midway associates arbitrary regions of shared data with locks, and ensures that shared data are consistent when the lock associated with the data is acquired. In this way, it successfully hides synchronization messages by combining them with data access messages. The reader-writer locks protecting the shared data are managed via an invalidation protocol. The Linda system provides operations that insert, read, and remove "tuples" from a shared tuple space. Sophisticated compiler analysis is typically required to analyze and optimize the communication in a Linda program. We do not know of a distributed-memory Linda implementation that provides dynamic caching of tuples (except for one which broadcasts all tuples to all processors [7]).

2.2 Design of SAM

SAM takes one step further than Orca and Midway in providing user control over communication on a distributed memory machine. SAM also communicates data at the level of user-defined data types. While most shared object systems differ primarily in the consistency schemes and implementations used, SAM is based on a significantly different set of primitives that are motivated by optimizations commonly used on distributed memory machines. Message-passing programs seldom incur extra communication just for the sake of synchronization, since synchronization is tied with the arrival of messages that also contain data. Furthermore, it is possible to relax synchronization by taking advantage of the explicit copies made on distributed address space machines. For example, a write to a local copy of shared data need not wait for all reads of the older version of the data to complete as long as a copy of the original version exists. Finally, message-passing programs can hide the latency of communication by sending data to remote processors before they require the data. SAM preserves these advantages of message-passing systems while providing the ease of programming associated with shared memory machines.

The basic principle of SAM is to require the programmer to designate the way in which data will be accessed. With this access information, SAM can combine synchronization and communication of data. There are two kinds of data in SAM, which correspond to the two kinds of data relationships (hence synchronization) in parallel programs:

values with a *single-assignment semantics*. Values make it simple to express producer-consumer relationships or precedence constraints; any read of a value must wait for the creation of the value.

accumulators [21], whose data accesses are *mutually exclusive*. Data are migrated automatically in turn to processors which request mutually exclusive access.

The explicit naming of all values makes it possible to eliminate anti-dependence constraints between processors; a processor can continue to read an older version of a data item while another processor generates another version (using a different name). The concept of single-assignment values have been used in a variety of parallel languages [10, 9, 13, 14, 20] as a way of exposing parallelism and synchronizing independent tasks. Such systems often must deal with problems of excessive memory usage and data copying as shared data items are created and modified. SAM avoids these problems by requiring that the programmer explicitly supply information on when a piece of data is no longer needed, and allowing the programmer to specify that one value should reuse the storage of another value. We have found that managing the names and memory of these values to be straightforward using the primitives provided by SAM.

SAM also provides access to stale, local copies of accumulator data, which can be used in *chaotic* algorithms which do not always need to use the most up-to-date data. Using a local, possibly older copy is sometimes sufficient and can reduce the total execution time of these algorithms. A number of systems have supported the notion of chaotic access. Agora [4] supports a memory model in which all accesses are chaotic, since all modifications to shared data structures are allowed to complete before holders of cached copies have been notified. Mether [19] and Clouds [22] support operations for accessing a read-only copy of a page (or segment) that will not be kept coherent even if the contents of the page (or segment) are changed by another processor.

Finally, besides minimizing communication, SAM also provides primitives for optimizing communication. SAM provides mechanisms for producers to *push* data to consumers, and for processes to *prefetch* a data item. All these optimizations are well integrated into SAM's shared memory model.

3 SAM Overview

In this section, we present a brief overview of SAM mainly via several examples. A more detailed description is provided in [24].

3.1 Basic Primitives

In SAM, all shared data are represented by either a *value* or an *accumulator*. (SAM deals only with the management and communication of shared data; data that are completely local to a processor can be managed by any appropriate method.) In Figure 1, we show several common idioms, as they would be expressed using semaphores on a shared address space machine and using SAM primitives.

In the first example, mutual exclusion is required to protect updates to shared data. In SAM, an accumulator is used to represent a piece of data that is to be updated a number of times, and whose final value is independent of the order in which the updates occurs. SAM automatically migrates the accumulator between processors as necessary and ensures that a process does not access the accumulator until mutual exclusion is obtained. Updates to an accumulator must be encapsulated by the SAM primitives begin_update_accum and end_update_accum. The call to begin_update_accum returns a pointer by which the accumulator can be accessed. SAM supports the idiom of chaotic computation via primitives which provide read access to a "recent" value of the accumulator, which is not guaranteed to be the most current value of the accumulator. SAM maintains a cache on each processor of versions of accumulators that have been recently accessed and therefore may be able to satisfy the chaotic request locally without communication.

In the second example, a consumer (right column) accesses data created by a producer (left column). In SAM, a value provides producer/consumer synchronization. Values have a single-assignment semantics: a value is atomically created once its initial contents are set and is henceforth immutable. The code to create a value, which may include arbitrary updates to different components of the value, is encapsulated by a pair of primitives begin_create_value and end_create_value. Similarly, code accessing a value is encapsulated by the primitives begin_use_value and end_use_value. A process that attempts to access a value will automatically be suspended until the value is created and has been brought to the local processor. Conversely, an access will succeed immediately if the value is already cached on the local processor, returning a pointer to the local copy.

In the third example, a consumer accesses a sequence of values created by a producer through a limited-sized buffer. To avoid memory usage problems that are associated with single-assignment values, SAM allows one value to reuse the storage of another value via the begin_rename_value primitive. This primitive pro-

Shared Address Space

1) Mutual Exclusion

```
wait(lock)
a[1] = ...;
a[34] = ...;
signal(lock)
```

2) Producer/consumer

```
i=i+1              wait(flag_j)
allocate a_i       j=j+1
a_i = ...          ... = a_j
signal(flag_i)
```

3) Finite buffer (size 4)

```
i=i+1 mod 4        j=j+1 mod 4
wait(buf_i)        wait(flag_j)
a[i] = ...         ... = a[j]
signal(flag_i)     signal(buf_j)
```

Distributed Address Space + SAM

```
begin_update_accum(a)
a[1] = ...;
a[34] = ...;
end_update_accum(a)
```

```
i=i+1                       j=j+1
begin_create_value(a_i)     begin_use_value(a_j)
a_i = ...                   ... = a_j
end_create_value(a_i)       end_use_value(a_j)
```

```
i=i+1                          j=j+1
begin_rename_value(a_{i-4}→a_i) begin_use_value(a_j)
a_i = ...                      ... = a_j
end_rename_value(a_i)          end_use_value(a_j)
                               free(a_j)
```

Figure 1: Example of Creating and Accessing Values

---

vides the necessary synchronization to ensure that the producer does not reuse the storage of a value before the consumer has accessed it. In a similar fashion, imperative data objects are easily represented in SAM via a sequence of values which can all share the same storage. SAM also allows a value to be converted to an accumulator and vice versa.

3.2 Memory Management

The creator of a value or an accumulator must specify the type of the new data. With the help of a preprocessor, SAM uses this type information to allocate space for, pack (for sending in a message), unpack, and free the storage of the data. The preprocessor can handle complex C data types, including types that contain pointers and therefore are not necessarily stored in one contiguous block in memory.[1] In heterogeneous environments, SAM also handles any necessary data conversion between dissimilar machines.

SAM maintains local copies of values fetched from remote processors in the form of a cache. Because all values have distinct names and are immutable, there is no consistency problem associated with maintaining this cache. SAM automatically frees up local copies that are not in use when the cache memory becomes filled. SAM must ensure that at least one copy of a value is maintained in the system, until it can determine that there will not be any other processes that will need to access the value. The SAM

programmer provides this information by specifying the number of accesses to the value that will occur or explicitly indicating when all accesses to the value have occurred.

3.3 Communication Optimizations

An important mechanism for tolerating the communication latency is support for asynchronous access. SAM provides the capability to fetch values and accumulators asynchronously. An asynchronous fetch succeeds immediately if a copy of the value is available on the local processor. However, if the value is not immediately available, the fetch operation returns an indication that the value is not available. The requesting process can proceed with other accesses or computation. When the value becomes available on the local processor, the requesting process is notified by calling a function specified when the request was made. For asynchronous access to an accumulator, the process is notified when the accumulator has been fetched to the local processor and mutual exclusion has been obtained.

Another method for optimizing communication is to send data directly from one processor to another processor which will need it. A copy of any specified value available on a processor can be explicitly sent ("pushed") to a remote processor via the push_value primitive. SAM's basic mechanisms combine smoothly to provide the buffering necessary to support a message-passing style. If a process attempts to access a piece of data before it has arrived, then the process suspends until the named value arrives. Conversely, if a value arrives at a processor before it is needed, it is automatically buffered by caching it as a local

---

[1]The preprocessor only handles simple hierarchical data types; it does not handle general data structures that contain multiple pointers to the same data.

copy. Note, however, that the push operation is only an optimization and does not change the correctness of a SAM program.

4 Applications

In this section, we describe the applications we have used in evaluating SAM, assess the ease of programming these applications using SAM, and give performance results on a variety of hardware platforms. For comparison purposes, we have chosen several complex applications that have been implemented previously either on shared-memory multiprocessors or distributed memory machines using message passing. The applications are:

- Block Cholesky - application that does a parallel Cholesky factorization of a sparse matrix by doing block updates in parallel.

- Barnes-Hut - application that simulates the evolution of an n-body system using a tree data structure to speed up the force calculations.

- Grobner Basis - application that computes the Grobner basis for a polynomial set by repeatedly processing pairs of polynomials and potentially adding new polynomials to the basis until no further polynomials need to be added.

	serial code	SAM code	DASH code	msg-pass. code
Block Cholesky	NA	6713	6813	NA
Barnes-Hut	1959	2896	2232	3973
Grobner Basis	3757	4082	NA	5747

Figure 2: Application Line Counts

Figure 2 gives approximate line counts for different versions of each application. The SAM version of the block Cholesky application is derived from the original code written for the DASH shared-memory multiprocessor [17]. Both the SAM and DASH versions of the Barnes-Hut application are derived from the original serial code. Warren and Salmon's message-passing Barnes-Hut code [27] is a completely separate code not based at all on the serial Barnes-Hut code. Chakrabarti's message-passing version of the Grobner basis algorithm for the CM-5 [8] is based on the original serial code, as is the SAM version. The line counts indicate the size of the applications and give a rough comparison of the difficulty in programming the different versions, which we will address further below.

Each of the SAM applications runs without modification on the CM-5, iPSC/860, Paragon, SP1, and networks of workstations. Below, we present performance results for a 64-processor CM-5 (running CMOST 7.3 and CMMD 3.2), a 32-processor iPSC/860, a 56-processor Paragon (running

OSF 1.0.4 and NX 1.2.1), a 16-processor SP1, and a 48-processor DASH.[2] In Figure 3, we give a summary of the important characteristics of each machine. The first five columns describe the processor at each node of the machine. (The third column reports peak *double-precision* megaflops.) The last three columns give the values that we have measured for bandwidth, one-way message send time, and round-trip message time between two nodes. By analyzing the performance of these applications on a variety of machines with different characteristics, we get a better understanding of the hardware and software factors that affect their performance.

4.1 Block Sparse Cholesky Factorization

The block Cholesky application [23] performs a Cholesky factorization of a sparse, symmetric matrix in parallel. It decomposes the sparse matrix into blocks and assigns work to processors at the granularity of updates to blocks. Such updates typically involve using two source blocks to update one destination block. The parallel algorithm involves executing updates to blocks in parallel while respecting the necessary data dependences. The block Cholesky algorithm benefits from dynamic caching, since each sparse block may be used many times by a processor to update other blocks.

The SAM implementation of the block Cholesky application is derived directly from a version for the DASH multiprocessor. Each individual block of the matrix is a SAM data item, and the matrix data structures remained largely unchanged. SAM's ability to deal with complex, non-contiguous data types as a single item is important, since each block actually contains a number of dynamically allocated index and data arrays. Each block in the matrix goes through three phases, which are readily apparent from the basic factorization algorithm. The first phase consists of a series of commutative updates (updates that can occur in any order). In the second phase (after the last update is done), the contents of the block are finalized by a matrix division. In the third and final phase, the block is not modified any further and is only used to update other blocks. Thus each block is represented as an accumulator in the first phase, and the second phase creates a value (using the same storage as the accumulator) that is used in the third phase.

Each processor is responsible for all the updates to a statically assigned set of blocks in the matrix. A task is created when one of the source blocks becomes available and is assigned to the processor that "owns" the destination block. The processor then accesses the second source block asynchronously. If the block is not immediately available, the processor continues computing with other data while the system fetches the block in the background.

---

[2]We were not able to get full numbers on the SP1 because of limited access to the machine. We were also not able to get 48-processor numbers for DASH for the block Cholesky application because of changes in the machine configuration.

Machine	processor	clock rate	peak MFLOPS[3]	I-Cache size	D-Cache size	network topology	measured bandwidth	send time	round-trip time
CM-5	Sparc	33 MHz	8	64KB	64KB	fat tree	8MB/s	$11\mu s$	$57\mu s$
iPSC/860	i860	40 MHz	60	4KB	8KB	hypercube	2.8MB/s	$47\mu s$	$154\mu s$
Paragon	i860	50 MHz	75	16KB	16KB	mesh	61MB/s	$50\mu s$	$125\mu s$
SP1	RS6000	62.5 MHz	125	32KB	64KB	multistage	7MB/s	$240\mu s$	$415\mu s$
DASH	R3000	33 MHz	10	64KB	64KB	bus/mesh	NA	NA	NA

Figure 3: Machine Characteristics

Figure 4 gives performance results for a sparse matrix BCSSTK15 (from the Harwell Boeing sparse matrix test set) and a dense matrix D1000, respectively.[3] The left graph gives parallel speedups with reference to an efficient left-looking, column-based serial factorization algorithm on the same machine; the right graph gives the corresponding absolute performance in double-precision megaflops. For these results, we use blocks of 32 by 32 double-precision numbers. For the sparse matrix, the average size of data transfer over a 32-processor run is 4233 bytes; for the dense matrix, it is 8384 bytes. (Because of the static task and data placement, these figures depend only on the input matrix and number of processors used.) Figure 5 gives information on the average time between shared data references in block Cholesky factorizations of the sparse matrix. To get these numbers, we have divided the serial run times (which represent useful work) by the total number of shared data accesses and the number of these accesses that must request their data remotely (i.e. that incur a cache miss), respectively.

The speedup trends are similar on all machines, indicating the success of SAM in providing portability across a range of distributed memory machines. As we discuss in Section 4.4, the low speedups for the sparse matrix are largely due to limited parallelism and poor load balancing in the parallel algorithm rather than SAM overheads; continued improvement in the parallel algorithm will result in better speedups on all machines.

The differences in the speedup curves reflect the different characteristics of the various machines. In particular, parallel performance can be limited by the available bandwidth between nodes on each machine. The Paragon and the DASH multiprocessor have the best speedups because of their high network bandwidth. The similar speedups of the Paragon and DASH suggest that performance is not significantly affected by the software shared memory implementation, because of the coarse granularity of shared data access. The SP1 reaches bandwidth limits for larger number of nodes, but has very high uniprocessor performance and achieves impressive parallel performance for a small number of nodes. The CM-5 and iPSC/860 also reach bandwidth limits, but at much larger numbers of processors.

---

[3]On the CM-5, we do not use the four vector units at each node to enhance floating-point performance, because significant additional programming is required to utilize them.

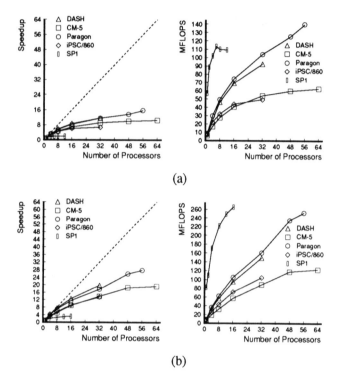

(a)

(b)

Figure 4: Block Cholesky Speedup (left) and Performance (right) for (a) BCSSTK15 and (b) D1000

4.2 Barnes-Hut Algorithm

The Barnes-Hut algorithm [2] is a fast algorithm for simulating the evolution of a system of astronomical bodies as they interact with each other via the gravitational force (the "n-body problem"). At each time step, the algorithm computes the gravitational forces between the n bodies, and determines the new position and velocity of each of the bodies. The Barnes-Hut application builds a tree data structure, called an *oct-tree*, at each time step to summarize the gravitational effects of nearby groups of bodies, so that the force calculation can be done more quickly. The structure of the oct-tree is complex and dependent on the input data, so the memory to hold the oct-tree structure cannot be statically allocated and partitioned across processors. However, the work of the force calculation phase can be partitioned so that there is extensive locality in each processor's access to the tree nodes [25]. The programmer only needs to worry about doing this partitioning correctly; SAM auto-

	number of processors	avg. useful work between accesses to shared data	avg. useful work between accesses to remote data
CM-5	32	$438\mu s$	$1910\mu s$
iPSC/860	32	$364\mu s$	$1588\mu s$
Paragon	32	$292\mu s$	$1274\mu s$
SP1	12	$76\mu s$	$409\mu s$

Figure 5: Frequency of Shared Data Access in Block Cholesky Factorization of BCSSTK15

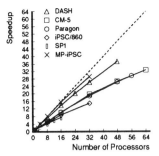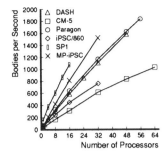

Figure 6: Barnes-Hut Speedup (left) and Absolute Performance (right) for 25000-body Simulation

matically exploits this locality by caching recently accessed tree nodes on each processor.

To reduce address translation and message-passing overhead for this application, we have experimented with blocking the nodes of the tree together. That is, as the oct-tree is built in each time step, we combine several nodes of the tree into one SAM data item. We have hidden the complexity of the blocking in an oct-tree library, and the user can specify the option of blocking or not blocking. When blocking, the tree library automatically brings over a whole block when the "top" node in the block is accessed. Such blocking increases the granularity and reduces the frequency of communication. It also does a form of prefetching, since it fetches a whole collection of nodes that are likely to be accessed in the near future when one of them is accessed. The disadvantage is that extra bandwidth and memory are used in bringing over nodes that are never accessed. In addition, for large blocks, the parallelism in some of the tree traversal phases is decreased, because only one processor can modify a block at a time.

Figure 6 shows speedup (measured against the efficient serial algorithm) and absolute performance (bodies processed per second) of our parallel version running on all machines for a simulation of a highly irregular distribution of 25000 bodies. We have also included performance numbers (labeled in the graph as MP-iPSC) for the message-passing Barnes-Hut code by Warren and Salmon [27]. We have ported this message-passing code to the iPSC/860 and run it on an identical problem.[4]

For these performance figures, tree blocking is used for the runs on the iPSC/860, Paragon, and SP1. Because of the low cost of sending and receiving messages on the CM-5, tree blocking is unnecessary and not used. The average granularity at which shared data are accessed depends on whether blocking is used or not. Each tree node has a size of 152 bytes. For typical 32-processor runs, the average size of messages that communicate data objects is about 220 bytes when blocking is not used, and 1340 bytes when blocking is used. Figure 7 gives information on the frequency of shared data references for the 25000-body simulation. These fig-

ures show that the granularity of access to shared data is much more fine-grain than in the block Cholesky application, but the locality of reference is also much higher.

	number of processors	avg. useful work between accesses to shared data	avg. useful work between accesses to remote data
CM-5	32	$27\mu s$	$3170\mu s$
iPSC/860	32	$39\mu s$	$8603\mu s$
Paragon	32	$32\mu s$	$7069\mu s$
SP1	16	$13\mu s$	$8848\mu s$

Figure 7: Frequency of Shared Data Access in 25000-body Barnes-Hut Simulation

The speedup curves scale for all versions of the application up to the maximum number of processors, though with different slopes. The message-passing version achieves the best speedups overall. However, as illustrated by the line counts in Figure 2, this version is much more complex and difficult to program than the original serial algorithm. It minimizes communication overhead by distributing tree nodes to all of the processors that will reference them in a single communication phase, and is highly dependent on the way that the Barnes-Hut algorithm uses the oct-tree. The SAM version is somewhat more complex than the serial version, but a large fraction of the increased number of lines is due to the tree blocking implementation, which is isolated in the tree library and reusable for other applications. By using SAM to program the Barnes-Hut algorithm, we have chosen to trade off some overall performance in return for considerably less programming effort and greater portability to newer machines.

The DASH shared-memory multiprocessor also achieves better speedups than the distributed memory machines using SAM. The performance of DASH benefits from its additional hardware that does address translation, caching, and communication without any software overheads. As we will see in Section 4.4, because of the finer granularity of shared data access in this application, software address translation and cache management take up a significant portion of each processor's time in the SAM versions. Nevertheless, the SAM versions scale well and achieve high ab-

---

[4]Because the error criterion in the message-passing version is different from the original serial version (and the SAM version), it does not do exactly the same computations as these versions, even for identical initial conditions. However, we have set the error parameters so that the work done in all runs is comparable.

solute performance. In addition, the use of machines with higher uniprocessor performance can compensate for the overheads of providing a shared name space in software. As with the block Cholesky algorithm, the SP1 achieves very good absolute performance with only a small number of processors. The low overhead of sending messages on the CM-5 allows us to get good speedups without blocking (and a much finer granularity of access to shared data). The SAM versions on the iPSC/860 and SP1 have the lowest speedups, because of the high cost of sending and receiving messages on these machines.

4.3 Grobner Basis Algorithm

We have used SAM to parallelize an important algorithm from symbolic algebra systems. The algorithm computes the Grobner basis [6] of a set of polynomials, which is used to solve systems of non-linear equations and determine implicit forms for parametric equations. This algorithm has been previously implemented on the CM-5 by Chakrabarti [8]. The basic structure of the algorithm is to start with the initial basis equal to the input set of polynomials. Then, each possible pair of polynomials from the basis is examined; potentially a new polynomial is produced that is added to the basis, and a new set of pairs between the new polynomial and the current members of the basis is generated. The algorithm continues until there are no more pairs left to be examined. All calculations of polynomial coefficients are done using an arbitrary-precision arithmetic package.

In the Grobner basis algorithm, each polynomial remains unchanged once added to the basis. In our parallel implementation of the Grobner basis algorithm using SAM, each polynomial is represented by a SAM value. The dynamic caching of the polynomials in the basis set that is automatically provided by SAM is crucial to good performance, since each processor repeatedly accesses these polynomials. The basis set is a monotonically growing set of polynomials. We represent the set by a linked list of polynomials and an accumulator which points to the polynomials at the head and tail of the list. Using SAM, we have built a distributed set abstraction, which allows polynomials to be added to the set and provides an operation to iterate over the current elements in the set. The set abstraction uses chaotic access to the head and tail pointers of the list when appropriate to reduce contention for these pointers.

Figure 8 shows the speedups and absolute performance of our Grobner basis program for a representative sample of input polynomial sets. The absolute performance is calculated as the number of polynomials tested in the serial execution divided by the parallel run times. The parallel algorithm is inherently non-deterministic due to different task orderings and can give superlinear speedup. In addition, the run times for comparable serial implementations can vary widely, depending on the heuristic used for ordering tasks. Speedups are determined by running the algorithm five times for a particular input set and number of processors, and dividing the average run time by the run time for an efficient serial algorithm with the same task ordering heuristic. For 32-processor runs, the average size of messages communicating data (mainly transmitting polynomials) varies from 200 to 1000 bytes depending on the input set. Figure 9 gives statistics on the frequency of shared data access in 32-processor runs using the Lazard input set. Because the parallel execution can do much more work than the serial execution, as we describe next, we give these figures in terms of the amount of time between accesses in the parallel execution.

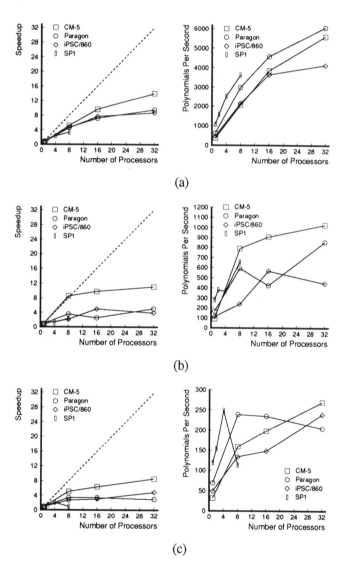

(a)

(b)

(c)

Figure 8: Grobner Speedups (left) and Performance (right) for Inputs (a) Lazard, (b) katsura4, and (c) trinks1

The actual speedups are limited for increasing numbers of processors in large part because the parallel algorithm almost always performs more work than the sequential counterpart. In the serial algorithm, as each polynomial is added to the basis set, it increases the fraction of the remain-

	number of processors	avg. parallel work between accesses to shared data	avg. parallel work between accesses to remote data
CM-5	32	$55\mu s$	$3188\mu s$
iPSC/860	32	$75\mu s$	$4315\mu s$
Paragon	32	$51\mu s$	$2947\mu s$
SP1	8	$30\mu s$	$7100\mu s$

Figure 9: Frequency of Shared Data Access in Grobner Basis Runs on Lazard

ing candidate polynomials that can be eliminated quickly. However, when the algorithm runs in parallel, each processor executes independently without the knowledge of the polynomials that are about to be added to the basis set by other processors. Therefore, the processors typically do more work and the basis set grows larger than it would in the serial execution. This effect increases with larger numbers of processors and with longer communication latencies.

Our implementation of the algorithm appears to have better heuristics for setting the priority of tasks than the Chakrabarti's message-passing implementation for the CM-5 [8]. In consequence, we have better absolute serial and parallel run times on the majority of the available polynomial benchmarks. Our uniprocessor and 10-processor times are better than those of the message-passing implementation for eight of the nine input sets whose timings are reported in [8]. For one input set, our 10-processor time is substantially slower than our 1-processor time, because our task-ordering heuristic happens not to work well for that input set. Our speedups are comparable to those in [8] for several of the benchmarks, but smaller for the other benchmarks because of our faster uniprocessor times.

As shown in Figure 2, the line count for the SAM version is not much larger than the line count of the serial version. The implementation of the distributed set abstraction accounts for most of the extra lines. On the other hand, the message-passing implementation has many more lines than the serial version, mainly because it implements an application-specific form of caching and consistency based on invalidation.

4.4 Parallelization and Communication Costs

In Figures 10 and 11, we give statistics on the parallelization and communication costs for 32-processor runs of our applications. Figure 10 displays the average values of the overheads, while each entry in Figure 11 has both an average value and a range over all the processors. In Figure 10, we have also included a segment (labeled *Application time*) that indicates the amount of work which would be done by each processor if there was perfect speedup (i.e. if each processor did 1/32 of the work done by the serial algorithm). The overheads divide naturally into those associated with the parallel algorithm (idle time), the communication

hardware (message and stall time), and the software shared memory layer (address translation and pack/unpack time):

- *Idle time* indicates the percentage of time that a processor was idle because of lack of work.

- *Message time* is the total time spent sending messages and responding to incoming messages (e.g. requests for a data item).

- *Stall time* is the time spent waiting for data from a remote processor, excluding time that is spent serving incoming messages.

- *Address translation time* is the percentage of time spent in the SAM system ensuring that a copy of a data item is available and determining the address of the local copy. This time includes the cost of a hash table lookup and LRU management of the cache of data items.

- *Pack/unpack time* is the total time spent packing and unpacking messages and has been separated out from the "message time". Packing and unpacking is necessary because SAM allows each data item to be an arbitrary non-contiguous data structure (connected by pointers).

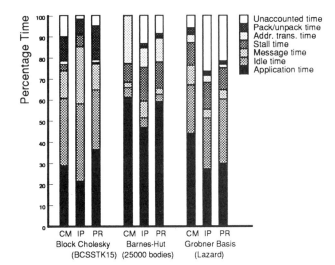

Figure 10: Parallelization and Communication Costs for 32-processor Runs on the CM-5 (CM), iPSC/860 (IP) and Paragon (PR)

In Figure 10, we have also shown the time that is not accounted for in any of the above categories. The biggest component of this unaccounted time is the extra computing done by the parallel application that is not done by the serial application. Some examples are the extra work done in the parallel Barnes-Hut algorithm to determine the appropriate partitioning of bodies across processors, and the extra work done in the parallel Grobner basis algorithm because the basis grows larger in parallel runs. The unaccounted time also covers some uncertainties in measuring the overheads.

Block Cholesky (BCSSTK15)	idle time (%)	message time (%)	stall time (%)	addr. trans. time (%)	pack/unpack time (%)
CM-5	31.8 (1.9-57.0)	13.2 (9.1-22.3)	3.0 (0.0-6.8)	1.7 (1.1-2.1)	11.5 (8.6-14.4)
iPSC/860	36.6 (15.4-55.4)	27.2 (17.0-38.9)	5.5 (0.0-12.6)	0.8 (0.6-1.0)	6.9 (5.1-8.5)
Paragon	28.2 (4.8 - 53.5)	12.4 (7.4-19.2)	0.7 (0.0-4.1)	1.3 (1.0-1.9)	16.2 (8.5-21.4)
Barnes-Hut (25000 part.)					
CM-5	4.6 (0.6 - 8.8)	2.5 (1.9-5.8)	9.0 (5.2-11.0)	22.7 (21.8-26.2)	2.0 (1.5-6.8)
iPSC/860	4.6 (0.2-10.6)	7.9 (6.1-13.8)	16.2 (4.7-18.6)	9.2 (7.9-10.2)	2.0 (1.3-2.4)
Paragon	3.6 (0.0-10.8)	2.9 (2.4-3.4)	12.5 (5.5-14.9)	11.2 (9.7-12.4)	2.3 (1.5-2.8)
Grobner Basis (Lazard)					
CM-5	23.1 (4.6 - 40.4)	9.3 (7.1 - 16.1)	10.8 (5.7 - 17.9)	3.8 (1.7 - 5.8)	3.2 (2.5 - 5.1)
iPSC/860	24.0 (0.0 - 54.9)	4.1 (2.0 - 13.0)	12.9 (6.6 - 19.4)	3.3 (2.8 - 4.4)	2.0 (1.6 - 4.6)
Paragon	30.3 (0 - 54.9)	4.6 (2.5 - 24.3)	10.5 (6.6 - 17.6)	1.7 (1.3 - 2.2)	1.5 (1.0 - 2.6)

Figure 11: Parallelization and Communication Costs for 32-processor Runs

All of the statistics are only approximate, since the timer calls used to measure the overheads may perturb the execution of the applications.[5] In addition, the message times given on the iPSC/860 and Paragon are only a lower bound, since much of the process of transmitting and receiving messages is handled via interrupts in system routines and are not instrumented.

We can make a number of general observations from the data. First, for applications with complex data structures and irregular parallelism like the ones we have used, the limited parallelism inherent in the underlying parallel algorithms can lead to large amounts of idle time that dominate other hardware and software overheads. In the block Cholesky application, the limited parallelism results from long critical paths and the static placement of tasks; in the Grobner basis application, the limited parallelism is due to difficulties in achieving good load balance as variable-sized tasks are dynamically created and distributed across processors.

For applications that must communicate a lot of data between processors, message sending and receiving can constitute a large fraction of the run time, as illustrated by the block Cholesky application. These overheads are largely governed by machine characteristics such as network bandwidth and can also limit performance regardless of other overheads. Note the high percentage of message time in the block Cholesky application for the iPSC/860, which has the least bandwidth of all the machines. The time for packing and unpacking complex objects (the blocks) is also significant in the block Cholesky application, because of the large amount of data communication. Much of this message handling time may be eliminated (or potentially offloaded to a message co-processor, as in the Paragon) with more efficient support for handling messages on newer machines.

The stall time is a function of both the parallel algorithm and machine characteristics. There are significant stall times in the Barnes-Hut algorithm, because of contention for nodes as the tree is built and frequent accesses to remote nodes. Similarly, the Grobner basis algorithm has significant stall times because of contention for the shared basis set. The percentage of stall time is larger in the iPSC/860 than in the other machines likely because of the higher cost of sending messages and the lower network bandwidth of the iPSC/860.

Finally, for applications with finer-grain access to shared data, the software address translation overhead can be significant. The SAM software overhead in the Barnes-Hut algorithm is substantial, especially for the CM-5, where we have not used tree blocking. However, because it depends only on the number of shared accesses and not on the amount of communication, software address translation is a fixed percentage overhead on each processor and does not affect the scalability of the parallel application.

In summary, the scalability of parallel applications is principally determined by the parallel algorithm used. The speedups of the block Cholesky and Grobner basis applications are limited by the characteristics of their underlying parallel algorithms. The Barnes-Hut application has good scalability because of its inherent parallelism and extensive locality of reference. SAM applications with fine-grain access to shared data, such as the Barnes-Hut application, may have significant software overhead in the form of address translation. The speedups of parallel applications can also be limited by machine characteristics such as network bandwidth.

---

[5]The instrumentation adds at most 11% to the execution time of all runs.

5 Evaluation of Communication Optimizations

In this section, we evaluate the usefulness of several aspects of SAM that allow for optimizing communication by measuring their effects on some of the applications we have described.

5.1 Caching

We are able to evaluate the usefulness of caching in the SAM system by measuring the performance of our applications when there is no caching (i.e. each object must be fetched from the processor on which it was created each time it is accessed). Figure 12 shows the improvements in 32-processor run times when caching is added. For reference, it also includes the serial times for the same applications. These figures do not include the pushing and chaotic optimizations of sections 5.3 and 5.4.

Block Cholesky (BCSSTK15)	serial time	32-processor time		
		without caching	with caching	factor improve.
CM-5	27.6s	4.13s	3.39s	1.22
iPSC/860	23.0s	5.14s	3.94s	1.30
Paragon	18.8s	2.62s	2.18s	1.20
Barnes-Hut (25000 bodies)				
CM-5	794.8s	618.5s	42.3s	14.6
iPSC/860	490.2s	2643.5s	42.4s	62.3
Paragon	402.8s	743.9s	27.2s	27.3
Grobner Basis (Lazard)				
CM-5	29.7s	50.60s	3.36s	15.1
iPSC/860	23.3s	87.25s	3.94s	22.1
Paragon	17.4s	45.56s	3.08s	14.8

Figure 12: Caching Performance for 32-processor Runs

The figures show that caching is important for all three applications, especially the Barnes-Hut and Grobner basis applications, which show a large amount of locality between the references of tasks executing on the same processor. The block Cholesky application does not show as much inter-task locality and benefits less from the caching provided by SAM, since any particular remote block may be used only a small number of times to update local blocks. However, the block Cholesky application has significant intra-task locality in block update operations themselves, which is already exploited well by the hardware caches of the nodes.

Many recent scientific algorithms use complex data structures and dynamic task placement and can benefit substantially from dynamic caching of remote data. Often, such caching functionality is implemented in an application-specific way in message-passing programs (for example, in [8]), at the cost of much programmer effort. SAM provides caching as a common functionality that is reusable in many applications and automatically exploits the locality of reference in these programs.

5.2 Synchronization

In a typical shared object system based on an imperative shared memory model, programmers express synchronization separately from data access. These explicit synchronization operations result in extra messages in addition to the messages used to transmit actual data. In contrast, SAM data access primitives directly express the mutual exclusion and producer/consumer data relationships in parallel program. No synchronization other than the synchronization implicit in shared data access is necessary to ensure correctness. For instance, during the parallel, post-order modification of the oct-tree in the Barnes-Hut algorithm, all synchronization occurs appropriately as nodes are accessed. In an imperative shared memory system, additional locks and flags would be necessary at each node to ensure that nodes are accessed in the proper order.

Figure 13 attempts to quantify the synchronizations that would be necessary for our applications in an imperative shared object system. In the first column, we show the number of barriers used in shared-memory implementations of our applications, and in the second column we show the total number of accesses to shared data objects. In the last two columns, we give the number of accesses (and percent of total shared accesses) that, in an imperative shared object system, would require extra synchronization not handled by the barriers. These figures are determined by classifying the types of accesses in runs of the SAM versions of the applications. The numbers show that there are a large number of synchronizations in our applications that would incur extra communication in imperative shared object systems.

Our applications include several common synchronization patterns which cannot be handled via barriers. For example, the producer/consumer synchronization necessary for the post-order tree modification in the Barnes-Hut algorithm is similar to the synchronization of a tree-based reduction, which occurs in many parallel programs. By combining synchronization with data access, SAM makes these important types of communication patterns more efficient.

5.3 Pushing Data

SAM provides a mechanism for sending values to remote processors that may require them. This "pushing" mechanism has the advantage of eliminating the latency for access to data if the pushed data item arrives at a processor before the processor requires the data. We were able to use this pushing mechanism in both the Barnes-Hut algorithm and in the block Cholesky application to improve performance. In the Barnes-Hut algorithm, we push the first few levels of the oct-tree to all processors after these levels have been

	barriers	total shared data accesses	est. non-barrier synchronizations prod/cons	est. non-barrier synchronizations mutual excl
Barnes-Hut (25000 bodies)	7	14649035	11210 (.08%)	27463 (.19%)
Block Cholesky (BCSSTK15)	2	93093	13197 (14%)	0
Grobner (Lazard)	2	1147680	0	17301 (1.5%)

Figure 13: Number of Synchronizations in 32-processor Runs

modified, since all processors will likely access the top part of the tree. In the block Cholesky algorithm, we push completed blocks of the matrix to (exactly) the processors that will access them, because a major limiting factor in the run time is the critical path of block dependencies. Anything that reduces this critical path by reducing latencies for accessing blocks improves the run time. Figure 14 shows the improvements in 32-processor run times when the push and chaotic (see Section 5.4) optimizations are used (with caching). In both applications, the push optimizations are simple additions to the code, and the pushes produce a substantial improvement in the run time of the computations where they are used. However, since the push optimizations are only used in certain phases of each application, the effects on the overall run times are lower.

5.4 Chaotic Access

In a variety of scientific applications, it is possible to use chaotic accesses to shared data to improve parallel performance, while still producing correct results. In the Barnes-Hut algorithm, we use chaotic accesses when traversing the tree to determine where an item should be inserted; the properties of the oct-tree allow this optimization as long as an exclusive access is used when a potential insertion point has been reached. In the Grobner basis algorithm, we use chaotic accesses in some references to the head and tail pointers of the shared polynomial basis. In Figure 14, we show the improvement in run times for 32-processors runs when chaotic accesses are used. (When not using chaotic access, we allow copies of data items to be cached, but force these copies to be invalidated when the items are modified.) The Barnes-Hut improvements are small but significant, because the chaotic optimization applies only to the tree building phase of the algorithm, not the main force calculation phase. The results show that significant performance improvement is possible by using application-specific knowledge to determine when accesses with relaxed consistency can be employed.

6 Conclusion

In this paper we have presented the design and evaluation of a shared object system for distributed memory machines called SAM. SAM is a portable run-time system that provides a global name space and automatic caching of shared data, but also provides the programmer with the ability to optimize communication when necessary. To evaluate SAM, we have used it to parallelize several complex scientific algorithms, each of which consists of thousands of lines of code. Programming these applications in SAM is significantly easier than writing message-passing code and provides portability across machines.

Our results show that the various communication optimizations provided by SAM are important for obtaining good performance results on these complex applications. SAM provides generic caching functionality that can be reused across applications and therefore simplifies programming effort. This caching is essential in a variety of complex applications for getting good performance by exploiting the dynamic locality of reference. By tying synchronization to data access, SAM improves communication efficiency in applications with complex synchronization patterns that cannot be managed via barriers. Our results also show that the use of "pushes" and chaotic accesses, when appropriate to the application, can provide significant performance improvements with minimal effort. We believe that software distributed shared memory system must address the problem of high communication overhead by providing flexible mechanisms for optimizing communication.

We find that the performance results achieved using the SAM system depend on a variety of factors. For the complex scientific algorithms we used, the largest factor can be the limited parallelism available in the parallel algorithms. Performance is also significantly affected by the limited communication capabilities of current distributed memory machines, which will improve in future machines. The amount of software overhead is a function of the granularity of access to shared data and is acceptable for moderately-grained applications. Overall, we found that SAM significantly eased programming of our applications and allowed us to achieve good performance for these applications on a variety of platforms.

Availability

The SAM system is available via anonymous FTP at `suif.stanford.edu` in `/pub/sam` and via the World Wide Web at `http://suif.stanford.edu`.

		with caching only	with pushes	percent speedup	with chaotic	percent speedup	with pushes and chaotic	percent speedup
Barnes-Hut	CM-5	42.3s	42.0s	1%	41.5s	2%	40.7	4%
(25000 bodies)	iPSC/860	42.4s	36.2s	17%	38.1s	11%	32.9	29%
	Paragon	27.2s	25.6s	6%	24.5s	11%	21.4	27%
Block Cholesky	CM-5	3.39s	3.20s	6%				
(BCSSTK15)	iPSC/860	3.94s	3.52s	12%	NA	NA	NA	NA
	Paragon	2.18s	1.66s	31%				
Grobner	CM-5	3.36s			1.98s	70%		
(Lazard)	iPSC/860	3.99s	NA	NA	2.68s	49%	NA	NA
	Paragon	2.54s			1.83s	39%		

Figure 14: Effects of Optimizations on 32-Processor Runs

Acknowledgments

We thank Ed Rothberg for his block Cholesky code, J.P. Singh for his DASH Barnes-Hut code, and Soumen Chakrabarti for his Grobner basis code. Evan Torrie ported the Barnes-Hut message-passing code to run on the iPSC/860. Some of the performance numbers were obtained using the CM-5 at Berkeley, which is supported by National Science Foundation Infrastructure Grant number CDA-8722788. The IBM SP1 was donated by IBM Corporation. We also thank the referees for comments that helped improve the paper.

References

[1] H. E. Bal, M. F. Kaashoek, and A. S. Tanenbaum. Orca: A Language for Parallel Programming of Distributed Systems. *IEEE Transactions on Software Engineering*, 18(3), Mar. 1992.

[2] J. E. Barnes and P. Hut. A Hierarchical O(NlogN) Force-Calculation Algorithm. *Nature*, 324(6096):446–449, Dec. 1986.

[3] B. N. Bershad, M. J. Zekauskas, and W. A. Sawdon. The Midway Distributed Shared Memory System. In *COMPCON 1993*, Mar. 1993.

[4] R. Bisiani and A. Forin. Multilanguage Parallel Programming of Heterogeneous Machines. *IEEE Transactions on Computers*, 37(8):930–945, Aug. 1988.

[5] R. D. Bjornson. *Linda on Distributed Memory Multiprocessors*. PhD thesis, Yale University, Department of Computer Science, Nov. 1992.

[6] B. Buchberger. Grobner Basis: an Algorithmic Method in Polynomial Ideal Theory. In N. K. Bose, editor, *Multidimensional Systems Theory*, chapter 6, pages 184–232. D. Reidel Publishing Company, 1985.

[7] N. Carriero. *Implementation of Tuple Space Machines*. PhD thesis, Yale University, Department of Computer Science, 1987.

[8] S. Chakrabarti and K. Yelick. Implementing an Irregular Application on a Distributed Memory Multiprocessor. In *Proceedings of the Fourth ACM/SIGPLAN Symposium on Principles and Practices and Parallel Programming*, pages 169–179, May 1993.

[9] K. M. Chandy and C. Kesselman. Composition C++: Compositional Parallel Programming. In *Fifth Workshop on Languages and Compilers for Parallel Computing*, pages 124–144, Aug. 1992.

[10] K. M. Chandy and S. Taylor. The Composition of Concurrent Programs. In *Proceedings of Supercomputing '89*, Reno, Nevada, Nov. 1989. ACM.

[11] J. S. Chase, F. G. Amador, E. D. Lazowska, H. M. Levy, and R. J. Littlefield. The Amber System: Parallel Programming on a Network of Multiprocessors. In *Proceedings of the Twelfth ACM Symposium on Operating Systems*, pages 147–158, Dec. 1989.

[12] A. L. Cox, S. Dwarkadas, P. Keleher, H. Lu, R. Rajamony, and W. Zwaenepoel. Software Versus Hardware Shared-Memory Implementation: A Case Study. In *Proceedings of the 21st Annual International Symposium on Computer Architecture*, pages 106–117, April 1994.

[13] M. J. Feeley and H. M. Levy. Distributed Shared Memory with Versioned Objects. In *1992 ACM SIGPLAN Conference on Object-Oriented Programming Systems, Languages, and Applications*, Oct. 1992.

[14] J. T. Feo, D. C. Cann, and R. R. Oldeheoft. A Report on the SISAL Language Project. *Journal of Parallel and Distributed Computing*, 10(4):349–366, Dec. 1990.

[15] J.B. Carter and J.K. Bennett and W. Zwaenepoel. Implementation and Performance of Munin. In *Proceedings of the 13th ACM Symposium on Operating Systems Principles*, pages 152–164, Oct. 1991.

[16] P. Keleher, A. L. Cox, S. Dwarkadas, and W. Zwaenepoel. TreadMarks: Distributed Shared

Memory on Standard Workstations and Operating Systems. In *Proceedings of the 1994 Winter Usenix Conference*, pages 115–132, January 1994.

[17] D. Lenoski, K. Gharachorloo, J. Laudon, A. Gupta, J. Hennessy, M. Horowitz, and M. Lam. The Stanford DASH Multiprocessor. *Computer*, 25(3):63–79, Mar. 1992.

[18] K. Li. IVY: A Shared Virtual Memory System for Parallel Computing. In *Proceedings of the 1988 International Conference on Parallel Processing*, pages II 94–101, Aug. 1988.

[19] R. G. Minnich and D. J. Farber. Reducing Host Load, Network Load, and Latency in a Distributed Shared Memory. In *Tenth International Conference on Distributed Computing Systems*, pages 468–475, June 1990.

[20] R. S. Nikhil. The Parallel Programming Language Id and Its Compilation for Parallel Machines. *International Journal of High Speed Computing*, 5(2):171–223, June 1993.

[21] K. Pingali and K. Ekanadham. Accumulators: New Logic Variable Abstractions for Functional Languages. *Theoretical Computer Science*, 81(2):201–221, Apr. 1991.

[22] U. Ramachandran, M. Yousef, and A. Khalidi. An Implementation of Distributed Shared Memory. *Software - Practice and Experience*, 21(5):443–464, May 1991.

[23] E. Rothberg and A. Gupta. An Efficient Block-Oriented Approach to Parallel Sparse Cholesky Factorization. In *Proceedings of Supercomputing '93*, pages 503–512, Nov. 1993.

[24] D. J. Scales and M. S. Lam. An Efficient Shared Memory System for Distributed Memory Machines. Technical Report CSL-TR-94-627, Computer Systems Laboratory, Stanford University, July 1994.

[25] J. P. Singh. Parallel Hierarchical N-body Methods and Their Implications for Multiprocessors. Technical Report CSL-TR-93-565, Stanford University, Mar. 1993.

[26] V. Sunderam. PVM: a Framework for Parallel Distributed Computing. *Concurrency: Practice and Experience*, 2(4):315–339, Dec. 1990.

[27] M. Warren and J. Salmon. An O(NlogN) Hypercube N-body Integrator. In *Third Conference on Hypercube Concurrent Computers and Applications*, pages II 971–975, Jan. 1988.

[28] W. Weihl et al. Prelude: A System for Portable Parallel Software. Technical Report MIT/LCS/TR-519, MIT, Oct. 1991.

PATHFINDER: A Pattern-Based Packet Classifier

Mary L. Bailey   Burra Gopal   Michael A. Pagels   Larry L. Peterson

Prasenjit Sarkar*

Department of Computer Science
University of Arizona
Tucson, AZ 85721

Abstract

This paper describes a pattern-based approach to building packet classifiers. One novelty of the approach is that it can be implemented efficiently in both software and hardware. A performance study shows that the software implementation is about twice as fast as existing mechanisms, and that the hardware implementation is currently able to keep up with OC-12 (622Mbps) network links and is likely to operate at gigabit speeds in the near future.

1 Introduction

A packet classifier is a mechanism that inspects incoming network packets, and based on the values found in select header fields, determines how each is to be processed. A classifier can be thought of as assigning a tag (type) to each packet, or alternatively, identifying the *flow* or *path* to which the packet belongs. We call this mechanism a packet classifier rather than a packet filter because it more accurately describes the function being performed—it classifies all packets, rather than filtering out select packets. Packet classifier is also becoming the accepted name in the networking community.

An operating system can take advantage of a classified packet in several ways. First, it can use this information to determine what code should be invoked to process the packet. For example, it might select a user-level protocol stack [5], or it might call a procedure that has been optimized to handle packets that follow a particular path through the system [8, 1]. Second, the OS can use the classification information to acquire the resources needed to process the packet. For example, it might select a buffer into which a packet should be placed [3], or it might determine the priority at which the packet should be processed.

The OS programs a classifier by giving it a set of *specifications*, each of which is bound to some identifier. When the classifier matches an incoming packet to a particular specification, it returns the corresponding classification identifier. The specification can either be given by a block of imperative code, in which case the classifier can be viewed as an interpretor (this is the case with three well-known systems, MPF [9], BPF [6] and CSPF [7]), or the specification can be declarative, that is, given by a pattern to be matched (this is the case for the classifier presented in this paper).

This paper describes a new packet classifier, called PATHFINDER, which maps incoming packets into an identifier for the *path* that the packet will traverse through the system. For the purpose of this paper, a path is an abstraction that encapsulates the code block and all the resources required to process the packet [8]. This paper concentrates on how PATHFINDER determines the path to which a packet belongs, and not on how the OS implements and exploits paths.

PATHFINDER has many of the same goals as existing packet classifiers, particularly MPF: it works for a wide range of protocols, it correctly handles fragmentation, it is able to process variable length headers, and it is efficiently implemented. In addition, PATHFINDER has two design goals that set it apart from existing packet classifiers. First, it is designed to support the composition of multiple independently specified patterns. The idea is that each protocol generates a protocol-specific pattern, and that by traversing the protocol graph at the time a network connection is opened and collecting a pattern from each protocol, a compound pattern that classifies packets for that entire path can be constructed. Second, PATHFINDER is designed so it can be efficiently implemented in both software and hardware. The importance of this goal is twofold: (1) it is important to classify a packet as early as possible so no resources are unnecessarily wasted, and sometimes this means running the classifier on the network adaptor; and (2) on high-speed networks, it might be necessary to implement the classifier in hardware in order to keep pace with network speeds.

This paper analyzes the merits of both implementations in terms of performance and functionality. The software implementation is twice as fast as any existing packet classifier, and is probably fast enough for all but the most demanding network loads. The only complication is whether or not

*This work supported in part by National Science Foundation Grant NCR-9204393 and ARPA Contract DABT63-91-C-0030. Additional information about this work, including software distribution, can be found at http://www.cs.arizona.edu/xkernel/www.

the host can make the classification decision soon enough to yield the maximum benefit. The hardware implementation is currently able to keep up with OC-12 (622Mbps) network links, and is likely to operate at gigabit speeds in the near future. A combination of both hardware and software implementations appears optimal, with the hardware acting as a cache for the software.

This paper is organized as follows. Section 2 gives an overview of PATHFINDER's design and Section 3 sketches how PATHFINDER has been implemented in both software and hardware. Section 4 then reports on the performance of these two implementations. Finally, Section 5 discusses several issues raised by this work, and Section 6 offers some concluding remarks.

2 Design Overview

This section describes PATHFINDER at an abstract level, focusing on how a specification is defined, and how PATHFINDER uses this specification to classify incoming packets. We start with PATHFINDER's most basic elements, and then incrementally add the machinery needed to handle more complicated cases.

```
# src port (2 bytes)
tcp_cell1 = (0, 2, 0xffff, 1234)
# dest port (2 bytes)
tcp_cell2 = (2, 2, 0xffff, 4321)
tcp_line = (tcp_cell1, tcp_cell2)
# 20 byte fixed size hdr
tcp_header = (FIXED, 20, 1)
tcp_pattern = (tcp_header, tcp_line, NULL)
```

Figure 1: TCP Example

```
# ip src addr 192.12.69.1 (4 bytes)
ip_cell1 = (12, 4, 0xffffffff, 0xc00c4501)
# IP more fragments bit (1 byte)
ip_cell2 = (6, 1, 0x20, 0x20)
# IP msg id (2 bytes)
ip_cell3 = (4, 2, 0xffff, NULL)
# TCP's protl id (1 byte)
ip_cell4 = (9, 1, 0xff, 6)
ip_line1 = (ip_cell1, ip_cell2, ip_cell4)
ip_line2 = (ip_cell1, ip_cell3)
# 20 byte fixed size hdr
ip_header = (FIXED, 20, 1)
# ip pattern for fragmented packets
ip_pattern = (ip_header, ip_line1, ip_line2)
```

Figure 2: IP Example

2.1 Basic Mechanism

The underlying primitive element in PATHFINDER is the *cell*. It is given by the tuple ⟨*offset, length, mask, value*⟩. Two operations are permitted on a cell: it can be compared to a packet, or it can be loaded from a packet. In the former case, *length* bytes at *offset* bytes from some reference point in the packet (more on this below) are masked out and compared to *value*. The cell is said to match if the masked packet contents equal the specified value. That is, the cell extracts some information from a packet and compares it with a known value stored in it. In the latter case, *length* bytes at the specified *offset* are masked and loaded into *value*. That is, the information extracted by a cell can be used to generate a new value to store in it.

A *line* corresponds to a set of cells. If all the cells in a line match a packet, then the line is said to match the packet. A line is said to be loaded when one or more of the cells that make up the line is loaded. Intuitively, a line attempts to match (is loaded from) a single protocol header; each cell matches (is loaded from) a different field in that header.

In the simplest case, a protocol specifies a *pattern* that it wants to match by giving a ⟨*hdrlen,line*⟩ pair, where *hdrlen* specifies the number of bytes in this protocol's header. This value is used to determine where the next protocol's header begins, that is, the sum of the *hdrlen*'s of all preceding protocols, plus a cell's *offset*, determines the absolute offset from the beginning of the packet for that cell. The pattern specified by a protocol is said to match when a packet that contains the header of the protocol matches the line in the pattern.

For example, Figure 1 gives a PATHFINDER specification tcp_pattern for the TCP protocol. It contains a header tcp_header which specifies that the TCP header is 20 bytes long (ignore the exact format for now), and a line tcp_line which contains cells that match packets meant for a particular TCP connection between source and destination ports 1234 and 4321. (Ignore the third component of tcp_pattern for now.) For simplicity, tcp_pattern is defined in several steps; it could also be given in a single, nested statement.

The full specification (*composite pattern*) that classifies packets on a particular path is constructed from the individual specifications (*patterns*) of each protocol that lie on that path. PATHFINDER associates each composite pattern with an identifier unique to that path. When PATHFINDER classifies a packet, it associates the packet with the identifier bound to the longest matching composite pattern.

In the x-kernel, for example, an EstablishPath operation is used to set up a path. This operation calls the sequence of protocols starting with the topmost protocol and ending at the device driver, and at each protocol in this chain, concatenates that protocol's pattern to the composite pattern. The device driver protocol then programs PATHFINDER with the resulting compound pattern, bound to an identifier for the path just traversed.

2.2 Fragmentation

To handle fragmentation, PATHFINDER actually associates a pair of lines with each pattern. (This corresponds to the third component of `tcp_pattern` in Figure 1.) This second line, which we sometimes call the *dual line*, is considered an *attribute* of the first (*primal*) line—it is an inactive template that contains cells to be loaded when the first line matches. The idea is that when the first line matches the first fragment of a multi-fragment sequence, some cells of the dual line are loaded with values found in that first fragment (e.g., a message id field), and this newly generated line becomes active and matches the subsequent fragments.

For example, Figure 2 gives a pattern specification for the IP protocol. To identify the individual fragments of a multi-fragment message, IP includes a unique message identifier *msgid* in the IP header of each fragment. The *morefrags* bit in the header of the first fragment indicates whether there are any other fragments in that message. In `ip_pattern`, `ip_line1` filters packets coming from the IP host 192.12.69.1. The dual line `ip_line2` contains cells to extract the IP source address and msgid from the first fragment of a multi-fragment message. Since no value is specified in `ip_cell3`, is is loaded from the initial fragment. Note that trailing fragments do not have the headers of the protocols above IP. Hence, without the dual line, PATHFINDER cannot associate them with the identifier bound to the longest matching composite pattern. However, when these fragments match the dual line, they can be correctly classified as falling on the same path as the first fragment.

Note that some of the cells that make up the first line are also present in the dual line. Also notice that in this IP example, the specified pattern expects only fragmented packets. In fact, both fragmented and non-fragmented packets can arrive. This is handled by having IP contribute two patterns to the composite pattern—one that matches unfragmented packets and one that matches fragmented packets—either of which might contribute to the IP portion of the composite pattern matching an incoming packet. In other words, each protocol submits one or more patterns that specify all the types of packets that they accept, where each pattern is defined by two lines.

2.3 Out-of-Order Delivery

If fragments of a message are delivered out-of-order, PATHFINDER might miss the longest matching composite pattern for later fragments that arrive before the first one. Usually, only the first fragment has the information that can trigger dual lines that correctly classify subsequent fragments. Hence, if the later fragments arrive before the first fragment, there must be a facility to *postpone* the classification of these fragments until the first fragment arrives. PATHFINDER handles this by associating a *postpone* attribute with each cell—if this attribute is set, then the classification of packets that do not match the cell is postponed until a packet that matches the cell arrives.

For example, IP might submit a pattern that sets the postpone attribute for the cell that checks for the *morefrags* bits of the IP header; i.e., `ip_cell2` in Figure 2.

2.4 Variable Length Headers

The last complication is that not all protocols have fixed headers, as suggested in the preceding two examples. To handle variable length headers, the *hdrlen* field can be given by a cell that is loaded from the message. Figure 3 extends the example specification for IP to include variable length headers (the TCP example would be extended similarly). Here, the length of the header is obtained from the `ip_hdrcell` cell in the packet header. In this case, the length is specified in words (4 bytes). Thus, we multiply this length by 4 (the third field in `ip_hdrcell`) to obtain the length in bytes.

```
# get lower 4 bits from offset 0
ip_hdrcell = (0, 1, 0x0f, NULL)
ip_header = (VARIABLE, ip_hdrcell, 4)
```

Figure 3: IP Example with Variable Length Header

2.5 Additional Features

In addition to the standard features just described, PATHFINDER also includes more advanced features that might prove useful in certain settings. For example, it includes the ability to handle range comparisons, handle multiple SIPP or XTP-style headers in a single protocol, and peek into the headers of other protocols. It is also possible to add more power to PATHFINDER by allowing a cell to perform more sophisticated operations than simple boolean comparisons.

3 Implementation

This section briefly sketches how PATHFINDER has been implemented in both software and hardware. Notice that the hardware implementation, by its very nature, must be viewed as a cache—finite space will limit the hardware to being programmed to match only a fixed number of patterns at a time. Given this limitation, we also considered the question of what other restrictions we might place on the hardware in an effort to improve its performance. The software version of PATHFINDER implements the full specification described in Section 2.

3.1 Software

The software version of PATHFINDER is implemented as a directed acyclic graph (DAG). Each node in the DAG corresponds to a cell. There are also special nodes, called *header nodes*, that act as demarcation points between the list of cells—i.e., a line—that make up patterns for different protocols. These header nodes contain information about header lengths, so absolute offsets can be computed correctly.

Translating the specification of a pattern to its DAG representation is straightforward: (1) a header node is created for the header-tuple, (2) a list of cell nodes is created for the primal line and then appended to the header node, and (3) a list of cells is created for the dual line and then added as an attribute of the *last cell* of the primal line. Note that until the dual line is activated by a match of all the cells of the primal line, it does not exist in the DAG; it is only an attribute of some cell in the DAG.

The DAG edges that link the header node and the list of cells corresponding to a single line are called *AND* edges. Figure 4 illustrates the set of cells that make up a TCP line, and the corresponding header node. It has only *AND* edges.

The DAG supports a second kind edge, called the *OR* edge, that allows the multiple lines that correspond to a single protocol to be linked together; either the first line or the second line yields the same path identifier. When a new pattern is inserted into the DAG, either by the OS or because the dual line in a protocol's pattern is activated, the DAG is traversed to determine the longest current prefix match. Only the remainder of the cells is added to the DAG by using the *OR* edge to separate this suffix from the cell that immediately follows the prefix. In this way, PATHFINDER avoids redundant computations that would have to be done if it tried to match a packet against multiple copies of the same cell. Note that if the longest prefix match is not identified, then the DAG degenerates into a linear list of patterns that must be checked one after the other. This would result in behavior similar to BPF.

Figure 5 shows a pair of lines that represent IP; *OR* edges are denoted by dashed lines. In this example, the bottom line, which is followed when the *morefrags* cell does not match, corresponds to a second pattern submitted by IP to capture non-fragmented packets. The ⟨line2⟩ associated with the *protid* cell is an attribute of the cell that represents the dual line for that pattern. A match on the first line triggers the dual line, which is then activated and added to the DAG.

When adding additional cells, attention is also paid to whether there currently exists a cell with exactly the same offset/length/mask triple, differing only in the value field. When this occurs, the two cells are merged into one, and implemented as a hash table that maps values into edges.

When classifying an incoming packet, the packet is matched against the cells in the nodes of the DAG until the longest matching line (*AND*-linked set of cells) is found. The corresponding path identifier is then returned. The DAG is constructed in such a way that the longest matching line can be obtained by simply traversing the

AND-edges whenever there is a match, and the *OR*-edges whenever there is no match, until a leaf node is reached.

If a packet does not match a cell and the cell has the postpone attribute set, PATHFINDER postpones the classification of that packet until a packet that matches the cell actually arrives (or a timer expires). The postponed classification is then attempted once more (or the packet is discarded). As explained earlier, this is sufficient to correctly classify a packet whose fragments are delivered out-of-order.

3.2 Hardware

The hardware prototype is implemented using an Altera 881152GC192 FPGA. The design was specified using Synario ABEL-HDL and verified using the Silos Simulator. It was then fit onto the device using Altera's MaxPlus-II device kit. Altera FPGA's were chosen because of their speed; other FPGA's can be used by simply using the appropriate device kit in the Synario environment. FPGA's were chosen for the prototype to facilitate quick evaluation of the design. A production version would likely be implemented using custom VLSI to increase both the speed and size of the circuit.

Each PATHFINDER feature was evaluated for its impact on the speed and utility of the prototype. Moreover, there were tradeoffs between the complexity of each cell, the number of cells per line, and the number of lines. The resulting prototype implements the basic cell functionality given by the tuple ⟨*offset, length, mask, value*⟩, and composes multiple cells to form a line. For speed, the prototype processes a 16-bit input stream rather than a byte stream. Because fragmentation is common and has reasonable complexity, the hardware prototype supports the handling of fragmentation. Other complexities are not handled due to their impact on the design, as discussed below.

Each cell contains an offset/mask/value triple; the length is fixed at 16 bits, the size of the input stream. As in the basic PATHFINDER mechanism, the offset, mask and value are used to compare the input stream with the stored data in the cell. The cell matches if the masked packet content equals the specified value at the correct offset in the packet. We considered having the value specified by ranges instead of matching on a single value. This would involve using two comparators in each cell, one for each of the upper and lower bound of the range, instead of the simple equality check. Due to the limited space in the Altera FPGA, we chose to implement more simple cells rather than fewer complex cells. Thus each cell matches a single value.

As stated above, the hardware prototype processes a 16-bit stream rather than a byte stream. This decision was made for performance considerations, and will be discussed in more detail in Section 4. It does place two restrictions on the classifier: (1) all cells have a fixed length of two bytes, and (2) all cells must start on even byte boundaries. These two restrictions only affect the way patterns are specified, and do not restrict the generality of the classifier, as the *mask*

Figure 4: Simple Line

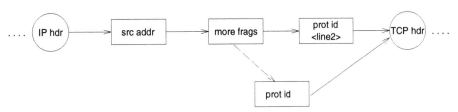

Figure 5: Pair of Lines

can always be used to ignore parts of the cell that are not of interest. It may mean that additional cells are required to handle the case where the two bytes of interest begin at an odd byte offset. Here, two cells are now required, instead of one. The 16-bit design does not preclude packets whose length in bytes are odd—we assume that network adaptors can pad such packets to make their length an even number of bytes.

To handle fragmentation, we initially planned to associate two complete lines for each pattern, one for the primal line and one for the dual line. However, we found that in most cases, there were some number of identical cells in the two lines, and thus, we saved space by using those cells in both lines, rather than replicating them. As a result, there are three types of cells: (1) those used to match both the primal and dual lines, (2) those used in just the primal line, and (3) those used in just the dual line.

The prototype does not handle out-of-order fragments using the POSTPONE facility, as this would require buffering on the network adaptor as packet processing cannot be done immediately. The synchronization logic for the POST-PONE facility would considerably slow the clock rate of the prototype, since it would require a relatively complex interface with the memory on the network adaptor board. In general, we did not feel that out-of-order packets are common enough to justify the increased complexity required in the hardware.

The prototype also *cannot* handle variable length headers; i.e., all headers are assumed to be fixed. This allows the byte offsets of all patterns for a single packet type to be determined when the patterns are loaded into the chip, which vastly simplifies the hardware design and allows for very high clock rates in the prototype. Once again, variable headers are not common enough to justify the necessary additional hardware.

The final restriction of the FPGA implementation is the fixed and limited amount of space available for each pattern. In the hardware, the patterns for all protocols in a given packet are combined to create a single (larger) pattern. The size of this pattern depends on the number of cells available

for each pattern. This limits the number of cells that can be implemented.

In spite of the fact that it handles only a subset of the PATHFINDER specification, the hardware prototype can handle handle the vast majority of network packets, including TCP/IP and RPC packets. In the current implementation, one FPGA contains a single pattern consisting of twelve 16-bit cells. As stated above, a custom VLSI implementation would increase both the number of cells and the resulting speed, and is likely the better candidate for a production implementation. As technology increases the size and speed of FPGA's, more space will be available for use in either adding more cells, more patterns, or more features.

The hardware prototype is designed to be placed on the network adaptor board. The application does not have to explicitly program the hardware; in fact, it need not be aware that the hardware exists. The PATHFINDER software accepts the pattern provided the application and checks whether it violates any of the restrictions imposed by the hardware implementation. After verification, the pattern can be downloaded onto the network adaptor board. The hardware prototype allows a pattern to be loaded while concurrent matching of other patterns take place, in order to maximize utility of the hardware.

When the hardware detects a pattern, it sets an output bit to indicate that a match has been detected. The network adaptor may have additional circuitry to place the packet in a specific buffer, either in host memory or in adaptor memory. If an incoming packet does not match any pattern in the hardware, then it is simply processed by the PATHFINDER software.

4 Performance

4.1 Software

The software version of PATHFINDER is about 5,000 lines of C code. We compiled it on each platform using the native C compiler with full optimization.

4.1.1 Lookup Costs

Table 1 compares the per-packet latency of PATHFINDER and MPF [9] on the DECStation 5000/200 for a TCP/IP protocol stack having ten open TCP/IP connections that wait for packets to arrive. The experiments were done with both cold and warm caches. They model the scenario where a total of 100000 TCP/IP packets that contain just the TCP/IP header with no data are recieved by a host machine. A given packet might be intended for any one of the 10 TCP/IP connections, and there is no way to determine which one it is without invoking a classifier. Hence, 1/100000-th of the time taken by PATHFINDER to classify all these packets exactly measures its per-packet latency. Note that since both PATHFINDER and MPF use hash-tables, these results do not vary as the number of connections increases. We see that PATHFINDER is about twice as fast as MPF with both cold and warm caches.

PATHFINDER performs better than MPF for three reasons. First, the DAG is carefully constructed so that just one path in it needs to be traversed to classify the packet. Second, the operations performed by a cell have simple semantics so that they can be implemented efficiently. Finally, the warm cache is implemented in a unique way: instead of storing the set of most recently matched composite patterns in a separate DAG and matching a packet against this DAG first, whenever a packet matches a composite pattern (either this is the first packet that matched that composite pattern, or the packet did not match the existing cache), a few key (unique/unchanging) fields in it are identified. These keys are then used to create a new *key*-pattern. It is associated with the same path-identifier as the corresponding composite pattern and is inserted into the original DAG in such a way that an incoming packet is matched against the key-pattern *before* it is matched against the composite pattern, i.e., the key-pattern acts like a cache for the composite pattern. Since key-patterns are chosen so that they typically have fewer cells than the composite pattern, the lookup latency of PATHFINDER which depends on the number of cells examined (see below) can also be reduced. Note that this is exactly how PATHFINDER handles fragmentation. In fact, the keys to be extracted can be specified explicitly in the dual line of a pattern even if the corresponding protocol does not handle fragmentation.

Classifier	Cache State	
	Cold	Warm
MPF	71	35
PATHFINDER	39	19

Table 1: PATHFINDER and MPF Per-Packet Latencies (μs)

We next examine how the cost varies with the *depth* of the protocol stack (number of protocols) when its breadth (number of open connections) at each level is kept constant at one. The results are given in Table 6. Here, we introduce

a series of dummy protocols, each with patterns that look at two header fields. The experimental conditions were similar to those above. They were again carried out on the DECStation 5000/200, this time with a cold cache only, since the warm cache does not show any variation with depth. We see that the per-cell latency of PATHFINDER on this machine is about 6 μs.

	Stack Depth						
	1	2	3	4	5	6	7
Lookup Latency	19	31	42	54	66	77	89

Table 2: PATHFINDER Lookup Latency (μs) versus Depth of Protocol Stack

Finally, we measured the lookup latency of PATHFINDER on various processors for a TCP/IP protocol stack having ten open connections. Both cold and warm caches were measured in a way similar to the first experiment. The results are given in Table 2.

4.1.2 Setup and Remove Costs

We also measured the time taken by PATHFINDER to setup a pattern for a new protocol and for an existing protocol, and compared them with the equivalent times in MPF. The results are given in Table 3. As can be seen, PATHFINDER takes significantly longer to set up a pattern than does MPF. There are several reasons for this. (These reasons also help to explain why PATHFINDER is faster than MPF in the lookup case.)

Classifier	Protocol State	
	New	Existing
MPF	33	< 2
PATHFINDER	78	45

Table 4: PATHFINDER and MPF Setup Costs (μs)

First, PATHFINDER has to see whether a prefix of the pattern matches any existing pattern before it can decide what suffix of the pattern must be inserted into the DAG. PATHFINDER also includes code that automatically orders cells in the DAG, so that it can retrieve the identifier corresponding to longest matching composite pattern even when two cells have masks/values that partially overlap.

Second, there is no way to determine ahead of time which part of a new pattern will get merged and which part will form a new branch in the DAG. This is why the time to setup a pattern for an existing protocol is not significantly lower than the corresponding time for a new protocol. This former time somewhat lower, however, since the DAG structure need not be modified when some parts of the new pattern get merged with the existing pattern(s) for that protocol. (If the new pattern is composite, then the patterns corresponding to the lower protocols always get merged into the DAG, but PATHFINDER cannot determine even this a priori.)

	Processor			
Cache State	SparcIPC 25 MHz	Sparc10/51 50 MHz	DS5000/200 25 MHz	DS3000/600 175 MHz
Cold Cache	63	15	39	10
Warm Cache	34	8	19	4

Table 3: PATHFINDER Lookup Latency (μs) on Various Processors

Third, the DAG structure has a common root-node (the header-node of the lowest protoccol) from which all insertions should begin: there is no 'handle' into the DAG where the header-cell of a given protocol begins, and as a consequence, insertions cannot 'start' from some interior point in the DAG. Moreover, a protocol can have multiple header-cells, and to handle that, it is necessary to traverse the DAG starting at the root to determine at which header-cell the insertions should start.

Finally, PATHFINDER has to allocate memory for every protocol-specified cell and make a copy of its contents before inserting it into the DAG. Similarly, it has to free memory after deleting a cell from the DAG.

The time it takes to remove the last pattern of a protocol from the DAG is about the same as the time it takes to setup a pattern for a new protocol. Similarly, the time it takes to remove other patterns of a protocol is about the same as the time it takes to setup a pattern for an existing protocol. Note, however, that setups and removes are not done frequently—lookups are most critical. The software implementation tries to trade setup/remove latencies for lookup latency.

4.1.3 Fragmentation Overhead

The fragmentation overhead of PATHFINDER is simply the time taken to: (1) activate a dual line by creating a new line from the template stored as an attribute of the last cell of the corresponding primal line, and (2) insert the new line into the DAG. Note that these steps automatically create a cache to speedup lookups for later fragments of the message. The fragmentation overhead for the IP protocol is 83 μs. Since step (2) simply sets-up a new pattern for an existing protocol, the overhead of step (1) comes to approximately 38 μs. Since the cost of handling fragmentation is slightly more than twice the time taken for a lookup with a cold cache, the automatic creation of a cache pays off if a message contains more than 3 fragments.

4.1.4 Space Requirements

The space required for the DAG implementation is minimal. On the DECStation 5000/200, each cell-node in the DAG occupies about 32 bytes, a cell-node with a hash-table occupies about 540 bytes, and a header-node occupies 8 to 16 bytes depending on whether the header is of fixed or variable length. Each TCP/IP pattern used in these experiments contains 6 cell-nodes and 2 header-nodes, and therefore occupies a modest 208 bytes.

4.2 Hardware

The hardware prototype was implemented using an Altera 881152GC192 FPGA. This FPGA was sufficiently large to hold twelve 16-bit cells, comprising a single pattern. The hardware prototype was tested for correctness with the following tests:

- Single Packet Testing: The lines were loaded with masks, offsets, and values, and a number of packets were streamed through to ensure that the matching portion of the chip functioned correctly.

- TCP/IP fragments back to back: This test case checks the dual line operation of the hardware prototype. A fragmented TCP packet stream was streamed through the circuit to ensure that fragmentation was implemented properly. The circuit was also tested in non-dual mode for correct behavior when the input stream consisted of unfragmented packets.

- Critical timing test: When two packets arrive back-to-back without delay, the start-in signal of the second packet should clear the state pertaining to the first packet and matching should proceed immediately.

- Concurrent Programming and Matching: The pattern was programmed while a packet was being processed to ensure that the current packet was processed correctly, and that the programming took effect in the following packet.

The implementation was tested at 50 and 100 MHz using simplified delay analysis. The design ran properly at 50 MHz, but did not completely function at 100 MHz. The major cause of failure at 100 MHz was asynchronous inputs. These errors may have been due to the simplified delay model. We are in the process of verifying the design using a more accurate timing model, and expect the circuit to function correctly at 100 MHz. Translating this into per-packet latency, it would take approximately 200ns to process a 40-byte TCP/IP message; i.e., one that contains a header and no data. This speed is sufficient to handle data rates of 1.2 Gbps.

5 Discussion

5.1 Putting Classifier Latency in Perspective

The first question raised by this work is "how fast is fast enough?". The issue is at what latency does the the time it takes to classify incoming packets become a limiting factor on network throughput. Table 4 provides the maximum amount of time available to classify packets in worse-case situations. For example, if a system is receiving back-to-back, minimal length IP packets on a 155 Mbps network, the next message will arrive within 1.25 microseconds. If we ignore the ability to buffer packets—that is, we think of data as streaming through the classifier—then the classifier must be able to keep up with the worse-case arrival rate.

Transfer item	Network fabric bandwidth (Mbs)				
	10	100	155	622	1244
8-bits	800	80	52	13	6.5
16-bits	1600	160	104	26	13
IP header	16000	1600	1040	260	130
TCP/IP header	32000	3200	1080	520	260

Table 5: Worse Case Arrival Periods (ns)

As can be seen, the current hardware implementation running at 50 MHz is sufficient to stream data through at OC-12 speeds (622 Mbps). Table 5 provides processing periods, on a per-byte basis, for various clock rates. It shows, for example, that a 1.2 Gbps network would require a processing period of $6.5ns$ per byte, which could be met by a 100 MHz implementation.

Data unit size	Clock frequency (MHz)			
	50	66	100	125
8-bits	10	7.5	5	4

Table 6: Hardware Processing Time (ns)

Unlike the hardware version, the software implementation has the luxury of buffering packets. Therefore, we can evaluate it in terms of processing complete packets, rather than just headers, in the allotted time. Even then, one can argue that if the classifier can't keep up with the incoming packets, then the host has little hope of dealing with the workload being generated by the application. However, it is interesting to note that if back-to-back 4KByte packets arrive on a 622 Mbps link, then the classifier has approximately $100\mu s$ to classify each packet. 1KByte packets would require $25\mu s$ per packet, which is near the limit of the software implementation.

5.2 Host versus Adaptor

Beyond the question of speed, however, there remain others issues pertaining to whether classifier functionality should be implemented on the host or on the network adaptor.

Putting the classifier on the host obviously implies the software implementation. This has the advantage of tracking improvements in host processor performance, but leaves the question of whether incoming packets are buffered in the host or on the adaptor. Buffering in the host is sufficient for determining what code should be invoked to process the packet (i.e., it makes user-level protocol stacks possible), but it is too late to affect all decisions as to what resources—in particular, memory buffers—are consumed by the packet. As a consequence, it does not support a mechanism like fbufs [3]. Buffering on the adaptor implies that incoming packets are held in adaptor memory and only header information is copied to host memory so the classifier can inspect it. Once the classifier makes a decision, the packet can be moved into host memory using either DMA or Programmed I/O. This approach has the complication of requiring the management of two disjoint buffer pools. It is also not clear how much adaptor buffering is sufficient.

The alternative is to locate PATHFINDER on the adaptor, where it could either be implemented as software running on a general-purpose processor, or as special-purpose hardware such as that described in Section 3.2. Both have the advantage of being able to classify packets soon enough to make the appropriate resource assignment decisions. A general-purpose processor would require buffering on the adaptor, since as illustrated in Section 5.1, even the fastest processors are not able to keep up with emerging network bandwidths. This approach also suffers from the problem of the adaptor's processor not necessarily keeping pace with the host's processor. The special-purpose hardware streams data through, and so must also keep up with network speeds. Fortunately, the data given in Section 4 suggests that is a reasonable expectation.

One final possibility is to put the classifier on both the host and the adaptor, and to treat the hardware implementation as a cache. We have experimented with this configuration on Sparc workstations connected by the ATOMIC network [2]. In this example, the ATOMIC adaptor has a 3-MIPS on-board processor, which was powerful enough to implement only a very restricted version of the software implementation of PATHFINDER. The adaptor-version was able to match only a very small set of patterns, with the on-host implementation catching those not flagged by the adaptor.

5.3 Future Considerations

ATM is an emerging standard for gigabit speed networks. Each ATM cell has a *virtual circuit identifier* (VCI) that can be used to demultiplex it [4]. One could argue that the availability of VCI's diminishes the need for a PATHFINDER-like classifier.

First, it is not yet settled how "plentiful" VCIs will be, that is, will VCIs be an abundant resource that can be cheaply allocated by the host operating system, or will the network control (and charge for) each VCI used by an end system.

If the latter scenario happens, one might aggregate multiple application-level connections onto a single VCI, and therefore need to employ a packet classifier.

Second, even if one can afford to allocate a a VCI to each connection, it is sometimes desirable to demultiplex incoming messages on an even finer level; e.g., program PATHFINDER to know about individual reply messages or messages of a particular type. Whether PATHFINDER can be programmed quickly enough to accommodate such fine-grain demultiplexing is a subject of further study.

Finally, even if ATM becomes a wide-spread network technology, other technologies, including ethernet, will still exist. In order to design an operating system to take advantage of the early demultiplexing made possible by VCIs—e.g., to support user-level protocols—it will be necessary to correctly and efficiently classify packets arriving on networks that do not support early demultiplexing.

6   Concluding Remarks

PATHFINDER is a pattern-based approach for building packet classifiers that can be implemented both in hardware and software. The software implementation is about twice as fast as any existing packet classifier, but cannot be expected to sustain gigabit network rates. The hardware implementation is currently able to keep up with 622Mbps network speeds, and can be expected to sustain gigabit speeds.

We envision two scenarios in which one or both of the implementations can be effectively employed. In the first, packets are buffered on the network adaptor, packet headers are loaded from the adaptor onto the host, the software implementation of PATHFINDER running on the host processes these headers, and the result of the classification governs how the rest of the packet is processed (e.g., where in host memory it copied to). In this scenario, the adaptor must have enough buffering to absorb bursts of data arriving at network bandwidth, but we assume the software implementation need not sustain network speeds for an arbitrarily long period of time. This is a valid assumption if the application program running on that host also cannot consume data at network speeds for an arbitrary period of time.

In the second scenario, a hardware implementation of PATHFINDER running on the network adaptor acts as a cache of the software implementation running on the host; any packets not classified by the hardware are processed by the software implementation. Because the hardware implementation can keep up with network speeds, this approach has the advantage of not requiring any buffering on the network adaptor. It also has the advantage of being able to sustain network speeds for an arbitrary length of time, but this would only be important if the application program does process the incoming data (e.g., it is simply copied to the framebuffer).

References

[1] M. B. Abbott and L. L. Peterson.   Increasing network throughput by integrating protocol layers. *IEEE/ACM Transactions on Networking*, 1(5):600–610, Oct. 1993.

[2] D. Cohen, G. Finn, R. Felderman, and A. DeSchon. ATOMIC: A low-cost, very-high-speed, local communications architecture. In *Proceedings of the 1993 Conference on Parallel Processing*, Aug. 1993.

[3] P. Druschel and L. L. Peterson.   Fbufs: A high-bandwidth cross-domain transfer facility. In *Proceedings of the Fourteenth ACM Symposium on Operating Systems Principles*, pages 189–202, Dec. 1993.

[4] P. Druschel, L. L. Peterson, and B. S. Davie. Experience with a high-speed network adaptor: A software perspective. In *Proceedings of the SIGCOMM '94 Symposium*, Aug. 1994.

[5] C. Maeda and B. Bershad. Protocol service decomposition for high-performance networking. In *Proceedings of the Fourteenth ACM Symposium on Operating Systems Principles*, Dec. 1993.

[6] S. McCnne and V. Jacobson.   The bsd packet filter: A new architecture for user-level packet capture. In *Proceedings of the USENIX '93 Winter Conference*, pages 259–269, Jan. 1993.

[7] J. C. Mogul, R. F. Rashid, and M. J. Accetta. The packet filter: An efficient mechanism for user-level network code. In *Proceedings of the Eleventh ACM Symposium on Operating Systems Principles*, pages 39–51, Nov. 1987.

[8] A. B. Montz, D. Mosberger, S. W. O'Malley, L. L. Petersonand, T. A. Proebsting, and J. H. Hartman. Scout: A communications-oriented operating system. Technical Report 94-20, Department of Computer Science, University of Arizona, June 1994.

[9] M. Yuhara, B. N. Bershad, C. Maeda, and J. E. Moss. Efficient packet demultiplexing for multiple endpoints and large messages. In *Winter 1994 Usenix Conference*, Jan. 1994.

Performance Issues in Parallelized Network Protocols

*Erich M. Nahum, David J. Yates, James F. Kurose, and Don Towsley**

Department of Computer Science
University of Massachusetts
Amherst, MA 01003

Abstract

Parallel processing has been proposed as a means of improving network protocol throughput. Several different strategies have been taken towards parallelizing protocols. A relatively popular approach is *packet-level parallelism*, where packets are distributed across processors.

This paper provides an experimental performance study of packet-level parallelism on a contemporary shared-memory multiprocessor. We examine several unexplored areas in packet-level parallelism and investigate how various protocol structuring and implementation techniques can affect performance. We study TCP/IP and UDP/IP protocol stacks, implemented with a parallel version of the *x*-kernel running in user space on Silicon Graphics multiprocessors.

Our results show that only limited packet-level parallelism can be achieved within a single connection under TCP, but that using multiple connections can improve available parallelism. We also demonstrate that packet ordering plays a key role in determining single-connection TCP performance, that careful use of locks is a necessity, and that selective exploitation of caching can improve throughput. We also describe experiments that compare parallel protocol performance on two generations of a parallel machine and show how computer architectural trends can influence performance.

1 Introduction

Parallel processing has been proposed as a means of improving network protocol throughput. Two trends motivate the use of parallelism in network processing. First, network bandwidths are increasing by orders of magnitude, with the advent of technologies such as ATM. Second, shared-memory multiprocessors are becoming more common, as

*This research supported in part by NSF under grant NCR-9206908 and ARPA under contract number F19628-92-C-0089. Erich Nahum was supported by an ARPA Research Assistantship in Parallel Processing. David Yates is the recipient of a Motorola Codex University Partnership in Research Grant. The authors can be reached at {nahum, yates, kurose, towsley}@cs.umass.edu.

shown by recent vendor introductions [1, 8, 9]. There is thus an opportunity to exploit the potential of parallelism in network protocol processing, and this has become a growing area of research.

The approach we study here is that of *packet-level parallelism*, sometimes referred to as thread-per-packet or processor-per-message parallelism. Originally proposed by Hutchinson and Peterson in the *x*-kernel [14], this approach distributes packets across processors, achieving speedup both with multiple connections and within a single connection. Packets can be processed on any processor, maximizing flexibility and utilization. Other systems using this approach include [5, 11].

Several other approaches to parallelism have also been proposed and are briefly described here; more detailed surveys can be found in [5, 11]. In *layered parallelism*, protocols are assigned to specific processors, and messages passed between layers through interprocess communication. Parallelism gains can be achieved mainly through pipelining effects. An example is found in [10]. *Connection-level parallelism* associates connections with a single processor or thread, achieving speedup with multiple connections. Multiprocessor STREAMS most closely matches this model [26, 27]. *Functional parallelism* decomposes functions within a single protocol and assigns them to processing elements. Examples include [19, 23, 25]. The relative merits of one approach over the others depends on many factors, including the host architecture, the number of connections, whether the implementation is in hardware or software, the thread scheduling policies employed, and the cost of primitives such as locking and context switching. Schmidt and Suda [28] show that packet-level parallelism and connection-level parallelism generally perform better than layer parallelism on a shared-memory multiprocessor, due to the context-switching overhead when crossing layers using layer parallelism.

This paper provides an experimental performance study of packet-level parallelism using TCP/IP and UDP/IP protocol stacks. We have conducted this study in the context of a multiprocessor implementation of the *x*-kernel, which runs in user space on Silicon Graphics shared-memory multiprocessors using the IRIX operating system.

Our results show that only limited packet-level parallelism can be achieved under TCP within a single connection, but that using multiple connections improves available parallelism. The effects of checksumming and packet size on speedup are also examined. We also find that ordering plays a key role in determining single-connection TCP performance, that careful use of locks is a necessity, and that selective exploitation of caching can improve throughput. Finally, we examine packet-level parallelism on three platforms: the current Challenge series using both 100 MHz and 150 MHz MIPS R4400 processors, and the older Power Series with 33 MHz MIPS R3000's.

The remainder of the paper is organized as follows: In Section 2, we describe our experimental environment, including the parallelized *x*-kernel and protocols. Section 3 gives our baseline results. Section 4 describes ordering issues and shows how ordering can impact performance. Section 5 examines locking strategies and techniques. Section 6 illustrates the effects of caching. Section 7 examines parallelized protocol performance on several different architectures. In Section 8 we summarize our results and conclude.

2 Experimental Environment

As stated earlier, our environment is based on a parallelized *x*-kernel, and as such, it is similar in several respects to the platform described by Bjorkman and Gunningberg at the Swedish Institute of Computer Science (SICS) [4, 5]. Our platform was, for the most part, developed independently, and for a different type of machine. The exception is the SICS MP TCP code, which we used to guide the design of our parallel TCP, as described in Section 5.1. The SICS platform, however, was based on the February 1992 release of the *x*-kernel, and ran on the Sequent Symmetry. Our environment is based on the December 1993 *x*-kernel release, and runs on the SGI Challenge. Given the differences in hardware, host operating systems, versions of the *x*-kernel infrastructure and protocols, a direct comparison is thus not possible. Where applicable, however, we describe differences between the systems.

2.1 Parallelized *x*-kernel

Our parallelized *x*-kernel was developed by adding locks into appropriate places in the *x*-kernel infrastructure. Like the SICS system, we placed locks protecting *x*-kernel infrastructure within the *x*-kernel, and placed locks concerning protocols within the protocols. Unlike the SICS system, which used a finite set of static, global locks, we instantiate locks on a finer-grained, per data-structure basis.

The *x*-kernel's *message tool* is a facility for managing packet data, analogous to Berkeley mbuf's. Messages are per-thread data structures, and thus required no locks. They point to allocated data structures called *MNodes* which are reference counted; these reference counts must be incremented and decremented atomically.

The *x*-kernel's *map manager* provides a mapping from an external identifier (e.g., a TCP port number) to an internal identifier (e.g., a TCP protocol control block), using chained-bucket hash tables with a 1-behind cache. Maps have many uses, but are primarily used for demultiplexing. They must be locked to insert, lookup, or remove entries. In addition, since the map manager provides an *iterator* function mapForEach(), the map manager can call itself recursively. To handle this recursion, counting locks are used, so that if a thread already owns the lock, it simply increments a count and proceeds. Similarly, an unlock decrements the count, and the lock is released when the count reaches zero.

The *event manager* uses a timing wheel [31] to manage events which are to occur in the future. The wheel is essentially another chained-bucket hash table, where the hashing function is based on the time that the event is scheduled to run. To protect this structure, we added per-chain locks, so that concurrent updates to the table were less likely to conflict with one another.

Other components of the *x*-kernel require locks for various reasons, most frequently for atomic addition and subtraction for object reference counts.

2.2 Parallelized Protocols

In order to experimentally study various performance-related issues in parallel protocols, we implemented multiprocessor versions of FDDI, IP, UDP, and TCP. This section briefly describes our parallel implementations of these protocols.

The FDDI protocol in the *x*-kernel is very simple; it essentially prepends headers to outgoing packets and removes headers from incoming packets. Locking is only necessary in two instances: during session creation and on packet demultiplexing (to determine the upper-layer protocol to which a message should be dispatched to). No locking is required for outgoing packets during data transfer.

The Internet Protocol is structured similarly to FDDI but has a slightly larger amount of state, which must be locked. On the send side, IP has a datagram identifier used for fragmenting packets larger than the network interface MTU. The identifier must be atomically incremented, per-datagram. On the receive side, if a packet is a fragment, a fragment table must be locked to serialize lookups and updates.

UDP is a connectionless transport protocol that provides little beyond simple multiplexing and demultiplexing. Like FDDI, locking is only required for session creation and packet demultiplexing.

TCP is a much more complex protocol than UDP. It provides reliable, in-order data delivery with no loss, error, or duplication, and has built in flow control and congestion control mechanisms. Our TCP is based upon the *x*-kernel's adaptation of the Berkeley Tahoe release, but was updated to be compliant with the BSD Net/2 release. In addition to adding header prediction, this involved updating the congestion control and timer mechanisms, as well as reordering code in the send side to test for the most frequent scenarios first [15]. The one change we made to the base Net/2 structure was to use 32-bit flow-control windows, rather than the 16-bit windows defined by the TCP specification. This turns out to be important for the high bandwidths generated by our experiments, and we note that 32-bit flow control information is used in both 4.4 BSD with large windows [16] and in the next-generation TCP proposals [6, 30].

Due to the semantics of TCP, the protocol consequently has a great deal of per-connection state, which must be locked to provide consistency and semantic correctness. For example, each connection has a retransmission queue, a reassembly queue, and various windows for both the send and receive sides. Given this large amount of state, several state locking strategies are possible. We thus implemented three Net/2-based versions of TCP, where each version uses a different locking granularity. These are described in more detail in section 5.1.

Checksumming has been identified as a potential performance issue in TCP/UDP implementations. We thus wished to examine the extent to which checksumming made a difference in protocol speedup and throughput. The checksum code used in our studies was the fastest available portable algorithm that we were aware of, which was from UCSD [18].

2.3   In-Memory Drivers

Since our platform runs in user space, accessing the FDDI adaptor involves crossing the IRIX socket layer, which is prohibitively expensive. Normally, in a user-space implementation of the *x*-kernel, a simulated device driver is configured below the media access control layer (in this case, FDDI). The simulated driver uses the socket interface to emulate a network device. To avoid this socket-crossing cost, we replaced the simulated driver with in-memory device drivers for both the TCP and UDP protocol stacks. The drivers emulate a high-speed FDDI interface, and support the FDDI maximum transmission unit (MTU) of slightly over 4K bytes. This is similar to the approaches taken in [5, 11, 21, 28].

The drivers act as senders or receivers, producing or consuming packets as fast as possible, to simulate the behavior of a simplex data transfer over an error-free network. To minimize execution time and experimental perturbation, the receive-side driver uses preconstructed packet templates, and does not calculate TCP and UDP checksums. Instead, in experiments that examine checksumming using a simulated sender, the actual TCP and UDP receivers calculate the checksum, but ignore the result.

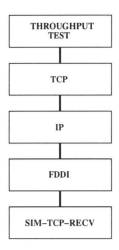

Figure 1: TCP Send-Side Configuration

Figure 1 shows an example of a test configuration. The example is of a send-side TCP throughput test, where a simulated TCP receiver sits below the FDDI layer. The simulated TCP receiver generates acknowledgement packets for packets sent by the actual TCP sender. The driver acknowledges every other packet, thus mimicking the behavior of Net/2 TCP when communicating with itself as a peer. Since spawning threads is expensive in user space in IRIX, the driver "borrows" the stack of a calling thread to send an acknowledgement back up.

The TCP receive-side driver (i.e., simulated TCP sender) produces packets in-order for consumption by the actual TCP receiver, and flow-controls itself appropriately using the acknowledgements and window information returned by the TCP receiver. Both simulated TCP drivers also perform their respective roles in setting up a connection.

3   Baseline Results

In this section we present a set of baseline results on our 8-processor 100 MHz Challenge machine. Our goal here is to illustrate the differences between the send and receive paths, and the impact of checksumming and packet size on scalability. The baseline protocol implementations which generated these results include message caching, atomic increment/decrement, and (in the case of TCP) a single lock on the TCP state. The locks used are the SGI supplied mutex locks. In sections 5 and 6 we describe these protocol structuring and implementation choices, and examine how they and various other alternative approaches effect and determine performance.

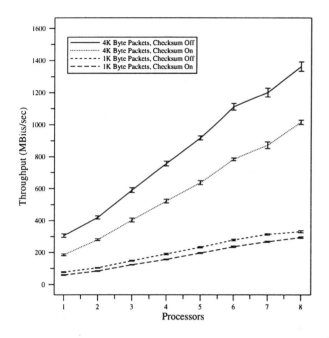

Figure 2: UDP Send Side Throughputs

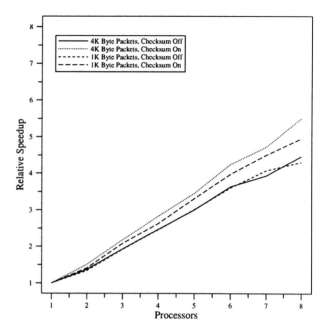

Figure 3: UDP Send Side Speedup

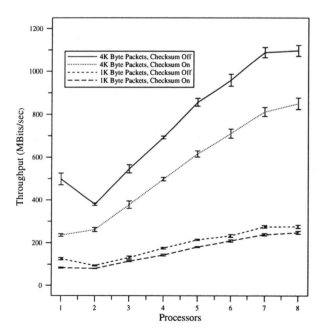

Figure 4: UDP Receive Side Throughputs

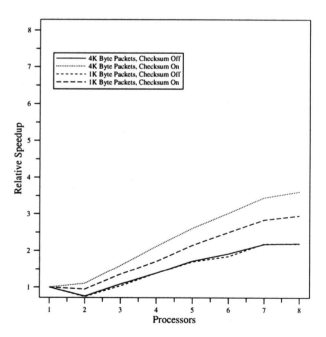

Figure 5: UDP Receive Side Speedup

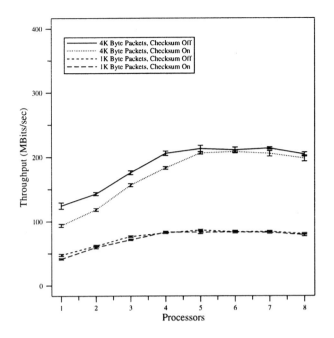

Figure 6: TCP Send Side Throughputs

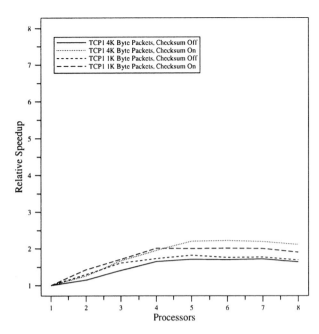

Figure 7: TCP Send Side Speedup

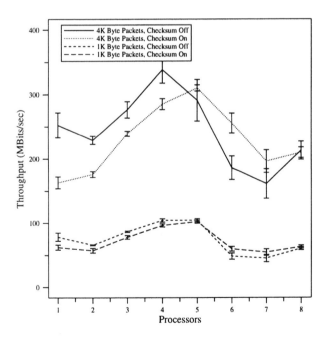

Figure 8: TCP Receive Side Throughputs

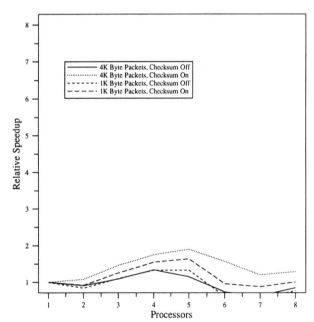

Figure 9: TCP Receive Side Speedup

In our experiments each processor has a single thread which is wired to that processor, similar to the method used by Bjorkman and Gunningberg. To see if wiring impacted our results, we ran several experiments without wiring threads to processors with TCP and UDP, send and receive side, with and without checksumming. The only change we observed was a small (approximately ten percent) difference on the send side for UDP above 4 processors. IRIX 5.2 schedules for cache affinity, and so we conclude that wiring has little perturbation of our experiments.

3.1 Send and Receive Side Processing

Figure 2 shows UDP send-side throughput, for a single UDP connection, in Megabits per second, measured on our 8-processor Challenge machine. Figure 3 shows relative speedup for the send side in UDP, where speedup is normalized relative to the uniprocessor throughput for that particular packet size. Figures 4 and 5 show UDP receive-side throughput and speedup, respectively. For these and all subsequent graphs, each data point is the average of 10 runs, where a run consists of measuring the steady-state throughput for 30 seconds, after an initial 30 second warmup period. In addition, we isolated our Challenge multiprocessor as much as possible by running experiments with no other user activity. All non-essential daemons were removed, and the machine did not mount or export any remote file systems. To check variance, we ran one 8-processor test 400 times, and observed that the data fit a normal bell-curve distribution. Throughput graphs include 90 percent confidence intervals.

The figures show that, as Bjorkman and Gunningberg discovered [5], UDP send-side performance scales well with larger numbers of processors. In our discussion, *scalability* means the first derivative of speedup as the last processor is added to the experiment. Note that a test can demonstrate high speedup to a point but exhibit poor scalability. We observe that send and receive side processing scale differently, but we do not wish to claim any inherent difference between their relative scalability. This is because our send-side experiments explicitly yield the processor on every packet, but the the receive side relies on the operating system to preempt the thread. This is partially a historical artifact of our implementation, and we plan a more detailed comparison between the two in the future.

One major difference between the send and receive paths is that a protocol's receive processing must demultiplex incoming packets to the appropriate upper layer protocol. At first, we thought that the locks used in the map manager for demultiplexing might be creating a bottleneck, but running the test without locking the maps yielded a small (approximately 10 percent) improvement in throughput.

The TCP throughput and speedup results, again for a single connection, are given in Figures 6-9 respectively. The TCP numbers here are from our baseline TCP, TCP-1, further described in section 5.1. Our results show that TCP does not scale nearly as well as UDP, in either the send or receive case. Locking state is the culprit here. For example, profiling with Pixie [29] shows that in an 8-processor receive-side test, 90 percent of the time is spent waiting to acquire the TCP connection state lock; on the send side, the amount is 85 percent.

Several unusual points warrant mentioning. Figure 6 shows that send-side throughput appears to level off at around 215 megabits/sec. Figure 8 shows that receive-side throughput levels off above 350 megabits/sec, but then drops off suddenly afterwards. This dip is caused by the combination of TCP packets being misordered when threads contend for the connection state lock, and the difference in processing times for in-order versus out-of-order packets in TCP. Section 4.1 discusses how this problem was discovered, as well as the solution.

3.2 Checksumming and Packet Size

As mentioned earlier, we were interested in how checksumming and packet size influence the performance of parallel protocols. Our expectations were that relative speedup would be greater when processing larger packets with checksumming, since checksumming occurs outside of locked regions and thus constant per-packet costs would constitute a smaller fraction of the processing time [17]. Figures 3, 5, 7, and 9 show that, in general, tests with larger packets have better speedup than those with smaller ones, and experiments for a particular packet size with checksumming have better speedup than those without, although the differences are not as pronounced as we had expected. The trends agree somewhat with those shown in [11], which showed better speedup with larger data units. However, their tests included presentation-layer conversion, which is much more compute-bound and data-intensive than checksumming.

Although the SGI documentation gives the aggregate bus bandwidth as 1.2 gigabytes/sec, we wished to see the read bandwidth limitations imposed by checksumming. To this end, we ran a micro-benchmark that checksummed over a large amount of data, to force cache misses. We observed that each processor could checksum at a rate of 32 MB/sec, or 256 megabits/sec, at least up to 8 processors. Assuming the bandwidth does not degrade as processors are added, this implies that the bus could support up to 38 processors doing nothing but checksumming.

4 Ordering Issues

4.1 Ordering Issues in TCP

Recall that in Figure 8, receive-side TCP throughput falls drastically beyond 4 or 5 processors. Further investigation showed large numbers of out-of-order arrivals at the TCP layer, a surprising result since data was being generated

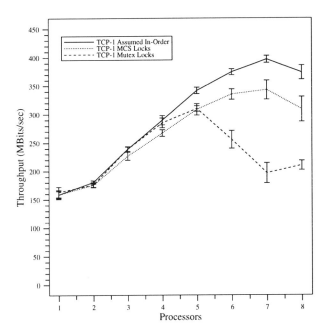

Figure 10: Ordering Effects in TCP

map lookups were serialized by MCS locks, and observed a slight reduction in throughput. Since MCS locks have a greater fixed-overhead cost without contention than the straight mutex locks (1.5 usec vs. 0.7 usec), we did not wish to simply replace all mutex locks in the system with MCS locks. However, as observed above, in the right scenario they can create an enormous performance win.

Processors	1	2	3	4	5	6	7	8
Mutex Locks	00	02	04	05	11	25	42	54
MCS Locks	00	02	04	06	09	11	14	18

Table 1. Percentage of packets out-of-order.

Table 1 also shows the impact of using FIFO locks. The table gives the percentage of packets received out-of-order in TCP with mutex locks and MCS locks, for a receive-side test using 4KB packets with checksumming. The table shows a large difference in the number of out-of-order packets between the two locking schemes as the number of processors increases.

An interesting side issue is the misordering that can occur on the send side when threads pass each other below TCP but before reaching the FDDI driver. This would cause packets to be placed out-of-order on the wire, and probably arrive out-of-order at the receiver. To quantify this potential problem, we measured the percentage of out-of-order packets in the send-side driver, and observed that fewer than one percent were misordered with up to eight processors.

4.2 Ordering and Correctness

We note that preserving order is a *semantic correctness* issue. If an application uses TCP and cannot cope with out-of-order delivery, packet order must also be preserved *above* TCP. When parallelism is introduced, an arriving packet cannot simply release the TCP connection state lock and continue; the moment the lock is relinquished, guarantees of ordered data above TCP are lost. Similarly, on the send side, the order of the data the application passes to TCP must be preserved, lest the order TCP preserves is different from the one the application observed. For some applications, this is not a problem. For example, NFS does not assume ordered packets, and can be configured to use TCP. In most cases, however, the application requires order to be preserved.

To examine this issue, we implemented a ticketing scheme similar to a bakery algorithm. Before releasing the TCP connection state lock, a receiving thread acquires an *up-ticket* for the next higher layer. The thread then releases the connection state lock, and continues up the stack. In the test application above TCP, at the point where the application requires order, the thread can then wait for its ticket to be called. The amount of mechanism required to implement this feature is not large, but restricts order, further limiting performance. Figure 11 shows a receive side TCP throughput test using 4KB packets, comparing an application that requires order preservation versus one that

in-order by the simulated TCP sender. As the TCP header prediction algorithm is dependent on the arrival of in-order packets, we hypothesized that out-of-order arrivals were reducing performance. To test this hypothesis, we ran a test using a version of TCP modified to treat *every* packet as if it were in-order. The result was the disappearance of the anomaly. The question then became how to bridge the gap between the observed behavior and the forced in-order experiment.

The Pixie results showed high contention for the connection state lock, and since the raw mutex locks provided by IRIX are not FIFO, this suggested that lock contention was causing threads, and thus packets, to be reordered. To preserve the original ordering, we implemented FIFO queueing using the MCS locks by Mellor-Crummey and Scott [22]. Their locking algorithm requires atomic swap and compare-and-swap functions, which we implemented using short R4000 assembler routines.

Figure 10 illustrates the effects, using 4 KB packets with checksumming on. The top curve in the figure is from the modified TCP where packets are *assumed* to be in order, a potential upper bound. The bottom curve is the baseline TCP-1 implementation using regular mutex locks for the connection state. The middle curve is TCP-1 using MCS locks. We see that using these locks bridges the majority of the gap between the baseline case and the "upper bound." In the case with checksumming off (not shown), there is no statistically discernible difference between the performance of the "upper bound" TCP and TCP with MCS locks. Closing the remainder of the gap with checksumming is not trivial. For example, we tried a receive-side test where

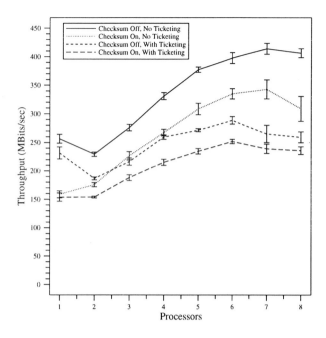

Figure 11: Ticketing Effects in TCP

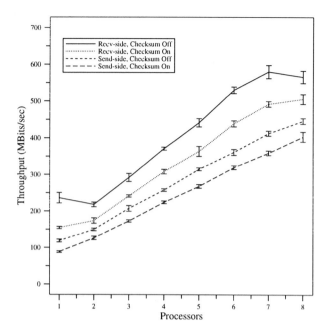

Figure 12: TCP with Multiple Connections

does not. In this example, the application is our test code, which simply counts packets that arrive. The application's critical section itself is small, a lock-increment-unlock sequence; the performance is lost preserving the order.

We are not the first to observe this problem [11, 13], but to our knowledge, previous work has not provided adequate solutions. For example, in [11], Goldberg et. al. use a ticketing scheme similar to ours, but assign tickets to packets at the driver for use in re-ordering at the application. However, this assumes a one-to-one correspondence between arriving packets and application data units. It does not address issues such as corrupted packets that are dropped, fragmented packets that are reassembled, or packets that are not data at all, such as acknowledgements.

The more general problem is to provide a mechanism that is correct in a general fashion, across several protocol layers. The solution we describe above only solves the problem when there is a one-to-one correspondence between a TCP connection and the application's notion of a connection. This is the case in the example of TCP and BSD sockets. However, if a TCP connection was multiplexed by several other higher-layer protocols, each message must be "re-ticketed" at each multiplexing or demultiplexing point[1]. A general solution that meshes with the x-kernel's infrastructure is an issue still under study.

4.3   Multiple Connections

Given the performance penalty exacted for maintaining order, and the single-connection performance limits in TCP,

we argue that if parallel applications are to reap the benefits of parallelized networking, they should perform their own ordering. Using either a connectionless protocol such as UDP or a connection-oriented protocol such as TCP with *multiple connections,* an application *must* be able to handle out-of order delivery. Lindgren et. al. [21] make a related argument that the parallel application must be tied closely to the parallel communication system.

To illustrate the benefits of using multiple connections, we ran send-side and receive-side experiments of TCP-1 with MCS locks, without ticketing, using 4KB packets with and without checksumming. In these tests, each processor was responsible for a separate connection. For example, the eight processor experiment examines throughput for eight connections. The simulated drivers were modified slightly to support multiple connections for these tests. The results are shown in Figure 12. The graph shows steadily increasing throughput as connections (and their associated processors) are added. This test is somewhat "idealized" in that the distribution of traffic across connections is relatively uniform. However, the point of the experiment is to show that the connection state lock is the major bottleneck for a single connection, and that it may be overcome by using multiple connections.

5   Locking Issues

5.1   Locking Granularity in TCP

Recall that TCP maintains a relatively large amount of state per connection. A question we wished to address was how

---

[1] Thanks to Mats Bjorkman for pointing this out.

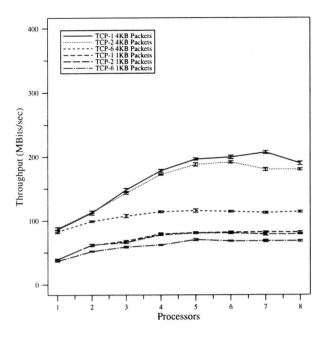

Figure 13: TCP Send-Side Locking Comparison

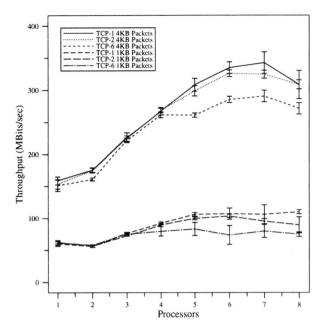

Figure 14: TCP Receive-Side Locking Comparison

that state should be locked in order to maximize performance and speedup. Towards this end, we produced three versions of our TCP, each with a different number of locks. For illustrative purposes, we call them TCP-N, where N indicates the number of locks involving connection state. The first version, the baseline given in Section 3, is TCP-1, which uses only a single lock to protect all connection information. The second version, TCP-2, uses two locks per connection: one to protect send-side state, and the other to protect receive-side state. The last version, TCP-6, uses the locking style from the SICS MP TCP, with six locks serializing access to various components of the connection state.

More specifically, TCP-6 has separate locks to protect the receive-side reassembly queue, the send-side retransmission buffer, the header prepend operation, header remove operation, send side window state, and receive side window state. In most cases, this locking is either redundant or unnecessary. For example, header manipulation occurs solely on the stack of the calling thread; thus, no locking is necessary. Similarly, the send and receive queues need to be locked at the same time as the send and receive window state, which is redundant.

Another concern we had with the SICS TCP implementation was that locks were being held where checksum calculation would have been done, on both incoming and outgoing packets.[2] In the *x*-kernel, this occurs where headers are prepended or removed, respectively, and the TCP-6 code is consistent with their implementation. However, we saw

that locking was not necessary here, and our two other TCP implementations reflect this. The key realization is that checksumming a packet is orthogonal to manipulating connection state. The only change needed was, in the case of the outbound processing in `tcp_output`, the checksum calculation had to be moved so that it was done outside the scope of the send window lock. This did not affect correctness, however.

The results for the three TCP implementations are given in Figures 13 and 14, which plot send and receive side throughput respectively with checksumming. The three TCP's measured here are based on the baseline version described in Section 3 with the addition of MCS locks. The goal here is simply to compare locking strategies. TCP-1 and TCP-2 both outperform TCP-6, particularly when checksumming is enabled. With checksumming off, the gaps are smaller, but the relative ordering between the three TCP's is the same. In all cases, send and receive side, with and without checksumming, the code with the simplest locking, TCP-1, performed the best. We also observed this behavior when the three TCP's did *not* include MCS locks. In retrospect, we can see how the single-lock version would perform the best, since the Net/2 TCP implementation manipulates send-side state on the receive path, and receive-side state on the send path. For example, in the TCP header prediction code (intended to be common-case processing), both the send and receive state locks must be acquired.

Another attractive feature of using a single lock is its simplicity. Implementation is easier, deadlock is easier to avoid, and atomicity of changes to protocol state is easier

---

[2]We note that Bjorkman and Gunningberg reported results for TCP without checksumming.

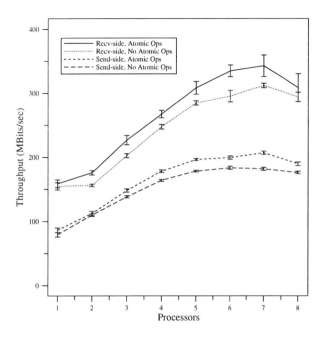

Figure 15: TCP Atomic Operations Impact

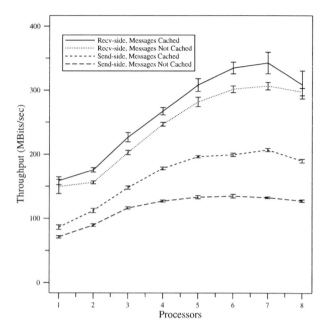

Figure 16: TCP Message Caching Impact

to guarantee.

We note that this result is specific to the BSD implementation, and that a TCP implementation designed around separating send and receive side processing may well yield better speedup with multiple locks. However, due to the widespread use of the BSD code, using the Net/2 example is applicable to many operating systems.

5.2 Atomic Increment and Decrement

Another locking issue we examined was using atomic increment and decrement functions that exploited the R4000's load-linked (LL) and store-conditional (SC) instructions. LL and SC allow programmers to produce *lock free* primitives [12]. A simple example of this is atomic increment, which replaces a lock-increment-unlock sequence.

We tried this for two reasons. First, the *x*-kernel's message tool relies on the notion that reference counts are atomically manipulated, and so the primitives map perfectly with the existing code. Thus, the primitives benefit the message tool, and subsequently all protocols that use it. Second, the *x*-kernel uses reference counts on session and protocol state in order to know when objects can be freed. When a packet is demultiplexed, these reference counts are incremented on the way up the stack and then decremented on the way down. This means that two locks are acquired and released *per-layer*, on the fast path of data transfer. Thus, atomic primitives again potentially benefit the entire protocol stack.

Replacing a lock-increment-unlock sequence with atomic increment pays off in two ways. First, a layer of procedure call is removed, which can affect performance

on the fast path. Second, in the best case, it reduces memory traffic by replacing three writes with a single one. We implemented these primitives with short R4000 assembler routines. Sample results are given in Figure 15, which shows the effects of atomic primitives on TCP throughputs with 4KB packets and checksumming on. Both TCP and UDP see improvements with the atomic primitives. The UDP receive-side obtains a larger benefit than the send side from atomic increments, due to the reference count manipulation that happens during demultiplexing. The benefits to the TCP send and receive sides were approximately equal, as the majority of the improvement is due to a more efficient message tool.

6 Per-Processor Resource Caching

As mentioned earlier, *x*-kernel protocols make heavy use of the message tool to manipulate packets. Since caching has been shown to be effective in data structure manipulations [2, 7], we decided to evaluate the use of simple per-thread resource caches in the message tool. Whenever a thread requires a new MNode (the message tool's internal data representation), it first checks a local cache, which can be done without locking. The cache is managed last-in first-out (LIFO) to maximize cache affinity. This avoids contention in two ways: first, the lock in `malloc` serializing memory allocation is avoided, reducing locking contention, and possible system calls (e.g., `sbrk`). Second, memory freed by a processor is re-used by that processor, avoiding memory contention. Figure 16 gives a sample of the results, displaying TCP throughputs with 4 KB packets with check-

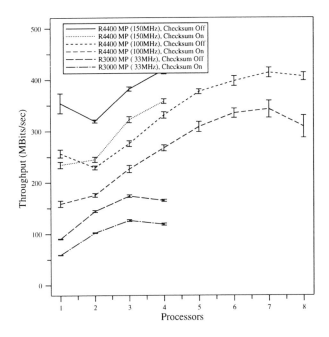

Figure 17: TCP Throughputs across Architectures

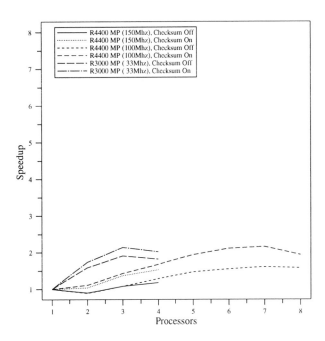

Figure 18: TCP Speedups across Architectures

summing. The improvement in TCP is significant, due to its heavy use of the message tool. The results are also positive for UDP send and receive side.

7 Architectural Trends

Of the experiments given in Section 3 that coincide with those given by Bjorkman and Gunningberg on the Sequent, we observed similar trends but relatively lower speedups. Drawing conclusions based on comparing speedups between two largely different architectures would most likely be inappropriate. Still, we were curious as to the differences that hardware made, since the Sequent used in their experiments was an older machine. Although we could not compare our results with theirs directly, we thought it would be illustrative to run our code on older hardware. To this end, we ran the same experiments on a Power Series, the previous generation Silicon Graphics multiprocessor, with four 33 MHz MIPS R3000's. We also ran our experiments on a faster version of our machine, a four-processor Challenge using 150 MHz R4400's. In all cases, the machines ran version 5.2 of the IRIX operating system. In these additional tests, we did not have exclusive access to the other machines, and so were not able to isolate them as carefully as with our Challenge experiments. However, we did run all our tests with minimal other activity on the systems, and the width of the confidence intervals on these graphs show that variance is low.

Examples of the architectural comparisons are given in Figures 17 and 18, which show receive-side throughput and speedup respectively for TCP on the three platforms. Space

constraints prevent us from showing all of our data, but in general, our findings were consistent across platforms. We do not wish to draw broad conclusions, especially from machines with only four processors, but we can summarize our observations:

- On all platforms, TCP-1 outperformed TCP-2 and TCP-6.

- On all platforms, UDP send-side scaled well, and TCP scaled poorly.

- On all platforms, the fastest machine had the highest throughput for a particular test.

- Speedup was consistently best on the Power Series (the oldest machine) and about the same on the two Challenge platforms.

- The two Challenge machines exhibited the receive-side drop in throughput at 2 processors, but the Power Series did not. In particular, UDP receive-side performance scales on the Power Series as far as could be observed, namely up to four processors.

The last item is perhaps the most interesting. Without more detailed information, we cannot assert any explanations for the behavior. We do note though, that the Power Series performs locking using a separate dedicated synchronization bus, similar to the Sequent. The Challenge, however, uses memory to synchronize, relying on the coherency protocol and the load-linked/store-conditional instructions [9]. Given that Bjorkman and Gunningberg did not observe the receive-side drop for their UDP receive side tests on the Sequent, we suspect that the difference in synchronization may be the cause of the anomaly. We are pursuing further studies along these dimensions.

Finally, the 100 MHz Challenge uniprocessor throughputs are roughly 25 to 50 percent better than those of the 33MHz Power Series. This is surprising, given that the former has a three times faster clock cycle, on-chip caches, and larger secondary caches. This is only one architectural comparison, with different generations of both the MIPS architecture and multiprocessor interconnects. Still, it suggests that network protocol processing speed may not be improving as fast as application performance, which agrees with the operating system trends shown in [3, 24]. We plan to investigate this further.

8 Conclusions and Future Work

We briefly summarize our findings as follows:

- *Preserving order pays.* We showed that, in cases where contention for locks perturbs order, simple FIFO queueing locks preserve this order, which improves performance.

- *Single-connection TCP parallelism is limited,* both on the receive side, and on the send side, even more so than shown by Bjorkman and Gunningberg.

- *Multiple-connection TCP parallelism can scale,* since contention for the connection state lock is avoided. However, the application must manage order across connections.

- *Exploiting cache affinity, and avoiding contention, is crucial.* This is demonstrated by the effectiveness of per-processor resource caching. Contemporary machines are memory-bound, due to the disparity between CPU and memory speeds, and the gap is only expected to grow.

- *Simpler locking is better.* We showed that, on a modern machine, locking structure impacts performance, and that a complex protocol with large connection state yields better speedup with a single lock than with multiple locks.

- *Atomic primitives can make a big difference.* Replacing sequences of lock-increment-unlock with an atomic increment improved receive-side TCP and UDP performance by about 20 percent on average, and send-side between 5 and 10 percent.

- *Checksumming has some influence on speedup.* This was demonstrated by the differences in relative speedup between experiments with and without checksumming.

These results indicate that packet-level parallelism is especially beneficial for connectionless protocols, but that connection-oriented protocols will have limited benefits in speedup within a single connection. Applications will need to use multiple connections to obtain parallel performance with connection-oriented protocols, which means they must manage order between connections. Due to time and space constraints, we have only been able to briefly address multiple connections in this paper. We plan to examine issues involving multiple connections more in-depth, and to examine another strategy of parallelizing protocols involving connection-level parallelism.

Acknowledgements

We are indebted to Larry Peterson and the *x*-kernel group at the University of Arizona for extending their help and hospitality, and allowing us to use their Power Series machine. Ed Menze and Hilarie Orman answered countless questions. Lawrence Brakmo assisted our understanding of TCP in general. Mats Bjorkman, Franklin Reynolds, and Franco Travostino discussed ordering issues with us. Special thanks to Mats Bjorkman for providing us with his original parallel TCP code, helping us with understanding it, and engaging in lively discussion. Thanks to David Oliver at the Center for Geometry Analysis Numerics and Graphics at the University of Massachusetts for letting us use their 150 MHz Challenge machine.

Many people contributed comments that improved the form and content of this paper, including Mats Bjorkman, Neal Nuckolls, and the anonymous reviewers.

References

[1] Brian Allison. DEC 7000/10000 Model 600 AXP multiprocessor server. In *Proceedings IEEE COMPCON*, pages 456–464, San Francisco CA, February 1993.

[2] Thomas E. Anderson, Edward D. Lazowska, and Henry M. Levy. The performance implications of thread management alternatives for shared-memory multiprocessors. *IEEE Transactions on Computers*, 38(12):1631–1644, December 1989.

[3] Thomas E. Anderson, Henry M. Levy, Brian N. Bershad, and Edward D. Lazowska. The interaction of architecture and operating system design. In *Fourth International Conference on Architectural Support for Programming Languages and Operating Systems*, pages 108–120, 1991.

[4] Mats Björkman. The xx-Kernel: an execution environment for parallel execution of communication protocols. Dept. of Computer Science, Uppsala University, June 1993.

[5] Mats Björkman and Per Gunningberg. Locking effects in multiprocessor implementations of protocols. In *ACM SIGCOMM Symposium on Communications Architectures and Protocols*, pages 74–83, San Francisco, CA, September 1993.

[6] Dave Borman. NTCP: A proposal for the next generation of TCP and UDP. In *Submission to the End2End-Interest mailing list*, pages 1–37, Eagan, MN, 1993. Cray Research. End2End archives available via FTP at ftp.isi.edu.

[7] Peter Druschel and Larry L. Peterson. Fbufs: A high-bandwidth cross-domain transfer facility. In *Proceedings of the Fourteenth ACM Symposium on Operating Systems Principles*, pages 189–202, Asheville, NC, Dec 1993.

[8] Michel Cekleov et. al. SPARCCenter 2000:Multiprocessing for the 90's! In *Proceedings IEEE COMPCON*, pages 345–353, San Francisco CA, February 1993.

[9] Mile Galles and Eric Williams. Performance optimizations, implementation, and verification of the SGI Challenge multiprocessor. Technical report, Silicon Graphics Inc., Mt. View, CA, May 1994.

[10] Dario Giarrizzo, Matthias Kaiserswerth, Thomas Wicki, and Robin C. Williamson. High-speed parallel protocol implementation. *First IFIP WG6.1/WG6.4 International Workshop on Protocols for High-Speed Networks*, pages 165–180, May 1989.

[11] Murray W. Goldberg, Gerald W. Neufeld, and Mabo R. Ito. A parallel approach to OSI connection-oriented protocols. *Third IFIP WG6.1/WG6.4 International Workshop on Protocols for High-Speed Networks*, pages 219–232, May 1993.

[12] Maurice Herlihy. A methodology for implementing highly concurrent data objects. *ACM Transactions on Programming Languages and Systems*, 15(5):6–16, November 1993.

[13] Norman C. Hutchinson. Protocols versus parallelism. In *Proceedings from the x-Kernel Workshop*, Tucson, AZ, November 1992. University of Arizona.

[14] Norman C. Hutchinson and Larry L. Peterson. The x-Kernel: An architecture for implementing network protocols. *IEEE Transactions on Software Engineering*, 17(1):64–76, January 1991.

[15] Van Jacobson. Efficient protocol implementation. In *ACM SIGCOMM 1990 Tutorial Notes*, Philadelphia, PA, September 1990.

[16] Van Jacobson, Robert Braden, and Dave Borman. TCP extensions for high performance. In *Network Information Center RFC 1323*, pages 1–37, Menlo Park, CA, May 1992. SRI International.

[17] Jonathan Kay and Joseph Pasquale. The importance of non-data touching processing overheads in TCP/IP. In *SIGCOMM Symposium on Communications Architectures and Protocols*, pages 259–269, San Francisco, CA, September 1993. ACM.

[18] Jonathan Kay and Joseph Pasquale. Measurement, analysis, and improvement of UDP/IP throughput for the DECStation 5000. In *USENIX Winter 1993 Technical Conference*, pages 249–258, San Diego, CA, 1993.

[19] Odysseas G. Koufopavlou and Martina Zitterbart. Parallel TCP for high performance communication subsystems. In *Proceedings of the IEEE Global Telecommunications Conference (GLOBECOM)*, pages 1395–1399, 1992.

[20] Samuel J. Leffler, Marshall Kirk McKusick, Michael J. Karels, and John S. Quarterman. *The Design and Implementation of the 4.3BSD UNIX Operating System*. Addison Wesley, Reading, Massachusetts, 1989.

[21] Bert Lindgren, Bobby Krupczak, Mostafa Ammar, and Karsten Schwan. An architecture and toolkit for parallel and configurable protocols. In *Proceedings of the International Conference on Network Protocols*, San Francisco, CA, October 1993.

[22] John M. Mellor-Crummey and Michael L. Scott. Algorithms for scalable synchronization on shared-memory multiprocessors. *ACM Transactions on Computer Systems*, 9(1):21–65, February 1991.

[23] Arun N. Netravali, W. D. Roome, and K. Sabnani. Design and implementation of a high-speed transport protocol. *IEEE Transactions on Communications*, 38(11):2010–2024, November 1990.

[24] John Ousterhout. Why aren't operating systems getting faster as fast as hardware? In *Proceedings of the Summer USENIX Conference*, pages 247–256, June 1990.

[25] Tom F. La Porta and Mischa Schwartz. A high-speed protocol parallel implementation: Design and analysis. *Fourth IFIP TC6.1/WG6.4 International Conference on High Performance Networking*, pages 135–150, December 1992.

[26] David Presotto. Multiprocessor streams for Plan 9. In *UKUUG*, January 1993.

[27] Sunil Saxena, J. Kent Peacock, Fred Yang, Vijaya Verma, and Mohan Krishnan. Pitfalls in multithreading SVR4 STREAMS and other weightless processes. In *Winter 1993 USENIX Technical Conference*, pages 85–96, San Diego, CA, January 1993.

[28] Douglas C. Schmidt and Tatsuya Suda. Measuring the impact of alternative parallel process architectures on communication subsystem performance. *Fourth IFIP WG6.1/WG6.4 International Workshop on Protocols for High-Speed Networks*, August 1994.

[29] Michael D. Smith. Tracing with Pixie. Technical report, Center for Integrated Systems, Stanford University, Stanford, CA, April 1991.

[30] Robert Ullman. TP/IX: The next internet. In *Network Information Center RFC 1475*, Menlo Park, CA, June 1993. SRI International.

[31] George Varghese and Tony Lauck. Hashed and hierarchical timing wheels: Data structures for the efficient implementation of a timer facility. In *The Proceedings of the 11th Symposium on Operating System Principles*, November 1987.

Experiences with Locking in a NUMA Multiprocessor Operating System Kernel

Ronald C. Unrau*   Orran Krieger   Benjamin Gamsa   Michael Stumm

Department of Electrical and Computer Engineering
Department of Computer Science
University of Toronto
Email: unrau@eecg.toronto.edu

Abstract

We describe the locking architecture of a new operating system, HURRICANE, designed for large scale shared-memory multiprocessors. Many papers already describe kernel locking techniques, and some of the techniques we use have been previously described by others. However, our work is novel in the particular combination of techniques used, as well as several of the individual techniques themselves. Moreover, it is the way the techniques work together that is the source of our performance advantages and scalability. Briefly, we use:

- a hybrid coarse-grain/fine-grain locking strategy that has the low latency and space overhead of a coarse-grain locking strategy while having the high concurrency of a fine-grain locking strategy;

- replication of data structures to increase access bandwidth and improve concurrency;

- a clustered kernel that bounds the number of processors that can compete for a lock so as to reduce second order effects such as memory and interconnect contention;

- Distributed Locks to further reduce second order effects, with modifications that reduce the uncontended latency of these locks to close to that of spin locks.

1 Introduction

The question of how to structure locks within an operating system is important, because it directly affects both the available concurrency and the latency of operating system services. The correct choice of locking strategy for a particular data structure or subsystem depends on the expected access pattern and the overall system workload. In a shared-memory multiprocessor environment, we need to efficiently support a workload consisting of either parallel applications or multiple sequential applications or both. These workloads result in four types of access behaviors for operating system data structures: 1) non-concurrent accesses, 2) concurrent accesses to independent data structures, 3) concurrent, read-shared accesses, and 4) concurrent, write-shared accesses.

A Unix application workload consisting of many sequential applications will primarily induce the first two types of access behaviors. Much of the existing work on operating system locking issues has focused on these types of workloads. Parallel applications, on the other hand, primarily induce the second and third type of behavior. The third and fourth types of behaviors are in some ways the most important, however, as these can induce worst-case behavior in the operating system.

In this paper, we describe a locking architecture that addresses all four types of access behaviors. It uses a *hybrid approach*, which combines properties of both coarse-grained and fine-grained locks. The coarse-grained locks minimize the number of atomic operations needed in the critical path of non-concurrent operations. Minimizing the latency of uncontended locks in the critical path is important, because it can constitute a significant portion of the overall response time of an operation. In our system, for example, the measured time for a simple page fault is 160 μsec, of which 40 μsec is attributable to lock overhead. Fine-grained locks, on the other hand, provide the high degree of concurrency needed for concurrent, independent operations. Further, we employ a technique called hierarchical clustering, which replicates data that is primarily read-shared so as to increase overall lock bandwidth, and bounds the contention on shared structures by constraining the number of processors that can access the structure. Finally, we make extensive use of Distributed Locks proposed by Mellor-Crummey and Scott [19], in order to reduce second-order effects for those cases where contention cannot be otherwise avoided. We have improved on the basic algorithm and optimized Distributed Locks for use in a kernel environment.

The design of a locking architecture is heavily dependent on the parameters of the system environment for which it is targeted. In our case, the design is influenced by

---

*currently at IBM Canada

the fact that 1) atomic operations are expensive relative to normal memory accesses, 2) `swap` is the only atomic operation supported, 3) our operating system is an exception-based micro-kernel (as opposed to process-based [6]), and 4) many of the kernel data structures are left uncached because our hardware does not support cache-coherence. Nevertheless, we believe that elements of our architecture are relevant to a wide variety of system architectures. It should also be noted that many of the techniques we use have been proposed previously. However, the strength of our approach lies in the particular combination of techniques used to efficiently support the four access patterns described above.

Section 2 of this paper describes our general locking architecture. Section 3 describes our improvements to, and experiences with, Distributed Locks. In Section 4 we present performance results from our system. This is followed in Section 5 by a discussion of how our approach to locking might generalize to other systems, and a discussion of our ongoing work. Finally, we conclude in Section 6 with a summary of this paper.

2 Locking Architecture

This section describes the locking architecture of the HURRICANE [8, 13, 25, 26] operating system. Three key features distinguish this architecture: a mix of coarse and fine grained locks are used to achieve low latency while still supporting high concurrency for independent operations; hierarchical clustering is used to limit contention by replicating data structures and constraining the number of processors that can directly access a particular data structure; and an optimistic deadlock avoidance protocol is used to reduce common case latency.

2.1 A Hybrid Approach

Our Hybrid approach uses coarse-grained locks, where a single lock may be used to protect several data structures but may only be held for short periods of time, and it uses "light-weight" fine-grained locks to protect data for longer periods of time but at a much finer granularity.

Consider the chained hash table of Figure 1. In a system using fine-grained locks (Figure 1a), each bin would have its own lock to serialize updates to the hash chains, and each hash entry would have one or more locks to protect the data therein. With our hybrid approach, the entire hash table might be protected by a single coarse-grained lock. Using coarse-grained locks in this way has both advantages and disadvantages with respect to space and time. Clearly the number of locks required to access a data structure is minimized, but that alone does not minimize the locking time, except in the case of no contention. The challenge is thus to keep locking time low as concurrency is increased, while

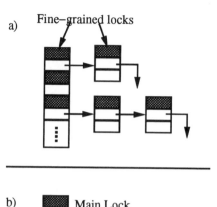

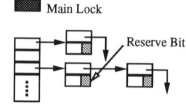

Figure 1: A chained hash table in a) a system with fine-grained locks, and b) the hybrid locking of HURRICANE. The boxes marked with the dark shading indicate locks that are set with atomic operations. The boxes marked with light shading are reserve bits.

still minimizing the number of locks held. The remainder of this section considers the trade-offs involved.

One disadvantage of a coarse-grained lock is that concurrent accesses to different elements are protected by the same lock, causing unnecessary contention for independent operations. Our first step to resolve this issue was to use Distributed Locks. Distributed Locks allow processors to spin locally while waiting for a lock, thereby removing the second order contention effects caused by spinning over the inter-connection network. The additional traffic on the network and memory caused by remote spinning not only slows down other non-contending processors, but also slows the processor that is holding the lock, extending the length of its critical section and exacerbating the contention problem. Although a Distributed Lock requires more space than a spin lock (an additional two words per actively spinning processor), a fine-grained approach would require one spin lock per hash element, a much higher total cost.

Figure 1b) shows how we allow increased concurrency by holding the main lock only long enough to search the hash table and set a *reserve* bit in the required element, after which the coarse-grained lock is released.[1] Other processors waiting for the reserved element spin on the reserve bit (with exponential back-off). When the bit is released, the waiting processors re-acquire the coarse-grained lock and search again.[2]

---

[1] Our hybrid locking approach is in some ways similar to the locking strategy used by Peacock, et al, for locking cache elements in a multiprocessor version of System V Release 4 [12, 21].

[2] Currently in our kernel, memory used for an object is always reused for objects of the same type. Hence, there is no danger that a process could

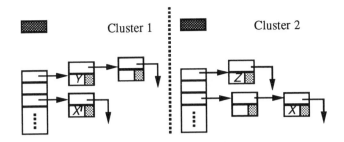

Figure 2: A chained hash table in a system with 2 clusters. Each cluster has a separate instantiation of the hash table and the locks that protect it. Deadlock must be avoided when a cluster requires a lock in two clusters simultaneously, for example, to instantiate a new copy of element Z on cluster 1.

The reserve bit is in essence a fine-grained spin lock, except that 1) it requires only one bit of storage instead of a whole word and is typically co-located with other needed status information, 2) multiple reserve bits can be acquired while the main lock is held, and atomic operations are not required to do so, and 3) it plays a special role in our deadlock avoidance strategy (described in Section 2.3). The fine-grained spin locks, however, can be subject to the contention effects that result from the bursty accesses we expect in a multiprocessor environment. We counteract this problem by controlling the number of processors that can simultaneously access the data structure and by replicating the data structure, as described next.

2.2   Hierarchical Clustering

To control the concurrency demands on the kernel data structures, we use a technique called hierarchical clustering. Briefly, hierarchical clustering is a framework for managing locality in a scalable shared-memory multiprocessor [25]. Instead of having one set of system data structures shared by all processors in the system, the processors are grouped into *clusters* and a complete set of system data structures are instantiated within each cluster. With this framework, the read-mostly data is replicated onto each cluster, and write-shared data exists on only one cluster, possibly being migrated from one cluster to another.

Figure 2 shows how the hash table of Figure 1 might appear in a two cluster system. A separate instance of the hash table, each with its own lock, exists in each cluster. The hash tables are used to hold both replicated entries (if they are primarily read-only) and non-replicated entries. In Figure 2, X is replicated to cluster 1 and cluster 2, while there is only a single copy of Y and Z in the system. Only

processors in the cluster may access the cluster-local hash table. To access entries of a hash table in another cluster, a remote procedure call (RPC) must be made to that cluster.[3]

Replicas of primarily read-shared data are typically made on demand. Hierarchical clustering supports efficient replication management by organizing the system into a tree. In the simplest case, the tree has three levels, with processors at the leaves, clusters forming intermediary nodes, and a logical top of tree for the entire system. The act of replication is made more efficient by combining multiple simultaneous requests from the processors in one cluster into a single request to the target cluster. This is accomplished by always first creating a local (reserved) instance before performing the replication. This local instance acts as a place-holder until the real data is obtained, preventing redundant replication requests from being issued. Combining is important because it is common that the many processes of a large SPMD program make concurrent demands that require the same (read shared) data.

The hierarchical clustering tree is also used to efficiently support the broadcast of modifications or invalidations when a replicated data structure is changed. For most data structures, the change is simply sent in parallel to each cluster. For data structures that are replicated per-processor, such as page tables in our system, the change is further broadcast within each cluster to each processor affected.

From the point of view of locking, hierarchical clustering provides two major benefits. First, it bounds contention for both coarse-grained locks and reserve bits, since RPCs are used instead of shared memory to access remote entries (Chaves et al discuss some of the trade-offs between using RPC and shared-memory [3]). Second, it increases lock bandwidth by i) instantiating per-cluster system data structures (such as the hash table in Figure 2), each with its own coarse-grained lock, and by ii) replicating read-shared objects (such as X in Figure 2), each with its own reserve bit.

Although hierarchical clustering bounds lock contention and increases lock bandwidth, it does complicate locking protocols [26]. For example, a needed data structure may not be present in the local cluster, requiring a remote operation to get it. If the data is replicated, then it must be kept consistent, which also requires remote operations. If the local kernel is holding any locks when initiating a remote operation, then some protocol must be established so that deadlock does not occur.

2.3   Deadlock Management Protocols

This section describes the protocol used to prevent deadlock across the clusters of a hierarchically clustered system. The protocol applies only to locks within the same class (e.g., the

---

spin indefinitely because the memory has been reallocated for another type of object that happens to have the same bit permanently set. If memory was arbitrarily recycled, then it would be necessary to either (i) periodically check, while spinning, that the data structure is still the one being sought, or (ii) use reference counts [1] to ensure that objects are not deallocated while a process is spinning on them.

---

[3]In theory, any processor of the target cluster may be used to execute the RPC. In our implementation, RPCs from the ith processor in the source cluster are always directed to the ith processor in the target cluster so as to roughly balance the RPC load.

---

class of process descriptor locks); we use a lock hierarchy across classes.

Consider again the clustered hash table of Figure 2. Assume a local copy of element Z is required by cluster 1. A search of the local hash table reveals that it is not present, at which point a data specific location resolution technique [25] indicates that the item resides in cluster 2. The kernel on cluster 1 then allocates a local instance of the element, Z', and initiates an RPC call to cluster 2 to retrieve the data. The local instance is created before the remote access is started so that other processors within the cluster that try to access Z while the remote operation is in progress will not also initiate (redundant) remote requests.

Because of the symmetric relationship between clusters, deadlock can result at this point if the RPC to retrieve Z is started without releasing the locally held locks. Our initial pessimistic deadlock prevention protocol required the initiator to release all locks before initiating the RPC, and then to re-acquire them once the remote operation had completed. This added considerable overhead to the code. Because the data structures were unprotected and could be modified or even removed while the local locks were released, the kernel had to search the hash table again to re-establish the continued existence of element Z after the RPC had completed. In addition, the kernel had to be prepared to handle the case where the data was no longer present. In the common case this re-establishment of state was unnecessary, since the probability of the data having been migrated or destroyed was very small.

To avoid the overhead of re-establishing state for the common case, we have implemented an optimistic algorithm that avoids deadlock and is similar to that described by Paciorek [20]. Before releasing the local locks, a reserve bit is set in any structure that might be needed after completing the call. The reserve bit may act as an exclusive lock or a reader-writer lock, depending on the data it protects. The local locks are then released and the RPC is initiated. If a reserve bit is encountered during processing in the remote cluster, the RPC operation fails and returns with an indication that a potential deadlock situation exists. The local reserve bits set earlier are then released and the remote operation is retried until it succeeds. Note that the local state must be re-established only if a retry is necessary.

Our optimistic approach saves us from having to re-establish state in the common case, although not for every case. In practice, we have found that retries are seldom needed, and the need to restart an operation because of modified state occurs even less frequently. Our approach does have two disadvantages, however. First, we have found that the deadlock avoidance algorithm required us to have two versions of code in many cases: one version has release/retry handling (used when executing as the target of a RPC); and one allows spinning without release/retry handling. Second, by requiring a remote request to continuously retry the RPC until it succeeds, the probability of being able to acquire a remote reserve bit is lower than for requesters that are in the target cluster and hence can spin directly on the reserve bit. Remote processors therefore have a greater potential of being starved for resources that are over-committed.

Remote operations must be retried even when the local locks and reserve bits have all been released, because the processor itself is effectively a locked resource (that could participate in a deadlock cycle) in an exception-based kernel. This is particularly apparent in our use of RPCs. Consider once again the hash table in Figure 2, and suppose processor P_1 in cluster 1 would like to modify X globally. Consider the situation where P_1 has dropped its local locks and reserve bits in order to retry the request, but the processor it directs the RPC to, say processor P_2, has the reserve bit for X set and is currently performing an RPC to another cluster. If the RPC from processor P_1 now executing on processor P_2 were to spin on X's reserve bit on processor P_2, deadlock would result. The deadlock cycle is caused by processor P_1's RPC holding the processor as it spins waiting for the reserve bit, while processor P_2 holds the reserve bit while waiting for the processor to be released.

Although our algorithm has been presented in the context of a clustered system, it is important to note that the same protocol could be applied to any system that requires multiple locks simultaneously. Also, we chose not to use the more common global ordering approach [22] within a particular class of locks, because the only ordering that makes sense in a clustered system is by cluster number. Since remote cluster operations are in general uniformly distributed across clusters, we would still have to release locks to preserve the correct ordering, and we would still require the ability to roll-back and restart.

We have observed two situations where modifications occur often to data required for the completion of the operation while their locks are released: copy-on-write page faults and program destruction. Both situations occur infrequently relative to other kernel operations, and of course are only a concern with large applications that span multiple clusters. Nevertheless, they will perform less efficiently on average because of the overhead of the retries.

2.4 Advantages of our Approach

The four classes of workload an operating system must handle are: 1) non-concurrent requests, 2) concurrent independent requests, 3) concurrent requests to read-shared operating system resources, and 4) concurrent requests to write-shared operating system resources. We have found that our hybrid locking approach, in conjunction with hierarchical clustering, allows us to effectively address all four workload classes.

Non-concurrent requests: The only important goal for this workload is to minimize latency. With our hybrid locking strategy, many kernel requests require only a single atomic operation. Hence, HURRICANE is able to achieve uncontended response times comparable to uniprocessor systems [14].

Concurrent independent requests: The important goal for this workload is to maximize concurrency, so an optimal strategy would be to use fine grain locks for these requests. With our hybrid locking strategy, the reserve bits serve as fine grain locks to maximize concurrency and minimize the time that the coarse-grained locks are held. By using hierarchical clustering, the number of processes concurrently contending for a coarse-grained lock is bounded, so, for this workload, HURRICANE is able to achieve performance comparable to systems structured using only fine grain locks. This is demonstrated in the results section.

Concurrent requests to read-shared resources:
Hierarchical clustering allows us to instantiate multiple instances of read-mostly data structures to increase the access bandwidth to the data. Since requests from SPMD applications to shared resources can be bursty, it is important that the replication be done efficiently; hierarchical clustering creates a combining tree to reduce the demand on the source data structure, should many processors wish to make copies of the data structure simultaneously.

Concurrent requests to write-shared resources:
Although kernel resources are seldom actively write-shared in our system, it is still important to minimize second order effects for those cases where write-sharing does occur. Since accesses to shared data in remote clusters typically occur via RPC calls, the number of processors competing for a write-shared data structure is bounded by the number of processors in the cluster.

2.5 Experiences using our approach

In the previous sections, we discussed our general locking methodology from an architectural perspective. Naturally, when applying a general methodology to a particular situation, one often makes adaptations and optimizations to accommodate particular uses. In this section we describe the more interesting lessons we learned from applying our general techniques to a full operating system implementation.

Pessimistic vs. Optimistic

In a number of cases we found it advantageous to use a pessimistic (i.e., release all locks, including reserve bits, prior to making a remote request) rather than an optimistic locking strategy, primarily for reasons of simplicity. For example, although we use an optimistic strategy for many data structures when creating local replicas, we typically use a pessimistic strategy for global updates. The optimistic approach is preferable for the former case, since it allows us to use the combining tree approach discussed in Section 2.2. The pessimistic approach is generally preferable for updates that may be broadcast to many clusters: if a processor in one cluster asks a processor in another cluster to broadcast modifications to data for which it also has a copy, then it is obviously better to have the local copy unlocked from the start.

Hybrid Compromises

Although we generally use the hybrid coarse-grain/fine-grain locking strategy as described, we do not follow it religiously. Our kernel has some data structures that are protected by coarse-grained locks and have no fine-grained locks, and in some cases, we have found it advantageous to split coarse-grained locks to achieve somewhat greater concurrency.

Retries

The rationale for using an optimistic approach is to trade off performance under contention (possibly requiring retries) for performance under light load (allowing locks to be safely held during remote operations). We found not only that retries are rarely required, but in those cases where they are required they would still have been required using a pessimistic approach.

For example, with SPMD programs, simultaneous faults to copy-on-write pages raise a number of potential deadlock situations that require retries with the optimistic approach. However, because a copy-on-write fault requires instantiating a new private page to replace the current shared page, the pessimistic approach would likely find that its copy of the page had disappeared by the time it completed its remote operation, requiring it to re-search its data structures and re-issue the request.

A second example can be found in the destruction of parallel programs containing many processes. Hurricane maintains a family tree of processes in the system, where the links of the tree run through the process descriptors. When a process in the application is to be destroyed, multiple process descriptors in different clusters must be updated to remove the process from the tree. Since all processes of an application are destroyed at approximately the same time, retries are common, independent of the strategy chosen.

Data structure design

One lesson we learned from the case of program destruction was that combining two structures with different locking characteristics into a single entity can lead to many concurrency control problems. In this particular case, the problem came from the fact that program destruction can involve up to three process descriptors and has a natural lock ordering that follows the structure of the tree, while process descriptors are also used to implement message passing which always involves two arbitrarily related processes, with no natural ordering. Had the family tree been implemented as a separate data structure, it would have been possible to exploit the hierarchy of the tree to enforce a lock ordering that would have allowed us to avoid the RPC retries described above.

3 Using Distributed Locks

Distributed Locks [19] are used in our system primarily for per-cluster coarse-grained locks, since cross-cluster interactions most often occur through RPCs. Distributed Locks are particularly well-suited for NUMA shared-memory multiprocessors and can substantially reduce the second-order effects stemming from the memory and inter-connection network contention that occurs when processors spin on remote memory. Distributed Locks build a queue of processors waiting to acquire a lock. Second-order contention effects are reduced because waiting processors spin on their local queue elements, instead of across the interconnection network. The queue also has the benefit that accesses to the lock are distributed fairly, since processors are queued in order of arrival. The remainder of this section describes several interesting lessons we have learned from using Distributed Locks.

3.1 Latency in the uncontended case

The high uncontended latency of Distributed Locks relative to spin locks was originally a concern to us, since other researchers had found that it could be as much as twice as high as that of simple spin locks [15]. One way to address this problem is to use an adaptive technique, where the locks switch between spin and distributed locks, depending on the amount of contention observed [2, 15]. We instead found that two simple modifications to the original distributed locking algorithm could improve the uncontended latency to make it competitive with that of simple spin locks (on our system), while preserving the advantages of distributed locks in the contended case.

The original and modified distributed locking algorithms are shown in Figures 3a and 3b, respectively. The first modification removes the code that initializes the per-processor local structure from the critical path of the uncontended case (i.e., the first dashed box in Figure 3a). This was done by requiring the per-processor queue structure to be initialized prior to the first request to the lock, and by re-initializing the structure when it is modified, which occurs only when there is contention for the lock. The code added is highlighted in Figure 3b.

The second modification to the Distributed Lock algorithm removes the condition in release_lock, which determines whether another processor has since added itself to the queue, and which is executed just prior the execution of the compare_and_swap to release the lock in the uncontended case (i.e., the second dashed box in Figure 3a). The check was there as an optimization for the contended case, assuming local memory accesses are much cheaper than remote accesses. However, this check degrades the performance of the common case where the lock is uncontended. Removing the check does not affect the scalability of the algorithm, since it adds only a constant overhead to the case where there is contention.

With these two modifications the uncontended latency on HECTOR improved from 5.40 μsec to 3.69 μsec — an improvement of 32%. The optimized time now compares favorably to the uncontended spin lock time of 3.65 μsec, the algorithm of which is shown in Figure 3c. These results are described in more detail in Section 4.1.1.

3.2 TryLock

As described by Mellor-Crummey and Scott, Distributed Locks do not support a *TryLock* operation. TryLock makes a single attempt to obtain a lock, and returns either with the lock held, or with a failure code if the lock is not free. In operating system kernels, TryLocks are typically used by the interrupt handlers, which cannot wait for a lock in case it is held by the pre-empted process. In our system, interrupts are used not only for devices, but also for invoking RPCs. In the case of an RPC, if a TryLock fails then the invoking processor is returned an error and retries the operation.

Our first attempt to extend the basic Distributed Locking algorithm to support TryLock took advantage of the fact that the local queue structures could be pre-allocated on a per-processor basis, one for each coarse-grained lock. The interrupt handler checks whether the pre-allocated local queue element is in use before it enqueues itself; if the queue element is free, then it is certain it did not interrupt a current holder of the lock and can therefore safely wait for the lock to be released. While this does not implement a true TryLock (because the interrupt handler will enqueue itself and wait rather than returning immediately if the lock is held), it does prevent deadlock and has the advantage of allowing the interrupt handler to acquire the lock under all conditions except when it clearly cannot, namely when it has interrupted the lock holder. Unfortunately, this implementation of TryLock required a flag in the local queue structure that had to be modified both when acquiring and releasing the lock, and hence had a negative impact on the base performance of our distributed locks in the uncontended case.

We developed a second variant of the Distributed Locking algorithm, which also supported TryLock (this time a true TryLock) but which only added overhead to release_lock in the contended case. The new algorithm is similar to acquire_lock of Figure 3b, except that it uses a separate local queue structure just for interrupt handlers. If an interrupt handler discovers that the lock is already held after

```
type qnode = record                    type qnode = record                  type lock = (unlocked, locked)
  next : ^qnode                          next : ^qnode
  locked : Boolean                       locked : Boolean                   procedure acquire_lock(L : ^lock)
type lock = ^qnode                     type lock = ^qnode                     while test_and_set( L ) = locked
                                                                                delay : integer := 1
procedure acquire_lock( L: ^lock, I : ^qnode )                                  while delay < MAX_DELAY
  I->next := nil                       procedure init_qnode( I : ^qnode )      Delay( delay )
  predecessor : ^qnode := fetch_and_store( L, I )   I->next := nil             if test_and_set( L ) != locked
  if predecessor != nil                                                          return
    I->locked := true                  procedure acquire_lock( L: ^lock, I : ^qnode )   delay := delay * 2
    predecessor->next := I               predecessor : ^qnode := fetch_and_store( L, I )
    while I->locked do <nothing>         if predecessor != nil              procedure release_lock(L : ^lock)
                                           I->locked := true                  lock^ := unlocked
procedure release_lock( L: ^lock, I: ^qnode )   predecessor->next := I
  if I->next = nil                         while I->locked  do <nothing>
    if compare_and_swap( L, I, nil )
      return                           procedure release_lock( L: ^lock, I: ^qnode )
    while I->next = nil do <nothing>     if compare_and_swap( L, I, nil )
  I->next->locked := false               return
                                         while I->next = nil do <nothing>
                                         I->next->locked := false
                                         I->next := nil

a) MCS distributed locks              b) modified distributed locks          c) exponential backoff locks
```

Figure 3: Locking algorithms used by HURRICANE

having enqueued itself, then it returns with an error code (rather than spinning), leaving its local queue structure still in the queue. The queue structures from failed TryLock requests are garbage collected by `Release_lock` operations. This implementation of TryLock is similar to the timeout mechanism for the queueing lock, developed independently by Craig [5].

Unfortunately, we found that this second variant of Try-Lock discriminated against RPC operations and favored local operations. In hindsight, we realized that this use of TryLock was fundamentally incompatible with Distributed Locks, since Distributed Locks are inherently fair, while retry-based locking is only probabilistically fair. That is, if a lock is saturated, then a Distributed Lock's `release_lock` operation will always hand-off the lock to some local processor that is waiting in the queue, keeping the lock permanently held; remote requests using TryLock will never see the lock free.

An alternative to using TryLock for RPCs is to disable interrupts while the lock is held, thus preventing RPCs from getting through. This way, the RPC interrupt handler can be sure it cannot deadlock with the processor it interrupted. Unfortunately, our hardware only provides the ability to enable and disable all interrupts, and for a number of reasons the HURRICANE kernel always runs with interrupts on. We therefore adapted a strategy first suggested by Stodolsky et al [23].

Inter-processor interrupts are treated as a separate interrupt class that can be logically masked. A per-processor flag is set whenever a lock is about to be acquired that could cause deadlock with an interrupt handler. An interrupt handler always first checks the flag, and if clear, can safely queue for the lock. If, on the other hand, the flag is set, then the interrupt handler enqueues a record of the work to be done on a per-processor work queue. When the flag

is cleared, the queue is checked and any pending work is immediately completed. Because the flag and the queue are accessed strictly locally, they can be cached effectively.

The per-processor flag acts as a lock for the processor, placed at the top of the lock hierarchy: it must be acquired before any other lock can be acquired. For RPCs, it allows fair access to the processor, because work is enqueued for later execution whenever the interrupt handler finds the processor locked in a manner similar to the way processors enqueue themselves on Distributed Locks.

In retrospect, it may have been better to combine the work queue with our second TryLock variant, rather than adding the additional per-processor flag to the top of the lock hierarchy.

4 Experimental Results

In this section, we use synthetic stress tests to demonstrate the performance of our locking architecture. The experiments were run on a fully configured version of HURRICANE with all servers active, but with no other applications running at the time. The operating system was running on a 16 processor HECTOR prototype with 16 MHz MC88100 processors [27]. The particular hardware configuration used in our experiments consists of 4 processor-memory modules per station (a shared bus) and 4 stations connected by a ring. This causes access times to vary from 10 cycles for a local (on-board) access, to 19 cycles for an on-station access, and 23 cycles for a cross-ring access.

4.1 Basic locking performance

We first present performance results for the three locking algorithms of Figure 3 in the absence of contention, and then show their performance as the locks become con-

	Atomic	Mem.	Reg.	Br.
MCS	2	2	3	5
H1-MCS	2	1	3	5
H2-MCS	2	0	3	4
Spin	2	0	1	3

Figure 4: Instruction counts required to execute a lock/unlock pair for the various routines in the absence of contention. MCS is the unmodified Mellor-Crummey and Scott Distributed Lock algorithm; H1-MCS is the MCS algorithm with our first modification, that removes the initialization code; H2-MCS is the H1-MCS algorithm with the conditional test in the unlock removed; Spin is the exponential backoff spin lock algorithm. *Atomic* are atomic read_modify_write instructions (swap instructions in our case); *Mem* are loads or stores to memory; *Reg* are single-cycle register-to-register instructions; *Br* are branch instructions (including return).

tended. Our processors only support fetch_and_store instructions (and not compare_and_swap). Therefore, we use Mellor-Crummey and Scott's fetch_and_store variant of their Distributed Lock algorithm in these experiments. Using this variant of the algorithm only impacts the performance of the contended case, as described in Section 4.1.2.

4.1.1 Uncontended performance

We measured the performance of the three locking algorithms by measuring the average time to acquire and release a lock 10^6 times. The uncontended latency of exponential backoff spin locks (Figure 3c) varies between 3.65 μsec and 4.63 μsec, depending on the distance between the process requesting the lock and the lock variable. The latency of the unmodified Distributed Locks (Figure 3a) varies between 5.40 μsec and 6.02 μsec. With our first modification that eliminates the initialization code, latency improves to between 4.56 μsec and 5.33 μsec, and with our second modification that also removes the condition code, the uncontended latency further improves to between 3.69 μsec and 4.63 μsec.

The instruction counts for the three locking algorithms, obtained by inspecting the assembly code, are shown in Figure 4.[4] While the modified Distributed Lock algorithm (H2-MCS) has the same number of atomic operations and memory accesses as the spin lock algorithm, it should have five additional cycles of latency due to branch instructions and register to register instructions. This expected latency is not reflected in the measured performance results, because the execution of these instructions is overlapped with the store part of the fetch_and_store instructions (the MC88100 processor can proceed as soon as the fetch portion of the fetch_and_store has completed). Hence, our

---

[4]On our system, all stores to a variable that might be modified with a fetch_and_store instruction must also occur using a fetch_and_store instruction. For this reason, the unlock operation for a spin lock releases the lock using a fetch_and_store rather than a store instruction.

modified Distributed Lock algorithm performs almost as well as the spin lock algorithm on our system.

4.1.2 Performance under contention

Figure 5 compares the response times of the different locking algorithms under contention, when p processors continuously acquire and release the same lock. Figure 5a and 5b show the performance for the case where the lock is held for 0 μsec and 25 μsec, respectively.

Because we use the fetch_and_store variant of Distributed Locks, it is possible that a *nil* will be stored to the lock variable in release_lock, even if there is some successor waiting for the lock. In this case, a performance penalty is incurred to repair the queue. From Figure 5a and 5b, we can see that the first modification we made to Distributed Locks does not degrade performance in the case of contention, while the second modification adds a constant overhead to release_lock, which is shown by that fact that the latency increases linearly with the number of contending processors. The extra latency for the second variant is a result of not checking for successors in the unlock operation, requiring the queue to always be repaired if there is a successor. If the lock is held for zero time, then this degradation has a significant effect on performance (Figure 5a), but if the lock is held for as little as 25 μsec, then the extra latency is much less significant (Figure 5b). Note that if compare_and_swap were available, then the performance differential would be significantly lower, although it would not be eliminated.

The Distributed Locks are compared against two variants of the exponential backoff spin locks in Figure 5, one where the maximum backoff is 35 μsec and the other where the maximum backoff is 2 msec. The former value is intended for lightly contended locks to reduce the latency in the case where the lock could not be acquired immediately, and is the value used internal to our operating system (for a cluster size of 4). The latter value was chosen because it yields optimal results for the experiments presented. With a maximum backoff of 2 msec, the performance of the spin locks is competitive with that of the Distributed Locks, since the memory contention becomes negligible. However, using this value makes the lock highly susceptible to starvation: with 16 processors contending for the lock and a lock hold time of 25 μsec, it took over 2 msec to acquire the lock in over 13% of the acquisition attempts.

4.2 General locking results

We use two synthetic page fault tests to demonstrate the effects of our locking architecture. In particular, the tests use soft page faults (i.e., faults to pages already in core), since such faults are fairly common in our system, both for mapping in cached files, and to support page-level cache coherence, page migration, and page replication. The tests model particular phases of real applications, stressing the

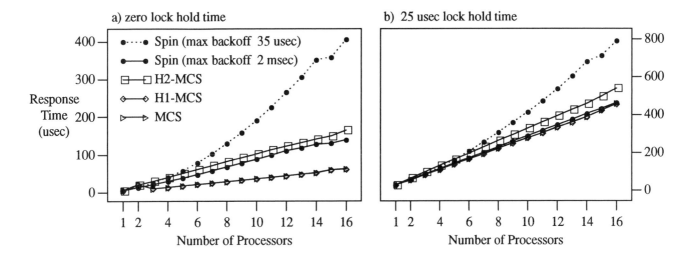

Figure 5: The average response times of a lock/unlock pair when p processes repeatedly access a critical section. The curves show the original Distributed Locking algorithm (MCS), the original algorithm with the initialization code removed (H1-MCS), the second algorithm with the conditional test also removed (H2-MCS), the exponential backoff spin lock with a maximum backoff of 35 μsec, and the exponential backoff spin lock with a maximum backoff of 2 msec.

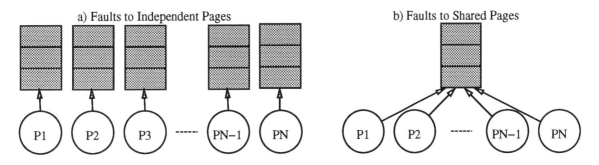

Figure 6: A schematic depiction of the programs that stress the memory management sub-system. (a) p processes repeatedly fault on a region of local memory. (b) p processes simultaneously write to the same small number of shared pages.

boundary cases. Using synthetic tests instead of real applications has the advantage that it allows us to focus our attention on results of interest to this paper. Application results on our system are presented in [25].

The two synthetic tests used are:

Independent faults (Figure 6a): p processes repeatedly fault on a per-process private region of local memory. Because the faults are to different physical resources (i.e., different pages) the only lock contention in this experiment is due to unnecessary locking conflicts in the kernel.

Shared faults (Figure 6b): p processes repeatedly 1) write to the same small number of shared pages, 2) barrier, and 3) unmap the pages from the processes' page tables. Because the faults from the different processes are all to the same shared pages, lock contention is implicit in the application demands.

Figures 7a and 7b show the response time of a page fault for the two tests on a single cluster of 16 processors, as p is varied from 1 to 16 processors. The different curves represent performance when either Distributed Locks or exponential backoff spin locks are used.

For the independent fault test (Figure 7a), there is little difference between the performance of Distributed and exponential backoff spin locks if the number of contending processors is between 1 and 4. However, if p is increased beyond four, then the use of spin locks degrades performance substantially, indicating that the coarse grain locks are a source of contention. With 16 processors faulting concurrently, the latency to handle a page fault is over twice as high when spin locks are used instead of Distributed Locks. These results demonstrate the dramatic impact that second order effects can have on the performance of kernel operations, since the latency increases are due almost entirely to contention at the memory and interconnection network.

For the shared fault test (Figure 7b), the difference in latency between Distributed Locks and spin locks is much smaller. This is because processes contend more for reserve bits, and less for the coarse grain locks. However,

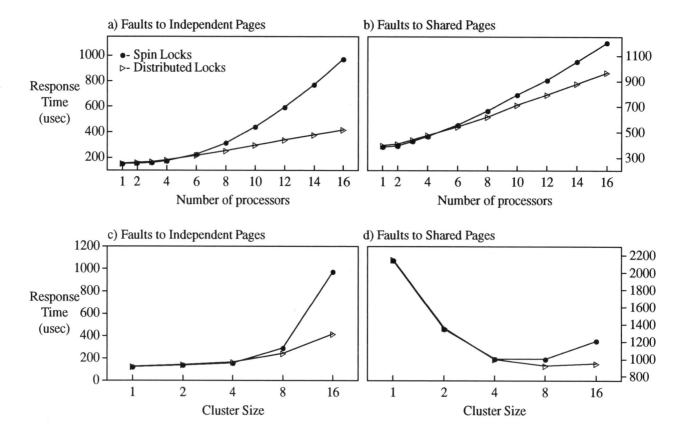

Figure 7: Page fault response times for the two synthetic page fault tests. Figures (a) and (b) demonstrate the effect of different amounts of contention in a fixed cluster size of 16 processors. Figures (c) and (d) demonstrate the impact of different cluster sizes given a fixed degree of contention caused by 16 processors.

it is apparent that there is at least some contention for the coarse grain locks as the number of contending processors increases. This stems from the fact that multiple processors simultaneously attempt to acquire the coarse grain lock that protects the reserve bit they are waiting on whenever a reserve bit is cleared, so there are bursts of heavy demand on the coarse grain locks.

Figures 7c and 7d show the response time with 16 processors as a function of the cluster size, which is varied between 1 and 16. For the independent page fault test, we expect small cluster sizes to result in the best performance. For the shared fault test, however, the situation is not so clear. We expect the sharing in this test to give larger cluster sizes an advantage. On the other hand, having a cluster size smaller than the system size means that the page descriptors are replicated to each cluster, increasing the lock bandwidth and bounding the contention on each page descriptor to the number of processors in the cluster.

Figure 7c shows that smaller cluster sizes do indeed lead to better performance for independent requests. For this experiment, performance does not degrade under contention if the cluster size is 4 or less.[5] Hence, it is clear that

the coarse-grained locks that protect the reserve bits do not constrain concurrency; i.e., they do as well as a fine grained locking strategy. Since this is a stress test that exerts demands on the kernel that are more extreme than that of any application, one can expect cluster sizes larger than 4 to perform as well with our hybrid locking strategy as with a fine grained locking strategy, assuming the requests are independent.

By comparing the results of Figure 7c to those of Figure 7a, we can see that the performance of 16 processes, faulting independently in 4 clusters of 4 processors each, is as good as the performance of 4 processes faulting in a single 16 processor cluster. From this we can conclude that hierarchical clustering is effective in localizing requests, allowing independent requests on different clusters to proceed concurrently without interference.

Figure 7d shows that moderate cluster sizes yield the best performance in the case of the shared fault test. For very small cluster sizes, the overhead of inter-cluster operations dominates performance.[6] As the cluster size increases, the cost of obtaining a local copy of the page descriptor with

---

[5]The difference between the performance of the 2 processor cluster and 4 processor cluster is due to NUMA affects rather than contention.

[6]A null Remote Procedure Call (RPC) requires 27 μsec, while the cost to perform a cluster-wide page lookup and replicate a page descriptor is approximately 88 μsec.

---

an RPC is amortized over more processors, since only one processor in each cluster must do so; the other processors in the same cluster can then service the fault using the local replica of the page descriptor. This is an example of increasing the lock bandwidth through replication, and merging requests using a combining tree. For very large cluster sizes, the page descriptors become shared by too many processors, and lock contention within the cluster becomes a problem.

A workload with a mix of real applications can be expected to have both independent and non-independent faults. The performance behavior can therefore be expected to be a combination of the behavior of both tests. From this, we conclude that a cluster size somewhere in the range of 4 to 16 processors could be optimal for our system. It is also interesting to note that results similar to those presented above were obtained for stress tests that exercised other portions of the kernel, such as the message passing subsystem.

5 Generalization of Experiences

Our experiences relate to one particular system. In this section we attempt to generalize our results to other hardware and software system architectures.

5.1 Other Operating System Designs

Process-based operating systems

Because our operating system is exception-based, as opposed to process-based [6], non-blocking locks are the most natural approach to locking, since there is no process in the kernel to block. While our approach can be applied directly to process-based kernels in those places where they use spin locks, process-based kernels can also use blocking locks which open up new opportunities to improve on our techniques. For example, by creating a process to handle interrupts and letting them block on locks, it is possible to remove the processor from the lock cycle and to provide greater fairness for remote requests, eliminating the problem described in Section 3.2.

Monolithic operating systems

Another question concerns how our locking strategy might apply to monolithic operating systems. We have applied the techniques described in this paper to several of our system servers, in particular the file system [13], and have found the benefits of reduced latency and increased concurrency that stem from the use of both hierarchical clustering and our hybrid locks apply. This gives us some confidence that our approach would be just as effective when applied to monolithic kernels.

5.2 Other Multiprocessor Designs

The system we used to test our ideas has only 16 relatively slow processors, does not support hardware cache coherence, and provides locking support that is relatively slow (requiring two remote memory accesses for a single read-modify-write sequence) and inflexible (supporting only atomic-swap). It is natural, therefore, to question how our results might apply to more modern systems, with faster processors and interconnection networks, cache-coherence or COMA (Cache-Only Memory Access [7,9]) support, and more powerful cache-based atomic primitives. Although such architectural changes will shift the tradeoff points, we believe that many of the techniques described in this paper would still apply to these systems. We address each of these issues in turn.

Larger and faster systems

Recent progress in processor design and manufacturing have allowed CPU performance to advance at a significantly greater rate than other components in multiprocessor systems. Although higher bandwidth can be achieved in other components by widening the data paths, the latency to access memory or transfer data between processor caches is a difficult problem to overcome. If one additionally considers the effect of larger systems, it becomes clear that contention for shared resources and the locks that protect them will only get worse. Therefore, techniques such as hierarchical clustering to bound the number of contending processors and lock replication to increase lock bandwidth, RPCs to increase locality, and distributed locks to reduce second-order effects, will become all the more important for such systems.

Cache-coherent systems

One of the more significant differences between our system and many others is our lack of hardware cache-coherence. As a general effect, the lack of cache-coherence makes physical locality more important in our kernel than in others, since we run with most of the kernel data uncached and hence cannot take advantage of temporal locality.

Cache-coherent NUMA and COMA systems have higher data access bandwidth and lower access latency when data is read shared, which suggests that our software techniques for increasing data bandwidth and reducing access latency would be less important in such systems. However, for many kernel data structures we do not believe this to be the case. For example, the HURRICANE memory manager modifies the reference count on page descriptors when a page is mapped into an application address space, and hence page descriptors cannot be replicated efficiently using hardware cache coherence; with hierarchical clustering, a separate local reference count is maintained for each instance of the page descriptor replicated by software. Also, it is still important to limit the number of processors that can contend for a lock, and distribute kernel data structures so that they are near requesting processors. Hence we believe that hierarchical clustering can help, even for systems with hardware cache coherence.

(As an aside, we believe that one might want to run with some portions of the kernel data uncached, even in a hardware cache-coherent system. Running uncached eliminates cache-line-based false sharing, and with it the cache-line ping-pong effects that often occur when data with different access patterns share cache lines. Also, temporal and spatial locality in current operating systems is often quite poor [4, 24], leading to very low cache hit rates, reducing the benefits of cache-coherence.)

Advanced atomic primitives

The atomic-swap operation supported by our processor requires two main memory accesses and is hence relatively slow compared to cache-based atomic operations which permit a lock to be acquired without going to memory (provided the cache-line is currently held in the exclusive state). Newer systems also provide more powerful atomic primitives, such as compare-and-swap (CAS) and load-linked/store-conditional (LL/SC), which allow a number of additional optimizations that were not available to us in our system.

The benefits of our hybrid locking strategy come primarily from the reduced number of atomic primitives required, their reduced space overhead, and their natural support for performing multiple simple atomic operations under a single lock. However, cache-based atomic primitives can reduce the cost of atomic operations to close to that of regular memory accesses, bringing into question our focus on reducing the number of atomic operations required for locking. The trade-off between atomic and regular memory accesses depends, however, on subtle implementation issues that can change from year to year. We believe that reducing the number of atomic operations will likely remain beneficial, although not at the expense of larger numbers of regular loads and stores, and hence this benefit of hybrid locking should still apply.

Both CAS and LL/SC instructions allow single bit locks to be implemented that can share a word with other data, thus eliminating another advantage of the hybrid locks. However, the hybrid-lock technique of using coarse-grained locks to protect large data structures has the advantage that multiple operations (such as dequeuing and locking an element) can be performed atomically under a single lock. Hence hybrid locks, with Distributed Locks as the coarse-grain locks, would remain a good choice.

Distributed Locks are affected by cache-based locks in a number of ways. The trade-off between regular spin locks, our version of MCS Distributed Locks, and newer cache-based queueing locks which are optimized for the contended case [5, 17] depends on three primary factors:

1) the degree of sharing of the locks (and thus its hit rate); 2) the amount of steady-state contention expected; and 3) the probability of bursts of very high contention. For low sharing, low steady-state contention, and low burstiness, spin locks would be the better choice, since they have the lowest latency. With higher degrees of sharing the savings from using spin locks are likely to be minimal, since the cost of the cache misses will swamp any savings. In addition, if occasional burstiness is a problem, spin locks must also be ruled out because of the second-order effects from cache-coherence traffic. If the steady-state contention is expected to be low, our modified MCS locks have the advantage, since they have lower latency than other queueing locks. Finally, if high contention is common, the cache-based queueing locks would be the better choice, since their contended-case performance is better than the MCS locks.

Finally, LL/SC or CAS instructions, whether cached or not, can be used to implement lock-free operations, which can remove the need for locks entirely [18]. Lock-free data structures have a number of benefits, both in terms of performance (by removing the extra space and time cost of locks) and in terms of functionality (they eliminate deadlock), but also have a number of disadvantages. Because only a single word (or double word) can be updated atomically, modifications often become more complex: either an entire data structure is copied, changes made to the copy, and a pointer to the copy atomically swapped in (provided the previous pointer still points to the original copy [11]); or the changes can be performed as a series of atomic operations on single words, but only if each change leaves the full data structures in a valid, consistent state [18]. The first approach can be very expensive if the data structure is large, while the second approach requires finding safe states for each atomic change, which can be difficult and error prone. Even when atomic modifications can be done with a small number of atomic primitives, it may still be more efficient to use regular locks depending on the true relative cost of the atomic primitives compared to regular loads and stores. Finally one must be careful about the possibility of starvation using the lock-free approach.[7]

5.3 Current Directions

We are currently in the process of redesigning our locking strategy for our next operating system, TORNADO, targeting a new, T5-based multiprocessor called NUMAchine. This multiprocessor will have an order of magnitude faster processors, cache-coherence support in hardware, cache-based LL/SC instructions, and network caches. Our initial design considerations include:

- Operating systems have traditionally had poor caching behavior [4, 24]. However, we believe this is primarily because caching and multiprocessor cache-coherence

---

[7]An alternative is to use a wait-free approach, but this is generally much more expensive [10].

effects have been largely ignored in the design of operating systems. Today's processor speeds relative to memory speeds make it imperative to seriously consider the caching effects. We believe it is possible to design the data structures and the locking architecture of an operating system to be cache friendly. Since 10 to 20 lock operations can be performed in the processor's primary cache in the time it takes to service a single cache miss, improving locality and reducing the sharing of locks is likely to be more important than reducing the number of locks.

- We are considering using lock-free data structures for simple leaf locks, particularly for data structures that are required by interrupt handlers and if the data to be modified is contained in a single word.

- Clustering to bound contention and increase lock bandwidth is a clear necessity and should prove to be even more beneficial in our new, larger and faster system.

- Although some of the benefits of our hybrid locks observed in our current system will no longer apply to our new system, their ability to reduce the number of critical sections and to simplify atomic operations involving multiple data structures is still valuable.

- We are currently investigating alternative deadlock management schemes such as the timestamp based approach used in the OSF/1 UFS implementation [16], to be used in conjunction with hierarchical clustering. We hope to be able to preserve the simplicity of the pessimistic approach, and the performance of the optimistic approach.

- Finally, we are starting with a more process-oriented kernel, in part to remove some of the complications of clustering and deadlock, and in part because we believe dynamic process creation can be made to be very fast [8]. We will be reducing our reliance on spin locks, choosing instead to use either lock-free data structures or spin-then-block locks, depending on the situation. As such, the benefits of distributed spin locks will likely be reduced, although it should be possible to support process blocking under distributed locks by building on some of the techniques described in Section 3.2 for handling TryLock.

6 Concluding Remarks

In this paper, we have described a new locking architecture designed for large-scale shared-memory multiprocessors. This architecture consists of a number of components that together provide high performance and scalability. First, a hybrid coarse-grain/fine-grain locking strategy is used that has the low latency and space overhead of a coarse-grained locking strategy, while having the high concurrency

of a fine-grained locking strategy. The coarse-grained locks protect large amounts of data, but may only be held for short periods of time. The fine-grained locks must be set under the protection of coarse-grained locks, but can protect individual objects, require only a single bit of storage, and may be held for longer periods of time.

Second, Hierarchical Clustering extends the effectiveness of the hybrid locking strategy to large systems. It organizes the processors into clusters, with separate instances of data structures and the locks that protect them on each cluster. Primarily read-shared data is replicated as needed to accessing clusters, increasing concurrency. Because only processors local to the cluster may access the data in the cluster (requiring an RPC to access remote data), the number of processors contending for a lock is bounded, limiting second-order contention effects on the fine-grained locks.

Finally, Distributed Locks are used to further reduce the second-order effects of lock contention. Our modifications to Distributed Locks bring their uncontended cost close to that of spin locks.

The results of our performance experiments clearly demonstrate the effectiveness of our strategy, at least for our current hardware base. The independent fault test showed little contention for the coarse-grained locks up to 4 processors, suggesting that this aspect of the hybrid locking strategy is appropriate for clusters with up to 8 or even 16 processors under more realistic workloads. However, for non-independent faults, which require greater cross-processor interactions, cluster sizes larger than 4 provided the best performance. Taken together these results suggest that with a mix of real applications having both independent and non-independent demands, a cluster size somewhere in the range of 4 to 16 processors would be optimal for our system.

Overall, we have found that the design of a locking architecture is largely an exercise in global optimization, as one tries to balance the strengths and weaknesses of both the techniques and the underlying hardware. However, we believe that many of the techniques presented in this paper will also apply to other systems.

References

[1] David L. Black, Avadis Tevanian Jr. , David B. Golub, and Michael W. Young. Locking and reference counting in the mach kernel. In *Proc. 1991 ICPP*, volume II, Software, pages II–167–II–173, Boca Raton, FL, August 1991. CRC Press.

[2] H.H.Y. Chang and B. Rosenburg. Experience porting mach to the RP3 large-scale shared-memory multiprocessor. *Future Generation Computer Systems*, 7(2–3):259–267, April 1992.

[3] E. Chaves, P.C Das, T. J. LeBlanc, B. D. Marsh, and M. L. Scott. Kernel-kernel communication in a shared-

memory multiprocessor. *Concurrency: Practice and Experience*, 5(3):171–191, May 1993.

[4] J. Bradley Chen and Brian N. Bershad. The impact of operating system structure on memory system performance. In *Proc. 14th ACM SOSP*, pages 120–133, 1993.

[5] Travis S. Craig. Building FIFO and priority-queuing spin locks from atomic swap. Technical Report TR 93-02-02, University of Washington, 02 1993. (ftp tr/1993/02/UW-CSE-93-02-02.PS.Z from cs.washington.edu).

[6] R. P. Draves, B. N. Bershad, R. F. Rashid, and R. W. Dean. Using continuations to implement thread management and communication in operating systems. In *Proc. 13th ACM SOSP*, page 122, Pacific Grove, CA, October 1991.

[7] S. Frank, J. Rothnie, and H. Burkhardt. The KSR1: Bridging the gap between shared memory and MPPs. In *IEEE Compcon 1993 Digest of Papers*, pages 285–294, 1993.

[8] B. Gamsa, O. Krieger, and M. Stumm. Optimizing IPC performance for shared-memory multiprocessors. In *Proc. 1994 ICPP*, pages 208–211, Boca Raton, FL, August 1994. CRC Press.

[9] Erik Hagersten, Anders Landin, and Seif Haridi. "DDM – A Cache-Only Memory Architecture". *IEEE Computer*, pages 44–54, September 1992.

[10] Maurice Herlihy. Wait-free synchronization. *ACM TOPLAS*, 13(1):124–149, January 1991.

[11] Maurice Herlihy. A methodology for implementing highly concurrent objects. *ACM TOPLAS*, 15(5):745–770, November 1993.

[12] J. Kent Peacock, S. Saxena, D. Thomas, F. Yang, and W. Yu. Experiences from multithreading system V release 4. In *SEDMS III*, pages 77–91. Usenix Assoc, March 1992.

[13] Orran Krieger. *HFS: A flexible file system for shared memory multiprocessors*. PhD thesis, Department of Electrical and Computer Engineering, University of Toronto, Toronto, Canada, 1994.

[14] Orran Krieger, Michael Stumm, and Ronald Unrau. The Alloc Stream Facility: A redesign of application-level stream I/O. Technical Report CSRI-275, Computer Systems Research Institute, University of Toronto, Toronto, Canada, M5S 1A1, October 1992.

[15] Beng-Hong Lim and Anant Agarwal. Reactive synchronization algorithms for multiprocessors. In *ASPLOS-VI*, 1994. To appear.

[16] Susan LoVerso, Noemi Paciorek, Alan Langerman, and George Feinberg. The OSF/1 UNIX filesystem (UFS). In *USENIX Conference Proceedings*, pages 207–218, Dallas, TX, January 21-25 1991. USENIX.

[17] Peter Magnussen, Anders Landin, and Erik Hagersten. Queue locks on cache coherent multiprocessors. In *8th IPPS*, pages 26–29, 1994.

[18] H. Massalin and C. Pu. A lock-free multiprocessor OS kernel. Technical Report CUCS-005-91, Department of Computer Science, Columbia University, February 1991.

[19] J.M. Mellor-Crummey and M.L. Scott. "Algorithms for Scalable Synchronization on Shared-Memory Multiprocessors". *ACM Transactions on Computer Systems*, 9(1):21–65, February 1991.

[20] Noemi Paciorek, Susan Lo Verso, and Alan Langerman. Debugging multiprocessor operating system kernels. In *SEDMS II*, pages 185–202. USENIX, Atlanta GA, March 21 - 22 1991.

[21] J. Kent Peacock. File system multithreading in system V release 4 MP. In *USENIX Conference Proceedings*, pages 19–30, San Antonio, TX, Summer 1992. USENIX.

[22] Abraham Silberschatz, James L. Peterson, and Peter Galvin. *Operating Systems Concepts*. Addison-Wesley, third edition edition, 1991.

[23] Daniel Stodolsky, J. Bradley Chen, and Brian N. Bershad. Fast interrupt priority management in operating system kernels. In *USENIX Microkernels Workshop*. USENIX, 1993.

[24] Josep Torrellas, Anoop Gupta, and John L. Hennessy. Characterizing the caching and synchronization performance of a multiprocessor operating system. In *ASPLOS-IV Proceedings*, pages 162–174, Boston, Massachusetts, 1992.

[25] R. Unrau, M. Stumm, O. Krieger, and B. Gamsa. Hierarchical clustering: A structure for scalable multiprocessor operating system design. *Journal of Supercomputing*. To appear. Also available as technical report CSRI-268 from ftp.csri.toronto.edu.

[26] Ronald C. Unrau. *Scalable Memory Management through Hierarchical Symmetric Multiprocessing*. PhD thesis, Department of Electrical and Computer Engineering, University of Toronto, Toronto, Canada, January 1993.

[27] Zvonko G. Vranesic, Michael Stumm, Ron White, and David Lewis. "The Hector Multiprocessor". *Computer*, 24(1), January 1991.

HiPEC: High Performance External Virtual Memory Caching

Chao-Hsien Lee[†], Meng Chang Chen[‡] and Ruei-Chuan Chang[††]

Department of Computer and Information Science[†]
National Chiao Tung University, Taiwan, ROC
paul@os.nctu.edu.tw

Institute of Information Science[‡]
Academia Sinica, Taiwan, ROC
{mcc,rc}@iis.sinica.edu.tw

Abstract

Traditional operating systems use a fixed LRU-like page replacement policy and centralized frame pool that cannot properly serve all types of memory access patterns of various applications. As a result, many memory-intensive applications, such as databases, multimedia applications and scientific simulators, induce excessive page faults and page replacement when running on top of existing operating systems.

This paper presents a High Performance External virtual memory Caching mechanism (HiPEC) to provide applications with their own specific page replacement management. The user specific policy, programmed in the HiPEC command set, is stored in user address space. When a page fault occurs, the kernel fetches and interprets the corresponding policy commands to perform the user-specific page replacement management. Experimental results show that HiPEC induces little overhead and can significantly improve performance for memory-intensive applications.

1 Introduction

Though technological advances have greatly improved the speed and enlarged the memory capacity of computer systems, because of the increasing size of applications, it is still impossible to load all applications and their data sets into physical memory at one time. Existing virtual memory management schemes can be used to compensate for limited memory size by sharing the physical frame pool among all applications. In current operating systems, a fixed LRU-like page replacement policy is usually used to handle memory sharing. This fixed LRU-like page replacement policy performs well when the applications have limited memory requirements or random memory access patterns, but it is unsuitable for many memory-intensive applications,

such as databases [27], multimedia applications [24], and scientific simulators [23].

The reasons for this are the following. First, a fixed LRU-like page replacement policy and centralized frame pool that cannot properly serve all types of memory access patterns of various applications. As a result, memory intensive applications tend to induce excessive page faults and page replacement. Since page replacement usually involves disk I/O operations that are far slower than processor computation and memory access, the performance of memory-intensive applications degenerates.

Second, the operating system kernel cannot predict application access patterns and user applications know nothing about their virtual memory caching status. Since all the applications share the same centralized frame pool, the lack of information sharing between the kernel and user applications leads to unnecessary paging activities. Ideally, if the kernel and user applications share information in page replacement decision-making, and each application manages its private frame pool, the system can achieve high performance virtual memory caching by reducing unnecessary page replacement. However, the information sharing induces expensive overhead if the kernel should transfer control to user applications, or user applications should transfer control to kernel.

In this paper, we present a new mechanism, HiPEC (High Performance External virtual memory Caching), to support application-controlled virtual memory page replacement management. HiPEC is based on the Mach 3.0 kernel but can easily be ported to other operating systems. Recent research has addressed similar virtual memory caching problems. This research will be reviewed in Section 2. The motivation for HiPEC and system design are described in Section 3. The overall architecture of HiPEC and the implementation are presented in Section 4. In Section 5, several measurements and experiments are used to evaluate the overhead of HiPEC and the performance improvement

The research described in this paper was partially supported by NSC under grant NSC83-0408-E-001-008.

for specific applications that using the HiPEC mechanism. Section 6 concludes the paper and presents suggestions for future work.

2 Related Work

Many advanced operating systems and research prototypes have addressed the virtual memory caching problems. Mach [1], V++ [8] [11], Spring [18], and SPIN [6] all put the external memory management into their designs. In Mach, an external pager [32] is responsible for paging in and paging out memory-mapped data, which can be shared in a distributed environment because each data object is represented as a Mach IPC port. External pager is powerful but it lacks interfaces for applications to handle page replacement management.

McNamee's PREMO extends the external pager interfaces so that the page replacement facility is exported to applications [21]. The system-maintained information, such as reference and modify bits for each page frame, can be obtained by invoking PREMO-created system calls. This simple and direct modification of Mach reduces the number of page faults by 15% in a synthetic benchmark program. However, PREMO does not take into account the interference from other applications. PREMO puts all the page frames in one pool, which makes specific applications susceptible to unnecessary paging activities because of interference between applications.

In addition, although PREMO provides reference and modify information, it does not supply other information, such as the number of physical frames under control, which is essential to the performance of specific applications. Moreover, the IPC overhead for communication between the kernel and external pager is high. Even if the communications are implemented by upcall, as Krueger suggested [17], it is still expensive to upcall from the kernel to the user application and then call back from the user to the kernel because of the runtime stack changes.

In Sechrest's work [28], the centralized frame pool is partitioned into separate private frame lists when new memory objects are created. Specific applications have their own PageOut Daemon (POD) to handle their own memory object management, while non-specific applications are handled by a default POD. The weakness of this approach is its lack of security: information is shared between the kernel and applications without protection. The strategy of [28] is to trust on specific application designers.

Spring [18] has an external paging mechanism similar to Mach except that it separates the memory object from the pager object. The caching objects are also controlled by the kernel without user participation.

V++ and SPIN are designed for application-controlled external page-cache management. V++ uses a segment manager to handle page faults and has interfaces to request and migrate page frames to and from different segment managers. It uses a memory market approach [10] to handle global memory allocation among segment managers. However, all the operations or requests involve transferring control among different address spaces. This incurs extra IPC overhead compared to an in-kernel integrated implementation.

SPIN is an extensible operating system for dynamic creation of system services. The dynamically created objects, called *spindles*, allow applications to have specific control of their allocated system resources, such as processors, memory, and network protocols. Using optimized compiling and dynamic linking skills, SPIN provides applications with full control of allocated system resources. Applications running under SPIN can achieve maximum performance without overhead from crossing the kernel/user boundary.

HiPEC is similar to SPIN in that it does not need to cross the kernel/user boundary when executing a user-specific page replacement policy. SPIN creates its application-specific control by linking the compiled object code into the kernel. It requires dynamic compiling and linking when new services are created. On the contrary, HiPEC does not create any object codes. Instead, HiPEC interprets the specific control codes placed in the user buffer area. This design provides more flexibility and requires less modification of the operating system kernel.

Mogul's work [22], the *packet filter*, is worth mentioned, although it is not related to user level memory management. The packet filter is a kernel-resident, protocol independent packet demultiplexer. Users can program their filters in the filter language, which is similar to, but simpler than, HiPEC commands. The filter is interpreted by the packet filter when system receives a packet. The goals of the packet filter are the reduction of the rate of context switches, and easy to port and test communication protocols.

3 Motivation and System Design

Due to the variety of memory access patterns of applications, operating systems must be flexible enough to support different page replacement strategies to meet the individual needs. When several page replacement strategies run at a time, it is important to reduce the interference from each other to maintain the performance of applications. One solution is to partition the centralized frame pool into separate lists that each list is allocated to a specific application* and managed

---

*A *specific application* is defined as an application uses HiPEC mechanism in this paper.

by the application. In addition, the kernel and specific applications need to cooperate with each other to make good allocation and replacement decisions.

There are several communication techniques available between kernel and applications. When an application needs information from kernel, it uses system calls or sends messages to communicate with kernel. Upcalls are often used by kernel to activate applications functions. Since requiring context switches, all the techniques are expensive. Another approach is to use shared memory to map shared data structures between kernel and user applications. Though this approach can speed up data access, the data has to be collected and mapped into fixed locations which is expensive too. Moreover, if the shared area is mapped with read/write permission, the security of the operating system kernel might be compromised. Consequently, kernel crossing is the source of overhead and potential problems.

Instead of finding an efficient technique for crossing the kernel boundary, HiPEC employs an integrated in-kernel implementation. In HiPEC, a specific application only needs to place its specific page replacement policy, coded as a sequence of commands in HiPEC command set, in the user space and store the pointer in an object known to the kernel. When page replacement is needed, the kernel fetches, decodes and interprets the command codes to perform the application specific page replacement policy.

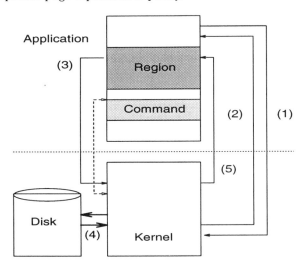

Figure 1: The Proposed Mechanism for Application Specific Control.

Figure 1 illustrates the proposed mechanism for application-specific control. The address space of specific application is partitioned into regions of continuous virtual memory. The region is the basic unit of specific control. The command codes implementing the application page replacement policy are stored in the command buffer. To activate HiPEC mechanism, the specific application first (1) calls the HiPEC-created system call with parameters including the starting address and size of the virtual memory region, and pointer to the command buffer. Normally, the specific application obtains the corresponding private frame list from the kernel, as in (2). When a page fault is generated inside the region, the application traps to the kernel as shown in the step (3). If a page replacement decision is needed, the kernel fetches the commands from the command buffer, decodes the commands and performs the required operations. After allocating physical frames for the faulted region, the kernel reads data from the disk and stores the data to the faulted address, as in step (4). Finally, in the step (5), the page fault is resolved and the application resumes its work.

This design has several advantages:

- A high degree of efficiency can be achieved because no need to cross the kernel boundary and the overhead for fetching and decoding commands is low.

- System security is guaranteed because the kernel data structure is accessed by the kernel-provided operations only. Applications cannot access protected information.

- The command codes can be treated as a portable interface for specific applications. The details of virtual memory management and system-maintained data structures are shielded from applications and designers. As a result, specific application designers do not need to consider tedious operating system internals in their design.

- High performance gain is obtainable if specific application designers know the access patterns of their applications and are able to program an efficient replacement policy in HiPEC command set.

4 HiPEC Implementation

HiPEC has been implemented on OSF/1 MK 5.0.2 operating system that extends the external memory management (EMM) interface of Mach kernel to support external virtual memory caching management. With this extension, applications can control the paging activities of memory-mapped data via the external pager [31] interface and handle the page replacement policy of a virtual memory region. Wang's implementation [30] shows that little performance overhead is incurred for running an EMM interface on BSD UNIX. This result implies that HiPEC can be ported to operating systems to support virtual memory caching management no matter whether there is an EMM interface embedded in the operating systems.

Though the current HiPEC virtual memory caching management is based on the Mach EMM interface, the concept and implementation of HiPEC is independent from the interface. Specific applications can use HiPEC to control dynamically created virtual memory regions without the help of an external pager. HiPEC has several constituents, including the *security checker, policy executor, command buffer, global frame manager, user-level pseudo code translator,* and *HiPEC command set.*

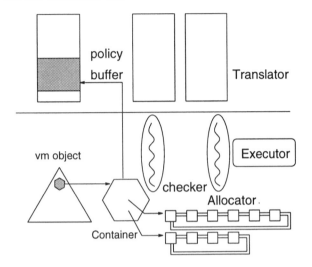

Figure 2: HiPEC Architecture.

4.1 Architecture Overview

HiPEC is composed of a set of kernel data structures, procedures, kernel threads, and user-level libraries and utilities. The architecture of HiPEC is illustrated in Figure 2. The global frame manager, implemented from Mach pageout daemon, is responsible for allocating free frames to and deallocating frames from applications. The VM object is used in the Mach kernel to represent a segment of virtual memory region that can be a memory-mapped data file or a segment of address space with the same protection attributes. One new kernel object, *container*, is added to record useful information for the HiPEC mechanism. Container is created from the zone system [29] and mounted under VM object when HiPEC is invoked by specific applications. A list of free frames, allocated by the global frame manager, is mounted under the container. The important information stored in the container includes pointer to next container, pointers to related VM objects and threads, pointers to the HiPEC command buffers, pointers to allocated free frame lists, operand array, and a timeout flag.

The command buffer is a wired down user-level area, used to store the application-specific page replacement policy. The buffer is set as read-only after a specific

application invokes HiPEC and the buffer is passed as a parameter to kernel. If applications attempt to modify the contents of the policy buffer, a write fault occurs. The page fault handling routines check the address of the fault, and terminate the application with a error message.

The policy executor, called by the page fault handler, fetches the HiPEC commands for the event, decodes them, and performs the operations. Since executor resides in kernel address space, it can fetch the commands without kernel crossing or stack changing. The overhead introduced is just the time for fetch and decode several HiPEC commands.

The security checker is implemented as a kernel thread to check illegitimate HiPEC commands and detect abnormal policy execution. In the current implementation, the checker checks whether HiPEC commands have an invalid format or are inconsistent. The checker is periodically awakened to detect timeouts of policy executions. Since policy execution is performed in kernel mode, bad policies from malicious users or due to program mistakes can compromise system integrity and degenerate performance. The security checker ensures the robustness of the system. The detailed structure of each component of HiPEC is discussed in the following subsections.

4.2 HiPEC Commands

Figure 3: The HiPEC Command Format.

A HiPEC command is a 32-bit long word that contains an 8-bit operator code and up to three operands, as depicted in Figure 3. The operand is an 8-bit long integer which is used as an index to one entry in the operand array. The operand array is stored in a container with up to 256 entries. Each entry in the operand array is a pointer to a variable. The types of the variable can be as simple as an unsigned integer, or as complex as the virtual memory page structure or page queue list.

There are 20 commands in the current implementation: *Return, Arith, Comp, Logic, EmptyQ, InQ, Jump, DeQueue, EnQueue, Request, Release, Flush, Set, Ref, Mod, Find, Activate, FIFO, LRU* and *MRU*. The syntax and semantics of each command are listed in Table 1.

Each command is implemented in the kernel as a macro or a procedure call. HiPEC commands range from complex commands, such as the page replacement policies FIFO, LRU, and MRU, to simple ones, such as Arith and Comp. The more complex a com-

Command	Binary	Op1	Op2	Flag	Operations
Return	00000000	op	—	—	The end of execution. Return value is stored in *op*.
Arith	00000001	op1	op2	flag	Arithmetic operations for integer operands.
Comp	00000010	op1	op2	flag	Comparison operations for integer operands.
Logic	00000011	op1	op2	flag	Logical operations for boolean operands.
EmptQ	00000100	op	—	—	Test if queue *op* is empty.
InQ	00000101	op1	op2	—	Test if page *op2* is in queue *op1*.
Jump	00000110	CC			Branch to next command. *CC* is the command counter.
DeQueue	00000111	op1	op2	flag	Move the page *op1* from queue *op2*.
EnQueue	00001000	op1	op2	flag	Add page *op1* to queue *op2*.
Request	00001001	Size			Request *Size* frames from frame manager.
Release	00001010	op	—	—	Release *op* frame to frame manager.
Flush	00001011	op	—	—	Flush page *op* to disk.
Set	00001100	op1	flag1	flag2	Set or reset reference or modify bit of page *op1*.
Ref	00001101	op	—	—	Test if page *op* is referenced or not.
Mod	00001110	op	—	—	Test if page *op* is modified or not.
Find	00001111	op1	op2	flag	Given virtual address *op2*, find the associated page frame *op1*.
Activate	00010000	op	—	—	Invoke another policy event. *op* is the event number.
FIFO	00010001	op	—	—	Execute FIFO page replacement policy for the *op* queue.
LRU	00010010	op	—	—	Execute LRU page replacement policy for the *op* queue.
MRU	00010011	op	—	—	Execute MRU page replacement policy for the *op* queue.

Table 1: The HiPEC Command Set.

mand is, the less overhead it creates because the policy executor does not need to fetch and interpret many commands during execution. While the simple commands induce more overhead in executing the page replacement policy, they are flexible for application designers to program a specific policy. Though only 20 commands are defined in the current implementation, they are powerful enough for many specific applications. Since the HiPEC command code is 8 bits long, there can be up to 256 different commands. It is easy to add new commands to HiPEC if more commands are needed to handle page replacement. A HiPEC program can be created by a user-level translator from a high-level pseudo code program or by hand coding.

When an event occurs, a segment of a HiPEC command program is called to handle the event. There is no limitation of the number of events that a specific application can define. However, a specific application at least has to handle the two HiPEC-defined events, **PageFault** and **ReclaimFrame**. When page faults occur, the HiPEC commands for PageFault event are interpreted to obtain free frames to handle the fault. The ReclaimFrame event happens when the system needs to retrieve physical frames from user jobs. The non-HiPEC-defined events are activated by other events, which can be viewed as procedure calls. Table 2 is a simple example that implements a FIFO with a second chance LRU-like page replacement policy.

4.3   Implementation

HiPEC mechanism is initialized by two HiPEC system calls, vm_map_hipec() and vm_allocate_hipec(), corresponding to vm_map() and vm_allocate() in Mach respectively. vm_map() maps a file into the application's address space and vm_allocate() allocates a region of unused virtual memory for dynamic or temporary data. When either of these two system calls are invoked, the kernel allocates and initializes the container, allocates free page frames from the global frame manager, and checks the validity of HiPEC commands stored in the policy buffers.

4.3.1   Pageout Daemon Serves as Global Frame Manager

In the HiPEC implementation, the pageout daemon acts as the global frame manager. It allocates free page frames to specific applications, and reclaims them when applications terminate, or when other specific applications request for page frames. Since specific applications and non-specific applications share the same global frame pool, it is important to balance the allocation of free page frames between them. The global frame manager performs four basic tasks: balance, allocation, deallocation, and I/O handling.

- *Balance.* The global frame manager is also the pageout daemon, which is responsible for page allocation and page replacement for non-specific applications when page faults occur. Since the page frame allocation should be fair for both spe-

The PageFault Event

CC	Command Code				The executed operations.
0	HiPEC Magic No				Magic number used for checking.
1	02	02	0C	01	if(_free_count > reserved_target)
2	06	00	00	05	/* else */ Jump to (CC==5)
3	07	0B	01	01	Get page from _free_queue by DeQueue.
4	00	0B	—	—	Return
5	10	02	—	—	Activate Lack_free_frame event.
6	06	00	00	03	Jump

The Lack_Free_Frame Event

CC	Command Code				The executed operations.
0	HiPEC Magic No				Magic number used for checking.
1	02	02	0A	02	if(_free_count < free_target)
2	06	00	00	0E	/* else */Jump to (14)
3	07	0B	00	01	Get page from _inactive_queue by DeQueue.
4	0D	0B	—	—	Judge if the page is referenced
5	06	00	00	09	/* else */Jump to (09)
6	08	0B	03	02	Put page to _active_queue by EnQueue
7	0C	0B	02	01	Reset the page reference bit
8	06	00	00	0E	Jump to (CC==14)
9	0E	0B	—	—	Judge if the page is modified
10	06	00	00	0C	/* else */Jump to (CC==12)
11	0B	0B	—	—	Flush page
12	08	0B	01	01	Put page to free queue by EnQueue
13	06	00	00	01	Jump to (CC==1)
14	02	06	09	02	if (inactive_count < inactive_target)
15	06	00	00	14	/* else */ Jump to (CC==20)
16	07	0B	03	01	Get page from _free_queue by DeQueue
17	0C	0B	02	01	Reset the page reference bit
18	08	0B	05	02	Put page to _inactive_queue
19	06	00	00	0E	Jump to (CC==14)
20	00	00	—	—	Return

Table 2: The FIFO with Second Chance Page Replacement Policy.

cific and non-specific applications, we define a watermark *partition_burst* to monitor the allocation. When the total pages allocated to all the specific applications exceed this watermark, the global frame manager will deallocate pages from specific applications.

Currently, partition_burst is defined as 50% of the available free page frames after the system starts up. This is under the assumption that about the same number of physical page frames are requested by specific and non-specific applications and they should have equal opportunity to be served by the global frame manager. An adaptable or dynamically adjustable partition burst will be studied in the future to investigate the impact on system performance. The effect of other frame allocation methods is also worth studying. However, it is beyond the scope of this paper.

- *Allocation.* When specific applications invoke the HiPEC mechanism, they must identify the size of their memory needs. The parameter *minFrame* is passed to the kernel to request the minimum number of page frames from the global frame manager. Specific applications will keep at least *minFrame* pages during their executions. If the *minFrame* request cannot be satisfied when HiPEC is initially invoked, an error code is returned. The specific application can either run as a non-specific application or terminate and retry later. The *minFrame* of each specific application is decided and administrated by designated privileged users who have the responsibility of system performance.

  If a specific application needs more page frames, the executor executes a *Request* command to request more pages. The global frame manager grants or rejects the request depending on the number of the remaining free page frames and the status of the requester. When the number of requested page frames is more than the available page frames, the request is rejected. The executor checks the returned code to know the status of frame allocation request. Upon request failure, the executor makes the specific page replacement policy to handle the shortage of page frames. Consequently, the HiPEC executor will not be hung indefinitely for waiting the return from the global frame manager.

- *Deallocation.* The global frame manager retrieves page frames from specific applications when their VM region is deallocated. The second situation is when global frame manager has fewer available free page frames than the *minFrame* requests from new specific applications. The last situation

of reclamation is when the total pages allocated to specific application exceed the *partition_burst*. The global frame manager reclaims page frames from specific applications with more pages than their minimal request(i.e. *minFrame* pages) only.

The reclamation of frames can be normal reclamation and forced reclamation. When HiPEC is invoked, the newly created container is added to the end of the list that links all containers. A simple policy, FAFR (First Allocated, First Reclaimed), is implemented to select the victims of reclamation. The procedure of normal reclamation is that the global frame manager follows the container list and selects the first container to release page frames until the request is satisfied. The global frame manager calls the policy executor to execute the **ReclaimFrame** event of a selected specific application to return pages to the system. This ReclaimFrame event allows specific applications to decide which pages are less important and can be released.

The global frame manager starts forced reclamation when it cannot retrieve enough page frames from normal reclamation. Since all the allocated page frames of all specific applications are linked in the sequence of the time of allocation, the global frame manager can reclaim frame pages from the list. The reclaimed dirty pages are linked to a VM object and are flushed to disk by the global frame manager later.

- *I/O Handling.* The global frame manager also performs page flushing for specific applications. When a policy executor wants to flush a page using *Flush* command, it releases the flushed page to a VM object of the global frame manager and receives a new free page from the global frame manager. The real flushing operation is done by the global frame manager later. This design prevents the executor from having to wait for disk I/O operations. Otherwise, the executor may timeout often and terminated by the checker when waiting for the time consuming disk I/O operations.

4.3.2 Application-Specific Policy Executor

When invoked by the page fault handler or global frame manager, the policy executor fetches commands from policy buffers, decodes them, and executes the corresponding operations. The policy executed depends on the type of event that occurs for the specific VM object. At the begin of execution, the policy executor first writes a timestamp into the container to record the starting time of execution. This timestamp is checked by security checker to detect timeout of policy execution. The container also contains a CC

(Command Counter) variable that is used to record the address of the next HiPEC command to be interpreted. Since the policy executor runs in kernel mode and can directly access both kernel and user address spaces, it does not need to transfer control from kernel to user applications when fetching the commands. The executor will keep running until it reads **Return** from the policy buffers.

4.3.3 In-Kernel Security Checker

The security checker is implemented as a kernel thread that checks the validity of application-specific page replacement policies. In the current version, the security checker only checks for illegal syntax of commands, such as the wrong number or illegal type of operands. Another duty of the checker is to detect timeouts of policy executions. The checker is awakened periodically by the timer. The length of sleeping time is adjusted according to whether a timeout is detected by the checker. Every time a timeout is detected, the sleeping time for the checker is halved. If no timeout execution is detected, the time is doubled. Since normally there are very few runaway policy executions, the checker sleeps most of the time and does not create enormous overhead to degenerate system performance. The formula of the sleeping time of the checker is described in the following equation:

$$
\text{WakeUp} = \begin{cases} WakeUp/2 & \text{if timeout detected} \\ WakeUp * 2 & \text{if no timeout detected} \\ 250msec & \text{if WakeUp} \leq 250 \text{ msec} \\ 8sec & \text{if WakeUp} \geq 8 \text{ sec} \end{cases}
$$

When the checker is awakened, it checks the stored timestamp of each container by traversing the container link list. A policy execution is treated as a timeout if the execution time is longer than the *TimeOut* period. Currently, the length of *TimeOut* period is determined manually by a privileged user. When the checker finds an executor has run longer than the timeout period, the corresponding specific application will be terminated by the checker.

4.3.4 Pseudo Code Translator and Library

It is not convenient for a programmer to design a page replacement policy by directly using the low-level HiPEC command set. We implement a pseudo code translator to assist application designers in their programming. The translator translates C language like pseudo codes into a stream of HiPEC command codes. The translator is implemented as a stand alone program and is also incorporated into the user level library. The HiPEC event is represented as a procedure call in the pseudo code program with the **Event** type. Figure 4 shows an example of a pseudo code program

```
Event PageFault() {
if (_free_count > reserve_target)
    page = de_queue_head(_free_queue)
else begin
    Lack_free_frame()
    page = de_queue_head(_free_queue)
endif
return(page)
}
Event Lack_free_frame() { /* FIFO with 2th Chance */
while (_inactive_count < inactive_target) {
        page = de_queue_head(_active_queue)
        reset(page.reference)
        en_queue_tail(_inactive_queue)
}
while (_free_count < free_target) {
        page = de_queue_head(_inactive_queue)
        if (page.reference) begin
          en_queue_tail(_active_queue,page)
          reset(page.reference)
          end
        else begin
            if (page.dirty) begin
              flush(page)
            end
            en_queue_head(_free_queue,page)
        end
}
}
Event ReclaimFrame() { ...... }
```

Figure 4: Pseudo Code Program for FIFO with Second Chance Caching Policy.

that implements a FIFO with a second chance page replacement policy.

5 Experiments and Performance Evaluation

The advantage of HiPEC over previous techniques is that it does not need to transfer control between kernel and applications. The cost is the time for fetching and decoding HiPEC commands, execution of security checker and miscellaneous processings. In this section, three experiments are designed to measure the overhead and evaluate the performance of HiPEC mechanism. The experimental results show that HiPEC induces little overhead and can significantly improve performance for memory-intensive applications.

The first experiment presents the measurements of HiPEC mechanism that are compared with other techniques. The second experiment shows negligible overhead of HiPEC for non-specific applications. The last

Evaluation	Average Time Overhead
40 Mbytes page fault	
Without disk I/O operations	
Running on Mach 3.0 Kernel	4016.5 msec
Running on HiPEC mechanism	4088.6 msec
HiPEC Overhead	1.8%
40 Mbytes page fault	
with disk I/O operations	
Running on Mach 3.0 Kernel	82485.5 msec
Running on HiPEC mechanism	82505.6 msec
HiPEC Overhead	0.024%

Table 3: Comparison — I.

Evaluation	Average Time
Null System Call	19 μ sec
Null IPC Call	292 μ sec
Simple HiPEC page fault overhead	$\cong$150 nsec

Table 4: Comparison — II.

experiment show the merit of HiPEC in allowing specific applications to have great performance improvement by using their specific page replacement policy. All the experiments are performed on an Acer Altos 10000 machine, which has two Intel 486-50 CPUs and 64 Megabytes main memory. One CPU is disabled during the experiments to prevent unexpected interference.

5.1 Measurements of HiPEC Mechanism

In this experiment, we want to find out the overhead created by HiPEC and compare with other techniques that are usually used to implement application-specific page replacement management. We measure the page fault handling time for accessing 40 Megabytes virtual address space both under Mach kernel and HiPEC. To make the comparison fair, the HiPEC environment has implemented the same FIFO with a second chance page replacement policy as in Mach kernel [13] and both request 40 Megabytes for their private management. In order to distinguish the effect of disk I/O on the overall execution time, we measure the elapsed time with and without disk I/O operations separately. From Table 3, the overhead incurred by HiPEC is so small that can be compensated by as few as one or two disk page I/O operations. In the experiment 3, it is shown that a specific application with right replacement policy can reduce unnecessary page replacements.

The common techniques used to provide application specific resource management are upcall and IPC. Upcalls are implemented as procedure invocations from the kernel to user applications. The overhead is mainly in allocating area for new user stack and changing stacks. In Mach, the IPC mechanism is implemented by message passing. The time for null system call is used to describe the upcall overhead. For IPC, we measure the execution time of a null IPC.

Since HiPEC overhead is mostly determined by the

programmed policy, we again use the FIFO with a second chance page replacement policy as the referenced policy. The overhead created by HiPEC mechanism in simple page fault is negligible, because it is only the time to fetch and decode *Comp, DeQueue, Return* commands. We use approximation notation to represent the simple page fault overhead for HiPEC mechanism, because the time measured is too small that can be easily affected by other system activities. It is concluded from Table 4 that HiPEC is more efficient than the upcall or IPC techniques.

5.2 The System Throughputs of Modified and Unmodified Mach Kernel

In this experiment, we want to find out the overhead of HiPEC to non-specific applications. We run a synthetic system benchmark, AIM, on the original Mach kernel and modified HiPEC kernel to compare the overall system throughput. The AIM suite III benchmark [3] is designed to compare the system performance of various platforms and operating systems. Users can tune the workload mix by giving weights to different kind of simulated jobs to measure system throughputs.

HiPEC implementation has added checking statements to Mach kernel in the page fault handling routines to decide whether the faulted virtual address is located in the regions controlled by the specific applications. Another HiPEC implementation overhead for non-specific applications is from the security checker. The checker is awakened periodically to check if there is any timeout of policy execution. The overhead of the checker depends on the number of specific applications running in the system and the frequency of timeout detected. When only non-specific applications run in the system, the overhead created by the checker is limited.

We use three different workload mixes to evaluate the system throughput. The first is the standard workload. The second workload emphasizes on the disk usage and the third emphasizes on the memory usage. The experimental results are illustrated in Figure 5. When the number of simulated concurrent users is larger than five or six, the throughput is degraded because the users jobs are competing the system resources. From the results in Figure 5, the original

Mach Kernel and modified HiPEC kernel almost provide the same throughput under these three different workload mixes. The overhead created from HiPEC does not have obvious influence on the system performance.

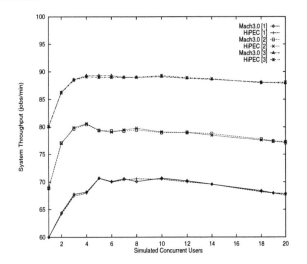

Figure 5: The Throughput on Mach Kernel and HiPEC Kernel.

5.3 Performance Evaluation of Join Operator

Join is one of the most important operations of relational database management systems. We implement a MRU page replacement policy in HiPEC for the nested-loops join operator to show the performance improvement. The other policy used is a LRU-like page replacement policy for its popularity in conventional operating systems. The inner table of the join operator is 4 K bytes and the size of outer table ranges from 20 Megabytes to 60 Megabytes. Both tables are composed of 64 bytes tuples. The output table is dumped immediately in this experiment since we want to focus on the page replacement behavior of outer table. In this experiment, the join operator is implemented as sequentially accessing the tuples in the 4 K inner table and doing join operation with every tuple in the outer table. The inner 4 K table is pinned in memory while the outer table is scanned as many times as the number of tuples in the inner table.

When the size of allocated memory is larger than the outer table, no page replacement will be needed. Otherwise, there are page replacement activities for each scan of outer table. LRU policy chooses the least recently used page frame as the page to be replaced that causes the cyclic faults for every outer loop scan. The number of page faults for LRU is

$$PF_l = \frac{OutLSize * Loop}{PageSize}$$

The $OutLSize$ represents the size of the outer table. The $Loop$ is the scanning times for the outer table. In our experiment, $Loop$ equals to 64. $PageSize$ is the physical page frame size, which is 4096 bytes for our machine.

MRU chooses the most recently used page frame to be replaced. The number of page faults for first scanning the outer table is the page number of outer table. But in the successive scanning, the number of page faults is just the page number difference between the outer loop table and the HiPEC allocated memory. The total number of page faults for MRU is

$$PF_m = \frac{(OutLSize - MSize) * (Loop - 1) + OutLSize}{PageSize}$$

The variable $MSize$ represents the allocated memory size, which is 40 Mega bytes in this experiment. Obviously, MRU is the right solution to the nested-loop join operation. The performance gain is

$$Gain = (PF_l - PF_m) * PFHandleTime$$
$$= \frac{(Loop - 1) * MSize}{PageSize} * PFHandleTime$$

Experimental results show that a great response time gap occurs when data size is larger than available frames, i.e. 40 Megabytes. Figure 6 shows the experimental results which match the analytic result.

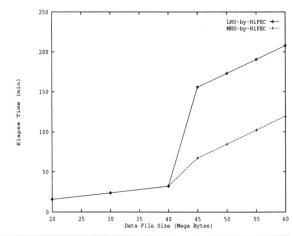

—	30	40	45	50	55	60
LRU	23.8	32.1	155.8	173.1	190.5	207.7
MRU	23.8	32.1	67.5	84.8	102.3	119.5

Figure 6: Elapsed Time (in min.) for The Join Operation.

6 Conclusions and Future Work

In this paper, we considered the virtual memory caching problem for specific applications. We presented the design and implementation of the HiPEC mechanism which provides efficient external page replacement management. The HiPEC mechanism does not require the kernel transfer control to the user applications when the kernel makes page replacement decisions to match the specific applications access patterns. Specific applications use HiPEC command codes to inform the kernel of their specific page replacement policies. The kernel fetches the commands, decodes them and does the corresponding operations.

The shared centralized frame pool is partitioned into private frame lists for each specific application. This separation can avoid interference from other jobs. HiPEC also implements a security checker to check the syntax of the HiPEC command sequence and detect any policy execution timeout. The security checker does not incur heavy overhead because it will sleep often if there is no frequent policy execution timeouts within the system. Several measurements and experiments are also presented to show that the HiPEC mechanism has little overhead as compared to the original integrated kernel services. Specific applications can achieve the maximum performance if the right page replacement policies are designed and managed by using HiPEC.

Though the current version of HiPEC shows successes in solving page replacement problem, there are some jobs that need more considerations in the future. First, we want to consider the page migration operations between relevant specific applications. In our current implementation, specific applications can only return the page frames to the global frame allocator. However migrating physical frames between the relevant jobs might be important and necessary. Relevant jobs can use physical frame migration to share information.

Second, we only define 20 HiPEC commands for doing application-specific control in our current implementation. They are sufficient in the current usage, but not claim they are complete. The new hardware architecture, such as flash RAM, can be managed efficiently if each specific application can control the device to meet its specific requirement. To manage these new hardware architecture, the HiPEC commands should be extended to meet the requirement. Fortunately, adding new HiPEC commands is easy in our implementation. Third, the security checker could do more than the current version in detecting malicious actions or mistakes from the specific applications. Fourth, the global frame allocation and deallocation are extremely important to the system performance. Though the current allocation policy works well, the allocation policy does not address the problems of effective resource usage and pays little attention to fairness.

Lastly, we plan to design a database management system that uses HiPEC to improve the performance and observe database requirements for future enhancement to HiPEC. This is important because the HiPEC mechanism is expected and designed for practical specific applications, not just an experimental product.

Acknowledgments

The authors would like to thank the paper shepherd, Brian Bershad, OSDI program committee as well as reviewers for their valuable comments in improving this paper.

References

[1] Accetta, M. J., Baron, R. V., Bolosky, W., Golub, D. B., Rashid, R. F., Tevanain, Jr. A., and Young, M. W. Mach: A New Kernel Foundation for UNIX Development. In *Proceedings of the Summer 1986 USENIX Conference*, July 1986.

[2] Anderson, Thomas E., Bershad, Brian N., Lazowska, Edward D. and Levy, Henry M. Scheduler Activations: Effective Kernel Support for the User-Level Management of Parallelism. In *Proceedings of the 13th ACM Symposium on Operating System Principles*, October 1991.

[3] AIM Technology AIM Benchmark Suite III User's Guide. 1986.

[4] Black, D. L. Scheduling and Resource Management Techniques for Multiprocessors. Ph.D. dissertation, Carnegie Mellon University, July 1990.

[5] Bershad, Brian N., Anderson, Thomas E., Lazowska, Edward D., and Levy, Henry M. User-Level Interprocess Communication for Shared Memory Multiprocessors. In *ACM Transactions on Computer Systems*, 9(2):175-198, May 1991.

[6] Bershad, Brian N., Chambers, C., Eggers, S., Maeda, C., McNamee, D., Pardyak, P., Savage, S., and Sirer, Emin Gün SPIN - An Extensible Microkernel for Application-specific Operating System Services. Tech. Report, University of Washington, Feburary 1994.

[7] Bolosky, William J., Fitzgerald, Robert P., Scott, Michael L. Simple But Effective Techniques for NUMA Memory Management. In *Proceedings of the 12th ACM Symposium On Operating Systems Principles*, December 1989.

[8] Cheriton, David R. The V Distributed System. In *Communications of the ACM*, 31(3):314-333, March 1988.

[9] Cheriton, David R., Goosen, Hendrik A. and Boyle, Patrick D. Pradigm : A Highly Scalable Shared Memory Multicomputer Architecture. *IEEE Computer*, February 1991.

[10] Cheriton, David R. and Harty, Kieran A Market Approach to Operating System Memory Allocation. Tech. Report, Stanford University, CA, March 1992.

[11] Harty, Kieran and Cheriton, David R. Application-Controlled Physical Memory Using External Page-Cache Management. In *Proceedings of 5th International Conference on Architectural Support for Programming Languages and Operating Systems,* October 1992.

[12] Date, C. J. An Introduction To Database Systems. In Addison-Wesley Systems Programming Series, Volume 1, Fifth Edition, 1990.

[13] Draves, Richard P. Page Replacement and Reference Bit Emulation in Mach. In *Proceedings of the USENIX Mach Symposium,* Monterey, CA, November 1991.

[14] Draves, Richard P., Bershad, Brian N., Rashid, Richard F. and Dean, Randall W. Using Continuations to Implement Thread Management and Communication in Operating Systems. In *Proceedings of the 13th ACM Symposium on Operating System Principles,* October 1991.

[15] Golub, David B. and Draves, Richard P. Moving the Default Memory Manager out of the Mach Kernel. In *Proceedings of the USENIX Mach Symposium,* Monterey, CA, November 1991.

[16] Graefe, Goetz Query Evaluation Techniques for Large Database. In *ACM Computing Surveys,* June 1993.

[17] Krueger, Keith and Loftesness, David and Vahdat, Amin and Anderson, Thomas Tools for the Development of Application-Specific Virtual Memory Management. In *Proceedings of the 1993 OOPSLA,* 1993.

[18] Khalidi, Youself A. and Nelson, Michael N. A Flexible External Paging Interface. In *Proceedings of USENIX Association Symposium on Microkernels and Other Kernel Architectures,* 1993.

[19] Lenoski, Dean, et al. The DASH prototype: Implementation and Performance. In *Proceedings of 19th Symposium on Computer Architecture,* May 1992.

[20] McCanne, S., Jacobson, V. The BSD Packet Filter: A New Architecture for User-Level Packet Capture. In *Proceedings of the Winter 1993 USENIX Conference,* January 1993.

[21] McNamee, Dylan and Armstrong, Katherine Extending The Mach External Pager Interface To Accommodate User-Level Page Replacement Policies. In *Proceedings of the USENIX Association Mach Workshop,* Burlington, Vermont, October 1990.

[22] Mogul, J. C., Rashid, R. F., and Accetta, M. J. The Packet Filter: An Efficient Mechanism for User-level Network Code. In *Proceedings of th 11th ACM Symposium on Operating Systems Principle,* November 1987.

[23] McDonald, Jeffrey D. Particle Simulation in a Multiprocessor Environment. In *Proceedings of AIAA 26th Thermophysics Conference,* June 1991.

[24] Muller, Keith and Pasquale, Joseph A High Performance Multi-Structured File System Design. In *Proceedings of the 13th ACM Symposium on Operating System Principles,* October 1991.

[25] Ritchie, D. Stuart and Neufeld, Gerald W. User Level IPC and Device management in the Raven Kernel. In *Proceedings of USENIX Association Symposium on Micro Kernels and Other Kernel Architectures,* 1993.

[26] Ruemmler, Chris and Wilkes, John An Introduction to Disk Drive Modeling. In *IEEE Computer,* March 1994.

[27] Stonebraker, Michael Operating System Support for Database Management. In *Communications of the ACM,* Vol. 24, No. 7, July 1981.

[28] Sechrest, Stuart and Park, Yoonho User-Level Physical Memory Management for Mach. In *Proceedings of the USENIX Mach Symposium,* Monterey, CA, November 1991.

[29] Sciver, James V. and Rashid, Richard F. Zone Garbage Collection. In *Proceedings of the USENIX Association Mach Workshop,* Burlington, Vermont, October 1990.

[30] Wang, Hsiao-Hsi., Lu, Pei-Ku, and Chang, Ruei-Chuan. An Implementation of an External Pager Interface on BSD UNIX. To appear in *The Journal of Systems and Software.*

[31] Young, M., Tevanian, A., Rashid, R., Golub, D., Eppinger, J., Chew, J., Bolosky, W., Black, D. and Baron, R. The Duality of Memory and Communication in the Implementation of a Multiprocessor Operating System. In *Proceedings of the 11th ACM Symposium on Operating System Principles,* November 1987.

[32] Young, Michael W. Exporting a User Interface to Memory Management from a Communication-Oriented Operating System. Ph.D. dissertation, Carnegie Mellon University, November 1989.

[33] Yuhara, Masanobu and Bershad, Brian N. Efficient Packet Demultiplexing for Multiple Endpoints and Large Messages. In *Proceedings of the Winter 1994 USENIX Conference,* January 1994.

Implementation and Performance of Application-Controlled File Caching

Pei Cao, Edward W. Felten, and Kai Li

Department of Computer Science
Princeton University
Princeton, NJ 08544 USA
{pc,felten,li} @cs.princeton.edu

Abstract

Traditional file system implementations do not allow applications to control file caching replacement decisions. We have implemented two-level replacement, a scheme that allows applications to control their own cache replacement, while letting the kernel control the allocation of cache space among processes. We designed an interface to let applications exert control on replacement via a set of directives to the kernel. This is effective and requires low overhead.

We demonstrate that for applications that do not perform well under traditional caching policies, the combination of good application-chosen replacement strategies, and our kernel allocation policy LRU-SP, can reduce the number of block I/Os by up to 80%, and can reduce the elapsed time by up to 45%. We also show that LRU-SP is crucial to the performance improvement for multiple concurrent applications: LRU-SP fairly distributes cache blocks and offers protection against foolish applications.

1 Introduction

File caching is a widely used technique in file systems. Cache management policy is normally centrally controlled by the operating system kernel. Recently, we have shown by simulation that application-controlled file caching can offer higher file cache hit ratios than the traditional approach [3]. This paper presents the design and implementation of an application-controlled file cache and reports its performance benefit under a real application workload.

The design of our application-controlled file cache is based on a two-level replacement scheme proposed in [3]. This method lets the kernel dynamically allocate cache blocks to user processes, and allows each user process to apply its favorite file caching policy to its blocks. A cache block allocation policy, called Least-Recently-Used with Swapping and Placeholders(LRU-SP), is used to guarantee the fairness of allocation.

We designed an interface of user-to-kernel directives to enable applications to control file cache replacement. The interface is designed to be sufficiently flexible for applications to express desired strategies in the common cases, and yet to have low overhead.

We implemented the application-controlled file cache for the Ultrix file system on the DEC 5000/240 workstation. We compared the performance of our file cache to that of the traditional, global LRU approach, using several real applications. First, we showed that a well-chosen caching policy can reduce cache misses (and hence disk I/Os) significantly. In our single-application experiments, good policies can reduce cache misses by between 10% and 80%. As a result, these policies can reduce the elapsed time of applications by up to 45%. Second, we measured the effectiveness and fairness of our LRU-SP allocation policy. Using various mixes of concurrent applications, we showed that our implementation can reduce their elapsed times by up to 30% over the global LRU approach.

We also compared our implementation with our earlier simulation study. This confirmed the result from our simulation study that the added features of LRU-SP (swapping and placeholders) are important for performance improvement. Although LRU-SP does not always provide *perfect* protection against foolish processes, it significantly reduces their effect, and it provides an easy way for the kernel to detect foolish or malicious behavior.

2 Two-Level Replacement and LRU-SP

This section presents some background material about two level block replacement and the LRU-SP global allocation policy. For a full discussion see [3].

The challenge in application-controlled file caching

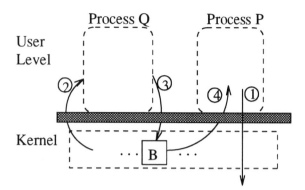

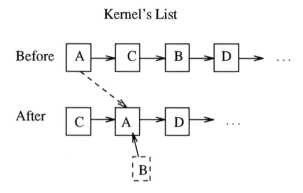

Figure 1: Interaction between kernel and user processes in two-level replacement: (1) P misses; (2) kernel consults Q for replacement; (3) Q decides to give up page B; (4) kernel reallocates B to P.

Figure 2: How LRU-SP keeps the "LRU" list. Here the kernel suggests block A as a candidate for replacement; the application overrules the kernel, and causes block B to be replaced instead. The figure shows the list before and after the replacement decision.

is to allow each user process to control its own caching *and* at the same time to maintain the dynamic allocation of cache blocks among processes in a fair way so that overall system performance improves.

To achieve this goal, we use *two level block replacement.* Two-level replacement splits the responsibility for allocation and replacement between the kernel and user level. The kernel is responsible for allocating cache blocks to processes, while each user process can control the replacement strategy on its share of cache blocks. When a user-level process misses in the cache, the kernel chooses a process to give up a cache block. The designated process is free to give up whichever block it likes. The kernel's *allocation policy* is used to decide which process will give up a block.

The interactions between the kernel and the controlling user process (called the manager process) are as follows: on a cache miss, the kernel first finds a candidate block to replace, based on its "global replacement" policy (step 1 in Figure 1). The kernel then identifies the manager process for the candidate. This manager process is given a chance to decide on the replacement (step 2). The candidate block is given as a hint, but the manager process may overrule the kernel's choice by suggesting an alternative block under that manager's control (step 3). Finally, the block suggested by the manager process is replaced by the kernel (step 4). (If the manager process does not exist or is uncooperative, then the kernel simply replaces the candidate block.)

Clearly, the kernel's "global replacement" policy is actually not a replacement policy at all (as it doesn't really decide which block to replace) but rather a global *allocation* policy. A sound global allocation policy is crucial to the success of two level replacement. It should satisfy these three criteria:

- Oblivious processes (those that do not want to

manage their share of the cache) should do no worse than they would have done under the existing LRU policy.

- Foolish processes should not hurt other processes.

- Smart processes should perform better than under the existing LRU policy whenever possible, and they should never perform worse.

In [3] we proposed a kernel policy called LRU-SP that satisfies these criteria. LRU-SP operates by keeping an LRU list of all cache blocks and having two extensions to the "basic LRU" scheme:

- If the kernel suggests block A for replacement and the user-level manager chooses to replace B instead, the kernel swaps the positions of A and B in the LRU list ("swapping"), then builds a record (a "placeholder") for B, pointing to A, to remember the manager's choice. (See Figure 2.)

- If a user process misses on a block B, and a placeholder for B exists, then the block pointed to by that placeholder is chosen as the candidate for replacement. Otherwise, the block at the end of the LRU list is picked as the candidate.

If an application never overrules the kernel's suggestions, then no swapping or placeholders are ever used for that application's blocks, so the application sees an LRU policy. If it uses a better policy than LRU to overrule the kernel's suggestion, then swapping is necessary so that it won't be penalized by the kernel. If it uses a worse policy than LRU, then placeholders are necessary to prevent it from hurting other processes. For more details please see [3].

3 Supporting Application Control

There are a variety of ways to implement the user-kernel interaction in two level block replacement, as discussed in [3]. The main design challenge is to devise an interface that allows applications to exert the control they need, without introducing the overhead that would result from a totally general mechanism.

Our approach was to first consider common file access patterns reported in the literature (e.g. [24, 1, 6]) as well as patterns that we observed in the applications discussed below. We then chose a simple interface that was sufficient to compose caching strategies to support these access patterns.

An Interface for Application Control

The basic idea in our interface is to allow applications to assign priorities to files and to specify file cache replacement policies for each priority level. The kernel always replaces blocks with the lowest priority first. (This rule applies only within the blocks of a single process. Inter-process allocation decisions are made using LRU-SP, as explained above.) The calls for applications are:

- set_priority(file, prio) and get_priority(file) set and get the long-term cache priority of a file.

- set_policy(prio, policy) and get_policy(prio) set and get the file cache replacement policy of a priority level. At present, we offer only two policies: least-recently-used (LRU) and most-recently-used (MRU). The default policy is LRU.

Since files with the same priority belong to the same caching "pool" with the same replacement policy, application or library writers can use a combination of priorities and policies to deal with various file access patterns. They can apply a single policy to all files, can apply different policies for different pools of files, and can change priorities to tell the kernel to replace some files before others.

Our interface also has a primitive for applications to assign temporary priorities to file blocks:

set_temppri(file,startBlock,endBlock,prio)

This is a mechanism to allow applications to temporarily change the priority of a set of blocks within a file. This temporary change affects only those blocks that are presently in the cache, and a block's priority change only lasts until the next time the block is either referenced or replaced. When the temporary priority ends, the block reverts to its long-term priority as set by set_priority.

These five operations are multiplexed through a single new fbehavior system call, in the same way that the Unix ioctl system call multiplexes several operations.

Supporting Common Access Patterns

We now illustrate how our interface can be used to support a variety of common file access patterns. Further examples are found in section 5, in which we discuss how we used our interface to control caching for a set of real applications.

Sequential Applications often read a file sequentially from beginning to end. If the file is accessed sequentially repeatedly, it can be assigned a low priority and MRU replacement policy. If the file is accessed only once, it can be assigned priority -1 to flush its block from cache quickly.

Cyclic access Some applications repeat the same sequence of accesses several times. These applications can assign a low priority, and MRU replacement policy, to the relevant file or files.

Access to many small files Some applications access many small files. Since our interface treats all files of the same priority as being in a single "pool" when making replacement decisions, these applications can control the caching of these blocks. (An interface that allowed control only within individual files would be useless for tiny files.)

Hot and cold files Some applications have particular files that are accessed unusually often, or with unusually good temporal locality. Such files can be assigned high priority.

Future access prediction Some applications can predict that certain blocks are especially likely to be accessed in the near future. These blocks can be given a temporary increase in priority, to keep them in the cache longer.

Done-with blocks An application may know that it is finished with a block, and will not be accessing it again for a long time. For example, this can happen in temporary files, which are often written once and then read once. When such a file is being read, the priority of a block can be decreased temporarily when the file pointer moves past the end of the block. This will flush the block quickly from the cache.

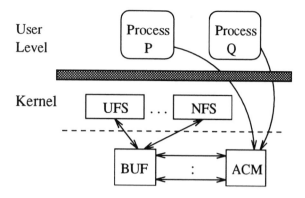

Figure 3: Implementation of Application Controlled Caching.

4 Kernel Implementation

The kernel implementation of two-level replacement is done by breaking the existing buffer cache code into two modules. The buffer cache module (BUF) handles cache management and bookkeeping and implements the allocation policy. The application control module (ACM) implements the interface calls and acts as a proxy for the user-level managers. Both of these modules sit below the VFS interface and communicate via procedure calls. The implementation is done on a Ultrix 4.3 kernel. [1]

When a block must be replaced, BUF picks a candidate block and asks ACM which block to replace, giving the candidate block as a suggestion. ACM then acts on behalf of the appropriate user-level manager to make the decision. The structure is shown in Figure 3.

ACM implements the calls from user level in a straightforward way. It allocates a "manager" structure for any process that wants to control its own caching. Then for each priority level it allocates a header to keep the list of blocks in that level. It also allocates a file record if a file has a non-zero long-term priority. The implementation imposes a limit on kernel resources consumed by these data structures and fails the calls if the limit would be exceeded.

Every block, upon entering the cache, is linked into the appropriate list based on its file's long-term priority. The lists are always kept in LRU order, and LRU (MRU, respectively) chooses blocks from the head (tail) of the list. Blocks may move among lists by set_priority or set_temppri. The implementation uses the rule that blocks moving into a list will be put at the end that causes them to be replaced later (the MRU end if the policy is LRU, or the LRU end if the policy is MRU). The opposite effect can be achieved by appropriate use of set_temppri.

BUF and ACM communicate by using five proce-

dure calls. They serve the purpose of notifying ACM about replacement decisions and mistakes, informing ACM about changes in cache state and accesses, and asking ACM for replacement decisions. The calls are:

- new_block(block): informs ACM that block was loaded into cache buffer;

- block_gone(block): informs ACM that block was removed from the cache;

- block_accessed(block, offset, size): informs ACM that block was accessed;

- replace_block(candidate, missing_block): asks ACM which block to replace;

- placeholder_used(block, placeholder): informs ACM that a previous decision to replace block was erroneous.

Changes are needed in the replacement procedure in BUF to implement LRU-SP. Instead of replacing the LRU (Least-Recently-Used) block, the procedure first checks if the missing block has a placeholder, then takes the LRU block or the block pointed to by the placeholder (if there is one) as the candidate. BUF calls replace_block if the candidate block's caching is application-controlled, and finally BUF swaps block positions and builds a placeholder. The interface is well defined, and the procedures are called with no lock held.

Since BUF and ACM sit below the VFS interface, our implementation works for both UFS [18] and NFS [26]. In all our following experiments, however, we put all files on local disks to avoid impact on performance from network traffic.

We believe this interface could be used if one wanted to implement two level replacement using upcalls or dropped-in-kernel "user-level handlers" [2]. In particular user-level handlers could know which blocks are in cache by keeping track of new_block and block_gone calls.

Our current implementation adds negligible overhead to file accesses. For processes that do not control their own caching, there is no added overhead on cache hits. On a cache miss, there are two sources of overhead: we have to keep track of which file's data are in a cache block because Ultrix does not remember this; and if the candidate block belongs to a process that manages its own cache, replace_block and block_gone have to be called. Since these procedures are cheap and are implemented in the kernel, both overheads are small; indeed they are negligible compared to the disk latency.

For processes that control their own caching, the extra overhead on a cache miss is similar to the above case except that new_block is called as well. The

---

[1] Contact the authors for portions of the code that are not vendor-proprietary.

overhead on a cache hit depends on the work done in `block_accessed`, which in our current implementation only involves updating counters and moving a few blocks around in lists. These overheads are often smaller than the potential reduction in system CPU time caused by reducing the number of misses.

5 Performance Results

Beneficiaries of application controlled caching include applications that use large file data sets (i.e. they do not fit in cache), because LRU is often not the right policy for them. Examples include: database systems, including text retrieval software; trace-driven simulations, as the trace files are often large; graphics and image-processing applications; and I/O-intensive UNIX utilities.

We chose a set of such applications for our experiments. Below we first describe the applications that we chose and the replacement strategies they use; then we present performance results for single and multiple application experiments.

5.1 Applications

We chose the following applications:

cscope [cs1-3] Cscope is an interactive C-source examination tool written by Joe Steffen. It builds a database of all source files, then uses the database to answer queries about the program. There are two kinds of queries for cscope: symbol-oriented ones, mostly questions about where C-symbols occur; and egrep-like text search, mostly asking where patterns of text occur. We used cscope on two software packages (in fact, two kernel sources), one about 18MB and one about 10MB, and did two sets of queries: searching for eight symbols, and searching for four text patterns. The three runs are: **cs1** — symbol search on the 18MB source; **cs2** — text search on the 18MB source; **cs3** — text search on the 10MB source.

Strategy: Symbol-oriented queries always read the database file "cscope.out" sequentially to search for records containing the requested symbols. Therefore for this kind of queries, the right policy is to use MRU on "cscope.out":

```
set_priority("cscope.out", 0);
set_policy(0, MRU);
```

Text searches involve reading all the source files in the same order on every query, so the right policy is MRU on all the source files. Since all source files have the default priority 0, the only necessary call is:

```
set_policy(0, MRU);
```

(When there is a mix of these queries, cscope can keep or discard "cscope.out" in cache when necessary by raising or lowering its priority.)

dinero [din] Dinero is a cache simulator written by Mark Hill and used in Hennessy and Patterson's architecture textbook [13]. The distribution package for the course material includes the simulator and several program trace files. We chose the "cc" trace (about 8MB) from the distribution package, and ran a set of simulations, varying the cache line size from 32 to 128 bytes, and set associativity from 1 to 4.

Strategy: Dinero reads the trace file sequentially on each simulation. Hence the right policy is MRU on trace file and the call is:

```
set_priority(trace, 0);
set_policy(0, MRU);
```

glimpse [gli] Glimpse is a text information retrieval system [17]. It builds approximate indexes for words to allow both relatively fast search and small index files. We took a snapshot of news articles in several comp.* newsgroups on May 22, 1994, about 40MB of texts. Then we `glimpseindex`ed it, resulting in about 2MB of indexes. The searches are for lines containing these keywords: scheduling, scheduling and disk, cluster, rendering and volume, DTM.

Strategy: The index files and data files naturally lead to two priority levels because index files are always accessed first on every query, but data files are not. Hence glimpse gives the index files long-term priority 1, and the articles the default long-term priority 0. Since index files are always accessed in the same order, and several groups of articles (called partitions [17]) are accessed in the same order, MRU is chosen for both levels. The calls are:

```
set_priority(".glimpse_index", 1);
set_priority(".glimpse_partitions", 1);
set_priority(".glimpse_filenames", 1);
set_priority(".glimpse_statistics", 1);
set_policy(1, MRU);
set_policy(0, MRU);
```

link editor [ldk] Ld is the Ultrix link-editor. We used it to build the Ultrix 4.3 kernel from about 25 MB of object files.

Strategy: Ld almost never accesses the same file data twice, but it does lots of small accesses, so the right thing to do is to free a block whenever its data have all been accessed by calling [2]:

```
set_temppri(file, blknum, blknum, -1);
```

---

[2]We can't obtain the source of the DEC MIPS link editor, so we implemented this policy in the kernel to simulate what the program would do and called it "access-once".

---

postgres join [pjn] Postgres is a relational database system from the University of California at Berkeley. We used version 4.0.1 for Ultrix 4.3. It uses the file system for I/O operations, and since it only has a small internal buffer, it relies heavily on file caching. We chose one query operation: a join between an indexed and a non-indexed relation, to illustrate how it can use application control on file caching.

The relations are a 200,000 tuple one, **twohundredk**, and a 20,000 tuple one, **twentyk**, from a scaled-up Wisconsin benchmark[10]. The join is on field **unique1**, which is uniquely random within 1-200,000 in **twohundredk**, and uniquely random within 1-1,000,020 in **twentyk**. The size of **twentyk** is roughly 3.2MB, **twohundredk** 32MB, and index **twohundredk_unique1** 5MB.

Strategy: Since there is a non-clustered index on **unique1** in **twohundredk**, and no index in **twentyk**, Postgres executes the join by using **twentyk** as the outer relation and using the index to retrieve tuples from **twohundredk**. The index blocks have a much higher probability of being accessed than data blocks. Therefore postgres uses two priority levels: the index file has long-term priority 1, while data files have default priority 0. LRU is used for both priority levels. The only call necessary is:

```
set_priority("twohundredk_unique1", 1);
```

sort [sort] Sort is the external sorting utility in UNIX. We used a 200,000-line, 17MB text file as input, and sorted numerically on the first field.

Sort has two phases: it first partitions the input file into sorted chunks that are stored in temporary files, then repeatedly merges the sorted files. Its access pattern has the following characteristics: input files are read once; temporary files are written once and then read once; merging is done eight files at a time, and temporary files are merged in the order in which they were created.

Strategy: Sort has two priority levels, -1 and 0. Input files have priority -1 as they are read once. Temporary files have default priority 0. MRU is chosen for both level -1 and level 0 (because temporary files created earlier will be merged first). The calls are:

```
set_policy(-1, MRU);
set_policy(0, MRU);
set_priority(input_file, -1);
```

In addition, the "readline" routine is changed to keep track of when the end of an 8K block is reached, and at the end of reading a block to free the block by calling:

```
set_temppri(file, blknum, blknum, -1);
```

We experimented with other strategies, and we found that the ones given here performed the best.

5.2 Single Applications

We compared the performance of each application under application-controlled file caching to that under the kernel-controlled file caching (the original, unmodified kernel). We used a DEC 5000/240 workstation with one RZ56 disk and one RZ26 disk. The RZ56 is a 665M SCSI disk, with average seek time of 16ms, average rotational latency of 8.3ms, and peak transfer rate of 1.875MB/s; the RZ26 is a 1.05GB SCSI disk, with average seek time of 10.5ms, average rotational latency of 5.54ms, and peak transfer rate of 3.3MB/s. The two disks are connected to one SCSI bus.

Applications **cs[1-3]**, **din**, **gli** and **ldk** were run on the RZ56 disk, and **pjn** and **sort** were run on the RZ26 disk.

We measured both the number of block I/Os, reflecting the cache misses, and the elapsed time, for several configurations of the buffer cache size (6.4MB[3], 8MB, 12MB, 16MB). Figure 4 shows the elapsed times and the number of block I/Os *normalized* to those under the original kernel. The raw data for this experiment appear in the appendix[4].

Application-specific policies reduce the number of block I/Os by an amount ranging from 9% to over 80%. This confirms our simulation result [3] that miss ratio is reduced by application controlled caching. The reduction in elapsed time ranges from 6% to over 45%. Elapsed time is not directly proportional to block I/Os because elapsed time is also affected by the amount of CPU computation time, and because the disk access latency is not uniform.

The performance improvement often depends on the relative size of the cache versus the data set. For example, for **cs1**, the improvement increases until the 9MB database file "cscope.out" fits in cache, at which point all policies perform the same. In some cases LRU makes a bigger cache useless — there is no benefit until the entire data set can fit in the cache. Application specific policies, on the other hand, can appropriately take advantage of a bigger cache and improve application performance. As DRAM density improves, we will see ever-larger caches, so the benefit of application control will become more significant.

5.3 Multiple Applications

In our previous paper we used simulations to show that our global allocation policy LRU-SP can properly take advantage of application control on replacement to improve the hit ratio of the whole system. Now

---

[3]This is 10% of the memory of our workstation, which is the default cache size under Ultrix.

[4]Raw data for all of our experiments are available at ftp.cs.princeton.edu: /pub/pc/OSDI/.

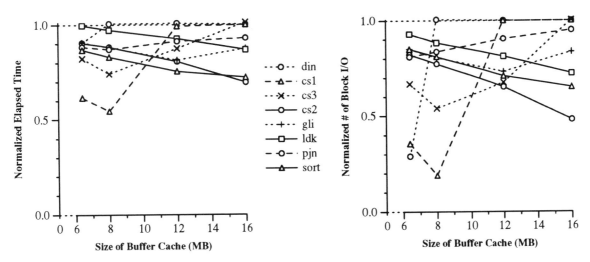

Figure 4: Normalized elapsed time and block I/Os of individual applications under LRU-SP, versus file cache size. Elapsed times under the original kernel are set to 1.0. All numbers are averages of five cold-start runs; variances are less than 2% with a few exceptions that are less than 5%.

that we've implemented the system, we'd like to see whether this is true in practice.

We ran several combinations of two or more of the above applications, with each application using its appropriate user-level replacement policy. The combinations were chosen to have various mixes of access patterns. For this purpose, we put the applications into categories based on their access patterns. We put **cs[1-3]** and **din** into the "cyclic" category, **gli** and **pjn** into the "hot/cold" category, and **ldk** and **sort** in two separate categories. We ran six two-application combinations, chosen to cover all combinations of the four categories. We also randomly chose two three-application combinations and one four-application combination.

The combinations are: **cs2+gli**, **cs3+ldk**, **gli+sort**, **din+sort**, **sort+ldk**, **pjn+ldk**, **din+cs2+ldk**, **cs1+gli+ldk**, and **din+cs3+gli+ldk**. Note that **gli+sort**, **din+sort**, **sort+ldk**, **pjn+ldk** are run using two disks, while all others are run using one disk.

We measured the total elapsed time and the total number of block I/Os for these concurrent applications. Figure 5 shows the *normalized* elapsed time and the number of block I/Os. As can be seen, LRU-SP indeed improves the performance of the whole system. The improvement becomes more significant as the file cache size increases.

6   Analysis of LRU-SP

In our simulation study [3] we found that both the **swapping** and **placeholders** techniques in LRU-SP are necessary, and that LRU-SP satisfies our allocation criteria as described in Section 2. In this section, we investigate these questions again with our real im-

plementation.

6.1   Comparison with ALLOC-LRU

LRU-SP keeps a basic LRU list of cache blocks to choose victim processes, but makes two variations, **swapping** and **placeholders**, to the list, as described in Section 2. In the following we first see whether swapping is necessary, then check whether placeholders are necessary.

Is swapping necessary? Let's call the basic scheme that simply uses the LRU list to choose victim processes the ALLOC-LRU (ALLOCation by LRU order) policy. With ALLOC-LRU as allocation policy in two level replacement, we randomly chose the following from our above experiments: **cs2+gli**, **cs3+ldk**, **din+cs2+ldk**, **cs1+gli+ldk**, and **din+cs3+gli+ldk**, and compared the results to those of LRU-SP. The results of this comparison are shown in Figure 6.

In most cases ALLOC-LRU performs worse. In fact, in a few cases, under ALLOC-LRU applications are better off not using smart policies — smarter allocation hurts their performance[5]! The problem is that ALLOC-LRU uses straight LRU order without swapping, and hence penalizes any process that does not replace the LRU block. These results show that swapping positions of candidate and alternative blocks is necessary.

Are placeholders necessary? To see whether placeholders are also necessary, we need an application that can have a replacement policy that does much

---

[5]For detailed data, see ftp.cs.princeton.edu: /pub/pc/OSDI.

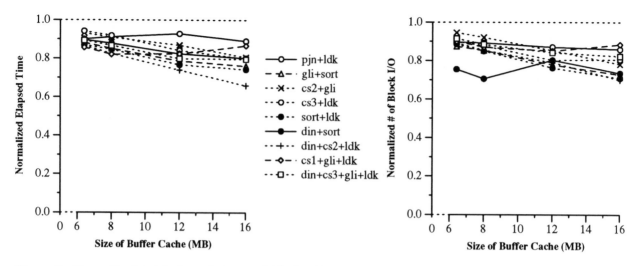

Figure 5: Normalized total elapsed time and block I/Os of multiple concurrent applications. Values under the original kernel are normalized to 1.0. All numbers are averages of three cold-start runs; variances are less than 2%.

worse than LRU [6], and an oblivious application whose performance is sensitive to the number of cache blocks it is given. We found a program "ReadN" that can serve both purposes.

ReadN sequentially reads the first N 8K-byte blocks from a file in sequence, repeating this sequence five times, then reads the next N blocks five times, and so on. MRU replacement policy is much worse than LRU for ReadN, so ReadN with MRU can be used as an example of a foolish application. ReadN also has the characteristic that under LRU, the cache miss ratio is low when it has at least N cache blocks, but is high when it has less than N cache blocks. Therefore we can compare the number of block I/Os done by ReadN in different situations as a way of measuring what share of the cache blocks it is getting.

To answer our question about the effectiveness of placeholders, we ran two versions of ReadN concurrently. One version, with N=300, is run with various replacement policies: the oblivious LRU policy (which is good but not optimal), and MRU (which is terrible). The other version of ReadN is used to detect changes in allocation of cache blocks. This version is run with various values of N: Read390, Read400, Read490, and Read500. These values are chosen because our cache size is 6.4MB, or 819 blocks, so Read300 and Read390 can comfortably fit in cache together with plenty of space to spare, while Read300 and Read500 can barely just fit in cache together.

We measured the performance (running time and number of I/Os) of the various ReadN's when the background Read300 uses both oblivious (LRU) and dumb (MRU) replacement policies. If processes are

protected from the foolishness of others, then the performance of the ReadN's should not get much worse when the background Read300's policy is changed from oblivious to foolish.

In the case where the background Read300 is foolish, we actually ran two experiments. In the "protected" experiment, the kernel uses our LRU-SP allocation policy. In the "unprotected" experiment, the kernel uses LRU-SP *without placeholders*. Thus there are three cases overall:

- Oblivious: the background Read300 uses the oblivious (LRU) policy;

- Unprotected: the background Read300 uses a foolish (MRU) policy, and the kernel uses LRU-SP *without placeholders* i.e. LRU-S;

- Protected: the background Read300 uses a foolish (MRU) policy, and the kernel uses LRU-SP;

The results are shown in Table 1. The data clearly shows that place-holders are necessary to protect the oblivious **readN** from losing its share of cache blocks. (For a detailed explanation of why placeholders provide this protection, see [3].) However, the data also shows that placeholders did not prevent the increasing in elapsed times of ReadN. The next subsection explains why.

6.2   Criteria Test

We have seen in Section 5 that smart processes improve their performance. The next two questions are: do foolish processes hurt other processes, and do smart processes hurt oblivious processes?

---

[6]We do not use the previous applications here because LRU works poorly for them.

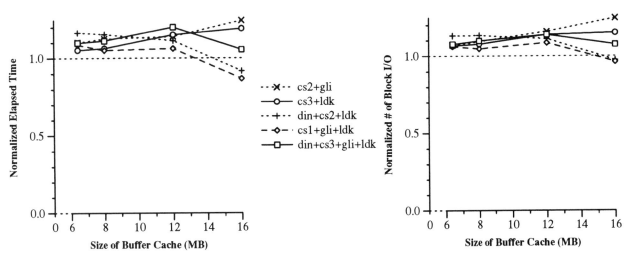

Figure 6: Normalized total elapsed time and block I/Os of multiple concurrent applications under **ALLOC-LRU**. Values under two level replacement with **LRU-SP** are normalized to 1.0. All numbers are averages of three cold-start runs; variances are less than 2%.

Settings	Elapsed Time of "ReadN"				Block I/Os of "ReadN"			
	Read390	Read400	Read490	Read500	Read390	Read400	Read490	Read500
Oblivious	53	58 (7%)	59	72 (14%)	1172	1181	1176	1481 (11%)
Unprotected	73 (23%)	89 (24%)	76	122 (27%)	1300 (19%)	1538 (21%)	1465	2294 (27%)
Protected	75	75	72	91 (12%)	1170	1170	1199	1580 (10%)

Table 1: Results from experiments done to test the effectiveness of placeholders. For descriptions of these experiments please see text. The first four columns show the running time in seconds, and the next four the number of block I/O's, for ReadN. Results are averaged over five runs. Variances are shown in parentheses; when omitted they are less than 5%.

"Read300"	Elapsed Time				Block I/Os			
Policy	din	cs2	gli	ldk	din	cs2	gli	ldk
Oblivious	155	225	156	112	3067	9760	9086	5201
Foolish	202	339	261	208	3495	10542	9759	5374

Table 2: Effect of a foolish process on smart applications. This table shows performance of various processes when run concurrently with a Read300 process, depending on whether the Read300 is oblivious (using LRU) or is foolish (using MRU). The first four columns shows elapsed time in seconds, and the next four the number of block I/Os. Numbers are averages of three runs with all variances < 3%.

Application	Elapsed time of "Read300"			
Policies	w. din	w. cs2	w. gli	w. ldk
Oblivious	87	88	60(7%)	78
Smart	67(8%)	83	64(9%)	76

Table 3: Elapsed time of "Read300" when run concurrently with oblivious and smart versions of other applications on one disk. Numbers are in seconds, averages of three runs with variances <4% except those shown in parenthesis. Read300's numbers of block I/Os are the same in all cases (about 1310) as they are all compulsory misses.

Do foolish processes hurt other processes? We have that seen placeholders at least limit the harm done to oblivious processes by foolish processes. To see whether smart processes are protected as well, we ran each of **din**, **cs2**, **gli** and **ldk**, all using smart policies, concurrently with "Read300". The results when "Read300" is oblivious and when it is foolish are shown in Table 2.

The data show that there are degradations in both the number of block I/Os and the elapsed time. This contradicts results from our simulation study. The reasons include the following:

- Foolish processes generate more I/O requests, and thus put a heavier load on the disk. This leads to longer queueing time for the disk, so non-foolish processes' I/O requests wait longer to be served.

- Foolish processes take longer to finish and therefore occupy cache blocks for a longer time. Processes that run concurrently with them and finish after them normally get an increase in available cache blocks after they are finished. If they finish later, this increase comes later.

The best way to provide protection from foolish processes is probably for the kernel to revoke the cache-control privileges of consistently foolish applications. Placeholders allow the kernel to tell when an application is foolish, so the kernel can keep track of how good the application's policy is. If it turns out that a certain percentage of the application's decisions are wrong, the kernel can revoke its right to control its caching [7].

Do smart processes hurt oblivious ones? To answer this we use "Read300" again, this time as an oblivious application. We run it with each of **din**, **cs2**, **gli**, **ldk**, both when they are oblivious and when they are smart. The results are summarized in Table 3.

In most cases smart processes do not hurt but rather help oblivious processes. Since these experiments are

[7]We are adding this in our implementation.

Application	Elapsed time of "Read300"			
Policies	w. din	w. cs2	w. gli	w. ldk
Oblivious	20	18	19	17
Smart	20	17.5	18	17

Table 4: Elapsed time of "Read300" when run concurrently with oblivious and smart versions of other applications on two disks. Numbers are in seconds, averages of three runs with variances <3%. Read300's number of block I/Os is the same in all cases (about 1310).

run on one disk (RZ56), the reduction in the number of I/Os from smart processes reduces the load on the disk, and speeds up the requests from "Read300".

The only exception is the experiments with **gli**, which have a high variance in the elpased time. Since the number of block I/Os from "Read300" did not increase, nor did its user and system times, we suspect that this is due to the RZ56 disk's internal scheduling or buffering. To test this, we also run this experiments on two disks, with "Read300" using RZ26 and others using RZ56. The results are summarized in Table 4.

As can be seen, the anomaly goes away, which suggests that the previous problem was due to the disk contention. The improvements in the elapsed times, however, are not as noticeable as before because "Read300" is using a seperate disk.

From these results we believe that both swapping and placeholders are necessary. Although placeholders do not completely eliminate the harm done by foolish processes, they at least help the kernel take administrative measures to solve the problem.

7 Related Work

There have been many studies on caching in file systems (e.g. [27, 4, 26, 14, 22, 15]), but these investigations were not primarily concerned with the performance impact of different replacement policies. Recently several research projects have tried to improve file system performance in a number of other ways, including prefetching[30, 25, 7, 5, 11], delayed writeback[21] and disk block clustering[20, 29]. Most of these papers still assume global LRU as the basic cache replacement policy, and they do not address how to use application control over replacement to improve cache hit ratio. Our work is complementary to these approaches; in other words, with application-controlled file caching, these approaches will improve file system performance even more.

The database community has long studied access patterns and buffer replacement policies [31, 6, 23]. In our experiments we used **pjn** (Postgres join) as an example of how database systems may use our interface to control file caching. We believe our interface is flexible enough to implement most of the policies a database system might want to use.

A very similar problem is application controlled physical memory management in virtual memory systems. Current operating systems provide limited facilities that are not adequate for application control. For example, the Berkeley UNIX system calls for pinning pages, `mpin` or `mlock`, are often only available to the superuser. Advisory calls like `vadvise` or `madvise` provide an interface for applications to advise the kernel about their access patterns over a memory object, including a mapped file. However, this interface is much more limited than ours, allowing specification of only a small number of basic patterns and no priorities.

As a result, in the past few years there has been a stream of research papers on application control of caching in the virtual memory context [19, 28, 12, 16]. Our work differs from that described in these papers in three significant ways:

- None of these papers (except [12]) addresses the global allocation policy problem. By contrast, we discuss this problem in detail, and provide a solution, LRU-SP, which we have simulated [3] and now have implemented.

- Most of these papers relied on RPC or upcalls for kernel-to-user communication, and consequently reported overhead as high as 10% of the total execution time [19, 28]. We provide a flexible interface for applications to issue primitives to exert control on cache replacement; we found that this is adequate most of the time and requires low overhead.

- Most of these papers do not adequately consider which replacement policy an application should use. In [3] we proposed that application replacement policies be based on the optimal replacement principle [8], and in this paper we discussed which policies to use for our example applications.

On the other hand, our work shares some common purposes with the existing work on application-controlled virtual memory. We believe that, with some minor modifications, our approach applies to virtual memory cache management as well.

First, swapping and placeholder techniques apply to the virtual memory caching problem — one can swap positions of pages on the two-hand-clock list, and can build placeholders to catch foolish decisions. Second, our interface can be modified to apply to virtual memory context, i.e. instead of files, we use a range of virtual addresses (or memory regions).

One important difference is that in the virtual memory context, the implementation cannot capture the exact reference stream as it does in the file caching context. It is still not clear to us what are the common policies applications may want to use for virtual memory caching and whether not capturing exact references is a serious problem.

Our implementation is for Ultrix 4.3 where there is a fixed amount of DRAM memory allocated for file caching. In modern operating systems the virtual memory system and the file system often share a common page buffer pool. We believe our approach to file caching fully applies to these systems as well, with only some minor changes in data structures.

Finally, the difference between this paper and the work described in [3] is that in [3] we proposed and simulated LRU-SP, and in this paper we proposed a concrete scheme for user-kernel interaction and implemented both the interaction scheme and application-controlled caching in a real kernel.

8 Conclusion and Future Work

Our main conclusion is that two level replacement with LRU-SP works. It can be implemented with low overhead, and it can improve performance significantly.

Applications with large data sets often do not perform well under traditional file caching. We have identified common access patterns of these applications, and have designed an interface for them to express control over cache replacement. The allocation policy LRU-SP fairly distributes cache blocks among applications. As a result, the number of disk I/Os can be significantly reduced, and the application's elapsed time and the system's throughput can improve.

We are working on improving our user-kernel interface, and on supporting user-level control over caching of concurrently shared files[3]. In addition, our current implementation ignores metadata blocks like inodes, partly because there is a separate caching scheme for them inside the file system. We plan to look more into metadata caching performance and investigate what should be done.

We also plan to look into the interaction between caching, prefetching, write-back and disk block clustering.

The search for better global allocation policies requires a clear definition of the goal and an examination of the interactions between caching and scheduling/management policies in other parts of the system, particularly process scheduling and disk scheduling[9]. This is a fruitful area for future work.

Acknowledgements

We are grateful to our paper shepherd Jay Lepreau and the anonymous referees for their valuable comments.

Keith Bostic and Randy Appleton also provided helpful feedback.

References

[1] Mary Baker, John H. Hartman, Michael D. Kupfer, Ken W. Shirriff, and John Ousterhout. Measurements of a distributed file system. In *Proceedings of the Thirteenth Symposium on Operating Systems Principles*, pages 198–211, October 1991.

[2] Brian N. Bershad, Craig Chambers, Susan Eggers, Chris Maeda, Dylan MaNamee, Przemystaw Pardyak, Stefan Savage, and Emin Gun Sirer. SPIN — an extensible microkernel for applicatoin-specific operating system services. Technical Report TR 94-03-03, Dept. of Computer Science and Engineering, University of Washington, 1994.

[3] Pei Cao, Edward W. Felten, and Kai Li. Application-controlled file caching policies. In *Conference Proceedings of the USENIX Summer 1994 Technical Conference*, pages 171–182, June 1994.

[4] David Cheriton. Effective use of large RAM diskless workstations with the V virtual memory system. Technical report, Dept. of Computer Science, Stanford University, 1987.

[5] Khien-Mien Chew, A. Jyothy Reddy, Theodore H. Romer, and Avi Silberschatz. Kernel support for recoverable-persistent virtual memory. Technical Report TR-93-06, University of Texas at Austin, Dept. of Computer Science, February 1993.

[6] Hong-Tai Chou and David J. DeWitt. An evaluation of buffer management strategies for relational database systems. In *Proceedings of the Eleventh International Conference on Very Large Databases*, pages 127–141, August 1985.

[7] Kenneth M. Curewitz, P. Krishnan, and Jeffrey Scott Vitter. Practical prefetching via data compression. In *Proc. 1993 ACM-SIGMOD Conference on Management of Data*, pages 257–266, May 1993.

[8] Edward G. Coffman, Jr. and Peter J. Denning. *Operating Systems Theory*. Prentice-Hall, Inc., 1973.

[9] Gregory R. Ganger and Yale N. Patt. The process-flow model: Examing I/O performance from the system's point of view. In *Proceedings of SIGMETRICS 1993*, pages 86–97, May 1993.

[10] Jim Gray. *The Benchmark Handbook*. Morgen-Kaufman, San Mateo, Ca., 1991.

[11] Jim Griffioen and Randy Appleton. Reducing file system latency using a predictive approach. In *Conference Proceedings of the USENIX Summer 1994 Technical Conference*, pages 197–208, June 1994.

[12] Kieran Harty and David R. Cheriton. Application-controlled physical memory using external page-cache management. In *The Fifth International Conference on Architectural Support for Programming Languages and Operating Systems*, pages 187–197, October 1992.

[13] John L. Hennessy and David A. Patterson. *Computer Organization & Design: The Hardware/Software Interface*. Morgan Kaufmann Publishers, Inc., 1994.

[14] John H. Howard, Michael Kazar, Sherri G. Menees, David A. Nichols, M. Satyanarayanan, Robert N. Sidebotham, and Michael J. West. Scale and performance in a distributed file system. *ACM Transactions on Computer Systems*, pages 6(1):51–81, February 1988.

[15] James J. Kistler and M. Satyanarayanan. Disconnected operation in the Coda file system. *ACM Transactions on Computer Systems*, pages 6(1):1–25, February 1992.

[16] Keith Krueger, David Loftesness, Amin Vahdat, and Tom Anderson. Tools for the development of application-specific virtual memory management. In *OOPSLA '93 Conference Proceedings*, pages 48–64, October 1993.

[17] Udi Manber and Sun Wu. GLIMPSE: A tool to search through entire file systems. In *Conference Proceedings of the USENIX Winter 1994 Technical Conference*, pages 23–32, January 1994.

[18] M. McKusick, W. Joy, S. Leffler, and R. Fabry. A fast file system for UNIX. *ACM Transactions on Computer Systems*, August 1984.

[19] Dylan McNamee and Katherine Armstrong. Extending the Mach external pager interface to accommodate user-level page replacement policies. In *Proceedings of the USENIX Association Mach Workshop*, pages 17–29, 1990.

[20] L. W. McVoy and S. R. Kleiman. Extent-like performance from a UNIX file system. In *1991 Winter USENIX*, pages 33–43, 1991.

[21] Jeffrey C. Mogul. A better update policy. In *Proceedings of 1994 Summer USENIX*, pages 99–111, June 1994.

[22] Michael N. Nelson, Brent B. Welch, and John K. Ousterhout. Caching in the Sprite file system. *ACM Transactions on Computer Systems*, pages 6(1):134–154, February 1988.

[23] Elizabeth J. O'Neil, Patrick E. O'Neil, and Gerhard Weikum. The LRU-K page replacement algorithm for database disk buffering. In *Proc. 1993 ACM-SIGMOD Conference on Management of Data*, pages 297–306, May 1993.

[24] J. K. Ousterhout, H. Da Costa, D. Harrison, J.A. Kunze, M. Kupfer, and J. G. Tompson. A trace-driven analysis of the UNIX 4.2 BSD file system. In *Proceedings of the Tenth Symposium on Operating Systems Principles*, pages 15–24, December 1985.

[25] Hugo Patterson, Garth Gibson, and M. Satyanarayanan. Transparent informed prefetching. *ACM Operating Systems Review*, pages 21–34, April 1993.

[26] R. Sandberg, D. Boldberg, S. Kleiman, D. Walsh, and B. Lyon. Design and implementation of the Sun network filesystem. In *Summer Usenix Conference Proceedings*, pages 119–130, June 1985.

[27] M. D. Schroeder, D. K. Gifford, and R. M. Needham. A caching file system for a programmer's workstation. *ACM Operating Systems Review*, pages 19(5):35–50, December 1985.

[28] Stuart Sechrest and Yoonho Park. User-level physical memory management for Mach. In *Proceedings of the USENIX Mach Symposium*, pages 189–199, 1991.

[29] Margo Seltzer, Keith Bostic, Marshall Kirk McKusick, and Carl Staelin. An implementation of a log-structured file system for UNIX. In *Proceedings of 1993 Winter USENIX*, January 1993.

[30] Alan Jay Smith. Cache memories. *ACM Computing Surveys*, 14(3):473–530, September 1982.

[31] Michael Stonebraker. Operating system support for database management. *Communications of the ACM, v. 24, no. 7*, pages 412–418, July 1981.

Appendix

These tables show raw performance data for our single application experiments.

Application		Buffer Cache Size			
		6.4MB	8MB	12MB	16MB
din	original	117	99	99	99
	LRU-SP	106	99	100	100
	ratio	0.90	1.01	1.01	1.00
cs1	original	62	61	28	28
	LRU-SP	38	33	27	28
	ratio	0.62	0.54	0.99	1.00
cs3	original	96	96	57	47
	LRU-SP	79	71	50	48
	ratio	0.82	0.74	0.87	1.01
cs2	original	191	190	188	184
	LRU-SP	172	168	152	128
	ratio	0.90	0.88	0.81	0.70
gli	original	126	123	113	97
	LRU-SP	114	108	92	84
	ratio	0.91	0.88	0.81	0.87
ldk	original	66	65	65	65
	LRU-SP	66	64	60	56
	ratio	1.00	0.97	0.93	0.87
pjn	original	225	220	202	187
	LRU-SP	199	192	185	174
	ratio	0.88	0.87	0.91	0.93
sort	original	339	338	339	336
	LRU-SP	294	281	256	243
	ratio	0.87	0.83	0.75	0.72

Table 5: Elapsed time in seconds with/without application-controlled cache. The numbers are average of five runs. Variances are less than 2% with a few exceptions that are less than 5%.

Application		Buffer Cache Size			
		6.4MB	8MB	12MB	16MB
din	original	8888	998	997	998
	LRU-SP	2573	1003	997	997
	ratio	0.29	1.01	1.00	1.00
cs1	original	8634	8630	1141	1141
	LRU-SP	3066	1628	1141	1141
	ratio	0.36	0.19	1.00	1.00
cs3	original	6575	6571	2815	1728
	LRU-SP	4394	3548	1903	1733
	ratio	0.67	0.54	0.68	1.00
cs2	original	11785	11762	11717	11647
	LRU-SP	9680	9091	7650	5597
	ratio	0.82	0.77	0.65	0.48
gli	original	10435	10321	9720	7508
	LRU-SP	8870	8308	7120	6275
	ratio	0.85	0.81	0.73	0.84
ldk	original	5395	5389	5397	5390
	LRU-SP	5011	4760	4385	3898
	ratio	0.93	0.88	0.81	0.72
pjn	original	7166	6738	5897	5257
	LRU-SP	5800	5635	5334	4993
	ratio	0.81	0.84	0.90	0.95
sort	original	14670	14671	14639	14520
	LRU-SP	12462	11884	10400	9460
	ratio	0.85	0.81	0.71	0.65

Table 6: The numbers of block I/Os with/without application-controlled cache. The numbers are average of five runs, variances are less than 2% with one exception which is less than 3%.

A Caching Model of
Operating System Kernel Functionality

David R. Cheriton and Kenneth J. Duda
Computer Science Department
Stanford University
Stanford, CA 94025
{cheriton,kjd}@cs.stanford.edu

Abstract

Operating system research has endeavored to develop micro-kernels that provide modularity, reliability and security improvements over conventional monolithic kernels. However, the resulting kernels have been slower, larger and more error-prone than desired. These efforts have also failed to provide sufficient application control of resource management required by sophisticated applications.

This paper describes a caching model of operating system functionality as implemented in the *Cache Kernel*, the supervisor-mode component of the V++ operating system. The Cache Kernel caches operating system objects such as threads and address spaces just as conventional hardware caches memory data. User-mode *application kernels* handle the loading and writeback of these objects, implementing application-specific management policies and mechanisms. Experience with implementing the Cache Kernel and measurements of its performance on a multiprocessor suggest that the caching model can provide competitive performance with conventional monolithic operating systems, yet provides application-level control of system resources, better modularity, better scalability, smaller size and a basis for fault containment.

1 Introduction

Micro-kernels to date have not provided compelling advantages over the conventional monolithic operating system kernel for several reasons.

First, micro-kernels are larger than desired because of the complications of a modern virtual memory system (such as the copy-on-write facility), the need to support many different hardware devices, and complex optimizations in communication facilities, all of which have been handled inside most micro-kernels. Moreover, performance problems have tended to force services originally implemented on top of a micro-kernel back into the kernel, increasing its size. For example, the Mach inter-machine network server has been added back into some versions of Mach for this reason.

Second, micro-kernels do not support domain-specific resource allocation policies any better than monolithic kernels, an increasingly important issue with sophisticated applications and application systems. For example, the standard page-replacement policies of UNIX-like operating systems perform poorly for applications with random or sequential access [17]. Placement of conventional operating system kernel services in a micro-kernel-based server does not generally give the applications any more control because the server is a fixed protected system service. Adding a variety of resource management policies to the micro-kernel fails to achieve the efficiency that application-specific knowledge allows and increases the kernel size and complexity.

Finally, micro-kernels are bloated with exception-handling mechanisms for the failure and unusual cases that can arise with the hardware and with other server and application modules. For example, the potential page-in exception conditions with external pagers introduces complications into Mach.

In this paper, we present an alternative approach to kernel design based on a caching model, as realized in the V++ Cache Kernel. The *V++ Cache Kernel* caches the active objects associated with the basic operating system facilities, namely the address spaces and threads associated with virtual memory, scheduling and IPC. In contrast to conventional micro-kernel design, it does not fully implement all the functionality associated with address spaces and threads. Instead, it relies on higher-level *application kernels* to provide the management functions required for a complete implementation, including the loading and writeback of these objects to and from the Cache Kernel. For example, on a page fault, the application kernel associated with the faulting thread loads a new page mapping descriptor into the Cache Kernel as part of a cached address space object. This new descriptor may cause another page mapping descriptor to be written back to another application kernel to make space for the new descriptor. Because the application kernel selects the physical page frame to use, it

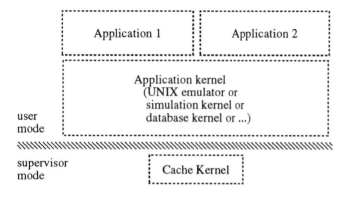

| user mode | Application 1 | Application 2 |
| Application kernel (UNIX emulator or simulation kernel or database kernel or ...) |

supervisor mode — Cache Kernel

Figure 1: Overall System Architecture in V++

fully controls physical page selection, the page replacement policy and paging I/O.

The following sections argue that this caching model reduces supervisor-level complexity, provides application control of resource management and provides application control over exception conditions and recovery, addressing the problems with micro-kernel designs to date (including a micro-kernel that we developed previously [4]).

The next section describes the Cache Kernel programming interface, illustrating its use by describing how an emulator application kernel would use this interface to implement standard UNIX-like services. Section 3 describes how sophisticated applications can use this interface directly by executing as part of their own application kernel. Section 3 describes how resources are allocated among competing applications. Section 4 describes our Cache Kernel implementation, and Section 5 describes its performance, which appears to provide competitive performance with conventional monolithic kernels. Section 6 describes previous research we see as relevant to this work. We close with a summary of the work, our conclusions and some indication of future directions.

2 The Cache Kernel Interface

In a Cache-Kernel-based system, one or more application kernels execute in user mode on top of the supervisor-mode Cache Kernel, as illustrated in Figure 1. Applications execute on top of the application kernel, either in separate address spaces or the same address space as the application kernel. For example, application 1 and 2 in the figure may be executing on top of, but in separate address spaces from, a UNIX kernel emulator.

The Cache Kernel acts as a cache for three types of operating system objects: address spaces, threads and kernels. It holds the descriptors for the active subset of these objects, executing the performance-critical actions on these objects. The rest of the service functionality typical in a modern operating system (e.g., virtual memory and scheduling) is implemented in application kernels. The application ker-

nel also provides backing store for the object state when it is unloaded from the Cache Kernel, just as data in a conventional cache has a backing memory area. For example, each application kernel maintains a descriptor for each of its threads, loads a thread descriptor into the Cache Kernel to make the thread a candidate for execution, and saves the updated state of that thread when the thread is written back to it.

The primary interface to the Cache Kernel consists of operations to load and unload these objects, signals from the Cache Kernel to application kernels that a particular object is missing, and writeback communication to the application kernel when an object is displaced from the Cache Kernel by the loading of another object.

Each loaded object is identified by an object identifier, returned when the object is loaded. This identifier is used to specify the object when another object is loaded that depends on it. For example, when a thread is loaded, its address space is specified by the identifier returned from the Cache Kernel when the corresponding address space object was loaded. If this identifier fails to identify a valid address space, such as can arise if the address space object is written back concurrently with the thread being loaded, the thread load operation fails, and the application kernel retries the thread load after reloading the address space object. Application kernels do not use the Cache Kernel object identifiers except across this interface because a new identifier is assigned each time an object is loaded. For example, the UNIX emulator provides a "stable" UNIX-like process identifier that is independent of the Cache Kernel address space and thread identifiers which may change several times over the lifetime of the UNIX process.

A small number of objects can also be *locked* in the Cache Kernel, protected from writeback. Locked objects are used to ensure that the application page fault handlers, schedulers and trap handlers execute and do not themselves incur page faults.

The following subsections describe this interface in more detail, illustrating its use by describing how an emulator application kernel would use this interface to implement UNIX-like operating system kernel services.

2.1 Address Space Objects

The Cache Kernel caches an address space object for each active address space. The address space state is stored as a root object and a collection of per-page virtual-to-physical memory mappings. The page mappings, one per mapped page, specify some access flags, a virtual address and the corresponding physical address.

An address space object is loaded by its application kernel with minimal state (currently, just the lock bit), returning a Cache Kernel identifier for the address space object. This identifier is used to specify this object for unloads, references and various query/modify operations. As an illustration of use, the UNIX emulation kernel executes a new process by loading an address space object into the Cache Kernel for the new process to run in and a new thread descriptor to execute this program. Its own data structures for the process record the Cache Kernel identifiers for the address space and thread objects as well as management information associated with the process, such as the bindings of virtual addresses to the program's code and data, which are typically contained in a file. The emulator may then explicitly load some per-page memory mappings for the new process or simply load them on demand, as described below.

When a new address space object is loaded, the Cache Kernel may write back another address space object to make space available for the new object. Before an address space object is written back, all the page mappings in the address space and all the associated threads are written back. For example, in response to address space writeback, the UNIX emulator (application kernel) marks the corresponding address space object as "unloaded," indicating that it must be loaded before the process it contains can be run again.

The page mappings associated with an address space object are normally loaded on demand in response to page faults. When a thread accesses a virtual address for which no mapping is cached, the Cache Kernel delivers a mapping fault to the kernel that owns the address space (and thread(s) contained therein), following the steps illustrated in Figure 2. In step 1, the hardware traps to the Cache Ker-

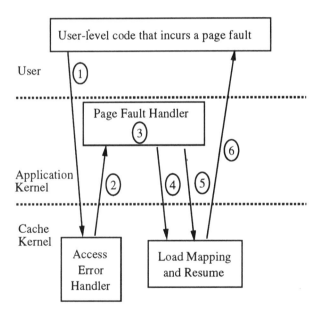

Figure 2: Page Fault Handling

nel access error handler. The handler stores the state of the faulting thread in its thread descriptor, switches the thread's address space to the thread's application kernel's address space, switches the thread's stack pointer to an exception stack provided by the application kernel, and switches the program counter to the address of the application kernel's

page fault handler, which is specified as an attribute of the kernel object corresponding to the application kernel. In step 2, the access error handler causes the thread to start executing the application-kernel-level page fault handler. The faulting address and the form of access (read or write) are communicated as parameters to the page fault handler. In step 3, the application kernel page fault handler navigates its virtual memory data structures, possibly locating a free page frame and reading the page from backing store. It constructs a page mapping descriptor and loads it into the Cache Kernel in step 4. (Alternatively, it may send a UNIX-style SEGV signal to the process. In this latter case, it resumes the thread at the address corresponding to the user-specified UNIX signal handler.) The loading of a new page descriptor may cause another page descriptor to be written back to the associated application kernel in order to make space for the new descriptor, the same as previously described for address space descriptors. In step 5, the faulting thread informs the Cache Kernel that exception processing is complete. The Cache Kernel then restores the stack pointer, program counter, and a few other registers, and resumes the thread in step 6. As an optimization, there is a special Cache Kernel call that both loads a new mapping and returns from the exception handler. To provide protection, the physical address and the access that the application kernel can specify in a new mapping are restricted by its authorized access to physical memory, as recorded in its corresponding kernel object loaded in the Cache Kernel.

Other exceptions are forwarded to the application kernel by the same mecahnism. In particular, exceptions arise from writing to a read-only page (protection fault), attempting to execute a privileged-mode instruction (privilege violation), and accessing a main-memory cache line that is held on a remote node (consistency fault)[1]. The application kernel has complete control of the faulting thread while handling the fault, just as a conventional operating system would. This approach allows the application kernel to handle these exceptions without complicating the Cache Kernel.

A page mapping is written back to the managing application kernel in response to an explicit request, such as when a page frame is reclaimed, as well as in response to another mapping being loaded. The writeback provides current state bits associated with the mapping including the "referenced" and "modified" bits. The application kernel uses this writeback information to update its records about the state of this page in the address space. In particular, it uses the "modified" bit to know whether the page contents need to be written to backing store before the page frame is reused. The page faulting and writeback mechanisms allow the Cache Kernel to cache only the active set of mappings, relying on the application kernel to store the other mappings.

---

[1] The *consistency fault* mechanism is used to implement a consistency protocol on a cache-line basis for distributed shared memory, providing a finer-grain consistency unit than pages. A consistency trap also occurs if a reference is made to a memory module that has failed.

The application kernel can explicitly unload inactive mappings, reducing the replacement interference on active mappings. For instance, the UNIX emulator may unload an address space descriptor (and thus all its page mappings) when the process is swapped to disk and no longer executing. In expected use, the Cache Kernel provides enough address space descriptors so that replacement interference in the Cache Kernel is primarily on the page mappings, not address space objects.

Page mappings are identified by address space and virtual address or virtual address range. This identification is adequate for mappings and avoids the space overhead of the general object identification scheme, which would require a separate field per page mapping descriptor. The size of page mapping descriptor is minimized because space for these descriptors dominates the space requirements for the Cache Kernel (see Section 5).

2.2 Interprocess Communication

All interprocess and device communication is provided in the caching model by implementing it as an extension of the virtual memory system using *memory-based messaging* [7]. With memory-based messaging, threads communicate through the memory system by mapping a shared region of physical memory into the sender and receiver address spaces, as illustrated in Figure 3. The sending thread

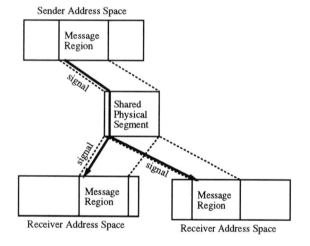

Figure 3: Memory-based Messaging

writes a message into this region and then delivers the address of the new message to the receiving threads as an *address-valued signal*. That is, the virtual address corresponding to the location of the new message is passed to the receiving threads' signal function, translated from the virtual address of the sending thread (using the normal inverted page table support). On receiving the address-valued signal, the receiving thread reads the message at the designated location in the virtual memory region. While the

thread is running in its signal function, additional signals are queued within the Cache Kernel.

To support memory-based messaging, the page mappings described in the previous section are extended to optionally specify a *signal thread* and also to specify that the page is in *message mode*. An application kernel interested in receiving signals for a given page specifies a signal thread in the mapping for the page. The signaling uses the same mapping data structures as the rest of the virtual memory system. This extension is simpler than the separate messaging mechanism for interprocess communication that arises with other micro-kernels. Also, the Cache Kernel is only involved in communication setup. The performance-critical data transfer aspect of interprocess communication is performed directly through the memory system. Moreover, with suitable hardware support, there is no software intervention even for signal delivery[2]. Thus, communication performance is limited primarily by the raw performance of the memory system, not the software overhead of copying, queuing and delivering messages, as arises with other micro-kernels.

Memory-based messaging is used for accessing devices controlled by the Cache Kernel. For example, the Ethernet device in our implementation is provided as memory-mapped transmission and reception memory regions. The client thread sends a signal to the Ethernet driver in the Cache Kernel to transmit a packet with the signal address indicating the packet buffer to transmit. On reception, a signal is generated to the receiving thread with the signal address indicating the buffer holding the new packet. This thread demultiplexes the data to the appropriate input stream, similar to conventional network protocol implementations.

Devices that fit into the memory-based messaging model directly require minimal driver code complexity of the Cache Kernel. They also provide the best performance. For example, our own network interface for a 266 Mb Fiber Channel interconnect is designed to fit into this memory-mapped model, and so requires relatively few (276) lines of code for the Cache Kernel driver. In particular, the driver only needs to support memory mapping the special device

---

[2]The ParaDiGM hardware [7] provides *automatic signal-on-write* to memory in message mode, delivering an *address-valued signal* to each processor managing a signal thread for the page when a thread writes a cache line in message mode. It also provides *message-oriented consistency* on pages in message mode, allowing a processor (presumably the sender) to write a cache line without requiring any "ownership" of the line. When the write completes, the cache controller updates other cached copies of the line as necessary. This specialized consistency minimizes the cache consistency overhead for memory used purely for messaging. The design also calls for hardware delivery of the signal using a per-processor reverse-TLB that maps physical addresses to the corresponding virtual address and signal handler function pairs so there is no software intervention on a reverse-TLB hit. At present, our hardware supports automatic signal generation but not delivery, so the missing portion is emulated in a tightly coded part of the Cache Kernel. Conventional hardware requires software support for generating the signal as well as signal delivery, but this software is a minor extension of the current Cache Kernel mapping mechanisms.

address space corresponding to the network interface. Data transfer and signaling is then handled using the general Cache Kernel memory-based messaging mechanism. The clock is also designed to fit this memory-based messaging model. In contrast, the Ethernet device requires a non-trivial Cache Kernel driver to implement the memory-based messaging interface because the Ethernet chip itself provides a conventional DMA interface.

An object-oriented RPC facility implemented on top of the memory-based messaging as a user-space communication library allows applications and services to use a conventional procedural communication interface to services. For instance, object writeback from the Cache Kernel to the owning application kernel uses a *writeback channel* implemented using this facility. This RPC facility is also used for high-performance communication between distributed application kernels, as described in Section 3. Memory-based messaging supports direct marshaling and demarshaling to and from communication channels with minimal copying and no protection boundary crossing in software. The implementation in user space allows application kernels control over communication resource management and exception handling, by, for example, overriding functions in the communication library.

2.3   Thread Objects

The Cache Kernel caches a collection of thread objects, one for each application kernel thread that should be considered for execution. The thread object is loaded with the values for all the registers and the location of the kernel stack to be used by this thread if it takes an exception (as described in Section 2.1). Other process state variables, such as signal masks and an open file table, are not supported by the Cache Kernel, and thus are stored only in the application kernel. As with address space objects, the Cache Kernel returns an object identifier when the thread is loaded which the application kernel can use later to unload the thread, to change its execution priority, or to force the thread to block. Each thread is associated with an address space which is specified (and must be already loaded) when loading the thread.

The Cache Kernel holds the set of active and response-sensitive threads by mechanisms similar to that used for page mappings. A thread is normally loaded when it is created, or unblocked and its priority makes it eligible to run. It is unloaded when the thread blocks on a long-term event, reducing the contention for thread descriptors in the Cache Kernel. For example, in the UNIX emulation kernel, a thread is unloaded when it begins to sleep with low priority waiting for user input. It is then reloaded when a "wakeup" call is issued on this event. (Reloading in response to user input does not introduce significant delay because the thread reload time (about 230 μs) is short compared to interactive response times.) A thread whose application has been swapped out is also unloaded until its application

is reloaded into memory. In this swapped state, it consumes no Cache Kernel descriptors, in contrast to the memory-resident process descriptor records used by the conventional UNIX kernel. A thread being debugged is also unloaded when it hits a breakpoint. Its state can then be examined and reloaded on user request.

A thread that blocks waiting on a memory-based messaging signal can be unloaded by its application kernel after it adds mappings that redirect the signal to one of the application kernel's internal (real-time) threads. The application-kernel thread then reloads the thread when it receives a redirected signal for this unloaded thread. This technique provides on-demand loading of threads similar to the on-demand loading of page mappings that occurs with page faults. A thread can also remain loaded in the Cache Kernel when it suspends itself by waiting on a signal so it is resumed more quickly when the signal arrives. An application kernel can handle threads waiting on short-term events in this way. It can also lock a small number of real-time threads in the Cache Kernel to ensure they are not written back. Retaining a "working set" of loaded threads allows rapid context switching without application kernel intervention.

Using this caching model for threads, an application kernel can implement a wide range of scheduling algorithms, including traditional UNIX-style scheduling. Basically, the application kernel loads a thread to schedule it, unloads a thread to deschedule it, and relies on the Cache Kernel's fixed priority scheduling to designate preference for scheduling among the loaded threads. For example the UNIX emulator per-processor *scheduling thread* wakes up on each rescheduling interval, adjusts the priorities of other threads to enforce its policies, and goes back to sleep. A special Cache Kernel call is provided as an optimization, allowing the scheduling thread to modify the priority of a loaded thread (rather than first unloading the thread, modifying its priority and then reloading it.) The scheduling thread is assured of running because it is loaded at high-priority and locked in the Cache Kernel. Real-time scheduling is provided by running the processes at high priority, possibly adjusting the priority over time to meet deadlines. Co-scheduling of large parallel applications can be supported by assigning a thread per processor and raising all the threads to the appropriate priority at the same time, possibly across multiple Cache Kernel instances, using inter-application-kernel communication.

A thread executing in a separate address space from its application kernel makes "system calls" to its kernel using the standard processor trap instruction. When a thread issues a trap instruction, the processor traps to the Cache Kernel, which then forwards the thread to start executing a trap handler in its application kernel using the same approach as described for page fault handling. This trap forwarding uses similar techniques to those described for UNIX binary emulation [8, 19, 1]. A trap executed by a thread executing in its application kernel (address space) is handled as a Cache Kernel call. An application that is linked directly in the same address space with its application kernel calls its application kernel as a library using normal procedure calls, and invokes the Cache Kernel directly using trap instructions.

The trap, page-fault and exception forwarding mechanisms provide "vertical" communication between the applications and their application kernels, and between the application kernels and the Cache Kernel. That is, "vertical" refers to communication between different levels of protection in the same process or thread, namely supervisor mode, kernel mode and conventional user mode. "Horizontal" communication refers to communication between processes, such as between application kernels and communication with other services and devices. It uses memory-based messaging, as described in the previous subsection.

2.4 Kernel Objects

The Cache Kernel caches a collection of kernel objects, one for each active application kernel. A kernel object designates the application kernel address space, the trap and exception handlers for the kernel and the resources that the kernel has been allocated, including the physical pages the kernel can map, the percentage of each processor the kernel is allowed to use, and the number of locked objects of each type the kernel can load. The address spaces and threads loaded by an application kernel are owned and managed by that application kernel.

For example, the UNIX emulator is represented by a kernel object in the Cache Kernel. Each new address space and thread loaded into the Cache Kernel by the UNIX emulator is designated as owned and managed by the UNIX emulator. Consequently, all traps and exceptions by threads executing in address spaces created by the UNIX emulator are forwarded to the UNIX emulator for handling, as described earlier.

A kernel object is loaded into the Cache Kernel when a new application kernel is executed. Kernel objects are loaded by, and written back to, the first application kernel, which is normally the *system resource manager* described in Section 3. This first kernel is created, loaded and locked on boot. As with all Cache Kernel objects, loading a new kernel object can cause the writeback of another kernel object if there are no free kernel object descriptors in the Cache Kernel. Unloading a kernel object is an expensive operation because it requires unloading the associated address spaces, threads, and memory mappings. The Cache Kernel provides a special set of operations for modifying the resource attributes of a kernel object, as an optimization over unloading a kernel object, modifying the kernel object attributes and reloading it. Currently, there are only three such specialized operations. The use of these operations is discussed further in Section 3.

Writeback of kernel objects is expected to be, and needs to be, infrequent. It is provided because it is simple to do in the Cache Kernel framework, ensures that the system resource manager need runs out of kernel descriptors, such as for large swapped jobs with their own kernels, and provides a uniform model for handling Cache Kernel objects.

This description covers the key aspects of the Cache Kernel interface. Other conventional operating system services are provided at the application kernel level, as illustrated by the UNIX emulator.

A key benefit of the Cache Kernel is that it allows execution of multiple application kernels simultaneously, both operating system emulators as well as application-specialized kernels, as described in the next section. In this mode, it supports system-wide resource management between these separate kernels, as covered in Section 3.

3 Other Application Kernels

A variety of application kernels can be run (simultaneously) on the Cache Kernel. For example, a large-scale parallel scientific simulation can run directly on top of the Cache Kernel to allow application-specific management of physical memory [16] (to avoid random page faults), direct access to the memory-based messaging, and application-specific processor scheduling to match program parallelism to the number of available processors. For example, we have experimented with a hypersonic wind tunnel simulator, MP3D [6], implemented using the particle-in-cell technique. This program can use hundreds of megabytes of memory, parallel processing and significant communication bandwidth to move particles when executed across multiple nodes and can significantly benefit from careful management of its own resources. For example, it can identify the portion of its data set to page out to provide room for data it is about to process. Similarly, a database server can be implemented directly on top of the Cache Kernel to allow careful management of physical memory for caching, optimizing page replacement to minimize the query processing costs. Finally, a real-time embedded system can be realized as an application kernel, controlling the locking of threads, address spaces and mappings into the Cache Kernel, and managing resources to meet response requirements.

An application kernel is any program that is written to interface directly to the Cache Kernel, handling its own memory management, processing management and communication. That is, it must implement the basic system object types and handle loading these objects into, and processing writeback from, the Cache Kernel. Moreover, to be efficient, it must be able to specialize the handling of these resources to the application requirements and behavior.

A C++ class library has been developed for each of the resources, namely memory management, processing and communication. These libraries allow applications to start

---

with a common base of functionality and then specialize, rather than provide all the required mechanism by itself. Application kernels can override general-purpose resource management routines in these libraries with more efficient application-specific ones. They can also override exception handling routines to provide application-specific recovery mechanisms.

The memory management library provides the abstraction of physical segments mapped into virtual memory regions, managed by a segment manager that assigns virtual addresses to physical memory, handling the loading of mapping descriptors on page faults. It bears some similarity to the library described by Anderson et al. [13]. The processing library is basically a thread library that schedules threads by loading them into the Cache Kernel rather than by using its own dispatcher and run queue. A communication library supports channels and channel management on top of the memory-based messaging, and interfaces to the stub routines of the object-oriented RPC facility mentioned earlier.

At the time of writing, we have implemented a simple subset of MP3D and a basic communication server using these libraries. In each of these cases, the application executes directly in the application kernel address space. We also have an initial design of a UNIX emulator, in which applications run in a separate address space from the application kernel for protection. We are also working to integrate a discrete-event simulation library we developed previously with these computational framework libraries. This simulation library provides temporal synchronization, virtual space decomposition of processing, load balancing and cache-architecture-sensitive memory management.

By allowing application control of resource management and exception handling, the Cache Kernel provides the basis for a highly scalable general-purpose parallel computer architecture that we have been developing in the ParaDiGM [5] project. The ParaDiGM architecture is illustrated in Figure 4. Each *multiprocessor module* (MPM) is a self-contained unit with a small number of processors, second-level cache and high-speed network interfaces, executing its own copy of the Cache Kernel out of its PROM and local memory. The high-speed network interfaces connect each MPM to other similarly configured processing nodes as well as to shared file servers. A shared bus connects the MPM to others in the same chassis and to memory modules.

The separate Cache Kernel per MPM limits the degree of parallelism that the Cache Kernel needs to support to the number of processors on one MPM, reducing contention for locks and eliminating the need for complex locking strategies. The MPM also provides a natural unit for resource management, further simplifying the Cache Kernel. Finally, the separate Cache Kernel per MPM provides a basis for fault-containment. A Cache Kernel error only disables its MPM and an MPM hardware failure only halts the local

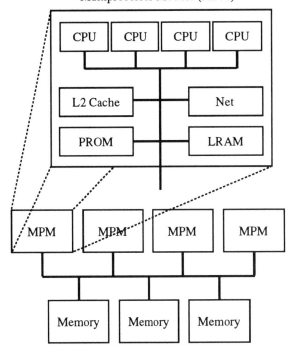

Figure 4: ParaDiGM Architecture

Cache Kernel instance and applications running on top of it, not the entire system. That is, a failure in one MPM does not need to impact other kernels. Explicit coordination between kernels, as required for distributed shared memory implementation, is provided by higher-level software.

The software architecture built on the ParaDiGM hardware architecture is illustrated in Figure 5. A sophisticated application can be distributed and replicated across several nodes, as suggested by the database query in the figure. The application can be programmed to recover from failures by restarting computations from a failed node on different nodes or on the original node after it recovers. One of our current challenges is extending the application kernel resource management class libraries to provide a framework for exception handling and recovery, facilitating the development of applications that achieve fault-tolerance on the basis provided by the Cache Kernel.

A variety of applications, server kernels and operating system emulators can be executing simultaneously on the same hardware as suggested in Figure 5. A special application kernel called the *system resource manager* (SRM), replicated one per Cache Kernel/MPM, manages the resource sharing between other application kernels so that they can share the same hardware simultaneously without unreasonable interference. For example, it prevents a rogue application kernel running a large simulation from disrupting the execution of a UNIX emulator providing timesharing services running on the same ParaDiGM configuration.

The SRM is instantiated when the Cache Kernel boots,

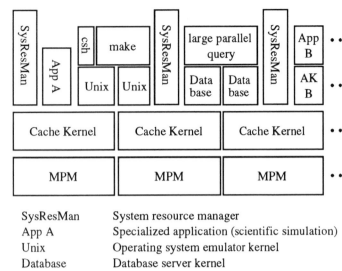

SysResMan	System resource manager
App A	Specialized application (scientific simulation)
Unix	Operating system emulator kernel
Database	Database server kernel
AK B	Kernel for specialized application B
App B	Specialized application B (user process)

Figure 5: Software Architecture

with its kernel descriptor specifying full permissions on all physical resources. It acts as the owning kernel for the other application kernel address spaces and threads as well as the application kernel objects themselves, handling writeback for these objects. The SRM initiates the execution of a new application kernel by creating a new kernel object, address space, and thread, granting an initial resource allocation, bringing the application's text and data into the address space, and loading these objects into the Cache Kernel. Later, it may swap the application kernel out, unloading its objects and saving its state on disk.

The SRM allocates processing capacity, memory pages and network capacity to application kernels. Resources are allocated in large units that the application kernel can then suballocate internally. Memory allocations are for periods of time from multiple seconds to minutes, chosen to amortize the cost of loading and unloading the memory from disk. Similarly, percentages of processors and percentages of network capacity are allocated over these extended periods of time rather than for individual time slices.

The SRM communicates with other instances of itself on other MPMs using the RPC facility, coordinating to provide distributed scheduling using techniques developed for distributed operating systems. In this sense, the SRM corresponds to the "first team" in V [4]. The SRM is replicated on each MPM for failure autonomy between MPMs, to simplify the SRM management, and to limit the degree of parallelism, as was discussed with other application kernels above. Our overall design calls for protection maps in the memory modules, so an MPM failure cannot corrupt memory beyond that managed by the SRM/Cache Kernel/MPM unit that failed. Application kernels that run across several MPMs can be programmed to recover from individual

MPM failures, as mentioned earlier.

In contrast to the general-purpose computing configurations supported by the SRM, a single-application configuration, such as real-time embedded control, can use a single application kernel executed as the first kernel. This application kernel, with the authorization to control resources of the first kernel, then has full control over system resources.

4 Internal Design Issues

The Cache Kernel has been implemented in C++ and is running on our multiprocessor ParaDiGM hardware. This hardware prototype uses an MPM with four Motorola 68040 processors running at 25Mhz, two megabytes of local memory and 512 kilobytes of PROM. The Cache Kernel manages four to eight megabytes of high-speed software-controlled second-level cache per MPM that is shared by all four processors, connecting to third-level memory and other MPMs using VMEbus. Each MPM also has two 266 Mb fiber optic channel connections, providing high-speed communication to other MPMs not on the same VMEbus. Although this hardware is not the highest performance at this time, it does provide interesting architectural support for our operating system research, including hardware support for memory-based messaging, hierarchical software-controlled caching, local memory and PROM per MPM, direct connection of high-speed networking to the second-level cache through the memory-based messaging facility, and cache-based locking support.

The Cache Kernel code is burned into PROM on each MPM together with a conventional PROM monitor and network boot program. It executes in supervisor mode with all its data structures in the local RAM of the MPM. The memory mapping is set to protect the Cache Kernel against corruption from application programs.

This section describes three key design issues that we encountered in its implementation, namely efficient mapping support, the object cache replacement mechanism and resource allocation control.

4.1 Mapping Data Structures

The Cache Kernel must efficiently support a large number of memory mappings to allow application kernels to map large amounts of memory with minimal overhead. The mapping needs to be space-efficient because they are stored in memory local to each instance of the Cache Kernel. The mappings must also support specification of a signal process and copy-on-write, although these occur with only a small percentage of the mappings. To meet these requirements, the information from a page mapping is stored across several data structures when it is loaded into the Cache Kernel.

The virtual-to-physical mapping is stored in conventionally structured page tables, one set per address space and logically part of the address space object. The mapping's flags, such as the writable and cachable bits, are also stored in the page table entry. The current implementation uses Motorola 68040 page tables as dictated by the hardware. However, this data structure could be adapted for use with a processor that requires software handling of virtual-to-physical translation, such as the MIPS requires on a TLB miss.

The physical-to-virtual mapping is stored in a physical memory map, using 16-byte descriptors per page, specifying the physical address, the virtual address, the address space and a hash link pointer. The physical memory map is used to delete all mappings associated with a given physical page as part of page reclamation as well as to determine all the virtual addresses mapping to a given physical page as part of signal delivery. The specifications of signal thread and source page for a copy-on-write for a page, if present, are also stored as similar descriptors in this data structure. This data structure is viewed as recording dependencies between objects, the physical-to-virtual dependency being a special but dominant case. That is, the descriptor is viewed as specifying a key, the dependent object and the context, corresponding to the physical address, virtual address and address space in the case of the physical-to-virtual dependency. A signal thread is recorded as a dependency record with the address of the physical-to-virtual mapping as the key, a pointer to the signal thread as the dependent, and a special signal context value as the context. Locating the threads to which a signal on a given physical page should be delivered requires looking up the physical-to-virtual dependency records for the page, and then looking up the signal dependency records for each of these records. A similar approach is used to record copy-on-write mappings.

This approach to storing page mapping information minimizes the space overhead because the common case requires 16 bytes per page plus a small overhead for the page tables. However, it does impose some performance penalty on signal delivery, given the two lookups required in this approach.

To provide efficient signal delivery in the common case, a per-processor reverse-TLB is provided that maps physical addresses to the corresponding virtual address and signal handler function pairs. When the Cache Kernel receives a signal on a given physical address, each processor that receives the signal checks whether the physical address "reverse translates" according to this reverse TLB. If so, the signal is delivered immediately to the active thread. Otherwise, it uses the two-stage lookup described above. Thus, signal delivery to the active thread is fast and the overhead of signal delivery to the non-active thread is more, but is dominated by the rescheduling time to activate the thread (if it is now the highest priority). The reverse-TLB is currently implemented in software in the Cache Kernel but is feasible to implement in hardware with a modest extension to the processor, allowing dispatch of signal-handling to the active thread with no software intervention.

As mentioned earlier, the ParaDiGM hardware provides a number of extensions that the Cache Kernel takes advantage of for performance. However, the Cache Kernel is designed to be portable across conventional hardware. These extensions are relatively easy to omit or provide in software and have relatively little impact on performance, especially with uniprocessor configurations.

4.2 Object Replacement

The Cache Kernel requires a more complex replacement mechanism than a conventional data cache because the objects it caches have relationships among themselves, between themselves and the hardware, and internally to each object. For example, when an address space is replaced in the Cache Kernel and written back to its application kernel, all of its associated threads must also be unloaded and written back. (The alternative of allowing a loaded thread to refer to a missing address space was considered but was rejected as being too complicated, error-prone, and inefficient.) The relationships between objects and the hardware must also be managed carefully. For example, when unloading an address space, the mappings associated with that address space must be removed from the hardware TLB and/or page tables. Similarly, before writing back an executing thread, the processor must first save the thread context and context-switch to a different thread. Objects also have a more complex structure than the typical fixed-size cache line. For example, an address space is represented as a variable number of page table descriptors linked into a tree, providing efficient virtual-to-physical address mapping. Thus, loading and unloading these objects requires several actions and careful synchronization to ensure that the object is loaded and unloaded atomically with respect to other modules in the Cache Kernel and the application kernels.

Figure 6 shows the dependencies between Cache Kernel objects. The arrows in the figure indicate a reference, and therefore a caching dependency, from the object at the tail of the arrow to the object at the head. For example, a signal mapping in the physical memory map references a thread which references an address space which references its owning kernel object. Thus, the signal mapping must be unloaded when the thread, the address space or the kernel is unloaded.

When an object is unloaded, either in response to an explicit application kernel request or as required to free a descriptor in the Cache Kernel to handle a new load request, the object first unloads the objects that directly depend on it. These objects first unload the objects that depend on them, and so on. Locked dependent objects are unloaded the same as unlocked objects. Locking only prevents an object from being unloaded by the object reclamation mechanism when the object and the objects on which it depends are locked. For example, a locked mapping can be reclaimed unless its

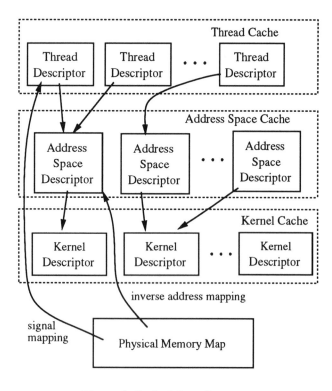

Figure 6: Cached Data Structures

address space, its kernel object and its signal thread (if any) are locked.

The Cache Kernel data structures use non-blocking synchronization techniques so that potentially long unload operations are performed without disabling interrupts or incurring long lock hold times. The version support that is used with the non-blocking synchronization also allows a processor to determine whether a data structure has been modified, perhaps by a unload, concurrently with its execution of a Cache Kernel operation. If it has been modified, the processor retries the operation. For example, a processor loading a new entry into the signal reverse TLB from the physical memory map can check that the version of the map has not changed before adding the entry, and can relookup the mapping if it has.

Memory-based messaging complicates the object replacement mechanism with the need for multi-mapping consistency. *Multi-mapping consistency* ensures that the sender's mapping for a message page is written back if any of the receivers' mappings are written back. This consistency avoids the situation of the sender signaling on the address and the receivers not being notified because their mappings are not loaded in the Cache Kernel. To enforce multi-mapping consistency, the Cache Kernel flushes all writable mappings associated with a physical page frame when it flushes any signal mapping for the page. Each application kernel is expected to load all the mappings for a message page when it loads any of the mappings. Thus, if the mappings are not loaded when the sender writes a mes-

sage, it generates a mapping trap, causing all the mappings to be loaded. When communication is between threads on separate Cache Kernel instances, the application kernels must coordinate to ensure multi-mapping consistency. Locking of active mappings in the Cache Kernel can be used in this case as part of this coordination. As an alternative to unloading all the mappings, an application kernel can redirect signals to another thread as described in Section 2.2.

4.3 Resource Allocation

The Cache Kernel provides resource allocation enforcement mechanisms to allow mutually distrustful application kernels to execute using shared resources without undue interference.

An application kernel's access to memory is recorded as read and write permission on *page groups* of physical memory. A *page group* is a set of contiguous physical pages starting on a boundary that is aligned modulo the number of pages in the group (currently 128 4k pages). The page group as a large unit of allocation minimizes the space required in the Cache Kernel to record access rights to memory and minimizes overhead allocating memory to application kernels. Using two bits per page group to indicate access, a two-kilobyte memory access array in each kernel object records access to the current four-gigabyte physical address space. Each time a page mapping is loaded into the Cache Kernel, it checks that the access for the specified physical page is consistent with the memory access array associated with the loading kernel. Typically, each kernel has read and write access on a page group or else no access (meaning the memory is allocated to another application kernel). However, we are exploring the use of page groups that are shared between application kernels for communication and shared data, where one or more of the application kernels may only have read access to the memory. As described in Section 3, only the SRM can change the memory access array for a kernel.

The kernel object also specifies the processor allocation that the kernel's threads should receive in terms of a percentage for each processor's time and the maximum priority it can specify for its threads, *i.e.,* its quota. The Cache Kernel monitors the consumption of processor time by each thread and adds that to the total consumed by its kernel for that processor, charging a premium for higher priority execution and a discounted charge for lower priority execution. Over time, it calculates the percentage of each processor that the kernel is consuming. If a kernel exceeds its allocation for a given processor, the threads on that processor are reduced to a low priority so that they only run when the processor is otherwise idle. The graduated charging rate provides an incentive to run threads at lower priority. For example, the UNIX emulator degrades the priority of compute-bound programs to low priority to reduce the effect on its quota when running what are effectively batch, not interactive, programs.

The specification of a maximum priority for the kernel's threads allows the SRM to prevent an application kernel from interfering with real-time threads in another application kernel. For example, a compute-bound application kernel that is executing well under its quota might otherwise use the highest priorities to accelerate its completion time, catastrophically delaying real-time threads. The Cache Kernel also implements time-sliced scheduling of threads at each priority level, so that a real-time thread cannot excessively interfere with a real-time thread from another application executing at the same priority. That is, a thread at a given priority should run after all higher priority threads have blocked (or been unloaded), and after each thread of the same priority ahead of this thread in the queue has received one time slice. This scheme is relatively simple to implement and appears sufficient to allow real-time processing to co-exist with batch application kernels.

I/O capacity is another resource for which controlled sharing between application kernels is required. To date, we have only considered this issue for our high-speed network facility. These interfaces provide packet transmission and reception counts which can be used to calculate network transfer rates. The channel manager for this networking facility in the SRM calculates these I/O rates, and temporarily disconnects application kernels that exceed their quota, exploiting the connection-oriented nature of this networking facility. There is currently no I/O usage control in the Cache Kernel itself.

There is no accounting and charging for cache misses or memory-based message signaling even though these events make significant use of shared hardware resources. For example, a large number of cache misses can significantly load the memory system and the interconnecting bus, degrading the performance of other programs. It may be feasible to add counters to the second-level cache to recognize and charge for this overhead. The premium charged for high priority execution of threads is intended in part to cover the costs of increased context switching expected at high priority. However, to date we have not addressed this problem further.

We have also not implemented quotas on the number of Cache Kernel objects that an application kernel may have loaded at a given time, although there are limits on the number of locked objects. Application kernels simply contend for cached entries, just like independent programs running on a shared physically mapped memory cache. Further experience is required to see if quotas on cache objects are necessary.

5 Evaluation

The Cache Kernel is evaluated from three major standpoints: code size, caching performance, and microbenchmarks of trapping, signaling and page fault handling. The code size measurements indicate the reduction in size

is a benefit of the caching approach while the other measurements indicate that the caching model has not detracted from performance over a conventional kernel structure.

5.1 Code Size

The Cache Kernel represents a significant reduction in size and complexity over previous kernels. For example, the virtual memory code in the Cache Kernel is a little under 1,500 lines of C++ code, whereas the V kernel virtual memory support for the same hardware is 13,087 lines of C/C++. The virtual memory system for Ultrix 4.1 for MIPS is 23,400 lines, for SunOS 4.1.2 for Sparc is 14,400 lines, and for Mach for MIPS is a little over 20,000 lines. In total, the Cache Kernel consists of 14,958 lines of C++ code, of which roughly 6000 lines (40 percent) is PROM monitor, remote debugging and booting support (including implementations of UDP, IP, ARP, RARP, and TFTP.) The second-level cache manager software requires a further 1262 lines of code, which would be eliminated if the second-level cache management was implemented entirely in hardware, as is the more conventional approach.

The Cache Kernel has a binary code and data size of 139 kilobytes allowing it to fit easily into the PROM. We expect the size of the Cache Kernel to grow somewhat as we extend and refine its functionality, but do not see it moving beyond 150 kilobytes.

Based on these measurements and our experience writing and debugging the code, we conclude that the caching model, the minimal object approach, and memory-based messaging significantly reduce the size and complexity of kernel code over conventional approaches, including our previous micro-kernel work.

5.2 Caching Performance

The Cache Kernel as a cache of descriptors can be expected to perform well with programs that are reasonably structured, and is not the key performance problem for those that are not, as argued below. First, as shown in Table 1, the size of the descriptors is relatively small, allowing the Cache Kernel to hold enough descriptors to avoid thrashing under reasonable application demands. For instance,

Object	Size (bytes)	Cache Size
Kernel	2160	16
AddrSpace	60	64
Thread	532	256
MemMapEntry	16	65536

Table 1: Cache Kernel Object Sizes(bytes)

our prototype configuration provides 256 thread descriptors for a space cost in local RAM of about 128 kilobytes. (The number designates the maximum number of thread descriptors that can be loaded in the Cache Kernel at one time.) A system that is actively switching among more than 256 threads is incurring a context switching overhead that would dominate the cost of loading and unloading thread descriptors from the Cache Kernel. With this number of thread descriptors, 64 address space descriptors and 16 kernel descriptors, these descriptors constitute about 10 percent of the 2 megabytes of local memory on our hardware prototype MPM.

Approximately 50 percent of the local RAM is used to store the `MemMapEntry` descriptors listed last in Table 1, providing roughly 65,000 descriptors. Assuming on average at least four cache lines (less than four percent) of each page mapped by these descriptors is accessed, then this number of mapping descriptors covers that accommodated in our 8-megabyte second-level cache[3]. Consequently, software that actively accesses more pages than there are mapping descriptors will thrash the second-level data cache as well as the Cache Kernel memory mappings. Moreover, a program that has poorer page locality than we have hypothesized (*i.e.*, less than four percent usage of pages) also suffers a significant performance penalty from TLB miss behavior on most architectures [3]. For example, we measured up to a 25 percent degradation in performance in the MP3D program mentioned above from processors accessing particles scattered across too many pages. The solution with MP3D was to enforce page locality as well as cache line locality by copying particles in some cases as they moved between processors during the computation. In general, reasonable page locality is necessary for performance, and programs with reasonable page locality execute with minimal replacement interference on page mappings in the Cache Kernel. With programs whose lack of locality leads to extra paging to disk or over the network, the Cache Kernel overhead for loading and unloading mappings is dominated by the page I/O overhead.

The mapping descriptors represent as little as 0.4 percent overhead on the space that they map, so the actual space overhead is acceptable, even considering some duplication of this information at the application kernel level.

The mapping descriptors typically require two to four times the space of the page table descriptors, which are also part of the space overhead. The top-level 512-byte page tables consume a small amount of space because their number is exactly equal to the number of address space descriptors. Assuming reasonable page clustering, the space for the 512-byte second-level tables is also small, bringing the space required for first- and second-level tables to about 5K per address space. Finally, the 256-byte third-level page tables map 64 pages each, *i.e.*, there is one third-level page table for up to 64 16-byte mapping descriptors. Assuming the table is at least half-full, at least two times as much space is used for mapping descriptors as for third-level page tables.

---

[3]Our hardware has 32-byte cache line size, 8 megabytes of cache, and a page size of 4k (128 lines).

The execution time costs of Cache Kernel object loading and unloading operations are shown in Table 2 for each type of object, with and without writeback occurring. The

Object Types	load No writeback	load Writeback	unload
Mappings	45	145	160
(optimized)	67	167	
Threads	113	489	206
AddrSpaces	101	229	152
Kernel	244	291	80

Table 2: Basic Operations — Elapsed Time in Microseconds

optimized mapping load operation combines loading a new mapping with restarting the faulting thread. This operation is an important optimization for page fault handling.

Cache Kernel loading and writeback overhead can be expected to be minimal in typical system operation. Loading page mappings is expected to be the most common operation, occurring as new page mappings are loaded, and it is also the least expensive. The time to load a mapping could be increased somewhat by the cost of reclamation if reclamation ended up scanning a large range of locked mappings, but the large number of mapping descriptors makes this situation unlikely. The thread loading and unloading corresponds more or less to blocking on long-term events and so occurs infrequently. The loading and unloading of address spaces and kernels typically corresponds to loading and unloading these entities to disk or over the network. Thus, their respective costs are not significant compared to the times associated with these disk/network operations. In the worst case, a kernel descriptor needs to be reclaimed, causing writeback of all the address spaces, threads and mappings associated with the kernel. While this operation can take several milliseconds, it is performed with interrupts enabled and very infrequently. Of course, with a real-time configuration in which objects are locked in the Cache Kernel, the overhead would be essentially zero.

5.3 Trap, Communication and Page Fault Times

The performance of applications using the Cache Kernel is most dependent on the trap handling, signal delivery and page fault handling times.

The cost of a simple trap from a UNIX program to its emulator is 37 microseconds, effectively the cost of a `getpid` operation. This time is 12 microseconds longer than the same operation performed in Mach 2.5 running on a NextStation with a comparable speed processor. For most system calls, the extra trap overhead is insignificant compared to the system call processing time, and that processing time is largely independent of the Cache Kernel.

The time to deliver a signal from one thread to another running on a separate processor is 71 microseconds, composed of 44 microseconds for signal delivery and 27 microseconds for the return from signal handler. These measurements are in agreement with (in fact slightly better than) those reported for a similar implementation of memory-based messaging [7]. Because the communication schemes are identical at the higher levels, and no Cache Kernel involvement occurs on data transfer, the communication using the Cache Kernel is as efficient as the communication in the V implementation of memory-based messaging.

The basic cost of page fault handling is 99 microseconds, which includes 32 microseconds for transfer to the application kernel and 67 microseconds for the optimized mapping load operation. This cost is comparable to the page fault cost of Ultrix and other conventional systems and also comparable to the cost of the comparable operation for external page cache management in the V kernel as described by Harty and Cheriton [16]. A page fault that entails page zeroing, page copying or page read from backing store incurs costs that make the Cache Kernel overhead insignificant. Extrapolating from the application-level performance measured by Harty and Cheriton [16] indicates that performance of applications on the Cache Kernel will be comparable to that of conventional operating systems on the same hardware.

6 Related Work

The Cache Kernel builds on the experience and insight gained in the previous work on micro-kernels, such as V [4] and Mach [21]. As demonstrated in Mach, a dominant contributor to the complexity of these kernels is the virtual memory mechanisms for recording shared mappings, such as shadow object chains. With the Cache Kernel, this complexity has been moved outside of the kernel, cleanly partitioned from the performance-critical mapping supported by the Cache Kernel.

The Cache Kernel interface and facilities for virtual memory support bear some similarity to Mach's "Pmap" interface [11, 15]. However, the Cache Kernel includes additional support for deferred copy as well as page group protection, which was not needed in Mach because the Pmap interface was only an internal interface. The Pmap interface also does not consider multi-mapping consistency support, as required for memory-based messaging. In contrast to the caching of operating system objects in the Cache Kernel, which writes back the objects to untrusted application kernels, KeyKOS [10] writes back objects to protected disk pages. That is, it is only caching the objects in the sense of paging those data structures.

A redesign of Multics [20] proposed the idea of virtual processes that were loaded and saved from a fixed number of "real processes," similar to the thread caching mechanism in the Cache Kernel, but this proposal was never implemented.

Finally, the Cache Kernel exploits memory-based messaging [7] and application-controlled physical memory [16] to minimize mechanism while providing performance and control to sophisticated applications that wish to provide their own operating system kernel. It also builds on experience in implementing binary UNIX emulation [8, 19]. In contrast to Chorus [14], which loads operating system emulator modules directly into the kernel, the Cache Kernel executes its emulators in a separate address space and in non-privileged mode. The lock-free implementation uses similar techniques to that used by Massalin and Pu [18]. These advances together with the caching approach reduce the complexity of the Cache Kernel such that it can be integrated with the PROM for further stability and reliability. They also provide application performance that is competitive with conventional monolithic operating systems.

In contrast to the highly optimized, same-CPU and cross-address space IPC in L3 [12] and KeyKOS [10], the Cache Kernel supports inter-CPU peer-to-peer "horizontal" communication through memory-based messaging. The Cache Kernel trap forwarding facility most closely resembles the sort of same-CPU IPC found in L3, providing efficient transfer of control in the special case of an application communicating with its kernel.

A different approach to application-specific customization is being explored by the SPIN micro-kernel effort [2]. In SPIN, untrusted users write kernel extensions in a pointer-safe language. The extensions are compiled by a trusted compiler and dynamically loaded into the micro-kernel, where they are activated by system events (such as context switch or page fault). They interact with the micro-kernel through protected interfaces but without paying the system call cost. Thus, SPIN allows user modifications to the kernel whereas the Cache Kernel does not. However, with SPIN, the integrity of the micro-kernel is highly dependent on the adequacy of the compiler checking. Customizability is also limited by the set of events one can hook into, and by the expressiveness of the protected interface. Moreover, these user customizations appear to require a complex framework in the micro-kernel, including a supervisor-level garbage collector to reclaim memory allocations made by these extensions and mechanisms to limit resource consumption by these extensions. In contrast, the Cache Kernel is protected from user programming by hardware, does not significantly depend on extended languages and trusted compilers, and implements a relatively simple resource management model, given the simple set of objects it provides. Moreover, the mechanisms in the user class libraries, such as the virtual memory support, are more readily user customizable using the C++ inheritance mechanism.

Like the Cache Kernel, the Aegis exokernel [9] enables application-specific customization through a micro-kernel implementing a minimal machine-dependent interface to the underlying hardware. Like SPIN, Aegis allows untrusted users to extend the supervisor-level portion of the operating system using a variety of techniques to achieve saftey, including code examination, sandboxing, and the use of type-safe languages. Most hardware-level traps are reflected to application-specific trap handlers. For example, an application can install its own TLB miss handler that navigates application-specific page tables. This approach depends on the benefits of application-specific page table structures justifying the cost of ensuring safety in the performance-critical TLB miss handler, and other similar examples.

In overall comparison to these last two competing approaches, the Cache Kernel places a hard protection boundary at a lower level than conventional micro-kernels and exports more control for user customizability while SPIN and Aegis allow controlled entry of supposedly "safe" user software through the protection boundary. We conjecture that a hard protection boundary is required for reliable systems (compilers have enough trouble just generating correct code, never mind checking it for safety), and that the control exported by the caching model is adequate to implement the required application mechanisms. However, further experience is required with all these approaches.

7   Concluding Remarks

The caching model of operating system kernel functionality has produced a small, fast micro-kernel, namely the V++ Cache Kernel, providing system performance that appears competitive with monolithic kernels and well-suited for building robust scalable parallel systems.

As realized in the V++ Cache Kernel, the caching model offers three key benefits. First, the low-level caching interface provides application control of hardware resource management. An application kernel can load and unload objects to implement any desired resource management policy, only relying on the Cache Kernel to handle the loaded active objects (over short time intervals) according to this policy.

Second, the low-level Cache Kernel interface and its forwarding of exceptions to the application kernel allows application-specific exception handling and recovery. The caching approach also means that an application never encounters the "hard" error of the kernel running out of thread or address space descriptors as can occur with conventional systems like UNIX. The Cache Kernel always allows more objects to be loaded, writing back other objects to make space if necessary.

Finally, the caching model has led to a fundamental reduction in the complexity of supervisor mode software compared to prior micro-kernel work, measured by both lines of code and binary code size. The plethora of query and modify operations of conventional operating systems are absent from the Cache Kernel. Instead, the application kernel unloads the appropriate object, examines its state, and, if a modify operation, loads a modified version of that state back into the Cache Kernel. With experience, we are adding a small number of special query and modify operations as optimizations of this basic mechanism, such as a kernel call to modify the page groups associated with a kernel. However, these few optimizations do not significantly increase the size or complexity of the Cache Kernel. The use of memory-based messaging further simplifies the Cache Kernel and minimizes data copying and traps across the kernel protection boundary. We have taken advantage of this smaller size and stable functionality by incorporating the Cache Kernel into the PROM monitor code.

The Cache Kernel's small size allows it to be used economically in embedded real-time systems as well as to be replicated on each node of a large-scale parallel architecture for fault containment. Exploiting the Cache Kernel facilities, sophisticated application kernels can support efficient, robust parallel computation, real-time processing and database management systems while sharing all or part of a multiprocessor with other application kernels.

We are currently developing application kernels and operating system emulators that exploit the Cache Kernel capabilities. In particular, we are developing a simulation kernel (running on the Cache Kernel) that supports applications such as the MP3D wind tunnel simulation [6]. The operating systems emulators, such as one for UNIX, allow simple applications to share the same hardware concurrently with these sophisticated applications. We are also exploring the use of the Cache Kernel and modular application kernels for fault-tolerant scalable parallel and distributed computing, as described in Section 3.

Looking ahead, hardware manufacturers might reasonably provide a Cache-Kernel-like PROM monitor for their future hardware. This approach would allow a wide range of applications and operating systems to use the hardware without introducing as many dependencies on low-level hardware characteristics. The result would be better portability as well as greater freedom for the hardware manufacturers to revise their implementation of the Cache Kernel abstraction. In fact, it would allow independently developed operating systems to execute concurrently on the same hardware, a situation similar to that provided by the *virtual machine* operating system efforts of the 1960's and 70's. However, the Cache Kernel "virtual machine" supports scalable high-performance parallel distributed systems, not just the conventional single processor, single-node configurations of yore.

8   Acknowledgements

This work was sponsored in part by ARPA under US Army contract DABT63-91-K-0001. Equipment and funding by IBM for the ParaDiGM hardware is also gratefully acknowledged. This paper has benefited considerably from the comments of the reviewers, our "shepherds" Brian Bershad and

Willy Zwaenepoel, and various colleagues, including Mary Baker, Fusun Ertemalp, Hugh Holbrook, Michael Greenwald, Tim Mann and Ross Finlayson.

References

[1] B.N. Bershad, T.E. Anderson, E.D. Lazowska, and H.M. Levy. Lightweight remote procedure call. *ACM Transactions on Computer Systems*, 8(1):37–55, February 1990.

[2] B.N. Bershad, C. Chambers, S. Eggers, C. Maeda, D. McNamee, P. Pardyak, S. Savage, and E. Gün Sirer. Spin — an extensible microkernel for application-specific operating system services. University of Washington Computer Science and Engineering Technical Report 94-03-03, February 1994.

[3] J.B. Chen, A. Borg, and N.P. Jouppi. A simulation-based study of TLB performance. In *Proc. 19th Annual Intl. Symposium on Computer Architecture*, pages 114–123. ACM SIGARCH, IEEE Computer Society, May 1992.

[4] D.R. Cheriton. The V distributed system. *Comm. ACM*, 31(3):314–333, March 1988.

[5] D.R. Cheriton, H. Goosen, and P. Boyle. ParaDiGM: A highly scalable shared-memory multi-computer architecture. *IEEE Computer*, 24(2), February 1991.

[6] D.R. Cheriton, H. Goosen, and P. Machanick. Restructuring a parallel simulation to improve shared memory multiprocessor cache behavior: A first experience. In *Shared Memory Multiprocessor Symposium*, pages 23–31. ACM, April 1991.

[7] D.R. Cheriton and R. Kutter. Optimizing memory-based messaging for scalable shared memory multiprocessor architectures. Stanford Computer Science Technical Report CS-93-123, December 1993.

[8] D.R. Cheriton, G.R. Whitehead, and E.W. Sznyter. Binary emulation of UNIX using the V kernel. In *USENIX Summer Conference*. USENIX, June 1990.

[9] D.R. Engler, M.F. Kaashoek, and J.W. O'Toole Jr. The operating system kernel as a secure programmable machine. *Proceedings of the ACM European SIGOPS Workshop*, September 1994.

[10] A.C. Bomberger et al. The KeyKOS nanokernel architecture. In *Proceedings of the USENIX Workshop on Micro-kernels and Other Kernel Architectures*. USENIX, April 1992.

[11] D. Black et al. Translation lookaside consistency: A software approach. In *Proc. 17th Int. Symp. on Computer Architecture*, pages 113–122, April 1989.

[12] J. Liedtke et al. Two years of experience with a micro-kernel based os. *Operating Systems Review*, 25(2):57–62, 1991.

[13] K. Anderson et al. Tools for the development of application-specific virtual memory management. In *OOPSLA*, 1993.

[14] M. Rozier et al. Overview of the CHORUS distributed operating system. In *Proceedings of the USENIX Workshop on Micro-kernels and Other Kernel Architectures*. USENIX, April 1992.

[15] R. Rashid et al. Machine-independent virtual memory management for paged unitprocessor and multiprocessor architectures. *IEEE Trans Comput.*, 37(8):896–908, August 1988.

[16] K. Harty and D.R. Cheriton. Application-controlled physical memory using external page cache management. In *ASPLOS*, pages 187–197. ACM, October 1992.

[17] J. Kearns and S. DeFazio. Diversity in database reference behavior. *Performance Evaluation Review*, 1989.

[18] H. Massalin and C. Pu. A lock-free multiprocessor OS kernel. Technical Report CUCS-005-91, Computer Science Department, Columbia University, October 1991.

[19] R. Rashid and D. Goluv. UNIX as an application process. In *USENIX Summer Conference*. Usenix, June 1990.

[20] M. Schroeder, D. Clark, and J. Saltzer. The MULTICS kernel design project. In *Proceedings of the 6th Symposium on Operating Systems Principles*, pages 43–56. ACM, November 1977.

[21] M. Young et al. The duality of memory and communication in the implementation of a multiprocessor operating system. In *11th Symp. on Operating Systems Principles*. ACM, November 1987.

Panel: Radical Operating Systems Structures for Extensibility

Paul Leach *(Microsoft)*, moderator

Brian Bershad *(Univ. of Washington)*
David Cheriton *(Stanford University)*
Frans Kaashoek *(MIT)*
Steven Lucco *(CMU)*
Larry Peterson *(Univ. of Arizona)*

Abstract

Why are there so many major new kernel efforts underway today — more than at any time in recent memory? What is spawning this upsurge in kernel development activity? Is it the information highway? ATM? Wireless? Do RISC processors make microkernels too slow? Is OS extensibility really required to cope with changing system requirements? Do we really need to insert untrusted application code into the kernel to get performance? In this panel, five leading OS researchers will explain what trends in computer systems make *their* new kernel necessary, and why their approach is better than the other four.

Some Issues in the Design of an Extensible Operating System

Stefan Savage and Brian N. Bershad
Department of Computer Science and Engineering
University of Washington
Seattle, WA 98195
{savage,bershad}@cs.washington.edu

Extensible operating systems are designed around the principle that the service and performance requirements of all applications cannot be met in advance by any operating system. Consequently, an extensible system strives to provide a dynamic software infrastructure which allows system interfaces and implementations to be adapted or replaced to best serve application demands. However, realizing this goal poses a number of unique problems which must be addressed. Foremost among these are:

- Incrementality. Small changes to the system's behavior can be affected with small amounts of code.

- Correctness. An extension provided by an application should not compromise the overall integrity of the system.

- Efficiency. The potential for an extension should incur no overhead. The use of an extension should have an overhead which is determined by the extension's code, and not the infrastructure that has enabled the extension.

A system's *incrementality* determines the ease of introducing a system extension. Systems with high degrees of incrementality have few policy decisions embedded in the implementation and provide fine grain "hooks" to allow extensions to interpose on, or replace, existing code.

High degrees of incrementality make a system flexible but they also present greater opportunities for system corruption. Traditional systems have a relatively easy job maintaining integrity because they have few trust relationships to enforce. Such systems reply on almost complete trust between different components of the operating system kernel and frequently share data directly. Untrusted clients are isolated through a combination of memory protection and run time verification of arguments passed through a small number of external interfaces. System extensions such as dynamically loadable device drivers or file systems are usually trusted in their entirely.

Extensible systems, by contrast, export potentially large numbers of interfaces to untrusted clients. These untrusted extensions must be isolated from misusing these interfaces in any way that might compromise the integrity of the overall system. Moreover, it is not possible to provide this isolation mechanically through memory protection. While reference isolation mechanisms can ensure that storage is not corrupted, they are not sufficient for enforcing more complicated restrictions, such as invariants about liveness or synchronization. For example, an extension may enter an infinite loop, or fail to follow a locking protocol on a shared resource, or invoke an operation with invalid parameters.

These invariants must be guaranteed using a combination of *a priori* verification, run-time protection mechanisms, and safe interface design techniques. We believe that much of this work is well suited to current compiler technology which allows for both the automation of such isolation mechanisms as well as opportunities to optimize their implementation based on high level information.

We are designing an extensible system called SPIN, which attempts to solve these issues using a combination of language and compiler support for the safe manipulation of objects and the design of careful resilient interfaces to share system resources.

Low and High Risk Operating System Architectures

David R. Cheriton
Computer Science Department
Stanford University
cheriton@cs.stanford.edu

An operating system is the manager of a computer system. Managers should ensure proper operation of an organization and its resources to provide good performance. To manage, operating systems need control. An unprotected operating system has no control. MS-DOS, MacOS are not operating systems; they are run-time libraries. They have no true control. Any application can take over the machine from these fake operating systems. Thus, an operating system must be protected from application programs, and must provide protection between application programs. Good protection is hard, judging by the number of times operating systems designers have abdicated from this task, or screwed up this aspect of the design.

One cop-out has been the single-user excuse, stated as: "No protection is needed because there is only one user on the computer." But experience suggests otherwise. Viruses show the need for protection between applications, and the operating system and the applications. Moreover, protection between users seems to follow easily from protection between applications, and thus need not be a direct operating system design goal. Thus, the single-user versus multi-user distinction is not relevant.

Operating system designers also have fallen for the temptation of trusting the language compiler to provide protection by compile-time checking. This tendency reoccurs periodically in the research community, along with the fantasy of a "safe" language. However, it is a high-risk approach. A compiler is a large, complex piece of software. It is hard enough to have confidence that it produces correct code. Believing its protection checking is correct takes more faith than I have. Moreover, real applications and modules are binaries, not source code. The operating system really deals with "bags of bits." When your operating system crashes at 3 am in the morning, the day before product launch, will you really believe that your protection provided by the compiler is adequate and correct?

We define a low-risk operating system architecture as one that implements protection with a simple hardware/software mechanism. It is then feasible to thoroughly test and inspect to gain confidence that this mechanism is right. Memory protection and privileged modes in hardware are common, simple and relatively well understood. The weak point is the size of the operating system kernel and its various escape mechanisms (/dev/kmem, etc.) that further increase the number of lines of code that are critical to protection. The V++ Cache Kernel requires a significantly smaller amount of protection-critical code and mechanism than many previous protected kernels, aided by the caching approach as well as the memory-based messaging and application-controlled page cache management we developed previously. As such, it provides an interesting point on the spectrum of protection risk for operating system architectures.

However, the Cache Kernel (and any kernel) is a fuzzy point to measure at best, because there are almost invariably additional code that is critical to ensuring protection. For example, in Unix, all su-uid programs are a critical aspect to consider for protection. The security community has a good term for what one needs to consider, namely the *trusted computing base*. We need to think in similar terms.

The operating system community should develop a standardized measure of protection risk for operating systems based on the number of lines of code and hardware design that is part of the trusted computing base, or whatever term we choose to consider. Just as with SpecMarks, it may not be the only figure of merit, but it should at least be known and considered.

The Exokernel Approach to Operating System Extensibility

Dawson R. Engler   M. Frans Kaashoek   James W. O'Toole Jr.

MIT Laboratory for Computer Science

To provide modularity and performance, operating system (OS) kernels should have only minimal embedded functionality. Today's operating systems are large, inefficient, and most importantly, inflexible. In our view, most OS performance and flexibility problems can be eliminated simply by pushing the OS interface lower. To achieve this goal, we have defined a new OS structure, *exokernel*, that safely exports only those resources defined by the underlying hardware. Our goal is to put abstractions traditionally implemented by the kernel out into user-space, where user-level libraries or servers abstract the exposed hardware resources.[1]

By moving management of resources out into user-space, an exokernel allows aggressive customization. We see three reasons for customization. The first is to tailor policies to given hardware configurations, allowing applications to advance with the hardware. The second is to tailor policies to given applications. For example, closer integration with virtual memory management can enable distributed shared memory systems and garbage collectors to run an order of magnitude faster. The third is to improve performance by reducing the overhead of interrupts, exceptions, context switches, and cache misses, which are the primary sources of overhead in today's OSs.

The exokernel's sole function is to allocate, deallocate, and multiplex physical resources in a secure way. Resource access is controlled through 64-bit capabilities. The resources exported by the exokernel include physical memory (divided into pages), the CPU (divided into time-slices), the TLB, context-identifiers, and disk memory (divided into blocks).

The exokernel performs two non-physical functions: exception forwarding and upcalls. The exokernel hands exceptions directly to applications, enabling efficient user-level exception handling. Upcalls implement synchronous cross-domain transfer of control. Operationally, an upcall transfers the program counter in one domain to an agreed upon value in another, and installs the called domain's exception context. This mechanism is light-weight (our unoptimized implementation takes 20 instructions on a MIPS R3000) and lets applications build their own IPC semantics (i.e., a client can trust a server to save and restore registers).

The exokernel can be *programmed* by down-loading application code into the kernel. This code is made safe by bounding wild jumps and memory operations through sandboxing. Execution time can be bounded through either code augmentation or interrupts. The ability to download code allows applications to perform operations not possible in user-space. For example, this code can access unmapped physical memory, which is important for handling TLB-miss exceptions. Additionally, by allowing user code and state to reside behind the supervisor barrier, the frequency of user/supervisor kernel crossings can be reduced.

The exokernel's low-level interface allows flexible user-level implementations of traditionally rigidly defined OS services. For instance, since the exokernel does not enforce a particular page-table structure, applications can aggressively specialize them. Since the address space of a "protected object" may contain just a few pages, it can be mapped using a small linear page-table, while a single 64-bit address-space subsystem may use inverted page-tables.

To summarize, the advantages of an exokernel-OS are: (1) ambitious systems can be built without fighting inappropriate OS abstractions by accessing physical resources directly, and (2) multiple implementations of OS abstractions can co-exist, allowing them to be less complex and more efficient through specialization to a given domain. Furthermore, as these libraries can reside in the same protection domain as an application, cross-domain calls may be avoided.

No other OS architecture allows this degree of flexibility in the definition and implementation of fundamental OS services.

---

[1] See http://www.pdos.lcs.mit.edu or "Aegis: a secure programmable exokernel" in the *Proc. of the Sixth European SIGOPS workshop*, Sept. 1994, Wadern, Germany., for more information.

High-Performance Microkernel Systems

Steven Lucco

School of Computer Science
Carnegie Mellon University
5000 Forbes Ave.
Pittsburgh, PA 15213
lucco@cs.cmu.edu

Many recently developed operating systems segregate traditional services such as file systems into *servers* that inhabit separate address spaces. A protected-mode *microkernel* provides basic services such as virtual memory and scheduling. This organization, while aiding flexibility and fault tolerance, has limited performance. In this talk, we make a case for the "integrated multiserver," an operating system organization that can provide high performance services while retaining and even enhancing the flexibility and fault tolerance offered by conventional microkernel systems. We outline the design of the Bridge operating system, an integrated multiserver being developed at CMU.

In a previous report we introduced a basic software system restructuring tool called *software fault isolation*. Software fault isolation provides a means for enforcing protection between two modules that share an address space. We can use software fault isolation to accomplish two restructuring goals. First, we can implement some system services entirely at user level, using software fault isolation to prevent corruption of metadata. Second, we can dynamically load servers directly into the operating system kernel, providing the flexibility of microkernel systems but avoiding the performance overhead of separate address space organizations.

Software fault isolation (SFI) modifies the object code of a distrusted module to limit its behavior. We can use this technique to restrict access to devices, memory, privileged instructions or CPU resources. SFI has three features that make it useful as an operating system restructuring tool. First, it incorporates new compiler optimization techniques that can eliminate most runtime checking, yielding checking overheads of under 3% on modern architectures. Second, checking is based on the instruction set architecture of the workstation. Hence SFI is language-independent. Further, the integrity of a software module can be verified using a simple linear algorithm, *independent of the compiler techniques used to produce the module*. Finally, because SFI enforces modularity within a single address space, it supports communication between modules that is 50 to 1000 times faster than RPC between separate address spaces. In a previous report, we demonstrated that this gain in communication speed could dramatically improve the performance of the extensible database system Postgres on the Sequoia 2000 benchmarks.

We have modified our user-level SFI system to support safe incorporation of diverse software modules into an operating system kernel. We are using this kernel extension mechanism in the development of an operating system called Bridge. Bridge is an integrated multiserver, a new operating system structure that offers the flexibility and reliability of a multiserver but is more efficient than conventional microkernel designs. We assert that, using a multiserver integrated into a single kernel address space, we can provide a least as much flexibility and reliability as separate address space designs. At the same time, we will provide performance competitive with state-of-the-art monolithic kernels.

To support Bridge, we have augmented our SFI system so that it can handle faults without trapping, can precisely identify the source of the fault, and can work directly on object code. We have also developed a hybrid scheme in which control transfers are limited through software whereas memory access is limited through conventional hardware. We have measured these SFI variants on three types of extensions, a scheduler modification, an ATM network protocol server, and a downloadable version of LFS. The results demonstrate that best performance is achieved when the SFI mechanism can be customized to the particular type of extension used.

Scout: A Communications-Oriented Operating System
(Abstract)

Allen B. Montz   David Mosberger   Sean W. O'Malley   Larry L. Peterson
Todd A. Proebsting   John H. Hartman

Department of Computer Science
University of Arizona
Tucson, AZ 85721

As the National Information Infrastructure (NII) evolves, and digital computer networks become ubiquitous, communication will play an increasingly important role in computer systems. In fact, a recent report on the NII rejects the term "computer" because of its emphasis on computation, and instead choses to call these systems "information appliances" that support communication, information storage, and user interactions [1]. We expect these information appliances to include video displays, cameras, Personal Digital Assistants (PDAs), thermostats, and data servers, as well as more conventional compute servers and desktop workstations. In many of these cases, computation will simply be viewed as something one does to I/O data as it passes through the system.

We are designing a new operating system, called Scout, for systems connected to the NII. Scout is a configurable, communication-oriented operating system, whose performance is both predictable and scales with processor performance. Claiming an operating system is suitable for the NII is easy. What makes Scout unique is the set of insights, experiences, and enabling technologies it leverages. The real innovation of this work comes from the following four forces that shape Scout.

Software Specialization: We envision the systems connected to the NII being constructed from inexpensive, commodity components, and then specialized in software to perform a particular task. Software specialization does not imply that each system must be built from scratch. Instead, the key is to provide a framework (toolkit) for configuring in the modules required by the application. Thus, Scout is designed to be configurable—a given instance contains exactly the functionality required by the system for which it is built.

Communication-Centric Design: A principal task of the OS running on the systems connected to the NII is to shuffle data between I/O sources and sinks, and possibly to compute on it, as efficiently as possible. To better support this communication-centric model,

Scout is designed around a new OS abstraction called the *path*. The path abstraction encapsulates the flow of data through the system, and provides a focal point for addressing resource allocation and enabling effective optimizations.

Managing System Entropy: A major force that shapes Scout is what we refer to as computer system entropy— the growing complexity of both operating systems and machine architectures, and the unpredictable (often inexplicable) artifact that results when the two are mixed. In reaction to this trend, Scout provides performance that both scales with processor performance, and is predictable—improvements to individual components of the system will lead to the expected improvement to the overall system.

Exploiting Compiler Technology: A key design principle in RISC architectures is that much of the responsibility for achieving good performance falls to the compiler. While this principle as been aggressively applied to application code, it is often given less attention in the case of operating system code. Scout addresses this deficiency by leveraging compiler technology for two purposes—to help put the OS on the processor performance curve, and to simplify the process of constructing and porting the OS.

Scout involves research at the intersection of operating systems, compilers, and networks. We plan to demonstrate and evaluate Scout on several information appliances, including multimedia workstations, scalable storage servers, and network devices.

References

[1] NIST. *R&D for the NII: Technical Challenges*. Gaithersburg, MD, Mar. 1994.

Distributed Filaments: Efficient Fine-Grain Parallelism on a Cluster of Workstations *

Vincent W. Freeh, David K. Lowenthal, Gregory R. Andrews
{vin,dkl,greg}@cs.arizona.edu
Department of Computer Science
University of Arizona
Tucson, AZ 85721

Abstract

A fine-grain parallel program is one in which processes are typically small, ranging from a few to a few hundred instructions. Fine-grain parallelism arises naturally in many situations, such as iterative grid computations, recursive fork/join programs, the bodies of parallel FOR loops, and the implicit parallelism in functional or dataflow languages. It is useful both to describe massively parallel computations and as a target for code generation by compilers. However, fine-grain parallelism has long been thought to be inefficient due to the overheads of process creation, context switching, and synchronization. This paper describes a software kernel, Distributed Filaments (DF), that implements fine-grain parallelism both portably and efficiently on a workstation cluster. DF runs on existing, off-the-shelf hardware and software. It has a simple interface, so it is easy to use. DF achieves efficiency by using stateless threads on each node, overlapping communication and computation, employing a new reliable datagram communication protocol, and automatically balancing the work generated by fork/join computations.

1 Introduction

One way to write a program for a parallel machine is to create a process (thread) for each independent unit of work. Although generally thought to be inefficient, such *fine-grain* programs have several advan-

*This research was supported by NSF grants CCR-9108412 and CDA-8822652

tages. First, they are architecture independent in the sense that the parallelism is expressed in terms of the application and problem size, not in terms of the number of processors that might actually be used to execute the program. This also makes fine-grain programs easier to write, because it is not necessary to cluster independent units of work into a fixed set of larger tasks; indeed, adaptive programs such as divide-and-conquer algorithms do not have an *a priori* fixed set of tasks. Third, the implicit parallelism in functional or dataflow languages is inherently fine-grain, as is the inner-loop parallelism extracted by parallelizing compilers or expressed in parallel variants of languages such as Fortran; using fine-grain threads simplifies code generation for such languages. Finally, when there are many more processes than processors, it is often easier to balance the total amount of work done by each processor; in a coarse-grain program, it is important that each processor be statically assigned about the same amount of work, but this is impossible if the computation is dynamic or if the amount of work per process varies.

We have developed a software kernel called Filaments that strives to support efficient execution of fine-grain parallelism and a shared-memory programming model on a range of multiprocessors. A *filament* is a very lightweight thread. Each filament can be quite small, as in the computation of an average in Jacobi iteration; medium size, as in the computation of an inner product in matrix multiplication; or large, as in a coarse-grain program with a process per processor. The Filaments package provides a minimal set of primitives that we have found sufficient to implement all the parallel computations we have examined so far. As an analogy, the goal of Filaments relative to other approaches to writing parallel programs is similar to the goal of RISC relative to other styles of processor architecture: to provide a least common denominator that is easy to use as a compiler target and that is efficiently implementable.

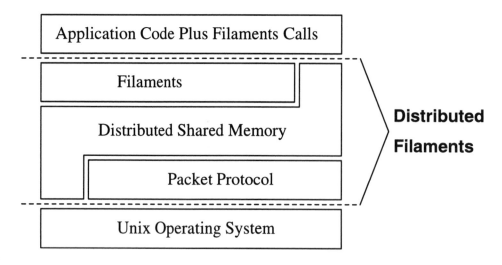

Figure 1: Distributed Filaments Components

Previous work has described the Shared Filaments (SF) package for shared-memory multiprocessors [EAL93]. We have used SF as a system-call library for a variety of applications; performance using SF is typically within 10% of that of equivalent coarse-grain programs, and it is sometimes even better (for load-imbalanced problems). We have also used SF as the back end for a modified Sisal compiler, thereby achieving efficient *forall* and function-call parallelism in a dataflow language [Fre94].

This paper addresses the issue of providing portable, efficient fine-grain parallelism on a cluster of workstations. Distributed Filaments (DF) extends SF and combines it with a distributed shared memory (DSM) customized for use with fine-grain threads. Figure 1 shows the components of DF and their inter-relation. The unique aspects of DF are:

- a multi-threaded DSM that implicitly overlaps communication and computation by executing new filaments while page faults are being serviced;

- a new page consistency protocol, implicit invalidate, for regular problems;

- a low overhead, reliable, datagram communication package, and

- an efficient implementation of the fork/join programming paradigm.

DF requires no special hardware support for a shared-memory address space or for multithreading. In addition, the only machine-dependent code in DF is a very small amount of context-switching code; hence, DF can easily be ported to different distributed-memory architectures (see below).

DF uses multithreading to overlap communication and computation, thereby masking communication latency due to "wire" and memory-access (DMA) time.

In particular, when a thread faults on a page, another thread can execute while the page request is still outstanding. In this way DF differs from DSMs such as IVY [LH89], Munin [CBZ91], Mirage [FP89], and Midway [BZS93], where a page fault blocks the entire node. (VISA [HB92], a DSM specifically supporting distributed SISAL programs, does some overlapping of computation and communication, but VISA's stack-based nature limits the overlap relative to the multithreading of DF.) Overlapping communication and computation is useful on both older (e.g. Ethernet) and newer (e.g. FDDI, ATM) network technologies. While FDDI and ATM provide higher bandwidth than Ethernet, there is still sufficient latency to make overlapping beneficial [TL93].

DF also uses a reliable datagram protocol built on UDP to reduce communication overhead. Our protocol buffers only short request messages, saving both time and space. This protocol provides reliable communication with the efficiency and scalability of UDP.

Another unique aspect of DF is its fork/join mechanism, which makes DF much easier to use for recursive applications. For adaptive quadrature and evaluating binary expression trees, for example, the simplest way to implement parallelism is to execute recursive procedure calls in parallel. However, it can be difficult to implement fork/join efficiently, because recursive parallelism can result in many small tasks, numerous messages to communicate arguments and results, and differing task workloads. DF solves each of these problems.

Distributed Filaments runs on a cluster of Sun workstations on top of SunOS; prototypes run on a cluster of DECstations running Mach and on an Intel Paragon running OSF. Performance on the Suns is such that an eight node version of Jacobi iteration—which has a large number of very small threads, and thus is a worst-case application—is within 8% of an equivalent coarse-grain program that uses explicit message-passing. DF achieves a speedup of 5.58 on 8 nodes relative to the sequential program. Moreover, overlapping communication and computation results in a 21% improvement over the equivalent non-overlapping program.

The rest of the paper is organized as follows. The next section gives an overview of the Filaments package. Section 3 describes our multi-threaded DSM, the datagram communication package, and the implicit-invalidate page consistency protocol. Section 4 summarizes performance results. Section 5 discusses related work. Finally, Section 6 gives concluding remarks.

2   Filaments Overview

The Filaments package supports fine-grain parallelism on both shared- and distributed-memory machines. The same user code (C plus Filaments calls) will run unchanged on either type of machine. However, the run-time systems that support the shared and distributed versions differ. Below we first describe elements common to both implementations and then describe the important elements of the distributed version. (We will refer to the shared and distributed implementations of Filaments as SF and DF, respectively.)

2.1   Common Elements

There are three kinds of filaments: run-to-completion, iterative, and fork/join. These are sufficient to support all the parallel applications we have examined, and hence we believe they are sufficient for most if not all applications.

A run-to-completion (RTC) filament executes once and then terminates; it is used in applications such as matrix multiplication. Iterative filaments execute repeatedly, with barrier synchronization occurring after each execution of all the filaments; they are used in applications such as Jacobi iteration. Fork/join filaments recursively fork new filaments and wait for them to complete; they are used in divide-and-conquer applications such as adaptive quadrature.

A filament does not have a private stack; it consists only of a code pointer and arguments. All filaments are independent; there is no guaranteed order of execution among them. Filaments are executed one at a time by server threads, which are traditional threads with stacks. Our threads package is based on the one used in the SR run-time system [AOC+88]. It is non-preemptive, and it employs a scheduler written specifically for DF.

Many Filaments programs attain good performance with little or no optimization. However, achieving good performance for applications that possess many small filaments requires three techniques: inlining, pruning, and pattern recognition. These techniques reduce the cost of creating and running filaments, reduce the working set size to make more efficient use of the cache, and produce code that is amenable to subsequent compiler optimizations of the Filaments code.

Inlining and pruning eliminate some of the overhead associated with creating and running filaments. Static inlining is performed for RTC and iterative filaments. Instead of calling the function specified by the filament each time, the body is inlined in a loop over all filaments. Dynamic pruning is performed for fork/join filaments. When enough work has been created to keep all nodes busy, forks are turned into procedure calls and joins into returns.

Inlining eliminates a function call, but DF still has to traverse the list of filament descriptors to obtain the arguments. The Filaments package can produce code that is amenable to compiler optimizations, improves cache performance, and eliminates additional overhead associated with running filaments. It does this by recognizing common patterns of RTC and iterative filaments at run-time. Currently, Filaments recognizes contiguous strips of one- or two-dimensional arrays of filaments assigned to the same node. For such strips of filaments the package dynamically switches to code that iterates over the assigned strip, generating the arguments in registers rather than reading the filament descriptors. This optimization supports a large subset of regular problems; we are working on supporting other common patterns.

2.2   Run-to-Completion and Iterative Filaments in DF

The possibility of a DSM page fault means filaments in DF must be able to block at unpredictable points. Hence, DF creates multiple server threads per node (as opposed to SF, which creates one server thread per node). A server thread runs filaments until either a page fault occurs or all eligible filaments have been executed. When a fault occurs, the state of the filament is saved on the stack of its server thread, and another server thread is executed. The faulting server thread is inserted in a queue for the appropriate page. On receipt of a page, all server threads waiting on that page are enabled.

Two important issues arise with RTC filaments in DF: avoiding excessive faulting and overlapping communication and computation as much as possible. DF provides *pools* to address both issues.

A pool is a collection of filaments that ideally reference the same set of pages. At creation time, the

Filaments program (user or compiler generated) assigns a filament to a pool. When a program is started, a server thread on each node starts executing a pool of filaments. On a page fault, a new server thread is started; it executes filaments in a different pool while the remote page is being fetched. Thus, an *entire* pool is suspended when any one of its filaments faults. This minimizes page faults if filaments in the same pool reference the same pages.

Iterative filaments are a generalization of RTC filaments. For iterative applications, DF ensures that after the first iteration the pools that are run first will be those that faulted on the previous iteration; i.e., the faults are frontloaded, which increases the potential for overlap of communication and computation. This is a useful optimization, as many iterative applications have constant sharing patterns. DF implements this in the following way. On a page reply, the enabled server threads are placed on the tail of the ready queue. This ensures that pools containing at least one filament that faults will finish execution after a pool that contains no filaments that fault, provided that the faulting pool is started before the non-faulting pool. To make sure all faulting pools are started first, when a server thread finishes executing an entire pool of filaments, it pushes the pool on a stack. On the next iteration, the pools are run starting at the top of the stack, which ensures that all faulting pools are run first. The combination of these two mechanisms effectively frontloads the faults, and the greatest overlap of communication and computation will be achieved.[1]

At present, it is up to the programmer or compiler to determine the number of pools on each node and to assign filaments both to a node and to a pool on that node. Both of these decisions can be nontrivial and have to be done well or performance will suffer (although correctness will not). The filaments should be assigned to nodes so that the load is balanced, and the filaments within a node should be assigned to pools so that faults are minimized and good overlap of computation and communication is achieved. Determining the correct node and pool for filaments can lead to some of the same difficulties that occur in writing a coarse-grain program. We are currently working on adaptive algorithms for making both of these decisions within DF at run time.

2.3 Fork/Join Filaments in DF

In recursive, fork/join applications, the computation starts on just one node, and other nodes are idle.

---

[1] We have not found iterative applications that possess a sharing pattern for which this algorithm is not optimal. However, if such an application does exist, we can frontload the faults by running one filament from each pool at the beginning of each iteration.

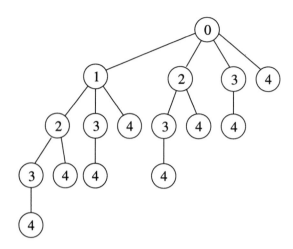

Figure 2: Logical tree of 16 nodes, for applications that create parallelism by the pattern of 2 forks and a join. At each step, the number of nodes with work doubles. The numbers in the figure indicates the step in which the node first gets a filament.

To get all nodes involved in the computation, new work (from forks) needs to be sent to idle nodes. Dynamic load balancing may then be required to keep the nodes busy, because different nodes can receive different amounts of work.

Load balancing can, however, have several negative effects. In DF, there are two significant ones. First, when a node starts executing a filament, it needs to get the data associated with the filament. At best this costs the time to acquire the working set of the filament, and at worst it can lead to thrashing. Second, the initial load-balancing phase can be very costly, as all nodes other than the one that starts the computation will either query other nodes with requests for work (most of which will be denied) or flood the initial node with requests (which can cause a bottleneck).

DF first uses a sender-initiated load-balancing scheme and then employs a simple receiver-initiated, dynamic load-balancing policy (which can be enabled and disabled by the application programmer or compiler). Suppose that a fork/join application creates parallelism by two forks and then a join. The initial load-balancing phase then works as follows. The nodes form a logical tree (see Figure 2). The root begins the computation; after forking the first two filaments, it sends one filament to its left child and keeps the other. Both nodes continue the computation. When the root forks another two filaments, it now sends one to its second child and keeps the other; the next time it sends a new filament to its third child and keeps the other; and so on. Each child node follows the same pattern. Consequently, in each step the number of nodes with work doubles. The initial phase continues in this way until a node has sent work to all of its children, after which it keeps all filaments it forks.

After the initial work-distribution phase, some applications will need to employ dynamic load balancing; in DF this is receiver initiated. When a node has no new filaments and none that are suspended waiting for a page, it queries other nodes in a round-robin fashion. For applications that do not exhibit much load imbalance—such as evaluating balanced binary expression trees, merge sort, or recursive FFT—the cost of acquiring pages outweighs the gain of load balancing. On the other hand, for applications such as adaptive quadrature—where evaluating intervals can take widely varying amounts of time—dynamic load balancing is absolutely necessary.

Another concern in implementing fork/join is avoiding thrashing, which can occur when two nodes write to the same page. Fork/join in DF uses two mechanisms. The first is similar to one used in the Mirage [FP89] system. A node will keep a page for a certain length of time before giving it up; during that time all requests for the page from other nodes are dropped (they will be retransmitted later). The Mirage timer can hurt system performance because it may delay sending a requested page. However, this problem is mitigated in Filaments by multithreading; if there is other work, the delay of the request is insignificant. The second mechanism used to control thrashing is that when a page arrives, all server threads waiting on the page are scheduled at the *front* of the ready queue. Hence the page that just arrived will be utilized as soon as the currently executing thread gives up control. This increases the probability that the page is still resident by the time the enabled threads are actually scheduled to run.

3   Distributed Shared Memory

Our multi-threaded distributed shared memory (DSM) is built on top of SunOS and therefore requires no specialized hardware or changes to the operating system kernel. In a single-threaded DSM implementation, all work on a faulting node is suspended until the fault is satisfied. In a multi-threaded implementation, other work is done while the remote fault is pending. This makes it possible to overlap communication and computation.

The address space of each node contains both shared and private sections. Shared user data (matrices, linked lists, etc.) are stored in the shared section, while local user data (program code, loop variables, etc.) and all system data structures (queues, page tables, etc.) are stored in the private sections. The shared section is replicated on all nodes in the same location so that pointers into the shared space have the same meaning on all nodes.

The shared address space is divided into individually protected pages of 4K bytes each (this is the granularity supported in SunOS). However, a user does not have to use all of the locations in a page. In particular, user data structures can be padded to distribute elements onto different pages. We have written a library routine that allocates a data structure in global memory and automatically pads (when necessary). Additionally, two or more pages can be grouped so that a request for any page in the group is a request for all of them. Thus our DSM supports pages that can have different sizes than the pages directly supported by the operating system.

There are two events in our DSM system: *remote page fault* and *message pending*. A remote page fault is generated when a server thread tries to access a remote memory location. It is handled by using the `mprotect` system call, which changes the access permission of pages, and by using a signal handler for segmentation violations. A message pending event is generated when a message arrives at a node; it is handled by an asynchronous event handler which is triggered by `SIGIO`.

When a filament accesses a remote page, the server thread executing the filament is interrupted by a signal. The signal handler inserts the faulted server thread in the suspended queue for that page, requests the remote page if necessary, and calls the scheduler, which will execute another server thread. When the request is satisfied, the faulted server thread is rescheduled, as are all other server threads that are waiting on that page. Because a new server thread is run after every page fault, the system can have several outstanding page requests.

There are any number of page consistency protocols (PCP) that could be implemented. We have found three PCPs to be sufficient to support the wide range of applications we have programmed in DF: *migratory* [CBZ91], *write-invalidate* [LH89], and a new protocol we call *implicit-invalidate*. The migratory PCP keeps only one copy of each page; the page moves from node to node as needed. Write-invalidate allows replicated, read-only copies; all are invalidated explicitly when any copy is written. Implicit-invalidate is similar to write-invalidate, but it is optimized to eliminate the invalidation messages. In particular, read-only copies of a page are *implicitly* invalidated at every synchronization point. Hence a read-only copy of a page has a very short lifetime and explicit invalidate messages are not needed. Implicit-invalidate works only for regular problems with a stable sharing pattern, such as Jacobi iteration.

A DSM requires reliable communication, ideally with low overhead. On a Unix system there are two communication choices: TCP and UDP. TCP is reliable, but it does not scale well with the number of

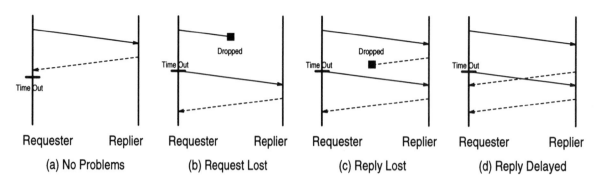

Figure 3: Possible scenarios in Packet

nodes; UDP is scalable, but it is not reliable. UDP is also slightly faster than TCP, and it supports message broadcast. Therefore we use UDP and an efficient reliability protocol to create Packet, a low overhead reliable datagram communication package.

In Packet there are two types of messages: *request* and *reply*. Communication always occurs in pairs: first a request and then the associated reply. When either the request or reply message is lost or delayed, the request message is retransmitted. All request messages are buffered; however, they are very short (20 bytes or less), so buffering consumes very little time and space. Packet is efficient because only small messages are buffered and, in the common case, only two messages are sent. (Figure 3 shows the four possible situations that can arise.) In an unreliable network where a lost packet is a likely event, a different reliability mechanism—such as the one in TCP—might perform better than Packet. However, in a highly reliable network, Packet adds essentially no additional overhead. In particular, the overhead consists of buffering request messages and, when a reply is received, removing the message from a list. The list is never longer than the number of messages that are sent between synchronization points.

With Packet we avoid the expense of buffering DSM page data. All page replies are constructed using the current contents of the page. Nodes delay at synchronization points until all outstanding page requests have been satisfied. Therefore, in a program without race conditions, a page request always returns a consistent copy of a page.

Packet is similar to the VMTP protocol [CZ83], which also does not buffer reply messages and retransmits request messages only when necessary. However, there is a fundamental difference: VMTP uses a synchronous send/receive/reply, whereas Packet uses an asynchronous send/receive/reply.

Because request messages are retransmitted until acknowledged, we can implement a very efficient mutual exclusion mechanism. When a server thread is in a critical section, all messages that cause critical data

(i.e., thread queues) to be modified are ignored—they will be retransmitted when the requester times out. (The servicing of some messages, such as a page request, will never modify critical data.) The entry and exit protocols for a critical section are simply a single assignment statement, so many, very small critical sections can be used efficiently. Our experience shows that an ignored message is so rare that it essentially never occurs.

A *reduction* in Filaments is a primitive that both (1) causes a value from each node to be accumulated and then disseminated to all nodes, and (2) ensures that no node continues until all nodes have completed the same reduction. Hence, a reduction also serves as a barrier synchronization point. (A "pure" barrier is a reduction that does not compute a value.) A reduction is a high-level mechanism that we have used in our application programs instead of low-level mechanisms like locks. Reductions are not necessarily a part of a DSM, although they are a necessary part of a parallel programming system. Implementing reductions as part of the DSM has the advantage that they can be an integral part of the page consistency protocol (PCP). This can reduce the number of messages required to maintain consistency and allows greater flexibility in the design of a PCP. For example, in our implicit-invalidate protocol, a node invalidates all its read-only copies before performing an inter-node barrier; hence, no invalidation messages are sent.

4 Performance

This section reports the performance of four programs: matrix multiplication, Jacobi iteration, adaptive quadrature, and evaluation of binary expression trees. For each we developed a sequential program, a coarse-grain program, and a Filaments program. All programs use similar computation code. The sequential programs are distinct from the others—they are not simply a parallel program run on one node. The coarse-grain (CG) programs have a single heavyweight process on each node and use explicit message-

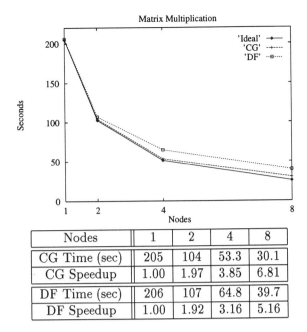

Nodes	1	2	4	8
CG Time (sec)	205	104	53.3	30.1
CG Speedup	1.00	1.97	3.85	6.81
DF Time (sec)	206	107	64.8	39.7
DF Speedup	1.00	1.92	3.16	5.16

Figure 4: Matrix multiplication, size 512×512. Sequential program: 205 sec.

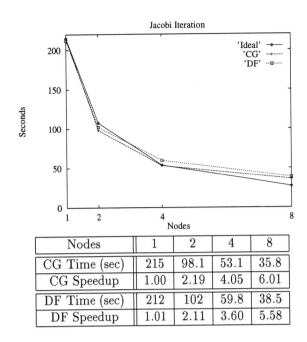

Nodes	1	2	4	8
CG Time (sec)	215	98.1	53.1	35.8
CG Speedup	1.00	2.19	4.05	6.01
DF Time (sec)	212	102	59.8	38.5
DF Speedup	1.01	2.11	3.60	5.58

Figure 5: Jacobi iteration, 256×256, $\epsilon = 10^{-3}$, 360 iterations. Sequential program: 215 sec.

passing. They use UDP for communication. The times reported are those of the tests in which all messages were delivered and the program completed; when a message was lost, the program hung and the test was aborted. All speedups are computed using the sequential program as the baseline. In the graphs that follow, the ideal time is the sequential time divided by the number of nodes.

Below, we briefly describe four applications, present the results of runs on 1, 2, 4, and 8 nodes, and examine the parallel speedup. In Section 4.5 we examine the overheads of Filaments in detail. All tests were run on a network of 8 Sun IPCs connected by a 10Mbs Ethernet. We used the gcc compiler, with the -O flag for optimization. The execution times reported are the median of at least three test runs, as reported by gettimeofday. The variance of the test runs was small. The tests were performed when the only other active processes were Unix daemons.

4.1 Matrix Multiplication

The execution times for matrix multiplication are shown in Figure 4. The programs compute $C = A \times B$, where A, B, and C are $n \times n$ matrices. Each node computes a horizontal contiguous strip of rows of the C matrix. A master node initializes the matrices and distributes all of B and the appropriate parts of A to the other nodes.

In the coarse-grain program, all slave nodes receive all the data they need before starting their computation. The distribution of the A and B matrices takes

5.1 seconds in the 8 node program. This initial overhead limits the speedup of the coarse-grain program.

The DF program for matrix multiplication uses run-to-completion filaments, one per point of the C matrix, and the write-invalidate PCP. Because there are no write conflicts in the C matrix, there is very little synchronization overhead (two barriers, one to ensure the master node initializes A and B before other nodes start computing, and one to ensure all nodes have computed their part of C before the master node prints it). However, in the problem tested each matrix requires 512 pages of 4K bytes each. All $p - 1$ slave nodes must receive all of B and $1/p$ of A, so the number of page requests is $O(pn^2)$ in the DF program. The master node must service all these page requests. The overhead to service 4032 page requests in the 8 node program is approximately 6.2 seconds, and the network is saturated by the large number of messages. This saturation results in an increase in the latency of acquiring pages and leads to workload imbalance. These factors explain the drop-off in speedup on 4 and 8 nodes for the DF program.

4.2 Jacobi Iteration

Laplace's equation in two dimensions is the partial differential equation $\nabla^2(\Phi) = 0$. Given boundary values for a region, its solution is the steady-state values of interior points. These values can be approximated numerically by using a finite difference method such as Jacobi iteration, which repeatedly computes new values for each point, then tests for convergence.

In Jacobi, one horizontal strip of each array is distributed to each node. The nodes in the coarse-grain program repeatedly send edges, update interior points, receive edges, update edges, and check for termination. In this way the coarse-grain program achieves maximal overlap of communication and computation.

The DF program uses iterative filaments—one per point—and three pools of filaments—one each for the top row, bottom row, and interior rows. Filaments in the top and bottom pools fault, generating a page request; those in the local pool do not fault. All communication latency will be overlapped provided that the latency of acquiring pages is less than the total execution time of filaments in the local pool; the DF program achieves full overlap. A reduction is needed on every iteration.

Figure 5 shows the main results of our Jacobi iteration programs.[2] The coarse-grain program gets better than linear speedup for 2 and 4 nodes (the primary reason is the size of the working set and its effect on the cache, etc. [SHG93]), and it gets reasonable speedup on 8 nodes. The gain of overlapping communication and computation in the coarse-grain program is 5.5% and 14% on 4 and 8 nodes, respectively.

The DF program uses the implicit-invalidate PCP, which eliminates invalidation messages. The speedup obtained is 3.60 on 4 nodes and 5.58 on 8 nodes. The running times increase by 10% and 26% on 4 and 8 nodes, respectively, if the communication latency is not overlapped.

4.3 Adaptive Quadrature

Adaptive quadrature is an algorithm to compute the area under a curve defined by a continuous function. It works by dividing an interval in half, approximating the areas of both halves, and then subdividing further if the approximation is not good enough. The programs tested evaluate a curve that causes workload imbalance.

Our coarse-grain approximation divides the interval into p subintervals and assigns one to each node. However, this can lead to severe load imbalance, as reflected in Figure 6. A second program that uses a bag-of-tasks [CGL86] has better speedup, but its absolute time is much worse. The overhead of accessing the centralized bag is extremely high due to the large number of small tasks. These coarse-grain programs

---

[2] The DF program should not run faster than the sequential program, but it does. Even though the C code for the computation of each point is identical in all three programs, the compiler generates different assembler code for DF than for the CG and sequential programs. The innermost computation (the average) is slightly faster in DF than in the other two programs. This anomaly, for which we have no explanation, also occurs on some other test programs.

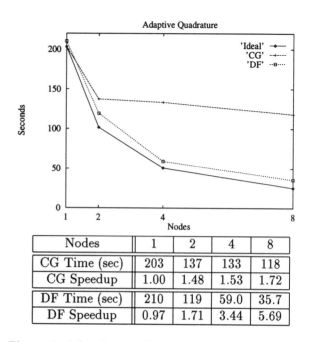

Nodes	1	2	4	8
CG Time (sec)	203	137	133	118
CG Speedup	1.00	1.48	1.53	1.72
DF Time (sec)	210	119	59.0	35.7
DF Speedup	0.97	1.71	3.44	5.69

Figure 6: Adaptive quadrature, interval of length 24. Sequential program: 203 sec.

illustrate the need for a low-overhead, decentralized load balancing mechanism.

The natural algorithm for this problem uses divide-and-conquer, so our DF program uses fork/join filaments. Speedups of 3.44 and 5.69 were obtained on four nodes and eight nodes, respectively. The speedup tapers off as the number of nodes increases because the two nodes evaluating the extreme intervals initially contain most of the work. With eight nodes, six complete their initial work quickly and make load-balancing requests. This not only increases the number of messages but increases the likelihood of a load-balance denial (because only two have sufficient work).

4.4 Binary Expression Trees

The fork/join paradigm can also be used to compute the value of a binary expression tree, an application described in [EZ93]. The leaves are matrices and interior operators are matrix multiplication; the tree is traversed in parallel and the matrices are multiplied sequentially. Figure 7 contains the results of running the matrix expression program with 70 by 70 matrices and a balanced binary tree of height 7. The maximum possible speedup that can be achieved for this application is limited by the tail-end load imbalance. In particular, near the top of the tree some nodes must remain idle. However, because the work doubles with each level of the tree, good speedup can still be achieved. For the problem tested, the maximum speedup is 3.85 and 7.06 on 4 and 8 nodes, respectively.

The coarse-grain program contains two phases. In

First Symposium on Operating Systems Design and Implementation (OSDI)   USENIX Association

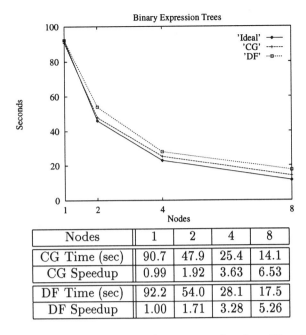

Binary Expression Trees

Nodes	1	2	4	8
CG Time (sec)	90.7	47.9	25.4	14.1
CG Speedup	0.99	1.92	3.63	6.53
DF Time (sec)	92.2	54.0	28.1	17.5
DF Speedup	1.00	1.71	3.28	5.26

Figure 7: Binary expression tree evaluation, 70 × 70 matrices, tree of height 7. Sequential program: 92.1 sec.

Nodes	2	4	8
Time (msec)	3.20	5.29	8.45

Figure 8: Barrier synchronization, 1000 barriers

Operation	Time (μs)	ops/sec
Filaments creation	2.10	457,000
Context switch		
Filaments	0.643	1,560,000
Fil. Inlined	0.126	7,950,000
Threads	48.8	20,500
Page faults	4,120	238.

Figure 9: Filaments overheads

the first, the program divides the work up evenly among the nodes. The second phase combines the intermediate values that each node calculated into a single result using a tree. Tail-end load imbalance is handled in this last phase. Proceeding towards the top of the combining tree, half of the active nodes become inactive at each level. There are very few messages in this algorithm (a total of $2(p-1)$ to transfer result matrices in the combining tree). The overhead is very low, so the speedup is very good.

This DF fork/join program uses the global (DSM) memory, unlike adaptive quadrature where all the information is contained in the function parameters. The migratory PCP is used, although in this particular application there is no performance difference between migratory and write-invalidate. The DF program sends many more messages than the coarse-grain program because (1) the parallelism begins from a single root filament and its children are distributed to the other nodes and (2) data is acquired implicitly by page faults (requiring a request and a reply).

4.5 Analysis of Overhead

DF introduces four categories of overheads relative to sequential programs: filaments execution, paging, synchronization, and workload imbalance. Filaments execution has the following costs: creating and running filaments, more memory for filament descriptors (and therefore less effective caching), and lost compiler optimizations. As discussed in Section 2.1, the Filaments

package has support for decreasing these costs. This support resulted in Filaments execution overhead of less than 5% in all the test programs.

The second source of DF overhead is due to DSM paging. The faulting node incurs the cost of faulting on the page and sending and receiving the resulting messages. The owner of the requested page incurs the cost of servicing the page request (receiving the request and sending the page). The paging overhead per node is application-dependent. In general it does not depend on the number of nodes but on the sharing of data. However, even with a constant paging overhead per node, the total number of messages in the system will increase linearly with the number of nodes. This can be a problem when the network becomes saturated, as is the case in Jacobi iteration on eight nodes.

The third DF overhead is due to synchronization, which results from barriers (in RTC and iterative filaments) or messages containing filaments and result values (in fork/join filaments). The overhead of barriers is a function of the number of nodes. DF uses a tournament barrier with broadcast dissemination, which has $O(p)$ messages and a latency of $O(\log p)$ messages [HFM88]. Barrier synchronization times are shown in Figure 8. This is the cost of the barrier only; in an actual application it is likely that the nodes arrive at the barrier at different times, which increases the time a particular node is at the barrier. The barrier time given includes message latency (wire time) as well as message processing overhead. Communication latency cannot be overlapped with computation during a barrier because a processor has no more work to do when it reaches a barrier. Therefore, a barrier is an expensive operation.

The final DF overhead is a result of nodes having differing workloads. This can occur in two ways: either nodes are given different amounts of work, or the work leads to different amounts of paging and synchronization overhead. Differing workload results in nodes

Node	Master	Interior	Tail
Work	22.3	22.9-24.4	22.6
Filament Exec	1.57	1.54-1.87	1.73
Data Transfer	7.75	2.31-3.02	1.53
Sync Overhead	0.99	1.51-2.14	1.12
Sync Delay	6.62	5.24-10.3	14.7

Figure 10: Analysis of overheads in Jacobi iteration, 8 nodes, 256×256, $\epsilon = 10^{-3}$, 360 iterations. Total execution time 42.1 seconds.

arriving at synchronization points at different times and hence leads to uneven and longer delays.

The coarse-grain programs also incur overheads due to data transfer, synchronization, and workload imbalance. The latter two overheads are roughly the same as DF; however, the data-transfer overhead is much less because the coarse-grain programs use explicit messages to transfer data.

Some of the filaments overheads are shown in Figure 9. Each overhead is shown both as the time per operation and as the number of operations per second. The cost of switching between filaments depends on whether or not they are inlined. Inlining filaments eliminates a function call (and return) and is more than five times faster than not inlining. For comparison purposes, context switch times for the light-weight server threads are shown as well. The page fault times assume the owner is known and the page is immediately available.

Figure 10 shows DF overheads in the specific case of Jacobi iteration. The nodes are split into three categories: the master node, the interior nodes, and the tail node. The master node and the tail node fault on one page and service one page request per iteration. Interior nodes incur two page faults and two page requests per iteration. In addition, the master node must service all the initial page requests. The execution time in Figure 10 is divided among five categories: work (the cost of the computation proper), filaments overhead, data transfer (page faulting and servicing), synchronization overhead (sending and receiving synchronization messages), and synchronization delay (differing barrier arrival times). A range is given for the times of the six interior nodes because of their different synchronization delays. The overall time is longer than that previously reported because this test was run using profiled code. Because the programs were started on each node in succession, and the system initialization and termination are included, the total time taken by each node in Figure 10 is not equal.

The Jacobi iteration times reported in section 4.2 take advantage of two performance enhancements: the implicit-invalidate page consistency protocol (PCP) and multiple pools. The communication overhead is

Nodes	1	2	4	8
DF Time (sec)	212	103	61.4	40.9
DF Speedup	1.01	2.09	3.50	5.26

Figure 11: Jacobi iteration, Write-Invalidate PCP, 256×256, $\epsilon = 10^{-3}$, 360 iterations. Sequential program: 215 sec.

Nodes	1	2	4	8
DF Time (sec)	212	104	65.5	48.5
DF Speedup	1.01	2.07	3.28	4.43

Figure 12: Jacobi iteration, Implicit-Invalidate PCP, single pool, 256×256, $\epsilon = 10^{-3}$, 360 iterations. Sequential program: 215 sec.

reduced by using the implicit-invalidate PCP, which has fewer messages than the write-invalidate PCP. The write-invalidate PCP requires invalidate messages to be sent, received, and acknowledged. The performance improvement, 3% and 6% on 4 and 8 nodes, can be seen by comparing the results in Figure 11 with those in Figure 5. The times for single-pool, non-overlapping Jacobi iteration are shown in Figure 12. Overlapping communication leads to a 9% and 21% improvement on 4 and 8 nodes, as can be seen by comparing the times in Figure 12 with those in Figure 5.

5 Related Work

There is a wealth of related work on threads packages. In general-purpose threads packages, such as uSystem [BS90], each thread has its own context. Consequently, the package has to perform a full context switch when it switches between threads. (This is true even in threads packages with optimizations such as those described in [ALL89]). The overhead of context switching is significant when threads execute a small number of instructions, as in Jacobi iteration. Hence, general-purpose threads packages are most useful for providing coarse-grain parallelism or for structuring a large concurrent system.

A few threads packages support efficient fine-grain parallelism, e.g., the Uniform System [TC88], Shared Filaments [EAL93] and Chores [EZ93]. The first two restrict the generality of the threads model. In particular, the Uniform System uses task generators to provide parallelism, much in the way a parallelizing compiler works, and in Shared Filaments a thread (filament) cannot block. On the other hand, Chores uses PRESTO threads as servers, so it can block a chore when necessary. However, Chores does not have a distributed implementation.

Support for the recursive programming style does

---

not generally exist on distributed-memory systems. For example, in Munin [CBZ91], the user must program recursive applications using a shared queue (bag) of unexecuted tasks and must explicitly implement and lock the queue. DF allows recursive programs to be written naturally and efficiently by means of fork/join filaments.

Several systems use overlapping to mask communication latency. Active Messages [vCGS92] accomplishes overlap explicitly by placing prefetch instructions sufficiently far in advance of use that the shared data will arrive before it is used. On the other hand, DF achieves overlap implicitly through multithreading. Both require some programmer support to achieve maximal overlap of communication and computation. In Active Messages, the user has to make sure the prefetch is started soon enough, and in DF the user must correctly place filaments in pools (although we are working on making the placement automatic). The Threaded Abstract Machine, TAM [CGSv93], uses Active Messages to achieve overlap of communication and computation in a parallel implementation of a dataflow language.

CHARM is a fine-grain, explicit message-passing threads package [FRS+91]. It provides architecture independence, overlap of communication and computation, and dynamic load balancing. CHARM has a distributed-memory programming model that can be run efficiently on both shared- and distributed-memory machines. DF provides functionality similar to CHARM using a shared-memory programming model.

The Alewife [KCA91], a large-scale distributed-memory multiprocessor, provides hardware support for overlapping communication and computation. It provides the user with a shared-memory address space and enforces a context-switch to a new thread on any remote reference. The Alewife and DF use similar ideas, except that DF is a software implementation requiring no specialized hardware.

VISA, a DSM written for the functional language Sisal, also uses overlapping [HB92]. Suspended threads are pushed on a stack, so there can be many outstanding page requests. The disadvantage of a stack-based approach is that threads are resumed in the inverse order in which they request pages. In DF a thread is scheduled as soon as the page it requested arrives, whereas in VISA a thread is executed when it is popped off the stack. Thus, in VISA a faulting thread cannot execute until after the page it requested arrives and after completion of all other threads that were subsequently started.

False sharing occurs when two nodes access locations within the same page, and hence it can cause thrashing. Mirage uses the *time window coherence protocol*

to control thrashing. In particular, a node keeps a page for some minimum time period to guarantee that it makes some progress each time it acquires the page [FP89]. Munin uses *release consistency* in the write-shared protocol to handle false sharing [CBZ91]. The memory is made consistent at synchronization points so there is no thrashing. TreadMarks provides lazy-release consistency on a network of Unix workstations [KDCZ94]. Simulation has shown that this greatly reduces the number of messages relative to the number of messages needed in systems like Munin. Some DSMs provide different granularities of memory consistency. For example, Clouds [DJAR91] and Orca [Bal90] provide shared memory objects. This provides consistency at the granularity of user-level objects instead of operating system pages, which can reduce thrashing. Blizzard [SFL+94] and Midway [BZS93] minimize false sharing by providing coherence at cache-line granularity. Midway keeps a dirty bit per cache line and propagates changes at synchronization points.

DF controls thrashing by using the Mirage window protocol and by providing the user control over the granularity of DSM pages. DF provides no support for concurrent writers to the same page; instead, the user must lay out the data such that thrashing will not occur. Currently, this must be solved at a higher level, such as by a compiler. We are investigating ways to simplify this task.

6 Conclusion

We have argued that fine-grain parallelism is useful and that it can be implemented quite efficiently on a workstation cluster without modifying either the hardware or the operating systems software. The Distributed Filaments package has a simple interface, and we have found it easy to use when programming parallel applications. DF achieves efficiency by overlapping communication with useful computation, by using a new datagram protocol that is both fast and reliable, and by automatically balancing the work generated by fork/join computations. The net result is that DF achieves good speedup on a variety of applications. In particular, as long as an application has a reasonable amount of computation per node, communication latency due to paging messages can be effectively masked. (However, if the cost of latency drops below that of context-switching, overlapping may no longer be beneficial.)

This paper describes DF, which is implemented on a cluster of Sun workstations running SunOS. We have prototypes running on a cluster of Sun workstations running Solaris, DEC workstations running Mach, and an Intel Paragon multicomputer running OSF. We are developing more application programs to provide a better basis for performance comparisons. We are also working on a number of improvements to the DF package itself: automatic clustering of filaments that share pages into execution pools, automatic data placement, experiments with different types of barriers for large numbers of processors, and support for explicit message passing as well as DSM.

Acknowledgements

Dawson Engler and David "the Kid" Koski provided numerous technical ideas and did lots of implementation work. Bart Parliman ported DF to the Mach operating system. Gregg Townsend provided comments on early drafts of the paper. The referees also made many constructive suggestions.

References

[ALL89] T.E. Anderson, E.D. Lazowska, and H.M. Levy. The performance implications of thread management alternatives for shared-memory multiprocessors. *IEEE Transactions on Computers*, 38(12):1631–1644, December 1989.

[AOC+88] Gregory R. Andrews, Ronald A. Olsson, Michael Coffin, Irving Elshoff, Kelvin Nilsen, Titus Pursin, and Gregg Townsend. An overview of the SR language and implementation. *ACM Transactions on Programming Languages and Systems*, 10(1):51–86, January 1988.

[Bal90] Henri E. Bal. Experience with distributed programming in Orca. *Proc. IEEE CS 1990 Int Conf on Computer Languages*, pages 79–89, March 1990.

[BS90] Peter A. Buhr and R.A. Stroobosscher. The uSystem: providing light-weight concurrency on shared memory multiprocessor computers running UNIX. *Software Practice and Experience*, pages 929–964, September 1990.

[BZS93] Brian N. Bershad, Matthew J. Zekauskas, and Wayne A. Sawdon. The Midway distributed shared memory system. In *COMPCON '93*, 1993.

[CBZ91] John B. Carter, John K. Bennett, and Willy Zwaenepoel. Implementation and performance of Munin. In *Proceedings of 13th ACM Symposium On Operating Systems*, pages 152–164, October 1991.

[CGL86] Nicholas Carriero, David Gelernter, and Jerry Leichter. Distributed data structures in Linda. In *Thirteenth ACM Symp. on Principles of Programming Languages*, pages 236–242, January 1986.

[CGSv93] David E. Culler, Seth Copen Goldstein, Klaus Erik Schauser, and Thorsten von Eicken. TAM—a compiler controlled threaded abstract machine. *Journal of Parallel and Distributed Computing*, 18(3):347–370, August 1993.

[CZ83] D.R. Cheriton and W. Zwaenepoel. The distributed V kernel and its performance for diskless workstations. In *Proceedings of the Ninth ACM Symposium on Operating Systems Principles*, pages 128–140, October 1983.

[DJAR91] Partha Dasgupta, Richard J. LeBlanc Jr., Mustaque Ahmad, and Umakishore Ramachandran. The Clouds distributed operating system. *Computer*, pages 34–44, November 1991.

[EAL93] Dawson R. Engler, Gregory R. Andrews, and David K. Lowenthal. Shared Filaments: Efficient support for fine-grain parallelism on shared-memory multiprocessors. TR 93-13, Dept. of Computer Science, University of Arizona, April 1993.

[EZ93] Derek L. Eager and John Zahorjan. Chores: Enhanced run-time support for shared memory parallel computing. *ACM Transactions on Computer Systems*, 11(1):1–32, February 1993.

[FP89] Brett D. Fleisch and Gerald J. Popek. Mirage: a coherent distributed shared memory design. In *Proceedings of 12th ACM Symposium On Operating Systems*, pages 211–223, December 1989.

[Fre94] Vincent W. Freeh. A comparison of implicit and explicit parallel programming. TR 93-30a, University of Arizona, May 1994.

[FRS+91] W. Fenton, B. Ramkumar, V. A. Saletore, A. B. Sinha, and L. V. Kale. Supporting machine independent programming on diverse parallel architectures. In *Proceedings of the 1991 International Conference on Parallel Processing*, volume II, Software, pages II-193–II-201, Boca Raton, FL, August 1991. CRC Press.

[HB92] Matthew Haines and Wim Bohm. The design of VISA: A virtual shared addressing system. Technical Report CS-92-120, Colorado State University, May 1992.

[HFM88] D. Hansgen, R. Finkel, and U. Manber. Two algorithms for barier synchronization. *Int. Journal of Parallel Programming*, 17(1):1–18, February 1988.

[KCA91] Kiyoshi Kurihara, David Chaiken, and Anant Agarwal. Latency tolerance through multithreading in large-scale multiprocessors. In *International Symposium on Shared Memory Multiprocessing*, pages 91–101, April 1991.

[KDCZ94] Pete Keleher, Sandhya Dwarkadas, Alan Cox, and Willy Zwaenepoel. TreadMarks: Distributed shared memory on standard workstations and operating systems. In *Proceedings of the 1994 Winter Usenix Conference*, pages 115–131, January 1994.

[LH89]   Kai Li and Paul Hudak. Memory coherence in shared virtual memory systems. *ACM Transactions on Computer Systems*, 7(4), November 1989.

[SFL+94]   Ioannis Schoinas, Babak Falsafi, Alvin R. Lebeck, Steven K. Reinhardt, James R. Larus, and David A. Wood. Fine-grain access control for distributed shared memory. In *Sixth International Conference on Architecture Support for Programming Languages and Operating Systems (to appear)*, October 1994.

[SHG93]   Jaswinder Pal Singh, John L. Hennessy, and Anoop Gupta. Scaling parallel programs for multiprocessors: Methodology and examples. *Computer*, 26(7):42–50, July 1993.

[TC88]   Robert H. Thomas and Will Crowther. The Uniform system: an approach to runtime support for large scale shared memory parallel processors. In *1988 Conference on Parallel Processing*, pages 245–254, August 1988.

[TL93]   Chanramohan A. Thekkath and Henry M. Levy. Limits to low-latency communication on high-speed networks. *ACM Transactions on Computer Systems*, 11(2):179–203, May 1993.

[vCGS92]   Thorsten von Eicken, David E. Culler, Seth Copen Goldstein, and Klaus Eric Schauser. Active Messages: a mechanism for intergrated communication and computation. In *Proceedings of the 19th International Symposium on Computer Architecture*, pages 256–266, May 1992.

Integrating Coherency and Recoverability in Distributed Systems

Michael J. Feeley, Jeffrey S. Chase, Vivek R. Narasayya, and Henry M. Levy

Department of Computer Science and Engineering, FR-35
University of Washington
Seattle, WA 98195
{feeley,chase,nara,levy}@cs.washington.edu

Abstract

We propose a technique for maintaining coherency of a *transactional* distributed shared memory, used by applications accessing a shared persistent store. Our goal is to improve support for fine-grained distributed data sharing in collaborative design applications, such as CAD systems and software development environments. In contrast, traditional research in distributed shared memory has focused on supporting parallel programs; in this paper, we show how distributed programs can benefit from this shared-memory abstraction as well.

Our approach, called *log-based coherency*, integrates coherency support with a standard mechanism for ensuring recoverability of persistent data. In our system, transaction logs are the basis of both recoverability and coherency. We have prototyped log-based coherency as a set of extensions to RVM [Satyanarayanan et al. 94], a runtime package supporting recoverable virtual memory. Our prototype adds coherency support to RVM in a simple way that does not require changes to existing RVM applications. We report on our prototype and its performance, and discuss its relationship to other DSM systems.

1 Introduction

Existing distributed shared memory (DSM) systems support *parallel programming* on distributed-memory multicomputers and workstation networks. Examples of such systems include IVY [Li & Hudak 89], Munin [Carter et al. 91], TreadMarks [Keleher et al.

94], and Midway [Zekauskas et al. 94]. These DSM systems maintain the illusion of a single shared memory by synchronizing data access and moving data between nodes when required, transparently to the application. DSM is useful in this context, because it simplifies programming of these distributed-parallel programs.

Parallel programs are not the only applications that can benefit from the concept of distributed shared memory; DSM can be applied to other application domains as well. Our goal is to support coherent virtual memory for programs that perform *transactional* updates to their shared memory space. While this style of programming is not ordinarily seen in parallel programs, it is standard for applications using a *persistent store*, a system that supports storage and retrieval of virtual memory data structures in disk files.

Our work explores the interactions between coherency and transactions. We describe *log-based coherency*, a simple technique for maintaining consistency of a transactional distributed virtual memory. The key idea behind log-based coherency is that log records used to support atomic transactions are also used as the basic mechanism for updating cached copies of the data on peer nodes. This unification of mechanisms allows us to add DSM support to systems that support persistence, without modifying existing persistent programs and without adding significant software overhead.

1.1 Persistent Stores

Persistent storage systems have evolved to meet the data management needs of design applications, including electronic and mechanical CAD systems and software development environments. These application environments consist of collections of programs that operate on persistent data structures representing design artifacts and derived information. Client programs navigate through the stored data by following pointers directly in virtual memory, with the sys-

This work is supported in part by the National Science Foundation (Grants No. CDA-9123308 and CCR-9200832), the Washington Technology Center, Digital Equipment Corporation, Boeing Computer Services, Intel Corporation, Hewlett-Packard Corporation, and Apple Computer. Both Feeley and Chase have been supported by Intel Foundation Graduate Fellowships. Chase's present address is: Department of Computer Science, Duke University, Durham, NC 27706 (chase@cs.duke.edu).

tem moving data between memory and the persistent store as needed. A number of persistent stores have been built; some are research systems [Cockshott et al. 84, Moss 90, Carey et al. 94] and others are commercial object-oriented database (OODB) products (e.g., [Butterworth et al. 92, Lamb et al. 91, O. Deux 92]), augmented with database features such as query processors, schema languages, and indexing facilities.

To prevent failures from corrupting persistent structures, updates to a persistent store are grouped together and applied "all or nothing" at *commit points* designated by the program during its execution. For our purposes, a *transaction* is a period of execution ending in a commit point. The key property of transactions is that each commit point atomically enters a set of updates that together transform the store from one durable consistent state to another. Failures may cause some uncommitted updates to be lost, but the last committed state can always be recovered. Database systems typically combine these requirements of atomicity and durability with additional assumptions about how concurrent transactions are synchronized, but this is not essential to our notion of a transaction.

Our work explores techniques for extending a persistent store to allow network access. For example, a persistent store that supports design applications can be extended to allow a group of collaborating designers to run CAD tools at their workstations, accessing the shared store through the network. In the simplest configuration, updates are written atomically to a centralized server that maintains the authoritative copy of the data in the store. Clients fetch data from the server in bulk, cache it locally, and operate directly on the cached image in virtual memory. In the database community this architecture is sometimes called a *client/server database*. We refer to it as a *cached persistent store* since the ideas generalize to persistent virtual memory systems that do not provide full database features. Note that cached persistent stores are distinct from transactional systems for reliable distributed programming (e.g., Argus [Liskov 88] and Camelot [Eppinger et al. 91]) in that the database itself is not distributed; each transaction updates a cached *image* of a centralized database in virtual memory on a single node. In particular, there is no need for two-phase commit, since each transaction commits or aborts within a single process.

1.2 Combining Coherency and Recoverability

A key problem for cached persistent stores is maintaining consistency of the data cached in memory on each client. While these systems are similar to distributed file systems, the caches should be viewed as a distributed shared memory, since each client process accesses the cache *directly* in its virtual address space. There are other important similarities with DSM systems. Fine-grained sharing is common in collaborative design environments, where changes made by one engineer must be quickly integrated into structures that are readable by the others. The caches of different clients will overlap considerably when clients access the same artifacts, more so as physical memories grow and data remains in client memory for longer periods. For these reasons, DSM techniques such as fine-grained client-client transfers are appropriate for maintaining coherency for cached persistent stores. In the past, distributed persistent systems have supported coherency in a manner similar to most distributed file systems: by reading and writing shared data through the server, usually in fixed-size blocks, and invalidating cached blocks when another client acquires the file token or lock.

In addition, there is commonality between the key implementation aspects for coherency and recoverability. To implement either property, the system must capture the updates made by the application, and propagate those updates — either to durable memory (e.g., disk) or to other memories in the network — in such a way that all clients see a consistent view of the data at all times. The key performance factors are the same: (1) the cost of capturing updates, and (2) the precision with which those updates are captured, which determines the amount of traffic to the disk or network. This synergy can be exploited when both properties are supported together, and optimizations that improve the performance of one may also improve the performance of the other.

This paper develops a combined approach that integrates coherency support with a mechanism for ensuring recoverability of persistent data. It differs from other DSM systems in that it accommodates a transactional programming model and exploits the capturing of updates for a transaction log. Section 2 outlines our approach and its variations, discusses some of the design issues, and sets our work in context with other systems that support distributed database access and distributed shared memory. Section 3 describes our prototype implementation, and Section 4 presents some performance results. In Section 5 we discuss additional related work, and we conclude in Section 6.

2 Log-Based Coherency for a Cached Persistent Store

Log-based coherency is an extension to *write-ahead redo logging*, a common mechanism for implementing atomic and durable transactions. This mechanism works by recording new values of data items modified by a transaction, and writing them to a log on durable memory when the transaction commits. The system ensures that commits are atomic by writing the log *before* writing the updated objects back to the permanent database file. In the event of failure, a recovery procedure restores the database to a consistent state by replaying the committed log records into the permanent database file. Many recoverable systems use write-ahead redo logging; for example, it is fundamental to the *pin/update/log* commit protocol used by Camelot [Eppinger et al. 91].

When multiple clients are accessing the store through a network, the log records are written to a logically centralized storage service that also holds the permanent database file. A client failure aborts all uncommitted transactions executing in that client. A server failure may abort uncommitted transactions in all clients and initiate the recovery procedure to bring the permanent database file to a consistent state, reflecting the committed updates made by all clients. (Note that the storage service could be transparently replicated to reduce the probability of a server failure.)

The key to log-based coherency is that the redo log generated by each client holds exactly the information needed to maintain consistency of distributed memory. The system need only transmit the committed log tails to peer nodes that are sharing the modified objects; the recipients apply the log records they receive to update their cached data images. There is no extra runtime cost for collecting the information needed to maintain coherency, since it is already collected to support recoverability. Thus, a common implementation technique for a recoverable store is extended to support coherency in a straightforward way. In fact, our approach can be viewed as transaction logging to remote memory instead of (or in addition to) the disk.

As an example, suppose that several nodes are sharing a persistent object, X; each has a copy of X cached in its primary memory. When one of the nodes executes a transaction modifying X, the updates are performed and logged locally; other nodes are neither updated nor invalidated at that time. When the transaction is complete, the generated log record contains exactly the information needed to transition to the current state of X from its initial state. Thus, to bring the other nodes up to date, it is sufficient to propagate this portion of the log to the peer nodes.

Within this broad framework, systems that use log-based coherency could vary in a number of details, including:

- when log records are transmitted to peer nodes,

- which peers receive the log records,

- how updates are applied to a recipient's cache,

- how updates are synchronized with client threads executing locally, and, in a recipient's cache.

In our prototype, described in Section 3, we have made choices for ease of implementation and for the workloads we expect. However, our approach is flexible enough to accommodate variations. The following subsections discuss underlying concepts, the design choices we made, and some alternative possibilities.

2.1 The Role of Synchronization

In DSM systems, the method and timing of update propagation is closely tied to synchronization events. The first DSM systems (Monads [Rosenberg & Abramson 85] and IVY [Li & Hudak 89]) used virtual page protections and reference traps to capture updates and synchronize access to shared pages. In these systems, page-grain locking and page-grain coherency led to performance problems caused by false sharing. Newer high-performance DSM systems based on *release consistency* [Gharachorloo et al. 90] (e.g., Munin), *lazy release consistency* [Keleher et al. 92] (TreadMarks) and *entry consistency* (Midway) have reduced this problem by supplying synchronization primitives that function independently of the coherency protocol, and drive the propagation of updates. These systems reduce false sharing by allowing concurrent accesses to a shared page. However, they assume a fully synchronized (*properly labeled*) application program; that is, the application must acquire and release the correct locks at the correct times. For all of these systems, the coherency algorithm will fail for programs that make synchronization errors.

Log-based coherency uses a similar approach resting on similar assumptions. Our prototype supplies standard mutex primitives that are acquired as a transaction executes and released at transaction commit (we currently assume that transactions use strict two-phase locking). The system propagates updates only after a writer has released all relevant locks at commit, and it ensures that all relevant updates are applied locally before a reader is permitted to acquire a lock. Our system differs from release consistency, and is similar to entry consistency (Midway), in that coherency operations initiated by a lock operation are restricted to the data under the scope of that lock. The store is partitioned into segments, each under the control of a separate lock. Segments can be large or small, presenting an obvious tradeoff between synchronization overhead and false lock conflicts. We expect locks to be relatively coarse-grained; most commercial persistent stores support coarse-grained locking as natural for collaborative design environments. Regardless of the locking grain, the updates made while a lock is held often involve only a small number of the bytes controlled by that lock. In fact, we expect that most updates will be fine-grained (e.g., "change this **and** to an **or**"), but that read operations will consume large amounts of data for input to functions such as design analysis or graphical display. For this reason, log-based coherency separates the coherency grain from the synchronization grain: the updates sent to peer nodes are determined not by the locks acquired, but by the values logged at transaction commit.

Transaction log records include information about the locks acquired during the transaction. Each lock has a unique lock number and a sequence number (timestamp) that is incremented on each **acquire**. When a transaction acquires a lock, its log record is tagged with the sequence number and lock number of that lock. The synchronization primitives contain embedded calls to logging routines to generate these tags. The tags are used to determine which nodes must receive the log records and when they must be applied. For example, updates for a segment need only be sent to nodes that have previously acquired the lock for the segment. The sequence numbers are also used to ensure that all relevant data has been rendered coherent before an **acquire** can succeed, and to preserve the global ordering of updates from multiple nodes during recovery, as described in Section 3.4.

We believe that alternative synchronization models can be implemented with a modest effort, by replacing the synchronization primitives and the calls they make to underlying logging and coherency routines. Several relaxed models have been proposed by researchers arguing that strict serializability is inappropriate for design transactions (e.g., [Hornick & Zdonik 87]). We are exploring a read/write model that permits readers to operate on a previous consistent version of the data while an update is in progress elsewhere; readers use an **accept** primitive to explicitly signal their willingness to move forward to a newer consistent version. In this scheme, pending log records must be buffered in the recipient until they can be applied. We have used a similar *version-based consistency* model in the past for a range of parallel applications [Feeley & Levy 92].

2.2 Propagating Log Records

Our prototype uses a simple eager policy for propagating updates. At each commit point, after the log records have been written to the storage server, the in-memory copies of the log records for each segment are eagerly propagated to all clients that have recently acquired the locks for the modified segments. We use eager updates because they are simple (i.e., no buffering of log records), they are tolerant of client failures, and they reduce the latency of data access on a client. However, eager updates may increase network traffic and cannot scale to large numbers of clients, particu-

larly on networks with point-to-point links that do not support broadcast or multicast.

We believe that alternative policies could be implemented transparently to the application by replacing the synchronization primitives and their embedded coherency code. For example, the system could propagate segment updates lazily, using an embedded call in the **acquire** primitive to fetch and apply pending log records. Segment updates could be fetched from the server, where all log records are cached in memory for a time, or passed with the lock by the last writer. In Midway, for example, the **acquire** primitive retrieves current versions of any stale objects in the requester's cache from the current lock holder. The acquire request includes a timestamp for the last time the lock was held by the requester; the lock holder determines which modified objects to return by comparing the timestamp against a modification timestamp for each object under the lock's scope.

For log-based coherency, lazy update propagation raises the question of how to determine when pending log records are no longer needed by peer nodes and can be discarded. One solution is to pass information about how many log records to hold for each segment along with the lock token, as each node acquires the lock in turn. Each node holds all log records up to and including the oldest records needed by the most out-of-date peer. Acquiring a lock brings new records, as well as an opportunity to discard records held locally. Note that discarding pending update records is not a concern with Midway's lazy propagation scheme, because no log records or captured updates are held; nodes do not save intermediate versions of objects that are modified repeatedly. In our case, these log records must be held in order to support the nonserializable read/write model described above. That is, a reader may acquire a previous version even if uncommitted writes are present in the writer's cache; the reader's cache must be updated to reflect the previous committed version.

2.3 Summary

In this section we presented an overview of log-based coherency. Built-in synchronization primitives are fundamental to our approach. Alternative coherency protocols — rules for propagating, applying, and releasing log records — can be realized by embedding calls to logging routines in the synchronization primitives. The locking routines can collect and maintain information about which peers must receive a given set of updates, and when.

3 Prototype Implementation

To experiment with our approach, we prototyped a simple implementation of log-based coherency by adding distribution support to CMU's Recoverable Virtual Memory (RVM) package [Satyanarayanan et al. 94]. RVM is a logging facility that supports transactional update and recovery of virtual-memory resident data structures. RVM is designed to be a lightweight and portable package for use with small databases that easily fit in physical memory: an RVM client copies the entire database into virtual memory when it starts up. This avoids the need to pin modified pages, but for large databases it causes double paging and unnecessary pageouts of clean pages by the virtual memory system. This limits RVM's usefulness for the collaborative design environments that interest us; however, it is an expedient vehicle for experimenting with log-based coherency.

In keeping with its minimalist philosophy, RVM does not support or rely upon any particular synchronization scheme. Though updates are transactional, multi-threaded updates may or may not be serializable. In a similar spirit, our RVM-based prototype separates the synchronization aspects of coherency and recoverability from the mechanisms for collecting, propagating, and applying redo log records. Our intent is to accommodate various policies for propagating updates as part of a synchronization scheme "plugged in" to RVM.

We use RVM as a client/server distributed database by placing the transaction log files and the database file on a central NFS server. Clients maintain caches of the central database in their local virtual memories by reading the entire database into memory at startup (as in centralized RVM), in this case using the NFS protocol. As write transactions execute, RVM produces redo log records that are written to the NFS server. Log-based coherency is implemented by sending the log tails to other nodes that have the region mapped, where they are applied to each recipient's cache. Each node recording such a transaction produces a separate log. We added an RVM utility that merges these into a single log for recovery (see Section 3.4).

Our application interface is summarized in Table 1. The left-hand column describes the procedures the application uses to initialize, begin, and commit a transaction; to acquire a segment lock; and to describe the data that is modified by the transaction. The right-hand column shows the RVM calls made by each of these procedures. We added a new procedure, called **rvm_setlockid_transaction**, to the standard RVM interface. This procedure is called by the **acquire** primitive, as described in Section 3.3.

3.1 Capturing Updates

Both DSM and recoverable systems must determine which bytes are modified by the application using either VM write faults, a write barrier inserted by the compiler, or explicit calls from the application. Like the RVM system, our prototype assumes explicit run-time calls to a **set_range** procedure in the runtime package. A call to this function indicates an intent to update a particular range of bytes. We expect that this range corresponds to an object, and that the call is made by code generated explicitly by the language compiler (such as the ML compiler that has been used with RVM [O'Toole et al. 93]). In contrast, most DSM systems use virtual page access faults to captue updates, though software-based write detection is also used in Midway [Zekauskas et al. 94]. This issue is discussed in more detail in Section 4.

RVM coalesces modified ranges that are adjacent or overlapping in order to avoid writing redundant bytes to the disk log. Overlapping ranges, however, are unlikely when calls to **set_range** are generated by a compiler, as is anticipated. To improve common-case performance, we modified **set_range** to coalesce only when there is an exact match with a previously added range. Thus, objects that are modified multiple times during a transaction are still coalesced but with a simpler and more efficient implementation; this reduces **set_range** overhead by a factor of five. The remaining per-update overhead is dominated by searching the binary tree that stores modified ranges (in order by their address). As a second optimization, we avoid this search in the special case where a sequence of **set_range** calls is ordered by address.

3.2 Propagating Log Records

In response to **set_range** calls, the RVM runtime library builds a data structure that describes the modifications made by a transaction. When the transaction commits, this data structure is used to build I/O vectors for the Unix **writev** system call. The **writev** causes the new values of all modified objects to be copied from virtual memory to a system buffer for writing to disk. RVM thus avoids building an object log in virtual memory that contains copies of the modified objects.

We modified the RVM commit procedure to broadcast the same new-value information that is written to disk. Coherency data is broadcast using TCP/IP by issuing a **writev** system call for each node that has the current region mapped. We use the OSF/1 PThreads facility [Mueller 93] to create *receiver* threads for each communication channel that connects a node to its peers. These threads block in **readv** system calls waiting for coherency messages and applying the updates

Log-Based Coherency Operation	RVM Routine Called
Trans.Init()	tid=rvm_malloc_tid()
Trans.Begin(rvm_mode)	rvm_begin_transaction(tid, rvm_mode)
Trans.Commit(rvm_mode)	rvm_end_transaction(tid, rvm_mode)
Trans.Acquire(lock)	rvm_setlockid_transaction(tid, lock.lockId, lock.sequenceNum)
Trans.SetRange(addr, size)	rvm_set_range(addr, size)

Table 1: *Log-based coherency interface.*

when they arrive.

The format of the coherency records data differs from the data sent to disk in two respects. First, some records that are needed only for recovery and log trimming are not included in the broadcast data; i.e., only new-value range records are needed for coherency. Second, the header information for each range record is compressed from 104 bytes to between 4 and 24 bytes. The standard RVM header contains fields that are not needed for coherency; our header contains only the range's type, address, and size. The header is further compressed when ranges are small (less than 4 Kbytes) or close together (fewer than 256 Kbytes apart) by using smaller fields and by replacing the range's address with its offset from the preceding range; our modified **set_range** orders modified ranges by their address.

3.3 Synchronization

We added distributed locks that provide mutually-exclusive access to non-overlapping portions of an RVM region. Locks are acquired inside of transactions in a two-phase manner; all locks are automatically released when a transaction commits. Applications must acquire a lock before reading or writing the data protected by that lock.

The lock implementation is token based with a centralized lock manager and a distributed waiter queue, an approach used in many distributed systems including TreadMarks. At all times, exactly one node owns the lock token. The lock can be acquired on that node without remote communication; nodes hold onto the token until they are requested to pass it to another node. Acquire operations at other nodes send a message to the lock manager to request the lock. The node number of the lock manager is determined from the lock identifier number. The manager maintains a distributed queue of nodes waiting to acquire the lock. It adds the requester to the tail of the queue and forwards its request to the previous tail which responds either by sending the lock token to the requester, if the lock is available, or by queueing the request until the lock is released.

Each lock has a unique identifier and a sequence number that is incremented on each **acquire**. The current sequence number is passed along with the lock token when ownership of the lock changes. The **acquire** primitive calls RVM to associate the lock with the current transaction. We added a new procedure to the RVM interface, **rvm_setlockid_transaction(tid, lockId, sequenceNum)**, for this purpose. Because locks follow a strict two-phase protocol, each lock is acquired at most once during a transaction.

3.4 Preserving Ordering

While synchronization is mostly independent of coherency and recovery, there is an important interaction. When a transaction commits, the lock information provided to RVM is used to generate *lock records* that are inserted in the log entry for the transaction. Lock records contain the lock identifier and sequence number. These lock records are used by both the coherency and recovery code to preserve the ordering of updates generated by different nodes.

For coherency, the lock records ensure that log records applied by a receiver thread are properly interleaved with those sent by other nodes. The lock records included with a received update are used to set the receiver's local sequence number for the lock. If necessary, receiver threads hold log records until the updates for the immediately preceding sequence number have been applied. Also, the sequence number must match the sequence number passed with the lock token before the lock can be acquired on that node. An application that tries to acquire the lock prematurely will wait on a condition variable until signaled by the receiver thread that applies the latest update. This interlock between coherency and synchronization is necessary because updates are broadcast asynchronously; the lock token could arrive at a node before all necessary coherency updates have been received and applied. For example, if the token passes in order through nodes A, B, and C, C might receive the token from B before A's updates arrive at C. The protocol ensures that, for updates made to data protected by the same lock, (1) none of B's updates are applied at C until C has applied A's updates and (2) C is not allowed to acquire the lock until B's updates have been applied.

For recovery, lock records are used to merge the individual RVM redo logs produced by each node. When applications share a segment, their logs may record interleaving updates to the same data. Thus, before any of these logs can be used by the standard RVM recovery procedure, they must be merged into a single log. We built a new RVM utility to do this. Our merge utility reads input logs from head to tail; transaction records from different logs are compared by comparing their lock records. Our current merge utility exploits the fact that our current synchronization model guarantees strictly serializable transactions. When merging records from different logs, it is sufficient to order transactions so that if two transactions acquired the same lock, the transaction with the earlier sequence number for that lock is ordered first.

3.5 Distributed Log Trimming

The current RVM log-trimming algorithm has an unfortunate interaction with our distribution implementation. In the current version of RVM, log records are trimmed from the head of the log using the standard recovery procedure to compute a new checkpoint. This operation, which runs asynchronously with normal transactions, is triggered when the number of records in the log reaches a high-water point. In our system, it is no longer possible to use the log generated by a single node to compute a new checkpoint; instead, log records from all nodes must first be merged. Our current prototype performs log trimming offline using the recovery procedure described above. Online trimming could be implemented using the merging procedure by coordinating checkpointing; one node would checkpoint at a time, broadcasting to other nodes when done to inform them of their new log head.

An improved log-trimming scheme for RVM is described in [Satyanarayanan et al. 94]. In this scheme, nodes checkpoint a page at a time by writing the current version of a page to the checkpoint file. Log records for updates made to a page before it was checkpointed can be discarded. This checkpointing scheme could be more easily incorporated into our prototype, because it does not require logs to be merged.

4 Performance

This section presents performance measurements of our prototype. While most DSM systems have used parallel programs for evaluation, our application domain — collaborative design applications accessing a distributed persistent store — requires a different benchmark. For this reason, we have chosen to use OO7 [Carey et al. 93], a standard object-oriented database benchmark. OO7 consists of a number of different traversals, updates, and queries of a synthetic object-oriented database. The database and the traversal tests are intended to be suggestive of typical engineering database applications.

We modified OO7 to run with RVM in standard virtual memory (i.e., no OODB) and integrated it with our log-based coherency prototype. We report timings and related overheads for several OO7 traversals using our prototype. These experiments were conducted using two Digital 3000-400 Alpha APX (133 Mhz, 74 SPECints) workstations with 8-Kbyte pages and separate 512-Kbyte direct-mapped instruction and data caches [Dig 92]. The machines are connected by a 100 Mbit/s AN1 network, an experimental switch-based network capable of sending message packets of up to 64 Kbytes [Rodeheffer & Schroeder 91]. Elapsed time measurements were taken using the Alpha cycle counter. For these experiments, we disabled RVM disk logging so that we could isolate the costs associated with coherency from the synchronous disk writes needed to support recovery. This is important in part because optimizations using non-volatile RAM can be used to eliminate synchronous disk writes from the commit critical path [Hagmann 86].

The figures also depict estimated lower bounds for alternative DSM implementations that use page access faults to capture updates. For log-based coherency, updates are captured by calls to the RVM set_range procedure. These calls are coded explicitly in our OO7 benchmarks, although other RVM applications have used compiler-generated set_range calls [O'Toole et al. 93]. In contrast, most DSM systems use page access faults to capture updates without involvement from the compiler or application. Early page-locking DSM systems, such as Monads and IVY, use page access faults to grant a writer exclusive access to a page while updates are in progress, then transmit the entire contents of each modified page to other nodes accessing the page. In newer multiple-writer "copy/compare" DSM systems, such as Munin and TreadMarks, updates are also detected a page at a time, but multiple nodes are permitted to make concurrent non-conflicting updates to any given page. In these systems, the first store to a unmodified page on each node delivers a write-access fault to the coherency software, which makes a copy of the page before enabling write access. Updates are collected by later comparing the modified page with its copy. The copy/compare technique could improve performance for some OODBs that use page-grained locking and updates today.

Our lower-bound estimates for page-locking (labeled *Page*) and multiple-writer (labeled *Cpy/Cmp*) DSM systems are computed from the measurements listed in Table 2. We measured the cost of using the OSF/1

Operation	Cost (μsec/page)	Throughput (MBytes/s)
page copy (cold cache)	171.9	43
page copy (warm cache)	57.8	135
page compare (cold cache)	281.0	28
page compare (warm cache)	147.3	53
page send (TCP/IP)	677.0	12 (96.8 Mbit/s)
handle signal and change protection	360.1	

Table 2: *Operation costs (per page) on Alpha/AN1.*

`mprotect` system call to change page protection, by storing to a read-only page to generate a protection fault, delivering the signal to a user-level procedure, calling `mprotect` again to enable writing, and returning from the signal handler. We also measured the time to copy and compare pages (we use the cold cache times in the figures). For page-grain DSM (Page), updated pages are not copied or scanned, so we assume no collection overhead. However, network I/O overhead for Page is greater because entire pages are transmitted instead of just the modified bytes. This time is estimated from the measured TCP throughput given in Table 2. Communication overhead for Cpy/Cmp is assumed to be the same as the measured times for log-based coherency (labeled *Log*), since both send only the modified bytes. Both Log and Cpy/Cmp also incur overhead at the receiver to *apply* the updates to the cache; however, this cost is too small to be clearly distinguished in any of the graphs below.

4.1 The OO7 Benchmark

The OO7 database is composed of a *design library* and an *assembly hierarchy*. The design library, which makes up the bulk of the database, is a set of 500 composite parts. A composite part corresponds to a design primitive, such as a register cell in a VLSI CAD application or a procedure in a CASE application. Each composite part is itself made up of a graph of 20 atomic parts. Composite and atomic part objects are each roughly 200 bytes long. Each atomic part contains an index field; a part index is maintained using a self-balancing tree.

Objects in the assembly hierarchy correspond to higher-level design constructs in the application. The assembly hierarchy is a tree of assembly objects with 729 leaf nodes. Each leaf node, called a base assembly, points to three composite parts that are chosen at random from the design library when the database is constructed.

There are two traversals in OO7 that update the database, T2 and T3. Both traverse the assembly hierarchy to visit all of the composite parts pointed to by each base assembly; thus, a total of 2187 compos-

ite parts are visited. When a composite part is visited, its atomic-part graph is traversed and updates are performed. There are three variants of the traversals (A, B, and C) that update different numbers of atomic parts. In A, one atomic part per composite part is modified; in B, every atomic part is modified; and in C, every atomic part is modified four times. An atomic part is updated by changing an eight-byte field. The difference between T2 and T3 is that T3 updates the atomic part's index field. Each time this field is changed, the part index is updated by deleting the index entry for the old value and adding an entry for the new value. This results in an average of seven index updates for each atomic-part update.

We added a third update traversal, called T12. T12 differs from the other update traversals in that it performs a sparse traversal of the database. It is similar to read-only traversal T6; for each composite part it visits only one atomic part. In T12, a higher percentage of overall running time is related to updating objects. This highlights the performance costs associated with coherency overhead.

In our RVM-based OO7 benchmark, the database elements are heap-allocated C++ objects and a threaded AVL-balanced tree is used for the part index. The atomic parts associated with a particular composite part tend to be clustered on the same page while atomic parts from different composite parts are usually on different pages. We ran each of the OO7 update traversals under our prototype. Each test consists of a single transaction (and a single segment lock) in which one node performs the traversal and another receives the log tail and installs the updates, bringing its copy of the database up to date.

4.2 Results

Figures 1, 2, and 3 show the results of running the various OO7 traversals, along with the associated coherency overhead. Write overhead consists of *detecting* and *collecting* updates and the *network I/O* costs of transmitting those updates to the other node. Table 3 summarizes the characteristics of these traversals, listing the number of updates performed by each, the

Traversal	Updates	Bytes Updated	Message Bytes	Pages Updated
T12-A	2,187	4,000	6,000	500
T12-C	8,748	4,000	6,000	500
T2-A	2,187	4,000	6,000	500
T2-B	43,740	80,000	120,000	618
T2-C	174,960	80,000	120,000	618
T3-A	16,924	31,300	39,000	552
T3-B	248,632	114,650	163,300	667
T3-C	1,502,708	115,100	163,800	670

Table 3: *Summary of OO7 update-traversal characteristics*

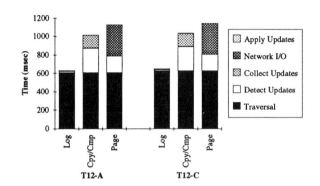

Figure 1: *OO7 Sparse-update traversals T12-A and T12-C.*

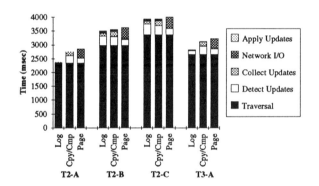

Figure 2: *OO7 Full-update traversals T2-A, T2-B, and T2-C, and index-update traversal T3-A.*

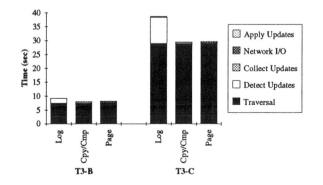

Figure 3: *OO7 Index-update traversals T3-B and T3-C.*

number of unique bytes updated, the number of bytes sent over the network, and the number of pages updated. (The difference between the number of bytes updated and the number transmitted is due to range-message overhead; each range is preceded by a header that describes the address of the range and its size.)

Based on the Alpha-OSF/1 measurements, our analysis shows that for the anticipated application workload, in which updates affect a large number of pages, software write detection (e.g., compiler-generated set_range calls) performs better than any form of hardware-based write detection. Our approach performs significantly better for traversals T12-A, T12-C, T2-A, and T3-A because they perform relatively few updates per page. Traversals T2-B and T2-C perform 71 and 283 update per page respectively; for these traversals, our approach performs about as well as Cpy/Cmp. However, the index-update traversals T3-B and T3-C perform significantly more updates per page, 373 and 2,243; as a result our approach performs poorly. This shows that when there are many updates per page, a page-based systems such as TreadMarks is preferred to a software-based approach such as log-based coherency.

4.3 Analysis

There is a performance tradeoff between the three approaches evaluated above that is a function of (1) the number of modified bytes per page and (2) the number of individual updates per page. The overhead of Log and Cpy/Cmp depends on the number of modified bytes, Cpy/Cmp and Page depend on the number of modified pages, and Log alone depends on the number of updates per page. Which approach works best depends on the workload. As we have seen, log-based coherency is preferred when there are few updates per page; similarly, Page performs best when most of a page is modified. Figures 4–7 below show where the breakeven points occur.

Figure 4 shows coherency overhead as a function of the number of modified bytes per page. This compares

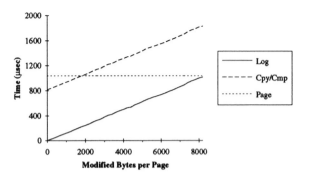

Figure 4: *Comparison of overhead as the number of modified bytes per page increases. For log-based coherency, per-update overhead is not included.*

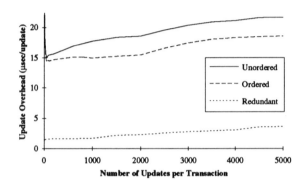

Figure 5: *The overhead associated with a single update for log-based coherency as the number of updates per transaction increases.*

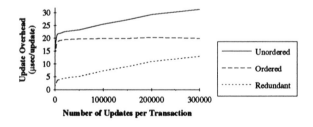

Figure 6: *Log-based coherency update overhead up to 300,000 updates per transaction.*

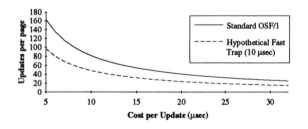

Figure 7: *Breakeven point for log-based coherency. For different update overheads, the number of updates per page at which log-based coherency performs better than Cpy/Cmp.*

the per-byte overhead of log-based coherency with the total overhead of copy/compare and page approaches. When more than 1037 bytes are modified per page, Page outperforms Cpy/Cmp. When there are few updates per page, Log outperforms the alternatives no matter how many bytes are modified. However, this graph does not include the per-update overhead associated with Log; this is shown in Figures 5–7.

Figures 5 and 6 show the log-based coherency overhead associated with detecting and collecting a single update as the number of updates per transaction increases. This is a measurement of the performance of RVM operations **set_range** and **rvm_commit**. The middle line is the cost for an update in an ordered sequence of **set_range** calls (taking advantage of the optimization described in Section 3.1). The lower line is the cost of detecting an update to a range that was modified previously in the same transaction.

Figure 7 shows the breakeven point at which log-based coherency and Cpy/Cmp have equivalent performance. For a given average per-update cost on the x-axis, the y-axis shows the maximum number of updates per page possible before Cpy/Cmp outperforms log-based coherency. For example, using Figures 5 and 7, we can determine that if there are 1000 updates per transaction, log-based coherency performs better when there are 45 or fewer updates per page (55 if the updates are ordered).

Recent work [Thekkath & Levy 94] has shown an order-of-magnitude reduction in exception-handling cost, which would make hardware-based write detection more attractive. Figure 7 shows how the performance tradeoff would be affected if signal handling overhead were 10 μsec instead of the 340 μsec measured for Alpha-OSF/1.

4.3.1 Increasing the Number of Nodes

Another important performance concern for log-based coherency is the effect of increasing the number of nodes using a segment to be kept coherent. In our prototype the *network I/O* overhead of the writer increases linearly with the number of peer nodes, because the writer node issues separate **writev** system calls for each peer. Since this overhead is relatively small, our approach will scale to a moderate number of nodes. Systems with a very large number of clients will perform better with multicast hardware or lazy coherency.

4.3.2 Impact of Coherency on Recoverability

Finally, we wanted to determine the impact of our modifications on the performance of standard RVM. Figure 8 shows four measurements of the coherency and recoverability overheads for the T12-A bench-

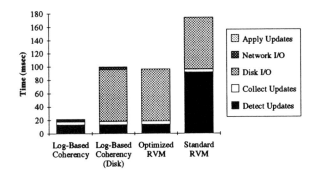

Figure 8: *Comparison of log-based coherency, disk logging, and standard RVM. Optimized RVM is standard RVM with our optimizations to* set_range.

mark. The first column is the overhead for log-based coherency presented in the previous section. The next column measures the overhead when disk logging is enabled; from this we see that the only additional overhead is due to writing the log tail to disk. The third and fourth columns were taken using standard RVM, without our log-based coherency modifications; the third column is standard RVM with our optimized set_range modification. This shows that the overhead added to RVM by log-based coherency is directly related to sending the modified bytes to peer nodes. This validates our assertion that there is a high degree of overlap between the mechanisms for recoverability and coherency.

5   Related Work

In the context of RVM, transaction logs have been used in a similar fashion to propagate updates between data spaces in a system with concurrent replicating garbage collection [O'Toole et al. 93]. Our contribution is to use this idea for maintaining coherency of client database caches. Log propagation has been used to maintain the consistency of replicas in replicated database systems. Replicated systems differ from log-based coherency in that the replicas are used to ensure availability of the data. In replicated systems, log records flow in one direction: from clients to servers (or from a client to a server, and then on to other servers). Servers cooperate to ensure that log records are applied in a consistent order at all locations. In our system, the replicas are caches that keep only enough data to meet the local client's needs; update propagation may be delayed until a client requests the new data.

Harp [Liskov et al. 92] file servers log received updates to peer servers in order to remove stable storage writes from the commit path. Similarly, Naughton and Li have used log propagation to keep a hot standby of

a main-memory database [Li & Naughton 88]. The standby keeps a complete copy of the database in its memory and receives updates from the primary in the form of log records sent at commit points. Their purpose is to allow checkpointing to take place in the standby, off-line, without interfering with clients executing on the primary copy of the database. Delis and Roussopoulos conducted a simulation study of client-server relational databases using a log-based approach for updating client caches [Delis & Roussopoulos 92]. Updates are centralized at the server; the server maintains a recovery log and a separate update log. Before a client accesses a data item in its cache, it first contacts the server to retrieve log records generated since the cached copy of the item was last updated. While several of these systems send log records from clients to one or more servers, log-based coherency sends log records from client to client.

Several groups have integrated coherency and recoverability by adding checkpointing to page-based DSM, without using transactions. This allows non-transactional applications such as parallel programs to be made recoverable. The main issue is to coordinate individual node checkpoints to attain a consistent global checkpoint, using a combination of dependency tracking, message logging, and replication. The first such system is due to Wu and Fuchs [Wu & Fuchs 90]. Stumm and Zhou describe a system that tolerates the failure of a single node by ensuring that every page resides in the caches of at least two nodes [Stumm & Zhou 90]. Richard and Singhal use page logging [Richard & Singhal 93]; a copy of a page is written to a local volatile log each time it is acquire for reading or writing. A node writes its volatile log to disk before transferring a modified page to another node.

Janssens and Fuchs added checkpointing to relaxed-consistency DSM [Janssens & Fuchs 93]. Instead of requiring checkpointing or other recoverability actions each time an application gains access to a page, their system checkpoints only when a node releases or acquires a lock.

Neves et al. added checkpointing to an entry-consistent DSM system similar to Midway, using object-grain locking [Neves et al. 94]. Their system tolerates single node failures by keeping old versions of modified objects in the volatile memory of the nodes that modify them. Each node checkpoints independently; a failed node recovers by replaying its execution starting with its most recent checkpoint. Information recorded at other nodes is sufficient for them to supply the recovering node with the same version of objects as it saw during normal execution. The impact on failure-free execution is minimized by piggy-backing recoverability information on coherency messages.

6 Conclusion

The key points of this paper are: (1) DSM techniques such as fine-grained client-client transfers are appropriate for maintaining cache coherency for distributed persistent stores, (2) there is a commonality between the implementation techniques for recoverability and coherency, and (3) this synergy can be exploited when both properties are supported together.

We have presented a new DSM approach called log-based coherency that uses recoverability mechanisms from persistent object systems as the basis for maintaining coherency of distributed objects. Our work extends previous work on DSM to exploit the notion of commit points in which a group of related updates become visible atomically. We extend work on persistent stores to support the fine-grained sharing made possible for parallel applications by DSM systems. In particular, log-based coherency separates the coherency grain from the synchronization grain. This is important for collaborative-design applications, where large data regions are shared among engineers at different nodes, but where updates are sparse and infrequent. With log-based coherency, locking overhead can be reduced by using coarse-grain locks without increasing coherency overhead; i.e., coarse-grain locks can support fine-grain sharing.

While log-based coherency provides an alternative to other DSM systems, the approaches are not mutually exclusive. Our measurements show that application behavior determines the best approach; e.g., if updates are highly clustered within a page, standard DSM techniques will perform better, while for sparse updates, the log-based approach will perform better. Therefore, adaptive hybrid approaches maybe be possible where application behavior can be predicted.

References

[Butterworth et al. 92] Butterworth, P., Otis, A., and Stein, J. The GemStone object database management system. *Communications of the ACM*, 34(10):64–77, October 1992.

[Carey et al. 93] Carey, M. J., Dewitt, D. J., and Naughton, J. F. The OO7 benchmark. *1993 ACM SIGMOD. International Conference on Management of Data*, 22(2):12–21, May 1993.

[Carey et al. 94] Carey, M. J., Dewitt, D. J., and Franklin, M. J. Shoring up persistent applications. *1994 ACM SIGMOD. International Conference on Management of Data*, May 1994.

[Carter et al. 91]
Carter, J., Bennet, J., and Zwaenepoel, W. Implementation and performance of Munin. In *Proceedings of the 13th ACM Symposium on Operating Systems and Principles*, pages 152–164, October 1991.

[Cockshott et al. 84] Cockshott, W., Atkinson, M., Chisholm, K., Bailey, P., and Morrison, R. Persistent object management system. *Software Practice and Experience*, 14(1), January 1984.

[Delis & Roussopoulos 92] Delis, A. and Roussopoulos, N. Performance and scalability of client-server database architectures. In *Proceedings of the 18th International Conference on Very Large Databases*, pages 610–623, August 1992.

[Dig 92] Digital Equipment Corporation, Maynard, MA. *Alpha Architecture Handbook*, 1992.

[Eppinger et al. 91] Eppinger, J., Mummert, L., and Spector, A. *Camelot and Avalon*. Morgan Kaufmann, 1991.

[Feeley & Levy 92] Feeley, M. J. and Levy, H. M. Distributed shared memory with versioned objects. In *Proceedings of the Conference on Object-Oriented Programming Systems, Languages, and Applications*, October 1992.

[Gharachorloo et al. 90] Gharachorloo, K., Lenoski, D., Laudon, J., Gibbons, P., Gupta, A., and Hennessy, J. Memory consistency and event ordering in scalable shared-memory multiprocessors. In *Proc. 17th Annual Symposium on Computer Architecture, Computer Architecture News*, pages 15–26. ACM, June 1990.

[Hagmann 86] Hagmann, R. B. A crash recovery scheme for a memory-resident database system. *IEEE Transactions on Computers*, C-35(9):839–843, September 1986.

[Hornick & Zdonik 87] Hornick, M. F. and Zdonik, S. B. A shared, segmented memory system for an object-oriented database. *A ACM Transactions on Office Informations Systems*, 5(1), January 1987.

[Hosking & Moss 93] Hosking, A. L. and Moss, J. E. B. Protection traps and alternatives for memory managemnt of an object-oriented language. In *Proceedings of the 14th ACM Symposium on Operating Systems Principles*, December 1993.

[Janssens & Fuchs 93] Janssens, B. and Fuchs, W. K. Relaxing consistency in recoverable distributed shared memory. In *Proceedings of the Twenty-Third Annual International Symposium on Fault-Tolerant Computing: Digest of Papers*, pages 155–163, June 1993.

[Keleher et al. 92]
Keleher, P., Cox, A., and Zwaenepoel, W. Lazy release consistency for software distributed shared memory. In *Proceedings of the 19th Annual Symposium on Computer Architecture*, pages 13–21, May 1992.

[Keleher et al. 94] Keleher, P., Cox, A. L., Dwarkadas, S., and Zwaenepoel, W. TreadMarks: Distributed shared memory on standard workstations and operating systems. In *Proceedings of the Winder 1994 USENIX Conference*, pages 115–132, January 1994.

[Lamb et al. 91] Lamb, C., Landis, G., Orenstein, J., and Weinreb, D. The ObjectStore database system. *Communications of the ACM*, 34(10):50–63, October 1991.

[Li & Hudak 89] Li, K. and Hudak, P. Memory coherence in shared virtual memory systems. *ACM Transactions on Computer Systems*, 7(4):321–359, November 1989.

[Li & Naughton 88] Li, L. and Naughton, J. F. Multiprocessor main memory transaction processing. In *Proceedings of the International Symposium on Databases in Parallel and Distributed Systems*, pages 177–187, December 1988.

[Liskov 88] Liskov, B. Distributed programming in Argus. *Communications of the ACM*, 31(3):300–312, March 1988.

[Liskov et al. 92] Liskov, B., Ghemawat, S., Gruber, R., Johnson, P., and Shrira, L. Replication in the Harp file system. In *Proceedings of the Thirteenth ACM Symposium on Operating Systems Principles*, pages 226–238, October 1992.

[Moss 90] Moss, J. E. B. Design of the Mneme persistent object store. *ACM Transactions on Information Systems*, 8(2):103–139, April 1990.

[Mueller 93] Mueller, F. A library implementation of POSIX threads under Unix. In *Proceedings of the Winter 1993 USENIX Conference*, pages 29–41, January 1993.

[Neves et al. 94] Neves, N., Castro, M., and Guedes, P. A checkpoint protocol for an entry consistent shared memory system. In *Proceedings of the 13th ACM Symposium on Principles of Distributed Computing*, August 1994.

[O. Deux 92] O. Deux. The O₂ system. *Communications of the ACM*, 34(10):34–48, October 1992.

[O'Toole et al. 93] O'Toole, J., Nettles, S., and Gifford, D. Concurrent compacting garbage collection of a persistent heap. In *Proceedings of the Fourteenth ACM Symposium on Operating Systems Principles*, pages 161–174, December 1993.

[Richard & Singhal 93] Richard, III, G. G. and Singhal, M. Using logging and asynchronous checkpointing to implement recoverable distributed shared memory. In *Proceedings of the 12th Symposium on Reliable Distributed Systems*, pages 58–67, October 1993.

[Rodeheffer & Schroeder 91] Rodeheffer, T. and Schroeder, M. D. Automatic reconfiguration in autonet. In *Proceedings of the Thirteenth ACM Symposium on Operating Systems Principles*, pages 183–197, October 1991.

[Rosenberg & Abramson 85] Rosenberg, J. and Abramson, D. A. MONADS-PC: A capability-based workstation to support software engineering. In *Proceedings of the 18th Hawaii International Conference on System Sciences*, 1985.

[Satyanarayanan et al. 94] Satyanarayanan, M., Mashburn, H. H., Kumar, P., Steere, D. C., and J.Kistler., J. Lightweight recoverable virtual memory. *ACM Transactions on Computer Systems*, 12(4):33–57, February 1994.

[Stumm & Zhou 90] Stumm, M. and Zhou, S. Fault tolerant distributed shared memory algorithms. In *Proceedings of the Second IEEE Symposium on Parallel and Distributed Processing*, pages 719–724, December 1990.

[Thekkath & Levy 94] Thekkath, C. and Levy, H. Hardware and software support for efficient exception handling. In *Proceedings of the 6th International Conference on Architectural Support for Programming Languages and Operating Systems*, October 1994.

[Wu & Fuchs 90] Wu, K.-L. and Fuchs, W. K. Recoverable disributed shared virtual memory. *IEEE Transactions on Computers*, 39(4):460–469, April 1990.

[Zekauskas et al. 94] Zekauskas, M. J., Sawdon, W. A., and Bershad, B. N. Software write detection for distributed shared memory. In *Proceedings of the First Symposium on Operating Systems Design and Implementation*, November 1994.

Garbage Collection and DSM Consistency[*]

Paulo Ferreira[†] *and* Marc Shapiro
INRIA - Projet SOR

Abstract

This paper presents the design of a copying garbage collector for persistent distributed shared objects in a loosely coupled network with weakly consistent distributed shared memory (DSM).

The main goal of the design for this garbage collector is to minimize the communication overhead due to collection between nodes of the system, and to avoid any interference with the DSM memory consistency protocol.

Our design is based on the observation that, in a weakly consistent DSM system, the memory consistency requirements of the garbage collector are less strict than those of the applications. Thus, the garbage collector reclaims objects independently of other copies of the same objects without interfering with the DSM consistency protocol. Furthermore, our design does not require reliable communication support, and is capable of reclaiming distributed cycles of dead objects.

1 Introduction

Garbage collection (GC) is a fundamental component for supporting persistent objects in distributed systems. The importance of garbage collection in such systems is twofold: first, the object graphs of applications, like financial or design databases, cooperative work and exploratory tools similar to the World-Wide-Web, are very intricate, which makes manual storage management increasingly difficult and error-prone, often resulting in dangling pointers and storage leaks. Second, garbage collection is necessary to support the property of persistence by reachability [2]; this property states that only objects reachable from the persistent root should be persistent. In other words, objects that are no longer reachable from the persistent root should not be stored on disk. Even in a persistent 64-bit address space, there is a need for memory reorganization and address recycling, otherwise the address space gets severely fragmented and secondary storage fills with garbage.

In addition, distributed shared memory systems have become popular because they support a simpler programming model for distributed applications than RPC-based systems [3]. Furthermore, weak consistency protocols seem to offer the best performance when compared to sequential consistency [4].

For these reasons, we have designed and implemented a platform, called BMX [8], that provides persistent weakly consistent shared distributed virtual memory and copying garbage collection. We chose a copying garbage collector because it can improve an application's locality [13], it contributes to reduce memory fragmentation, and it provides sufficient support to reclaim cycles of unreachable objects.

The paper focuses on the issue of how the garbage collector copies shared objects without interfering with the DSM consistency protocol. This is an important systems problem, since interference between the garbage collector and the consistency protocol could potentially nullify the advantages of using a weakly consistent DSM system. For example, when updating a reference inside an object, to reflect the new location of a live descendent that has already been copied, the garbage collector should not require exclusive write-access to modify the object. If exclusive write-access was needed, read-access to all other replicas of the object would have to be invalidated, therefore nullifying the advantage of using weak consistent DSM. Current distributed GC algorithms do not handle this problem; they implicitly assume the existence of a single object copy, which is not the case in a DSM system.

---

[*]This work has been done within the framework of the ES-PRIT Basic Research Action Broadcast 6360, and was partially supported by Digital Equipment Corporation.

[†]Full time Ph.D. student at *Université Pierre et Marie Curie (Paris VI)*. Supported by a JNICT Fellowship of Program *Ciência* (Portugal). Email: Paulo.Ferreira@inria.fr. Tel: +33 (1) 39 63 52 08. Fax: +33 (1) 39 63 53 30. Address: INRIA - Rocquencourt, B.P. 105 - 78153 Le Chesnay Cedex, FRANCE.

Besides the problem of avoiding interference with the DSM consistency protocol, the other two problems that need to be addressed in the design of a garbage collector for distributed shared objects are: (i) collection of acyclic distributed dead objects, and (ii) collection of distributed cycles of garbage. Due to space limitations, we only present a general overview of our solution to these two issues (see Ferreira[9] for more detail). As mentioned above, this paper focuses on the techniques used by the garbage collector to avoid interference between the collector and the DSM consistency protocol.

Our GC algorithm is orthogonal to DSM consistency, that is, it tolerates inconsistent objects, therefore it is generally applicable to other consistency protocols. Furthermore, our design is application- and language-independent. However, the compiler must be instrumented in order to interface with the algorithm support layer.

The paper is organized as follows. The next section presents the basic aspects of the BMX platform. Section 3 gives a global overview of the GC design. The collection of shared objects and its relation to the DSM consistency protocol is described in Sections 4 and 5. Sections 6 and 7 briefly describe acyclic and cyclic distributed garbage collection. Section 8 gives an overview of the implementation, and finally, the paper ends with related work and some conclusions.

2 BMX Overview

This section presents the aspects of the BMX platform that are relevant to the GC design described in this paper.

2.1 Objects, Segments, and Bunches

BMX offers a 64-bit single address space spanning all the nodes of a network, including secondary storage. The object, which consists of a contiguous sequence of bytes, is the basic unit of identification and invocation. An object is represented by its address; object references are therefore ordinary pointers. Each object has an header that precedes the object's data, which includes system information such as the object's size. We assume that objects are passive and generally small, that is, the size of most objects is much smaller than a virtual memory page.

Objects can become persistent by reachability, that is, they are persistent if reachable from the persistent root. Once mapped in main memory, such objects are shared through a DSM mechanism, just like any other non-persistent object.

For clustering purposes, objects are allocated within segments. A *segment* is a set of contiguous virtual memory pages with a constant size. BMX ensures that segments have non-overlapping addresses.

Segments are logically grouped into *bunches* because a single segment is not flexible enough to support solutions for situations like segment overflow. Each bunch has an associated owner, and protection attributes like the usual Unix read, write, and execute permissions.

BMX supports recovery for operations on bunches. Recovery is based on the recoverable virtual memory techniques proposed by Satyanarayanan et al. [19]. Therefore, after a bunch is mapped into memory, every modification performed on the bunch's range of addresses has an associated log entry and can be recovered after a system failure.

In summary, the user program, called the mutator in the GC literature [7], operates on a single, shared, persistent, possibly large graph of objects allocated from a number of bunches. These bunches can be simultaneously replicated on several nodes in the system and are kept weakly consistent by the DSM system described below.

2.2 DSM Support

The BMX system supports weakly consistent distributed shared memory based on the entry consistency protocol [4]. Applications do not send explicit messages. They only use the distributed shared memory paradigm for communication.

The entry consistency protocol provides the traditional model of multiple readers and a single writer. Thus, there can either be several read tokens, or one exclusive write token associated with each object. Nodes holding a read token are ensured to be reading a consistent version of the corresponding object. The possession of the write token means that there is no other consistent copy of the object at any other node of the network. The entry consistency protocol therefore guarantees that an object is consistent, with respect to previous operations on the object, as long as a node holds the corresponding read or write token. Otherwise the observed state of the object is undefined.

Every object has an *owner*, which is either the node currently holding the object's write token, or the node that last held the write token. A write token can only be obtained from the object's owner, while a read token can be obtained from any node already holding a read token. A token is obtained by performing a read or write token *acquire* operation and is freed by the corresponding *release*.

Tokens are managed with an algorithm similar to Li's dynamic distributed manager with distributed copy sets [16]. Thus, the copy-set of an object (list of nodes with a read token) is not centralized by its owner; rather, it is distributed among the owner and those nodes that have transitively granted a read token to other nodes.

In addition, there is a forwarding pointer mechanism indicating which node is the current object's owner. We call such a forwarding pointer an `ownerPtr`. Therefore, for each bunch there is a set of entering `ownerPtrs` that originate at nodes with non-owned replicas for the objects in this bunch, and a set of exiting `ownerPtrs` pointing to the owner node of each of the objects from this bunch.

3 Garbage Collection Design

The premise of our garbage collection algorithm is that an application's object graph can be enormous and widely distributed among the nodes of the system. It would therefore not be feasible to collect all objects of an application at the same time. Our algorithm collects each bunch of objects independently of any other bunch.

To be able to collect a bunch independently, it must be isolated from all other bunches. In other words, every copy of a bunch has to contain enough local information to independently make all reachability decisions for its objects, that is, without requesting information from any other bunch, nor from other copies of the same bunch. For this purpose each cached copy of a bunch holds two tables (in addition to the tables of entering and exiting `ownerPtrs`): the stub table and the scion table. The *stub table* contains information about outgoing links, that is, which objects referenced from within the bunch are allocated in some other bunch and the bunches to which they correspond. The *scion table* contains information about incoming references, that is, which local objects are referenced from other bunches and from where these references originate. Thus, for each stub there is a corresponding scion, these two entities form a stub-scion pair (SSP).

The bunch isolation provided by stubs and scions affects how inter-bunch reachability is propagated, and therefore how inter-bunch garbage is collected. For this reason, our GC design is based on three sub-algorithms that perform complementary tasks: the first component, called the *bunch garbage collector* (BGC), executes the collection on a local replica of a bunch, independently from the collection of any other bunch and other replicas of the same bunch; the second component, called the *scion cleaner*, uses information generated by the bunch garbage collectors of other bunches (stub tables and lists of outgoing `ownerPtrs`) to recognize which objects are no longer reachable from remote bunches or remote copies of the same bunch; and finally, the last component is called the *group garbage collector* (GGC), which is in charge of reclaiming inter-bunch cycles of garbage. Together, these sub-algorithms support an integral GC solution for a DSM system providing a high degree of scalability and parallelism.

This paper focuses on the garbage collection of a replicated bunch and how the BGC interacts with DSM consistency. However, for the sake of completeness, we will include an overview of both the scion cleaner and the group garbage collector (Sections 6 and 7).

3.1 Stubs and Scions

Figure 1 illustrates the use of stubs and scions. These stub-scion pairs are simpler than the ones used in RPC-based distributed systems [20], because: (i) they are not used for indirections, that is, they are just auxiliary data structures that describe relevant references, and (ii) stubs/scions do not perform any kind of marshaling/un-marshaling.

There are two kinds of slightly different SSPs: an *inter-bunch* SSP describes references that cross bunch boundaries, while an *intra-bunch* SSP records relevant dependencies between copies of the same bunch.

Inter-bunch SSPs have the same direction of the cross-bunch reference they represent (for example, O3→O5 in Figure 1). When an object becomes cached on multiple nodes, the inter-bunch stubs that represent the object's links to objects in other bunches do not have to be replicated. This is not problematic because a single SSP is enough to keep the target object alive in the whole system, as will be described further on. Figure 1 illustrates this situation: in spite of the fact that O3 is cached on N1 and N2, there is only one inter-bunch stub due to O3→O5 that is kept at N2.

Intra-bunch SSPs have the opposite direction of the corresponding `ownerPtr`, and are used to preserve an object's replica at a node that stores inter-bunch stubs created when the node was previously the owner of the object, but is no longer so. Intra-bunch SSPs are necessary because **inter**-bunch SSPs do not move with the ownership of an object, instead the **intra**-bunch SSP serves as a forwarding link. For example, in spite of being unreachable by the mutator at N2, object O3 must be kept alive at this node because: (i) there is an inter-bunch reference in O3 for which the corresponding stub is allocated at N2, and (ii) a copy of O3 is reachable by a mutator at N1. Object O3 can be collected in N2 only after becoming unreachable in N1.

3.2 Creation of Stub-Scion Pairs

An inter-bunch SSP is automatically constructed immediately after detecting the creation of the corresponding inter-bunch reference. This detection is done with a write-barrier [10] associated with every write performed by an application.

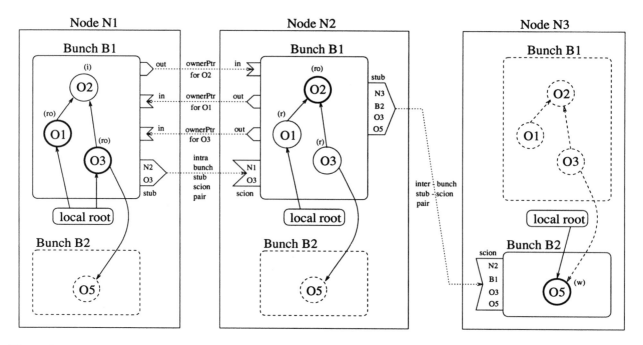

Figure 1: Bunch B1 is mapped on nodes N1 and N2, and bunch B2 is mapped only on N3; mapped bunches are represented with a solid line, unmapped bunches are represented with a dashed line. Stub and scion tables contain inter-bunch and intra-bunch SSPs. For each object, the state of its token is indicated as follows: letters r and w indicate that the node has a read or a write token respectively; o means that the node is the object's owner (thicker objects); i is used for inconsistent copies. The local root includes mutator stacks. No GC has taken place on any node.

When an inter-bunch reference is created, either both the source and target bunches are already mapped on the local node, or only the target bunch has not yet been locally mapped. In the first case, the corresponding stub and scion get created locally. The second case requires that a message be sent to a node where the target bunch is mapped. This message is called a *scion-message* and is used to inform the target bunch about the necessity of creating the scion corresponding to the the new cross-node inter-bunch reference.

Figure 1 shows a cross-node inter-bunch SSP required by the link O3→O5 from N2 to N3. Node N3 gets a scion-message from N2 when the inter-bunch reference O3→O5 is created and creates the matching scion for the stub on N2.

Intra-bunch scions are created when the ownership of an object moves from one node to another and the old owner holds an inter-bunch stub for this object. In other words, the old owner created a link to an object in a different bunch and the information required by the garbage collector for this purpose, that is the inter-bunch stub, needs to be preserved after the object's ownership is transferred. The intra-bunch SSP takes care of creating a forwarding link between the new owner and the inter-bunch stub at the old owner. Therefore, in the example illustrated by Figure 1, when O3's write token goes from N2, where the

inter-bunch reference was created, to N1, the corresponding intra-bunch SSP from N1 to N2 is created.

We decided to use intra-bunch SSPs, instead of replicating inter-bunch SSPs, in order to reduce the number of scion messages and the amount of memory consumed for GC purposes. In fact, if inter-bunch SSPs were replicated, each time object ownership changes, a new inter-bunch SSP would have to be created, which would imply sending the corresponding scion-message. By using intra-bunch SSPs, no extra messages are needed, because the information is piggy-backed onto consistency protocol messages. In addition, an inter-bunch SSP occupies more memory than an intra-bunch SSP.

4 Bunch Garbage Collection

This section describes the garbage collection of a bunch with multiple, possibly inconsistent, cached copies on several nodes. We first present the main aspects of the algorithm; then, we describe the algorithm in more detail, focusing on how live objects are copied and scanned, how reachability information is regenerated by the BGC, how references are updated and how the from-space is reused. Each of these issues is discussed in light of what is needed for the collector not to interfere with the DSM consistency protocol.

4.1 Outline

The BGC is based on the algorithm by O'Toole et. al [17] for three main reasons: (i) the time to *flip*[1] is very small and therefore not disruptive to applications, (ii) portability (no virtual memory manipulations), and (iii) objects are non-destructively copied (suitable for recovery purposes). However, any other copying algorithm could be used.

When a bunch has several copies on different nodes, a separate local BGC operates on each copy. The local collection of a bunch proceeds independently of the collection of other bunches, and of the collection of copies of the same bunch at other nodes. The roots of the BGC are located in the mutators stack, intra-bunch and inter-bunch scions, and list of entering `ownerPtrs`.

Each time the local BGC is executed, it reconstructs a new version of the bunch's stub table, and a new set of exiting `ownerPtrs`. The new stubs and exiting `ownerPtrs` will later be sent to the scion cleaner of all nodes that either have cached copies of the same bunch or contain the scions corresponding to the stubs of both old and reconstructed stub tables. On those nodes, the scion cleaner discovers and removes all local intra-bunch and inter-bunch scions that are no longer reachable from any stub, and all incoming `ownerPtrs` for local copies of objects that are no longer live remotely.

To avoid synchronizing all nodes in an object's copyset, a local BGC only copies the objects that are locally owned. Non-locally owned objects are simply scanned. This asynchronous collection of different copies of the same bunch can cause inconsistent views of object's addresses across cached replicas. However, as explained in the following sections, the asynchronous collection of object replicas is not a problem, because addresses on other nodes can be updated when these nodes synchronize on behalf of application's DSM consistency needs. Thus, applications designed for weakly consistent DSM systems will work correctly.

4.2 Copying/Scanning Live Objects

A local BGC copies live objects from the from-space segment to the to-space segment, independently of other BGCs of the same bunch. The first challenge of such an algorithm is to avoid that two BGCs, simultaneously executing on different replicas of a bunch, move the same live object to different memory locations. One obvious solution to this problem would be to acquire the write token of every live object before copying it. However, this solution is undesirable, since it would trigger memory consistency actions that

could disrupt the application's working-set. For example, each readable copy would be invalidated.

Our solution avoids this drawback by only copying those objects that are locally owned. Thus, if the node holds the write token or was the last one to hold it, the corresponding object is copied to to-space and scanned, and a forwarding pointer is written into the object's header, which is left in from-space. This header modification is strictly local and does not imply acquiring the object's write token because, at this time, only the local node has to be aware of the object's new location. As explained later in this section, other nodes will eventually be informed of the object's new location.

Other live objects, that is, those not locally owned, are simply scanned. An important aspect of this design is that these objects can be scanned, even though their copy might not be consistent with the owner's. In fact, an inconsistent copy of the object is sufficient, because scanning an old version results in making a more conservative decision about the referenced objects reachability, ensuring that they will not be erroneously collected if not dead.

The header with the forwarding pointer, left in place of an object copied to to-space, is deleted only when every reference to that object has been updated with the new address. These references can be local or remote, as shown in Figure 2: object O2 has been copied to the to-space segment by the BGC in N2; thus, pointers inside O1 and O3 must be updated accordingly, on both nodes.

After updating the local references to a copied object, and before performing the same operation on remote references to the object, the copied object will be at different addresses on different nodes. However, this is not a problem. The data inside the copied object is kept consistent from the applications point of view, as guaranteed by the consistency protocol. Thus, remote references can be updated lazily. As an example, consider Figure 2: after updating the references to O2 in N2, and before performing the same operation in N1, object O2 will exist in different addresses on these two nodes. However, mutators in both nodes continue to work correctly.

Applications perform correctly because they are implemented for a weakly consistent DSM. Remember that applications do not send explicit messages that could, for example, reference objects with a new address not known to the receiver. Furthermore, to account for the existence of forwarding pointers, a special operation is provided to perform pointer comparison. The conditions that need to be upheld at DSM synchronization points (read or write token acquires) to ensure the proper execution of applications are described in Section 5.

---

[1] Time during which an application is stopped due to garbage collection.

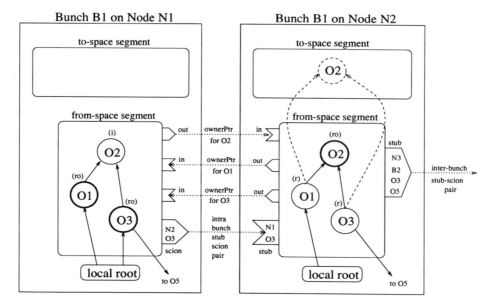

Figure 2: Zooming into Figure 1, we show more detail of bunch B1 on nodes N1 and N2. The BGC on N2 only copies locally-owned live objects, that is, O2. The update of pointers to O2 is represented by dashed arrows. Node N1 has not yet been informed of the O2's new address, and the local BGC of B1 has not been executed.

4.3 Creating new Stub and Outgoing ownerPtr Tables

As mentioned earlier, a local execution of the BGC scans all objects that are reachable from the mutators stacks, scions, and entering ownerPtrs, and creates a new table of inter-bunch and intra-bunch stubs, as well as a new list of outgoing ownerPtrs. The new stub table and list of outgoing ownerPtrs represents all objects in other bunches or in other nodes that are accessible from the local copy of the bunch. An object that has been locally garbage collected will neither add a stub nor an outgoing ownerPtr to the new tables. An inter-bunch stub will not be added to the new stub table if the corresponding local object no longer includes the inter-bunch reference associated with the stub. When the BGC scans a live object containing an inter-bunch reference, three actions may be taken (see Figure 1):

- if the inter-bunch reference has been created at the local node (as is the case of O3 at N2), than the corresponding inter-bunch stub is added to the new stub table,

- if the inter-bunch reference has not been created locally, but the scanned object is locally owned (as is the case of O3 at N1), than the corresponding intra-bunch stub is added to the new stub list, and

- if neither the inter-bunch reference has been created locally, nor the local node is the object's owner, than no stub is added to the new stub list.

Furthermore, for objects that can only be accessed via an intra-bunch scion the exiting ownerPtr will be omitted from the new outgoing list (see Section 6.2).

The new intra-bunch stubs and the new set of exiting ownerPtrs constructed by the local BGC are eventually sent to other nodes where the corresponding objects are mapped.

4.4 Updating References

The next challenge in designing our garbage collector is how to update all local and remote references to an object that has been copied to to-space, without interfering with the DSM consistency protocol and without incurring in high communication overhead between nodes.

At first, it may seem impossible to update a reference without interfering with the consistency protocol, because it implies updating the object that contains the reference. Normally to update an object it is necessary to acquire the write token for the object, which would in turn make outstanding readable copies stale. However, the same way it was possible to copy an object without exclusive-access, the object can also be modified without acquiring the corresponding write token, because the modification is visible only to the local node, and does not affect the applications behavior on other nodes, which might be accessing another copy of the object. Hence, reference updating can be done without interfering with the consistency protocol. For example, in Figure 2, updating O1 in N2 with O2's new address can be done without acquiring O1's write token. In spite of the difference between O1 on both nodes, mutators at N1 and at N2 still *see* a copy of O1 that is consistent with the application's requirements.

For the purpose of updating remote references to locally copied objects we want to avoid sending an explicit message from the node where an object was copied to the node holding the remote reference. Furthermore, we want to avoid blocking an application while such an update is taking place.

Because remote references can be updated lazily, an object's new address can be communicated to other nodes by piggy-backing such information onto messages due to the consistency protocol, which are performed on behalf of applications. Thus, no extra message is used. For instance (see Figure 2), O2's new address can be sent from N2 to N1 in a message due to the consistency protocol exchanged between these two nodes. After N1 receives O2's new address, O2 is copied to the indicated address, and all the local references are updated accordingly without requiring any token.

Reference updating does not have to be done immediately after receiving the corresponding message with an object's new location. In fact, it can be postponed until a bunch garbage collection takes place at the local node. Therefore, there is a tradeoff on how consistent the addresses are going to be and the overhead of immediately executing the updates at the remote nodes.

It is important to note, that if there is no communication between nodes on behalf of applications, then there is no need for updating references unless the from-space needs to be reused. In this case, as explained in the next section, explicit messages must be used.

4.5 Reusing From-Space

Since during bunch garbage collection only locally owned objects are copied to to-space, it may happen that some live objects and forwarding pointers remain in the from-space after the local BGC has completed. Thus, immediately after a local bunch garbage collection, the from-space segment might not be fully reused nor freed. This is the case of B1's from-space segment after the BGC on N2 has finished (see Figure 2): objects O1 and O3 are live and remain in the from-space segment. These objects will eventually be copied by B1's local BGC running on node N1. Before reusing or freeing a from-space segment, it is therefore necessary to ensure that no live objects remain in the segment

and that the forwarding pointers are no longer necessary.

It is worthy to note that a from-space segment will be reused for allocating new objects only after the corresponding to-space segment becomes full. Until then, non-owned objects remaining in the from-space segment may either die or be copied by their owners. Furthermore, all the space that was occupied by dead objects could be completely reused.

Nevertheless, suppose that we want to fully reuse or discard a from-space segment. In that case, we must ensure that it contains neither forwarding pointers to already copied objects nor non-locally owned live objects. Both conditions are guaranteed by informing all other nodes affected by the address changes in this segment about these changes, and by asking the owner nodes to copy those live objects still allocated in the from-space segment. Once the local node receives the replies to the above messages, the from-space segment can be fully reused or freed.

Since the address-change messages are exchanged in the background, applications can make progress without having to process them immediately. From the point of view of the application, processing these messages is part of the garbage collection overhead, and is no more disruptive than garbage collection itself.

For example, consider Figure 2: node N2 informs N1 of O2's new address, asks the BGC in N1 to copy its locally owned live objects (O1 and O3), and updates its local references to O1's and O3's new location. After that, B1's from-space segment can be freed or reused in its entirety.

Note that the list of nodes where an object's reference must be updated is already kept in the object's owner node for the purpose of the DSM mechanism: nodes from where the set of entering ownerPtrs originate. This implies that there is no extra memory overhead due to the GC.

5 DSM Acquires and the BGC

As explained before, since remote object references are updated lazily, different replicas of the same object can be located at different addresses on different nodes after the execution of a BGC. We also mentioned that mutators on these nodes will operate correctly, because the data held by the objects is consistent with respect to the guarantees made by the DSM consistency protocol. However, after synchronization points in the application, that is, read or write token acquires, the system has to ensure that the synchronizing nodes reference objects with the same addresses. In this section we describe three invariants that the garbage collector has to ensure for this purpose.

1. *The acquisition of a read or write token for an object can complete only after ensuring that the object's address and all references inside it are valid at the acquiring node.*

This invariant avoids erroneous situations such as the following: suppose that object O1 points to O2, both objects are allocated from bunch B and nodes N1 and N2 hold replicas of the objects.

   (a) Node N1 is the owner of both objects.

   (b) Bunch B is collected at N1, therefore O1's copy at N1 will point to the new location of object O2.

   (c) Node N2 issues a read or write token acquire request for O1 to N1.

   (d) If invariant 1 was not maintained, the new copy of O1 at N2 could point to the new address of O2, while O2 was still at the old address.

This first invariant prevents the situation described above, by ensuring that N2 is aware of O2's new location before the acquire request completes. The invariant is easily maintained by piggy-backing information with the new locations of the object being acquired and of every object directly referenced from it, onto the reply to the acquire message.

2. *A node that receives a message with the new location for an object forwards this information to all the nodes that are in the local copy-set for the object, that is, to which it has granted a read token.*

This second invariant is necessary because a distributed copy-set algorithm is used for token management. Remember that a read token for an object can be obtained from a node already holding a read token. Therefore, a node with a read token for an object, that is not the object's owner, is responsible for forwarding messages containing an object's new location. The mechanism, to forward new location information to all nodes with a read token, is similar to the one used to invalidate all read copies of an object when some node acquires the object's write token.

3. *The acquisition of a write token for an object completes only after all necessary intra-bunch SSPs have been created.*

This invariant ensures that the appropriate intra-bunch SSP is created between the new owner of the object and an old owner, when ownership is transferred from a node holding either inter-bunch

stubs or an intra-bunch stub for the object. Remember that the intra-bunch SSPs serve as forwarding pointers from the new owner to inter-bunch stubs located at previous owners of the object.

The three invariants can be maintained without incurring in extra communication overhead, by taking advantage of the messages transferred by the DSM system on behalf of the applications at synchronization points, that is, replies to acquire messages. For a DSM system that does not require applications to synchronize on accesses to shared objects, the invariants can be guaranteed by ensuring that whenever a node faults on the access to an object O, the node that supplies O also sends all the necessary location updates and intra-bunch SSP information.

Now, let us present a detailed example of the specific operations that are executed to satisfy the invariants presented above before a write token acquire is completed (see Figure 3). Suppose that a write token for object O1 is requested by node N2 from node N1:

- If neither O1 nor any of the objects referenced directly by O1 have been copied to to-space at either node (situation represented by case (a) and (c)), no special operation has to be performed.

- On the other hand, if either O1 or an object pointed at by O1 have been copied to to-space at N1 (situation represented by case (b) and (c)), their new locations are piggy-backed in the message granting the token to N2 and are processed at N2 before the application returns from the token request.

  In addition, the new locations of O1 and of the objects directly referenced by O1 are forwarded by N2 to all nodes to which it had granted a read token for those objects. Nodes to which N2 granted a read token are listed in the corresponding object's copy-set.

- If any of the objects pointed at by O1 gets copied to to-space at N2 prior to the write token acquire operation (situation represented by case (d)), when N2 receives the valid copy of O1 from N1 with the token, it updates all references in O1 pointing to forwarding pointers in from-space, to point to the new addresses in to-space directly.

- If any inter-bunch stubs exist for O1 at N1 (not represented in Figure 3), before the write token acquire can complete, an intra-bunch SSP for O1 has to be created, pointing from N2 to N1. N1 creates the intra-bunch scion before it replies with the token-grant message, and piggy-backs a request for N2 to create the appropriate intra-bunch stub upon reception of the message.

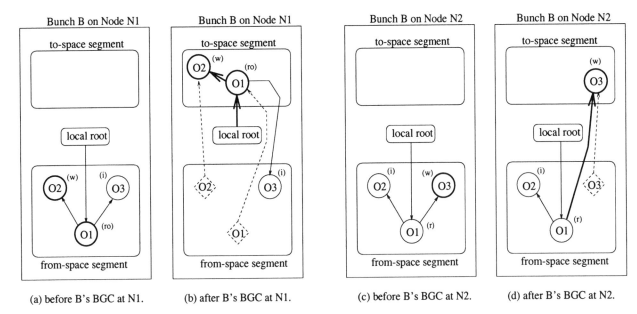

Figure 3: Bunch B is mapped on nodes N1 and N2 (before and after the execution of the BGC). Thicker arrows represent references locally updated by the BGC. Dashed lines are used to represent forwarding pointers left in place of copied objects.

This set of operations, executed when a write token is acquired, ensures that, after synchronizing, a pair of nodes sees consistent addresses for objects in the DSM system, by guaranteeing the three invariants described earlier.

6 Scion Cleaner

This section presents an overview of the scion cleaner and then describes in detail how intra-bunch SSPs are deleted when no longer necessary.

6.1 Overview

The scion cleaner locally processes the reachability information (stubs and outgoing ownerPtrs) that has been constructed by the execution of a BGC on other bunches. This process is identical for information received from a bunch with or without a local replica. There is a scion cleaner service per node that operates on all bunches of that node. The cleaner recognizes and removes all scions that are no longer reachable from any stub and all entering ownerPtrs that correspond to remote replicas that have been garbage collected. In essence, the scion cleaner, updates the roots for the next execution of the local BGC.

The main advantage of sending messages with tables containing all the reachability information, over sending increment/decrement messages [5], is that the former are idempotent. In case of message loss they can be resent without the need for a reliable communication protocol. However, messages with reach-

ability information must be received in FIFO order. Otherwise, the scion cleaner may use an old stub table that does not match the scions being considered. Such an inconsistency could result in the erroneous deletion of a scion. Since the messages with stub and ownerPtr information are exchanged between a pair of nodes (point-to-point communication), FIFO ordering is easily guaranteed by numbering the messages. In Ferreira[9] we describe some race situations that can occur between stub table messages and scion-messages; however, the description of these race conditions is beyond the scope of this paper.

Messages with the reachability information can be piggy-backed onto messages used by the DSM consistency protocol, or exchanged in the background. Thus, they are not disruptive in the sense that applications do not depend on the scion cleaner having finished to continue their execution. Note that the scion cleaner does not have to process each new message it receives immediately; messages can be accumulated and their processing can be postponed until the start of the next local BGC.

6.2 Deletion of Intra-bunch SSPs

This section describes how an object with copies on several nodes is collected and the corresponding intra-bunch SSPs and ownerPtrs are deleted, once all replicas become unreachable.

An object that becomes unreachable from all mutators at all nodes will end up not being referenced by any inter-bunch scion at any node and by any entering

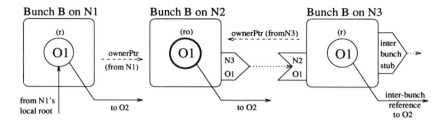

Figure 4: O1 is cached on nodes N1, N2, and N3 and is reachable from a single mutator in N1.

ownerPtr at its owner node. Thus, when the BGC is executed on the owner node, the mentioned object will not be *seen*. Should the object have any intra-bunch stub(s) on the owner node, these will not become part of the new stub table. Transitively, the scion cleaner running on the other nodes will delete the unreachable intra-bunch scion(s) and the object will be reclaimed by the next BGC at those nodes as well.

For example, consider Figure 4 and suppose that the BGC of B is executed at N3; the new set of exiting ownerPtrs will not include the one from N3 to N2, because O1 is not reachable from the mutator at N3. However, O1 remains alive at N3 due to the intra-bunch scion. Note that if the ownerPtr from N3 to N2 was included in the list of outgoing pointers, O1 could never be reclaimed because of the following cycle: O1 on N2 → intra-bunch SSP → O1 on N3 → ownerPtr from N3 to N2 → O1 on N2. By not including the outgoing ownerPtr from N3 the cycle is broken and the scion-cleaner at N2 deletes the entering ownerPtr for N3.

The BGC running on N2 considers O1 alive because of the entering ownerPtr, which originates at N1. Now, imagine that O1 becomes unreachable at N1, that is, the reference to O1 is deleted from the local root of the mutator at N1. Then, a BGC is executed for B on N1. Object O1 can be reclaimed at N1, and the ownerPtr pointing from N1 to N2 will not be part of the new set of ownerPtrs exiting B on N1.

Finally, when N2 receives the new information generated by the BGC at N1, the scion cleaner at N2 deletes the last entering ownerPtr for O1. Therefore, during the next execution of B's BGC at N2, object O1 is no longer reachable, which in turn will drop the intra-bunch stub pointing to O1 at N3 from the new stub table. Thereafter, when N3 receives this new information from N2 and runs its own BGC on B, object O1 will no longer be reachable on N3 either, and will also be garbage collected there.

7 Group Garbage Collector

The GGC is used to reclaim inter-bunch cycles of garbage. There is one GGC per node and it operates on groups of bunches local to that node. The algo-

rithm used by the GGC is identical to the one used by the BGC, only that it operates on a group of bunches, rather than on one bunch at a time.

The root of the GGC includes: mutator stacks, intra-bunch scions, entering ownerPtrs, and inter-bunch scions identifying source bunches that are *not* members of the group being collected. The inter-bunch scions corresponding to SSPs that originate within the group that is being collected are not part of the root. Therefore, objects in the group, which are not reachable from any sources other than these SSPs, will be collected. In particular, objects that form an inter-bunch cycle, but are non-reachable from bunches outside the group or the mutator's stack, will be collected, because they are not artificially held over by SSPs from within the group.

The significance of the group garbage collector is that it can collect an arbitrary subset of the distributed and persistent objects on a single site, independently of the rest of the address space. Bunches are grouped based on a heuristic that maximizes the amount of inter-bunch garbage that is collected and minimizes the cost of performing the collection. Currently, we use a locality-based heuristic, that is, we collect all bunches that are in memory at the site where the GGC is going to run. This heuristic avoids disk input-output overheads.

This locality-based heuristic does not collect cycles of garbage that partially reside on disk, that is, cycles with objects allocated in bunches not currently mapped in memory. Collecting such a cycle involves input-output costs that need to be balanced against the expected gain. In addition, if an application does not move bunches around the nodes there is a possibility that some dead cycles may not ever be removed at all. We believe that some of these cycles can be collected by improving the grouping heuristic. However, we intend to do that only after having experimented with the locality-based heuristic. If experimental results mandate it, we will explore more complex heuristics. Dynamic grouping of collection spaces was first proposed by Lang[14]. However, our solution is much simpler because a group collection occurs at a single site, instead of spanning multiple nodes. Therefore, we expect our solution to be more scalable.

8   Implementation

The current prototype of BMX is implemented in C++ for a network of DEC Alpha workstations. The prototype implementation was simplified by placing the following constraints on the system: first, a bunch is shared only by processes on different nodes, in other words, there is only one process per node accessing a bunch; second, the copy-set of an object is centralized at the object's owner node, instead of being distributed among those nodes that have transitively granted a read token to other nodes; and finally, persistence is supported by associating each segment with a Unix file.

The current prototype is based on BMX-servers and BMX-clients. A BMX-server runs on every node in the system and provides basic services, such as allocation of non-overlapping segments. The BMX-client is a library that is linked with each application and is used to interact with the BMX system internals, in particular with the BMX-server.

Bunches are mapped into shared virtual memory. The BGC runs as a thread inside the process that is accessing the corresponding bunch. This particular implementation of the BGC is facilitated by our simplification of allowing only one process per node to have access to a bunch. The scion cleaner and the GGC each run as a privileged process on each node. Because these processes are privileged they have access to all bunches local to the node.

Recovery is based on the recoverable virtual memory (RVM) techniques proposed by Satyanarayanan et al. [19]. RVM provides simple recoverable transactions with no support for nesting, distribution, or concurrency control. Recovery in RVM is implemented with a disk-based log. In our prototype we use the approach proposed by O'Toole et al. [17], in which the from-space and the to-space are each supported by a file. Changes to mapped segments are atomically transferred to disk by RVM.

As previously mentioned, inter-bunch pointers are described by inter-bunch SSPs that are automatically allocated whenever an inter-bunch reference is created. We detect the creation of cross-bunch references using a write barrier technique, that is, write barriers are inserted into applications by instrumenting every write with a C++ macro. Another macro is provided to perform pointer comparison. This macro is necessary to account for the use of forwarding pointers left by the execution of a garbage collection. Currently, the programmer must include these macros explicitly. In the future, we expect to modify the pre-processor to insert these macros automatically.

The contents of a bunch are described by two special data structures that contain information needed for garbage collection: an *object-map*, which describes the location of objects inside the bunch, and a *reference-map*, which indicates where pointers are located inside each object. These data structures are implemented as bit arrays; each bit describes the contents of a 4-byte address range inside the bunch. A set bit in the object-map means that at the corresponding address is an object; a set bit in the reference-map means that at the corresponding address is a pointer to some object.

One of the performance goals of our design is to support replication of bunches on several nodes without increasing the cost of the bunch garbage collection, when compared to a system without support for bunch replication. From the point of view of the application, the cost of the BGC should be the same whether the bunch is replicated or not. We believe we can ensure this cost property by avoiding the interference between the garbage collector and the DSM mechanisms. This expectation is based on two observations: (i) the BGC never acquires a token for any object, and consequently does not interfere with the DSM consistency protocol, and (ii) information exchanged among nodes is either piggy-backed onto messages due to the consistency protocol, or exchanged in the background.

9   Related Work

A large amount of literature exists in the area of concurrent GC either for multiprocessors [1, 6], or for RPC-based distributed systems (see Plainfossé[18] for a survey). On the contrary, to our knowledge, little work has been done on garbage collecting objects in a loosely coupled network with weakly consistent DSM.

The fundamental difference between our system and a multiprocessor system, with respect to GC, is that of scale and synchronization overhead. This difference implies that, if we apply a GC algorithm designed for multiprocessors (for instance, Appel[1]) to our case, the overhead will be unacceptable due to communication and synchronization costs. These costs are due to the fact that current multiprocessor GC algorithms implicitly assume the existence of strongly consistent objects. In fact, communication and synchronization overhead arises because of the necessity of providing strongly consistent objects and the interference with applications' consistency needs. Note that the overhead is not due to the synchronization between the mutator and the GC algorithm, as is usually the case in non-distributed settings.

Furthermore, GC in DSM is more difficult than in distributed RPC-based systems (for example, Juul[11]) due to the existence of multiple copies of the same object on several nodes, and the problem of consistency interference.

Le Sergent[15] describes an extension of a copying garbage collector first developed for a multiprocessor, to a DSM system. Objects are kept strongly consistent, the entire address space is collected at the same time, which is not scalable, and the garbage collector locks pages while scanning, which interferes with the consistency protocol.

Kordale's GC design for distributed shared memory [12] is very complex and relies on a large amount of auxiliary information. This GC algorithm is based on the mark & sweep technique, and objects are kept strongly consistent.

10   Conclusion

We have presented a copying garbage collector algorithm for objects accessed via DSM in a loosely coupled network. Objects are allocated from bunches of non-overlapping segments in a single 64-bit address space spanning the whole network, including secondary storage. Objects are kept weakly consistent by the entry consistency protocol.

Our design goals were that the garbage collector neither interfere with the consistency protocol, nor introduce high communication overheads. Therefore, in our garbage collection design: (i) a cached copy of a bunch can be collected independently of any other copy of that same bunch on other nodes, (ii) only locally-owned live objects are copied by a bunch garbage collector; not owned live objects are simply scanned, and (iii) references to copied objects are lazily updated, either by taking advantage of messages sent on behalf of the consistency protocol (piggy-backing), or in the background. In any circumstance, the garbage collector acquires neither a read nor a write token.

The fundamental observation that guided our design is that GC consistency needs are less strict than applications'. Thus, the garbage collector can work with objects that are inconsistent from the point of view of the consistency protocol. This allows the GC to be performed without interfering with applications' consistency needs and requiring very little synchronization or communication.

We are currently in the process of evaluating the performance of BMX. In future work, we hope to generalize our design to other consistency protocols and other GC algorithms, in addition, to evaluating the impact of the consistency granularity on our approach. We are also extending the current GC design to incorporate a weakly consistent distributed shared memory system with full support for transactions.

Acknowledgments: We are grateful to our shepherd, Karin Petersen, and to the anonymous referees for their help with improving this paper.

References

[1] Andrew W. Appel, John R. Ellis, and Kai Li. Real-time concurrent collection on stock multiprocessors. In *SIGPLAN'88 - Conference on Programming Language Design and Implementation*, pages 11–20, Atlanta (USA), June 1988.

[2] M. P. Atkinson, P. J. Bailey, K. J. Chisholm, P. W. Cockshott, and R. Morrison. An approach to persistent programming. *Computer*, 26(4):360–365, 1983.

[3] John K. Bennett, John B. Carter, and Willy Zwaenepoel. Munin: Distributed shared memory based on type-specific memory coherence. In *Proc. 2nd Annual Symp. on Principles and Practice of Parallel Programming*, Seattle, WA (USA), March 1990. ACM SIGPLAN. In SIGPLAN Notices 25(3).

[4] Brian N. Bershad and Matthew J. Zekauskas. The Midway distributed shared memory system. In *Proceedings of the COMPCON'93 Conference*, pages 528–537, February 1993.

[5] D. I. Bevan. Distributed garbage collection using reference counting. In *PARLE'87—Parallel Architectures and Languages Europe*, number 259 in Lecture Notes in Computer Science, pages 117–187, Eindhoven (the Netherlands), June 1987. Springer-Verlag.

[6] Hans-J. Boehm, Alan J. Demers, and Scott Shenker. Mostly parallel garbage collection. In *Proc. of the SIGPLAN'91 Conf. on Programming Language Design and Implementation*, pages 157–164, Toronto (Canada), June 1991. ACM.

[7] E. Dijkstra, L. Lamport, A. J. Martin, C. S. Scholten, and E. F. M. Steffens. On-the-fly garbage collection: an exercise in cooperation. *Comm. of the ACM*, 21(11):966–975, November 1978.

[8] Paulo Ferreira and Marc Shapiro. Distribution and persistence in multiple and heterogeneous address spaces. In *Proc. of the International Workshop on Object Orientation in Operating Systems*, Ashville, North Carolina, (USA), December 1993. IEEE Comp. Society Press.

[9] Paulo Ferreira and Marc Shapiro. Garbage collection of persistent objects in distributed shared memory. In *Proc. of the 6th International Workshop on Persistent Object Systems*, Tarascon (France), September 1994. Springer-Verlag.

[10] Antony L. Hosking, J. Eliot B. Moss, and Darko Stefanoviè. A comparative performance evaluation of write barrier implementations. In *Conf. on Object-Oriented Programming Systems, Languages, and Applications*, volume 27 of *SIGPLAN Notices*, pages 92–109, Vancouver (Canada), October 1992. ACM Press.

[11] Niels C. Juul. *Comprehensive, Concurrent, and Robust Garbage Collection in the Distributed, Object-Based System Emerald*. PhD thesis, Dept. of Computer Science, Univ. of Copenhagen, Denmark, February 1993.

[12] R. Kordale, M. Ahamad, and J. Shilling. Distributed/concurrent garbage collection in distributed shared memory systems. In *Proc. of the International Workshop on Object Orientation and Operating Systems*, Ashville, North Carolina (USA), December 1993. IEEE Comp. Society Press.

[13] M. S. Lam, P. R. Wilson, and T. G. Moher. Object type directed garbage collection to improve locality. In *Proc. Int. Workshop on Memory Management*, number 637 in Lecture Notes in Computer Science, pages 404–425, Saint-Malo (France), September 1992.

[14] Bernard Lang, Christian Queinnec, and José Piquer. Garbage collecting the world. In *Proc. of the 19th Annual*

ACM SIGPLAN-SIGACT Symp. on Principles of Programming Lang., Albuquerque, New Mexico (USA), January 1992.

[15] T. Le Sergent and B. Berthomieu. Incremental multi-threaded garbage collection on virtually shared memory architectures. In *Proc. Int. Workshop on Memory Management*, number 637 in Lecture Notes in Computer Science, pages 179–199, Saint-Malo (France), September 1992. Springer-Verlag.

[16] Kai Li and Paul Hudak. Memory coherence in shared virtual memory systems. *ACM Transactions on Computer Systems*, 7(4):321–359, November 1989.

[17] James O'Toole, Scott Nettles, and David Gifford. Concurrent compacting garbage collection of a persistent heap. In *Proceedings of the 14th ACM Symposium on Operating Systems Principles*, pages 161–174, Asheville, NC (USA), December 1993.

[18] David Plainfossé. *Distributed Garbage Collection and Reference Management in the Soul Object Support System*. PhD thesis, Université Paris-6, Pierre-et-Marie-Curie, Paris (France), June 1994. Available from INRIA as TU-281, ISBN-2-7261-0849-0.

[19] M. Satyanarayanan, Henry H. Mashburn, Puneet Kumar, David C. Steere, and James J. Kistler. Lightweight recoverable virtual memory. In *Proceedings of the 14th ACM Symposium on Operating Systems Principles*, pages 146–160, Asheville, NC (USA), December 1993.

[20] Marc Shapiro, Peter Dickman, and David Plainfossé. SSP chains: Robust, distributed references supporting acyclic garbage collection. Rapport de Recherche 1799, Institut National de la Recherche en Informatique et Automatique, Rocquencourt (France), nov 1992. Also available as Broadcast Technical Report #1.

Software Prefetching and Caching
for
Translation Lookaside Buffers

Kavita Bala *   M. Frans Kaashoek *   William E. Weihl*

MIT Laboratory for Computer Science
Cambridge, MA 02139, USA

Abstract

A number of interacting trends in operating system structure, processor architecture, and memory systems are increasing both the rate of translation lookaside buffer (TLB) misses and the cost of servicing a miss. This paper presents two novel software schemes, implemented under Mach 3.0, to decrease both the number and the cost of *kernel* TLB misses (*i.e.*, misses on kernel data structures, including user page tables). The first scheme is a new use of prefetching for TLB entries on the IPC path, and the second scheme is a new use of software caching of TLB entries for hierarchical page table organizations.

For a range of applications, prefetching decreases the number of kernel TLB misses by 40% to 50%, and caching decreases TLB penalties by providing a fast path for over 90% of the misses. Our caching scheme also decreases the number of nested TLB traps due to the page table hierarchy, reducing the number of kernel TLB miss traps for applications by 20% to 40%. Prefetching and caching, when used alone, each improve application performance by up to 3.5%; when used together, they improve application performance by up to 3%. On synthetic benchmarks that involve frequent communication among several different address spaces (and thus put more pressure on the TLB), prefetching improves overall performance by about 6%, caching improves overall performance by about 10%, and the two used together improve overall performance by about 12%.

Our techniques are very effective in reducing kernel TLB penalties, which currently range from 1% to 5% of application runtime for the benchmarks studied. Since processor speeds continue to increase relative to memory speeds, our schemes should be even more effective in improving application performance in future architectures.

1 Introduction

A number of interacting trends in operating system structure, processor architecture, and memory systems are increasing both the rate of translation lookaside buffer (TLB) misses and the relative cost of servicing a miss. Microkernel-based operating systems achieve modularity and flexibility by providing OS functionality in user-level server processes. Frequent communication between client processes, the kernel, and server processes results in more TLB misses than in monolithic-kernel systems [17]. Furthermore, many microkernel-based systems use virtual memory rather than physical memory for most OS data structures. This increases the number of pages in the active working set that require TLB entries.

Several modern RISC architectures (*e.g.*, the MIPS R2000/3000, the DEC Alpha, and the HP PA-RISC) handle TLB misses in software. This simplifies the hardware considerably, and provides greater flexibility to the operating system. However, the penalty for a TLB miss increases. This penalty becomes even more significant as CPU speeds increase relative to memory speeds, since the cost of accessing page table entries is growing [18].

As researchers continue to improve inter-process communication (IPC) performance [4, 15], TLB penalties will become an increasing fraction of the IPC cost [3, 11]. In addition, recent commercial standards, such as OLE [9] and OpenDoc [21], place an increasing emphasis on inter-application communication. The net effect of all these factors is that the impact of TLB misses on overall system performance is increasing [1, 7].

While TLB penalties have been recognized as a problem, proposed solutions typically require expensive hardware [17, 16]. We present two schemes to address this problem that rely only on software mechanisms; no additional hardware is required. Our techniques reduce both the number and cost of TLB misses.

The first technique involves *prefetching* TLB entries during IPC. This well-known technique has not been applied before in the context of TLB management. After an IPC, many page table accesses that cause TLB misses are highly predictable. By prefetching these entries in the kernel during the IPC, many misses can be avoided.

The second technique introduces a software cache for the TLB, called the *software TLB* (STLB). On several architectures, handling some types of TLB traps is quite expensive (on the order of several hundred cycles). By introducing a large software cache for TLB entries and checking it early in the TLB miss trap handler, this approach reduces the time for servicing expensive misses. In addition, in systems with hierarchical page table organizations, page tables

---

*E-mail: {kaybee, kaashoek, weihl}@lcs.mit.edu. World Wide Web URL: http://www.psg.lcs.mit.edu/. Prof. Weihl is currently supported by DEC while on sabbatical at DEC SRC. This research was supported in part by the Advanced Research Projects Agency under Contract N00014-94-1-0985, by grants from AT&T and IBM, and by an equipment grant from DEC. The views and conclusions contained in this document are those of the authors and should not be interpreted as representing the official policies, either expressed or implied, of the U.S. government.

themselves are mapped. A hit in the STLB avoids further references to the page tables. Preventing cascaded misses reduces the total number of TLB misses significantly. To the best of our knowledge, this paper is the first to present a technique to reduce nested TLB traps in hierarchical page table organizations. A scheme similar to the STLB was simulated with a different organization of the hardware TLB and the page tables [12], and is discussed with related work in Section 7.

We have implemented our prefetching and caching techniques in the Mach 3.0 kernel running on a MIPS R3000-based DECstation 5000/240. Prefetching TLB entries benefited the entire range of applications we examined, decreasing the number of *kernel TLB misses* (*i.e.*, misses on kernel data structures, user page tables, and kernel page tables) by 40% to 50%. This improves overall application performance by up to 3.5%. The penalties of kernel TLB misses for these applications range from 1% to 5% [16]; benchmarks in other studies have higher TLB penalties [12]. Thus, prefetching eliminates a significant fraction of kernel TLB penalties. The software TLB achieves high hit rates for kernel TLB misses that range from 90% to nearly 100%. It also decreases the number of kernel TLB misses by eliminating nested TLB traps. As with prefetching, this improves performance by up to 3.5%.

Using our two techniques together improves application performance by up to 3%. On synthetic benchmarks that involve frequent communication among several different address spaces (and thus put more pressure on the TLB), prefetching improves overall performance by about 6%, caching improves overall performance by about 10%, and the two used together improve overall performance by about 12%. Thus, for systems that use more frequent communication, we expect our techniques to provide increasing benefits, and provide even greater benefits when used together.

Although currently the impact of TLB miss handling on overall application performance is small, TLB miss handling penalties are expected to have a larger impact on overall application performance on newer architectures. Our proposed techniques reduce both the number of misses and the cost of each miss, and we expect both techniques to provide increasing benefits on future architectures.

Our experiments assume a microkernel-based operating system. However, our techniques can be applied to other operating system organizations, such as large single address space systems [6] and systems with software segmentation [24]. Furthermore, with the current emphasis on application-controlled resource management [2, 10], our prefetching techniques could become even more effective, since the prefetching strategy can be tailored for individual applications. Prefetching can also be integrated with other VM functions such as prefetching cache entries.

Section 2 presents some background material on page table organizations and VM management. Section 3 describes our prefetching scheme, implementation details,

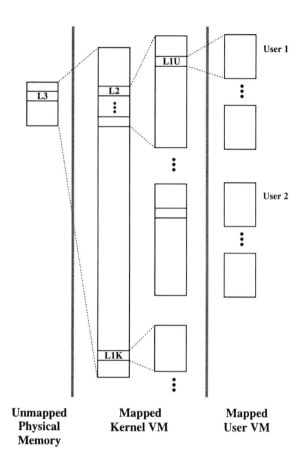

Figure 1: **Mach 3.0 Page Table Hierarchy.** Mach 3.0 implements a 3-level page table hierarchy on the DECstation 5000/240.

and results. In Section 4, we present our software caching scheme, implementation details, and results. In Section 5, results for the integration of our two schemes are presented. In Section 6, we discuss the benefits of our schemes in the context of client-server database applications. We also present a model for TLB penalties on faster architectures. In Section 7 we discuss related work, and we summarize our conclusions in Section 8.

2 Background

Architectures such as the DEC Alpha, the HP PA-RISC, and the MIPS R2000/3000 provide software-managed TLBs. This provides greater flexibility to the operating system and eliminates hardware complexity. For example, different operating systems can implement different page table organizations for the same architecture. Some common page table organizations are inverted page tables and forward-mapped page tables. For example, HP-UX implements an inverted page table for the PA-RISC [12], while Mach 3.0 implements a 3-level page table hierarchy for the MIPS R2000/3000 [23].

Type of miss	Penalty (cycles)
L1U	10 or 30-40
L1K	512
L2	555
L3	407
TLB-invalid	338

Table 1: **Average TLB Miss Penalties.** Average penalties, measured in CPU cycles, for TLB misses under Mach 3.0 on a 40 MHz R3000-based DECstation. These averages were measured using the IOASIC counter. The cycles counts for the misses exhibited fairly high variability.

Figure 1 depicts the page table hierarchy implemented by Mach 3.0 for an R3000-based machine. There are four types of page table entries (PTEs): L1U, L2, L1K, and L3. L1U PTEs map the pages of user address spaces. L2 PTEs map the user page tables. L1K PTEs map kernel data structures. L3 PTEs map the pages containing L2 and L1K PTEs. A page pinned down in physical memory at the root of the hierarchy holds L3 PTEs [17].

There are five types of TLB misses: L1U, L1K, L2, and L3 misses, as well as TLB-invalid misses. A TLB-invalid miss takes place on user addresses that are marked invalid by the virtual memory system. These misses are handled identically by the VM system both in Mach and in our modified versions of Mach.

Table 1 gives the the average cost of each miss type, in CPU cycles, for a 40MHz R3000-based architecture running Mach 3.0. The cycle counts reported in the table were measured using the IOASIC counter on the 25 MHz system bus. The counter is a free-running 32 bit counter that is incremented once per TURBOchannel clock cycle (40 ns for the DECstation 5000/240). The time to service TLB traps exhibited fairly high variability, on the order of a couple hundred cycles. We also observed that the trap time was related to the time between consecutive traps. We believe that trap times are significantly affected by cache misses.

Since L1U misses are the most frequent, the architecture provides a special trap handler, making them fast. The L1U special trap handler executes 9 instructions and one memory load. If the memory load hits in the cache the handler executes in 10 cycles; otherwise, the L1U miss handler executes in about 30-40 cycles. All other misses are slow, since they are serviced by a generic trap handler that handles all traps except for L1U TLB misses.

Our prefetching and caching schemes decrease the number of L1K, L2, and L3 misses, from now on referred to as the *kernel TLB misses*. Kernel TLB misses typically account for greater than 50% of TLB penalties [17]. Since L1U miss handling is extremely fast, and TLB-invalid misses require the intervention of the VM system, our schemes do not service these types of TLB misses.

3 Prefetching TLB Entries

One software approach to decrease TLB overheads is to prefetch page table entries. Successful prefetching reduces the number of TLB misses and thus eliminates the overhead of invoking TLB miss handlers. As a beneficial side-effect, prefetching decreases the pollution of caches caused by executing trap handlers. When prefetching TLB entries, three issues must be resolved: where to place the prefetching code, what entries to prefetch, and how many entries to prefetch at a time.

Prefetching can be done on IPCs, or context switches between different protection domains or even between different threads running in a single large address space. Communication between concurrently executing protection domains significantly increases the number of TLB misses in the system, since several protection domains must be mapped at the same time. In this situation, prefetching on the communication path can be useful. Communication takes place very frequently between clients and servers in Mach; therefore, we decided to prefetch entries on the IPC path.

A process is typically structured such that its stack segment and code segment are allocated at opposite ends of the address space, while the data segment is allocated somewhere in the middle of the process virtual address space. This means that more than one L2 TLB entry is required to map the process. Therefore, prefetching the L2 entries mapping the process stack, code, and data segments on IPCs can be beneficial. For communicating processes, prefetching TLB entries that map message buffers and those that map IPC data structures is useful. Therefore, we decided to prefetch L1K entries mapping IPC data structures. We also prefetch L2 entries mapping message buffers and their associated L3 entries, and L2 entries mapping the process stack and code segments.

There is a trade-off between the benefits of aggressive prefetching and the overheads added to the system. Prefetching entries that are not subsequently used can evict useful entries from the TLB and thus increase the total number of TLB misses. Therefore, aggressive prefetching can result in performance degradation. In our experiments, the remaining TLB misses were not frequent enough to warrant the overhead added by prefetching. Therefore, more aggressive prefetching was not worthwhile.

3.1 Implementation

Our implementation maintains TLB entries to be prefetched in a separate *Prefetch TLB* (PTLB). The PTLB is a table maintained in unmapped, cached physical memory, to avoid a cascade of TLB misses while prefetching. PTLB entries are kept consistent with the kernel page tables efficiently, by invalidating them when the kernel invalidates page table entries. The PTLB can hold up to 4K entries and stores L1K, L2, and L3 TLB entries. TLB entries are

Application	Kernel TLB misses (thousands)			
	Total	L1K	L2	L3
mpeg_play	245.5	46.8	116.0	82.7
jpeg_play	25.6	6.2	10.0	9.4
video_play	211.0	41.5	98.4	71.1
IOzone	5.9	2.9	0.1	2.9
ousterhout	43.0	11.2	16.3	15.5
mab	89.6	33.3	22.4	33.9

Table 2: **Baseline application statistics.** This figure gives the breakdown of the different types of kernel TLB misses under unmodified Mach 3.0. The counts are in thousands.

prefetched on the IPC path between different protection domains. On the first IPC call between a pair of protection domains, TLB misses are handled through the generic trap handler. The hardware TLB is then probed on the IPC path and the TLB entries are entered into the PTLB. On subsequent IPC calls, a hashed lookup is done into the PTLB to prefetch the entries. Thus, the PTLB does not add overhead to the TLB trap handler, but only to the IPC path; however, this overhead is not significant (adding only about 25-60 cycles to a path of length 3500-4000 cycles).

Trace data collected during experiments indicated that prefetching L1K entries mapping kernel data structures eliminates about 20% of kernel TLB misses. Prefetching L2 entries mapping the code and stack segments of processes eliminates about 15%, while prefetching L2 entries mapping server message buffers and their associated L3 entries eliminates another 15%. We decided to dynamically prefetch these entries on the IPC path between processes.

TLB misses on L2 entries for the data segment of processes were also frequent. Mach supports sparse memory allocation, and therefore permits allocation of memory in non-contiguous locations of the virtual address space of a process [5]. While this is a useful feature of the VM system, it is not easy to dynamically determine the location of the data segment of a process. Therefore, we did not prefetch L2 entries mapping the data segment of a process.

3.2 Experimental Environment

Our experimental platform consists of Mach 3.0 running on an R3000-based DECstation 5000/240. MK82 is the Mach 3.0 microkernel used in our experiments with the user-level server, UX41, to provide Unix functionality. Xcfbpmax is the X11R5 server used in our experiments. Thus, our experiments consist of three user-level processes: the Unix server, the X server, and the client application, all communicating through the kernel using IPC.

The R3000 has a 64-entry fully associative TLB. The hardware supports using the TLB in two partitions. The upper partition of 56 entries supports a random replacement policy and Mach uses it to hold L1U, L1K, and L3 entries.

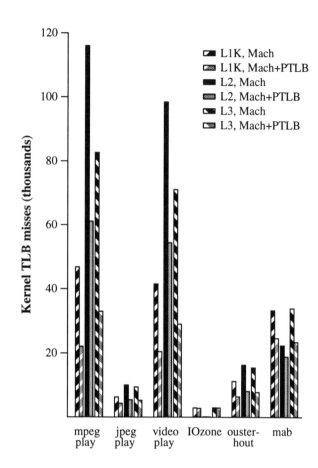

Figure 2: **Kernel TLB misses: Mach, Mach+PTLB.** Kernel misses under unmodified Mach are shown in black; misses under Mach+PTLB are shown in gray.

Mach uses the lower partition of 8 entries to hold L2 entries with a FIFO policy.

The benchmarks studied were mpeg_play, jpeg_play, video_play, which are X applications, and ousterhout, IOzone, and mab (modified Andrew benchmark), which are file-system-oriented applications. Table 2 lists some relevant statistics for each benchmark. For a full description of the benchmarks refer to [16].

Network traffic, Mach's random page replacement policy [7], and the "aging" of the kernel [22], result in variability in application runtimes. The machine was taken off the network to eliminate variability due to network traffic. As the system stays up for a long time, the number of L1K misses increases. This happens because the kernel starts allocating kernel data structures from mapped virtual memory. To eliminate this effect, all timings were taken with freshly booted kernels. However, our schemes will give increasing benefits as the number of L1K misses in the system increases with the aging of the kernel. In order to obtain accurate timings, 50 data points were collected for each benchmark. This decreased the variability in the average time to acceptable amounts.

	Kernel TLB Misses		
Application	Mach	Mach+ PTLB	Removed
mpeg_play	245.4	116.1	52.7%
jpeg_play	25.6	14.9	42.0%
video_play	211.0	103.9	50.8%
IOzone	5.9	5.7	4.1%
ousterhout	43.0	22.2	48.5%
mab	89.6	67.0	25.2%

Table 3: **Kernel TLB miss counts: Mach, Mach+PTLB.** Total kernel TLB miss counts, in thousands, and the percentage of kernel TLB misses eliminated by prefetching.

	Kernel TLB Penalty (million cycles)		Application Speedup
Application	Mach	Mach+ PTLB	
mpeg_play	124.6	48.2	1.69%
jpeg_play	13.0	6.0	0.91%
video_play	108.0	41.6	3.52%
IOzone	3.4	2.7	0.19%
ousterhout	28.6	17.4	0.77%
mab	52.0	29.8	0.96%

Table 4: **Kernel TLB penalties: Mach, Mach+PTLB.** The TLB penalties are reported in millions of CPU cycles. The last column gives the percentage of application time saved by prefetching.

We measured average application runtimes ($\bar{X}$) and standard deviations (σ), for all our experiments. For all the data presented in this paper, we found that for jpeg_play $\sigma/\bar{X}$ is less than 0.3%, for video_play it is less than 0.8%, for mpeg_play $\sigma/\bar{X}$ is less than 1.0%, for mab it is less than 1.2%, for IOzone it is less than 1.5%, and for ousterhout it is less than 4.0%. Since TLB penalties are a relatively small percentage of overall application runtime, it is important that $\sigma/\bar{X}$ be small.

3.3 Prefetching Results

Figure 2 shows the decrease in the number of kernel TLB misses for each of the three types of misses – L1K, L2, and L3. Table 3 gives the counts of kernel TLB misses under unmodified Mach and Mach+PTLB and the percentage of kernel TLB misses eliminated by prefetching.

Prefetching TLB entries on the IPC path eliminates 40% to 50% of the kernel TLB misses for all benchmarks except IOzone and mab. Neither of these benchmarks is IPC-intensive, and therefore they derive little benefit from the PTLB.

Figure 3 shows kernel TLB miss penalties under unmodified Mach in black. The striped bars represent kernel

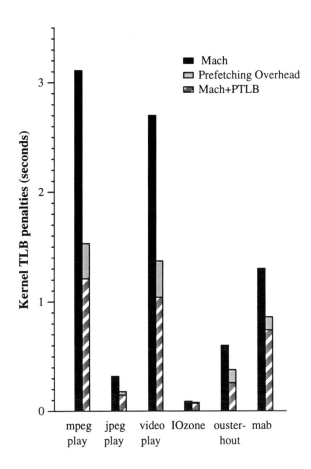

Figure 3: **Prefetching costs and benefits.** The measured timing contributions of kernel TLB misses in unmodified Mach and Mach+PTLB. The solid gray bars show the measured overhead added on the IPC path due to prefetching.

TLB miss penalties under Mach+PTLB, and the solid gray bars indicate the prefetching overheads added to the IPC path. Prefetching an entry into the TLB takes about 60 cycles, while probing the TLB and not prefetching an entry because it already exists takes about 25 cycles (this case occurs about twice as often as successful prefetching).

Table 4 presents the measured kernel TLB penalties, in millions of CPU cycles, for applications under Mach and Mach+PTLB. The last column presents the application speedup due to prefetching; speedup is measured as the decrease in application runtime as a percentage of the application runtime under unmodified Mach. Prefetching results in speedups of up to 3.5% of overall application run time. Kernel TLB misses typically constitute greater than 50% of the overall TLB penalties in an application[1]. Kernel TLB miss penalties constitute 1% to 5% of the overall application time for the benchmarks studied [17]. Thus, prefetching decreases a significant fraction of the kernel TLB penalties.

---

[1] The remaining penalties are due to L1U and TLB-invalid misses. Even though L1U misses are highly optimized, their frequency is so high that they significantly contribute to overall TLB penalties.

Application	Mach Total	DM 1K Total	DM 1K Hit rate	DM 4K Total	DM 4K Hit rate
mpeg_play	245.4	197.5	82.5%	173.8	97.2%
jpeg_play	25.6	20.2	84.4%	17.4	99.8%
video_play	211.0	202.4	70.9%	163.3	100.0%
IOzone	5.9	4.4	98.5%	4.3	99.3%
ousterhout	43.0	33.2	85.9%	29.0	99.3%
mab	89.6	88.0	70.6%	63.9	92.5%

Table 6: **TLB miss counts and hit rates under Mach and STLB.** Total kernel misses in thousands under unmodified Mach 3.0, and the two direct-mapped STLB configurations, DM 1K and DM 4K. Hit rates are included for the STLB configurations. DM 1K is the direct-mapped STLB with 1K entries, while DM 4K is the direct-mapped STLB with 4K entries.

	Penalty (cycles)		
	STLB		
Miss Type	Hit	Miss	Mach
L1K	105	582	512
L2, Path 1	114	625	555
L2, Path 2	160	625	555
L3	105	408	338

Table 5: **Average STLB penalties.** An STLB miss adds about 70 cycles to the TLB trap path. The first L2 path through the STLB is more frequent than the second L2 path, and has been optimized to take less time.

	Nested Misses (thousands)		
Application	Mach	DM 1K	DM 4K
mpeg_play	72.3	13.1	3.3
jpeg_play	7.9	1.0	0.0
video_play	61.4	35.8	0.0
IOzone	1.7	0.0	0.0
ousterhout	13.1	2.9	0.0
mab	26.4	12.6	0.2

Table 7: **Nested TLB misses.** Nested TLB misses in thousands under unmodified Mach 3.0, and the two direct-mapped STLB configurations, DM 1K and DM 4K. The nested misses are caused because of the page table hierarchy.

In summary, prefetching benefits all applications and decreases TLB overheads significantly, usually eliminating about 50% of the kernel TLB miss penalties. Although TLB penalties are currently only a few percent of overall application runtime, prefetching will provide increasing benefits as TLB penalties increase in the future.

4 Software Cache of TLB Entries

Architectures with software managed TLBs incur large penalties in TLB miss handling. This is due not only to the use of generic trap handlers but also to cascaded TLB misses resulting from hierarchical page table organizations. We address this problem by providing a large second-level software cache of TLB entries (STLB).

L1K, L2, and L3 entries that have been evicted from the hardware TLB are stored in the STLB. The STLB code branches off the generic trap handler path at the beginning and does a quick lookup in the STLB. On an STLB hit, the entry is inserted into the hardware TLB. On an STLB miss, the code branches back to the generic trap handler path.

Thus, the first benefit of the STLB is that it provides a fast trap path for TLB misses, and on an STLB hit this avoids the overhead (such as saving and restoring registers) of the generic trap handler. The second benefit of the STLB is that it eliminates cascaded TLB misses. Cascaded TLB misses

occur because the page tables are hierarchically organized with the lower levels in mapped memory. The TLB trap handler code tries to resolve a TLB miss by looking in the next higher level in the page table hierarchy. However, this lookup can itself cause a TLB miss (up to a depth of three in Mach's page table organization), resulting in a cascade of TLB misses. The STLB provides a flat space of TLB entries in unmapped physical memory, and thus prevents such cascaded TLB misses.

As with any cache, the STLB can be organized in many different ways – direct-mapped, direct-mapped with a victim cache [14], n-way associative, or fully associative [18]. The organization and the size of the STLB affect its hit rate.

4.1 Implementation

Like the PTLB, the STLB resides in unmapped, cached physical memory, and therefore does not occupy page table entries in the hardware TLB. Since the STLB code branches off the generic trap handler path, it adds some overhead to other traps. However, this code has been optimized so that it adds only 4 cycles to system calls and interrupts, which are by far the most frequent kinds of traps[2].

---

[2] The STLB code adds only 11 cycles to the other traps, such as Bus Error, Address Error, and Floating Point exceptions, which are relatively infrequent.

Application	TLB penalty (million cycles)			Speedup	
	Mach	DM 1K	DM 4K	DM 1K	DM 4K
mpeg_play	124.6	41.7	21.4	0.27%	1.73%
jpeg_play	13.0	4.2	1.9	0.15%	0.21%
video_play	108.0	60.7	15.7	2.18%	3.53%
IOzone	3.4	0.7	0.6	0.85%	0.59%
ousterhout	24.0	7.9	3.9	0.76%	1.53%
mab	52.0	31.6	13.2	0.76%	0.80%

Table 8: **Kernel TLB penalties: Mach, STLB.** Kernel TLB penalties under Mach 3.0, and the two direct-mapped STLB configurations, DM 1K and DM 4K, in millions of CPU cycles. The last two columns present the percentage of application time saved by the STLB configurations.

We studied the following organizations of the STLB: direct-mapped with 1K entries (DM 1K), direct-mapped with 4K entries (DM 4K), 2-way set-associative with 1K and 4K entries, and 4-way set-associative with 1K and 4K entries. The direct-mapped organizations index into the STLB and check only one entry to find a match with the faulting address, whereas the set-associative organizations check more than one entry of the STLB in software to find a match.

4.2 STLB results

Preliminary experiments with direct-mapped organizations showed high hit rates, comparable to the set-associative organizations, but with lower access times because sequential checks in software for matches are avoided in a direct-mapped organization. Therefore, we present only the results for the direct-mapped configurations of the STLB. Table 5 presents the average time, in CPU cycles, that the direct-mapped STLB takes to service TLB misses[3]. An STLB hit takes about 115-160 cycles for L2 hits and about 100 cycles for L1K and L3 hits. The difference in timings is because Mach 3.0 replaces L2 entries using a FIFO policy, and a random replacement policy is followed for L1K and L3 entries. An STLB miss adds about 70 cycles to the trap path. Thus, on an STLB hit, this scheme decreases the overhead of the generic trap handler by providing fast access to a large number of page table entries.

The experimental environment and benchmarks for the STLB are the same as those for the PTLB which are described in Section 3.2. Table 6 presents the number of kernel TLB misses for the two STLB configurations and the associated STLB hit rates. The number of kernel TLB misses under unmodified Mach 3.0 has been included for comparison. The hit rates achieved by DM 1K range from 70% to 99% while the hit rates achieved by DM 4K are close to 100%. The larger STLB (DM 4K) services more TLB misses than the smaller DM 1K STLB. This configuration

also results in an overall decrease in the number of kernel TLB misses. This is because the cascade of TLB misses to higher levels of the page table hierarchy is eliminated

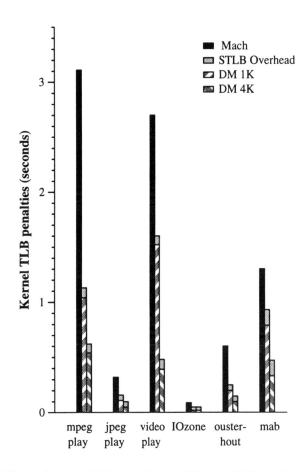

Figure 4: **Total TLB penalties for different STLB configurations.** This figure gives the kernel TLB penalties, in seconds, with the different STLB configurations and compares them with TLB penalties under Mach. The overhead added by the STLB is represented by the solid gray bars. The overhead is the same for both STLB configurations, since it depends on the number of system calls and is independent of the STLB size.

---

[3]The two different L2 paths correspond to L2 misses that take place when in user space, and L2 misses that take place when in kernel space.

Application	Kernel TLB Misses			
	Mach	**PTLB+ STLB**	**Percent Removed**	**Hit Rate**
mpeg_play	245.4	128.6	47.6%	96.2%
jpeg_play	25.6	13.8	46.2%	99.7%
video_play	211.0	111.8	47.0%	100.0%
IOzone	5.9	4.1	31.2%	99.3%
ousterhout	43.0	21.1	50.9%	99.1%
mab	89.6	52.8	41.1%	90.9%

Table 9: **Kernel TLB miss counts: Mach, PTLB+STLB.** Total kernel TLB miss counts, in thousands, under Mach and PTLB+STLB. The third column presents the percentage of kernel TLB misses eliminated by the software TLB and prefetching, and the last column gives the hit rate for the STLB.

Application	Kernel TLB Penalty (million cycles)		
	Mach	**PTLB+ STLB**	**Speedup**
mpeg_play	124.6	18.4	1.09%
jpeg_play	13.0	1.6	0.27%
video_play	108.0	11.4	3.04%
IOzone	3.4	0.6	0.99%
ousterhout	24.0	3.4	1.65%
mab	52.0	13.6	0.25%

Table 10: **Kernel TLB penalties: Mach, PTLB+STLB.** The kernel TLB penalties are measured in millions of CPU cycles. The last column gives the percentage of application time saved by using the integrated scheme with prefetching and the STLB.

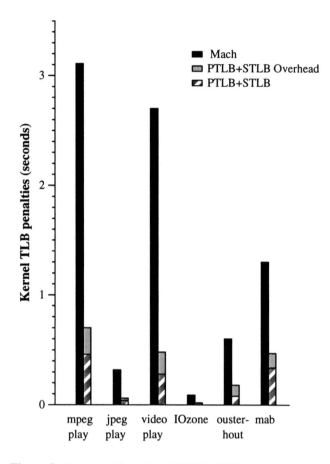

Figure 5: **Costs and benefits of PTLB+STLB.** The measured timing contributions of kernel TLB misses in unmodified Mach and PTLB+STLB. The solid gray bars give the measured overhead added to the IPC path due to prefetching, and the trap handler path due to the STLB.

when a TLB miss hits in the STLB; and as Table 7 shows, under Mach 3.0 nearly 30% of the kernel TLB misses for each application are such nested misses. The larger STLB eliminates almost all of these cascaded misses.

Figure 4 presents the total TLB penalties under the different STLB configurations and unmodified Mach. The gray bars represent the overhead imposed by the STLB on system calls. As is evident from the figure, DM 4K reduces TLB penalties significantly.

Table 8 presents TLB penalties under unmodified Mach and the two STLB configurations, and the percentage of application time saved by using the STLB. The speedups obtained by using the larger STLB, DM 4K, go up to 3.5%, a significant fraction of application kernel TLB penalties. DM 1K does not perform as well for all applications, due to its lower hit rate.

5 Prefetching with the Software TLB

The direct-mapped organization of the PTLB and the STLB make integrating the two schemes fairly straightforward. Using the STLB decreases the number of cascaded TLB traps. Therefore, prefetching L3 entries is not very useful. In fact, it has the negative effect of evicting useful entries from the TLB. Therefore, only L1K and L2 entries are prefetched. Since the DM 4K organization of the STLB performed well, the PTLB+STLB implementation uses a direct-mapped STLB, with 4K entries.

Table 9 gives the counts of kernel TLB misses under unmodified Mach and PTLB+STLB and the percentage of kernel TLB misses eliminated. The STLB hit rates are given in the last column. The hit rates are lower than those obtained for the STLB configuration DM 4K in Table 6. This is because the total number of kernel TLB misses is decreased due to prefetching. Figure 5 shows kernel TLB miss penalties under unmodified Mach in black. The striped bars represent the kernel TLB miss penalties under the PTLB+STLB, and the solid gray bars indicate the overheads added by prefetching and the STLB.

Table 10 presents the measured kernel TLB penalties, in millions of CPU cycles, for applications under Mach and the PTLB+STLB. The last column gives the percentage of overall application time saved due to the integrated scheme. As seen in Figure 5 and Table 10, the integrated scheme performs well, improving application performance by up to 3% of overall application runtime. However, it does not do better than the prefetching scheme alone or the STLB scheme alone for these applications. This is because while prefetching and the STLB are both very effective at reducing TLB penalties, they eliminate opportunities to reduce TLB costs from each other. However, integrating the two schemes adds the overhead of both schemes. Therefore, it does not provide greater benefits than the two schemes do independently for these benchmarks.

6 Discussion

6.1 Multiple Clients and Servers

All the benchmarks presented above involve a single client application communicating though IPC to the UX server and the X server. To study the benefits of our schemes with multiple clients and servers and more frequent IPC, we ran a small synthetic database application that consists of several clients making requests in a loop to a database server. The database server receives a request from each client to query a fixed number of records randomly distributed in the memory-resident database file. The server touches each record requested and returns to the requesting client. This application is IPC-intensive and tests TLB behavior with several communicating processes. Since it includes several clients, it puts significantly more pressure on the TLB than the benchmarks presented earlier.

We ran the benchmark with three clients communicating with one server. Prefetching eliminates about 30% to 35% of the kernel TLB misses. This improves overall application performance by 6%. The STLB exhibits a hit rate of about 90% and eliminates about 20% of the kernel TLB misses by avoiding cascaded TLB misses. Using DM 4K, this improves overall application performance by 10%. The integrated PTLB+STLB scheme achieves an STLB hit rate of about 86%. It eliminates about 40% of kernel TLB misses, and improves application performance by about 12%.

Thus, as the number of clients and servers increases, TLB penalties represent a larger fraction of the runtime of IPC-intensive applications. Our prefetching and caching schemes both provide increasing benefits under these circumstances. This benchmark also demonstrates the usefulness of the integrated scheme. The PTLB+STLB provides greater benefits than either technique used alone.

6.2 Model for Future Architectures

To study the benefits of our schemes on future architectures we modelled trap time as a function of the caching behavior of the TLB miss handler code. We use the following notation: i denotes the number of instructions executed by the trap handler, m denotes the number of cache misses during trap execution, and t denotes the time to service a cache miss. Therefore we have, Trap time $= i + m \times t$.

The time to service a cache miss on the DECstation 5000/240 is $t = 24$ cycles [8]. On a machine with a clock speed of 200 MHz and the same memory system, the time to service a cache miss will be $(200/40) \times 24 = 120$ cycles. On such a machine, TLB penalties will become:

$$
\begin{aligned}
STLB\ fail &= 29 + 2 \times 120 &= 269\ \text{cycles} \\
STLB\ L2,\ path1 &= 61 + 2 \times 120 &= 301\ \text{cycles} \\
STLB\ L2,\ path2 &= 76 + 3 \times 120 &= 436\ \text{cycles} \\
STLB\ L1K,\ L3 &= 52 + 2 \times 120 &= 292\ \text{cycles}
\end{aligned}
$$

and for unmodified Mach,

$$
\begin{aligned}
L1K &= 167 + 14 \times 120 &= 1847\ \text{cycles} \\
L2 &= 207 + 14 \times 120 &= 1887\ \text{cycles} \\
KPT &= 161 + 10 \times 120 &= 1361\ \text{cycles}
\end{aligned}
$$

Thus, TLB miss penalties increase by approximately 1500 cycles, from 500 cycles to nearly 2000 cycles. STLB penalties increase only by about 300 cycles, from 100 cycles to 400 cycles. Referring to Table 5, an L1K miss that hits in the STLB on the current architecture eliminates approximately $(512 - 105) = 407$ cycles. Based on the above model for a 200MHz architecture, an L1K hit in the STLB would eliminate $(1847 - 292) = 1555$ cycles. Prefetching entirely eliminates the penalty of the TLB miss. Thus, prefetching and the STLB should decrease TLB miss handling penalties significantly on faster, newer architectures, and should have an even greater impact on overall application performance.

7 Related Work

Prefetching and caching are two well-known techniques that have been widely applied in computer systems [19, 20], but have not been applied to software management of TLBs. Most of the previous work has focussed on hardware caches.

Huck and Hays [12] have explored an idea similar to the STLB in the context of the HP PA-RISC. Their *Hashed Page Table* (HPT) is a page table organization suited for large address spaces. The faulting virtual address is used to index into the HPT and a match is attempted between the faulting address and the HPT entry. If no match is found, a fault is taken to the OS. Collision entries are then looked up in software. This scheme replaced an earlier one in the HP-UX operating system, which used an inverted page table organization. Huck and Hays simulated both hardware and software implementations of the HPT.

Our work, which has been implemented on a different architecture, complements their work in a number of ways.

Our entirely software-based implementation is in the context of hierarchically-organized forward-mapped page tables and it studies the effect of nested TLB traps. We obtained measurements from a running system for a range of applications and found that a direct-mapped organization of the STLB was very effective. Our experiments showed that a 2-way set-associative software STLB adds more overhead, as compared to a simple direct-mapped organization. Further, our work studies the benefit of prefetching TLB entries in the context of a microkernel-based OS environment with several communicating processes, where TLB performance is more critical.

Another approach to decreasing TLB miss handling costs is to provide variable-sized pages that use a single TLB entry to map large contiguous regions of memory. This scheme is used by the PowerPC architecture [13]. Prefetching of TLB entries is still useful for dynamically allocated data structures. As operating systems move to modular organizations supporting finer grained processes interacting with each other, the number of L2 TLB misses will increase. Thus, although each process could be mapped by a single TLB entry with a larger page size, the number of such entries is still large. Since the TLB is a shared resource, contention for the TLB will be high. Therefore, although each entry maps more pages of an address space, prefetching such entries should continue to be useful. Also, in systems supporting garbage collection, ensuring that all important data structures are contiguous in physical memory is not easy. Thus, our schemes can complement the variable-sized pages solution in reducing TLB miss penalties.

8 Conclusions

This paper presents two entirely software-based solutions to decrease TLB penalties. The first scheme, prefetching TLB entries on the IPC path, decreases kernel TLB miss penalties by about 50%. The second scheme uses a large software cache to provide fast path access to entries on a TLB miss. The hit rates achieved are high, ranging from 90% to nearly 100%.

Both prefetching and software caching perform well for all applications. The integration of the two schemes also performs well, though it provides less benefits than any one scheme independently for the benchmarks studied. For a synthetic benchmark that involves several processes communicating frequently, however, using the two techniques together provides greater benefits than either technique alone.

Although TLB penalties are currently only a few percent of overall application runtime, they will probably increase in the future, both because processor speeds are increasing more rapidly than memory speeds, and because of changes in operating system structure that are resulting in more frequent communication. Analysis and experiments indicate that our techniques should improve application runtime by more than 10% in the future.

9 Acknowledgments

Thanks to Wilson Hsieh and Carl Waldspurger for their contribution to early ideas in this work. Special thanks to Carl for his invaluable suggestions, advice, time and support. Thanks also to Don Yeung for our fruitful discussions, Anthony Joseph for his help with X and Rich Uhlig, Alessandro Forin and Mary Thompson for their help with Mach. Thanks to Anthony, Debby Wallach, Don, Eric Brewer, Ulana Legedza, and Wilson for their useful comments on the drafts. Thanks to Paul Leach and the anonymous referees for their helpful comments.

References

[1] T. Anderson, H. Levy, B. Bershad, and E. Lazowska. The interaction of architecture and operating system design. In *Proceedings of the 4th Conference on Architectural Support for Programming Languages and Systems*, pages 108–119, Santa Clara, CA, April 1991.

[2] B. Bershad, C. Chambers, S. Eggers, C. Maeda D., McNamee, P. Pardyak, S. Savage, and E. Sire. SPIN - an extensible microkernel for application-specific operating system services. Technical Report TR94-03-03, University of Washington, February 1994.

[3] B.N. Bershad. The increasing irrelevance of IPC performance for microkernel-based operating systems. In *USENIX Workshop on Microkernels and Other Kernel Architectures*, pages 205–211, Seattle, WA, April 1992.

[4] B.N. Bershad, T.E. Anderson, E.D. Lazowska, and H.M. Levy. Lightweight remote procedure call. In *Proceedings of the 12th Symposium on Operating Systems Principles*, pages 102–113, Litchfield Park, AZ, December 1989.

[5] J. Boykin, D. Kirschen, A. Langerman, and S. LoVerso. *Programming under Mach*. Addison-Wesley Publishing Company, 1993.

[6] J.S. Chase, H.M. Levy, E.D. Lazowska, and M. Baker-Harvey. Lightweight shared objects in a 64-bit operating system. In *Proceedings of the Conference on Object-Oriented Programming Systems, Languages and Applications*, pages 397–413, Vancouver, Canada, October 1992.

[7] B. Chen and B. Bershad. The impact of operating system structure on memory system performance. In *Proceedings of the 14th Symposium on Operating Systems Principles*, pages 120–133, Asheville, NC, December 1993.

[8] Digital Equipment Corporation. *DECstation and DECsystem 5000 Model 240 Technical Overview*. 1991.

[9] Microsoft Corporation. *Microsoft OLE programmer's reference*. Microsoft Press, 1993.

[10] D. Engler, M. F. Kaashoek, and J. O'Toole. The operating system kernel as a secure programmable machine. In *Proceedings of the 6th European SIGOPS Workshop*, Germany, September 1994.

[11] W. Hsieh, M. F. Kaashoek, and W. E. Weihl. The persistent relevance of IPC performance: New techniques for reducing the IPC penalty. In *Proceedings of the 4th Workshop on Workstation Operating Systems*, pages 186–190, Napa, CA, October 1993.

[12] J. Huck and J. Hays. Architectural support for translation table management in large address space machines. In *Proceedings of the 20th International Symposium on Computer Architecture*, pages 39–50, San Diego, CA, May 1993.

[13] Motorola Inc. *PowerPC 601: RISC Microprocessor User's Manual*. Prentice-Hall, Inc., 1993.

[14] N. Jouppi. Improving direct-mapped cache performance by the addition of a small fully-associative cache and prefetch buffers. In *Proceedings of the 17th International Symposium on Computer Architecture*, pages 364–373, Seattle, WA, May 1990.

[15] J. Liedtke. Improving IPC by kernel design. In *Proceedings of the 14th Symposium on Operating Systems Principles*, pages 175–188, Asheville, NC, December 1993.

[16] D. Nagle, R. Uhlig, T. Mudge, and S. Sechrest. Optimal allocation of on-chip memory for multiple-API operating systems. In *Proceedings of the 21st International Symposium on Computer Architecture*, pages 358–369, Chicago, IL, April 1994.

[17] D. Nagle, R. Uhlig, T. Stanley, S. Sechrest, T. Mudge, and R. Brown. Design tradeoffs for software managed TLBs. In *Proceedings of the 20th International Symposium on Computer Architecture*, pages 27–38, San Diego, CA, May 1993.

[18] D. Patterson and J. Hennessy. *Computer architecture: a quantitative approach*. Morgan Kaufman Publishers, 1989.

[19] D. Patterson and J. Hennessy. *Computer organization and design: the hardware/software interface*. Morgan Kaufman Publishers, 1993.

[20] A. S. Tanenbaum. *Modern Operating Systems*. Prentice-Hall, Inc., 1992.

[21] OpenDoc Design Team. OpenDoc technical summary. In *Apple's World Wide Developers Conference Technologies CD*, San Jose, CA, April 1994.

[22] R. Uhlig. Private communication, 1993.

[23] R. Uhlig, D. Nagle, T. Mudge, and S. Sechrest. Software TLB management in OSF/1 and Mach 3.0. Technical report, University of Michigan, 1993.

[24] R. Wahbe, S. Lucco, T. Anderson, and S. Graham. Efficient software-based fault isolation. In *Proceedings of the 14th Symposium on Operating Systems Principles*, pages 203–216, Asheville, NC, December 1993.

Dynamic Page Mapping Policies for Cache Conflict Resolution on Standard Hardware

Theodore H. Romer
Dennis Lee
Brian N. Bershad

*Department of Computer Science
and Engineering
University of Washington
Seattle, WA 98195*

{romer,dlee,bershad}@cs.washington.edu

J. Bradley Chen

*Division of Applied Sciences
29 Oxford Street
Harvard University
Cambridge MA 02138*

bchen@das.harvard.edu

Abstract

In computer systems with large, physically-indexed, direct-mapped caches, a poor mapping from virtual to physical pages causes excessive cache conflict misses. In a previous paper we proposed a simple hardware device, the Cache Miss Lookaside (CML) Buffer, which identifies pages that are suffering from conflict misses. The operating system can use this information to implement a dynamic page mapping policy that resolves conflicts by performing an in-memory copy of one of the conflicting pages, and updating the virtual to physical mappings. In this paper, we propose several dynamic page mapping policies that detect and resolve cache conflicts using hardware available in existing systems, such as a TLB and cache miss counter, to locate possible cache conflicts. We evaluate the simulated performance of a variety of mapping policies, and show that a dynamic page mapping policy using standard hardware can improve upon the performance of a static policy, but is not as effective as special-purpose hardware such as an associative cache or a CML buffer. We also describe the implementation and performance of a software-based dynamic policy on a DEC Alpha workstation running DEC OSF/1.

1 Introduction

Modern workstations typically include a large direct-mapped second-level cache to reduce the latency of

This research was sponsored by a grant from the Office of Naval Research, and an equipment grant from Digital Equipment Corporation. Bershad was partially supported by a National Science Foundation Presidential Young Investigator Award. Romer was supported by a National Science Foundation Graduate Student Fellowship. Lee was supported by a gift from the Intel Corporation. Part of the research was conducted by Chen, Lee, and Romer at the DEC Western Research Laboratory. The views and conclusions contained in this document are those of the authors and should not be interpreted as representing the official policies, either expressed or implied, of the University of Washington, Harvard University, the Digital Equipment Corporation, the Intel Corporation, or the U.S. Government.

memory accesses. A direct mapped cache may suffer from *conflict misses*, which occur when two memory locations compete for the same cache line, even though the cache is large enough to hold the current working set [Hill 87]. Conflict misses cause programs to run slowly and with unpredictable execution time. In a physically indexed cache the mapping from a virtual address to a cache line is determined by the physical address to which the virtual address is mapped. This mapping provides an opportunity for the operating system to eliminate cache conflicts by dynamically relocating pages in physical memory and updating the virtual to physical mapping.

In order to eliminate cache conflicts, a dynamic page mapping policy must determine when and where conflicts are occurring, and resolve them. In an earlier paper [Bershad et al. 94] we proposed a simple hardware device called the Cache Miss Lookaside (CML) Buffer, which monitors memory traffic to identify pages that are incurring large numbers of cache misses. Pages are likely to be conflicting with each other if they exhibit large numbers of misses in a short period of time and they map to the same *color*, that is, the pages map to the same page in the cache. The operating system resolves conflicts by copying frequently conflicting pages elsewhere in physical memory. The destination of the copy is a physical page with a color different from the source page. The application's virtual pages are remapped so that the copy is transparent. We use the term *recolor* to describe the process of copying and remapping a conflicting page. Our simulations showed that the CML buffer eliminates many conflicts in a large direct mapped cache, and compares favorably to a more expensive two-way set associative cache of equivalent size. Although the CML buffer is not a complicated piece of hardware, it does not exist on current workstations.

In this paper, we explore alternative techniques that rely on software to detect and eliminate cache conflicts. Our goal is to emulate the function of the CML buffer using features such as a TLB and a cache miss counter that are available on many modern machines. With these, we can construct an approximation of the current working set to infer the location of cache conflicts. We first simulate a collection of software-based techniques using trace-based simulation. This allows us to precisely evaluate a range of policies, to explore the tradeoffs between overhead and effectiveness, and to compare the performance of software-based policies to policies that rely on hardware, including the CML buffer and a two-way set associative cache. We then implement and measure the most promising simulated dynamic policy on a modern workstation.

Our simulation results lead us to conclude that dynamic mapping strategies based on standard hardware can improve performance, but are not as effective as those based on the CML buffer hardware, which has greater precision and lower overhead. We also show that the dynamic policies can reduce execution time variability by removing cache conflicts that occur when the operating system makes a poor initial mapping of a virtual page.

The rest of this paper

In Section 2, we discuss related work. In Section 3, we describe several dynamic page mapping policies that can be implemented using existing hardware. In Section 4, we evaluate their impact on performance. In Section 5, we describe an implementation and the performance of the most promising dynamic page mapping policy on a DEC Alpha workstation running Version 2.0 of the DEC OSF/1 operating system. Finally, we present our conclusions in Section 6.

2   Related Work

The interaction between caches and memory management has been heavily studied [Chiueh & Katz 92, Kessler & Hill 92, Lynch 93], mostly in the context of *static mapping policies*. A static mapping policy assigns a page frame to a virtual page at page-in time, but unlike the dynamic policies described in this paper, does not change that mapping as a program executes. Static policies are simple to implement and have low overhead. However, they cannot adapt to changing program and system conditions, leading to unpredictable cache performance [Hosking & Moss 93, Wahbe et al. 93, Chaiken & Agarwal 94]. Moreover, static policies do not address the problem of conflicts between a user-level task and the operating system or between multiple user-level tasks [Chen 94, Mogul & Borg 91].

In this paper, we discuss two static policies that have been described in the literature and are used in current systems: Page Coloring and Bin Hopping. Page Coloring exploits spatial locality by mapping consecutive virtual pages to consecutive colors, so that pages close together in the virtual address space do not conflict in the cache. Operating systems that implement Page Coloring generally hash the virtual page number with the process ID before choosing a color to avoid conflicts between tasks that use the virtual address space in similar ways [Chiueh & Katz 92]. Bin Hopping [Kessler & Hill 92] cycles through the available colors sequentially as pages are faulted in so that pages first used close together in time will map to different locations in the cache.

3   Dynamic policies

A dynamic page mapping policy updates the mappings between virtual and physical pages in order to minimize the number of cache conflicts. As an example, a simple policy might maintain the invariant that no two physical pages of the same color be mapped by the TLB simultaneously. If satisfying a TLB miss would cause two pages of the same color to be in the TLB, one of the pages is copied to a physical page of a different color. This policy, though simple, can incur excessive overhead due to a more complicated TLB miss path and frequent recoloring. No consideration is given to questions such as "is the potentially conflicting page actually in conflict with other pages that are in use?" or "are cache misses currently a problem?" A good policy eliminates conflicts, has low overhead, and recolors only when necessary. A bad policy can degrade performance because it fails to eliminate conflicts, has excessive overhead, or recolors unnecessarily.

In this section, we explore two sets of policies that use the TLB to approximate the system's current working set in order to detect conflicts. The first set of policies continuously monitor TLB activity in order to detect conflicts as they occur. The second set of policies periodically inspect the TLB to detect potential conflicts. We refer to the first set of policies as *active* and the second set of policies as *periodic*. We first describe a simple active policy that is easy to understand and accurately detects conflict misses, but has high overhead. We will then progressively refine this policy by trading away accuracy for reduced overhead.

The policies we explore require that the operating system monitor references to pages and arrange for notification on references to specific pages. Modern systems satisfy these requirements. In a system with a software-filled TLB [Kane 88, Digital Equipment Corporation 92], these mechanisms are easy to support. In other systems, virtual memory page protection can be used. We will consider one policy that relies on a cache miss counter to determine when the cache conflict detection software should be activated. This type of simple performance monitoring hardware is becoming increasingly common on high-performance processors [Digital Equipment Corporation 92, Singhal & Goldberg 94, Glew & Wang 94, Shippy 94].

3.1 Active policies

An active policy attempts to prevent conflicts by rearranging pages in physical memory whenever a conflict might occur. The active policies discussed in this section do so by maintaining the invariant that all pages appearing in the TLB be of different colors. The simplest active policy, which we will call *Active-Naive*, maintains this invariant by recoloring any page which would violate the invariant on every TLB miss. This policy can reduce conflicts by distributing the CPU's references over the cache, but it will recolor excessively. Data on pages of the same color but not in long-term competition for cache space may be unnecessarily copied.

To avoid resolving false conflicts, or conflicts that are short-lived, the *Active-Delay* policy allows potential conflicts to persist briefly. Pages of the same color are still not allowed to appear in the TLB, but rather than immediately recoloring, the older TLB entry is invalidated, and a counter is incremented on each TLB miss to one of the two competing pages. Recoloring is delayed until the counter reaches a given threshold. In effect, this policy uses the TLB to monitor the memory reference stream. Using the TLB this way can reduce the frequency of recoloring, but at the cost of increased TLB and conflict misses relative to the Active-Naive policy.

Recolor overhead can be reduced further by increasing the delay, but delaying too long eliminates useful recolor operations as well as useless ones, and also increases TLB overhead. The *Active-Throttle* policy instead caps the number of recolors in any given time interval. Since it is unnecessary to detect conflicts when the throttling mechanism prevents pages from being recolored, Active-Throttle allows conflicting pages to appear in the TLB once the cap has been reached. After a suitable delay, the policy is re-enabled and conflicting pages are evicted from the TLB. The Active-Throttle policy limits recolor and TLB overhead per unit time, but will not resolve conflicts that occur while the recolor rate is being throttled.

3.2 Periodic policies

Periodic policies poll the TLB in search of conflicts that may already be occurring, rather than preventing conflicts that have not yet occurred. A periodic policy can have lower TLB and recolor overhead than an active policy since its intrusiveness is limited by the rate of polling. With frequent polling, a periodic policy approximates an active one. As polling becomes less frequent, overhead drops, but the number of outstanding unresolved conflicts may increase.

A simple periodic policy is *Periodic-Random*, which periodically recolors one randomly chosen page that appears in the TLB. Since it may recolor pages that do not conflict, Periodic-Random may introduce as many conflicts as it removes. The *Periodic-Color* policy is more selective, scanning the TLB and recoloring one page from a set of pages that conflict.

The Periodic-Random and Periodic-Color policies assume that the contents of the TLB accurately reflect the current working set. In practice, inactive pages can appear in the TLB, causing unnecessary recolors. The *Snapshot* policy is similar to Periodic-Color, but filters out these inactive pages. A "snapshot" of the working set is periodically taken by flushing the TLB, and observing which pages incur TLB misses over a short interval. By definition, the working set consists of these pages. The Snapshot policy recolors one page from the set of pages that appear to conflict with other pages in the snapshot.

The Snapshot policy assumes that conflicting pages will continue to conflict long enough to justify recoloring. If conflicts are short-lived, the policy will recolor excessively. To confirm that a conflict is long-lived, the *Snapshot-Delay* policy takes a second "confirmation" snapshot after a specified delay time, and only recolors a page when it is found to conflict in both the original and confirmation snapshots. In Section 4.2, we will show that no one setting of the period and delay parameters satisfies all applications.

The periodic policies invoke the cache conflict detection mechanisms at a fixed rate, whether or not cache misses are occurring. This may lead to excessive recoloring when the cache miss rate is naturally low, or delayed conflict resolution when the cache miss rate is high. The *Snapshot-Miss* policy addresses these problems and can be used on systems that provide a register containing a count of cache misses. Snapshot-Miss is a variant of Snapshot-Delay in which the policy parameters are measured in cache misses rather than machine cycles. An interrupt is generated when the cache miss counter reaches a given threshold, at which point the policy takes a snapshot of the working set as described above. In effect, this policy uses the cache miss counter to determine *when* excessive cache misses are occurring, and only then monitors the TLB to determine if those misses are due to conflicts, and if so, where they are occurring.

Policy	Summary	Advantages	Disadvantages
Active-Naive	Recolor on every TLB miss to conflicting pages.	Detects all cache conflicts in mapped memory.	Excessive recoloring.
Active-Delay	Recolor after several TLB misses to conflicting pages.	Detects most persistent cache conflicts.	Excessive TLB overhead.
Active-Throttle	Recolor after several TLB misses to conflicting pages, but with a cap on the recoloring rate.	Bounded copy overhead.	Many conflicts may not be detected.
Periodic-Random	Periodically recolor a randomly selected page that appears in the TLB.	Repairs poor initial mappings.	Destroys good initial mappings.
Periodic-Color	Periodically recolor one of a set of pages that conflict and appear in the TLB.	Repairs poor initial mappings.	May recolor inactive pages.
Snapshot	Periodically flush the TLB. Recolor when two conflicting pages reappear in the TLB.	Recolors only active pages.	Recolors in response to short-lived conflicts.
Snapshot-Delay	Recolor when two pages conflict in two consecutive snapshots.	Recolors in response to persistent conflicts.	Difficult to determine good period and delay values.
Snapshot-Miss	Measure snapshot interval and length in cache misses rather than cycles.	Adapts to cache miss rate.	Requires cache miss counter.

Table 1: *Some dynamic page mapping policies. A poor mapping is one which results in excessive cache conflicts.*

3.3 Summary

Table 1 reviews the policies presented in this section, and summarizes some of their advantages and disadvantages. Although not shown in the table, all of the policies share two disadvantages. First, they may interpret pages on which there are no actual cache conflicts as conflicting. For example, suppose that physical pages P1 and P2 have the same color, and that both are being referenced by the CPU. Even if no reference to P1 actually conflicts with those to P2 (suppose that only the top half of P1 and only the bottom half of P2 are active), the policies may conclude that P1 and P2 conflict. Snapshot-Miss is the least likely to exhibit this behavior, because it only activates during periods of high cache miss activity. Nevertheless, all the software policies are subject to "spoofing" because they do not use information about actual cache misses, only apparent ones. A policy that relies on information about true memory traffic, that is, one that uses hardware to collect reference information, is unlikely to be similarly misled.

The second disadvantage of the software policies is that they are unable to resolve conflicts between mapped and unmapped pages. A system with a CML buffer can detect these conflicts because the CML buffer snoops on the memory bus, seeing misses to both mapped and unmapped pages. The operating system can then resolve these conflicts by recoloring the mapped page. Since unmapped pages do not appear in the TLB, the software approach cannot even detect that conflicts are occuring on these pages.

4 Simulation methodology and results

We use trace-driven simulation of ten benchmark programs described in Table 4 to evaluate the effectiveness of different dynamic policies. We will first describe our methodology and then will describe two groups of measurements. The first group compares all of the dynamic policies from Section 3. The second group compares the best of these policies to static and hardware-based policies.

4.1 Methodology

We collected our traces, which include user and system references, using epoxie [Wall 92] on a DECstation 5000/200 running Ultrix 4.2A. The simulated memory system, described in Table 2, is based on the DEC 3000/500 Alpha workstation [Dutton et al. 92], which contains an Alpha 21064 processor [Digital Equipment Corporation 92]. Memory references due to TLB misses are not traced directly, but are injected into the reference stream during the simulation. The simulated TLB miss handler includes any overhead incurred by the dynamic policies. The simulations assume infinite memory, and do not include paging effects. Additional information about our trace methodology can be found in [Bershad et al. 94].

Policy	Max recoloring rate	Delay
Active-Naive	Unbounded	None
Active-Delay	Unbounded	100 TLB misses
Active-Throttle	$1/(1 \times 10^6)$ cycles	100 TLB misses
Periodic-Random	$1/(2 \times 10^6)$ cycles	None
Periodic-Color	$1/(2 \times 10^6)$ cycles	None
Snapshot	$1/(2 \times 10^6)$ cycles	None
Snapshot-Delay	$1/(2 \times 10^6)$ cycles	200×10^3 cycles
Snapshot-Miss	$1/(10 \times 10^3)$ L2 misses	1×10^3 L2 misses

Table 3: *Parameters of simulated dynamic page mapping policies.*

Page size	8KB
Line size	32 bytes
First level cache (L1)	8KB Instruction, 8KB Data physically indexed direct-mapped
Policy	write-through, read-allocate
Write buffer	4 entries
Miss penalty	5 cycles
TLB	16-line ITLB, 32-line DTLB no "large" entries fully associative
Second level cache (L2)	512 KB, unified, physically indexed, direct-mapped
Policy	write-back, read/write-allocate
Miss penalty	25 cycles

Table 2: *The simulated memory system.*

Our primary evaluation metric is Memory Cycles Per Instruction (MCPI), which is the total number of cycles spent servicing cache misses, write buffer stalls, and memory management (including TLB misses and page mapping policy), divided by the number of user and system instructions (excluding memory management). References due to the operating system's idle loop are excluded, since the idle loop has good locality and artificially lowers MCPI. Since the first-level caches on the Alpha 21064 are each the same size as a page of physical memory, first-level cache performance is largely independent of the mapping policy. Hence we focus on memory cycles per instruction due to second level cache misses and memory management overhead (L2 plus Policy MCPI).

4.2 Evaluation of dynamic policies

We simulated static Page Coloring (the default Ultrix policy) alone, and combined with each of the dynamic policies described in Section 3. We used the parameters shown in Table 3 to drive the simulator for each policy. We selected parameter values that balanced conflict elimination with policy overhead. This resulted in values that were neither extremely large (too conservative) or extremely small (too aggressive).

Figure 1 shows the results of these measurements. The figure decomposes MCPI into L2, Recolor, and TLB MCPI. L2 MCPI is the actual memory penalty due to misses in the second level cache. If a policy has lower L2 MCPI than Page Coloring for a particular application, then the policy eliminates cache conflicts. Recolor MCPI is due to the actual copying of pages from one portion of physical memory to another. For example, Active-Naive, as expected, has a high recolor overhead. TLB MCPI reflects the TLB management penalty for the given policy. The dynamic policies have increased TLB MCPI compared to Page Coloring because they use the TLB to collect information about the current working set.

The three active policies perform worse than static Page Coloring for the workloads except for *strawman, doduc,* and *tomcatv*. Active-Delay and Active-Throttle eliminate some of the recolor overhead of Active-Naive, and reduce L2 MCPI for most of the benchmarks. However, they incur many additional TLB misses because the TLB is used to monitor the memory reference stream. The additional TLB overhead overwhelms the improvement in L2 MCPI. For example, both Active-Delay and Active-Throttle reduce the L2 MCPI of *gcc-a*, but degrade overall performance.

Periodic policies address the high overhead of the active policies by monitoring the TLB periodically rather than continuously. However, conflicts may persist for a longer time before resolution. This delay results in a larger L2 MCPI component than the active policies in some cases, most notably *strawman* and *tomcatv*. The figure shows that for most of the programs and with most of the periodic policies, the reduction in overhead compensates for the small increase in conflict misses.

Despite the reduced overhead, Periodic-Random and Periodic-Color still perform worse than Page Coloring in several cases, including *gcc-b*, *splot*, and *gs*. The problem with these policies is that some of the pages recolored are not currently active. Snapshot attempts to address this problem, and slightly outperforms both policies for six of the ten benchmarks. Snapshot-Delay further improves performance by re-

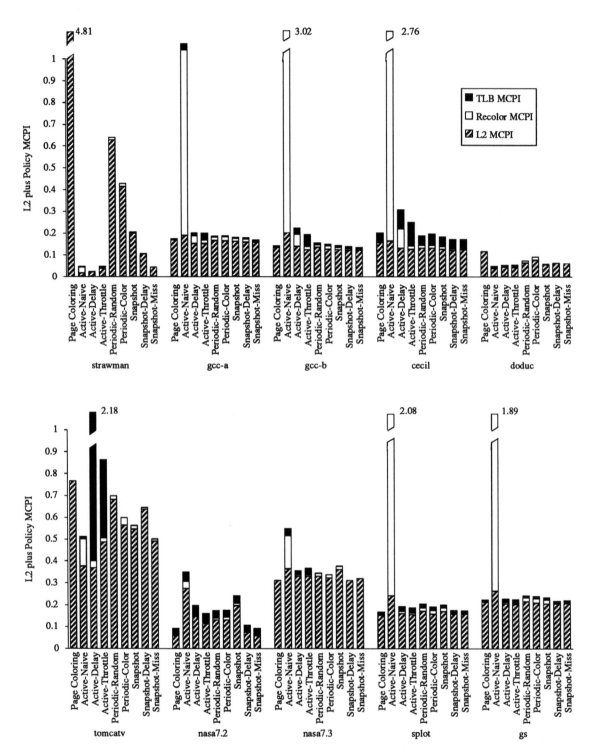

Figure 1: *Software-Based Dynamic Policies. This figure shows the impact that software-based dynamic page mapping policies have on second level cache performance. L2 MCPI is the cost of second level cache misses incurred by the application under the given policy. Recolor MCPI includes all cycles spent in dynamic page mapping policy code, including the instructions executed and cache misses incurred when recoloring pages. TLB MCPI includes all overhead due to TLB misses. Changes in TLB MCPI relative to Page Coloring reflect the overhead of software-based conflict detection.*

Benchmark	Description	Memory References (millions)	MCPI	L2 MCPI
strawman	a program that repeatedly alternates references to two conflicting cache-pages.	16	5.79	4.81
gcc-a	gcc compiling a 17 KB pre-processed program into Sun-3 assembly code.	41	0.81	0.17
gcc-b	gcc compiling a 149 KB program into Sun-3 assembly code.	279	0.50	0.13
cecil	a 6000-line unoptimized Cecil program, including the 20-queens problem, Towers of Hanoi, the game of Life, and compiler test code. (Cecil is a pure object oriented language being developed at the University of Washington [Chambers 93].)	248	0.56	0.16
doduc	Monte-Carlo simulation of the time evolution of a nuclear reactor component described by an 8K input file. (Fortran.)	368	0.38	0.12
tomcatv	a program that generates a vectorized mesh. (Fortran.)	278	1.09	0.77
nasa7.2	Fast fourier transform component of the SPEC Nasa7 floating point benchmark. (Fortran)	255	0.46	0.06
nasa7.3	Cholesky factorization. (Fortran)	128	0.79	0.31
splot	the X11 program splot run four times on four different input files. Total input file size is 94 KB.	259	0.99	0.15
gs	an X11 Postscript previewer on a 251 KB input file.	667	1.09	0.22

Table 4: *Experimental workloads. Memory references, MCPI, and L2 MCPI (MCPI due to second level cache misses) were measured on our simulated memory system when using static page coloring as the mapping policy. Most programs are written in C. Traces of gs and splot include client, X11 server, and operating system references.*

coloring only when a conflict persists. We were able to tune Snapshot-Delay to perform well for different applications, but there was no single set of parameter values that worked well for all of the benchmarks. The problem is best illustrated by considering *doduc* and *tomcatv*. Both applications incur conflict misses, but at very different rates. Using a short period will allow the policy to identify closely spaced conflicts in *tomcatv* but not to identify the relatively infrequent conflicts in *doduc*; using a long period in order to identify the widely spaced conflicts in *doduc* will cause many of the conflicts in *tomcatv* to remain unresolved. This leads us to conclude that elapsed time is not a good metric for determining when the dynamic policy should be activated.

The Snapshot-Miss policy uses the count of cache misses instead of elapsed time to determine when to take action. The policy is invoked quickly during periods of high cache miss activity, which is when it is needed. Moreover, the frequency with which it is invoked reflects the number cache misses and hence it can capture conflicts whether they show up frequently or infrequently. With a single setting of the parameters, the policy detects and resolves conflicts for both *doduc* and *tomcatv*. The figure shows that for all the benchmarks, Snapshot-Miss either outperforms or does as well as all the other software-based policies.

4.3 Software-based and hardware-based policies

We now compare the performance of a good software-based dynamic policy to alternative strategies for reducing conflicts. We measured the performance of the two static policies described in Section 2, Page Coloring and Bin Hopping, alone, combined with the Snapshot-Miss policy, combined with a policy based on a CML buffer (CML), and combined with a 2-way associative cache (A2). Figure 2 shows the results of these simulations. Comparing just the unaugmented static policies, we see that neither Bin Hopping nor Page Coloring performs best across all applications. For example, Page Coloring performs better for *nasa7.2* and *splot*, while Bin Hopping performs better for *doduc* and *tomcatv*. The difficulty in choosing the correct static policy is a key motivation for using a dynamic policy.

The dynamic policies and the associative cache outperform the static policies for the majority of programs because they can adjust to conflicts in the memory reference stream. While the three techniques differ in the cost of conflict resolution, the most important difference is the speed with which they identify and resolve conflicts. The associative cache resolves conflicts immediately with no direct cost[1] and has the best performance. The CML buffer incurs a small delay be-

---

[1] However, an associative cache may require an increased cache access time. For this discussion, we assume that the access time is unaffected by the increased associativity.

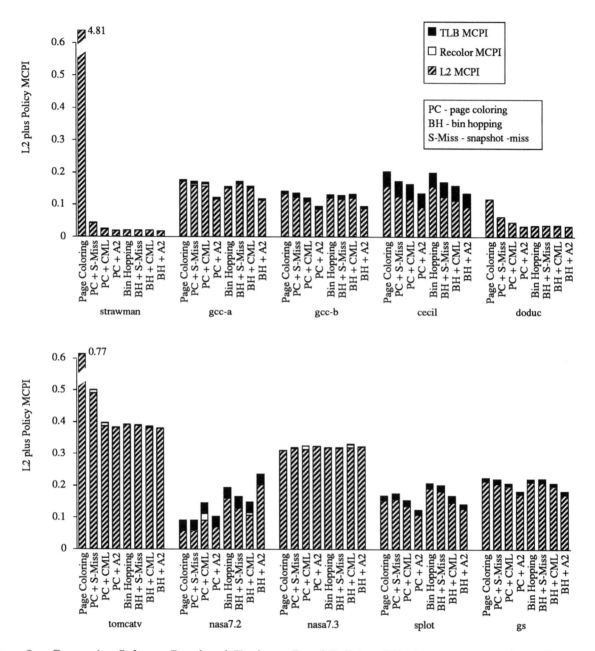

Figure 2: *Comparing Software-Based and Hardware-Based Policies. This figure compares the performance of software-based and hardware-based mapping policies. For each benchmark two sets of four policies are shown, one set based on Page Coloring and one based on Bin Hopping. CML is a policy based on a CML buffer. A2 is a two-way associative cache. The categories are as shown in Figure 1.*

fore recoloring a page and suffers from some conflict misses that would be resolved by the associative cache. Finally, the Snapshot-Miss policy may be delayed by as much as the snapshot interval (1,000 cache misses for the policy we simulated) and hence incurs conflict misses that would have been resolved by a CML buffer. As a result, for each static policy, performance is generally good for Snapshot-Miss, better for CML, and best for A2.

While most of the programs benefit from added associativity, *nasa7.2* and *nasa7.3* do not. For these programs, L2 MCPI is dominated by capacity and compulsory misses rather than conflict misses. As a result, they can perform worse with dynamic policies because capacity misses are misidentified as conflict misses, resulting in analysis and recoloring that pollute the cache and increase overhead.

4.4   Summary

The simulations showed that no one static policy works best, and that a dynamic policy based on software or a CML buffer can improve the performance of a static policy. The Snapshot-Miss policy approaches the performance of the CML buffer, and has the advantage that it can be implemented in existing systems that provide the appropriate mechanisms.

Although the dynamic policies can improve second level cache performance, this is only one component of overall execution time. Comparing the MCPI numbers in Table 4 to the L2 numbers in Figure 2, we see that the magnitude of the differences among different policies may not be very pronounced, and so end-to-end execution time may not be significantly affected except in cases of pathological mappings. As the penalty for accessing memory increases, the value of eliminating conflicts will also increase.

5   Implementation and performance

In this section, we describe the implementation and performance of the Snapshot-Miss policy on a DEC Alpha workstation running Version 2.0 of the DEC OSF/1 operating system. The Alpha provides sufficient support for a software-based dynamic mapping policy in the form of cache miss counters and software-filled TLBs. The cache miss counters can be configured to deliver an interrupt to the processor after every 4,096 misses to the second level cache[2]. Our implementation of Snapshot-Miss operates as follows: every 32,768 misses, two snapshots are collected, separated in time by 4,096 misses. A snapshot is collected by

---

[2]The Alpha cache miss register operates at a granularity of 4,096 misses, which is the same order of magnitude as the delay setting of 1,000 misses from our simulations of Snapshot-Miss.

flushing the TLB and recording the first 16 pages to incur TLB misses. If two or more pages conflict in both the first and second snapshots, one of the pages is recolored.

The implementation required minimal changes to the vendor's operating system. The policy code is contained in a module devoted to analyzing the snapshots and deciding which page, if any, to recolor. Conflict detection is triggered by a cache miss counter interrupt, which required that we define a simple interrupt handler to initiate a snapshot. A modified TLB miss handler collects the snapshots during periods of high cache miss rates. The implementation complexity and overhead of the dynamic policy is summarized in Table 5.

Operation	Avg. Cost	Code Size
Deliver cache miss counter interrupt	70 cycles	20 lines of C
Determine whether to record TLB miss	6.5 cycles	4 PAL instructions
Record TLB miss	10 cycles	10 PAL instructions
Analyze TLB miss info	11,000 cycles	200 lines of C
Recolor page and update page tables	29,000 cycles	30 lines of C

Table 5: *Dynamic Policy Operations. The cost of delivering cache miss counter interrupts was estimated by comparing the execution time of programs with cache miss counter interrupts enabled and then disabled. The other overheads were measured with the Alpha cycle counter. On the Alpha, TLB misses are handled in PAL code, which is essentially programmable microcode.*

5.1   Performance

We measured the performance of the two static mapping policies described earlier: Page Coloring and Bin Hopping (the policy that ships with DEC OSF/1 [Woodman 94]). We then augmented those basic policies with the Snapshot-Miss policy. We first describe the effect on a synthetic benchmark that is poorly served by static mapping policies. We then describe the end-to-end performance of several applications. The trends reflected by our measured end-to-end times are not always consistent with our simulations, which focus only on second level cache behavior. Moreover, our simulations rely on traces from the MIPS architecture, which can introduce differences in the trends.

A synthetic workload

The program *stab* is a symbol table library that uses a standard shared library routine to compute a hash function. This code is drawn from the Cecil compiler [Chambers 93]. If the shared library code and the calling routine are mapped to the same cache page and are linked at overlapping page offsets within the page, performance will suffer. In this case, with a static policy, the program executes in 18.3 seconds, whereas with Snapshot-Miss, execution time drops to 9.0 seconds. With a non-conflicting initial mapping, execution time is 8.6 seconds. This synthetic benchmark represents a worst-case scenario, with conflicts that static policies cannot avoid. For this benchmark, the relative location in the virtual address space of the pages in conflict is arbitrary, and the time separating page frame allocations for the conflicting pages is large. As such, the assumptions about relative spatial and temporal distance between pages in the same working set do not hold, and the mappings created by Bin Hopping and Page Coloring are essentially random. The dynamic policy serves to correct those poor mapping choices which are impossible for the static policy to avoid.

Application workloads

We measured a subset of the applications presented in the Section 4 to evaluate end-to-end performance. The workloads, together with elapsed execution times, are described in Table 6 along with relative improvements and overheads. The differences between the policies are due to the difference in page mapping and, in the case of the dynamic policies, the overhead due to monitoring the TLB and recoloring pages. The first only affects the performance of the L2 cache, while the second only increases execution time. Thus any improvement in execution time with the dynamic policies can be attributed to fewer conflict misses in the L2 cache.

The table shows that no one static policy performs best for all the benchmarks. Bin Hopping does better than Page Coloring for four of the eight benchmarks (*gcc1*, *tomcatv*, *gs*, and *mpeg*), but Page Coloring outperforms Bin Hopping for *doduc*, *nasa7.3*, and *nasa7.6*. Both policies do about the same for *nasa7.2*. The dynamic policy had only a small effect on overall performance for *mpeg*, *gs*, and *gcc1*. In three cases (*doduc* with Bin Hopping, *tomcatv* with Page Coloring and *nasa7.6* with Bin Hopping) the dynamic policy improves execution time by removing conflicts. However, *nasa7.2* and *nasa7.3* are slowed down by the dynamic policy. These programs have a working set much larger than the second level cache. The result is that the dynamic policy is invoked frequently in response to capacity misses, and the interrupt handler and policy

software pollute the cache, degrading performance.

5.2 Summary

Our implementation of Snapshot-Miss for the DEC Alpha workstation shows that it is possible to implement a dynamic page mapping policy that has low overhead for most applications. The policy has measurable and sometimes significant performance benefits when a mismatch occurs between the static policy used for the initial page mapping and the reference patterns of the application. In essence, the dynamic policy helps to recover from "mistakes" made by the initial (static) policy. Snapshot-Miss is useful for reducing variability between program executions, making it a viable alternative for system designers who wish to avoid the pathological behavior that can occur with static policies but do not want the variations in execution time that a random policy tends to cause.

6 Conclusion

Dynamic page mapping policies attempt to improve application performance by detecting and removing conflicts in a large physically indexed cache. We compared static mapping policies to dynamic policies that used hardware available on existing systems. We found that a policy that uses a cache miss counter to detect when conflicts are a problem and the TLB to determine the location of these conflicts improves performance in several cases. Performance is most improved when this accounting function is performed by specialized hardware such as a CML buffer. As the performance disparity between the CPU and memory increases, resulting in larger on-chip caches and greater off-chip miss penalties, we expect that mechanisms that can dynamically adapt to a program's cache access patterns will become increasingly important.

Acknowledgments

We could not have completed this project without the support of the people at DEC WRL. Alan Eustace of DEC WRL provided invaluable assistance throughout the course of implementing the dynamic software policy on the DEC Alpha workstations. Marc Fiuczynski helped us understand the networking code in DEC OSF/1. Jeffrey Dean, Anthony LaMarca, David Grove, Larry Peterson, and Wayne Wong offered suggestions on an early draft of this paper.

References

[Bershad et al. 94] Bershad, B. N., Chen, J. B., Lee, D., and Romer, T. H. Avoiding Cache Misses Dynamically in Large Direct-Mapped Caches. In *Proc. 6th International Conference on Architectural Support for*

Bench-mark	Description	Page Coloring							Bin Hopping						
		Static		Dynamic					Static		Dynamic				
		time	σ	time	σ	improve-ment	over-head	recolors	time	σ	time	σ	improve-ment	over-head	recolors
gcc1	The full gcc1 SPEC benchmark.	112,079	128	112,388	319	-0.3%	135	143	111,548	75	111,335	158	0.2%	103	60
doduc	Nuclear reactor simulation.	23,160	210	23,077	119	0.4%	8	9	23,986	1	23,093	157	3.7%	8	7
tomcatv	The full tomcatv SPEC benchmark.	33,339	6	26,380	53	20.9%	220	345	25,071	24	25,368	32	-1.2%	185	111
nasa7.2	Fast fourier transform.	26,913	3	27,457	344	-2.0%	33	15	26,912	5	28,296	853	-5.1%	63	35
nasa7.3	Cholesky factorization.	31,571	49	32,540	125	-3.1%	142	55	31,651	3	32,748	162	-3.5%	139	34
nasa7.6	Matrix manipulation.	6,900	11	6,906	21	-0.1%	4	2	7,301	4	6,954	36	4.7%	5	6
gs	ghostscript with a 363 KB input file.	23,236	173	23,109	60	0.5%	20	11	23,188	139	23,017	127	0.7%	19	10
mpeg	mpeg_play with a 217 KB input file.	18,958	591	18,698	409	1.4%	27	19	17,990	117	17,929	114	0.3%	18	5

Table 6: *Static vs. Dynamic Policies. This table shows performance for Page Coloring and for the native OSF/1 mapping policy (Bin Hopping), each with and without a dynamic mapping policy. The programs mpeg and gs displays images through the X11 server. The columns labeled time and σ show the mean and standard deviation of the execution time for five runs in milliseconds. The improvement column shows the percentage improvement of the dynamic policy over the static policy. The overhead column shows the time attributed to dynamic policy overhead in milliseconds. The recolors column shows the total number of pages recolored.*

Programming Languages and Operating Systems, pages 158–170. ACM, 1994.

[Chaiken & Agarwal 94] Chaiken, D. and Agarwal, A. Software-Extended Coherent Shared Memory: Performance and Cost. In *Proc. 21st International Symposium on Computer Architecture*, pages 314–324. IEEE, 1994.

[Chambers 93] Chambers, C. The Cecil Language: Specification and Rationale. Technical Report 93-03-05, University of Washington, March 1993.

[Chen 94] Chen, J. B. Memory Behavior For An X11 Window System. In *Proc. Winter 1994 USENIX Conference*, pages 189–200, January 1994.

[Chiueh & Katz 92] Chiueh, T. and Katz, R. H. Eliminating the Address Translation Bottleneck for Physical Address Cache. In *Proc. 5th International Conference on Architectural Support for Programming Languages and Operating Systems*, pages 137–148. ACM, 1992.

[Digital Equipment Corporation 92] Digital Equipment Corporation. *DECchip 21064-AA Microprocessor, Hardware Reference Manual*, 1992. Order Number: EC-N0079-72.

[Dutton et al. 92] Dutton, T., Eiref, D., Kurth, H., Reisert, J., and Stewart, R. The Design Of The DEC 3000 AXP Systems, Two High-Performance Workstations. *Digital Technical Journal*, 4(4):66–81, 1992. Special Issue.

[Glew & Wang 94] Glew, A. and Wang, W. Personal communication, 1994.

[Hill 87] Hill, M. D. *Aspects of Cache Memory and Instruction Buffer Performance*. PhD dissertation, University of California at Berkeley, Computer Sciences Division, November 1987. Number UCB/CSD 87/381.

[Hosking & Moss 93] Hosking, A. L. and Moss, J. E. B. Protection Traps and Alternatives for Memory Management of an Object Oriented Language. In *Proc. 14th ACM Symposium on Operating System Principles*, pages 106–119. ACM, December 1993.

[Kane 88] Kane, G. *MIPS RISC Architecture*. Prentice-Hall, Englewood Cliffs, NJ, 1988.

[Kessler & Hill 92] Kessler, R. and Hill, M. D. Page Placement Algorithms for Large Real-Indexed Caches. *ACM Transactions on Computer Systems*, 10(4), November 1992.

[Lynch 93] Lynch, W. L. *The Interaction of Virtual Memory and Cache Memory*. PhD dissertation, Computer Systems Laboratory, Stanford University, November 1993. Technical Report CSL-TR-93-587.

[Mogul & Borg 91] Mogul, J. C. and Borg, A. The Effect Of Context Switches On Cache Performance. In *Proc. 4th International Conference On Architectural Support For Programming Languages And Operating Systems*, pages 75–84, April 1991.

[Shippy 94] Shippy, D. The Power2+ Processor. In *Symposium Record, Hot Chips VI*, pages 9–18. IBM, August 1994. Slides.

[Singhal & Goldberg 94] Singhal, A. and Goldberg, A. J. Architectural Support for Performance Tuning: A Case Study on the SPARCcenter 2000. In *Proc.*

21st International Symposium on Computer Architecture, pages 48–59. IEEE, 1994.

[Wahbe et al. 93] Wahbe, R., Lucco, S., Anderson, T. E., and Graham, S. L. Efficient Software-Based Fault Isolation. In *Proc. 14th ACM Symposium on Operating Systems Principles*, pages 203–216. ACM, 1993.

[Wall 92] Wall, D. W. *Systems for Late Code Modification*, pages 275–293. Springer-Verlag, 1992.

[Woodman 94] Woodman, L. Personal communication, 1994.

Cooperative Caching: Using Remote Client Memory to Improve File System Performance

Michael D. Dahlin, Randolph Y. Wang, Thomas E. Anderson,
David A. Patterson

University of California at Berkeley
{dahlin, rywang, tea, patterson}@cs.berkeley.edu

Abstract

Emerging high-speed networks will allow machines to access remote data nearly as quickly as they can access local data. This trend motivates the use of *cooperative caching*: coordinating the file caches of many machines distributed on a LAN to form a more effective overall file cache. In this paper we examine four cooperative caching algorithms using a trace-driven simulation study. These simulations indicate that for the systems studied cooperative caching can halve the number of disk accesses, improving file system read response time by as much as 73%. Based on these simulations we conclude that cooperative caching can significantly improve file system read response time and that relatively simple cooperative caching algorithms are sufficient to realize most of the potential performance gain.

1. Introduction

Cooperative caching seeks to improve network file system performance by coordinating the contents of client caches and allowing requests not satisfied by a client's local in-memory file cache to be satisfied by the cache of another client.

Two technology trends push us to consider cooperative caching. First, processor performance is increasing much more rapidly than disk performance. This divergence makes it increasingly important to reduce the number of disk accesses by the file system. Second, emerging high-speed low-latency switched networks can supply file system blocks across the network much faster than standard Ethernet as indicated in Figure 1. Where fetching data from remote memory over an older network might be only three times faster than getting the data from remote disk, remote memory may now be accessed ten to twenty times as quickly as disk, increasing the payoff for cooperative caching.

Existing file systems use a three-level memory hierarchy, implementing a limited form of "cooperative caching" by locating a shared cache in server memory to supplement the other two memory levels, client memory and server disk. Although we can often reduce disk accesses by increasing the fraction of the system's RAM that resides in the server, four factors make cooperative caching more attractive than physically moving memory from clients to the server. First, cooperative caching can provide better performance: although either approach can improve the global hit rate and thus reduce the system's disk accesses, cooperative caching leaves large memories at the clients and so can also maintain high hit rates in the clients' local caches, saving network latencies compared to going to the server. Second, the server in the cooperative caching system will be less loaded since it can satisfy

	Ethernet		155 Mbit/s ATM	
	Remote Memory	**Remote Disk**	**Remote Memory**	**Remote Disk**
Mem. Copy	250 μs	250 μs	250 μs	250 μs
Net Overhead	400 μs	400 μs	400 μs	400 μs
Data	6250 μs	6250 μs	400 μs	400 μs
Disk	--	14,800 μs	--	14,800 μs
Total	**6,900** μs	**21,700** μs	**1050** μs	**15,850** μs

Figure 1. Time to service a file system local cache miss from remote memory or disk for a slow network, *Ethernet*, and a faster network, *155 MBit/s ATM*. Local memory copy time is the measured time to read 8 KB from the file cache on a DEC AXP 3000/400. Network overhead times indicate round trip small packet latencies based on TCP times reported in [Mart94] for a Hewlett-Packard 9000/735 workstation. Ethernet data transfer figures makes the unrealistically optimistic assumption that data is transferred at the full 10 Mbit/s link speed (in reality, transfer times would likely be at least double those listed above for unswitched Ethernet). The ATM transfer time assumes the full 155 Mbit/s bandwidth is attained (also an optimistic assumption, but one likely to be met in a year or two as processor speeds continue to increase.) The disk transfer time is based on measured physical disk time (excluding queueing) for the fastest of three systems measured under real workloads by Ruemmler and Wilkes [Ruem93].

This work is supported in part by the Advanced Research Projects Agency (N00600-93-C-2481), the National Science Foundation (CDA 8722788), California MICRO, the AT&T Foundation, Digital Equipment Corporation, Hewlett Packard, Siemens Corporation, Sun Microsystems, and Xerox Corporation. Dahlin was also supported under a National Science Foundation Graduate Research Fellowship. Anderson was also supported by a National Science Foundation Young Investigator Award.

many requests with small packets to forward requests rather than large data transfers. Third, cooperative caching allows more flexible use of memory: since the memory is still physically located at the clients, it can also be used for client virtual memory as system demands warrant [Nels88]. Finally, cooperative cache systems are more cost effective than building a system with an extremely large server cache. For example, it would be significantly cheaper to add 16 MB of industry-standard SIMM memory to each of one hundred clients than it would be to buy a specialized server machine capable of holding the additional 1.6 GB of memory. We quantify the trade-offs between centralized and distributed memory in more detail at the end of Section 4.

Cooperative caching introduces a fourth level in the network file system's cache hierarchy. Not only can data be found in local memory, in server memory, or on server disk, but it can also be found in another client's memory. Depending on the cooperative caching algorithm used, this new level may be found between a client's local memory and the server memory or between the server memory and the disk. Note that we are examining cooperative caching assuming that clients cache file system data in their local memories but not on their local disks. For the fast networks of the future, it will be much faster for a client to fetch data from another client's memory than to fetch that data from local disk.

In this paper we make the assumption that all clients in the system are equally secure. We believe this to be a fair assumption in most LAN environments where all machines are administered in the same way. Our trust is no stronger than that given to clients in currently popular file systems like NFS; in either case, if the client's operating system is compromised, the client can issue unauthorized file system requests. The increasing availability of process migration among networks of workstations [Nich87, Doug91, Litz92, Zhou93] is likely to speed the trend towards trust within an administrative domain—if a system allows a user's jobs to be migrated among machines, that user's data may be cached in the memories of many machines regardless of cooperative caching.

This study has two goals. Our first goal is to ascertain whether cooperative caching can provide significant benefits under real workloads. Our trace-driven simulation approach contrasts with previous efforts to evaluate cooperative caching using synthetic workloads [Leff93a, Fran92]. Our second goal is to evaluate a range of algorithms to find practical algorithms to implement effective cooperative caching. Previous studies have focused on algorithms requiring global knowledge of client cache contents [Leff93a] or on algorithms that sacrifice performance by not coordinating the contents of client caches [Fran92].

Our primary result is that cooperative caching can improve file read performance by as much as 73% for the configurations and workloads studied. We further conclude that an algorithm called *N-Chance Forwarding* is a practical algorithm that achieves nearly all of the potential performance gains for these workloads.

Cooperative caching is designed to improve cache performance for file system reads. This technique does not address issues such as write performance and large file performance that are also important to end users of the file system. To study these and other issues, we are implementing cooperative caching as a part of the xFS project [Wang93, Dahl94]. Cooperative caching illustrates a primary design philosophy of xFS, the use of the vast aggregate resources of the system's clients to improve performance.

Section 2 describes the four cooperative caching algorithms we examine. Section 3 describes our simulation methodology and Section 4 examines our simulation results. We compare our work to previous efforts to improve file cache performance in Section 5. Finally, Section 6 summarizes our conclusions.

2. Cooperative Caching Algorithms

This paper examines four variations of cooperative caching in detail, covering a range of algorithm design decisions. Cooperative caching creates a new level in the file system storage hierarchy: remote client memory. Different cooperative caching algorithms could manage this new level in many different ways. Figure 2 illustrates four fundamental design questions and the relationship of the four algorithms to these questions. Although the algorithms we examine are by no means an exhaustive set of

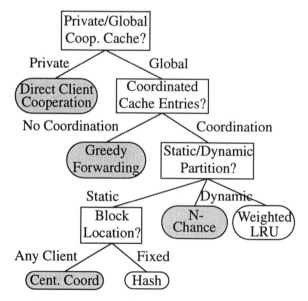

Figure 2. Cooperative caching algorithm design space. Each box represents a design decision while each oval represents an algorithm examined in this study. We focus on the four highlighted algorithms and do not consider the other two in detail due to space constraints.

cooperative caching algorithms, the subset contains representative examples from large portion of the design space and includes a practical algorithm with close to optimal performance.

Note that the algorithms examined do not affect data storage reliability since they do not alter the write-through, write-delay, or write-back policy of the file system. Clients still send modified data to the server when they would have without cooperative caching, and the server commits data to disk as it would in a traditional system.

The rest of this section describes the four algorithms under scrutiny and then briefly discusses two other algorithms.

2.1. Direct Client Cooperation

A very simple cooperative caching approach, *Direct Client Cooperation,* allows an active client to use an idle client's memory as backing store. The active client forwards cache entries that overflow its local cache directly to an idle machine. The active client can then access this private remote cache to satisfy its read requests until the remote machine becomes active and evicts the cooperative cache. The system must define criteria for designating active and idle clients and must provide a mechanism for the former to locate the latter.

Direct Client Cooperation is appealing because of its simplicity—it can be implemented without server modification. As far as the server is concerned, a client utilizing remote memory appears to have a temporarily enlarged local cache. A drawback of this lack of server coordination is that active clients do not benefit from the contents of other active clients' memories. A client's data request must go to disk if the desired block no longer happens to be in the limited server memory even if another client is caching that block. As a result, the performance benefits of Direct Client Cooperation are limited, motivating the next algorithm.

2.2. Greedy Forwarding

Another simple cooperative caching approach, called *Greedy Forwarding,* treats the cache memories of all clients in the system as a global resource that may be accessed to satisfy any client's request, but the algorithm does not attempt to coordinate the contents of these caches. As for traditional file systems, each client manages its local cache greedily, without regard to the contents of the other caches in the system or the potential needs of other clients. If a client does not find a block in its local cache, it asks the server for the data. If the server has the required data in its memory cache, it supplies the data. Otherwise, the server consults a data structure listing the contents of the client caches. If any client is caching the required data, the server forwards the request to that client. The client receiving the forwarded request sends the data directly to the client that made the request. Note that the block is not sent back through the server since that would

unnecessarily increase latency and add to the server's workload. If no client is caching the data, the request is satisfied by the server disk as it would have been if there were no cooperative caching.

With Greedy Forwarding the only change to the file system is that the server needs to be able to forward requests and the clients need to be able to handle forwarded requests; this support is also needed by the next two algorithms discussed. This server forwarding can be implemented with the data structures already present in systems implementing write-consistency with call backs [Howa88] or cache disabling [Nels88]. In those systems the server tracks the files being cached by each client so that it can take appropriate action to guarantee consistency when a file is modified. In this study we assume that cooperative caching extends a call back data structure to track the individual file blocks cached by each client to allow forwarding. For systems such as NFS whose servers do not maintain precise information about what clients are caching [Sand85], implementation of this directory may be simplified if its contents are taken as hints; some forwarded requests may be sent to clients no longer caching the desired block. In that case the client would inform the server of the mistake and the server would either forward the request to another client or get the data from disk.

Although the per-block forwarding table is larger than traditional per-file callback lists, the additional server memory overhead is reasonable since each entry allows the server to leverage a block of client cache. For instance, if the forwarding table is implemented as a hash table with each hash entry containing a four byte file identifier, a four byte block offset, a four byte client identifier, a four byte pointer for linked-list collision resolution, and two four byte pointers for a doubly linked LRU list, the server would require 24 bytes for every block of client cache. For a system caching 8 KB file blocks, such a data structure would consume 0.3% as much memory as it indexes. For a system with 64 clients each with 32 MB of cache, the server could track the contents of the 2 GB distributed cache with a 6 MB index.

Greedy Forwarding is also appealing because it preserves fairness—clients manage their local resources for their local good while still deriving benefit from the other clients. On the other hand, this lack of coordination among cache contents may cause unnecessary data duplication, not taking the best advantage of the system's memory to avoid disk accesses [Leff91, Fran92]. The next two algorithms attempt to address this lack of coordination.

2.3. Centrally Coordinated Caching

Centrally Coordinated Caching adds coordination to the Greedy Forwarding algorithm by statically partitioning each client's cache into a locally managed section, managed greedily by that client, and a globally managed section, coordinated by the server as an extension of its central cache. If a client does not find a block in its locally managed cache, it sends the request to the server. If the server has the desired data in memory, it supplies the data. Otherwise the server checks to see if it has stored the block in centrally coordinated client memory. If it locates the data in client memory, it forwards the request to the client storing the data. If all else fails, the server supplies the data from disk.

Centrally Coordinated Caching behaves very much like physically moving memory from the clients to the server. The server manages the globally managed fraction of each client's cache using a global replacement algorithm. When the server evicts a block from its local cache to make room for data fetched from disk, it sends the victim block to replace the least recently used block among all of the blocks in the centrally coordinated distributed cache. When the server forwards a client request to a distributed cache entry, it renews the entry on its LRU list for the global distributed cache. Unless otherwise noted we simulate a policy where the server manages 80% of each client's cache.

The primary advantage of Centrally Coordinated Caching is the high global hit rate that it can achieve through global management of the bulk of its memory resources. The main drawbacks to this approach are that the clients' local hit rates may be reduced since their local caches are effectively made smaller and also that the central coordination may impose significant load on the server.

2.4. N-Chance Forwarding

The final algorithm that we quantitatively evaluate, *N-Chance Forwarding*, dynamically adjusts the fraction of each client's cache managed cooperatively, depending on client activity. The N-Chance algorithm modifies the Greedy Forwarding algorithm to have clients cooperate to preferentially cache *singlets*, blocks stored in only one client cache. Except for singlets, N-Chance Forwarding works like Greedy Forwarding.

N-Chance Forwarding attempts to avoid discarding singlets from client memory. When a client discards a block, it checks to see if that block is the last copy cached by any client. This check may require a message to the server or it may be done by consulting some flags associated with each block as described below. If the block is a singlet, rather than throw the block away, the client sets the block's *recirculation count* to n, forwards the data to a random peer, and then sends the server a message telling it that the block has moved. The peer that receives the data adds the block to its LRU list as if the block had been recently referenced. If a recirculating block reaches the end of the LRU list, its count is decremented and it is forwarded again unless the count is now zero, in which case it is simply discarded. If a client references a singlet, it resets the block's recirculation count and caches the data normally while the client that had been cooperatively caching the singlet discards the block from its cache.

The parameter n indicates how many times a singlet should be allowed to recirculate through different clients' LRU lists without being referenced before finally being discarded. Greedy forwarding is simply the degenerate case of this algorithm with $n = 0$. Unless otherwise noted we use $n = 2$ for our simulations.

This algorithm provides a dynamic trade-off for each client cache's allocation between local data, data being cached because the client referenced it, and global data, singlets being cached for the good of aggregate system performance. Active clients will tend to force any global data sent to them out of their caches quickly as local references displace global data. Idle clients will tend to accumulate global blocks and hold them in memory for long periods of time. An enhancement to this algorithm might be to preferentially forward singlets to idle clients to avoid disturbing active clients. For this study, however, clients forward singlets uniformly randomly to the other clients in the system.

An implementation of this algorithm must prevent a ripple effect where a block forwarded from one client displaces a block to another client and so on. Note that in the common case, the displaced block is not the last copy of data and so no ripple occurs, however we simulate a policy that prevents deep recursion from ever occurring: a client receiving a recirculating block is not allowed to forward a block to make space. When a client receives such a block, it uses a modified replacement algorithm, discarding its oldest duplicated block. If the cache contains no duplicated blocks, the client discards the oldest recirculating block with the fewest recirculations remaining.

Several optimizations to this algorithm reduce the amount of communication with the server. First, on a cache miss, the client combines its messages to the server, updating the server's directory of client cache contents in the same message that requests data to satisfy the miss. This update indicates what block the client has discarded from its cache and where, if anywhere, that block has been forwarded.

The second set of optimizations reduces the number of messages asking the server if a block is the last cached copy when a client is deciding if a block should be recirculated or discarded. First, any block whose recirculation count is set must be a singlet, so no server message is necessary to decide its fate. For non-recirculating blocks, the client must usually send a message to the server, but once it has determined if the block is a singlet the client will discard or forward it, so only one message is needed during a block's lifetime in a cache. In the special case where the client is making space for a singlet that was kicked out of another client's cache, it will not discard blocks that it discovers to be singlets, but it will mark those blocks as singlets (without setting the recirculation count) so that it will not need to ask the server again unless another client references the block. If another client references such a block, the server forwards the request to the singlet, and the client resets the singlet flag.

The main advantage of N-Chance Forwarding is that it provides a simple dynamic trade-off between each client's private cache data and the data being cached for the good of the overall system. Favoring singlets provides better performance than the simple Greedy algorithm since discarding a singlet is potentially more expensive than discarding a duplicated block; later references to the duplicate can still be satisfied from another client's memory [Leff91]. A potential disadvantage of this approach is that a given block may be bounced among multiple caches while living in the "cooperative" portion of the caches, resulting in unnecessary system load.

2.5. Other Algorithms

We considered two other cooperative caching algorithms. Performance measurements for these algorithms are omitted from this report because each performed similarly to one of the other algorithms we examined.

Hash-Distributed Caching differs from Centrally Coordinated Caching in that Hash-Distributed Caching partitions the centrally managed cache based on block identifiers, with each client managing one partition of the cache. The central server sends blocks displaced from its local cache to a client selected by hashing on the block's identifier. On a local miss a client accesses this distributed cache by sending its request directly to the appropriate client. That client supplies the data if it is currently caching that block, or forwards the request to the server if it does not have that block. Our simulations indicate that Hash-Distributed caching provides nearly identical hit rates compared to Centrally Coordinated caching; fixed partitioning of the centrally managed cache does not hurt the hit rate. The main advantage of Hash-Distributed caching over Centrally Coordinated Caching is that Hash-Distributed caching significantly reduces server load since many requests satisfied by the cooperative cache don't go through the server.

We also examined *Weighted LRU*, a dynamic algorithm that attempts to replace the object with the globally lowest value/cost ratio. As with N-Chance, objects that are duplicated in multiple client caches are not very valuable since even if one copy is discarded, the data may be fetched from another client's memory. On the other hand the last cached copy of a block is very valuable since its loss might cause a disk access. The opportunity cost of keeping an object in memory is the cache space it consumes until the next time the block is referenced [Smit81], approximately the time since the last reference. Thus, weighted LRU explicitly balances keeping frequently used duplicates to avoid network accesses against keeping less frequently used singlets to avoid disk accesses. For our traces, however, response time was slightly worse than for the substantially simpler N-Chance Forwarding.

3. Simulation Methodology

We use trace-driven simulation to evaluate the cooperative caching algorithms. Our simulator tracks the state of all caches in the system and monitors the requests and hit rates seen by each client. We assume a cache block size of 8 KB, and we do not allow partial blocks to be allocated even for files smaller than 8 KB. We verified our simulator by using the synthetic workload described in [Leff93a] as input.

We calculate response times by multiplying the local memory, remote client memory, server memory, and disk hit rates by the times it takes to access those memories. Our baseline technology assumptions are the same as for the 155 Mbit/s ATM columns of Figure 1, that an 8 KB block can be fetched from local memory in 250 μs, that a fetch from remote memory takes an additional 400 μs plus 200 μs per network hop, and that an average disk access takes a further 14,800 μs. Figure 3 summarizes access times to different resources for the algorithms. In Section 4.3 we examine the sensitivity of our results to technology changes. Note that we do not include any queueing delays in our response time figures. Since the most attractive algorithms studied do not increase server load and since emerging high performance networks use a switched topology, we would not expect queueing to significantly alter our results.

To maintain data consistency on writes, we assume that data modifications are written through to the central server and that client caches are kept consistent using a write-invalidate protocol [Arch86]. Since we focus on read performance, a delayed write or write back policy would not affect our results.

For most of the results in this paper, we use traces five and six from the Sprite workload, described in detail by Baker et al. [Bake91]. The Sprite user community included about 30 full time and 40 part time users of the system. These users included operating systems researchers, computer architecture researchers, VLSI designers, and "others" including administrative staff and graphics

	Local Mem.	Remote Client Mem.	Server Mem.	Server Disk
Direct	250 μs	1050 μs	1050 μs	15,850 μs
Greedy	250 μs	1250 μs	1050 μs	15,850 μs
Central	250 μs	1250 μs	1050 μs	15,850 μs
N-Chance	250 μs	1250 μs	1050 μs	15,850 μs

Figure 3. Access times for the different levels in the memory hierarchy for different cooperative caching algorithms. The differences among the Remote Client times for the different algorithms depends on the number of network hops to reach the data for the algorithm.

researchers. These traces list the activity of 42 client machines and one server over a two day period measured under the Sprite operating system.[1] They contain over 700,000 read and write block accesses, and we use the first 400,000 accesses (a little over a day) to warm the simulated caches. Section 4.4 describes simulation results for an additional workload.

When reporting our results, we compare against a set of baseline cache management assumptions and against an unrealistic best case model. The *base case* assumes that each client has a cache and that the central server also has a cache, but that no cooperative caching is used. The unrealizable *best case* assumes that the cooperative caching algorithm is able to achieve a global hit rate as high as if all client memory were managed as a single global cache, but that the local hit rates are as if all client memory were managed as a private local cache. This best case provides a lower bound for the response time for cooperative caching algorithms that physically distribute client memory equally to each client and that use LRU replacement. We simulate this algorithm by doubling each client's local cache and allowing the clients to manage half of it locally and allowing the server to manage half of it globally as it does for the centrally coordinated case. For the best case we assume that data found in remote client memory is fetched with three network hops (request, forward, and reply) for a total of 1250 μs per remote memory hit.

4. Simulation Results

This section presents the main results from our simulation studies of cooperative caching. Section 4.1 compares the different cooperative caching algorithms to the base case, to each other, and to the unrealizable best case. For clarity, this comparison is made assuming a particular set of parameters for each algorithm, for a given set of technology and memory assumptions, and under a single workload. Section 4.2 examines the individual algorithms more closely, studying different values for the algorithms' parameters. Section 4.3 examines the sensitivity of our results to technology and memory assumptions such as the client cache size, server cache size, and hardware performance. Section 4.4 examines the algorithms under an additional workload. Finally, Section 4.5 summarizes our results, highlights our conclusions, and compares cooperative caching to moving more of the system's memory to the server.

4.1. Comparison of Algorithms

This section compares the algorithms' response times, hit rates, server loads, and impact on individual clients. Our initial comparison of the algorithms fixes the client caches to be 16 MB per client and fixes the server cache to be 128 MB for the Sprite workload. For the Direct Cooperation algorithm we made the optimistic assumption that

clients do not interfere with each other when they use remote caches; we simulate this assumption by allowing each client to maintain a permanent remote cache of a size equal to its local memory size, effectively doubling the size of each client's cache. For the Central Coordination algorithm, we assume that 80% of each client's cache memory is dedicated to the cooperative cache and that 20% is managed locally. For the N-Chance algorithm, we choose a recirculation count of two; unreferenced data will be passed to two random caches before being purged from memory. We will examine why these are appropriate parameters in Section 4.2.

Figure 4 illustrates the response times for each of the four algorithms being examined and compares these times to the base case on the left and the best case on the right. Direct Cooperation provides only a small speedup of 1.05[2] compared to the base case despite our optimistic assumptions for this algorithm. Greedy Forwarding shows a modest but significant performance gain, with a speedup of 1.22. The two algorithms that coordinate cache contents to reduce redundant cache entries show more impressive gains. Central Coordination provides a speedup of 1.64 and N-Chance Forwarding provides a performance improvement of 1.73. Both coordinated algorithms are within 10% of the ideal cooperative caching response time.

Two conclusions seem apparent from Figure 4. First, disk accesses are the dominant source of latency for the base case, so efforts like cooperative caching that improve the overall hit rate will be beneficial. Second, the most dramatic improvements in performance come from the

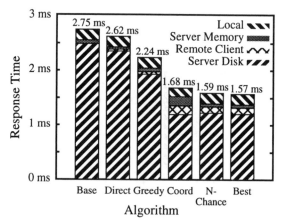

Figure 4. Average block read time. Each bar represents the time to complete an average read for one of the algorithms. The segments of the bars show the fraction of the total read time for data accesses satisfied by *Local* memory, *Server Memory*, *Remote Client* memory, or *Server Disk*.

[1.] Baker et al.'s traces also included requests to three auxiliary servers. We just used accesses to the main server, 81% of the trace.

[2.] All speedup and performance improvement figures in this paper use the terminology in [Henn90]. Speedup is defined as the execution time of the slower algorithm divided by the execution time for the faster algorithm. Performance improvement percentages are calculated by subtracting 1.00 from the speedup and then multiplying by 100 to get a percentage.

coordinated algorithms, where the system makes an effort to reduce the duplication among cache entries to improve the overall hit rate.

Figure 5 provides additional insight into the performance of the algorithms by illustrating the access rates at different levels of the memory hierarchy. The total height of each bar represents the miss rate for each algorithm's local cache. The base, Direct Cooperation, Greedy, and best case algorithms all manage their local caches greedily and so have identical local miss rates of 22%.[3] Central Coordination has a local miss rate of 36%, over 60% higher than the baseline local miss rate. This algorithm makes up for this local deficiency with aggressive coordination of most of the memory in the system, providing combined memory miss rates essentially identical to those achieved in the best case, with just 7.6% of all requests going to disk. This disk access rate is less than half of the 15.7% rate for the base caching scheme. The N-Chance algorithm's emphasis on holding onto the last data copies hurts the local miss rate by a surprisingly small amount; recirculation increases the local miss rate from 22% to 23%. N-Chance also provides a very low overall disk access rate of 7.7%.

A comparison between the static memory partition algorithm, Centralized Coordination, and the dynamic partition algorithm, N-Chance Forwarding, illustrates that both the local and global miss rates must be considered in evaluating these algorithms. Although the static algorithm provides the lower disk access rates, it provides this low miss rate at significant cost to its local cache performance.

The N-Chance algorithm coordinates a smaller fraction of the client cache contents, protecting the local cache hit rate but sacrificing some global hits.

Another important metric of comparison is the server load imposed by the algorithms. If a cooperative caching algorithm significantly increases server load, increased queueing delays might reduce the performance gains. Figure 6 illustrates the relative server loads for the algorithms.

Since we are primarily interested in verifying that cooperative caching's increased server coordination doesn't greatly increase server load, we make a number of simplifications in our server load calculations. First, we do not include the load for write-backs, deletes, file attribute requests, or other sources of server load in the load comparison. Including these loads would add equally to the load for each algorithm, reducing the relative differences among them.

Also, we base the server load calculations on the network messages and disk transfers made by the server for each algorithm. We assume that a network message overhead costs one load unit and that a block data transfer costs two load units. A small network message therefore costs one unit; a network data transfer costs one for overhead plus two for data transfer for a total of three units. We also charge the server two load units for a disk data transfer.

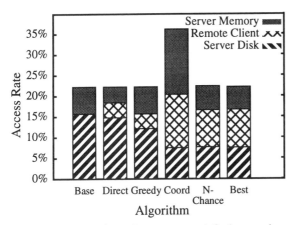

Figure 5. Fraction of requests satisfied at each level of the memory hierarchy for different algorithms. The total height of the bar is the local miss rate for each algorithm. The sum of the *Server Disk* and *Remote Client* segments shows the miss rate for the combined local and server memories. The bottom segment shows the miss rate once all memories are included, i.e. the disk access rate.

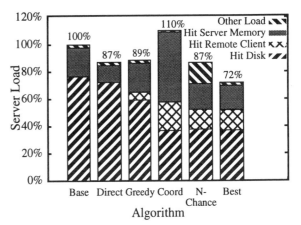

Figure 6. Server loads for the algorithms as a percentage of the baseline no cooperative caching server load. The *Hit Disk* segment includes both the network and disk load for all requests satisfied at the server disk. The *Hit Remote Client* segment shows the server load for receiving and forwarding requests to remote clients. The *Hit Server Memory* segment includes the cost of receiving requests and supplying data from the server's memory. Local hits generate no server load. The *Other Load* segment includes server overhead for invalidating client cache blocks and for answering client queries (e.g. N-Chance asks, "Is this block the last cached copy").

[3.] The simulated local miss rate is lower than the 40% miss rate measured for the Sprite machines in [Bake91] because we simulate larger caches than the average 7 MB caches observed in that study and because these larger caches service requests to only one server.

The results of the server load measurements suggest that most of the cooperative caching algorithms will not significantly increase server load and that our response time approximation of ignoring queueing delay should provide valid comparisons with the base case. The Centralized Coordinated algorithm does appear to increase server load somewhat, at least under these simple assumptions. This increase is because the centralized algorithm significantly increases the local miss rate, and all local misses are sent to the server. More detailed measurements would have to be made to determine if the centralized algorithm can be implemented without increasing server queueing delays.

A final comparison among the algorithms examines individual client performance rather than the aggregate average performance. Figure 7 illustrates the relative performance for individual clients under each cooperative caching algorithm compared to that client's performance in the base case. The graph positions data points for the clients so that inactive clients appear on the left of the graph and active clients on the right. Speedups or slowdowns for inactive clients may not be significant both because the clients are spending relatively little time waiting for the file system in either case and because these inactive clients' response times can be significantly affected by adding just a few disk accesses.

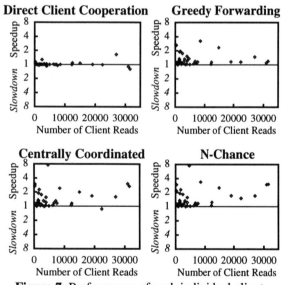

Figure 7. Performance of each individual client. Each point represents the speedup or slowdown seen by one client for a cooperative caching algorithm compared to that client's performance in the base case. Speedups are above the line and slowdowns are below it. A client's slowdown is defined as the inverse of its speedup if its speedup is less than one. The x-axis indicates the number of read requests made by each client; relatively inactive clients appear near the left edge of the graph, and active clients appear on the right.

One important aspect of individual performance is fairness: are any clients significantly worse off because they contribute resources to the community rather than managing their local caches greedily? Fairness is important because even if the average client performance is improved, some clients may refuse to participate in cooperative caching if their performance would be worse.

The data in Figure 7 suggest that fairness is not a widespread problem for this workload. Direct Client Cooperation and Centrally Coordinated Caching each slow a few clients by modest amounts. Greedy Forwarding and N-Chance Forwarding do no harm to any clients in this workload.

Although we would expect the two algorithms with greedy client cache management to always be fair, Direct Client Cooperation causes a few clients to suffer up to 25% worse performance than they had without the additional cooperative cache memory. These clients do not benefit greatly from their cooperative cache memory but have lower server cache hit rates under Direct Client Cooperation than in the base case. The lower server hit rates occur because the accesses to the server cache by all the clients in the system are filtered by their effectively larger local caches, reducing the correlation among client access streams at the server.

Although both the N-Chance and Centrally Coordinated algorithms disturb local greedy caching, their significant improvements in global caching provide a net benefit to almost all clients. N-Chance Forwarding hurts no clients for this workload, and Centrally Coordinated Caching damages the response of one client by 19%. Neither of these algorithms help a client whose working set fits completely into its local cache, but such a client can be hurt by interference with its local cache contents. Since N-Chance Forwarding interferes with local caching less than Centrally Coordinated Caching as was indicated in Figure 5, it is less likely to be unfair to individual clients. Other algorithms that statically partition client memory, such as Hash Distributed Caching or physically moving cache from the clients to the server, would suffer from the same vulnerability as Centrally Coordinated Caching.

4.2. Detailed Algorithm Analysis

This subsection examines the cooperative caching algorithms in more detail and evaluates their sensitivity to algorithm-specific parameters.

4.2.1 Direct Client Cooperation

Although Direct Client Cooperation is appealingly simple, achieving even the modest 5% response time improvement seen above may be difficult. We based the above results on the optimistic assumption that clients could recruit sufficient remote cache memory to double their caches without interfering with each other. In reality the algorithm must meet three challenges to provide even these modest gains.

The first difficulty for Direct Client Cooperation is that clients may not be able to find enough remote memory to significantly affect performance. Figure 8 plots Direct Cooperation response time as a function of the amount of remote memory recruited by each client. If, for instance, clients can only recruit enough memory to increase their cache size by 25% (4 MB), the response time improvement drops to under 1%. Significant speedups of 40% are only achieved if each client is able to recruit about 64 MBs—four times the size of its local cache.

Interference from other clients is likely to further limit Direct Client Cooperation benefits. When a client donating memory becomes active, it will flush any other client's data from its memory. A client trying to take advantage of remote memory sees a series of temporary caches, reducing its hit rate since a new cache will not be warmed with its data. Studies of workstation activity [Nich87, Thei89, Doug91, Mutk91, Arpa94] suggest that although many idle machines are usually available, the length of their idle periods can be relatively short. A possible solution to this problem would be to send the evicted data to a new idle client rather than discarding it, but that would increase the system's complexity.

A final challenge for Direct Client Cooperation is dynamically selecting which clients should donate memory and which should utilize remote memory. This problem appears solvable; if only the most active 10% of clients are able to recruit a cooperative cache they would achieve 85% of the maximum benefits available to Direct Client Cooperation for this trace. On the other hand, the implementation of a recruiting mechanism detracts from the algorithm's simplicity and may require server involvement.

4.2.2 Greedy Forwarding

Although the performance gains for the greedy algorithm are modest, the greedy algorithm may still be attractive because of its simplicity, because it does not increase server load, and because it is fair. In other words, this 22% performance improvement comes essentially for free once the clients and server have been modified to forward requests and the server's callback state is expanded to track individual blocks.

4.2.3 Centrally Coordinated Caching

Centrally Coordinated Caching can provide significant speedups and very high global hit rates. On the other hand, devoting a large fraction of each client's cache to Centrally Coordinated Caching reduces the local hit rate, potentially increasing the server load and reducing overall performance for some of the clients.

The fraction of each client's cache that is treated as a centralized resource determines the effectiveness of the algorithm. Figure 9 plots the overall response time as the centrally coordinated fraction is increased. As the fraction is increased, the global hit rate improves, reducing the time spent fetching data from disk. At the same time, the local hit rate decreases, driving up the time spent fetching from remote caches. These two trends create a response time plateau when 40% to 90% of each client's local cache is managed as a global resource. Note that these measurements do not take increased server load into account; increasing the centrally managed cache fraction also increases the load on the central server as local caches satisfy fewer requests. This effect may increase queueing delays at the server as the centrally-managed fraction is

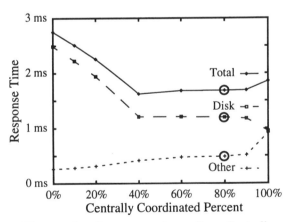

Figure 9. Response time for Centrally Coordinated Caching depends on the percent of the cache that is centrally coordinated. 0% corresponds to the baseline no cooperative caching case. The *Total* time is the sum of the time for requests that are satisfied by the *Disk* and the time for *Other* requests that are satisfied by a local or remote memory. The rest of this study uses a centrally coordinated fraction of 80% for this algorithm, indicated by the circled points.

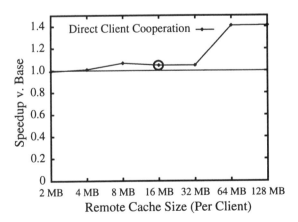

Figure 8. Direct Client Cooperation speedup compared to the base case as a function of each client's remote cache size. The circle indicates the result for the 16 MB per client remote cache assumed for this algorithm in the previous section.

increased, reducing the overall speedups and pushing the "break-even" point towards smaller centrally managed fractions.

We chose to use 80% as the default centrally managed fraction because that appears to be the more "stable" part of the plateau under different workloads and cache sizes. For instance, the plateau runs from 60% to 90% for the same workload but with 8 MB client caches. A high centrally managed fraction tends to achieve good performance because of the large disparity between disk and network memory access times compared to the gap between network and local memory. If the network were slower, a smaller percentage would be appropriate.

4.2.4 N-Chance Forwarding

N-Chance Forwarding also provides very good overall performance, but it does so by improving overall hit rates without significantly reducing local hit rates. This algorithm also has good server load and fairness characteristics.

Figure 10 plots response time against the recirculation count parameter, n, for this algorithm. The largest improvement comes when n is increased from zero (the Greedy algorithm) to one. Increasing the count from one to two also provides a small improvement while larger values make little difference. Relatively low values for n are effective since data that is recirculated through a random cache often lands in a relatively idle cache and so remains in memory for a significant period of time before being flushed. When the parameter is two, the random forwarding almost always gives a block at least one relatively long period of time in a mostly idle cache. Higher values make little additional difference both because few blocks need a third try to find an idle cache and because the algorithm

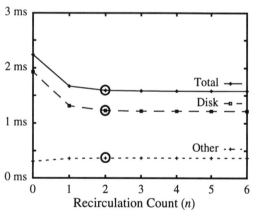

Figure 10. Response time for N-Chance algorithms depends on number of times unreferenced blocks are recirculated through random caches. Zero corresponds to the Greedy algorithm (no recirculation). The *Total* time is the sum of the time for requests that are satisfied by going to *Disk* and *Other* requests that are satisfied by a local or remote memory. The rest of this study uses a recirculation count of two for this algorithm, indicated by the circled points.

sometimes discards old cache items without recirculating them all n times to avoid a "ripple" effect among caches.

4.3. Sensitivity

This subsection explores the sensitivity of the results we present here to assumptions about each client's cache size, the central server's cache size, and the performance of the LAN over which the machines are connected.

Figure 11 plots the performance of the algorithms as a function of the size of each client's local cache. The graph shows that the two coordinated algorithms, Centralized Coordination and N-Chance Forwarding, perform well as long as caches are reasonably large. If caches are too small, however, coordinating the contents of client caches provides little benefit because borrowing any client memory causes a large increase in local misses with little aggregate benefit in reducing disk accesses. The simple Greedy algorithm also performs relatively well over the range of cache sizes.

Figure 12 illustrates the effect of varying the size of the cache at the central server. Increasing the server cache

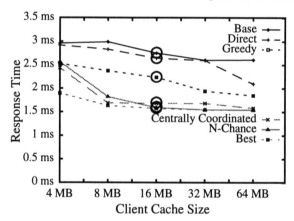

Figure 11. Response time as a function of client cache memory for the algorithms. Other graphs in this study have assumed a client cache size of 16 MB (circled).

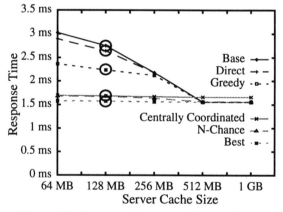

Figure 12. Response time v. total central server cache size. The circled points highlight the results for the default 128 MB server assumption.

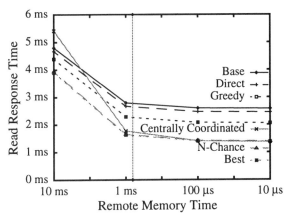

Figure 13. Response time as function of network speed. The X axis is the round trip time to request and receive an 8 KB packet. Disk access time is held constant at 15 ms and the memory access time is held constant at 250 μs. For the rest of this study we have assumed 200 us per hop plus 400 us per block transfer for a total remote fetch time of 800 us (request-reply excluding memory copy time), indicated by the vertical bar. The *N-Chance* and *Best* lines nearly overlap over the entire range of the graph.

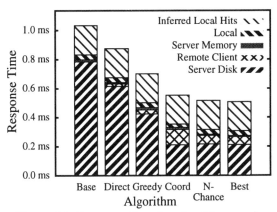

Figure 14. Response time for algorithms under the Auspex workload. The *Inferred Local Hits* segment indicates an estimate of the amount of time spent processing local hits that do not appear in the incomplete Auspex traces assuming that the traced system had an 80% local hit rate.

size significantly improves the base no cooperative caching case, while only modestly improving the performance of the cooperative algorithms that already have good global hit rates. For sufficiently large server caches, cooperative caching provides no benefit once the server cache is about as large as the aggregate client caches. Such a large cache, however, would double the system's memory cost compared to using cooperative caching. Note that when the server cache is very large Centrally Coordinated Caching performs poorly because of its degraded local hit rate.

The emergence of fast networks means that the time is ripe to begin utilizing cooperative caching in file systems. Although Ethernet-speed networks are too slow to get large benefits from cooperative caching, emerging ATM networks promise to be fast enough to see significant improvements. Figure 13 plots response time as a function of the network time to fetch a remote block. For an Ethernet-speed network, where a remote data access can take nearly 10 ms, the maximum speedup seen for a cooperative caching algorithm is 20%. If network fetch time were reduced to 1 ms, for instance by using a fast ATM network, the peak speedup increases to 70%. This graph shows little benefit from reducing network block fetch time below 100 μs because once the network is that fast, network times are not a significant source of delay compared to the constant memory and disk times.

Although either coordinated algorithm can provide nearly ideal performance when the network is fast, N-Chance Forwarding appears to be much less sensitive to network speed than Centrally Coordinated Caching. Centrally Coordinated Caching only makes sense in environ-

ments where accessing remote data is much closer to accessing local data than going to disk. Otherwise, its reduced local hit rate outweighs the increased global hit rate.

4.4. Berkeley Auspex Workload

The response time results for a second workload, called Berkeley Auspex, appear in Figure 14. The Berkeley Auspex workload traces the NFS file system network requests for 237 clients in the U.C. Berkeley Computer Science Division that are serviced by an Auspex file server. This workload is interesting because it follows the activity of a larger number of clients and includes a longer period of time than any of the Sprite traces. The large number of clients provide an extremely large pool of memory for cooperative caching to exploit. The traces cover a 6 day period and include five million read and write events of which we use the first million to warm the caches.

The trace was taken by snooping on the network; because it does not include local hits, we must adjust the simulation to account for the missing local accesses. We use Smith's Stack Deletion method [Smit77] to approximate the response time results based on this incomplete trace. Smith found that omitting references that hit in a small cache makes little difference in the number of faults seen when simulating a larger cache. The actual miss rate can be accurately approximated by dividing the number of faults seen when simulating the reduced trace by the actual number of references in the full trace.[4] As a further refinement, we utilize the *read attribute* requests present in our trace to more accurately simulate the local client LRU lists. NFS uses read attribute requests to validate cached blocks before referencing them. We can therefore use read attribute requests as a hint that the cached blocks of a file are being referenced even though the block requests do not appear in our trace. The attribute requests still provide only an approximation—an attribute cache hides attribute requests validated in the previous three seconds, and not all read attribute requests really signify that a file's cached blocks are about to be referenced—but they do allow us to infer some of the "missing" block hits.

Although the results for the Auspex workload are only approximate, they support the results seen for the Sprite workloads. The relative ranking of the algorithms under the Auspex workload is the same as it was for the Sprite workload: Centrally Coordinated Caching and N-Chance Forwarding work nearly as well as the best case, and the Greedy algorithm also provides significant speedups. Direct Cooperation provides more modest gains. This result is insensitive to the hit rate assumed. The predicted speedup factors for the Auspex workload does depend on the hit rate assumed but is significant over a wide range of assumed local hit rates.

4.5. Summary

N-Chance Forwarding is a relatively simple algorithm that appears to provide very good performance over a wide range of conditions. Centrally Coordinated Caching and the omitted Hash Distributed Caching can also provide very good performance, but they are more likely to degrade the performance of individual clients and depend heavily on fast network performance to make up for the reduced local hit rates they impose. The Weighted LRU algorithm (results omitted) performs similarly to the N-Chance algorithm, but it is more complicated and may also load the server with requests for information about global state.

The Greedy Forwarding algorithm appears to be the algorithm of choice if simplicity is the primary concern. Although the Direct Cooperation algorithm is also simple, satisfying the demands of cooperative caching without interfering with other client activities may be difficult, particularly since the Direct algorithm would have to locate 32 MB to 64 MB of remote memory per active client to equal the Greedy algorithm's performance.

Finally, consider the alternative to cooperative caching: physically moving more memory to the central server. This approach is very similar to the Centrally Coordinated algorithm and provides similar performance; moving 80% of client memory to the server yields improvements of 66% and 93% over the standard memory distribution for the Sprite and Auspex workloads respectively. These speedups are nearly equal to the speedups for the N-Chance algorithm, but fall short of equalling the N-Chance

---

4. Unfortunately, the Auspex trace does not indicate the total number of references. For the results in Figure 14 we assume a "hidden" hit rate of 80% (to approximate the 78% rate simulated for the Sprite trace), giving a maximum speedup of 2.00 for N-Chance Forwarding. If the local hit rate were higher, all of the bars would have a slightly larger constant added and the differences among the algorithms would be smaller (e.g. a 90% local hit rate reduces the N-Chance speedup to 1.67). If the local hit rate were lower, the differences would be magnified (e.g. a 70% local hit rate gives an N-Chance speedup of 2.20).

algorithm because of the reduced local hit rates resulting from smaller local caches. Moving large fractions of the clients' caches to the server has a number of other disadvantages compared to a good cooperative caching algorithm such as N-Chance Forwarding:

- Static allocation of the global/local caches is more likely to provide bad performance for some individual clients as was seen for Centrally Coordinated Caching in Figure 7.

- A system with more cache memory at the server and less at the clients would be very sensitive to network speed as was seen for Centrally Coordinated Caching in Figure 13. As the ratio of network performance to local memory performance is reduced, moving memory to the server becomes less attractive.

- Reducing the size of client local caches and transferring more data from the server can increase server load. The read load for a traditional caching system with the enlarged central cache is 50% higher than for N-Chance Forwarding under the Sprite workload.

- Memory physically moved for use as central server file system cache cannot be used by clients for other activities. Cooperative caching, on the other hand, may allow client cache memory to be released for use as client virtual memory as system demands warrant [Nels88].

- Configuring servers with large amounts of memory may be less cost-effective than spreading the same amount of memory among the clients. For instance, 80% of the 16 MB of cache memory for the 237 clients in the Auspex trace would be 3 GB of memory, demanding an extremely expandable and potentially expensive server.

5. Related Work

This paper evaluates the performance benefits and implementation issues of cooperative caching. Its primary contributions are evaluating realistic management algorithms under real file system workloads and a systematic exploration of implementation options.

Leff et al. [Leff91, Leff93a, Leff93b] investigate remote caching architectures, a form of cooperative caching, using analytic and simulation-based models under a synthetic workload. Two important characteristics of their workload were that the access probabilities for each object by each client were fixed over time and that each client knew what these distributions were. Leff found that if clients base their caching decisions on global knowledge of what other clients are caching, they could achieve nearly ideal performance, but that if clients made decisions on a strictly local basis, performance suffered greatly.

This paper differs from the Leff studies in a number of important ways. First, this paper uses actual file system reference traces as a workload, allowing us to quantify the benefits of cooperative caching realizable under real workloads. A second major feature of this study is that we have focused on getting good performance while controlling the amount of central coordination and knowledge required by the clients rather than focusing on optimal replacement algorithms.

Franklin et al. [Fran92] examined cooperative caching in the context of client-server data bases where clients were allowed to forward data to each other to avoid disk accesses. The study used synthetic workloads and focused on techniques to reduce replication between the clients' caches and the server cache. The server did not attempt to coordinate the contents of the clients' caches to reduce replication of data among the clients. Their "Forwarding—Sending Dropped Pages" algorithm is similar to our N-Chance Forwarding algorithm, but they send the last copy of a block to the server cache rather than to another client.

Blaze [Blaz93] proposed allowing file system clients to supply hot data to each other from their local on-disk file caches. The focus of this work was on reducing server load rather than improving responsiveness. He found that the use of client-to-client data transfers allowed *dynamic hierarchical caching* and avoided the store and forward delays experienced by static hierarchical caching systems [Munt92].

The idea of forwarding data from one cache to another has also been used to build scalable shared memory multiprocessors. DASH hardware implements a scheme similar to Greedy Forwarding for dirty cache lines [Leno90]. This policy avoids the latency of writing dirty data back to the server when it is shared. The same optimization could be used for a cooperative caching file system that uses delayed writes. Several "Cache Only Memory Architecture" (COMA) designs have also relied on cache to cache data transfers [Hage92, Rost93].

Other researchers have examined the idea of using remote client memory rather than disk for virtual memory paging. Felten and Zahorjan [Felt91] examined this idea in the context of traditional LANs. Schilit and Duchamp [Schi91] scrutinized using remote memory paging to allow diskless portable computers, and Iftode, Li, and Petersen [Ifto93] explored using memory servers in parallel supercomputers. Comer and Griffioen propose a communications protocol for remote paging in [Come92].

6. Conclusions

The advent of high-speed networks provides the opportunity for clients to work closely together to significantly improve the performance of file systems. We have investigated the technique of cooperative caching and conclude that cooperative caching can reduce read response times by nearly a factor of two for the workloads studied and that a relatively simple algorithm allows clients to efficiently manage their shared cache.

Acknowledgments

We owe special thanks to David Black of OSF for working as the OSDI shepherd for this paper. We would also like to thank Fred Douglis, John Howard, Edward Lee, John Ousterhout, and the anonymous OSDI referees whose comments improved both the content and the presentation of this paper. We are grateful to Mary Baker, John Hartman, Michael Kupfer, Ken Shirriff, and John Ousterhout for making the Sprite traces available. Finally, we thank Matt Blaze for providing the rpcspy tools we used to gather the Auspex traces.

References

[Arch86] James Archibald and Jean-Loup Baer. Cache Coherence Protocols: Evaluation Using a Multiprocessor Simulation Model. *ACM Transactions on Computer Systems*, 4:273–298, November 1986.

[Arpa94] Remzi Arpaci, Amin Vahdat, Thomas Anderson, and David Patterson. Combining Parallel and Sequential Workloads on a Network of Workstations. Technical report, Computer Science Division, University of California at Berkeley, 1994.

[Bake91] Mary G. Baker, John H. Hartman, Michael D. Kupfer, Ken W. Shirriff, and John K. Ousterhout. Measurements of a Distributed File System. In *Proc. of the 13th Symposium on Operating Systems Principles*, pages 198–212, October 1991.

[Blaz93] Matthew Addison Blaze. *Caching in Large-Scale Distributed File Systems*. PhD thesis, Princeton University, January 1993.

[Come92] Douglas Comer and James Griffioen. Efficient Order-Dependent Communication in a Distributed Virtual Memory Environment. In *Symp. on Experiences with Distributed and Multiprocessor Systems III*, pages 249–262, March 1992.

[Dahl94] Michael D. Dahlin, Clifford J. Mather, Randolph Y. Wang, Thomas E. Anderson, and David A. Patterson. A Quantitative Analysis of Cache Policies for Scalable Network File Systems. In *Proc. of 1994 SIGMETRICS*, pages 150–160, May 1994.

[Doug91] Fred Douglis and John Ousterhout. Transparent Process Migration: Design Alternatives and the Sprite Implementation. *Software: Practice and Experience*, 21(7), July 1991.

[Felt91] Edward W. Felten and John Zahorjan. Issues in the Implementation of a Remote Memory Paging System. Technical Report 91-03-09, Dept. of Computer Science, University of Washington, March 1991.

[Fran92] Michael J. Franklin, Michael J. Carey, and Miron Livny. Global Memory Management in Client-Server DBMS Architectures. In *Proc. of the International Conference on Very Large Data Bases*, pages 596–609, August 1992.

[Hage92] Erik Hagersten, Anders Landin, and Seif Haridi. DDM–A Cache-Only Memory Architecture. *IEEE Computer*, 25(9):45–54, September 1992.

[Henn90] John L. Hennessy and David A. Patterson. *Computer Architecture A Quantitative Approach*. Morgan Kaufmann Publishers, Inc., 1990.

[Howa88] John H. Howard, Michael L. Kazar, Sherri G. Menees, David A. Nichols, M. Satyanarayanan,

Robert N. Sidebotham, and Michael J. West. Scale and Performance in a Distributed File System. *ACM Transactions on Computer Systems*, 6(1):51–81, February 1988.

[Ifto93] Liviu Iftode, Kai Li, and Karin Petersen. Memory Servers for Multicomputers. In *Proc. of COMPCON93*, pages 538–547, 1993.

[Leff91] Avraham Leff, Philip S. Yu, and Joel L. Wolf. Policies for Efficient Memory Utilization in a Remote Caching Architecture. In *Proc. First International Conf. on Parallel and Distributed Information Systems*, pages 198–207, December 1991.

[Leff93a] Avraham Leff, Joel L. Wolf, and Philip S. Yu. Replication Algorithms in a Remote Caching Architecture. *IEEE Trans. on Parallel and Distributed Systems*, 4(11):1185–1204, November 1993.

[Leff93b] Avraham Leff, Philip S. Yu, and Joel L. Wolf. Performance Issues in Object Replication for a Remote Caching Architecture. *Computer Systems Science and Engineering*, 8(1):40–51, January 1993.

[Leno90] D. Lenoski, J. Laudon, K. Gharachorloo, A. Gupta, and J. Hennessy. The Directory-Based Cache Coherence Protocol for the DASH Multiprocessor. In *Proc. of the 17th International Symposium on Computer Architecture*, pages 148–159, May 1990.

[Litz92] Michael Litzkow and Marvin Solomon. Supporting Checkpointing and Process Migration Outside the UNIX Kernel. In *Proc. of the Winter 1992 USENIX*, pages 283–290, January 1992.

[Mart94] Richard P. Martin. HPAM: An Active Message Layer for a Network of HP Workstations. In *Proc. 1994 Hot Interconnects*, August 1994.

[Munt92] D. Muntz and P. Honeyman. Multi-level Caching in Distributed File Systems or Your cache ain't nuthin' but trash. In *Proc. of the Winter 1992 USENIX*, pages 305–313, January 1992.

[Mutk91] Matthew M. Mutka and Miron Livny. The Available Capacity of a Privately Owned Workstation Environment. *Performance Evaluation*, 12(4):269–84, July 1991.

[Nels88] Michael N. Nelson, Brent B. Welch, and John K. Ousterhout. Caching in the Sprite Network File System. *ACM Transactions on Computer Systems*, 6(1), February 1988.

[Nich87] David A. Nichols. Using Idle Workstations in a Shared Computing Environment. In *Proc. of the 9th Symposium on Operating Systems Principles*, pages 5–12, October 1987.

[Rost93] E. Rosti, E. Smirni, T. D. Wagner, A. W. Apon, and L.W. Dowdy. The KSR1: Experimentation and Modeling of Poststore. In *Proc. of 1993 ACM SIGMETRICS*, pages 74–85, June 1993.

[Ruem93] Chris Ruemmler and John Wilkes. UNIX Disk Access Patterns. In *Proc. of the Winter 1993 USENIX*, pages 405–420, January 1993.

[Sand85] Russel Sandberg, David Goldberg, Steve Kleiman, Dan Walsh, and Bob Lyon. Design and Implementation of the Sun Network Filesystem. In *Proc. of the Summer 1985 USENIX*, pages 119–130, June 1985.

[Schi91] Bill N. Schilit and Dan Duchamp. Adaptive Remote Paging for Mobile Computers. Technical Report CUCS-004-91, Dept. of Computer Science, Columbia University, February 1991.

[Smit77] Alan Jay Smith. Two Methods for the Efficient Analysis of Memory Address Trace Data. *IEEE Transactions on Software Engineering*, SE-3(1):94–101, January 1977.

[Smit81] Alan Jay Smith. Long Term File Migration: Development and Evaluation of Algorithms. *Computer Architecture and Systems*, 24(8):521–532, August 1981.

[Thei89] Marvin M. Theimer and Keith A. Lantz. Finding Idle Machines in a Workstation-Based Distributed System. *IEEE Transactions on Software Engineering*, 15(11):1444–57, November 1989.

[vE92] Thorsten von Eicken, David E. Culler, Seth Copen Goldstein, and Klaus Erik Schauser. Active Messages: A Mechanism for Integrated Communication and Computation. In *Proc. of 1992 ASPLOS*, pages 256–266, May 1992.

[Wang93] Randolph Y. Wang and Thomas E. Anderson. xFS: A Wide Area Mass Storage File System. In *Fourth Workshop on Workstation Operating Systems*, pages 71–78, October 1993.

[Zhou93] Songnian Zhou, Jingwen Wang, Xiaohu Zheng, and Pierre Delisle. Utopia: A Load Sharing Facility for Large, Heterogeneous Distributed Computer Systems. *Software - Practice and Experience*, 23(12):1305–1336, December 1993.